Jonathan Dymond

Essays on the Principles of Morality

And on the private and political Rights and Obligations of Mankind. Ninth Edition

Jonathan Dymond

Essays on the Principles of Morality
And on the private and political Rights and Obligations of Mankind. Ninth Edition

ISBN/EAN: 9783337132682

Printed in Europe, USA, Canada, Australia, Japan

Cover: Foto ©ninafisch / pixelio.de

More available books at **www.hansebooks.com**

ON THE

PRINCIPLES OF MORALITY

AND ON THE

PRIVATE AND POLITICAL

RIGHTS AND OBLIGATIONS OF MANKIND

BY

JONATHAN DYMOND

AUTHOR OF "AN ENQUIRY INTO THE ACCORDANCY OF WAR WITH THE
PRINCIPLES OF CHRISTIANITY," ETC.

"As the Will of God is our rule; to inquire what is our duty, or what we are obliged to do, in any instance, is, in effect, to inquire what is the Will of God in that instance? which consequently becomes the whole business of morality."—PALEY.

NINTH EDITION

DUBLIN: EASON AND SON, LIMITED
LONDON
SAMUEL BAGSTER AND SONS, LIMITED
SIMPKIN MARSHALL, HAMILTON, KENT & CO., LIMITED
EDWARD HICKS, JUN., 14, BISHOPSGATE WITHOUT

1894

TO THAT

SMALL BUT INCREASING NUMBER

WHETHER IN THIS COUNTRY OR ELSEWHERE

WHO

MAINTAIN IN PRINCIPLE, AND ILLUSTRATE BY THEIR PRACTICE

THE GREAT DUTY

OF

CONFORMING TO THE LAWS OF CHRISTIAN MORALITY

WITHOUT REGARD TO

DANGERS OR PRESENT ADVANTAGES

𝔗his 𝔐ork

IS

RESPECTFULLY DEDICATED

PREFACE

The Author of this Work died in the spring of 1828, leaving in manuscript the three Essays of which it consists. We learn from himself that the undertaking originated in a belief (in which he probably is far from being alone) that the existing treatises on Moral Philosophy did not exhibit the principles nor enforce the obligations of morality in all their perfection and purity; that a work was yet wanted which should present a true and authoritative standard of rectitude— one by an appeal to which the moral character of human actions might be rightly estimated. This he here endeavours to supply.

Rejecting what he considered the false grounds of duty, and erroneous principles of action which are proposed in the most prominent and most generally received of our extant theories of moral obligation, he proceeds to erect a system of morality upon what he regards as the only true and legitimate basis—the WILL OF GOD. He makes, therefore, the authority of the Deity the sole ground of duty, and His communicated Will the only ultimate standard of right and wrong; and assumes, "that wheresoever this Will is made known, human duty is determined;—and that neither the conclusions of philosophers, nor advantages, nor dangers, nor pleasures, nor sufferings, ought to have any opposing influence in regulating our conduct."

The attempt to establish a system of such uncompromising morality, must necessarily bring the writer into direct collision with the advocates of the utilitarian scheme, particularly with Dr. Paley; and accordingly it will be found that he frequently enters the lists with this great champion of Expediency. With what success—how well he exposes the fallacies of that specious but dangerous doctrine —how far he succeeds in refuting the arguments by which it is sought to be maintained, and in establishing another system of obligations and duties and rights upon a more stable foundation, must be left to the reader to determine.

In thus attempting to convert a system of Moral Philosophy, dubious, fluctuating, and inconsistent with itself, into a definite and harmonious code of Scripture Ethics, the Author undertook a task for which, by the original structure of his mind and his prevailing habits of reflection, he was, perhaps, peculiarly fitted. He had sought for himself, and he endeavours to convey to others, clear perceptions of the true and the right; and in maintaining what he regarded as truth and rectitude, he shows everywhere an unshackled independence of mind, and a fearless, unflinching spirit. The work will be found, moreover, if we mistake not, to be the result of a careful study of the writings of moralists, of much thought, of an intimate acquaintance with the genius of the Christian religion, and an extensive observation of human life in those spheres of action which are seldom apt to attract the notice of the meditative philosopher.

In proceeding to illustrate his principles, the Author has evidently sought, as far as might be, to simplify the subject, to disencumber it of abstruse and metaphysical appendages, and, rejecting subtleties and needless distinctions, to exhibit a standard of morals that should be plain, perspicuous, and practicable.

Premising thus much, the work must be left to its own merits. It is the last labour of a man laudably desirous of benefiting his fellow-men; and it will fulfil the Author's wish, if its effect be to raise the general tone of morals, to give distinctness to our perceptions of rectitude, and to add strength to our resolutions to virtue.

INTRODUCTORY NOTICES

Of the two causes of our deviations from Rectitude—want of Knowledge and want of Virtue—the latter is undoubtedly the more operative. Want of Knowledge is, however, sometimes a cause; nor can this be any subject of wonder when it is recollected in what manner many of our notions of right and wrong are acquired. From infancy, every one is placed in a sort of moral school, in which those with whom he associates, or of whom he hears, are the teachers. That the learner in such a school will often be taught amiss, is plain.—So that we want *information* respecting our duties. To supply this information is an object of Moral Philosophy, and is attempted in the present work.

When it is considered by what excellences the existing treatises on Moral Philosophy are recommended, there can remain but one reasonable motive for adding yet another—the belief that these treatises have not exhibited the Principles and enforced the Obligations of Morality in all their perfection and purity. Perhaps the frank expression of this belief is not inconsistent with that deference which it becomes every man to feel when he addresses the public; because, not to have entertained such a belief, were to have possessed no reason for writing. The desire of supplying the deficiency, if deficiency there be; of exhibiting a true and authoritative Standard of Rectitude, and of estimating the moral character of human actions by an appeal to that Standard, is the motive which has induced the composition of these Essays.

In the FIRST ESSAY the writer has attempted to investigate the Principles of Morality. In which term is here included, first, the Ultimate Standard of Right and Wrong; and, secondly, those Subordinate Rules to which we are authorised to apply for the direction of our conduct in life. In these investigations he has been solicitous to avoid any approach to curious or metaphysical inquiry. He has endeavoured to act upon the advice given by Tindal, the Reformer, to his friend John Frith: "Pronounce not or define of hid secrets, or things that neither help nor hinder whether it be so or no; but stick you stiffly and stubbornly in earnest and necessary things."

In the SECOND ESSAY these Principles of Morality are applied in the determination of various questions of personal and relative duty. In making this application, it has been far from the writer's desire to deliver a *system* of Morality. Of the unnumbered particulars to which this Essay might have been extended, he has therefore made a selection : and in making it, has chosen those subjects which appeared peculiarly to need the inquiry, either because the popular or philosophical opinions respecting them appeared to be unsound, or because they were commonly little adverted to in the practice of life. Form has been sacrificed to utility. Many great duties have been passed over, since no one questions their obligation ; nor has the author so little consulted the pleasure of the reader as to expatiate upon duties simply because they are great. The reader will also regard the subjects that have been chosen as selected, not only for the purpose of elucidating the subjects themselves, but as furnishing illustration of the General Principles—as the compiler of a book of mathematics proposes a variety of examples, not merely to discover the solution of the particular problem, but to familiarise the application of his general rule.

Of the THIRD ESSAY, in which some of the great questions of Political Rectitude have been examined, the subjects are in themselves sufficiently important. The application of sound and pure Moral Principles to questions of Government, of Legislation, of the Administration of Justice, or of Religious Establishments, is manifestly of great interest ; and the interest is so much the greater because these subjects have usually been examined, as the writer conceives, by other and very different standards.

The reader will probably find, in each of these Essays, some principles or some conclusions respecting human duties to which he has not been accustomed —some opinions called in question which he has habitually regarded as being indisputably true, and some actions exhibited as forbidden by morality which he has supposed to be lawful and right. In such cases I must hope for his candid investigation of the truth, and that he will not reject conclusions but by the detection of inaccuracy in the reasonings from which they are deduced. I hope he will not find himself invited to alter his opinions or his conduct without being shown why ; and if he is conclusively shown this, that he will not reject truth because it is new or unwelcome.

With respect to the present influence of the Principles which these Essays illustrate, the author will feel no disappointment if it is not great. It is not upon the expectation of such influence that his motive is founded or his hope rests. His motive is, to advocate truth without reference to its popularity ; and his hope is, to promote, by these feeble exertions, an approximation to that state of purity, which he believes it is the design of God shall eventually beautify and dignify the condition of mankind.

INTRODUCTORY WORDS

BY THE

RIGHT HON. JOHN BRIGHT.

I know of no better book dealing with morals as applied to nations than Dymond's Essays. As the world becomes more Christian, this book will be more widely read, and the name of its author more revered.

I have been asked on several occasions, "What do you think about the doctrine of the Peace Society, or of your own Religious Body, in their opposition to all War however necessary or however just it may seem to be, or however much you are provoked and injured?" I think every man must make up his own mind on that abstract principle; and I would recommend him, if he wants to know a book that says a good deal upon it, to study the New Testament, and make up his mind from that source.

It will be time enough perhaps to discuss that question when we have abandoned everything that can be called unjust and unnecessary in the way of War. Now, I believe, that with wise counsels, great statesmen, large knowledge of affairs combined with Christian principle, there is probably not a single war in which we have been engaged from the time of William III., that might not have been without difficulty avoided: and our military system might have been kept in great moderation, our National Debt would never have accumulated, our population would have been a great deal less barbarous and less ignorant than they are, and everything that tends to the true grandeur and prosperity and happiness of the people, would have been infinitely advanced beyond or above what we see now in our own time.

I think we ought to begin to ask ourselves how it is that Christian nations—that this Christian nation—should be involved in so many wars. If we may presume to ask ourselves, what, in the eye of the Supreme Ruler, is the greatest crime which His creatures commit, I think we may almost with certainty conclude that it is the crime of War. Somebody has described it as "the sum of all villanies;" and it has been the cause of sufferings, misery, and slaughter, which neither tongue nor pen can ever describe. And all this has been going on for eighteen hundred years after men have adopted the religion whose Founder and whose Head is denominated the Prince of Peace. It was announced as a religion which was intended to bring "Peace on earth, and goodwill towards men;" and yet, after all these years, the peace on earth has not come, and the goodwill among men is only partially and occasionally exhibited; and amongst nations we find almost no trace of it century after century.

Now in this country we have a great institution called the Established Church. I suppose that great institution numbers twenty thousand or more places of worship in various parts of the kingdom. I think this does not include what there are in Scotland, and what there are in Ireland. With these twenty thousand churches there are at least twenty thousand men, educated and for the most part Christian men, anxious to do their duty as teachers of the religion of peace; and besides these, there are twenty thousand other churches which are not connected with the Established institution, but have been built, and are maintained, by that large portion of the people who go generally under the name of Dissenters or Nonconformists: and they have their twenty thousand ministers; also men, many of them, as well educated, as truly Christian and devoted men, as the others; and they are at work continually from day to day, and they preach from Sabbath to Sabbath what they believe to be the doctrines of the Prince of Peace; and yet, notwithstanding all that, we have more than £30,000,000 a year spent by this country in sustaining armies and navies, in view of wars which, it is assumed, may suddenly and soon take place. Now, why is this, I should like to ask: for all these teachers and preachers profess to be the servants of the Most High God, and teachers of the doctrines of His Divine Son; and being such, may I not appeal to them and say—What have you, forty or fifty thousand men, with such vast influence, what have you been doing with this great question during all the years that you have ministered, and called yourselves the ministers of the Prince of Peace?

And I would not confine my appeal to the ministers only, but to the devout men of every church and every chapel, who surround the minister and uphold his hands; who do in many things his bidding, and who join him heartily and conscientiously in his work—I say, what are they doing? Why is it that there has never been a combination of all religious and Christian teachers of the country, with a view of teaching the people what is true, what is Christian, upon the subject?

I believe it lies within the power of the churches to do far more than statesmen can do in matters of this kind. I believe they might so bring this question home to the hearts and consciences of the Christian and good men and women of their congregations, that a great combination of public opinion might be created, which would wholly change the aspect of this question in this country and before the world, and would bring to the minds of statesmen that they are not the rulers of the people of Greece, or of the marauding hordes of ancient Rome, but that they are, or ought to be, the Christian rulers of a Christian people.

CONTENTS

ESSAY I.—PART I.
PRINCIPLES OF MORALITY.

CHAP. I.—MORAL OBLIGATION . . . 1
Foundation of Moral Obligation.

CHAP. II.—STANDARD OF RIGHT AND WRONG 1
The Will of God—Notices of Theories—The communication of the Will of God—The supreme authority of the expressed Will of God—Causes of its practical rejection—The principles of expediency fluctuating and inconsistent—Application of the principles of expediency—Difficulties—Liability to abuse—Pagans.

THE WILL OF GOD 1
THE COMMUNICATION OF THE WILL OF GOD 3

CHAP. III.—SUBORDINATE STANDARDS OF RIGHT AND WRONG 8
Foundation and limits of the authority of subordinate moral rules.

CHAP. IV.—COLLATERAL OBSERVATIONS . 9
IDENTICAL AUTHORITY OF MORAL AND RELIGIOUS OBLIGATIONS . . . 9
Identical authority of moral and religious obligations—The Divine attributes—Of deducing rules of human duty from a consideration of the attributes of God—Virtue: "Virtue is conformity with the standard of rectitude"—Motives of action.

THE DIVINE ATTRIBUTES . . . 10
VIRTUE 10

CHAP. V.—SCRIPTURE 11
The morality of the Patriarchal, Mosaic, and Christian dispensations—Their moral requisitions not always coincident—Supremacy of the Christian morality—Of variations in the Moral Law—Mode of applying the precepts of Scripture to questions of duty—No formal moral system in Scripture—Criticism of Biblical morality—Of particular precepts and general rules—Matt. vii. 12.—1 Cor. x. 31.—Rom. iii. 8.—Benevolence, as it is proposed in the Christian Scriptures.

THE MORALITY OF THE PATRIARCHAL, MOSAIC, AND CHRISTIAN DISPENSATIONS 11
MODE OF APPLYING THE PRECEPTS OF SCRIPTURE TO QUESTIONS OF DUTY . 14
BENEVOLENCE, AS IT IS PROPOSED IN THE CHRISTIAN SCRIPTURES . . 18

CHAP. VI.—THE IMMEDIATE COMMUNICATION OF THE WILL OF GOD . . 19
Conscience—Its nature—Its authority—Review of opinions respecting a moral sense—Bishop Butler—Lord Bacon—Lord Shaftesbury Watts—Voltaire—Locke—Southey—Adam Smith—Paley—Rousseau—Milton—Judge Hale—Marcus Antoninus—Epictetus—Seneca —Paul—That every human being possesses a moral law—Pagans—Gradations of light—Prophecy—The immediate communication of the Divine Will perpetual—Of national vices: Infanticide: Duelling—Of savage life.

SECTION I.—CONSCIENCE, ITS NATURE AND AUTHORITY 20
REVIEW OF OPINIONS RESPECTING A MORAL SENSE 23
THE IMMEDIATE COMMUNICATION OF THE WILL OF GOD 27

ESSAY I.—PART II.
SUBORDINATE MEANS OF DISCOVERING THE DIVINE WILL.

CHAP. I.—THE LAW OF THE LAND . . 32
Its authority—Limits to its authority—Morality sometimes prohibits what the law permits.

CHAP. II.—THE LAW OF NATURE . . 34
Its authority—Limits to its authority—Obligations resulting from the Rights of Nature—Incorrect ideas attached to the word Nature.

CHAP. III.—UTILITY 37
Obligations resulting from Expediency—Limits to these obligations.

CHAP. IV.—THE LAW OF NATIONS—THE LAW OF HONOUR . . . 39

SECTION I.—THE LAW OF NATIONS . 39
Obligations and authority of the Law of Nations—Its abuses, and the limits of its authority—Treaties.

SECTION II.—THE LAW OF HONOUR . 41
Authority of the Law of Honour—Its character.

ESSAY II.
PRIVATE RIGHTS AND OBLIGATIONS.

CHAP. I.—RELIGIOUS OBLIGATIONS . . 43
Factitious semblances of devotion—Religious conversation—Sabbatical institutions—Nonsanctity of days — Of temporal employments; Travelling; Stage-coaches; "Sunday papers;" Amusements — Holydays — Ceremonial institutions and devotional formularies —Utility of forms—Forms of prayer—Extempore prayer — Scepticism — Motives to Scepticism.

SABBATICAL INSTITUTIONS . . . 45
CEREMONIAL INSTITUTIONS AND DEVOTIONAL FORMULARIES 47

CHAP. II.—PROPERTY 51
Foundation of the Right to Property—Insolvency; Perpetual obligation to pay debts; Reform of public opinion; Examples of integrity—Wills, Legatees, Heirs; Informal Wills; Intestates — Charitable Bequests — Minor's Debts—A Wife's Debts—Bills of Exchange—Shipments—Distraints—Unjust Defendants—Extortion —Slaves — Privateers — Confiscations—Public Money—Insurance — Improvements on Estates — Settlements— Houses of infamy—Literary property—Rewards.

CHAP. III.—INEQUALITY OF PROPERTY . 63
Accumulation of Wealth; its proper limits—Provision for Children; "Keeping up the Family."

CHAP. IV.—LITIGATION—ARBITRATION . 66
Practice of early Christians—Evils of Litigation —Efficiency of Arbitration.

CHAP. V.—THE MORALITY OF LEGAL PRACTICE, ... 68
Complexity of Law—Professional Untruths—Defences of Legal Practice—Effects of Legal Practice; Seduction; Theft; Peculation—Pleading—The Duties of the Profession—Effects of Legal Practice on the Profession, and on the Public

CHAP. VI.—PROMISES—LIES . . . 75
PROMISES.—Definition of a Promise—Parole— Extorted Promises—John Fletcher.
LIES.—Milton's Definition—Lies in War; to Robbers; to Lunatics; to the Sick—Hyperbole—Irony—Complimentary Untruths— "Not at Home "—Legal Documents.

CHAP. VII.—OATHS 80
THEIR MORAL CHARACTER -- THEIR EFFICACY AS SECURITIES OF VERACITY—THEIR EFFECTS 80
A Curse—Immorality of oaths—Oaths of the ancient Jews — Milton—Paley—The High Priest's adjuration—Early Christians—Inefficacy of oaths—Motives to veracity—Religious sanctions; Public opinion; Legal penalties—Oaths in Evidence; Parliamentary Evidence; Courts Martial—The United States—Effects of Oaths; Falsehood—General obligations.

CHAP. VIII.—THE MORAL CHARACTER, OBLIGATIONS, AND EFFECTS OF PARTICULAR OATHS 88
SUBSCRIPTION TO ARTICLES OF RELIGION 88
Oath of Allegiance—Oath in Evidence—Perjury —Military oath — Oath against Bribery at Elections—Oath against simony—University oaths—Subscription to articles of religion— Meaning of the 39 Articles literal—Refusal to subscribe.

CHAP. IX.—IMMORAL AGENCY . . . 94
Publication and circulation of books—Seneca— Circulating Libraries—Public-houses—Prosecutions—Political affairs.

CHAP. X.—THE INFLUENCE OF INDIVIDUALS UPON PUBLIC NOTIONS OF MORALITY 97
Public notions of morality—Errors of public opinion; their effects — Duelling — Scottish Bench—Glory — Military virtues — Military talent—Bravery — Courage — Patriotism not the soldier's motive—Military fame—Public opinion of unchastity; In women; In men— Power of character—Character in Legal men —Fame—Faults of Great Men—The Press —Newspapers— History; Its defects; Its power.

CHAP. XI.—INTELLECTUAL EDUCATION . 110
Ancient Classics — London University — The Classics in Boarding-schools—English grammar — Science and Literature — Improved system of Education—Orthography; Writing; Reading; Geography; Natural History; Biography; Natural Philosophy; Political Science—Indications of a revolution in the system of Education—Female Education— The Society of Friends

CHAP. XII.—MORAL EDUCATION . . 117
Union of Moral Principle with the Affections— Society—Morality of the Ancient Classics— The supply of motives to virtue—Conscience —Subjugation of the Will—Knowledge of our own Minds—Offices of public worship.

CHAP. XIII.—EDUCATION OF THE PEOPLE 122
Advantages of extended Education — Infant Schools—Habits of inquiry.

	PAGE		PAGE
CHAP. XIV.—AMUSEMENTS	124	CHAP. XVI.—SUICIDE	130

CHAP. XIV.—AMUSEMENTS
The Stage—Religious Amusements—Masquerades—Field Sports—The Turf—Boxing—Wrestling—Opinions of Posterity—Popular amusements needless.

CHAP. XVI.—SUICIDE
Unmanliness of Suicide—Forbidden in the New Testament—Its folly—Legislation respecting suicide—Verdict of *Felo de se*.

CHAP. XV.—DUELLING 127
Pitt and Tierney—Duelling the offspring of intellectual meanness, fear, and servility—"A fighting man"—Hindoo immolations—Wilberforce—Seneca.

CHAP. XVII.—RIGHTS OF SELF-DEFENCE 132
These rights not absolute—Their limits—Personal attack—Preservation of property—Much resistance lawful—Effects of forbearance—Sharpe—Barclay—Ellwood.

ESSAY III.

POLITICAL RIGHTS AND OBLIGATIONS.

CHAP. I.—PRINCIPLES OF POLITICAL TRUTH, AND OF POLITICAL RECTITUDE 137

I. "Political Power is rightly exercised only when it is possessed by consent of the community"—Governors officers of the Public—Transfer of their rights by a whole people—The people hold the sovereign power—Right of Governors—A conciliating system.

II. "Political Power is rightly exercised only when it subserves the welfare of the community"—Interference with other nations—Present expedients for present occasions—Proper business of Governments.

III. "Political Power is rightly exercised only when it subserves the welfare of the community by means which the Moral Law permits"—The Moral Law alike binding on nations and individuals—Deviation from rectitude impolitic—"The Holy Alliance"—Durable fame.

I. "POLITICAL POWER IS RIGHTLY POSSESSED ONLY WHEN IT IS POSSESSED BY CONSENT OF THE COMMUNITY". 137

II. "POLITICAL POWER IS RIGHTLY EXERCISED ONLY WHEN IT SUBSERVES THE WELFARE OF THE COMMUNITY" 140

III. "POLITICAL POWER IS RIGHTLY EXERCISED ONLY WHEN IT SUBSERVES THE WELFARE OF THE COMMUNITY BY MEANS WHICH THE MORAL LAW PERMITS" 142

CHAP. II.—CIVIL LIBERTY . 144
Loss of Liberty—War—Useless laws.

CHAP. III.—POLITICAL LIBERTY . 146
Political Liberty the right of a community—Public satisfaction.

CHAP. IV.—RELIGIOUS LIBERTY . 147
Civil disabilities—Interference of the Magistrate—Pennsylvania—Toleration—America—Creeds—Religious Tests—"The Catholic Question."

CHAP. V.—CIVIL OBEDIENCE . . 150
Expediency of Obedience—Obligations to Obedience—Extent of the Duty—Resistance to the Civil Power—Obedience may be withdrawn—King James—America—Non-compliance—Interference of the Magistrate—Oaths of Allegiance.

CHAP. VI.—FORMS OF GOVERNMENT 156
Some general principles—Monarchy—Balance of interests and passions—Changes in a constitution—Popular government—The world in a state of improvement—Character of legislators.

CHAP. VII.—POLITICAL INFLUENCE-PARTY—MINISTERIAL UNION . 160
Influence of the Crown—Effects of influence—Incongruity of public notions—Patronage—American States—Dependency on the mother country—Party—Ministerial Union—"A party man"—The council board and the senate—Resignation of offices.

CHAP. VIII.—BRITISH CONSTITUTION . 166
Influence of the Crown—House of Lords—Candidates for a peerage—Sudden creation of peers—The bench of Bishops—Proxies—House of Commons—The wishes of the People—Extension of the elective franchise—Universal suffrage—Frequent elections—Modes of election—Annual parliaments—Qualification of voters and representatives—Of choosing the clergy—Duties of a representative—Systematic opposition—Placemen and pensioners—Posthumous fame.

CHAP. IX.—MORAL LEGISLATION . . 176
Duties of a Ruler—The two objects of moral legislation—Education of the People—Bible Society—Lotteries—Public-houses—Abrogation of bad laws—Primogeniture—Accumulation of property.

CHAP. X.—ADMINISTRATION OF JUSTICE 181
Substitution of justice for law—Court of Chancery—Of fixed laws—Their inadequacy—They increase litigation—Delays—Expenses

CONTENTS.

Informalities — Precedents — Verdicts — Legal proof—Courts of arbitration—An extended system of arbitration—Arbitration in criminal trials—Constitution of courts of arbitration—Their effects—Some alterations suggested—Technicalities—Useless laws.

CHAP. XI.—OF THE PROPER SUBJECTS OF PENAL ANIMADVERSION . . . 190
Crimes regarded by the Civil and the Moral Law—Created offences—Seduction—Duelling — Insolvents — Criminal debtors — Gradations of guilt in Insolvency — Libels; mode of punishing—Effects of the laws respecting Libels—Effects of public censure Libels on the Government—Advantages of a free statement of the truth—Freedom of the Press.

CHAP. XII.—OF THE PROPER ENDS OF PUNISHMENT 200
The three Objects of Punishment: Reformation of the Offender: Example: Restitution—Punishment may be increased as well as diminished.

CHAP. XIII.—PUNISHMENT OF DEATH . 202
Of the three objects of punishment, the punishment of death regards but one—Reformation of minor offenders; Greater criminals neglected- Capital punishments not efficient as examples — Public executions — Paul—Grotius—Murder—The punishment of death irrevocable—Rousseau—Recapitulation.

CHAP. XIV.—RELIGIOUS ESTABLISHMENTS 207
The primitive church—The established church of Ireland—America—Advantages and disadvantages of established churches—Alliance of a church with the state — An established church perpetuates its own evils —Persecution generally the growth of religious establishments- State religions injurious to the civil welfare of a people— Legal provision for Christian teachers—Voluntary payment—Advancement in the church — The appointment of religious teachers.

CHAP. XV.—THE RELIGIOUS ESTABLISHMENTS OF ENGLAND AND IRELAND . 219
The English Church the offspring of the Reformation, the Church *establishment*, of Papacy—Alliance of Church and State—"The Priesthood averse from Reformation" —Noble Ecclesiastics—Purchase of advowsons—Non-residence — Pluralities — Parliamentary Returns—The Clergy fear to preach the truth—Moral Preaching—Recoil from Works of Philanthropy — Tithes — "The Church is in Danger"—The Church *establishment* is in danger — Monitory suggestion.

CHAP. XVI.—OF LEGAL PROVISION FOR CHRISTIAN TEACHERS. — OF VOLUNTARY PAYMENT, AND OF UNPAID MINISTRY 232
Compulsory payment—America—Legal provision for *one* church unjust—Payment of Tithes by dissenters—Tithes a "property of the church " — Voluntary payment — The system of remuneration—Qualifications of a minister of the gospel—Unpaid ministry—Days of greater purity.

CHAP. XVII.—PATRIOTISM . . . 239
Patriotism as it is viewed by Christianity—A Patriotism which is opposed to general benignity—Patriotism not the soldier's motive.

CHAP. XVIII.—SLAVERY 241
Requisitions of Christianity professedly disregarded—Persian law—The slave system a costly iniquity.

CHAP. XIX.—WAR 244
CAUSES OF WAR 245
Want of inquiry: Indifference to human misery: National irritability: Interest: Secret motives of Cabinets: Ideas of glory —Foundation of military glory.

CONSEQUENCES OF WAR . . . 250
Destruction of human life: Taxation: Moral depravity: Familiarity with plunder: Implicit submission to superiors: Resignation of moral agency: Bondage and degradation —Loan of armies—Effects on the community.

LAWFULNESS OF WAR 255
Influence of habit—Of appealing to antiquity —The Christian Scriptures — Subjects of Christ's benediction—Matt. xxvii. 52—The Apostles and Evangelists—The Centurion—Cornelius—Silence not a proof of approbation—Luke xxii. 36—John the Baptist—Negative evidence—Prophecies of the Old Testament—The requisitions of Christianity of present obligation—Primitive Christians —Example and testimony of the early Christians—Christian soldiers—Wars of the Jews —Duties of individuals and nations—Offensive and defensive war—Wars always aggressive—Paley—War *wholly* forbidden.

OF THE PROBABLE AND PRACTICAL EFFECTS OF ADHERING TO THE MORAL LAW IN RESPECT TO WAR . 272
Quakers in America and Ireland—Colonisation of Pennsylvania — Unconditional reliance on Providence—Recapitulation—General Observations.

CONCLUSION 277

APPENDIX . 279

INDEX . 283

ESSAY I.—PART I.

PRINCIPLES OF MORALITY.

CHAPTER I.
Moral Obligation.

Foundation of Moral Obligation.

1. There is little hope of proposing a definition of Moral Obligation which shall be satisfactory to every reader ; partly because the phrase is the representative of different notions in individual minds. No single definition can, it is evident, represent various notions ; and there are probably no means by which the notions of individuals respecting Moral Obligation can be adjusted to one standard. Accordingly, whilst attempts to define it have been very numerous, all probably have been unsatisfactory to the majority of mankind.

2. Happily this question, like many others upon which the world is unable to agree, is of little practical importance. Many who dispute about the definition, coincide in their judgments of what we are obliged to do and to forbear ; and so long as the individual knows that he is actually the subject of Moral Obligation, and actually responsible to a superior power, it is not of much consequence whether he can critically explain in what Moral Obligation consists.

3. The writer of these pages, therefore, makes no attempts at strictness of definition. It is sufficient for his purpose that man is under an obligation to obey his Creator ; and if any one curiously asks "Why ?"—he answers, that *one* reason at least is, that the Deity possesses the power, and evinces the intention, to call the human species to account for their actions, and to punish or reward them.

4. There may be, and I believe there are, higher grounds upon which a sense of Moral Obligation may be founded ; such as the love of goodness for its own sake, or love and gratitude to God for His beneficence : nor is it unreasonable to suppose that such grounds of obligation are especially approved by the Universal Parent of mankind.

CHAPTER II.
Standard of Right and Wrong.

The Will of God—Notices of theories—The communication of the Will of God—The supreme authority of the expressed Will of God—Causes of its practical rejection—The principles of expediency fluctuating and inconsistent—Application of the principles of expediency—Difficulties—Liability to abuse—Pagans.

5. It is obvious that to him who seeks the knowledge of his duty, the first inquiry is, What is the Rule of Duty ? What is the Standard of Right and Wrong ? Most men, or most of those with whom we are concerned, agree that this Standard consists in the Will of God. But here the coincidence of opinion stops. Various and very dissimilar answers are given to the question, How is the Will of God to be discovered ? These differences lead to differing conclusions respecting human duty. *All* the proposed modes of discovering His Will cannot be the best nor the right ; and those which are not right are likely to lead to erroneous conclusions respecting what His Will is.

6. It becomes therefore a question of very great interest—How is the Will of God to be discovered ? and if there should appear to be more sources than one from which it may be deduced—What is that source which, in our investigations, we are to regard as paramount to every other ?

The Will of God.

7. When we say that most men agree in referring to the Will of God as the Standard of Rectitude, we do not mean that all those who have framed systems of moral philosophy have set out with this proposition as their fundamental rule ; but we mean that the majority of mankind do really believe (with whatever indistinctness) that they *ought* to obey the Will of God ; and that, as it respects the systems of philosophical men, they will commonly be found to involve, directly or indirectly, the same belief. He who says that the "Understanding"[1] is to be our moral guide, is not far from saying that we

---

[1] Dr. Price : Review of Principal Questions in Morals.

are to be guided by the Divine Will, because the understanding, however we define it, is the offspring of the Divine counsels and power. When Adam Smith resolves moral obligation into propriety arising from feelings of "Sympathy,"[1] the conclusion is not very different; for these feelings are manifestly the result of that constitution which God gave to man. When Bishop Butler says that we ought to *live according to nature*, and make conscience the judge whether we do so live or not, a kindred observation arises, for the existence and nature of conscience must be referred ultimately to the Divine Will. Dr. Samuel Clarke's philosophy is, that moral obligation is to be referred to the *eternal and necessary differences of things*. This might appear less obviously to have respect to the Divine Will, yet Dr. Clarke himself subsequently says, that the duties which these eternal differences of things impose "are also the express and unalterable will, command, and law of God to His creatures, which He cannot but expect should be observed by them in obedience to His supreme authority."[2] Very similar is the practical doctrine of Wollaston. His theory is, that moral good and evil consist in *a conformity or disagreement with truth*—"*in treating everything as being what it is.*" But then he says, that to act by this rule "must be agreeable to the Will of God, and if so, the contrary must be disagreeable to it, and, since there must be perfect rectitude in His Will, certainly *wrong*."[3] It is the same with Dr. Paley in his far-famed doctrine of Expediency. "It is the *utility* of any action alone which constitutes the obligation of it;" but this very obligation is deduced from the Divine Benevolence; from which it is attempted to show that a regard to utility is enforced by the Will of God. Nay, he says expressly, "Every duty is a duty towards God, since it is *His Will* which *makes* it a duty."[4]

8. Now there is much value in these testimonies, direct or indirect, to the truth—that the Will of God is the Standard of Right and Wrong. The indirect testimonies are perhaps the more valuable of the two. He who gives undesigned evidence in favour of a proposition is less liable to suspicion in his motives.

9. But whilst we regard these testimonies, and such as these, as containing satisfactory evidence that the Will of God is our Moral Law, the intelligent inquirer will perceive that many of the proposed Theories are likely to lead to uncertain and unsatisfactory conclusions respecting what that Will requires.

[1] Theory of Moral Sentiments.
[2] Evidence of Natural and Revealed Religion.
[3] Religion of Nature Delineated.
[4] Moral and Political Philosophy.

They prove that His Will is the Standard, but they do not clearly inform us how we shall bring our actions into juxtaposition with it.

10. One proposes the *Understanding* as the means; but every observer perceives that the understandings of men are often contradictory in their decisions. Indeed, many of those who now think their understandings dictate the rectitude of a given action, will find that the understandings of the intelligent pagans of antiquity came to very different conclusions.

11. A second proposes *Sympathy*, regulated indeed and restrained, but still Sympathy. However ingenious a philosophical system may be, I believe that good men find, in the practice of life, that these emotions are frequently unsafe, and sometimes erroneous guides of their conduct. Besides, the emotions are to be regulated and restrained: which of itself intimates the necessity of a regulating and restraining, that is, of a *superior* power.

12. To say we should act according to the "eternal and necessary differences of things," is to advance a proposition which nine persons out of ten do not understand, and of course cannot adopt in practice; and of those who do understand it, perhaps an equal majority cannot apply it, with even tolerable facility, to the concerns of life. Why indeed should a writer propose these eternal differences, if he acknowledges that the rules of conduct which result from them are "the express will and command of God?"

13. To the system of a fourth, which says that virtue consists in a "conformity of our actions with truth," the objection presents itself—What is truth? or how, in the complicated affairs of life, and in the moment perhaps of sudden temptation, shall the individual discover what truth is?

14. Similar difficulties arise in applying the doctrine of *Utility* in "adjusting our actions so as to promote in the greatest degree the happiness of mankind." It is obviously *difficult* to apply this doctrine in practice. The welfare of mankind depends upon circumstances which, if it were possible, it is not *easy* to foresee. Indeed, in many of those conjunctures in which important decisions must instantly be made, the computation of tendencies to general happiness is wholly impracticable.

15. Besides these objections which apply to the systems separately, there is one which applies to them all—That they do not refer us *directly* to the Will of God. They interpose a medium, and it is the inevitable tendency of all such mediums to render the

truth uncertain. They depend not indeed upon hearsay evidence, but upon something of which the tendency is the same. They seek the Will of God not from positive evidence, but by implication; and we repeat the truth, that every medium that is interposed between the Divine Will and our estimates of it, diminishes the probability that we shall estimate it rightly.

16. These are considerations which, antecedently to all others, would prompt us to seek the Will of God directly and immediately; and it is evident that this direct and immediate knowledge of the Divine Will can in no other manner be possessed than by His own Communication of it.

The Communication of the Will of God.

17. That a direct communication of the Will of the Deity respecting the conduct which mankind shall pursue, must be very *useful* to them, can need little proof. It is sufficiently obvious that they who have had no access to the written revelations have commonly entertained very imperfect views of right and wrong. What Dr. Johnson says of the ancient epic poets will apply generally to pagan philosophers : They "were very unskilful teachers of virtue," *because* "they wanted the light of revelation." Yet these men were inquisitive and acute, and it may be supposed they would have discovered moral truth if sagacity and inquisitiveness had been sufficient for the task. But it is unquestionable that there are many ploughmen in this country who possess more accurate knowledge of morality than all the sages of antiquity. We do not indeed sufficiently consider for *how much* knowledge respecting the Divine Will we are indebted to His own Communication of it. "Many arguments, many truths, both moral and religious, which appear to us the products of our understandings, and the fruits of ratiocination, are in reality nothing more than emanations from Scripture ; rays of the Gospel imperceptibly transmitted, and as it were conveyed to our minds in a side-light."[1] Of Lord Herbert's book, *De Veritate*, which was designed to disprove the validity of Revelation, it is observed by the editor of his "Life," that it is "a book so strongly embued with the light of revelation relative to the moral virtues and a future life, that no man ignorant of the Scriptures or of the knowledge derived from them could have written it."[2] A modern system of moral philosophy is founded upon the duty of doing good to man, because it appears, from the *benevolence* of God Himself, that such is His Will. Did those philosophers then, who had no access to the written expression of His Will, discover with any distinctness this seemingly obvious *benevolence* of God? No. "The heathens failed of drawing that deduction relating to morality, to which, as we should now judge, the most obvious parts of natural knowledge, and such as certainly obtained among them, were sufficient to lead them, namely, the *goodness of God.*"[1] We are, I say, much more indebted to revelation for moral light than we commonly acknowledge, or indeed commonly perceive.

18. But if, in fact, we obtain from the *communication* of the Will of God knowledge of wider extent and of a higher order than was otherwise attainable, is it not an argument that that communicated Will should be our *supreme* law, and that, if any of the inferior means of acquiring moral knowledge lead to conclusions in opposition to that Will, they ought to give way to its higher authority ?

19. Indeed, the single circumstance that an Omniscient Being, and who also is the Judge of mankind, has expressed His Will respecting their conduct, appears a sufficient evidence that they should regard that expression as their paramount rule. They cannot elsewhere refer to so high an authority. If the *expression* of His Will is not the ultimate standard of right and wrong, it can only be on the supposition that His Will itself is not the ultimate standard ; for no other means of ascertaining that Will can be equally perfect and authoritative.

20. Another consideration is this, that if we examine those sacred volumes in which the written expression of the Divine Will is contained, we find that they habitually proceed upon the supposition that the Will of God being expressed, is *for that reason* our final law. They do not set about formal proofs that we ought to sacrifice inferior rules to it, but conclude, as of course, that if the Will of God is made known, human duty is ascertained. "It is not to be imagined that the Scriptures would refer to any other foundation of virtue than the true one, and certain it is that the foundation to which they constantly do refer is the *Will of God.*"[2] Nor is this all : they refer to the *expression* of the Will of God. We hear nothing of any other ultimate authority —nothing of " Sympathy"—nothing of the " eternal fitness of things"—nothing of the " production of the greatest sum of enjoyment ;"—but we hear, repeatedly, constantly, of the Will of God ; of the voice of God ; of the commands of God. To " be obedient unto *His voice,*"[3] is the condition of favour.

---

[1] Balguy : Tracts Moral and Theological :—Second Letter to a Deist.
[2] 4th Ed., p. 336.

[1] Pearson : Remarks on the Theory of Morals.
[2] Pearson : Theory of Mor., c. 1.   [3] Deut. iv. 30.

To hear the "*sayings of Christ* and do them,"[1] is the means of obtaining His approbation. To "fear God and keep *His commandments*, is the whole duty of man."[2] Even superior intelligences are described as "doing *His commandments*, hearkening unto the *voice of His word*."[3] In short, the whole system of moral legislation, as it is exhibited in Scripture, is a system founded upon *authority*. The *propriety*, the *utility* of the requisitions are not made of importance. That which *is* made of importance is, the authority of the Being who legislates. "Thus saith the Lord," is regarded as constituting a sufficient and a final law. So also is it with the moral instructions of Christ. "He put the truth of what He taught upon *authority*."[4] In the Sermon on the Mount, *I say unto you*, is proposed as the sole, and sufficient, and ultimate ground of obligation. He does not say, "My precepts will promote human happiness, therefore you are to obey them;" but He says, "They are *My* precepts, therefore you are to obey them." So habitually is this principle borne in mind, if we may so speak, by those who were commissioned to communicate the Divine Will, that the *reason* of a precept is not often assigned. The assumption evidently was, that the Divine Will was all that it was *necessary* for us to know. This is not the mode of enforcing duties which one man usually adopts in addressing another. He discusses the reasonableness of his advices and the advantages of following them, as well as, perhaps, the authority from which he derives them. The difference that exists between such a mode and that which is actually adopted in Scripture, is analogous to that which exists between the mode in which a parent communicates his instructions to a young child, and that which is employed by a tutor to an intelligent youth. The tutor recommends his instructions by their reasonableness and propriety: the father founds his upon his own authority. Not that the father's instructions are not also founded in propriety, but that this, in respect of young children, is not the ground upon which he expects their obedience. It is not the ground upon which God expects the obedience of man. We can, undoubtedly, in general perceive the wisdom of His laws, and it is doubtless right to seek out that wisdom; but whether we discover it or not, does not lessen their authority nor alter our duties.

21. In deference to these reasonings, then, we conclude, that the *communicated* Will of God is the Final Standard of Right and Wrong —that wheresoever this Will is made known, human duty is determined—and that neither the conclusions of philosophers, nor advantages, nor dangers, nor pleasures, nor sufferings, ought to have any opposing influence in regulating our conduct. Let it be remembered that in morals there can be no equilibrium of authority. If the expressed Will of the Deity is not our supreme rule, some other is superior. This fatal consequence is inseparable from the adoption of any other ultimate rule of conduct. The Divine law becomes the decision of a certain tribunal—the adopted rule, the decision of a superior tribunal—for that must needs be the superior which can reverse the decisions of the other. It is a consideration, too, which may reasonably alarm the inquirer, that if once we assume this power of dispensing with the Divine law, there is no limit to its exercise. If we may supersede one precept of the Deity upon one occasion, we may supersede every precept upon all occasions. Man becomes the greater authority, and God the less.

22. If a proposition is proved to be true, no contrary reasonings can show it to be false; and yet it is necessary to refer to such reasonings, not indeed for the sake of the truth, but for the sake of those whose conduct it should regulate. Their confidence in truth may be increased if they discover that the reasonings which assail it are fallacious. To a considerate man it will be no subject of wonder that the supremacy of the expressed Will of God is often not recognised in the writings of moralists or in the practice of life. The speculative inquirer finds, that of some of the questions which come before him, Scripture furnishes no solution, and he seeks for some principle by which all may be solved. This indeed is the ordinary course of those who erect systems, whether in morals or in physics. The moralist acknowledges, perhaps, the authority of revelation; but in his investigations he passes away from the precepts of revelation to some of those subordinate means by which human duties may be discovered—means which, however authorised by the Deity as subservient to His great purpose of human instruction, are wholly unauthorised as ultimate standards of right and wrong. Having fixed his attention upon these subsidiary means, he practically loses sight of the Divine law which he acknowledges; and thus without any formal, perhaps without any conscious, rejection of the expressed Will of God, he really makes it subordinate to inferior rules. Another influential motive to pass by the Divine precepts operates both upon writers and upon the public:—the rein which they hold upon the desires and passions of mankind, is more tight than they are willing to bear. Respecting some of these precepts we feel as the rich man of old felt: we hear the injunction and go away, if not with sorrow, yet without obedience. Here again is an obvious motive to the writer to endeavour to substitute some

[1] Matt. vii. 24. [2] Eccl. xii. 13. [3] Ps. ciii. 20.
[4] Paley: Evid. of Chris., p. 2, c. 2.

less rigid rule of conduct, and an obvious motive to the reader to acquiesce in it as true without a very rigid scrutiny into its foundation. To adhere with fidelity to the expressed Will of Heaven requires greater confidence in God than most men are willing to repose, or than most moralists are willing to recommend.

23. But whatever have been the causes, the fact is indisputable, that few or none of the systems of morality which have been offered to the world, have uniformly and consistently applied the communicated Will of God in determination of those questions to which it is applicable. Some insist upon its supreme authority in general terms ; others apply it in determining *some* questions of rectitude : but where is the work that applies it always ? Where is the moralist who holds everything, Ease, Interest, Reputation, Expediency, " Honour " personal and national—in subordination to this Moral Law ?

24. One source of ambiguity and of error in moral philosophy has consisted in the indeterminate use of the term " the Will of God." It is used without reference to the mode by which that will is to be discovered, and it is in this *mode* that the essence of the controversy lies. We are agreed that the Will of God is to be our rule : the question at issue is, What mode of discovering it should be primarily adopted ? Now the term, " the Will of God," has been applied, interchangeably, to the precepts of Scripture, and to the deductions which have been made from other principles. The consequence has been that the imposing sanction," the Will of God," has been applied to propositions of very different authority.

25. To inquire into the validity of all those principles which have been proposed as the standard of rectitude would be foreign to the purpose of this essay. That principle which appears to be most recommended by its own excellence and beauty, and which obtains the greatest share of approbation in the world, is the principle of directing "every action so as to produce the greatest happiness and the least misery in our power." The particular forms of defining the doctrine are various, but they may be conveniently included in the one general term—*Expediency*.

26. We say that the apparent beauty and excellence of this rule of action are so captivating, its actual acceptance in the world is so great, and the reasonings by which it is supported are so acute, that if it can be shown that *this* rule is not the ultimate standard of right and wrong, we may safely conclude that none other which philosophy has proposed can make pretensions to such authority. The truth indeed is, that the objections to the doctrine of *expediency* will generally be found to apply to *every* doctrine which lays claim to moral supremacy—which application the reader is requested to make for himself as he passes along.

27. Respecting the principle of *Expediency*—the doctrine that we should, in every action, endeavour to produce the greatest sum of human happiness—let it always be remembered that the only question is, whether it ought to be the *paramount* rule of human conduct. No one doubts whether it ought to influence us, or whether it is of great importance in estimating the duties of morality. The sole question is this :—When an expression of the Will of God, and *our* calculations respecting human happiness, lead to different conclusions respecting the rectitude of an action—whether of the two shall we prefer and obey ?

28. We are concerned only with Christian writers. Now, when we come to analyse the principles of the Christian advocates of Expediency, we find precisely the resu't which we should expect—a perpetual vacillation between two irreconcilable doctrines. As Christians, they necessarily acknowledge the authority, and, in words at least, the *supreme* authority of the Divine Law : as advocates of the universal application of the law of Expediency, they necessarily sometimes set aside the Divine Law, because they sometimes cannot deduce, from both laws, the same rule of action. Thus there is induced a continual fluctuation and uncertainty both in principles and in practical rules : a continual endeavour to "serve two masters."

29. Of these fluctuations an example is given in the article "Moral Philosophy" in Rees's Encyclopædia—an article in which the principles of Hartley are in a considerable degree adopted. "The Scripture precepts," says the writer, "are in themselves the rule of life."—"The supposed tendency of actions can never be put against the law of God as delivered to us by revelation, and should not therefore be made our chief guide." This is very explicit. Yet the same article says that the first great rule is, that "we should aim to direct every action so as to produce the greatest happiness and the least misery in our power." This rule, however, is somewhat difficult of application, and therefore " instead of this most general rule, we must *substitute* others, less general and *subordinate* to it :" of which subordinate rules, to "obey the *Scripture precepts*" is one ! I do not venture to presume that these writers do really mean what their words appear to mean—that the law of God is supreme and yet that it is subordinate ; but one thing is perfectly clear, that either they make the vain attempt to "serve two masters," or that they employ language very laxly and very dangerously.

30. The high language of Dr. Paley respecting *Expediency* as a paramount law is well known :—" *Whatever* is expedient is right."[1] —" The obligation of *every* law depends upon its ultimate utility."[2]—"It is the utility of any moral rule *alone* which constitutes the obligation of it."[3] Perjury, Robbery, and Murder, "are not useful, and for that reason, and that reason *only*, are not right."[4] It is obvious that this language affirms that utility is a higher authority than the expressed Will of God. If the utility of a moral rule *alone* constitutes the obligation of it, then is its obligation not constituted by the Divine command. If murder is wrong *only* because it is not useful, it is not wrong because God has said, "Thou shalt not kill."

31. But Paley was a Christian, and therefore could neither *formally* displace the Scripture precepts from their station of supremacy, nor avoid *formally* acknowledging that they were supreme. Accordingly he says, "There are two methods of coming at the Will of God on any point : First, By His *express declarations*, when they are to be had, and which must be sought for in Scripture."[5] Secondly, By *Expediency*. And again, When Scripture precepts "are clear and positive, there is an end to all further deliberation."[6] This makes the expressed Will of God the final standard of right and wrong. And here is the vacillation, the attempt to serve two masters of which we speak : for this elevation of the express declarations of God to the supremacy, is absolutely incompatible with the doctrines that are quoted in the preceding paragraph.

32. These incongruities of principle are sometimes brought into operation in framing practical rules. In the chapter on Suicide it is shown that *Scripture* disallows the act. Here then we might conclude that there was "an end to all further deliberation ;" and yet, in the same chapter, we are told that suicide would nevertheless be justifiable *if it were expedient.* Respecting Civil Obedience he says, the *Scriptures* "inculcate the duty" and "enforce the obligation ;" but notwithstanding this, he pronounces that the "*only* ground of the subjects' obligation" consists in *Expediency.*[7] If it consists only in expediency, the Divine law upon the subject is a dead letter. In one chapter he says that murder would be right if it was useful ;[8] in another, that "one word" of prohibition "from Christ is *final.*"[9] The words of Christ cannot be final if we are afterwards to inquire whether murder is "useful" or not. One other illustration will suffice. In laying down the rights of the magistrate as to making laws respecting religion, he makes *Utility* the ultimate standard ; so that whatever the magistrate thinks it *useful* to ordain, that he has a *right* to ordain. But in stating the subjects' duties as to obeying laws respecting religion, he makes the *commands of God* the ultimate standard.[1] ,The consequence is inevitable that it is *right* for the magistrate to command an act, and r*ight* for the subject to refuse to obey it. In a sound system of morality such contradictions would be impossible. There is a contradiction even in terms. In one place he says, " *Wherever* there is a right in one person, there is a *corresponding obligation* upon others."[2] In another place, " The right of the magistrate to ordain, and the obligation of the subject to obey, in matters of religion, may be *very different.*"[3]

33. Perhaps the reader will say that these inconsistencies, however they may impeach the skilfulness of the writer, do not prove that his system is unsound, or that Utility is not still the ultimate standard of rectitude. We answer, that to a Christian writer such inconsistencies are unavoidable. He is obliged, in conformity with the principles of his religion, to acknowledge the Divine, and therefore the *supreme* authority of Scripture ; and if, in addition to this, he assumes that any other is supreme, inconsistency must ensue. For the same consequence follows the adoption of any other ultimate standard —whether sympathy, or right reason, or eternal fitness, or nature. If the writer is a Christian, he cannot, without falling into inconsistencies, assert the supremacy of any of these princip'es : that is to say, when the precepts of Scripture dictate one action, and a reasoning from his principle dictates another, he must make his election. If he prefers his principle, Christianity is abandoned : if he prefers Scripture, his principle is subordinate : if he alternately prefers the one and the other, he falls into the vacillation and inconsistency of which we speak.

34. Bearing still in mind that the rule "to endeavour to produce the greatest happiness in our power" is objectionable only when it is made an *ultimate* rule, the reader is invited to attend to these short considerations.

35. I. In computing human happiness, the advocate of Expediency does not sufficiently take into the account our happiness in futurity. Nor indeed does he always take it into account at all. One definition says, "The test of the morality of an act is its tendency to promote the *temporal* advantage

---

[1] Mor. and Pol. Phil., B. 2, c. 6. [2] B. 6, c. 12.
[3] B. 2, c. 6. [4] B. 2, c. 6.
[5] Mor. and Pol. Phil., B. 2, c. 4. [6] B. 2, c. 4 ; Note.
[7] B. 6, c. 3. [8] B. 2, c. 6. [9] B. 3, p. 3, c. 2.

[1] B. 6, p. 3, c. 10. [2] B. 2, c. 9. [3] B. 6, p. 3, c. 10.

of the greatest number in the society to which we belong." Now many things may be very expedient if death were annihilation, which may be very inexpedient now ; and therefore it is not unreasonable to expect, nor an unreasonable exercise of humility to act upon the expectation, that the Divine laws may sometimes impose obligations of which we do not perceive the expediency or the use. " It may so fall out," says Hooker, " that the reason why some laws of God were given, is neither opened nor possible to be gathered by the wit of man."[1] And Pearson says, " There are many parts of morality, as taught by revelation, which are entirely independent of an accurate knowledge of nature."[2] And Gisborne, " Our experience of God's dispensations by no means permits us to affirm that He always thinks fit to act in such a manner as is productive of particular expediency ; much less to conclude that He wills us always to act in such a manner as *we* suppose would be productive of it."[3] All this sufficiently indicates that Expediency is wholly inadmissible as an *ultimate* rule.

36. II. The doctrine is altogether unconnected with the Christian revelation, or with any revelation from heaven. It was just as true, and the deductions from it just as obligatory, two or five thousand years ago as now. The alleged supreme law of morality— "Whatever is expedient is right"—might have been taught by Epictetus as well as by a modern Christian. But are we then to be told that the revelations from the Deity have conveyed no moral knowledge to man? that they make no act obligatory which was not obligatory before ? that he who had the fortune to discover that "whatever is expedient is right," possessed a moral law just as perfect as that which God has ushered into the world, and much more comprehensive ?

37. III. If some subordinate rule of conduct were proposed—some principle which served as an auxiliary moral guide—I should not think it a valid objection to its truth, to be told that no sanction of the principle was to be found in the written revelation ; but if some rule of conduct were proposed as being of *universal* obligation, some moral principle which was paramount to every other—and I discovered that this principle was unsanctioned by the written revelation, I should think this want of sanction was conclusive evidence against it ; because it is not credible that a revelation from God, of which one great object was to teach mankind the moral law of God, would have been silent respecting a rule of conduct which was to be an universal guide to man. We apply these considerations to the doctrine of Expediency : *Scripture contains not a word upon the subject.*

38. IV. The principles of Expediency necessarily proceed upon the supposition that we are to investigate the future, and this investigation is, as every one knows, peculiarly without the limits of human sagacity : an objection which derives additional force from the circumstance that an action, in order to be expedient, " must be expedient on the whole, at the long-run, in all its effects, collateral and remote."[1] I do not know whether, if a man should sit down expressly to devise a moral principle which should be uncertain and difficult in its application, he could devise one that would be more difficult and uncertain than this. So that, as Dr. Paley himself acknowledges, " It is impossible to ascertain every duty by an immediate reference to public utility."[2] The reader may therefore conclude with Dr. Johnson, that " by presuming to determine what is fit and what is beneficial, they presuppose more knowledge of the universal system than man has attained, and therefore depend upon principles too complicated and extensive for our comprehension : and *there can be no security in the consequence when the premises are not understood.*"[3]

39. V. But whatever may be the propriety of investigating all consequences, " collateral and remote," it is certain that such an investigation is possible only in that class of moral questions which allows a man time to sit down and deliberately to think and compute. As it respects that large class of cases in which a person must decide and act in a moment, it is wholly useless. There are thousands of conjunctures in life in which a man can no more stop to calculate effects collateral and remote than he can stop to cross the Atlantic ; and it is difficult to conceive that any rule of morality can be absolute and universal which is totally inapplicable to so large a portion of human affairs.

40. VI. Lastly, the rule of Expediency is deficient in one of the first requisites of a moral law—obviousness and palpability of *sanction.* What is the process by which the sanction is applied ? Its advocates say, the Deity is a Benevolent Being : as He is benevolent Himself, it is reasonable to conclude He wills that His creatures should be benevolent to one another : this benevolence is to be exercised by adapting every action to the promotion of the " universal interest " of man : " Whatever is expedient is right :" or, God wills that we should consult Expediency. Now we say that there are so many considerations placed between the rule

[1] Eccles. Polity, B. 3, s. 10. [2] Theory of Morals, c. 3.
[3] Principles of Mor. Phil.

[1] Mor. and Pol. Phil., B. 2, c. 8. [2] B. 6, c. 12.
[3] Western Isles.

and the act, that the practical authority of the rule is greatly diminished. It is easy to perceive that the authority of a rule will not come home to that man's mind who is told, respecting a given action, that its effect upon the universal interest is the only thing that makes it right or wrong. All the doubts that arise as to this effect are so many diminutions of the sanction. It is like putting half a dozen new contingencies between the act of thieving and the conviction of a jury; and every one knows that the want of certainty of penalty is a great encouragement to offences. The principle too is liable to the most extravagant abuse—or rather extravagant abuse is, in the present condition of mankind, inseparable from its general adoption. "Whatever is expedient is right," soliloquises the moonlight adventurer into the poultry-yard : "it will tend more to the sum of human happiness that my wife and I should dine on a capon, than that the farmer should feel the satisfaction of possessing it ;"—and so he mounts the hen-roost. I do not say that this hungry moralist would reason soundly, but I say that he would not listen to the philosophy which replied, "Oh, your reasoning is incomplete : you must take into account all consequences collateral and remote; and then you will find that it is more expedient, upon the whole and at the long-run, that you and your wife should be hungry, than that hen-roosts should be insecure."

41. It is happy, however, that this principle never *can* be generally applied to the private duties of man. Its abuses would be so enormous that the laws would take, as they do in fact take, better measures for regulating men's conduct than this doctrine supplies. And happily, too, the Universal Lawgiver has not left mankind without more distinct and more influential perceptions of His Will and His authority than they could ever derive from the principles of Expediency.

42. But an objection has probably presented itself to the reader, that the greater part of mankind have no access to the written expression of the Will of God ; and how, it may be asked, can that be the final standard of right and wrong for the human race, of which the majority of the race have never heard ? The question is reasonable and fair.

43. We answer then, first, that supposing most men to be destitute of a communication of the Divine Will, it does not affect the obligations of those who do possess it. That communication is the final law to me, whether my African brother enjoys it or not. Every reason by which the supreme authority of the law is proved, is just as applicable to those who do enjoy the communication of it, whether that communication is enjoyed by many or by few ; and this, so far as the argument is concerned, appears to be a sufficient answer. If any man has no direct access to his Creator's will, let him have recourse to "eternal fitnesses," or to "expediency ;" but his condition does not affect that of another man who does possess this access.

44. But our real reply to the objection is, that they who are destitute of Scripture are not destitute of a direct communication of the Will of God. The proof of this position must be deferred to a subsequent chapter ; and the reader is solicited for the present to allow us to assume its truth. This direct communication may be limited, it may be incomplete, but some communication exists; enough to assure them that some things are acceptable to the Supreme Power, and that some are not; enough to indicate a distinction between right and wrong ; enough to make them moral agents, and reasonably accountable to our Common Judge. If these principles are true, and especially if the amount of the communication is in many cases considerable, it is obvious that it will be of great value in the direction of individual conduct. We say of *individual* conduct, because it is easy to perceive that it would not often subserve the purposes of him who frames public rules of morality. A person may possess a satisfactory assurance in his own mind that a given action is inconsistent with the Divine Will, but that assurance is not conveyed to another, unless he participates in the evidence upon which it is founded. That which is wanted in order to supply public rules for human conduct is a publicly avouched authority ; so that a writer, in deducing those rules, has to apply, ultimately, to that Standard which God has publicly sanctioned.

CHAPTER III.

Subordinate Standards of Right and Wrong.

Foundation and limits of the authority of subordinate moral rules.

45. The written expression of the Divine Will does not contain, and no writings can contain, directions for our conduct in every circumstance of life. If the precepts of Scripture were multiplied a hundred or a thousand fold, there would still arise a multiplicity of questions to which none of them would specifically apply. Accordingly, there are some subordinate authorities, to which, as can be satisfactorily shown, it is the Will of God that we should refer. He who does

AUTHORITY OF MORAL AND RELIGIOUS OBLIGATIONS.

refer to them, and regulate his conduct by them, conforms to the Will of God.

46. To a son who is obliged to regulate all his actions by his father's will, there are two ways in which he may practise obedience—one, by receiving upon each subject his father's direct instructions; and the other, by receiving instructions from those whom his father commissions to teach him. The parent may appoint a governor, and enjoin that upon all questions of a certain kind the son shall conform to his instructions; and if the son does this, he as truly and really performs his father's will, and as strictly makes that will the guide of his conduct, as if he received the instructions immediately from his parent. But if the father have laid down certain general rules for his son's observance, as that he shall devote ten hours a day to study, and not less—although the governor should recommend or even command him to devote fewer hours, he may not comply; for if he does, the governor, and not his father, is his supreme guide. The subordination is destroyed.

47. This case illustrates, perhaps, with sufficient precision, the situation of mankind with respect to moral rules. Our Creator has given direct laws, some general, and some specific. These are of final authority. But he has also sanctioned or permitted an application to other rules; and in conforming to these, so long as we hold them in subordination to His laws, we perform His will.

48. Of these subordinate rules it were possible to enumerate many. Perhaps, indeed, few principles have been proposed as "the fundamental Rules of Virtue" which may not rightly be brought into use by the Christian in regulating his conduct in life; for the objection to many of these principles is not so much that they are useless, as that they are unwarranted as *paramount* laws. "Sympathy" may be of use, and "Nature" may be of use, and "Self-love" and "Benevolence;" and to those who know what it means, "Eternal fitnesses" too.

49. Some of the subordinate rules of conduct it will be proper hereafter to notice, in order to discover, if we can, how far their authority extends, and where it ceases. The observations that we shall have to offer upon them may conveniently be made under these heads: The Law of the Land, The Law of Nature, The Promotion of Human Happiness or Expediency, The Law of Nations, The Law of Honour.

50. These observations will, however, necessarily be preceded by an inquiry into the great principles of human duty as they are delivered in Scripture, and into the reality of that communication of the Divine Will to the mind, which the reader has been requested to allow us to assume.

CHAPTER IV.

Collateral Observations.

The reader is requested to regard the present chapter as parenthetical. The parenthesis is inserted here, because the writer does not know where more appropriately to place it.

Identical Authority of Moral and Religious Obligations.

Identical authority of moral and religious obligations—The Divine Attributes—Of deducing rules of human duty from a consideration of the attributes of God—Virtue: "Virtue is conformity with the standard of rectitude"—Motives of action.

51. This *identity* is a truth to which we do not sufficiently advert either in our habitual sentiments or in our practice. There are many persons who speak of *religious* duties, as if there was something sacred or imperative in their obligation that does not belong to duties of morality—many who would perhaps offer up their lives rather than profess a belief in a false religious dogma, but who would scarcely sacrifice an hour's gratification rather than violate the moral law of love. It is therefore of importance to remember that *the authority which imposes moral obligations and religious obligations is one and the same*—the Will of God. Fidelity to God is just as truly violated by a neglect of His moral laws as by a compromise of religious principles. Religion and Morality are abstract terms, employed to indicate different classes of those duties which the Deity has imposed upon mankind; but they are all imposed by Him, and all are enforced by equal authority. Not indeed that the violation of every particular portion of the Divine Will involves equal guilt, but that each violation is equally a disregard of the Divine Authority. Whether, therefore, fidelity be required to a point of doctrine or of practice, to theology or to morals, the obligation is the same. It is the Divine requisition which constitutes this obligation, and not the nature of the duty required; so that, whilst I think a Protestant does no more than his duty when he prefers death to a profession of the Roman Catholic faith, I think also that every Christian who believes that Christ has prohibited swearing, does no more than his duty when he prefers death to taking an oath.

52. I would especially solicit the reader to bear in mind this principle of the identity of the authority of moral and religious obliga-

tions, because he may otherwise imagine that, in some of the subsequent pages, the obligation of a moral law is too strenuously insisted on, and that fidelity to it is to be purchased at "too great a sacrifice" of ease and enjoyment.

The Divine Attributes.

53. The purpose for which a reference is here made to these sacred subjects, is to remark upon the unfitness of attempting to deduce human duties from the attributes of God. It is not indeed to be affirmed that no illustration of those duties can be derived from them, but that they are too imperfectly cognisable by our perceptions to enable us to refer to them for specific moral rules. The truth indeed is, that we do not accurately and distinctly know what the Divine Attributes are. We say that God is merciful; but if we attempt to define, with strictness, what the term merciful means, we shall find it a difficult, perhaps an impracticable task; and especially we shall have a difficult task if, after the definition, we attempt to reconcile every appearance which presents itself in the world, with our notions of the attribute of mercy. I would speak with reverence when I say that *we* cannot always *perceive* the mercifulness of the Deity in His administrations, either towards His rational or His irrational creation. So, again, in respect of the attribute of Justice, who can determinately define in what this attribute consists? Who, especially, can *prove* that the Almighty designs that *we* should always be able to trace His justice in His government? We believe that He is unchangeable; but what is the sense in which we understand the term? Do we mean that the attribute involves the necessity of an unchanging system of moral government, or that the Deity cannot make alterations in, or additions to, His laws for mankind? We cannot mean this, for the evidence of revelation disproves it.

54. Now, if it be true that the Divine Attributes, and the uniform accordancy of the Divine dispensations with our notions of those attributes, are not sufficiently within our powers of investigation to enable us to frame accurate premises for our reasoning, it is plain that we cannot always trust with safety to our conclusions. We cannot deduce rules for our conduct from the Divine Attributes without being very *liable* to error ; and the liability will increase in proportion as the deduction attempts critical accuracy.

55. Yet this is a rock upon which the judgments of many have suffered wreck, a quicksand where many have been involved in inextricable difficulties. One, because he cannot reconcile the commands to exterminate a people with his notions of the attribute of mercy, questions the truth of the Mosaic writings. One, because he finds wars permitted by the Almighty of old, concludes that, as He is unchangeable, they cannot be incompatible with His present or His future Will. One, on the supposition of this unchangeableness, perplexes himself because the dispensations of God and His laws have been changed; and vainly labours, by classifying these laws into those which result from His attributes, and those which do not, to vindicate the immutability of God. We have no business with these things, and I will venture to affirm that he who will take nothing upon trust—who will exercise no faith—who will believe in the Divine authority of no rule, and in the truth of no record, which *he* is unable to reconcile with the Divine Attributes—must be consigned to hopeless Pyrrhonism.

56. The lesson which such considerations teach is a simple but an important one : that our exclusive business is to discover the actual present Will of God, without inquiring why His Will is such as it is, or why it has ever been different; and without seeking to deduce, from our notions of the Divine Attributes, rules of conduct which are more safely and more certainly discovered by other means.

Virtue.

57. The definitions which have been proposed of Virtue have necessarily been both numerous and various, because many and discordant standards of rectitude have been advanced ; and Virtue must, in every man's system, essentially consist in conforming the conduct to the standard which he thinks is the true one. This must be true of those systems, at least, which make Virtue consist in doing right. Adam Smith indeed says that "Virtue is excellence ; something uncommonly great and beautiful, which rises far above what is vulgar and ordinary."[1] By which it would appear that Virtue is a relative quality, depending not upon some perfect or permanent standard, but upon the existing practice of mankind. Thus the action which possessed no Virtue amongst a good community, might possess much in a bad one. The practice which "rose far above" the ordinary practice of one nation, might be quite common in another ; and if mankind should become much worse than they are now, that conduct would be eminently virtuous amongst them which now is not virtuous at all. That such a definition of Virtue is likely to lead to very imperfect practice is plain ; for what is the

[1] Theo. Mor. Sent.

probability that a man will attain to that standard which God proposes, if his utmost estimate of Virtue rises no higher than to an indeterminate superiority over other men.

58. Our definition of Virtue necessarily accords with the Principles of Morality which have been advanced in the preceding chapter : *Virtue is conformity with the Standard of Rectitude;* which standard consists, primarily, in the expressed Will of God.

59. Virtue, as it respects the meritoriousness of the agent, is another consideration. The quality of an action is one thing, the desert of the agent is another. The business of him who illustrates moral rules is not with the agent, but with the act. He must state what the moral law pronounces to be right and wrong : but it is very possible that an individual may do what is right without any Virtue, because there may be no rectitude in his motives and intentions. He does a virtuous act, but he is not a virtuous agent.

60. Although the concern of a work like the present is evidently with the moral character of actions, without reference to the motives of the agent ; yet the remark may be allowed, that there is frequently a sort of inaccuracy and unreasonableness in the judgments which we form of the deserts of other men. We regard the act too much, and the intention too little. The footpad who discharges a pistol at a traveller and fails in his aim, is just as wicked as if he had killed him ; yet we do not feel the same degree of indignation at his crime. So, too, of a person who does good. A man who plunges into a river and saves a child from drowning, impresses the parents with a stronger sense of his deserts than if, with the same exertions, he had failed. We should endeavour to correct this inequality of judgment, and in forming our estimates of human conduct, should refer, much more than we commonly do, to what the agent *intends.* It should habitually be borne in mind, and especially with reference to our *own* conduct, that to have been unable to execute an ill intention deducts nothing from our guilt ; and that at that tribunal where intention and action will be both regarded, it will avail little if we can only say that we have *done* no evil. Nor let it be less remembered, with respect to those who desire to do good but have not the power, that their Virtue is not diminished by their want of ability. I ought, perhaps, to be as grateful to the man who feelingly commiserates my sufferings but cannot relieve them, as to him who sends me money or a physician. The mite of the widow of old was estimated even more highly than the greater offerings of the rich.

CHAPTER V.

Scripture.

The morality of the Patriarchal, Mosaic, and Christian dispensations—Their moral requisitions not always coincident—Supremacy of the Christian morality—Of variations in the Moral Law Mode of applying the precepts of Scripture to questions of duty—No formal moral system in Scripture—Criticism of Biblical morality—Of particular precepts and general rules—Matt. vii. 12 - 1 Cor. x. 31—Rom. iii. 8—Benevolence as it is proposed in the Christian Scriptures.

The Morality of the Patriarchal, Mosaic, and Christian Dispensations.

61. One of the very interesting considerations which are presented to an inquirer in perusing the volume of Scripture, consists in the *variations* in its morality. There are three distinctly defined periods, in which the moral government and laws of the Deity assume, in some respects, a different character. In the first, without any system of external instruction, He communicated His Will to some of our race, either immediately or through a superhuman messenger. In the second, He promulgated, through Moses, a distinct and extended code of laws, addressed peculiarly to a selected people. In the third, Jesus Christ and His commissioned ministers delivered precepts, of which the general character was that of greater purity or perfection, and of which the obligation was universal upon mankind.

62. That the records of all these dispensations contain declarations of the Will of God is certain : that their moral requisitions are not always coincident is also certain ; and hence the conclusion becomes inevitable, that *to us* one is of primary authority :—that when all do not coincide, one is paramount to the others. That a coincidence does not always exist may easily be shown. It is manifest, not only by a comparison of precepts and of the general tenor of the respective records, but from the express declarations of Christianity itself.

63. One example, referring to the Christian and Jewish dispensations, may be found in the extension of the law of Love. Christianity, in extending the application of this law, requires us to abstain from that which the law of Moses permitted us to do. Thus it is in the instance of duties to our "neighbour," as they are illustrated in the parable of the Samaritan.[1] Thus, too, in the Sermon on the Mount : " It hath been said *by them of old time,* Thou shalt love thy neighbour and hate thine enemy ; but *I* say unto you, Love your enemies."[2] It is indeed some-

[1] Luke x. 30.   [2] Matt. v. 43.

times urged that the words "hate thine enemy," were only a gloss of the expounders of the law: but Grotius writes thus—"What is there repeated as said to those of old, are *not* the words of the teachers of the law, but of Moses, either literally or in their meaning. They are cited by our Saviour as his express words, not as interpretations of them."[1] If the authority of Grotius should not satisfy the reader, let him consider such passages as this: "An Ammonite or a Moabite shall not enter into the congregation of the Lord. Because they met you not with bread and with water in the way, when ye came forth out of Egypt. *Thou shalt not seek their peace nor their prosperity* all thy days for ever."[2] This is not coincident with, "*Love* your enemies," or with "*Do good* to them that hate you," or with that temper which is recommended by the words, "To him that smiteth thee on one cheek, turn the other also."[3]

64. "Pour out Thy fury upon the heathen that know Thee not, and upon the families that call not on Thy name,"[4] is not coincident with the reproof of Christ to those who, upon similar grounds, would have called down fire from heaven.[5] "The Lord look upon it and require it,"[6] is not coincident with, "Lord, lay not this sin to their charge."[7] "Let me see Thy vengeance on them,"[8]—"Bring upon them the day of evil, and destroy them with double destruction,"[9]—is not coincident with "Forgive them, for they know not what they do."[10]

Similar observations apply to Swearing, to Polygamy, to Retaliation, to the *motives* of murder and adultery.

65. And as to the express assertion of the want of coincidence:—"The *law* made nothing perfect, but the bringing in of a *better hope* did."[11] "There is verily a disannulling of the commandment going before, *for the weakness and unprofitableness* thereof."[12] If the commandment now existing is not weak and unprofitable, it must be because it is superior to that which existed before.

66. But although this appears to be thus clear with respect to the Jewish dispensation, there are some who regard the moral precepts which were delivered before the period of that dispensation, as imposing permanent obligations: they were delivered, it is said, not to one peculiar people, but to individuals of many; and, in the persons of the immediate survivors of the deluge, to the whole human race. This argument assumes a ground paramount to all questions of subsequent abrogation. Now it would appear a sufficient answer to say—If the precepts of the Patriarchal and Christian dispensations are coincident, no question needs to be discussed; if they are not, we *must* make an election; and surely the Christian cannot doubt what election he should make. Could a Jew have justified himself for violating the Mosaic law by urging the precepts *delivered* to the patriarchs? No. Neither then can we justify ourselves for violating the Christian law by urging the precepts delivered to Moses.

67. We indeed have, if it be possible, still stronger motives. The moral law of Christianity binds us, not merely because it is the *present* expression of the Will of God, but because it is a portion of His *last* dispensation to man—of that which is avowedly not only the last, but the highest and the best. We do not find in the records of Christianity that which we find in the other Scriptures, a reference to a greater and purer dispensation yet to come. It is as true of the Patriarchal as of the Mosaic institution that "it made nothing perfect," and that it referred us from the first to "the bringing in of that better hope which did." If then the question of supremacy is between a perfect and an imperfect system, who will hesitate in his decision?

68. There are motives of gratitude, too, and of affection, as well as of reason. The clearer exhibition which Christianity gives of the attributes of God, its distinct disclosure of our immortal destinies, and above all, its wonderful discovery of the *love* of our Universal Father, may well give to the moral law with which they are connected an authority which may supersede every other.

69. These considerations are of practical importance; for it may be observed of those who do not advert to them, that they sometimes refer indiscriminately to the Old Testament or the New, without any other guide than the apparent greater applicability of a precept in the one or the other to their present need; and thus it happens that a rule is sometimes acted upon less perfect than that by which it is the good pleasure of God we should now regulate our conduct. It is a fact which the reader should especially notice, that *an appeal to the Hebrew Scriptures is frequently made when the precepts of Christianity would be too rigid for our purpose.* He who insists upon a pure morality, applies to the New Testament: he who desires a little more indulgence, defends himself by arguments from the Old.

70. Of this indiscriminate reference to all the dispensations, there is an extraordinary example in the newly discovered work of Milton. He appeals, I believe, almost uniformly to

---

[1] Rights of War and Peace. [2] Deut. xxiii. 3, 4, 6.
[3] Matt. v. 39. [4] Jer. x. 25.
[5] Luke ix. 54. [6] 2 Chron. xxiv. 22.
[7] Acts vii. 60. [8] Jer. xx. 12.
[9] Jer. xvii. 18. [10] Luke xxiii. 34.
[11] Heb. vii. 19. [12] Heb. vii. 18.

the precepts of all, as of equal present obligation. The consequence is what might be expected—his moral system is not *consistent*. Nor is it to be forgotten, that in defending what may be regarded as less pure doctrines, he refers mostly, or exclusively, to the Hebrew Scriptures. In all his disquisitions to prove the lawfulness of untruths, he does not once refer to the New Testament.[1] Those who have observed the prodigious multiplicity of texts which he cites in this work will peculiarly appreciate the importance of the fact. Again: "Hatred," he says, "is in some cases a religious duty."[2] A proposition at which the Christian may reasonably wonder. And how does Milton prove its truth? He cites from Scripture *ten* passages, of which eight are from the Old Testament and two from the New. The reader will be curious to know what these two are:—"If any man come to Me, and *hate* not his father and mother, he cannot be My disciple."[3] And the rebuke to Peter: "Get thee behind Me, Satan."[4] The citation of such passages shows that no passages to the purpose could be found.

71. It may be regarded therefore as a general rule, that none of the injunctions or permissions which formed a part of the former dispensations can be referred to as of authority to us, except so far as they are coincident with the Christian law. To our own Master we stand or fall, and our Master is Christ. And in estimating this coincidence, it is not requisite to show that a given rule or permission of the former dispensations is *specifically* superseded in the New Testament. It is sufficient if it is not accordant with the general spirit; and this consideration assumes greater weight when it is connected with another which is hereafter to be noticed— that it is by the general spirit of the Christian morality that many of the duties of man are to be discovered.

72. Yet it is always to be remembered, that the laws which are thus superseded were, nevertheless, the laws of God. Let not the reader suppose that we would speak or feel respecting them otherwise than with that reverence which their origin demands, or that we would take anything from their present obligation but that which is taken by the Lawgiver Himself. It may indeed be observed, that in all His dispensations there is a harmony, a one pervading principle, which, without other evidence, indicates that they proceeded from the same authority. The variations are circumstantial rather than fundamental; and, after all, the great principles in which they accord far outweigh the particular applications in which they differ.

[1] Christian Doctrine, p. 660. [2] P. 641.
[3] Luke xiv. 26. [4] Mark viii. 33.

The Mosaic dispensation was "a schoolmaster" to bring us, not merely through the medium of types and prophecies, but through its moral law, to Christ. Both the one and the other were designed as preparatives; and it was probably as true of these moral laws as of the Prophecies, that the Jews did not perceive their relationship to Christianity as it was actually introduced into the world.

73. Respecting the variations of the moral law, some persons greatly and very needlessly perplex themselves by indulging in such questions as these. "If," say they, "God be perfect, and if all the dispensations are communications of His Will, how happens it that they are not uniform in their requisitions? How happens it that that which was required by Infinite Knowledge at one time was not required by Infinite Knowledge at another?" I answer—I cannot tell. And what then? Does the inquirer think this a sufficient reason for rejecting the authority of the Christian law? If inability to discover the reasons of the moral government of God be a good motive to doubt its authority, we may involve ourselves in doubts without end. Why does a Being who is infinitely pure permit moral evil in the world? Why does He who is perfectly benevolent permit physical suffering? Why did He suffer our first parents to fall? Why, after they had fallen, did He not *immediately* repair the loss? Why was the Messiah's appearance deferred for four thousand years? Why is not the religion of the Messiah universally known and universally operative at the present day? To all these questions and to many others, no answer can be given: and the difficulty arising from them is as great, if we choose to make difficulties for ourselves, as that which arises from variations in His moral laws. Even in infidelity we shall find no rest: the objections lead us onward to atheism. He who will not believe in a Deity unless he can reconcile all the facts before his eyes with his notions of the Divine Attributes, must deny that a Deity exists. I talked of *rest*—Alas! there is no rest in infidelity or in atheism. To disbelieve in revelation or in God is not to *escape* from a belief in things which you do not comprehend, but to *transfer* your belief to a new class of such things. Unbelief is credulity. The infidel is more credulous than the Christian, and the atheist is the most credulous of mankind: that is, he believes important propositions upon less evidence than any other man, and in opposition to greater.

74. It is curious to observe the anxiety of some writers to reconcile some of the facts before us with the "moral perfections" of the Deity; and it is *instructive* to observe into what doctrines they are led. They tell us that

all the evil and all the pain in the world are parts of a great system of Benevolence. "The moral and physical evil observable in the system, according to men's limited views of it, are necessary parts of the great plan; all tending ultimately to produce the greatest sum of happiness upon the whole, not only with respect to the system in general, but to each individual, according to the station he occupies in it."[1] They affirm that God is an "all-wise Being, who directs all the movements of nature, and who is determined, by His own unalterable perfections, to maintain in it at all times the greatest possible quantity of happiness."[2] The Creator found, therefore, that to inflict the misery which now exists was the best means of promoting this happiness—that to have abated the evil, the suffering, or the misery would be to have diminished the sum of felicity—and that men could not have been better or more at ease than they are, without making them on the whole more vicious or unhappy! These things are beacons which should warn us. The speculations show that not only religion, but reason, dictates the propriety of acquiescing in that degree of ignorance in which it has pleased God to leave us; because they show that attempts to acquire knowledge may conduct us to folly. These are subjects upon which *he* acts most rationally who says to his reason —Be still.

Mode of applying the Precepts of Scripture to Questions of Duty.

75. It is remarkable that many of these precepts, and especially those of the Christian Scriptures, are delivered, not systematically, but *occasionally*. They are distributed through occasional discourses and occasional letters. Except in the instance of the Law of Moses, the speaker or writer rarely set about a formal exposition of moral truth. The precepts were delivered as circumstances called them forth or made them needful. There is nothing like a system of morality; nor, consequently, does there exist that completeness, that distinctness in defining and accuracy in limiting, which, in a system of morality, we expect to find. Many rules are advanced in short absolute prohibitions or injunctions, without assigning any of those exceptions to their practical application which the majority of such rules require. The inquiry, in passing, may be permitted —Why are these things so? When it is considered what the Christian dispensation is, and what it is designed to effect upon the conduct of man, it cannot be supposed that the incompleteness of its moral precepts happened by inadvertence. The precepts of the former dispensation are much more precise; and it is scarcely to be supposed that the more perfect dispensation would have had a less precise law, unless the deficiency were to be compensated from some other authoritative source:—which remark is offered as a reason, *a priori*, for expecting that, in the present dispensation, God would *extend* the operation of His law written in the heart.

76. But whatever may be thought of this, it is manifest that considerable care is requisite in the application of precepts, so delivered, to the conduct of life. To apply them in all cases literally, were to act neither reasonably nor consistently with the design of the Lawgiver: to regard them in all cases as mere general directions, and to subject them to the unauthorised revision of man, were to deprive them of their proper character and authority as *divine* laws. In proposing some grounds for estimating the practical obligation of these precepts, I would be first allowed to express the conviction that the simple fact that such a disquisition is needed, and that the moral duties are to be gathered rather by implication or general tenor than from specific and formal rules, is one indication amongst the many that the dispensation of which these precepts form a part stands not in words but in power: and I hope to be forgiven, even in a book of morality, if I express the conviction that none can fulfil their requisitions—that none indeed can appreciate them—without some participation in this "power." I say he cannot *appreciate* them. Neither the morals nor the religion of Christianity can be adequately estimated by the man who sits down to the New Testament, with no other preparation than that which is necessary in sitting down to Euclid or Newton. There must be some preparation of heart as well as integrity of understanding—or, as the appropriate language of the volume itself would express it, it is necessary that we should become, in some degree, the "sheep" of Christ before we can accurately "know His voice."

77. There is one clear and distinct ground upon which we may limit the application of a precept that is couched in absolute language—the unlawfulness, in any given conjuncture, of obeying it. "Submit yourselves to every ordinance of man."[1] This, literally, is an unconditional command. But if we were to obey it unconditionally, we should sometimes comply with human, in opposition to Divine laws. In such cases, then, the obligation is clearly suspended; and this distinction the first teachers of Christianity

---

[1] This is given as the belief of Dr. Priestly. See Memoirs, Ap. No. 5.
[2] Adam Smith: Theory of Moral Sentiments. See also T. Southwood Smith's Illustrations of the Divine Government, in which unbridled license of speculation has led the writer into some instructive absurdities.

[1] 1 Pet. ii. 13.

recognised in their own practice. When an "ordinance of man" required them to forbear the promulgation of the new religion, they refused obedience, and urged the befitting expostulation—"Whether it be right in the sight of God to hearken unto you more than unto God, judge ye."[1] So, too, with the filial relationship: "Children, obey your parents in all things."[2] But a parent may require his child to lie or steal; and therefore when a parent requires obedience in such things, his authority ceases, and the obligation to obedience is taken away by the moral law itself. The precept, so far as the present ground of exception applies, is virtually this: Obey your parents in all things, unless disobedience is required by the Will of God. Or the subject might be illustrated thus: The Author of Christianity reprobates those who love father or mother more than Himself. The paramount love to God is to be manifested by obedience.[3] So, then, we are to obey the commands of God in preference to those of our parents. "All human authority ceases at the point where obedience becomes criminal."[4]

78. Of some precepts, it is evident that they were designed to be understood conditionally. "When thou prayest, enter into thy closet, and when thou hast shut thy door, pray to thy Father which is in secret."[5] This precept is conditional. I doubt not that it is consistent with His will that the greater number of the supplications which man offers at His throne shall be offered in secret; yet, that the precept does not exclude the exercise of public prayer, is evident from this consideration, if from no other, that Christ and His apostles themselves practised it.

79. Some precepts are figurative, and describe the spirit and temper that should govern us, rather than the particular actions that we should perform. Of this there is an example in, "Whosoever shall compel thee to go a mile, go with him twain."[6] In promulgating some precepts, a principal object appears to have been to supply sanctions. Thus in the case of Civil Obedience, we are to obey *because* the Deity authorises the institution of Civil Government—*because* the magistrate is the minister of God for good; and, accordingly, we are to obey not from considerations of necessity only, but of duty; "not only for wrath, but for conscience sake."[7] One precept, if we accepted it literally, would enjoin us to "hate" our parents; and this acceptation Milton appears actually to have adopted. One would enjoin us to accumulate no property: "Lay not up for yourselves treasures upon earth."[1] Such rules are seldom mistaken in practice; and, it may be observed, that this is an indication of their practical wisdom, and their practical adaptation to the needs of man. It is not an *easy* thing to pronounce, as occasions arise, a large number of moral precepts in unconditional language, and yet to secure them from the probability of even great misconstructions. Let the reader make the experiment. Occasionally, but it is only occasionally, a sincere Christian, in his anxiety to conform to the moral law, accepts such precepts in a more literal sense than that in which they appear to have been designed to be applied. I once saw a book that endeavoured to prove the unlawfulness of accumulating any property, upon the authority, primarily, of this last quoted precept. The principle upon which the writer proceeded was just and right—that it is necessary to conform, unconditionally, to the expressed Will of God. The defect was in the criticism; that is to say, in ascertaining what that Will did actually require.

80. Another obviously legitimate ground of limiting the application of absolute precepts is afforded us in just biblical criticism. Not that critical disquisitions are often necessary to the upright man who seeks for the knowledge of his duties. God has not left the knowledge of His moral law so remote from the sincere seekers of His Will. But in deducing public rules as authoritative upon mankind, it is needful to take into account those considerations which criticism supplies. The construction of the original languages and their peculiar phraseology, the habits, manners, and prevailing opinions of the times, and the *circumstances* under which a precept was delivered, are evidently amongst these considerations. And literary criticism is so much the more needed, because the great majority of mankind have access to Scripture only through the medium of translations.

81. But in applying all these limitations to the absolute precepts of Scripture, it is to be remembered that we are not subjecting their authority to inferior principles. We are not violating the principle upon which these essays proceed, that the expression of the Divine Will is our ultimate law. We are only ascertaining what that expression is. If, after just and authorised examination, any precept should still appear to stand imperative in its absolute form, we accept it as obligatory in that form. Many such precepts there are; and being such, we allow no considerations of convenience, nor of expediency,

---
[1] Acts iv. 19. [2] Col. iii. 20.
[3] "If ye love Me, ye will keep My commandments."—John xiv. 15.
[4] Mor. and Pol. Phil. [5] Matt. vi. 6.
[6] Matt. v. 41. [7] Rom. xiii 5.

[1] Matt. vi. 19.

nor considerations of any other kind, to dispense with their authority.

82. One great use of such inquiries as these is to vindicate to the apprehensions of men the authority of the precepts themselves. It is very likely to happen, and to some negligent inquirers it does happen, that seeing a precept couched in unconditional language, which yet cannot be unconditionally obeyed, they call in question its general obligation. Their minds fix upon the idea of some consequences which would result from a literal obedience, and feeling assured that *those* consequences ought not to be undertaken, they set aside the precept itself. They are at little pains to inquire what the proper requisitions of the precept are—glad, perhaps, of a specious excuse for not regarding it at all. The careless reader, perceiving that a literal compliance with the precept to *give the cloak to him who takes a coat*, would be neither proper nor right, rejects the whole precept of which it forms an illustration; and in doing this, rejects one of the most beautiful, and important, and sacred requisitions of the Christian law.[1]

83. There are two modes in which moral obligations are imposed in Scripture — by particular precepts and by general rules. The one prescribes a duty upon one subject, the other upon very many. The applicability of general rules is nearly similar to that of what is usually called the *spirit* of the Gospel, the *spirit* of the moral law: which spirit is of very wide embrace in its application to the purposes of life. "In estimating the value of a moral rule, we are to have regard not only to the particular duty, but the general spirit; not only to what it directs us to do, but to the character which a compliance with its direction is likely to form in us."[2] In this manner, some particular precepts become, in fact, general rules; and the duty that results from these rules, from this spirit, is as obligatory as that which is imposed by a specific injunction. Christianity requires us to maintain universal benevolence towards mankind; and he who, in his conduct towards another, disregards this benevolence, is as truly, and sometimes as flagrantly, a violator of the moral law, as if he had transgressed the command, "Thou shalt not steal." This doctrine is indeed recommended by a degree of utility that makes its adoption almost a necessity; because no number of specific precepts would be sufficient for the purposes of moral instruction: so that, if we were destitute of this species of general rules, we should frequently be destitute, so far as external precepts are concerned, of any. It

appears by a note to the work which has just been cited, that in the Mussulman code, which proceeds upon the system of a precise rule for a precise question, there have been promulgated *seventy-five thousand* precepts. I regard the wide practical applicability of some of the Christian precepts as an argument of great wisdom. They impose many duties in few words; or rather, they convey a great mass of moral instruction within a sentence that all may remember and that few can mistake. "All things whatsoever ye would that men should do to you, do ye even so to them,"[1] is of greater utility in the practice of life, and is applicable to more circumstances, than a hundred rules which presented the exact degree of kindness or assistance that should be afforded in prescribed cases. The Mosaic law, rightly regarded, conveyed many clear expositions of human duty; yet the quibbling and captious scribes of old found, in the literalities of that law, more plausible grounds for evading its duties than can be found in the precepts of the Christian Scriptures.

84. There are a few precepts of which the application is so extensive in human affairs that I would, in conformity with some of the preceding remarks, briefly inquire into their practical obligation. Of these, that which has just been quoted for another purpose, "All things whatsoever ye would that men should do to you, do ye even so to them,"[2] is perhaps cited and recommended more frequently than any other. The difficulty of applying this precept has induced some to reject it as containing a moral maxim which is not sound: but perhaps it will be found that the deficiency is not in the rule, but in the non-applicability of the cases to which it has often been applied. It is not applicable when the act which another *would that we should do to him* is in itself unlawful or adverse to some other portion of the moral law. If I seize a thief in the act of picking a pocket, he undoubtedly "would" that I should let him go; and I, if our situations were exchanged, should wish it too. But I am not *therefore* to release him; *because*, since it is a Christian obligation upon the magistrate to punish offenders, the obligation descends to me to secure them for punishment. Besides, in every such case I must do as I would be done unto with respect to *all* parties concerned—the public as well as the thief. The precept, again, is not applicable when the *desire* of the second party is such as a Christian cannot lawfully indulge. An idle and profligate man asks me to give him money. It would be wrong to indulge such a man's desire, and therefore the precept does not apply.

---

[1] Matt. v. 38. [2] Evidences of Christianity, p. 2, c. 2.   [1] Matt. vii. 12.   [2] Ibid.

85. The reader will perhaps say, that a person's duties in such cases are sufficiently obvious without the gravity of illustration. Well,—but are the principles upon which the duties are ascertained thus obvious? This is the important point. In the affairs of life, many cases arise in which a person has to refer to such principles as these, and in which, if he does not apply the right principles, he will transgress the Christian law. The law appears to be in effect this, Do as you would be done unto, except in those instances in which to act otherwise is permitted *by Christianity*. Inferior grounds of limitation are often applied; and they are always wrong; because they always subject the moral law to suspension by inferior authorities. To do this, is to reject the authority of the Divine Will, and to place this beautiful expression of that Will at the mercy of every man's inclination.

86. "Whether ye eat, or drink, or whatsoever ye do, do all to the glory of God."[1] I have heard of the members of some dinner club who had been recommended to consider this precept, and who, in their discussions over the bottle, thought perhaps that they were arguing soundly when they held language like this: "Am I, in lifting this glass to my mouth, to do it for the purpose of bringing glory to God? Is that to be my motive in buying a horse or shooting a pheasant?" From such moralists much sagacity of discrimination was not to be expected; and these questions delighted and probably convinced the club. The mistake of these persons, and perhaps of some others, is, that they misunderstand the rule. The promotion of the Divine glory is not to be the *motive* and *purpose* of all our actions, but, having actions to perform, we are *so* to perform them that this glory shall be advanced. The precept is in effect, Let your actions and the motives of them be such, that others shall have reason to honour God:[2] and a precept like this is a very sensitive test of the purity of our conduct. I know not whether there is a single rule of Christianity of which the use is so constant and the application so universal. To do as we would be done by, refers to relative duties; Not to do evil that good may come, refers to particular circumstances: but, To do all things *so* that the Deity may be honoured, refers to almost every action of a man's life. Happily the Divine glory is thus promoted by some men even in trifling affairs—almost whether they eat or drink, or whatsoever thing they do. There is, in truth, scarcely a more efficacious means of honouring the Deity, than the observing a constant Christian *manner* of conducting our intercourse with men. He who habitually maintains his allegiance to religion and to purity, who is moderate and chastised in all his pursuits, and who always makes the prospects of the future predominate over the temptations of the present, is one of the most efficacious recommenders of goodness,—one of the most impressive "preachers of righteousness,"—and by consequence, one of the most efficient promoters of the glory of God.

87. By a part of Paul's Epistle to the Romans, it appears that he and his coadjutors had been reported to hold the doctrine, that it is lawful "to do evil that good may come."[1] This report he declares is *slanderous;* and expresses his reprobation of those who act upon the doctrine, by the short and emphatic declaration—*their condemnation is just.* This is not critically a prohibition, but it is a prohibition in effect; and the manner in which the doctrine is reprobated, induces the belief that it was so flagitious that it needed very little inquiry or thought: in the writer's mind the transition is immediate, from the idea of the doctrine to the punishment of those who adopt it.

88. Now the "evil" which is thus prohibited, is, anything and all things discordant with the Divine Will; so that the unsophisticated meaning of the rule is, that nothing which is contrary to the Christian law may be done for the sake of attaining a beneficial end. Perhaps the breach of no moral rule is productive of more mischief than of this. That "the end justifies the means" is a maxim which many, who condemn it as a maxim, adopt in their practice: and in political affairs it is not only habitually adopted, but is indirectly, if not openly, defended as right. If a senator were to object to some measure of apparent public expediency, that it was not consistent with the Moral Law, he would probably be laughed at as a fanatic or a fool: yet perhaps some who are flippant with this charge of fanaticism and folly may be in perplexity for a proof. If the expressed Will of God is our paramount law, no proof can be brought; and in truth it is not often that it is candidly attempted. I have not been amongst the least diligent inquirers into the moral reasonings of men, but honest and manly reasoning against this portion of Scripture I have never found.

Of the rule, "not to do evil that good may come," Dr. Paley says, that it "is, for the most part, a salutary caution." A person might as well say that the rule "not to commit murder" is a *salutary caution.* There is no caution in the matter, but an imperative law. But he proceeds:—"Strictly speaking,

---
[1] 1 Cor. x. 31.
[2] "Let your light so shine before men that they may see your good works, and glorify your Father which is in heaven."—Matt. v. 16.

[1] Rom. iii. 8.

that cannot be *evil* from which *good* comes."¹ Now let the reader consider :—Paul says, *You may not do evil that good may come: Aye, but*, says the philosopher, *if good does come, the acts that bring it about are* NOT *evil*. What the apostle would have said of such a reasoner, I will not trust my pen to suppose. The reader will perceive the foundation of this reasoning. It assumes that good and evil are not to be estimated by the expressions of the Will of God, but by the *effects* of actions. The question is clearly fundamental. If expediency be the ultimate test of rectitude, Dr. Paley is right; if the expressions of the Divine Will are the ultimate test, he is wrong. You must sacrifice the one authority or the other. If this Will is the greater, consequences are not: if consequences are the greater, this Will is not. But this question is not now to be discussed: it may however be observed, that the interpretation which the rule has been thus made to bear, appears to be contradicted by the terms of the rule itself. The rule of Christianity is, Evil may not be committed for the purpose of good : the rule of the philosophy is, Evil may not be committed *except* for the purpose of good. Are these precepts identical? Is there not a fundamental variance, an absolute contrariety between them? Christianity does not speak of evil and good as contingent, but as fixed qualities. You cannot convert the one into the other by disquisitions about expediency. In morals, there is no philosopher's stone that can convert evil into good with a touch. Our labours, so long as the authority of the Moral Law is acknowledged, will end like those of the physical alchymist : after all our efforts at transmutation, lead will not become gold—evil will not become good. However, there is one subject of satisfaction in considering such reasonings as these. They prove, negatively, the truth which they assail ; for that against which nothing but sophistry can be urged, is undoubtedly true. The simple truth is, that if evil may be done for the sake of good, all the precepts of Scripture which define or prohibit evil are laws no longer ; for that cannot in any rational use of language be called a law in respect of those to whom it is directed, if they are at liberty to neglect it when they think fit. These precepts may be advices, recommendations, "salutary cautions," but they are not *laws*. They may suggest hints, but they do not impose duties.

89. With respect to the legitimate grounds of exception or limitation in the application of this rule, there appear to be few or none. The only question is, What actions *are* evil? Which question is to be determined, ultimately, by the Will of God.

¹ Mor. and Pol. Phil., b. 2, c. 8.

Benevolence, as it is Proposed in the Christian Scriptures.

90. In inquiring into the great principles of that moral system which the Christian revelation institutes, we discover one remarkable characteristic, one pervading peculiarity by which it is distinguished from every other —the paramount emphasis which it lays upon the exercise of pure Benevolence. It will be found that this preference of "Love" is wise as it is unexampled, and that no other general principle would effect, with any approach to the same completeness, the best and highest purposes of morality. How easy soever it be for us, to whom the character and obligations of this benevolence are comparatively familiar, to perceive the wisdom of placing it at the foundation of the Moral Law, we are indebted for the capacity, not to our own sagaciousness, but to light which has been communicated from heaven. That schoolmaster the law of Moses never taught, and the speculations of philosophy never discovered, that Love was the fulfilment of the Moral Law. Eighteen hundred years ago this doctrine was a new commandment.

91. Love is made the test of the validity of our claims to the Christian character—"By *this* shall all men know that ye are my disciples."¹ Again,—"Love one another. He that loveth another hath fulfilled the law. For this, Thou shalt not commit adultery, Thou shalt not kill, Thou shalt not bear false witness, Thou shalt not covet ; and if there be any other commandment, it is briefly comprehended in this saying, namely, Thou shalt love thy neighbour as thyself. Love worketh *no* ill to his neighbour : therefore Love is the fulfilling of the law."² It is not therefore surprising that after an enumeration, in another place, of various duties, the same dignified apostle says, "*Above all these things* put on charity, which is the bond of *perfectness*."³ The inculcation of this Benevolence is as frequent in the Christian Scriptures as its practical utility is great. He who will look through the volume will find that no topic is so frequently introduced, no obligation so emphatically enforced, no virtue to which the approbation of God is so specially promised. It is the theme of all the "apostolic exhortations, that with which their morality begins and ends, from which all their details and enumerations set out and into which they return."⁴ "He that dwelleth in love dwelleth in God, and God in him."⁵ More emphatical language cannot be employed. It exalts to the utmost the character of the virtue, and in effect, promises its possessor the utmost

¹ John xiii. 35.   ² Rom. xiii. 9.
³ Col. iii. 14.   ⁴ Evid. Christianity, p. 2, c. 2.
⁵ 1 John iv. 16.

favour and felicity. If then, of Faith, Hope, and Love, Love be the greatest; if it be by the test of love that our pretensions to Christianity are to be tried; if all the relative duties of morality are embraced in one word, and that word is Love; it is obviously needful that, in a book like this, the requisitions of Benevolence should be habitually regarded in the prosecution of its inquiries. And accordingly the reader will sometimes be invited to sacrifice inferior considerations to these requisitions, and to give to the law of Love that paramount station in which it has been placed by the authority of God.

92. It is certain that almost every offence against the relative duties has its origin, if not in the malevolent propensities, at least in those propensities which are incongruous with love. I know not whether it is possible to disregard any one obligation that respects the intercourse of man with man, without violating this great Christian law. This universal applicability may easily be illustrated by referring to the obligations of *Justice*, obligations which, in civilised communities, are called into operation more frequently than almost any other. He who estimates the obligations of justice by a reference to that Benevolence which Christianity prescribes, will form to himself a much more pure and perfect standard than he who refers to the law of the land, to the apprehension of exposure, or to the desire of reputation. There are many ways in which a man can be unjust without censure from the public, and without violating the laws; but there is no way in which he can be unjust without disregarding Christian Benevolence. It is an universal and very sensitive test. He who does regard it, who uniformly considers whether his conduct towards another is consonant with pure goodwill, cannot be voluntarily unjust; nor can he who commits injustice do it without the consciousness, if he will reflect, that he is violating the law of Love. That integrity which is founded upon Love, when compared with that which has any other basis, is recommended by its honour and dignity as well as by its rectitude. It is more worthy the man as well as the Christian, more beautiful in the eye of infidelity as well as of religion.

93. It were easy, if it were necessary, to show in what manner the law of Benevolence applies to other relative duties, and in what manner, when applied, it purifies and exalts the fulfilment of them. But our present business is with principles rather than with their specific application.

94. It is obvious that the obligations of this Benevolence are not merely prohibitory— directing us to avoid " working ill " to another, but mandatory,—requiring us to do him good. That benevolence which is manifested only by doing no evil, is indeed of a very questionable kind. To abstain from injustice, to abstain from violence, to abstain from slander, is compatible with an extreme deficiency of love. There are many who are neither slanderous, nor ferocious, nor unjust, who have yet very little regard for the benevolence of the Gospel. In the illustrations therefore of the obligations of morality, whether private or political, it will sometimes become our business to state, what this Benevolence requires as well as what it forbids. The legislator whose laws are contrived only for the detection and punishment of offenders, fulfils but half his duty: if he would conform to the *Christian* standard, he must provide also for their reformation.

CHAPTER VI.

The Immediate Communication of the Will of God.

Conscience—Its nature—Its authority—Review of opinions respecting a moral sense—Bishop Butler—Lord Bacon—Lord Shaftesbury—Watts—Voltaire—Locke—Southey—Adam Smith—Paley—Rousseau—Milton—Judge Hale—Marcus Antoninus—Epictetus—Seneca—Paul—That every human being possesses a moral law—Pagans—Gradations of light—Prophecy—The immediate communication of the Divine Will perpetual—Of national vices: Infanticide: Duelling—Of savage life.

95. The reader is solicited to approach this subject with that mental seriousness which its nature requires. Whatever be his opinions upon the subject, whether he believes in the reality of such communication or not, he ought not even to *think* respecting it but with feelings of seriousness.

96. In endeavouring to investigate this reality, it becomes especially needful to distinguish the communication of the Will of God from those mental phenomena with which it has very commonly been intermingled and confounded. The want of this distinction has occasioned a confusion which has been greatly injurious to the cause of truth. It has occasioned great obscurity of opinion respecting Divine instruction; and by associating error with truth, has frequently induced scepticism respecting the truth itself. —When an intelligent person perceives that *infallible* truth or *Divine* authority is described as belonging to the dictates of "Conscience," and when he perceives, as he must perceive, that these dictates are various and sometimes contradictory; he is in danger of concluding that no unerring and no divine guidance is accorded to man.

97. Upon this serious subject it is therefore peculiarly necessary to endeavour to attain distinct ideas, and to employ those words only which convey distinct ideas to other men. The first section of the present chapter will accordingly be devoted to some brief observations respecting the Conscience, its nature, and its authority; by which it is hoped the reader will see sufficient reason to distinguish its dictates from that higher guidance, respecting which it is the object of the present chapter to inquire.

98. For a kindred purpose, it appears requisite to offer a short review of popular and philosophical opinions respecting a Moral Sense. These opinions will be found to have been frequently expressed in great indistinctness and ambiguity of language. The purpose of the writer in referring to these opinions, is to inquire whether they do not generally involve a recognition—obscurely perhaps, but still a recognition—of the principle, that God communicates His Will to the mind. If they do this, and if they do it without design or consciousness, no trifling testimony is afforded to the truth of the principle : for how should this principle thus secretly recommend itself to the minds of men, except by the influence of its own evidence?

SECTION I.

Conscience, its Nature and Authority.

99. In the attempt to attach distinct notions to the term "Conscience," we have to request the reader not to estimate the accuracy of our observations by the notions which he may have habitually connected with the word. Our disquisition is not about terms but truths. If the observations are in themselves just, our principal object is attained. The secondary object, that of connecting truth with appropriate terms, is only so far attainable by a writer, as shall be attained by an uniform employment of words in determinate senses in his own practice.

100. Men possess notions of right and wrong; they possess a belief that, under given circumstances, they *ought* to do one thing or to forbear another. This belief I would call a *conscientious* belief. And when such a belief exists in a man's mind in reference to a number of actions, I would call the sum or aggregate of his notions respecting what is right and wrong, his *Conscience*.

101. To possess notions of right and wrong in human conduct,—to be convinced that we *ought* to do or to forbear an action,—implies and supposes *a sense of obligation* existent in the mind. A man who feels that it is wrong for him to do a thing, possesses a sense of obligation to refrain. Into the origin of this sense of obligation, or how it is induced into the mind, we do not inquire : it is sufficient for our purpose that it exists ; and there is no reason to doubt that its existence is consequent of the Will of God.

102. In most men—perhaps in all—this sense of obligation refers, with greater or less distinctness, to the will of a superior being. The impression, however obscure, is in general fundamentally this : I must do so or so, because God requires it.

103. It is found that this sense of obligation is sometimes connected, in the minds of separate individuals, with different actions. One man thinks he ought to do a thing from which another thinks he ought to forbear. Upon the great questions of morality there is indeed in general a congruity of human judgment ; yet subjects do arise respecting which one man's conscience dictates an act, different from that which is dictated by another's. It is not therefore essential to a conscientious judgment of right and wrong, that that judgment should be in strict accordance with the Moral Law. Some men's consciences dictate that which the Moral Law does not enjoin ; and this law enjoins some points which are not enforced by every man's conscience. This is precisely the result which, from the nature of the case, it is reasonable to expect: Of these judgments respecting what is right, with which the sense of obligation becomes from time to time connected, some are induced by the instructions or example of others ; some by our own reflection or inquiry ; some perhaps from the written law of revelation ; and some, as we have cause to conclude, from the direct intimations of the Divine Will.

104. It is manifest that if the sense of obligation is sometimes connected with subjects that are proposed to us merely by the instruction of others, or if the connection results from the power of association and habit, or from the fallible investigations of our own minds—that sense of obligation will be connected, in different individuals, with different subjects. So that it may sometimes happen that a man can say, I conscientiously think I ought to do a certain action, and yet that his neighbour can say, I conscientiously think the contrary. "With respect to particular actions, opinion determines whether they are good or ill ; and Conscience approves or disapproves, in consequence of this determination, whether it be in favour of truth or falsehood."[1]

105. Such considerations enable us to account for the diversity of the dictates of the

[1] Adventurer, No. 91.

conscience in individuals respectively. A person is brought up amongst Catholics, and is taught from his childhood that flesh ought not to be eaten in Lent. The arguments of those around him, or perhaps their authority, satisfy him that what he is taught is truth. The *sense of obligation* thus becomes connected with a refusal to eat flesh in Lent ; and thenceforth he says that the abstinence is dictated by his conscience. A Protestant youth is taught the contrary. Argument or authority satisfies him that flesh may lawfully be eaten every day in the year. *His* sense of obligation therefore is not connected with the abstinence ; and thenceforth he says that eating flesh in Lent does not violate his conscience. And so of a multitude of other questions.

106. When therefore a person says, My conscience dictates to me that I ought to perform such an action, he means—or in the use of such language he ought to mean—that the sense of obligation which subsists in his mind, is connected with that action ; that, so far as his judgment is enlightened, it is a requisition of the law of God.

107. But not *all* our opinions respecting morality and religion are derived from education or reasoning. He who finds in Scripture the precept, "Thou shalt love thy neighbour as thyself," derives an opinion respecting the duty of loving others from the discovery of this expression of the Will of God. His sense of obligation is connected with benevolence towards others, in consequence of this discovery ; or, in other words, his understanding has been informed by the Moral Law, and a new duty is added to those which are dictated by his conscience. Thus it is that Scripture, by informing the judgment, extends the jurisdiction of conscience ; and it is hence, in part, that in those who seriously study the Scriptures, the conscience appears so much more vigilant and operative than in many who do not possess, or do not regard them. Many of the mistakes which education introduces, many of the fallacies to which our own speculations lead us, are corrected by this law. In the case of our Catholic, if a reference to Scripture should convince him that the judgment he has formed respecting abstinence from flesh is not founded on the Law of God, the sense of obligation becomes detached from its subject ; and thenceforth his conscience ceases to dictate that he should abstain from flesh in Lent. Yet Scripture does not decide every question respecting human duty, and in some instances individuals judge differently of the decisions which Scripture gives. This, again, occasions some diversity in the dictates of the conscience ; it occasions the sense of obligation to become connected with dissimilar, and possibly incompatible, actions.

108. But another portion of men's judgments respecting moral affairs is derived from immediate intimations of the Divine Will. (This we must be allowed for the present to assume.) These intimations inform, sometimes, the judgment ; correct its mistakes ; and increase and give distinctness to our knowledge :—thus operating, as the Scriptures operate, to connect the sense of obligation more accurately with those actions which are conformable with the Will of God. It does not, however, follow, by any sort of necessity, that this higher instruction must correct *all* the mistakes of the judgment ; that because it imparts some light, that light must be perfect day ; that because it communicates some moral or religious truth, it must communicate all the truths of religion and morality. Nor, again, does it follow, that individuals must each receive the same access of knowledge. It is evidently as possible that it should be communicated in different degrees to different individuals, as that it should be communicated at all. For which plain reasons we are still to expect, what in fact we find, that although the judgment receives light from a superhuman intelligence, the degree of that light varies in individuals ; and that the sense of obligation is connected with fewer subjects, and attended with less accuracy, in the minds of some men than of others.

109. With respect to the *authority* which properly belongs to Conscience as a director of individual conduct, it appears manifest, alike from reason and from Scripture, that it is great. When a man believes, upon due deliberation, that a certain action is right, that action is right *to him*. And this is true, whether the action be or be not required of mankind by the Moral Law.[1] The fact that in his mind the sense of obligation attaches to the act, and that he has duly deliberated upon the accuracy of his judgment, makes the dictate of his conscience upon that subject an *authoritative* dictate. The individual is to be held guilty if he violates his conscience.—if he does one thing, whilst his sense of obligation is directed to its contrary. Nor, if his judgment should not be accurately informed, if his sense of obligation should not be connected with a proper subject, is the guilt of violating his conscience taken away. Were it otherwise, a person might be held virtuous for acting in opposition to his apprehensions of duty ; or guilty, for doing what he believed to be right. " It is happy for us that our title to the character of virtuous beings, depends not upon the justness of our opinions or the constant objective rectitude of all we do, but upon the conformity of our actions to the sincere convictions of our minds."[2] Dr. Fur-

[1] "By Conscience, all men are restrained from intentional ill :—it infallibly directs us to avoid guilt, but is not intended to secure us from error."—Advent., No. 91.   [2] Dr. Price.

neaux says, "To secure the favour of God and the rewards of true religion, we must follow our own consciences and judgments *according to the best light* we can attain."[1] And I am especially disposed to add the testimony of Sir William Temple, because he recognises the doctrine which has just been advanced, that our judgments are enlightened by superhuman agency. "The way to our future happiness must be left, at last, to the *impressions made upon every man's belief and conscience*, either by natural or *supernatural* arguments and means."[2]—Accordingly there appears no reason to doubt that some will stand convicted in the sight of the Omniscient Judge, for actions which his Moral Law has not forbidden; and that some may be uncondemned for actions which that law does not allow. The distinction here is the same as that to which we have before had occasion to allude, between the desert of the agent and the quality of the act. Of this distinction an illustration is contained in Isaiah x. It was the Divine Will that a certain specific course of action should be pursued in punishing the Israelites. For the performance of this the king of Assyria was employed:—"I will give him a charge to take the spoil, and to take the prey, and to tread them down like the mire of the streets." This charge the Assyrian monarch fulfilled; he did the Will of God: but then his *intention* was criminal; he "meant not so:" and therefore, when the "whole work" is performed, "I will *punish*," says the Almighty, "the fruit of the stout heart of the king of Assyria, and the glory of his high looks."

But it was said, that these principles respecting the authority of Conscience were recognised in Scripture.—"One believeth that he may eat all things; another who is weak eateth herbs. One man esteemeth one day above another: another esteemeth every day alike." Here then are differences, nay contrarieties of conscientious judgments. And what are the parties directed severally to do? —"Let every man be fully persuaded in his own mind;" that is, let the full persuasion of his own mind be every man's rule of action. The situation of these parties was, that one *perceived the truth* upon the subject, and the other did not; that in one the sense of obligation was connected with an accurate, in the other with an inaccurate opinion. Thus again:—"*I* know, and am persuaded by the Lord Jesus, that there is nothing unclean of itself;"—therefore, absolutely speaking, it is lawful to eat all things: "but *to him that esteemeth* any thing to be unclean, to him it is unclean." The question is not whether his judgment was correct, but what that judgment actually was. To the doubter, the uncleanness, that is, the *sin* of eating, was certain,

though the act was right. Again: "All things indeed are pure; but it is evil *for that man* who eateth with offence." And, again, as a general rule: "He that doubteth is condemned if he eat, *because* he eateth not of faith; for *whatsoever* is not of faith, is sin."[1]

110. And here we possess a sufficient answer to those who affect to make light of the authority of Conscience, and exclaim, "Every man pleases his conscientious opinions, and that he is bound in conscience to do this or that; and yet his neighbour makes the same plea and urges the same obligation to do just the contrary." But what then? These persons' judgments differed: that we might expect, for they are fallible; but their sense of obligation was in each case really attached to its subject, and was in each case authoritative.

111. One observation remains; that although a man ought to make his conduct conform to his conscience, yet he may sometimes justly be held criminal for the errors of his opinion. Men often judge amiss respecting their duties in consequence of their own faults: some take little pains to ascertain the truth; some voluntarily exclude knowledge; and most men would possess more accurate perceptions of the Moral Law if they sufficiently endeavoured to obtain them. And therefore, although a man may not be punished for a given *act* which he ignorantly supposes to be lawful, he may be punished for that ignorance in which his supposition originates. Which consideration may perhaps account for the expression, that he who ignorantly failed to do his master's will "shall be beaten with few stripes." There is a degree of wickedness, to the agents of which God at length "sends strong delusion" that they may "believe a lie." In this state of strong delusion, they perhaps may, without violating any sense of obligation, do many wicked actions. The principles which have been here delivered, would lead us to suppose that the punishment which awaits such men, will have respect rather to that intensity of wickedness of which delusion was the consequence, than to those particular acts which they might ignorantly commit under the influence of the delusion itself. This observation is offered to the reader because some writers have obscured the present subject, by speculating upon the moral deserts of those desperately bad men, who occasionally have committed atrocious acts under the notion that they were doing right.

112. Let us then, when we direct our serious inquiry to the Immediate Communication of the Divine Will, carefully distinguish that

---

[1] Essay on Toleration, p. 8.
[2] Works: v. 1, p. 55, f. 1740.

[1] Rom. xiv.

Communication from the dictates of the conscience. They are separate and distinct considerations. It is obvious that those positions which some persons advance;— "Conscience is our infallible guide,"—"Conscience is the voice of the Deity," &c., are wholly improper and inadmissible. The term may indeed have been employed *synonymously* for the voice of God; but this ought never to be done. It is to induce confusion of language respecting a subject which ought always to be distinctly exhibited; and the necessity for avoiding ambiguity is so much the greater, as the consequences of that ambiguity are more serious: it is obvious that, on these subjects, inaccuracy of language gives rise to serious error of opinion.

Review of Opinions respecting a Moral Sense.

113. The purpose for which this brief review is offered to the reader, is explained in very few words. It is to inquire, by a reference to the written opinions of many persons, whether they do not agree in asserting that our Creator communicates some portions of His Moral Law immediately to the human mind. These opinions are frequently delivered, as the reader will presently discover, in great ambiguity of language; but in the midst of this ambiguity there appears to exist one pervading truth,— a truth in testimony to which these opinions are not the less satisfactory because, in some instances, the testimony is undesigned. The reader is requested to observe, as he passes on, whether many of the difficulties which inquirers have found or made, are not solved by the supposition of a Divine communication, and whether they can be solved by any other. "The Author of nature has much better furnished us for a virtuous conduct than our moralists seem to imagine, by almost as *quick* and *powerful instructions* as we have for the preservation of our bodies."[1] "It is manifest, great part of common language and of common behaviour over the world, is formed upon the supposition of a moral faculty, whether called conscience, moral reason, moral sense, or Divine reason; whether considered as a sentiment of the understanding, or as a perception of the heart, or, which seems the truth, as including both."[2] Is it not remarkable that for a "faculty" so well known "over the world," even a name has not been found, and that a Christian bishop accumulates a multiplicity of ambiguous epithets to explain his meaning? Bishop Butler says again of Conscience, "To preside and govern, from the very economy and constitution of man, belongs to it. This faculty was placed within to be our proper governor, to direct and regulate all undue principles, passions, and motives of action.— It carries its own authority with it, that it is our natural guide, the guide assigned us by the Author of our nature." Would it have been unreasonable to conclude, that there was at least *some* connection between this reprover of "all undue principles, passions, and motives," and that law of which the New Testament speaks, "All things that are reproved are made manifest by the light"?[1]

114. Blair says, "Conscience is felt to act as the delegate of an invisible Ruler;"— "Conscience is the guide, or the enlightening or directing principle of our conduct.'[2] In this instance, as in many others, Conscience appears to be used in an indeterminate sense. Conscience is not an *enlightening* principle, but a principle which is enlightened. It is not a legislator, but a repository of statutes. Yet the reader will perceive the fundamental truth, that man is in fact illuminated, and illuminated by an invisible Ruler. In the thirteenth sermon there is an expression more distinct: "God has invested Conscience with authority to promulgate His laws." It is obvious that the Divine Being must have *communicated* His laws, before they could have been promulgated by Conscience. In accordance with which the author says in another place, "Under the tuition of God let us put ourselves."—"A Heavenly Conductor vouchsafes His aid."—"Divine light descends to guide our steps."[3] It were to be wished that such sentiments were not obscured by propositions like these: "A sense of right and wrong in conduct, or of moral good and evil, *belongs to human nature*."—"Such sentiments are *coeval with human nature*; for they are the remains of a law which was originally written in our heart."[4]

115. I do not know whether the reader will be able to perceive with distinctness the ideas of Lord Bacon and of Dr. Rush in the following quotations, but I think he will perceive that they involve a recognition—obscure and indeterminate, but still a recognition of the doctrine, that the Deity communicates His laws to the minds of men. Dr. Rush says, "It would seem as if the Supreme Being had preserved the *Moral Faculty* in man from the ruins of his fall, on purpose *to guide him back again to paradise*: and at the same time had constituted the *Conscience*, both in man and fallen spirits, a kind of royalty in his moral empire, on purpose to show His property in all intelligent creatures, and their original resemblance to Himself." And Lord Bacon says, "*The light of nature* not only *shines upon the human mind* through the medium of a rational faculty, but *by an*

---
[1] Dr. Hutcheson: Inquiry concerning Moral Good and Evil.
[2] Bishop Butler: Inquiry on Virtue.

[1] Eph. v. 13.   [2] Sermons.
[3] Sermon 7.   [4] Sermon 13.

internal instinct according to the law of conscience, which is a sparkle of the purity of man's first estate."

116. "The faculties of our minds are so formed by nature, that as soon as we begin to reason, we may also begin, in some measure, to distinguish good from evil."—"We prefer virtue to vice on account of the seeds planted in us."[1]

117. The following is not the less worthy notice because it is from the pen of Lord Shaftesbury: "Sense of right and wrong, being as natural to us as natural affection itself, and being a first principle in our constitution and make, there is no speculation, opinion, persuasion, or belief, which is capable, immediately or directly, to exclude or destroy it."[2] Sentiments such as these are very commonly expressed; and what do they imply? If sense of right and wrong is *natural* to us, it is because He who created us has placed it in our minds. The conclusion too is inevitable, that this sense must indicate the Divine Law by which right and wrong are discriminated. Now we do not say that these sentiments are absolutely just, or that a sense of right and wrong is strictly "natural" to man, but we say that the sentiments involve the supposition of some mode of Divine Guidance —some mode in which the Moral Law of God, or a part of it, is communicated by Him to mankind. And if this be indeed true, it may surely, with all reason, be asked, *why* we should not assent to the reality of that mode of communication, of which, as we shall hereafter see, Christianity asserts the existence?

118. "The first principles of morals are the *immediate dictates* of the moral faculty."— "By the moral faculty, or conscience, solely, we have the original conception of right and wrong."—"It is evident that this principle has, from its nature, authority to direct and determine with regard to our conduct; to judge, to acquit or condemn, and even to punish; an authority which belongs to no other principle of the human mind."—"The Supreme Being has given us this light within to direct our moral conduct."—"It is the candle of the Lord, set up within us to guide our steps."[3] This is *almost* the language of Christianity, "That was the true Light, which lighteth every man that cometh into the world."[4] I do not mean to affirm that the author of the essays speaks *exclusively* of the same Divine Guidance as the apostle; but surely, if Conscience operates as such a "light within," as "the candle of the Lord,"

[1] John Le Clerc. [2] Characteristics.
[3] Dr. Reid: Essays on the Powers of the Human Mind, Essay 3, c. 8, &c.
[4] John i. 9.

it can require no reasoning to convince us that it is illuminated from heaven. The indistinctness of notions which such language exhibits, appears to arise from inaccurate views of the nature of Conscience. The writer does not distinguish between the recipient and the source; between the enlightened principle and the enlightening beam. The apostle speaks only of the last; the uninspired inquirer speaks, without discrimination, of both;—and hence the ambiguity.

119. Dr. Beattie appears to maintain the same general principle, the same essential truth, under other phraseology. Common sense, he says, is "that power of the mind which *perceives truth* or commands belief by an instantaneous, instinctive, and irresistible impulse, neither derived from education nor from habit, but *from nature*."—"Every man may find the evidence of moral science in his own breast." An "instinctive" perception of truth derived from nature, must necessarily be tantamount to a power of perception imparted by the Deity. "Whatsoever nature does, God does," says Seneca: and Dr. Beattie himself explains his own meaning— "The dictates of nature, that is, the voice of God."[1] We have no concern with the justness of Beattie's philosophy, intellectual or moral, but the reader will perceive the recognition of the truth, or of something like the truth, to which we have so often referred.

120. "What is the power within us that perceives the distinctions of right and wrong? My answer is, The Understanding."—"Of every thought, sentiment, and subject, the Understanding is the natural and ultimate judge." This is the language of Dr. Price, but he does not seem wholly satisfied with his own definition. He says, "The truth seems to be, that in contemplating the actions of moral agents, we have *both* a perception of the understanding, and a feeling of the heart." And again, "It is to *intuition* that we owe our moral ideas." He speaks too of "the virtuous principle,"—"the inward spring of virtue;" and says, "Goodness is the power of reflection, raised to its due seat of direction and sovereignty in the mind." These various expressions do not appear to represent very distinct notions, but after the "Understanding" has been stated to be the ultimate judge, we are presented with the idea of Conscience, and then we perceive in Dr. Price's language, that which we find in the language of so many others, "Whatever our consciences dictate to us, that *He* (the Deity) *commands more evidently and undeniably*, than if by a voice from heaven we had been called upon to

[1] Essay on Truth.

do it.[1] Dr. Watts says that the mind "contains in it the plain and general principles of morality, not explicitly as propositions, but only as *native principles*, by which it judges, and cannot but judge, virtue to be fit and vice unfit."[2] And Dr. Cudworth: "The anticipations of morality do not spring merely from notional ideas, or from certain rules or propositions arbitrarily printed upon the soul as upon a book, but from some other more inward and vital principle in intellectual beings as such, whereby they have a natural determination in them to do some things and to avoid others."[3] Voltaire in his Commentary on Beccaria[4] says, "I call natural laws those which nature *dictates, in all ages, to all men*, for the maintenance of that Justice which she (say what they will of her) hath implanted in our hearts." "And this law is that innate sense of right and wrong, of virtue and vice, which every man carries in his own bosom."—"These impressions, operating on the mind of man, bespeak *a law written on his heart.*"—"This secret sense of right and wrong, for wise purposes so deeply implanted by our Creator on the human mind, has the nature, force, and effect of a law."[5] Locke: "The Divine law, that law which God has set to the actions of men, whether promulgated to them by the light of nature or the voice of revelation, is the measure of sin and duty. That God has given a rule whereby men should govern themselves, I think there is nobody so brutish as to deny."[6] The reader should remark, that revelation and "the light of nature" are here represented as being jointly and equally the law of God. "Actions, then, instead of being tried by the eternal standard of right and wrong, on which the *unsophisticated heart unerringly pronounces*, were judged by the rules of a pernicious casuistry."[7] This may not be absolutely true; but there must be some truth *which it is like*, or such a proposition would not be advanced. Who ever thought of attributing to the unsophisticated heart the power of unerringly pronouncing on questions of *prudence?* Yet questions of right and wrong are not, *in their own nature*, more easily solved than those of prudence.

121. "Boys do not listen to sermons. *They need not be told what is right; like men, they all know their duty sufficiently;* the grand difficulty is to practise it."[8] Neither may this be true; and it is not true. But upon what species of knowledge would any writer think of affirming that boys need not

[1] Review of Principal Questions in Morals.
[2] Philosophical Essays.
[3] Eternal and Immutable Morality.
[4] Crimes and Punishments, Com. c. 14.
[5] Dr. Shepherd's Discourse on Future Existence.
[6] Essay, b. 2, c. 28.
[7] Dr. Southey: Book of the Church, c. 10.
[8] West Rev. No. 1.

be instructed, except upon the single species, *the knowledge of duty?* And how should they know this without instruction unless their Creator has taught them? Dr. Rush exhibits the same views in a more determinate form: "Happily for the human race, the intimations of duty and the road to happiness are not left to the slow operations or doubtful inductions of reason. It is worthy of notice, that while second thoughts are best in matters of judgment, *first thoughts* are always to be preferred *in matters that relate to morality.*"[1] Adam Smith: "It is altogether absurd and unintelligible, to suppose that the first perceptions of right and wrong can be derived from reason. These first perceptions cannot be the object of reason, but of immediate sense and feeling."—"Though man has been rendered the immediate judge of mankind, an appeal lies from his sentence to a much higher tribunal, to the tribunal of their own consciences, to that of the man within the breast, the great judge and arbiter of their conduct." In some cases in which censure is violently poured upon us, "the judgments of the man within, are, however, much shaken in the steadiness and firmness of their decision. In such cases, this demigod within the breast appears, like the demigods of the poets, though partly of immortal, yet partly too of mortal extraction." Our moral faculties "were set up within us to be the supreme arbiters of all our actions." "The rules which they prescribe are to be regarded as the commands and laws of the Deity, promulgated by those vicegerents which He has thus set up within us." "Some questions must be left altogether to the decision of the man within the breast." And let the reader mark what follows: If we "listen with diligent and reverential attention to what he suggests to us, his voice will never deceive us. We shall stand in no need of casuistic rules to direct our conduct." How wonderful that such a man, who uses almost the language of Scripture, appears not even to have *thought* of the truth,—"The Anointing which ye have received of Him abideth in you, and ye need not that any man teach you!" for he does not appear to have *thought* of it. He intimates that this vicegerent of God, this undeceiving Teacher to whom we are to listen with reverential attention, is some "contrivance or mechanism within;" and says that to examine what contrivance or mechanism it is, "is a mere matter of philosophical curiosity."[2] A matter of philosophical curiosity, Dr. Paley seems to have thought a kindred inquiry to be. He discusses the question whether there is such a thing as a Moral Sense or not; and thus sums up the argument: "Upon the whole it seems to me, either that there exist no such instincts as

[1] Influence of Physical Causes on the Moral Faculty.
[2] Theory of Mor. Sent.

compose what is called the moral sense, or that they are not now to be distinguished from prejudices and habits."—"This celebrated question therefore becomes, in our system, a question of pure curiosity; and as such, we dismiss it to the determination of those who are more inquisitive than we are concerned to be, about the natural history and constitution of the human species."[1] But in another work, a work in which he did not bind himself to the support of a philosophical system, he holds other language: "Conscience, our own conscience, is to be our guide in all things." "It is through the whisperings of conscience that the Spirit speaks. If men are wilfully deaf to their consciences they cannot hear the Spirit. If, hearing, if being compelled to hear the remonstrances of conscience, they nevertheless decide and resolve and determine to go against them, then they grieve, then they defy, then they do despite to, the Spirit of God." Is it superstition? Is it not, on the contrary, a just and reasonable piety to implore of God the guidance of His Holy Spirit, when we have any thing of great importance to decide upon or undertake?"—"It being confessed that we cannot ordinarily distinguish, at the time, the suggestions of the Spirit from the operations of our minds, it may be asked, How are we to listen to them? The answer is, by attending, universally, to the admonitions within us."[2] The tendency of these quotations to enforce our general argument, is plain and powerful. But the reader should notice here another and a very interesting consideration. Paley says, "Our own conscience is to be our guide *in all things.*"—We are to attend *universally* to the admonitions within us. Now he writes a book of moral philosophy, that is, a book that shall "teach men their duty and the reasons of it," and from this book he *absolutely excludes* this law which men should universally obey, this law which should be their "guide in all things."

"Conscience, Conscience," exclaims Rousseau in his *Pensées,* "Divine Instinct, Immortal and Heavenly Voice, sure Guide of a being ignorant and limited but intelligent and free, infallible Judge of good and evil, by which man is made like unto God!" Here are attributes which, if they be justly assigned, certainly cannot belong to humanity; or if they do belong to humanity, an apostle certainly could not be accurate when he said that in us, that is, in our flesh, "*dwelleth no good thing.*" Another observation of Rousseau's is worth transcribing: "Our own conscience is the most enlightened philosopher. There is no need to be acquainted with Tully's Offices to make a man of probity; and perhaps the most virtuous woman in the world is the least acquainted with the definition of virtue."

"And I will place within them as a guide, My Umpire, Conscience; whom if they will hear, Light after light, well used, they shall attain."[1]

This is the language of Milton; and we have thus his testimony added to the many, that God has placed within us an Umpire which shall pronounce His own laws in our hearts. Thus in his "Christian Doctrine" more clearly: "They can lay claim to nothing more than human powers, assisted by *that spiritual illumination which is common to all.*"[2] Judge Hale: "Any man that sincerely and truly fears Almighty God, and calls and relies upon Him for His direction, has it as really as a son has the counsel and direction of his father; and though the voice be not audible nor discernible by sense, yet it is equally as real as if a man heard a voice saying, This is the way, walk in it."

122. The sentiments of the ancient philosophers, &c., should not be forgotten, and the rather because their language is frequently much more distinct and satisfactory than that of the refined inquirers of the present day.

123. Marcus Antoninus: "He who is well disposed will do everything dictated by the Divinity,—*a particle or portion of Himself, which God has given to each as a guide and a leader.*"[3]—Aristotle: "The mind of man hath a near affinity to God: *there is a Divine ruler in him.*"—Plutarch: "The light of truth is a law, not written in tables or books but dwelling in the mind, always as a living rule which never permits the soul to be destitute of an interior guide."—Hieron says that the universal light, shining in the conscience, is "a domestic God, a God within the hearts and souls of men."—Epictetus: "God has assigned to each man a director, his own good genius, a guardian whose vigilance no slumbers interrupt, and whom no false reasonings can deceive. So that when you have shut your door, say not that you are alone, for your God is within.—What need have you of outward light to discover what is done, or to light to good actions, who have God or that genius or divine principle for your light?"[4] Such citations might be greatly multiplied, but one more must suffice. Seneca says, "We find felicity—in a pure and untainted mind, which *if it were not holy were not fit to entertain the Deity.*" How like the words of an apostle!—"If any man defile the temple of God, him shall God destroy; for the temple of God is holy, which temple ye are."[5] The philosopher again: "There is a holy spirit in us;"[6] and

---

[1] Mor. and Pol. Phil., b. 1, c. 5. [2] Sermons.

[1] Par. Lost, iii. 194. [2] P. 81.
[3] Lib. 5, Sect. 27. [4] Lib. 1, c. 14.
[5] 1 Cor. iii. 17. [6] De Benef., c. 17, &c.

again the apostle: "Know ye not that" the "Spirit of God dwelleth in you?"[1]

124. Now respecting the various opinions which have been laid before the reader, there is one observation that will generally apply,—that they unite in assigning certain important attributes or operations to some principle or power existent in the human mind. They affirm that this principle or power possesses wisdom to direct us aright,—that its directions are given instantaneously as the individual needs them,—that it is inseparably attended with unquestionable *authority* to command. That such a principle or power does, therefore, actually exist, can need little further proof; for a concurrent judgment upon a question of personal experience cannot surely be incorrect. To say that individuals express their notions of this principle or power by various phraseology, that they attribute to it different degrees of superhuman intelligence, or that they refer for its origin to contradictory causes, does not affect the general argument. The great point for our attention is, not the designation or the supposed origin of this guide, but its *attributes;* and these attributes appear to be *divine*.

The Immediate Communication of the Will of God.

125. 1. That every reasonable human being is a moral agent,—that is, that every such human being is *responsible* to God, no one perhaps denies. There can be no responsibility where there is no knowledge: "Where there is no law there is no transgression." So then every human being possesses, or is furnished with, moral knowledge and a moral law. "If we admit that mankind, without an outward revelation, are nevertheless sinners, we must also admit that mankind, without such a revelation, are nevertheless in possession of the law of God."[2]

126. Whence then do they obtain it?—a question to which but one answer can be given: From the Creator Himself. It appears therefore to be almost demonstratively shown, that God does communicate His Will immediately to the minds of those who have no access to the external expression of it. It is always to be remembered that, as the majority of mankind do not possess the *written* communication of the Will of God, the question, as it respects them, is between an *Immediate* Communication and none; between such a communication and the denial of their responsibility in a future state; between such

[1] 1 Cor. iii. 16.
[2] Gurney: Essays on Christianity. p. 516.

a communication and the reducing them to the condition of the beasts that perish.

127. II. No one perhaps will imagine that this argument is confined to countries which the external light of Christianity has not reached. "Whoever expects to find in the Scriptures a specific direction for every moral doubt that arises, looks for more than he will meet with:"[1] so that even in Christian countries there exists some portion of that necessity for other guidance, which has been seen to exist in respect of pagans. Thus Adam Smith says, that there are some questions which it "is perhaps altogether impossible to determine by any precise rules," and that they "must be left altogether to the decision of the man within the breast."—But, indeed, when we speak of living in Christian countries, and of having access to the external revelation, we are likely to mislead ourselves with respect to the actual condition of "Christian" people. Persons talk of possessing the Bible, as if every one who lived in a Protestant country had a Bible in his pocket and could read it. But there are thousands, perhaps millions, in Christian and in Protestant countries, who know very little of what Christianity enjoins. They probably do not possess the Scriptures, or if they do, probably cannot read them. What they do know they learn from others,— from others who may be little solicitous to teach them, or to teach them aright. Such persons therefore are, to a considerable extent, practically in the same situation as those who have not heard of Christianity, and there is therefore to them a corresponding need of a direct communication of knowledge from heaven. But if we see the need of such knowledge extending itself thus far, who will call in question the doctrine, that it is imparted to the whole human race?

128. These are offered as considerations involving an antecedent probability of the truth of our argument. The reader is not required to give his assent to it as to a dogma of which he can discover neither the reason nor the object. Here is probability very strong; here is usefulness very manifest and very great;—so that the mind may reasonably be open to the reception of evidence, whatever Truth that evidence shall establish.

129. If the written revelation were silent respecting the immediate communication of the Divine Will, that silence might perhaps rightly be regarded as conclusive evidence that it is not conveyed; because it is so intimately connected with the purposes to which that revelation is directed, that scarcely

[1] Mor. and Pol. Phil., b. 1, c. 4.

any other explanation could be given of its silence than that the communication did not exist. That the Scriptures declare that God has communicated light and knowledge to some men by the immediate exertion of His own agency, admits not of dispute: but this it is obvious is not sufficient for our purpose; and it is in the belief that they declare that God imparts some knowledge to all men, that we thus appeal to their testimony.

130. Now here the reader should especially observe, that where the Christian Scriptures speak of the existence and influence of the Divine Spirit on the mind, they commonly speak of its higher operations; not of its office as a moral guide, but as a purifier, and sanctifier, and comforter of the soul. They speak of it in reference to its sacred and awful operations in connection with human salvation: and thus it happens that very many citations which, if we were writing an essay on religion, would be perfectly appropriate, do not possess that distinct and palpable application to an argument which goes no further than to affirm that it is a moral guide. And yet it may most reasonably be remarked, that if it has pleased the Universal Parent thus, and for these awful purposes, to visit the minds of those who are obedient to His power—He will not suffer them to be destitute of a moral guidance. The less must be supposed to be involved in the greater.

131. Our argument does not respect the degrees of illumination which may be possessed, respectively, by individuals,[1] or in different ages of the world. There were motives, easily conceived, for imparting a greater degree of light and of power at the introduction of Christianity than in the present day: accordingly there are many expressions in the New Testament which speak of high degrees of light and power, and which, however they may affirm the general existence of a Divine Guidance, are not descriptive of the general nor of the present condition of mankind. Nevertheless, if the records of Christianity, in describing these greater "gifts," inform us that a gift, similar in its nature but without specification of its amount, is imparted to all men, it is sufficient. Although it is one thing for the Creator to impart a general capacity to distinguish right from wrong, and another to impart miraculous power; one thing to inform His accountable creature that lying is evil, and another to

[1] I am disposed to offer a simple testimony to what I believe to be a truth;—that even in the present day, the Divine illumination and power is sometimes imparted to individuals in a degree much greater than is necessary for the purposes of mere moral direction; that on subjects connected with their own personal condition or that of others, light is sometimes imparted in greater brightness and splendour than is ordinarily enjoyed by mankind, or than is necessary for our ordinary direction in life.

enable him to cure a leprosy; yet this affords no reason to deny that the nature of the gift is not the same, or that both are not divine. "The degree of light may vary according as one man has a greater measure than another. But the light of an apostle is not one thing and the light of the heathen another thing, distinct in principle. They differ only in degree of power, distinctness, and splendour of manifestation."[1]

132. So early as Gen. vi. there is a distinct declaration of the moral operation of the Deity on the human mind; not upon the pious and the good, but upon those who were desperately wicked, so that even "every imagination of the thoughts of their heart was only evil continually."—"My Spirit shall not always strive with man." Upon this passage a good and intelligent man writes thus: "Surely, if His Spirit had striven with them until that time, until they were so desperately wicked, and wholly corrupted, that not only some, but every imagination of their hearts was evil, yes, *only* evil, and that continually, we may well believe the express Scripture assertion, that 'a manifestation of the Spirit is given to every man to profit withal.'"[2]

133. Respecting some of the prophetical passages in the Hebrew Scriptures, it may be observed that there appears a want of complete adaptation to the immediate purpose of *our* argument, because they speak of *that*, prospectively, which our argument assumes to be true retrospectively also. "*After those days*, saith the Lord, I will put My law in their inward parts and write it in their hearts;"[3] from which the reader may possibly conclude that before those days no such internal law was imparted. Yet the preceding paragraph might assure him of the contrary, and that the prophet indicated an increase rather than a commencement of internal guidance. Under any supposition it does not affect the argument as it respects the present condition of the human race; for the prophecy is twice quoted in the Christian Scriptures, and is expressly stated to be fulfilled. Once the prophecy is quoted almost at length, and in the other instance the important clause is retained, "I will put My laws into their hearts, and in their minds will I write them."[4]

134. "And *all* thy children," says Isaiah, "shall be taught of the Lord." Christ Himself quotes this passage in illustrating the nature of His own religion: "It is written in

[1] Hancock: Essay on Instinct, &c., p. 2, c. 7, s. 1. I take this opportunity of acknowledging the obligations I am under to this work, for many of the "Opinions" which are cited in the last section.
[2] Job Scott's Journal, c. i.   [3] Jer. xxxi. 33.
[4] Heb. viii. 10; and x. 16.

the Prophets, And they shall be *all* taught of God."[1]

135. "Thine eyes shall see thy teachers: and thine ears shall hear a word behind thee, saying, This is the way, walk ye in it; when ye turn to the right hand, and when ye turn to the left."[2]

136. The Christian Scriptures, if they be not more explicit, are more abundant in their testimony. Paul addresses the "*foolish* Galatians." The reader should observe their character; for some Christians who acknowledge the Divine influence on the minds of eminently good men, are disposed to question it in reference to others. These foolish Galatians had turned again to "weak and beggarly elements," and their dignified instructor was afraid of them, lest he had bestowed upon them labour in vain. Nevertheless to them he makes the solemn declaration, "God hath sent forth the Spirit of His Son into your hearts."[3]

137. John writes a *General* Epistle, an epistle which was addressed, of course, to a great variety of characters, of whom some, it is probable, possessed little more of the new religion than the name. The apostle writes —"Hereby we know that He abideth in us, by the Spirit which He hath given us."[4]

138. The solemn declarations which follow are addressed to large numbers of recent converts, of converts whom the writer had been severely reproving for improprieties of conduct, for unchristian contentions, and even for greater faults: "Ye are the temple of the living God, as God hath said, I will dwell in them and walk in them."—"What, know ye not that your body is the temple of the Holy Ghost which is in you?"[5] "Know ye not that ye are the temple of God, and that the Spirit of God dwelleth in you? If any man defile the temple of God, him shall God destroy; for the temple of God is holy, which temple ye are."[6]

139. And with respect to the moral operations of this sacred power:—"As touching brotherly love, ye need not that I write unto you: for ye yourselves are taught of God to love one another;"[7] that is, *taught a duty of morality*.

140. Thus also:—"The grace of God that bringeth salvation hath appeared to all men, teaching us that, denying ungodliness and worldly lusts, we should live soberly, righteously, and godly, in this present world;"[8]

or in other words, teaching *all* men moral laws—laws both mandatory and prohibitory, teaching both what to do and what to avoid.

141. And very distinctly:—"The manifestation of the Spirit is given to every man to profit withal."[1] "A Light to lighten the Gentiles."[2] "I am the Light of the world."[3] "The true Light which lighteth every man that cometh into the world."[4]

"When the Gentiles, which have not the law, do by nature the things contained in the law, these having not the law, are a law unto themselves, which show the work of the law written in their hearts,"[5]—written, it may be asked, by whom but by that Being who said, "I will put My law in their inward parts, and write it in their hearts?"[6]

142. To such evidence from the written revelation, I know of no other objection which can be urged than the supposition that this Divine instruction, though existing eighteen hundred years ago, does not exist now. To which it appears sufficient to reply, that it existed not only eighteen hundred years ago, but before the period of the Deluge; and that the terms in which the Scriptures speak of it are incompatible with the supposition of a temporary duration: "*all* taught of God:" "in you *all*:" "hath appeared unto *all* men:" "given to *every* man:" "*every man that cometh into the world*." Besides, there is not the most remote indication in the Christian Scriptures that this instruction would not be perpetual; and their silence on such a subject, a subject involving the most sacred privileges of our race, must surely be regarded as positive evidence that this instruction would be accorded to us for ever.

143. How clear soever appears to be the evidence of reason, that man, being universally a moral and accountable agent, must be possessed, universally, of a moral law; and how distinct soever the testimony of revelation, that he does universally possess it— objections are still urged against its existence.

144. Of these, perhaps the most popular are those which are founded upon the varying dictates of the "Conscience." If the view which we have taken of the nature and operations of the conscience be just, these objections will have little weight. That the dictates of the conscience should vary in individuals respectively, is precisely what, from the circumstances of the case, is to be expected; but this variation does not impeach the existence of that purer ray which, whether in less or greater brightness, irradiates the heart of man.

---

[1] John vi. 45. [2] Isa. xxx. 20, 21
[3] Gal. iv. 6. [4] 1 John iii. 24.
[5] 1 Cor. vi. 19. [6] 1 Cor. iii. 16.
[7] 1 Thess. iv. 9. [8] Tit. ii. 11, 12.

[1] 1 Cor. xii. 7. [2] Luke ii. 32.
[3] John viii. 12. [4] John i. 9.
[5] Rom. ii. 14. [6] Jer. xxxi. 33.

145. I am, however, disposed here to notice the objections[1] that may be founded upon national derelictions of portions of the Moral Law. "There is," says Locke, "scarce that principle of morality to be named, or rule of virtue to be thought on, which is not somewhere or other slighted and condemned by the general fashion of whole societies of men, governed by practical opinions and rules of living quite opposite to others."—And Paley: "There is scarcely a single vice which, in some age or country of the world, has not been countenanced by public opinion: in one country it is esteemed an office of piety in children to sustain their aged parents, in another to despatch them out of the way: suicide in one age of the world has been heroism, in another felony; theft, which is punished by most laws, by the laws of Sparta was not unfrequently rewarded: you shall hear duelling alternately reprobated and applauded according to the sex, age, or station of the person you converse with: the forgiveness of injuries and insults is accounted by one sort of people magnanimity, by another meanness."[2]

146. Upon all which I observe, that to whatever purpose these reasonings are directed, they are defective in an essential point. They show us indeed what the external actions of men have been, but give no proof that these actions were conformable with the secret internal judgment: and this last is the only important point. That a rule of virtue is "slighted and condemned by the *general fashion*," is no sort of evidence that those who joined in this general fashion did not still know that it *was* a rule of virtue. There are many duties which, in the present day, are slighted by the general fashion, and yet no man will stand up and say that they are not duties. "There is scarcely a single vice which has not been countenanced by public opinion;" but where is the proof that it has been approved by private and secret judgment? There is a great deal of difference between those sentiments which men seem to entertain respecting their duties when they give expression to "public opinion," and when they rest their heads on their pillows in calm reflection. "Suicide in one age of the world has been heroism, in another felony;" but it is not every action which a man says is heroic, that he believes is *right*. "Forgiveness of injuries and insults is accounted by one sort of people magnanimity, by another meanness;" and yet they who thus vulgarly employ the word meanness, do not imagine that forbearance and placability are really wrong.

[1] Not urged specifically, perhaps, against the Divine Guidance; but they will equally afford an illustration of the truth.
[2] Mor. and Pol. Phil., b. 1, c. 5.

147. I have met with an example which serves to confirm me in the judgment, that public notions or rather public actions are a very equivocal evidence of the real sentiments of mankind. "Can there be greater barbarity than to hurt an infant? Its helplessness, its innocence, its amiableness, call forth the compassion even of an enemy.—What then should we imagine must be the heart of a parent who would injure that weakness which a furious enemy is afraid to violate? Yet the exposition, that is, the murder of new-born infants, was a practice allowed of in almost all the states of Greece, even among the polite and civilised Athenians." This seems a strong case against us. But what were the grounds upon which this atrocity was defended?—"Philosophers, instead of censuring, supported the horrible abuse, by far-fetched considerations of public utility."[1]

148. *By far-fetched considerations of public utility!* Why had they recourse to such arguments as these? Because they found that the custom could not be reconciled with direct and acknowledged rules of virtue: because they felt and knew that it was *wrong*. The very circumstance that they had recourse to "far-fetched" arguments, is evidence that they were conscious that clearer and more immediate arguments were against them. They knew that infanticide was an immoral act.

149. I attach some importance to the indications which this class of reasoning affords of the comparative uniformity of human opinion, even when it is nominally discordant. One other illustration may be offered from more private life. Boswell, in his Life of Johnson, says that he proposed the question to the moralist, "Whether duelling was contrary to the *laws of Christianity?*" Let the reader notice the essence of the reply: "Sir, as men become in a high degree refined, various causes of offence arise which are considered to be of such importance that life must be staked to atone for them, though in reality they are not so. In a state of highly-polished society, an affront is held to be a serious injury. It must therefore be resented, or rather a duel must be fought upon it, as men have agreed to banish from their society one who puts up with an affront without fighting a duel. Now, sir, it is never unlawful to fight in self-defence. He then who fights a duel, does not fight from passion against his antagonist, but out of self-defence, to avert the stigma of the world, and to prevent himself from being driven from society.—While such notions prevail, no doubt a man may lawfully fight a duel." The question was, the consistency of duelling with the laws of

[1] Theory Mor. Sent., p. 5, c. 2.

Christianity; and there is not a word about Christianity in the reply. Why? Because its laws can never be shown to allow duelling; and Johnson doubtless knew this. Accordingly, like the philosophers who tried to justify the kindred crime of infanticide, he had recourse to "far-fetched considerations," —to the high polish of society,—to the stigma of the world,—to the notions that prevail. Now, whilst the readers of Boswell commonly think they have Johnson's authority in favour of duelling, I think they have his authority against it. I think that the mode in which he justified duelling, evinced his consciousness that it was not compatible with the Moral Law.

150. And thus it is, that with respect to Public Opinions, and general fashions, and thence descending to private life, we shall find that men very usually know the requisitions of the Moral Law better than they seem to know them; and that he who estimates the moral knowledge of societies or individuals by their common language, refers to an uncertain and fallacious standard.

151. After all, the uniformity of human opinion respecting the great laws of morality is very remarkable. Sir James Mackintosh speaks of Grotius, who had cited poets, orators, historians, &c., and says, "He quotes them as witnesses, whose conspiring testimony, mightily strengthened and confirmed by their discordance on almost every other subject, is a conclusive proof of the unanimity of the whole human race, on the great rules of duty and fundamental principles of morals."[1]

152. From poets and orators we may turn to savage life. In 1683, that is, soon after the colonisation of Pennsylvania, the founder of the colony held a "council and consultation" with some of the Indians. In the course of the interview it appeared that these savages believed in a state of future retribution; and they described their simple ideas of the respective states of the good and bad. The vices that they enumerated as those which would consign them to punishment are remarkable, inasmuch as they so nearly correspond to similar enumerations in the Christian Scriptures. They were "theft, swearing, lying, whoring, murder, and the like;"[1] and the New Testament affirms that those who are guilty of adultery, fornication, lying, theft, murder, &c., shall not inherit the kingdom of God. The same writer having on his travels met with some Indians, stopped and gave them some good and serious advices. "They wept," says he, "and tears ran down their naked bodies. They smote their hands upon their breasts and said, 'The Good Man *here* told them what I said was all good.'"[2]

153. But reasonings such as these are in reality not necessary to the support of the truth of the Immediate Communication of the Will of God; because, if the variations in men's notions of right and wrong were greater than they are, they would not impeach the existence of that communication. In the first place, we never affirm that the Deity communicates *all* His law to every man: and in the second place, it is sufficiently certain that multitudes *know* His laws, and yet neglect to fulfil them.

154. If, in conclusion, it should be asked, What assistance can be yielded, in the investigation of publicly authorised rules of virtue, by the discussions of the present chapter? we answer, Very little. But when it is asked, Of what importance are they as illustrating the Principles of Morality? we answer, Very much. If there be two sources from which it has pleased God to enable mankind to know His Will,—a law written externally, and a law communicated to the heart,—it is evident that both must be regarded as Principles of Morality, and that, in a work like the present, both should be illustrated as such. It is incidental to the latter mode of moral guidance, that it is little adapted to the formation of external rules; but it is of high and solemn importance to our species for the secret direction of the individual man.

[1] Disc. on Study of Law of Nature and Nations.   [1] John Richardson's Life.   [2] Ibid.

ESSAY I.—PART II.

SUBORDINATE MEANS OF DISCOVERING THE DIVINE WILL.

CHAPTER I.

The Law of the Land.

Its authority—Limits to its authority—Morality sometimes prohibits what the law permits.

1. The authority of civil government as a director of individual conduct, is explicitly asserted in the Christian Scriptures:—"Be subject to principalities and powers,—Obey magistrates,"[1]—"Submit yourselves to every ordinance of man for the Lord's sake: whether it be to the king, as supreme; or unto governors, as unto them that are sent by him for the punishment of evil-doers, and for the praise of them that do well."[2]

2. By this general sanction of civil government, a multitude of questions respecting human duty are at once decided. In ordinary cases, he upon whom the magistrate imposes a law, needs not to seek for knowledge of his duty upon the subject from a higher source. The Divine Will is sufficiently indicated by the fact that the magistrate commands. Obedience to the law is obedience to the expressed Will of God. He who, in the payment of a tax to support the just exercise of government, conforms to the law of the land, as truly obeys the Divine Will, as if the Deity had regulated questions of taxation by express rules.

3. In thus founding the authority of civil government upon the precepts of revelation, we refer to the ultimate, and for that reason to the most proper sanction. Not, indeed, that if revelation had been silent, the obligation of obedience might not have been deduced from other considerations. The utility of government—its tendency to promote the order and happiness of society—powerfully recommend its authority; so powerfully, indeed, that it is probable that the worst government which ever existed was incomparably better than none; and we shall hereafter have occasion to see that considerations of Utility involve actual moral obligation.

4. The purity and practical excellence of the *motives* to civil obedience which are proposed in the Christian Scriptures, are especially worthy of regard. "Submit *for the Lord's sake.*" "Be subject, not only for wrath, but *for conscience'* sake." Submission for wrath's sake, that is, from fear of penalty, implies a very inferior motive to submission upon grounds of principle and duty; and as to practical excellence, who cannot perceive that he who regulates his obedience by the motives of Christianity, acts more worthily, and honourably, and consistently, than he who is influenced only by fear of penalties? The man who obeys the laws for conscience' sake, will obey always; alike when disobedience would be unpunished and unknown, as when it would be detected the next hour. The magistrate has a security for such a man's fidelity, which no other motive can supply. A smuggler will import his kegs if there is no danger of a seizure—a Christian will not buy the brandy though no one knows it but himself.

5. It is to be observed, that the obligation of civil obedience is enforced, whether the particular command of the law is in itself sanctioned by morality or not. Antecedently to the existence of the law of the magistrate respecting the importation of brandy, it was of no consequence in the view of morality whether brandy was imported or not; but the prohibition of the magistrate involves a moral obligation to refrain. Other doctrine has been held; and it has been asserted, that unless the particular law is enforced by morality, it does not become obligatory by the command of the state.[1] But if this were true—if no law was obligatory that was not previously enjoined by morality, *no* moral obligation would result from the law of the land. Such a question is surely set at rest by, "Submit yourselves to every *ordinance of man.*"

6. But the authority of civil government is a *subordinate* authority. If, from any cause, the magistrate enjoins that which is prohibited by the Moral Law, the duty of obedience is withdrawn. "All human authority ceases at the point where obedience becomes criminal." The reason is simple; that

---
[1] Tit. iii. 1.   [2] 1 Pet. ii. 13.   [1] See Godwin's Political Justice.

when the magistrate enjoins what is criminal, he has exceeded his power: "the minister of God" has gone beyond his commission. There is, in our day, no such thing as a moral *plenipotentiary*.

7. Upon these principles, the first teachers of Christianity acted when the rulers "called them, and commanded them not to speak at all nor teach in the name of Jesus."— "Whether," they replied, "it be right in the sight of God, to hearken unto you more than unto God, judge ye."[1] They accordingly "entered into the temple early in the morning and taught:" and when, subsequently, they were again brought before the council and interrogated, they replied, "We ought to obey God rather than men;" and notwithstanding the renewed command of the council, "daily in the temple and in every house, they ceased not to teach and preach Jesus Christ."[2]—Nor let any one suppose that there is anything *religious* in the motives of the apostles, which involved a peculiar obligation upon them to refuse obedience: we have already seen that the obligation to conform to religious duty and to moral duty, is *one*.

8. To disobey the civil magistrate is, however, not a light thing. When the Christian conceives that the requisitions of government and of a higher law are conflicting, it is needful that he exercise a strict scrutiny into the principles of his conduct. But if, upon such scrutiny, the contrariety of requisitions appears real, no room is left for doubt respecting his duty, or for hesitation in performing it. With the consideration of consequences he has then no concern: whatever they may be, his path is plain before him.

9. It is sufficiently evident that these doctrines respect non-compliance only. It is one thing not to comply with laws, and another to resist those who make or enforce them. He who thinks the payment of tithes unchristian, ought to decline to pay them; but he would act upon strange principles of morality, if, when an officer came to distrain upon his property, he forcibly resisted his authority.[3]

10. If there are cases in which the positive injunctions of the law may be disobeyed, it is manifest that the mere *permission* of the law to do a given action, conveys no sufficient authority to perform it. There are, perhaps, no disquisitions connected with the present subject, which are of greater practical utility than those which show, that not everything which is legally right is morally right; that

[1] Acts iv. 18.   [2] Acts v. 29, 42.
[3] We speak here of private obligations only. Respecting the political obligations which result from the authority of civil government, some observations will be found in the chapter on Civil Obedience. Ess. iii. c. v.

a man may be entitled by law to privileges which morality forbids him to exercise, or to possessions which morality forbids him to enjoy.

11. As to the possession, for example, of property: the general foundation of the right to property is the Law of the Land. But as the law of the land is itself subordinate, it is manifest that the right to property must be subordinate also, and must be held in subjection to the Moral Law. A man who has a wife and two sons, and who is worth fifteen hundred pounds, dies without a will. The widow possesses no separate property, but the sons have received from another quarter ten thousand pounds apiece. Now, of the fifteen hundred pounds which the intestate left, the law assigns five hundred to the mother, and five hundred to each son. Are these sons morally permitted to take each his five hundred pounds, and to leave their parent with only five hundred for her support? Every man I hope will answer, No: and the reason is this; that the Moral Law, which is superior to the Law of the Land, forbids them to avail themselves of their legal rights. The Moral Law requires justice and benevolence, and a due consideration for the wants and necessities of others; and if justice and benevolence would be violated by availing ourselves of legal permissions, those permissions are not sufficient authorities to direct our conduct.

12. It has been laid down, that "so long as we keep within the design and intention of a law, that law will justify us, *in foro conscientiæ* as *in foro humano*, whatever be the equity or expediency of the law itself."[1] From the example which has been offered, I think it sufficiently appears that this maxim is utterly unsound: at any rate, its unsoundness will appear from a brief historical fact. During the Revolutionary war in America, the Virginian Legislature passed a law, by which "it was enacted, that all merchants and planters in Virginia who owed money to British merchants, should be exonerated from their debts, if they paid the money due into the public treasury instead of sending it to Great Britain; and all such as stood indebted, were invited to come forward and give their money, in this manner, towards the support of the contest in which America was then engaged." Now, according to the principles of Paley, these Virginian planters would have been justified, *in foro conscientiæ*, in defrauding the British merchants of the money which was their due. It is quite clear that the "design and intention of the law" was to allow the fraud—the planters were even *invited* to commit it; and yet the heart

[1] Mor. and Pol. Phil., b. iii. p. 1, c. 2.

of every reader will tell him, that to have availed themselves of the legal permission, would have been an act of flagitious dishonesty. The conclusion is therefore distinct —that legal decisions respecting property are not always a sufficient warrant for individual conduct. To the extreme disgrace of these planters it should be told, that although at first, when they would have *gained* little by the fraud, few of them paid their debts into the treasury, yet afterwards many large sums were paid. The Legislature offered to take the American paper money; and as this paper money, in consequence of its depreciation, was not worth an hundredth part of its value in specie, the planters, in thus paying their debts to their own government, paid but one pound instead of a hundred, and kept the remaining ninety-nine in their own pockets! Profligate as these planters and as this Legislature were, it is pleasant for the sake of America to add, that in 1796, after the Supreme Court of the United States had been erected, the British merchants brought the affair before it; and the judges directed that every one of these debts should again be paid to the rightful creditors.

13. It might be almost imagined that the moral philosopher designed to justify such conduct as that of the planters. He says, when a man "refuses to pay a debt of the reality of which he is conscious, he cannot plead the intention of the statute, *unless* he could show that the law intended to interpose its supreme authority to acquit men of debts of the existence and justice of which they were themselves sensible."[1] Now the planters *could* show that this was the intention of the law, and yet they were not justified in availing themselves of it. The error of the moralist is founded in the assumption, that there is "*supreme* authority" in the law. Make that authority, as it really is, *subordinate*, and the error, and the fallacious rule which is founded upon it, will be alike corrected.

14. In applying to the Law of the Land as a moral guide, it is of importance to distinguish its intention from its letter. The intention is not, indeed, as we have seen, a final consideration, but the *design* of a legislature is evidently of greater import, and consequent obligation, than the literal interpretation of the words in which that design is proposed to be expressed. The want of a sufficient attention to this simple rule occasions many snares to private virtue, and the commission of much practical injustice. In consequence, partly of the inadequacy of all language, and partly of the inability of those who frame laws, accurately to provide for cases which subsequently arise, it happens that the literal application of a law sometimes frustrates the intention of the legislator, and violates the obligations of justice. Whatever be the cause, it is found in practice, that courts of law usually regard the letter of a statute rather than its general intention; and hence it happens that many duties devolve upon *individuals* in the application of the laws in their own affairs. If legal courts usually decide by the letter, and if decision by the letter often defeats the objects of the legislator and the claims of justice, how shall these claims be satisfied except by the conscientious and forbearing integrity of private men? Of the cases in which this integrity should be brought into exercise, several examples will be offered in the early part of the next Essay.

CHAPTER II.

The Law of Nature.

Its authority—Limits to its authority—Obligations resulting from the Rights of Nature—Incorrect ideas attached to the word Nature.

15. We here use the term, the Law of Nature, as a convenient title under which to advert to the authority, in moral affairs, of what are called Natural Instincts and Natural Rights.

16. "They who rank Pity amongst the original impulses of our nature, rightly contend that when this principle prompts us to the relief of human misery, it *indicates the divine intention and our duty*. Indeed, the same conclusion is deducible from the existence of the passion, whatever account be given of its origin. Whether it be an instinct or a habit, it is in fact a property of our nature which God appointed."[1]

17. I should reason similarly respecting Natural Rights--the right to life—to personal liberty—to a share of the productions of the earth. The *fact* that life is given us by our Creator—that our personal powers and mental dispositions are adapted by Him to personal liberty—and that He has constituted our bodies so as to need the productions of the earth, are satisfactory indications of the Divine Will, and of human duty.

18. So that we conclude the general proposition is true— that a regard to the Law of Nature, in estimating human duty, is accordant with the Will of God. There is little necessity for formally insisting on the authority of the Law of Nature, because few are disposed to dispute that authority, at least when their own interests are served by appealing

---

[1] Mor. and Pol. Phil., b. 3, p. 1, c. 4.

[1] Mor. and Pol. Phil., b. 3, p. 2, c. 5.

to it. If this authority were questioned, perhaps it might be said that the expression of the Divine Will tacitly sanctions it, because that expression is addressed to us under the supposition that our constitution is such as it is; and because some of the Divine precepts appear to specify a point at which the authority of the Law of Nature stops. To say that a rule is only in some cases wrong, is to say, that in many it is right: to which may be added the consideration, that the tendency of the Law of Nature is manifestly beneficial. No man questions that the "original impulses of our nature" tend powerfully to the well-being of the species.

19. In speaking of the Instincts of Nature, we enter into no curious definitions of what constitutes an instinct. Whether *any* of our passions or emotions be properly instinctive, or the effect of association, is of little consequence to the purpose, so long as they actually subsist in the human economy, and so long as we have reason to believe that their subsistence there is in accordance with the Divine Will.

20. But the authority of the Law of Nature, like every other authority, is subordinate to that of the Moral Law. This indeed is sufficiently indicated by those reasonings which show the universal supremacy of that law. Yet it may be of advantage to remember such expressions as these: "Be not afraid of them that kill the body, and after that have no more that they can do. But fear Him which, after He hath killed, hath power to cast into hell."[1] This appears distinctly to place an instinct of nature in subordination to the Moral Law. The "fear of them that kill the body" results from the instinct of self-preservation; and by this instinct we are not to be guided when the Divine Will requires us to repress its voice.

21. Parental affection has been classed amongst the instincts.[2] The declaration, "He that loveth son or daughter more than Me, is not worthy of Me,"[3] clearly subjects this instinct to the higher authority of the Divine Will: for the "love" of God is to be manifested by obedience to His law. Another declaration to the same import subjects also the instinct of self-preservation: "If a man hate not (that is by comparison) his *own life* also, he cannot be My disciple."[4] And here it is remarkable, that these affections or instincts are adduced *for the purpose* of inculcating their subordination to the Moral Law.

22. Upon one of the most powerful instincts of nature, the restraints of revelation are emphatically laid. Its operation is restricted, not to a few of its possible objects,

[1] Luke xii. 4.
[2] Dr. Price.
[3] Matt. x. 37.
[4] Luke xiv. 26.

but exclusively to one; and to that one upon an express and specified condition.[1]

23. The propriety of holding the natural impulses in subjection to a higher law, appears to be asserted in this language of Dugald Stewart: "The dictates of reason and conscience inform us, in language which it is impossible to mistake, that it is sometimes *a duty* to check the most amiable and pleasing emotions of the heart; to withdraw, for example, from the sight of those distresses which stronger claims forbid us to relieve, and to deny ourselves that exquisite luxury which arises from the exercise of humanity. Even that morality which is not founded upon religion, recommends the same truth. Godwin says, that if Fenelon were in his palace and it took fire, and it so happened that the life either of himself or of his chambermaid must be sacrificed, it would be the *duty* of the woman to repress the instinct of self-preservation, and sacrifice hers—because Fenelon would do more good in the world.[2] If the morality of scepticism inculcates this subjugation of our instincts to indeterminate views of advantage, much more does the morality of the New Testament teach us to subject them to the determinate Will of God.

24. It is upon these principles that some of the most noble examples of human excellence have been exhibited—those of men who have died for the testimony of a good conscience. If the strongest of our instincts—if that instinct, excited to its utmost vigour by the apprehension of a dreadful death, might be of weight to suspend the obligation of the Moral Law, it surely might have been suspended in the case of those who thus proved their fidelity.

25. Yet, obvious as is the propriety and the duty of thus preferring the Divine Law before all, the dictates or the rights of nature are continually urged as of paramount obligation. Many persons appear to think that if a given action is dictated by the *law of nature*, it is quite sufficient. Respecting the instinct of self-preservation, especially, they appear to conclude that to whatever that instinct prompts, it is lawful to conform to its voice. They do not surely reflect upon the *monstrousness* of their opinions; they do not surely consider that they are absolutely superseding the Moral Law of God, and superseding it upon considerations resulting merely from the animal part of our constitution. The Divine Laws respect the whole human economy—our prospects in another world as well as our existence in the present.

26. Some men, again, speak of our rights

[1] See Matt. iv. 9; 1 Cor. vi. 9, vii. 1, 2; Gal. v. 19, &c.
[2] Political Justice.

in a *state of nature*, as if to be in a state of nature was to be without the jurisdiction of the Moral Law. But if man be a moral and responsible agent, that law applies everywhere; to a state of nature as truly as to every other state. If some other human being had been left with Selkirk on Juan Fernandez, and if that other seized an animal which Selkirk had ensnared, would Selkirk have been justified in asserting his natural right to the animal *by whatever means?* It is very possible that no means would have availed to procure the restoration of the rabbit or the bird short of *killing* the offender. Might Selkirk kill the man in assertion of his natural rights? Every one answers, No—because the unsophisticated dictates in every man's mind assure us that the rights of nature are subordinate to higher laws.

27. Situations similar to those of a state of nature sometimes arise in society;[1] as where money is demanded, or violence is committed by one person on another, where no third person can be called in to assistance. The injured party, in such a case, cannot go to *every* length in his own cause by virtue of the law of nature: he can go only *so far* as the Moral Law allows. These considerations will be found peculiarly applicable to the rights of self-defence; and it is pleasant to find these doctrines supported by that sceptical morality to which we just now referred. The author of *Political Justice* maintains that *man possesses no rights;* that is, no absolute rights—none, of which the just exercise is not conditional upon the permission of a higher rule. That rule, with him, is "Justice"—with us it is the law of God; but the reasoning is the same in kind.

28. Nevertheless, the natural rights of man ought to possess extensive application both in private and political affairs. If it were sufficiently remembered, that these rights are abstractedly possessed in equality by all men, we should find many imperative claims upon us with which we do not now comply. The artificial distinctions of society induce forgetfulness of the circumstance that we are all brethren: not that I would countenance the speculations of those who think that all men should be now practically equal; but that these distinctions are such, that the general rights of nature are invaded *in a degree* which nothing can justify. There are natural claims of the poor upon the rich, of dependants upon their superiors, which are very commonly forgotten: there are endless acts of superciliousness, and unkindness, and oppression in private life, which the Law of Nature emphatically condemns. When, sometimes, I see a man of fortune speaking in terms of supercilious command to his servant, I feel that he needs to go and learn some lessons of the Law of Nature. I feel that he has forgotten what he is, and what he is not, and what his brother is: he has forgotten that by nature he and his servant are in strictness equal; and that although, by the permission of Providence, a various allotment is assigned to them now, he should regard every one with that consideration and respect which is due to a man and a brother. And when to these considerations are added those which result from the contemplation of our relationship to God—that we are the common objects of His bounty and His goodness, and that we are heirs to a common salvation, we are presented with such motives to pay attention to the rights of nature, as constitute an imperative obligation.

29. The *political* duties which result from the Law of Nature, it is not our present business to investigate; but it may be observed here, that a very limited appeal to facts is sufficient to evince, that by many political institutions the Rights of Nature have been grievously sacrificed; and that if those Rights had been sufficiently regarded, many of these vicious institutions would never have been exhibited in the world.

30. It appears worth while at the conclusion of this chapter to remark, that a person when he speaks of "Nature," should know distinctly what he means. The word carries with it a sort of indeterminate authority; and he who uses it amiss, may connect that authority with rules or actions which are little entitled to it. There are few senses in which the word is used, that do not refer, however obscurely, to God; and it is for that reason that the notion of authority is connected with the word. "The very name of nature implies, that it must owe its birth to some prior agent, or, to speak properly, signifies in itself nothing."[1] Yet, unmeaning as the term is, it is one of which many persons are very fond;—whether it be that their notions are really indistinct, or that some purposes are answered by referring to the obscurity of nature rather than to God. "*Nature* has decorated the earth with beauty and magnificence,"—"*Nature* has furnished us with joints and limbs,"—are phrases sufficiently unmeaning; and yet I know not that they are likely to do any other harm than to give currency to the common fiction. But when it is said that "*Nature* teaches us to adhere to truth"—"*Nature* condemns us for dishonesty or deceit"—"Men are taught by *nature* that they are responsible beings"—there is considerable danger that we have both fallacious and injurious notions of the authority which

---

[1] See Locke on Gov., b. 2, c. 7.   [1] Milton: Christian Doct., p. 14.

thus teaches or condemns us. Upon this subject it were well to take the advice of Boyle: "Nature," he says, "is sometimes, indeed commonly, taken for a kind of semi-deity. In this sense it is best not to use it at all."[1] It is dangerous to induce confusion into our ideas respecting our relationship with God.

31. A *law of nature* is a very imposing phrase; and it might be supposed, from the language of some persons, that nature was an independent legislatress, who had sat and framed laws for the government of mankind. Nature is nothing: yet it would seem that men do sometimes practically imagine, that a "law of nature" possesses proper and independent authority; and it may be suspected that with some the notion is so palpable and strong, that they set up the authority of "the law of nature" without reference to the Will of God, or perhaps in opposition to it. Even if notions like these float in the mind only with vapoury indistinctness, a correspondent indistinctness of moral notions is likely to ensue. Every man should make to himself the rule, never to employ the word *Nature* when he speaks of ultimate moral authority. A law possesses no authority; the authority rests only in the legislator: and as nature makes no laws, a law of nature involves no obligation but that which is imposed by the Divine Will.

CHAPTER III.
Utility.
Obligations resulting from Expediency—Limits to these obligations.

32. That in estimating our duties in life we ought to pay regard to what is useful and beneficial to what is likely to promote the welfare of ourselves and of others—can need little argument to prove. Yet, if it were required, it may be easily shown that this regard to Utility is recommended or enforced in the expression of the Divine Will. That Will requires the exercise of pure and universal benevolence;—which benevolence is exercised in consulting the interests, the welfare, and the happiness of mankind. The dictates of Utility, therefore, are frequently no other than the dictates of benevolence.

33. Or, if we derive the obligations of Utility from considerations connected with our reason, they do not appear much less distinct. To say that to consult Utility is right, is almost the same as to say, it is right to exercise our understandings. The daily and hourly use of reason is, to discover what is fit to be done; that is, what is useful and expedient: and since it is manifest that the Creator, in endowing us with the faculty, designed that we should exercise it, it is obvious that in this view also a reference to expediency is consistent with the Divine Will.

34. When (higher laws being silent) a man judges that of two alternatives one is dictated by greater utility, that dictate constitutes an *obligation* upon him to prefer it. I should not hold a landowner *innocent*, who knowingly persisted in adopting a bad mode of raising corn; nor should I hold the person innocent who opposed an improvement in shipbuilding, or who obstructed the formation of a turnpike road that would benefit the public. These are questions, not of prudence merely, but of morals also.

35. Obligations resulting from Utility possess great extent of application to political affairs. There are, indeed, some public concerns in which the Moral Law, antecedently, decides nothing. Whether a duty shall be imposed, or a charter granted, or a treaty signed, are questions which are perhaps to be determined by expediency alone: but when a public man is of the judgment that any given measure will tend to the general good, he is *immoral* if he opposes that measure. The immorality may indeed be made out by a somewhat different process:—such a man violates those duties of benevolence which religion imposes: he probably disregards, too, his sense of obligation; for if he be of the judgment that a given measure will tend to the general good, conscience will scarcely be silent in whispering that he ought not to oppose it.

36. It is sufficiently evident, upon the principles which have hitherto been advanced, that considerations of Utility are only so far obligatory as they are in accordance with the Moral Law. Pursuing, however, the method which has been adopted in the two last chapters, it may be observed, that this subserviency of Utility to the Divine Will, appears to be required by the written revelation. That habitual preference of futurity to the present time, which Scripture exhibits, indicates that our interests here should be held in subordination to our interests hereafter: and as these higher interests are to be consulted *by the means* which revelation prescribes, it is manifest that those means are to be pursued, whatever we may suppose to be their effects upon the present welfare of ourselves or of other men. "If in this life only we have hope in God, then are we of all men most miserable." It certainly is not, in the usual sense of the word, expedient

---
[1] Free Inquiry into the vulgarly received Notions of Nature.

to be most miserable. And why did they thus sacrifice expediency? Because the communicated Will of God required that course of life by which human interests were *apparently* sacrificed. It will be perceived that these considerations result from the truth (too little regarded in talking of "Expediency" and "General Benevolence"), that Utility, as it respects mankind, cannot be properly consulted without taking into account our interests in futurity. "Let us eat and drink, for to-morrow we die," is a maxim of which all would approve if we had no concerns with another life. That which might be very expedient if death were annihilation, may be very inexpedient now.

37. "If ye say, We will not dwell in this land, neither obey the voice of the Lord your God, saying, No ; but we will go into the land of Egypt, where *we shall see no war ;*" "*nor have hunger of bread;* and there will we dwell ; it shall come to pass, that the sword, which ye feared, shall overtake you there in the land of Egypt ; and the famine, whereof ye were afraid, shall follow close after you in Egypt ; and there ye shall die."[1]—"We will burn incense unto the queen of heaven, and pour out drink-offerings unto her ; for then had we *plenty of victuals, and were well, and saw no evil.* But since we left off, we have wanted all things, and have been consumed by the sword, and by the famine."—Therefore, "I will watch over them for evil, and not for good."[2] These reasoners argued upon the principle of making expediency the paramount law ; and it may be greatly doubted whether those who argue upon that principle now, have better foundation for their reasoning than those of old. Here was the prospect of advantage founded, as they thought, upon experience. One course of action had led (so they reasoned) to war and famine, and another to plenty, and health, and general well-being ; yet still our Universal Lawgiver required them to disregard all these conclusions of expediency, and simply to conform to His will.

38. After all, the general experience is, that what is most expedient with respect to another world is most expedient with respect to the present. There may be cases, and there have been, in which the Divine Will may require an absolute renunciation of our present interests ; as the martyr who maintains his fidelity, sacrifices all possibility of advantage now. But these are unusual cases ; and the experience of the contrary is so general, that the truth has been reduced to a proverb. Perhaps in nineteen cases out of twenty, he best consults his present welfare, who endeavours to secure it in another world. "By the wise contrivance of the Author of nature, Virtue is upon all ordinary occasions, even with regard to this life, real wisdom, and the surest and readiest means of obtaining both safety and advantage."[1] Were it however otherwise, the truth of our principles would not be shaken. Men's happiness, and especially the happiness of good men, does not consist merely in external things. The promise of a hundredfold in this present life may still be fulfilled in mental felicity ; and if it could not be, who is the man that would exclude from his computations the prospect, in the world to come, of life everlasting?

39. In the endeavour to produce the greatest sum of happiness, or which is the same thing, in applying the dictates of Utility to our conduct in life, there is one species of utility that is deplorably disregarded both in private and public affairs—that which respects the *religious* and *moral* welfare of mankind. If you hear a politician expatiating upon the good tendency of a measure, he tells you how greatly it will promote the interests of commerce, or how it will enrich a colony, or how it will propitiate a powerful party, or how it will injure a nation whom he dreads ; but you hear probably not one word of inquiry whether it will corrupt the character of those who execute the measure, or whether it will introduce vices into the colony, or whether it will present new temptations to the virtue of the public. And yet these considerations are perhaps by far the most important in the view even of enlightened expediency ; for it is a desperate game to endeavour to benefit a people by means which may diminish their virtue. Even such a politician would probably assent to the unapplied proposition, " the virtue of a people is the best security for their welfare." It is the same in private life. You hear a parent who proposes to change his place of residence, or to engage in a new profession or pursuit, discussing the comparative conveniences of the proposed situation, the prospect of profit in the new profession, the pleasures which will result from the new pursuit ; but you hear probably not one word of inquiry whether the change of residence will deprive his family of virtuous and beneficial society which will not be replaced—whether the contemplated profession will not tempt his own virtue or diminish his usefulness—or whether his children will not be exposed to circumstances that will probably taint the purity of their minds. And yet this parent will acknowledge, in general terms, that "nothing can compensate for the loss of religious and moral character." Such persons surely make very inaccurate computations of Expediency.

---

[1] Jer. xlii.   [2] Jer. xliv.   [1] Dr. Smith : Theo. Mor. Sent.

40. As to the actual conduct of political affairs, men frequently legislate as if there was no such thing as religion or morality in the world ; or as if, at any rate, religion and morality had no concern with affairs of state. I believe that a sort of shame (a false and vulgar shame no doubt) would be felt by many members of senates, in directly opposing religious or moral considerations to prospects of advantage. In our own country, those who are most willing to do this receive, from vulgar persons, a name of contempt for their absurdity ! How inveterate must be the impurity of a system, which teaches men to regard as ridiculous that system which only is sound !

CHAPTER IV.

The Law of Nations — The Law of Honour.

Although the subjects of this chapter can scarcely be regarded as constituting rules of life, yet we are induced briefly to notice them in the present Essay, partly on account of the importance of the affairs which they regulate, and partly because they will afford satisfactory illustration of the principles of Morality.

SECTION I.

The Law of Nations.

Obligations and authority of the Law of Nations— Its abuses, and the limits of its authority — Treaties.

41. The Law of Nations, so far as it is founded upon the principles of morality, partakes of that authority which those principles possess ; so far as it is founded merely upon the mutual conventions of states, it possesses that authority over the contracting parties which results from the rule, that men ought to abide by their engagements. The principal considerations which present themselves upon the subject, appear to be these : 1. That the Law of Nations is binding upon those states who knowingly allow themselves to be regarded as parties to it. 2. That it is wholly nugatory with respect to those states which are not parties to it. 3. That it is of no force in opposition to the Moral Law.

42. 1. The obligation of the Law of Nations upon those who join in the convention is plain —that is, it rests, generally, upon all civilised communities which have intercourse with one another. A tacit engagement only is, from the circumstances of the case, to be expected ; and if any state did not choose to conform to the Law of Nations, it should publicly express its dissent. The Law of Nations is not wont to tighten the bonds of morality ; so that probably most of its positive requisitions are enforced by the Moral Law : and this consideration should operate as an inducement to a conscientious fulfilment of these requisitions. In time of war, the Law of Nations prohibits poisoning and assassination, and it is manifestly imperative upon every state to forbear them ; but whilst morality thus enforces many of the requisitions of the Law of Nations, that law frequently stops short, instead of following on to whither morality would conduct it. This distinction between assassination and some other modes of destruction that are practised in war, is not perhaps very accurately founded in considerations of morality : nevertheless, since the distinction is made, let it be made, and let it by all means be regarded. Men need not add arsenic and the private dagger to those modes of human destruction which war allows. The obligation to avoid private murder is clear, even though it were shown that the obligation extends much further. Whatever be the reasonableness of the distinction, and of the rule that is founded upon it, it is perfidious to violate that rule.

43. So it is with those maxims of the Law of Nations which require that prisoners should not be enslaved, and that the persons of ambassadors should be respected. Not that I think the man who sat down, with only the principles of morality before him, would easily be able to show, *from those principles*, that the slavery was wrong whilst other things which the Law of Nations allows are right—but that, as these principles actually enforce the maxims, as the observance of them is agreed on by civilised states, and as they tend to diminish the evils of war, it is imperative on states to observe them. Incoherent and inconsistent as the Law of Nations is, when it is examined by the Moral Law, it is pleasant to contemplate the good tendency of some of its requisitions. In 1702, previous to the declaration of war by this country, a number of the anticipated "enemy's" ships had been seized and detained. When the declaration was made, these vessels were released, "in pursuance," as the proclamation stated, "of the Law of Nations." Some of these vessels were perhaps shortly after captured, and irrecoverably lost to their owners : yet, though it might perplex the Christian moralist to show that the release was right and that the capture was right too, still he may rejoice that men conform, even *in part*, to the purity of virtue.

44. Attempts to deduce the maxims of international law as they now obtain, from principles of morality, will always be vain. Grotius seems as if he would countenance the attempt when he says, "Some writers

have advanced a doctrine which can never be admitted, maintaining that the Law of Nations authorises one power to commence hostilities against another, whose increasing greatness awakens her alarms. As a matter of expediency," says Grotius, " such a measure may be adopted ; but the principles of justice can never be advanced in its favour."¹ Alas ! if principles of justice are to decide what the Law of Nations shall authorise, it will be needful to establish a new code to-morrow. A great part of the code arises out of the conduct of war ; and the usual practices of war are so foreign to principles of justice and morality, that it is to no purpose to attempt to found the code upon them. Nevertheless, let those who refer to the Law of Nations, introduce morality by all possible means ; and if they think they cannot appeal to it always, let them appeal to it where they can. If they cannot persuade themselves to avoid hostilities when some injury is committed by another nation, let them avoid them when "another nation's greatness merely awakens their alarms."

45. II. That the Law of Nations is wholly nugatory with respect to those states which are not parties to it, is a truth which, however sound, has been too little regarded in the conduct of civilised nations. The state whose subjects discover and take possession of an uninhabited island, is entitled by the Law of Nations quietly to possess it. And it ought quietly to possess it : not that in the view of reason or of morality, the circumstance of an Englishman's first visiting the shores of a country, gives any very intelligible right to the King of England to possess it rather than any other prince, but that, such a rule having been agreed upon, it ought to be observed ; but by whom ? By those who are parties to the agreement. For which reason, the discoverer possesses no sufficient claim to oppose his right to that of a people who were not parties to it. So that he who, upon pretence of discovery, should forcibly exclude from a large extent of territory a people who knew nothing of European politics, and who in the view of reason possessed an equal or a greater right, undoubtedly violates the obligations of morality. It may serve to dispel the obscurity in which habit and self-interest wrap our perceptions, to consider, that amongst the states which were nearest to the newly-discovered land, a Law of Nations might exist which required that such land should be equally divided amongst them. Whose Law of Nations ought to prevail ? That of European states, or that of states in the Pacific or South Sea ? How happens it that the Englishman possesses a sounder right to exclude all other nations, than surrounding nations possess to partition it amongst them ?

46. Unhappily, our Law of Nations goes much further ; and by a monstrous abuse of power, has acted upon the same doctrine with respect to *inhabited* countries ; for when these have been discovered, the Law of Nations has talked, with perfect coolness, of setting up a standard, and thenceforth assigning the territory to the nation whose subjects set it up ; as if the previous inhabitants possessed no other claim or right than the bears and wolves. It has been asked (and asked with great reason), what we should say to a canoe full of Indians who should *discover* England, and take possession of it in the name of their chief?

47. Civilised states appear to have acted upon the maxim, that no people possess political rights but those who are parties to the Law of Nations ; and accordingly the history of European settlements has been, so far as the aborigines were concerned, too much a history of outrage, and treachery, and blood. Penn acted upon sounder principles : he perfectly well knew that neither an established practice, nor the Law of Nations could impart a right to a country which was justly possessed by former inhabitants ; and therefore, although Charles II. "granted" him Pennsylvania, he did not imagine that the gift of a man in London could justify him in taking possession of a distant country without the occupiers' consent. What was "granted" therefore by his sovereign, he purchased of the owners ; and the sellers were satisfied with their bargain and with him. The experience of Pennsylvania has shown that integrity is politic as well as right. When nations shall possess greater expansion of knowledge, and exercise greater purity of virtue, it will be found that many of the principles which regulate international intercourse are foolish as well as vicious ; that whilst they disregard the interests of morality they sacrifice their own.

48. III. Respecting the third consideration, that the Law of Nations is of no force in opposition to the Moral Law, little needs to be said here. It is evident that, upon whatever foundation the Law of Nations rests, its authority is subordinate to that of the Will of God. When, therefore, we say that amongst civilised states, when an island is discovered by one state, other states are bound to refrain, it is not identical with saying that the discoverer is at liberty to keep possession *by whatever means.* The mode of asserting all rights is to be regulated in subordination to the Moral Law. Duplicity and fraud, and violence, and bloodshed, may perhaps sometimes be the only means of availing

¹ Rights of War and Peace.

ourselves of the rights which the Law of Nations grants: but it were a confused species of morality which should allow the commission of all this, because it is consistent with the Law of Nations.

49. A kindred remark applies to the obligation of treaties. Treaties do not oblige us to do what is morally wrong. A treaty is a string of engagements; but those engagements are no more exempt from the jurisdiction of the Moral Law, than the promise of a man to assassinate another. Does such a promise morally bind the ruffian? No: and for this reason, and for no other, that the *performance* is unlawful. And so it is with treaties. Two nations enter into a treaty of offensive and defensive alliance. Subsequently one of them engages in an unjust and profligate war. Does the treaty morally bind the other nation to abet the profligacy and injustice? No: if it did, any man might make any action lawful to himself by previously *engaging* to do it. No doubt such a nation and such a ruffian have done wrong; but their offence consisted in making the engagement, not in breaking it. Even if ordinary wars were defensible, treaties of offensive alliance that are unconditional with respect to time or objects, can never be justified. The state, however, which, in the pursuit of a temporary policy, has been weak enough, or vicious enough to make them, should not hesitate to refuse fulfilment, when the act of fulfilment is incompatible with the Moral Law. Such a state should decline to perform the treaty, and retire with shame—with shame, not that it has violated its engagements, but that it was ever so vicious as to make them.

SECTION II.

The Law of Honour.

Authority of the Law of Honour—Its character.

50. The Law of Honour consists of a set of maxims, written or understood, by which persons of a certain class agree to regulate, or are expected to regulate, their conduct. It is evident that the obligation of the Law of Honour, as such, results exclusively from the agreement, tacit or expressed, of the parties concerned. It binds them *because* they have agreed to be bound, and for no other reason. He who does not choose to be ranked amongst the subjects of the Law of Honour, is under no obligation to obey its rules. These rules are precisely upon the same footing as the laws of freemasonry, or the regulations of a reading-room. He who does not choose to subscribe to the room, or to promise conformity to masonic laws, is under no obligation to regard the rules of either.

51. For which reasons, it is very remarkable that at the commencement of his Moral Philosophy, Dr. Paley says, "*The rules of life* are, the Law of Honour, the Law of the Land, and the Scriptures.*" It were strange indeed, if *that* were a rule of life which every man is at liberty to disregard if he pleases; and which, in point of fact, nine persons out of ten do disregard without blame. Who would think of taxing the writer of these pages with violating a "rule of life," because he pays no attention to the Law of Honour? "The Scriptures" communicate the Will of God; "the Law of the Land" is enforced by that Will; but where is the sanction of the Law of Honour?—It is so much the more remarkable that this law should have been thus formally proposed as a rule of life, because, in the same work, it is described as "unauthorised." How can a set of unauthorised maxims compose a rule of life? But further: the author says that the Law of Honour is a "capricious rule which abhors deceit, yet applauds the address of a successful intrigue."—And further still: "it allows of fornication, adultery, drunkenness, prodigality, duelling, and of revenge in the extreme." Surely then it cannot, with any propriety of language, be called a rule of life.

52. Placing, then, the obligation of the Law of Honour, as such, upon that which appears to be its proper basis—the duty to perform our lawful engagements—it may be concluded, that when a man goes to a gaming-house or a race-course, and loses his money by betting or playing, he is morally bound to pay: not because morality adjusts the rules of the billiard-room or the turf, not because the Law of the Land sanctions the stake, but because the party *previously promised* to pay it. Nor would it affect this obligation, to allege that the stake was itself both illegal and immoral. So it was; but the payment is not. The payment of such a debt involves no breach of the Moral Law. The guilt consists not in paying the money, but in staking it. Nevertheless, there may be prior claims upon a man's property which he ought first to pay. Such are those of lawful creditors. The practice of paying debts of honour with promptitude, and of delaying the payment of other debts, argues confusion or depravity of principle. It is not honour, in any virtuous and rational sense of the word, which induces men to pay debts of honour instantly. Real honour would induce them to pay their lawful debts *first:* and indeed it may be suspected that the motive to the prompt payment of gaming debts is usually no other than the desire to preserve a fair name with the world. Integrity of principle has often so little to do with it, that this principle is sacrificed in order to pay them.

53. With respect to those maxims of the Law of Honour which require conduct that the Moral Law forbids, it is quite manifest that they are utterly indefensible. "If unauthorised laws of honour be allowed to create exceptions to divine prohibitions, there is an end of all morality as founded in the Will of the Deity, and the obligation of every duty may at one time or other be discharged."[1] These observations apply to those foolish maxims of honour which relate to duelling. These maxims can never justify the individual in disregarding the obligations of morality. He who acts upon them acts *wickedly*; unless indeed he be so little informed of the requisitions of morality, that he does not, upon this subject, perceive the distinction between right and wrong. The man of honour, therefore, should pay a gambling debt, but he should not send a challenge or accept it. The one is permitted by the Moral Law, the other is forbidden.

54. Whatever advantages may result from the Law of Honour, it is, as a system, both contemptible and bad. Even its advantages are of an ambiguous kind; for although it may prompt to rectitude of conduct, that conduct is not founded upon rectitude of principle. The motive is not so good as the act. And as to many of its particular rules, both positive and negative, they are the proper subject of reprobation and abhorrence. We ought to reprobate and abhor a system which enjoins the ferocious practice of challenges and duels, and which allows many of the most flagitious and degrading vices that infest the world.

55. The practical effects of the Law of Honour are probably greater and worse than we are accustomed to suppose. Men learn, by the power of association, to imagine that *that* is lawful which their maxims of conduct do not condemn. A set of rules which inculcates some actions that are right, and permits others that are wrong, practically operates as a sanction to the wrong. The code which attaches disgrace to falsehood, but none to drunkenness or adultery, operates as a sanction to drunkenness and adultery. Does not experience verify these conclusions of reason? Is it not true that men and women of honour indulge, with the less hesitation, in some vices, in consequence of the tacit permission of the Law of Honour? What then is to be done but to reprobate the system as a whole? In this reprobation the man of sense may unite with the man of virtue; for assuredly the system is contemptible in the view of intellect, as well as hateful in the view of purity.

---

[1] Mor. and Pol. Phil., b. 3, c. 9.

ESSAY II.

PRIVATE RIGHTS AND OBLIGATIONS.

THE division which has commonly been made of the private obligations of man, into those which respect himself, his neighbour, and his Creator, does not appear to be attended with any considerable advantages. These several obligations are indeed so involved the one with the other, that there are few personal duties which are not also in some degree relative, and there are no duties, either relative or personal, which may not be regarded as duties to God. The suicide's or the drunkard's vice injures his family or his friends: for every offence against morality is an injury to ourselves, and a violation of the duties which we owe to Him whose law is the foundation of morality. Neglecting, therefore, these minuter distinctions, we observe those only which separate the Private from the Political Obligations of Mankind.

CHAPTER I.

Religious Obligations.

Factitious semblances of devotion—Religious conversation—Sabbatical institutions—Non-sanctity of days—Of temporal employments: Travelling: Stage-coaches: "Sunday papers:" Amusements—Holydays—Ceremonial institutions and devotional formularies—Utility of forms—Forms of prayer—Extempore prayer—Scepticism—Motives to Scepticism.

1. Of the two classes of Religious Obligations—that which respects the exercise of piety towards God, and that which respects visible testimonials of our reverence and devotion, the business of a work like this is principally with the latter. Yet at the risk of being charged with deviating from this proper business, I would adventure a few paragraphs respecting devotion of mind.

2. That the worship of our Father who is in heaven consists, *not* in assembling with others at an appointed place and hour; *not* in joining in the rituals of a Christian church, or in performing ceremonies, or in participating of sacraments,[1] all men will agree; because all men know that these things may be done whilst the mind is wholly intent upon other affairs, and even without any belief in the existence of God. "Two attendances upon public worship is a form, complied with by thousands who never kept a Sabbath in their lives."[2] Devotion, it is evident, is an operation of the mind; the sincere aspiration of a dependent and grateful being to Him who has all power both in heaven and in earth: and as the exercise of devotion is not necessarily dependent upon external circumstances, it may be maintained in solitude or in society, in the place appropriated to worship or in the field, in the hour of business or of quietude and rest. Even under a less spiritual dispensation of old, a good man "worshipped, leaning upon the top of his staff."

3. Now it is to be feared that some persons, who acknowledge that devotion is a mental exercise, impose upon themselves some feelings as devotional which are wholly foreign to the worship of God. There is a sort of spurious devotion—feelings, having the resemblance of worship, but not possessing its nature, and not producing its effects. "Devotion," says Blair, "is a powerful principle, which penetrates the soul, which purifies the affections from debasing attachments, and by a fixed and steady regard to God, subdues every sinful passion, and forms the inclinations to piety and virtue."[1] To purify the affections and subdue the passions, is a serious operation: it implies a sacrifice of inclination; a subjugation of the will. This mental operation many persons are not willing to undergo: and it is not therefore wonderful that some persons are willing to satisfy themselves with the exercise of a species of devotion that shall be attained at less cost.

4. A person goes to an oratorio of sacred music. The majestic flow of harmony, the exalted subjects of the hymns or anthems, the full and rapt assembly, excite, and warm, and agitate his mind: sympathy becomes powerful; he feels the stirring of unwonted emotions; weeps, perhaps, or exults; and when he leaves the assembly, persuades himself that he has been worshipping and glorifying God.

5. There are some preachers with whom

---
[1] It is to be regretted that this word, of which the origin is so exceptionable, should be used to designate what are regarded as solemn acts of religion.
[2] Cowper's Letters.

[1] Sermons, No. 10.

it appears to be an object of much solicitude to excite the hearer to a warm and impassioned state of feeling. By ardent declamation or passionate displays of the hopes and terrors of religion, they arouse and alarm his imagination. The hearer, who desires perhaps to experience the ardours of religion, cultivates the glowing sensations, abandons his mind to the impulse of feeling, and at length goes home in complacency with his religious sensibility, and glads himself with having felt the fervours of devotion.

6. Kindred illusion may be the result of calmer causes. The lofty and silent aisle of an ancient cathedral, the venerable ruins of some once honoured abbey, the boundless expanse of the heaven of stars, the calm immensity of the still ocean, or the majesty and terror of a tempest, sometimes suffuses the mind with a sort of reverence and awe; a sort of "philosophic transport," which a person would willingly hope is devotion of the heart.

7. It might be sufficient to assure us of the spuriousness of these semblances of religious feeling, to consider, that emotions very similar in their nature are often excited by subjects which have no connection with religion. I know not whether the affecting scenes of the drama and of fictitious story want much but *association with ideas of religion* to make them as devotional as those which have been noticed: and if, on the other hand, the feelings of him who attends an oratorio were excited by a military band, he would think not of the Deity or of heaven, but of armies and conquests. Nor should it be forgotten, that persons who have habitually little pretension to religion, are perhaps as capable of this factitious devotion as those in whom religion is constantly influential; and surely it is not to be imagined, that those who rarely direct reverent thoughts to their Creator, can suddenly adore Him for an hour and then forget Him again, until some new excitement again arouses their raptures, to be again forgotten.

8. To religious feelings as to other things, the truth applies —" By their *fruits* ye shall know them." If these feelings do not tend to "purify the affections from debasing attachments;" if they do not tend to "form the inclinations to piety and virtue," they certainly are not devotional. Upon him whose mind is really prostrated in the presence of his God, the legitimate effect is, that he should be impressed with a more sensible consciousness of the Divine presence: that he should deviate with less facility from the path of duty; that his desires and thoughts should be reduced to Christian subjugation; that he should feel an influential addition to his dispositions to goodness; and that his affections should be expanded towards his fellow-men. He who rises from the sensibilities of seeming devotion, and finds that effects such as these are not produced in his mind, may rest assured that, in whatever he has been employed, it has not been in the pure worship of that God who is a spirit. To the real prostration of the soul in the Divine presence, it is necessary that the mind should be still:—"Be still, and know that I am God." Such devotion is sufficient for the whole mind: it needs not perhaps in its purest state it admits not—the intrusion of external things. And when the soul is thus permitted to enter as it were into the sanctuary of God; when it is humble in His presence; when all its desires are involved in the one desire of devotedness to Him; then is the hour of acceptable *worship*—then the petition of the soul is *prayer*—then is its gratitude *thanksgiving*—then is its oblation *praise.*

9. That such devotion, when such is attainable, will have a powerful tendency to produce obedience to the Moral Law, may justly be expected: and here indeed is the true connection of the subject of these remarks with the general object of the present essays. Without real and efficient piety of mind, we are not to expect a consistent observance of the Moral Law. That law requires, sometimes, sacrifices of inclination and of interest, and a general subjugation of the passions, which religion, and religion only, can capacitate and induce us to make. I recommend not enthusiasm or fanaticism, but that sincere and reverent application of the soul to its Creator, which alone is likely to give either distinctness to our perceptions of His Will, or efficiency to our motives to fulfil it.

10. A few sentences will be indulged to me here respecting Religious Conversation. I believe both that the proposition is true, and that it is expedient to set it down—that religious conversation is one of the banes of the religious world. There are many who are really attached to religion, and who sometimes feel its power, but who allow their better feelings to evaporate in an ebullition of words. They forget how much religion is an affair of the mind and how little of the tongue: they forget how possible it is to live under its power without talking of it to their friends; and some, it is to be feared, may forget how possible it is to talk without feeling its influence. Not that the good man's piety is to live in his breast like an anchorite in his cell. The evil does not consist in speaking of religion, but in speaking too much; not in manifesting our allegiance to God; not in encouraging by exhortation, and amending by our advice; not in placing the light upon a candlestick — but in making religion a

common topic of discourse. Of all species of well-intended religious conversation, that perhaps is the most exceptionable which consists in narrating our own religious feelings. Many thus intrude upon that religious quietude which is peculiarly favourable to the Christian character. The *habit* of communicating "experiences" I believe to be very prejudicial to the mind. It may sometimes be right to do this: in the great majority of instances I believe it is not beneficial, and not right. Men thus dissipate religious impressions, and therefore diminish their effects. Such observation as I have been enabled to make, has sufficed to convince me that, where the religious character is solid, there is but little religious talk; and that, where there is much talk, the religious character is superficial, and, like other superficial things, is easily destroyed. And if these be the attendants, and in part the *consequences* of general religious conversation, how peculiarly dangerous must that conversation be, which exposes those impressions that perhaps were designed exclusively for ourselves, and the use of which may be frustrated by communicating them to others. Our solicitude should be directed to the invigoration of the religious character in our own minds; and we should be anxious that the plant of piety, if it had fewer branches, might have a deeper root.

Sabbatical Institutions.

11. "Not forsaking the assembling of ourselves together, as the manner of some is."[1] The divinely authorised institution of Moses respecting a weekly Sabbath, and the practice of the first teachers of Christianity, constitute a sufficient recommendation to set apart certain times for the exercise of public worship, even were there no injunctions such as that which is placed at the head of this paragraph. It is, besides, manifestly proper that beings who are dependent upon God for all things, and especially for their hopes of immortality, should devote a portion of their time to the expression of their gratitude, and submission, and reverence. Community of dependence and of hope dictates the propriety of *united* worship; and worship to be united, must be performed at times previously fixed.

12. From the duty of observing the Hebrew Sabbath, we are sufficiently exempted by the fact, that it was actually not observed by the apostles of Christ. The early Christians met, not on the last day of the week, but on the first. Whatever reason may be assigned as a motive for this rejection of the ancient Sabbath, I think it will tend to discountenance the observance of any day, *as such*: for if that day did not possess perpetual sanctity, what day does possess it?

13. And with respect to the general tenor of the Christian Scriptures as to the sanctity of particular days, it is, I think, manifestly adverse to the opinion that one day is obligatory rather than another. "Let no man therefore judge you in meat or in drink, or in respect of an holy day, or of the new moon or of the sabbath days; which are a shadow of things to come; but the body is of Christ."[1] Although this "sabbath day" was that of the Jews, yet the passage indicates the writer's sentiments, generally, respecting the sanctity of specific days: he classes them with matters which all agree to be unimportant;—with meats, and drinks, and new moons; and pronounces them to be alike "*shadows*." That strong passage addressed to the Christians of Galatia is of the same import: "How turn ye again to the weak and beggarly elements whereunto ye desire again to be in bondage? Ye observe days, and months, and times, and years. I am afraid of you, lest I have bestowed upon you labour in vain."[2] That which, in writing to the Christians of Colosse, the apostle called "shadows," he now, in writing to those of Galatia, calls "beggarly elements." The obvious tendency is to discredit the observance of particular times; and if he designed to except the first day of the week, it is not probable that he would have failed to except it.

14. Nevertheless, the question whether we are obliged to observe the first day of the week *because it is the first*, is one point—whether we ought to devote it to religious exercises, *seeing that it is actually set apart for the purpose*, is another. The early Christians met on that day, and their example has been followed in succeeding times; but if for any sufficient reason (and such reasons, however unlikely to arise, are yet conceivable), the Christian world should fix upon another day of the week instead of the first, I perceive no grounds upon which the arrangement could be objected to. As there is no sanctity in any day, and no obligation to appropriate one day rather than another, that which is actually fixed upon is the best and the right one. Bearing in mind, then, that it is right to devote *some* portion of our time to religious exercises, and that no objection exists to the day which is actually appropriated, the duty seems very obvious—so to employ it.

15. Cessation from labour on the first day

[1] Heb. x. 25.

[1] Col. ii. 16, 17. In Rom. xiv. 5, 6, there is a parallel passage.
[2] Gal. iv. 10, 11.

of the week is nowhere enjoined in the Christian Scriptures. Upon this subject, the principles on which a person should regulate his conduct appear to be these: He should reflect that the whole of the day is not too large a portion of our time to devote to public worship, to religious recollectedness, and sedateness of mind; and therefore that occupations which would interfere with this sedateness and recollectedness, or with public worship, ought to be forborne. Even if he supposed that the devoting of the whole of the day was not necessary for himself, he should reflect, that since a considerable part of mankind are obliged, from various causes, to attend to matters unconnected with religion during a *part* of the day, and that one set attends to them during one part and another during another—the whole of the day is necessary for the community, even though it were not for each individual: and if every individual should attend to his ordinary affairs during that portion of the day which he deemed superabundant, the consequence might soon be that the day would not be devoted to religion at all.

16. These views will enable the reader to judge in what manner we should decide questions respecting attention to temporal affairs on particular occasions. The *day* is not sacred, therefore business is not necessarily sinful; the day ought to be devoted to religion, therefore other concerns which are not necessary are, generally, wrong. The remonstrance, "Which of you shall have an ass or an ox fallen into a pit, and will not straightway pull him out on the sabbath day?" sufficiently indicates that, when reasonable calls are made upon us, we are at liberty to attend to them. Of the reasonableness of these calls every man must endeavour to judge for himself. A tradesman ought, as a general rule, to refuse to buy or sell goods. If I sold clothing, I would furnish a surtout to a man who was suddenly summoned on a journey, but not to a man who could call the next morning. Were I a builder, I would prop a falling wall, but not proceed in the erection of a house. Were I a lawyer, I would deliver an opinion to an applicant to whom the delay of a day would be a serious injury, but not to save him the expense of an extra night's lodging by waiting. I once saw with pleasure on the sign-board of a public-house, a notice that "none but travellers could be furnished with liquor on a Sunday." The medical profession, and those who sell medicine, are differently situated; yet it is not to be doubted that both, and especially the latter, might devote a smaller portion of the day to their secular employments, if earnestness in religious concerns were as great as the opportunities to attend to them. Some physicians in extensive practice attend almost as regularly on public worship as any of their neighbours. Excursions of pleasure on this day are rarely defensible: they do not comport with the purposes to which the day is appropriated. To attempt specific rules upon such a subject were, however, vain. Not everything which partakes of relaxation is unallowable. A walk in the country may be proper and right, when a party to a watering-place would be improper and wrong.[1] There will be little difficulty in determining what it is allowable to do and what it is not, if the inquiry be not, how much secularity does religion allow? but, how much can I, without a neglect of duty, avoid?

17. The habit which obtains with many persons of travelling on this day, is peculiarly indefensible; because it not only keeps the traveller from his church or meeting, but keeps away his servants, or the postmen on the road, and ostlers, and cooks, and waiters. All these may be detained from public worship by one man's journey of fifty miles. Such a man incurs some responsibility. The plea of "saving time" is not remote from irreverence; for if it has any meaning it is this, that our time is of more value when employed in business, than when employed in the worship of God. It is discreditable to this country that the number of carriages which traverse it on this day is so great. The evil may rightly and perhaps easily be regulated by the Legislature. You talk of difficulties: —you would have talked of many more, if it were now, for the first time, proposed to shut up the General Post-Office one day in seven. We should have heard of parents dying before their children could hear of their danger; of bills dishonoured and merchants discredited for want of a post; and of a multitude of other inconveniences which busy anticipation would have discovered. Yet the General Post-Office is shut; and where is the evil? The journeys of stage-coaches may be greatly diminished in number; and though twenty difficulties may be predicted, none would happen but such as were easily borne. An increase of the duty per mile on those coaches which travelled *every* day, might perhaps effect the object. Probably not less than forty persons are employed on temporal affairs, in consequence of an ordinary stage-coach journey of a hundred miles.[2]

[1] The scrupulousness of the "Puritans" in the reign of Charles I., and the laxity of Laud, whose ordinances enjoined sports after the hours of public worship, were both really, though perhaps not equally, improper. The Puritans attached sanctity to the *day*; and Laud did not consider, or did not regard the consideration, that his sports would not only discredit the notion of sanctity, but preclude that recollectedness of mind which ought to be maintained throughout the whole day.
[2] There is reason to believe that, to the numerous class of coachmen, waiters, &c., the alteration would be most ac-

18. A similar regulation would be desirable with respect to "Sunday papers." The ordinary contents of a newspaper are little accordant with religious sobriety and abstraction from the world. News of armies, and of funds and markets, of political contests and party animosities, of robberies and trials, of sporting, and boxing, and the stage, with merriment, and scandal, and advertisements —are sufficiently ill adapted to the cultivation of religiousness of mind. An additional twopence on the stamp-duty would perhaps remedy the evil.

19. Private, and especially public amusements on this day, are clearly wrong. It is remarkable that *they* appear least willing to dispense with their amusements on this day, who pursue them on every other: and the observation affords one illustration amongst the many of the pitiable effects of what is called—though it is only *called*—a life of pleasure.

20. Upon every kind and mode of negligence respecting these religious obligations, the question is not simply, whether the individual himself sustains moral injury, but also whether he occasions injury to those around him. The *example* is mischievous. Even supposing that a man may feel devotion in his counting-house, or at the tavern, or over a pack of cards, his neighbours who know where he is, or his family who see what he is doing, are encouraged to follow his example, without any idea of carrying their religion with them. " My neighbour amuses himself—my father attends to his ledgers—and why may not I?"—So that, if such things were not intrinsically unlawful, they would be wrong because they are inexpedient. Some things might be done without blame by the lone tenant of a wild, which involve positive guilt in a man in society.

21. Holy-days, such as those which are distinguished by the names of Christmas Day and Good Friday, possess no sanction from Scripture: they are of human institution. If any religious community thinks it is desirable to devote more than fifty-two days in the year to the purposes of religion, it is unquestionably right that they should devote them; and it is amongst the good institutions of several Christian communities, that they do weekly appropriate some additional hours to these purposes. The observance of the days in question is however of another kind: here, the observance refers to *the day as such;* and I know not how the censure can be avoided which was directed to those Galatians who "observed

ceptable. I have been told by an intelligent coachman that they would gladly unite in a request to their employers if it were likely to avail.

days, and months, and times, and years." Whatever may be the sentiments of enlightened men, those who are not enlightened are likely to regard such days as sacred in themselves. This is turning to beggarly elements: this partakes of the character of superstition; and superstition of every kind and in every degree is incongruous with that "glorious liberty" which Christianity describes, and to which it would conduct us.

Ceremonial Institutions and Devotional Formularies.

22. If God have made known His Will that any given ceremony shall be performed in His church, that expression is sufficient: we do not then inquire into the reasonableness of the ceremony, nor into its utility. There is nothing in the act of sprinkling water in an infant's face, or of immersing the person of an adult, which recommends it to the view of reason, any more than twenty other acts which might be performed: yet, if it be clear that such an act is required by the Divine Will, all further controversy is at an end. It is not the business, any more than it is the desire, of the writer here to inquire whether the Deity *has* thus expressed His Will respecting any of the rites which are adopted in some Christian churches; yet the reader should carefully bear in mind what it is that constitutes the obligation of a rite or ceremony, and what does not. Setting utility aside, the obligation must be constituted by an *expression* of the Divine Will: and he who inquires into the obligation of these things, should reflect that they acquire a sort of adventitious sanctity from the power of association. Being connected from early life with his ideas of religion, he learns to attach to them the authority which he attaches to religion itself; and thus perhaps he scarcely knows, because he does not inquire, whether a given institution is founded upon the law of God, or introduced by the authority of men.

23. Of some ceremonies or rites, and of almost all formularies and other appendages of public worship, it is acknowledged that they possess no proper sanction from the Will of God. Supposing the written expression of that Will to contain nothing by which we can judge either of their propriety or impropriety, the standard to which they are to be referred is that of Utility alone.

24. Now it is highly probable that benefits result from these adjuncts of religion, because, in the present state of mankind, it may be expected that some persons are impressed with useful sentiments respecting religion through the intervention of these adjuncts, who might otherwise scarcely regard religion

at all: it is probable that many are induced to attend upon public worship by the attraction of its appendages who would otherwise stay away. Simply to be present at the font or the communion-table may be a means of inducing many religious considerations into the mind. And as to those who are attracted to public worship by its accompaniments, they may at least be *in the way* of religious benefit. One goes to hear the singing, and one the organ, and one to see the paintings or the architecture; a still larger number go because they are sure to find *some* occupation for their thoughts; some prayers or other offices of devotion, something to hear, and see, and do. " The transitions from one office of devotion to another, from confession to prayer, from prayer to thanksgiving, from thanksgiving to 'hearing of the word,' are contrived, like scenes in the drama, to supply the mind with a succession of diversified engagements."[1] These diversified engagements I say attract some who would not otherwise attend; and it is better that they should go from imperfect motives than that they should not go at all. It must, however, be confessed that the groundwork of this species of utility is similar to that which has been urged in favour of the use of images by the Romish Church. "Idols," say they, "are laymen's books; and a *great means to stir up pious thoughts and devotion* in the learnedest."[2] Indeed, if it is once admitted that the prospect of advantage is a sufficient reason for introducing objects addressed to the senses into the public offices of worship, it is not easy to define where we shall stop. If we may have magnificent architecture, and music, and chanting, and paintings; why may we not have the yet more imposing pomp of the Catholic worship? I do not say that this pomp is useful and right, but that the *principle* on which such things are introduced into the worship of God furnishes no satisfactory means of deciding what amount of external observances should be introduced, and what should not. If figures on canvas are lawful because they are useful, why is not a figure in marble or in wood? Why may we not have images by way of laymen's books, and of stirring up pious thoughts and devotion?

25. But it is to be apprehended of such things, or of "contrivances like scenes in a drama," that they have much less tendency to promote devotion than some men may suppose. No doubt they may possess an imposing effect, they may powerfully interest and affect the imagination; but does not this partake too much of that factitious devotion of which we speak? Is it certain that such things have much tendency to purify the mind, and raise up within it a power that shall efficiently resist temptation?

26. Even if some benefits do result from the employment of these appendages of worship, they are not without their dangers and their evils. With respect to those which are addressed to the senses, whether to the eye or ear, there is obviously a danger that like other sensible objects they will withdraw the mind from its proper business—the cultivation of pure religious affections towards God. And respecting the formularies of devotion, it has been said by a writer, whom none will suspect of overstating their evils, "The arrogant man, as if like the dervise in the Persian fable, he had shot his soul into the character he assumes, repeats, with complete self-application, *Lord, I am not highminded:* the trifler says, *I hate vain thoughts:* the irreligious, *Lord, how I love Thy law:* he who seldom prays at all, confidently repeats, *All the day long I am occupied in Thy statutes.*"[1] These are not light considerations: here is insincerity and untruths; and insincerity and untruths, it should be remembered, in the place and at the time when we profess to be humbled in the presence of God. The evils, too, are inseparable from the system. Wherever preconcerted formularies are introduced, there will always be some persons who join in the use of them without propriety, or sincerity, or decorum. Nor are the evils much extenuated by the hope which has been suggested, that "the holy vehicle of their hypocrisy may be made that of their conversion." It is very Christian-like to indulge this hope, though I fear it is not very reasonable. Hypocrisy is itself an offence against God; and it can scarcely be expected that anything so immediately connected with the offence will often effect such an end.

27. It is not, however, in the case of those who use these forms in a manner positively hypocritical, that the greatest evil and danger consists: "There is a kind of mechanical memory in the tongue, which runs over the form without any aid of the understanding, without any concurrence of the will, without any consent of the affections; for do we not sometimes implore God to hear a prayer to which we are ourselves not attending?"[2] We have sufficient reason for knowing that to draw nigh to God with our lips whilst our hearts are far from Him, is a serious offence in His sight; and when it is considered how powerful is the tendency of oft-repeated words to lose their practical connection with feelings and ideas, it is to be feared that this class of evils, resulting from the use of forms, is of very wide extent. Nor is it to be forgotten,

---

[1] Mor. and Pol. Phil., b. 5, c. 5.
[2] Milton's Prose Works, v. 4, p. 226.

[1] More's Moral Sketches, 3rd Ed, p. 429.
[2] Ibid., p. 327.

that as even religious persons sometimes employ "the form without any aid of the understanding," so others are in danger of *substituting* the form for the reality, and of imagining that if they are exemplary in the observance of the externals of devotion, the work of religion is done.

28. Such circumstances may reasonably make us hesitate in deciding the question of the propriety of these external things, as a question of *expediency*. They may reasonably make us do more than this; for does Christianity allow us to invent a system of which some of the consequences are so bad, for the sake of a beneficial end?

29. Forms of *prayer* have been supposed to rest on an authority somewhat more definite than that of other religious forms. "The Lord's Prayer is a precedent, as well as a pattern, for forms of prayer. Our Lord appears, if not to have prescribed, at least to have authorised the use of fixed forms, when He complied with the request of the disciple who said unto Him, Lord, teach us to pray, as John also taught his disciples."[1] If we turn to Matt. vi., where the fullest account is given of the subject, we are, I think, presented with a different view. Our Saviour, who had been instituting His more perfect laws in place of the doctrines which had been taught of old time, proceeded to the prevalent mode of *giving alms*, of *praying*, of *fasting*, and of *laying up wealth*. He first describes these modes, and then directs in what manner *Christians* ought to give alms, and pray and fast. Now, if it be contended that He requires us to employ that particular form of prayer which He then dictated, it must also be contended that He requires us to adopt that particular mode of giving money which He described, and those particular actions, when fasting, which He mentions. If we are obliged to use the form of prayer, we are obliged to give money *in secret*; and when we fast, *to put oil upon our heads*. If these particular modes were not enjoined, neither is the form of prayer; and the Scriptures contain no indication that this form was ever used at all, either by the apostles or their converts. But if the argument only asserts that fixed forms are "authorised" by the language of Christ, the question becomes a question merely of expediency. Supposing that they are authorised, they are to be employed only if they are useful. Even in this view, it may be remarked that there is no reason to suppose, from the Christian Scriptures, that either Christ Himself or His apostles ever used a fixed form. If He had designed to authorise, and therefore to recommend, their adoption.

[1] Mor. and Pol. Phil. p. 3. b. 5. c. 5.

is it not probable that some indications of their having been employed would be presented? But instead of this, we find that every prayer which is recorded in the volume was delivered extempore, upon the then occasion, and arising out of the then existing circumstances.

30. Yet after all, the important question is not between preconcerted and extempore prayer as such, but whether any prayer is proper and right but that which is elicited by the influence of the Divine power. The inquiry into this solemn subject would lead us too wide from our general business. The truth, however, that "we know not what to pray for as we ought," is as truly applicable to extempore as to formal prayer. Words merely do not constitute prayer, whether they be prepared beforehand, or conceived at the moment they are addressed. There is reason to believe that he only offers perfectly acceptable supplications, who offers them "according to the Will of God," and "of the ability which God giveth:"—and if such be indeed the truth, it is scarcely compatible either with a prescribed form of words or with extempore prayer at prescribed times. Yet if any Christian, in the piety of his heart, believes it to be most conducive to his religious interests to pray at stated times or in fixed forms, far be it from me to censure this the mode of his devotion, or to assume that his petition will not obtain access to the Universal Lord.

31. Finally, respecting uncommanded ceremonials and rituals of all kinds, and respecting all the appendages of public worship which have been adopted as helps to devotion, there is one truth to which perhaps every good man will assent - that if religion possessed its sufficient and rightful influence, if devotion of the heart were duly maintained without these things, they would no longer be needed. He who enjoys the vigorous exercise of his limbs is encumbered by the employment of a crutch. Whether the Christian world is yet prepared for the relinquishment of these appendages and "helps",— whether an equal degree of efficacious religion would be maintained without them — are questions which I presume not to determine: but it may nevertheless be decided, that this is the state of the Christian Church to which we should direct our hopes and our endeavours—and that Christianity will never possess its proper influence, and will not effect its destined objects, until the internal dedication of the heart is universally attained.

32. To those who may sometimes be brought into contact with persons who profess scepticism respecting Christianity, and

especially to those who are conscious of any tendency in their own minds to listen to the objections of these persons, it may be useful to observe, that the grounds upon which sceptics build their disbelief of Christianity are commonly very slight. The number is comparatively few whose opinions are the result of any tolerable degree of investigation. They embraced sceptical notions through the means which they now take of diffusing them amongst others,—not by arguments but jests ; not by objections to the historical evidence of Christianity, but by conceits and witticisms ; not by examining the nature of religion as it was delivered by its Founder, but by exposing the conduct of those who profess it. Perhaps the seeming paradox is true, that no men are so credulous, that no men accept important propositions upon such slender evidence, as the majority of those who reject Christianity. To believe that the religious opinions of almost all the civilised world are founded upon imposture, is to believe an important proposition ; a proposition which no man, who properly employs his faculties, would believe without considerable weight of evidence. But what is the evidence upon which the "unfledged witlings who essay their wanton efforts" against religion, usually found their notions ? Alas ! they are so far from having rejected Christianity upon the examination of its evidences, that they do not know what Christianity is. To disbelieve the religion of Christianity upon grounds which shall be creditable to the understanding, involves no light task. A man must investigate and scrutinise ; he must examine the credibility of testimony ; he must weigh and compare evidence ; he must inquire into the reality of historical facts. If, after rationally doing all this, he disbelieves in Christianity—be it so. I think him, doubtless, mistaken, but I do not think him puerile and credulous. But he who professes scepticism without any of this species of inquiry, is credulous and puerile indeed : and such most sceptics actually are. "Concerning unbelievers and doubters of every class, one observation may *almost universally* be made with truth, that they are little acquainted with the nature of the Christian religion, and still less with the evidence by which it is supported."[1] In France, scepticism has extended itself as widely perhaps as in any country in the world, and its philosophers, forty or fifty years ago, were ranked amongst the most intelligent and sagacious of mankind. And upon what grounds did these men reject Christianity ? Dr. Priestley went with Lord Shelburne to France, and he says, " I had an opportunity of seeing and conversing with every person of eminence wherever we came : " I found "all the philosophical persons to whom I was introduced at Paris, unbelievers in Christianity, and even professed atheists. As I chose on all occasions to appear as a Christian, I was told by some of them that I was the only person they had ever met with, of whose understanding they had any opinion, who professed to believe in Christianity. But on interrogating them on the subject, I soon found that *they had given no proper attention to it, and did not really know what Christianity was*. This was also the case with a great part of the company that I saw at Lord Shelburne's."[1] If these philosophical men rejected Christianity in such contemptible and shameful ignorance of its nature and evidences, upon what grounds are we to suppose the ordinary striplings of infidelity reject it ?

33. How then does it happen that those who affect scepticism are so ambitious to make their scepticism known ? Because it is a short and easy road to distinction ; because it affords a cheap means of gratifying vanity. To "rise above vulgar prejudices and superstitions"—"to entertain enlarged and liberal opinions", are phrases of great attraction, especially to young men ; and how shall they show that they rise above vulgar prejudices, how shall they so easily manifest the enlargement of their views, as by rejecting a system which all their neighbours agree to be true ? They feel important to themselves, and that they are objects of curiosity to others : and they are objects of curiosity, not on account of their own qualities, but on account of the greatness of that which they contemn. The peasant who reviles a peasant, may revile him without an auditor, but a province will listen to him who vilifies a king. I know not that an intelligent person should be advised to *reason* with these puny assailants : their notions and their conduct are not the result of reasoning. What they need is the humiliation of vanity and the exposure of folly. A few simple interrogations would expose their folly ; and for the purposes of humiliation, simply pass them by. The sun that shines upon them makes them look bright and large. Let reason and truth withdraw their rays, and these seeming stars will quickly set in silence and in darkness.

34. More contemptible motives to the profession of infidelity cannot perhaps exist, but there are some which are more detestable. Hartley says that "the strictness and purity of the Christian religion in respect to sexual licentiousness, is probably the chief thing which makes vicious men first fear and hate, and then vilify and oppose it."[2]

[1] Gisborne's Duties of Men.

[1] Memoirs of Dr. Priestley.
[2] Observations on Man.

35. Whether therefore we regard the motives which lead to scepticism, or the reasonableness of the grounds upon which it is commonly founded, there is surely much reason for an ingenious young person to hold in contempt the jests, and pleasantries, and sophistries respecting revelation with which he may be assailed.

CHAPTER II.

Property.

Foundation of the Right to Property—Insolvency: Perpetual obligation to pay debts: Reform of public opinion: Examples of integrity—Wills, Legatees, Heirs: Informal Wills: Intestates—Charitable Bequests—Minors' debts—A Wife's debts--Bills of Exchange—Shipments—Distraints—Unjust defendants—Extortion—Slaves—Privateers—Confiscations—Public money—Insurance—Improvements on estates—Settlements—Houses of infamy—Literary property—Rewards.

36. Disquisitions respecting the *Origin* of Property appear to be of little use; partly because the origin can scarcely be determined, and partly because, if it could be determined, the discovery would be little applicable to the present condition of human affairs. In whatever manner an estate was acquired two thousand years ago, it is of no consequence in inquiring who ought to possess it now.

37. The foundation of the *Right* to Property is a more important point. Ordinarily, the foundation is the law of the land. Of Civil Government—which institution is sanctioned by the Divine Will—one of the great offices is, to regulate the distribution of property; to give it, if it has the power of giving; or to decide between opposing claimants, to whom it shall be assigned.

38. The proposition therefore, as a general rule, is sound :—*He possesses a right to property to whom the law of the land assigns it.* This, however, is only a *general* rule. It has been sufficiently seen that some legal possessions are not permitted by the Moral Law. The occasional opposition between the moral and the legal right to property, is inseparable from the principle on which law is founded—that of acting upon general rules. It is impossible to frame any rule the application of which shall, in every variety of circumstances, effect the requisitions of Christian morality. A rule which in nine cases proves equitable, may prove utterly unjust in the tenth. A rule which in nine cases promotes the welfare of the citizen, may in the tenth outrage reason and humanity.

39. It is evident that in the present state of legal institutions, the evils which result from laws respecting property must be prevented, if they are prevented at all, by the exercise of virtue in *individuals*. If the law assigns a hundred pounds to me, which every upright man perceives ought in equity to have been assigned to another, that other has no means of enforcing his claim. Either therefore the claim of equity must be disregarded, or *I* must voluntarily satisfy it.

40. There are many cases connected with the acquisition or retention of property, with which the decisions of law are not immediately connected, but respecting which it is needful to exercise a careful discrimination, in order to conform to the requisitions of Christian rectitude. The whole subject is of great interest, and of extensive practical application in the intercourse of life. The reader will therefore be presented with several miscellaneous examples, in which the Moral Law appears to require greater purity of rectitude than is required by statutes, or than is ordinarily practised by mankind.

Insolvency.

41. Why is a man obliged to pay his debts? It is to be hoped that the morality of few persons is lax enough to reply—Because the law compels him. But why then is he obliged to pay them? Because the Moral Law requires it. That this is the primary ground of the obligation is evident : otherwise the payment of any debt which a vicious or corrupt legislature resolved to cancel, would cease to be obligatory upon the debtor. The Virginian statute, which we noticed in the last Essay, would have been a sufficient justification to the planters to defraud their creditors.

42. A man becomes insolvent and is made a bankrupt : he pays his creditors ten shillings instead of twenty, and obtains his certificate. The law therefore discharges him from the obligation to pay more. The bankrupt receives a large legacy, or he engages in business and acquires property. Being then able to pay the remainder of his debts, does the legal discharge exempt him from the obligation to pay them? No : and for this reason, that the legal discharge is not a moral discharge : that as the duty to pay at all was not founded primarily on the law, the law cannot warrant him in withholding a part.

43. It is, however, said that the creditors have relinquished their right to the remainder by signing the certificate. But why did they accept half their demands instead of the whole? Because they were obliged to do it : they could get no more. As to granting the

certificate, they do it because to withhold it would be only an act of gratuitous unkindness. It would be preposterous to say that creditors relinquish their claims *voluntarily;* for no one would give up his claim to twenty shillings on the receipt of ten, if he could get the other ten by refusing. It might as reasonably be said that a man parts with a limb voluntarily, because, having incurably lacerated it, he submits to an amputation. It is to be remembered, too, that the necessary relinquishment of half the demand is occasioned by the debtor himself: and it seems very manifest that when a man, by his own act, deprives another of his property, he cannot allege the consequences of that act as a justification of withholding it after restoration is in his power.

The *mode* in which an insolvent man obtains a discharge, does not appear to affect his subsequent duties. Compositions, and bankruptcies, and discharges by an insolvent act are in this respect alike. The acceptance of a part instead of the whole is not voluntary in either case; and neither case exempts the debtor from the obligation to pay in full if he can.

44. If it should be urged that when a person entrusts property to another, he knowingly undertakes the risk of that other's insolvency, and that if the contingent loss happens, he has no claims to justice on the other, the answer is this: that whatever may be thought of these claims, they are not the grounds upon which the debtor is obliged to pay. The debtor always engages to pay, and the engagement is enforced by morality: the engagement therefore is binding, whatever risk another man may incur by relying upon it. The *causes* which have occasioned a person's insolvency, although they greatly affect his character, do not affect his obligations; the duty to repay when he has the power, is the same whether the insolvency were occasioned by his fault or his misfortune. In all cases, the reasoning that applies to the debt, applies also to the interest that accrues upon it; although, with respect to the acceptance of both, and especially of interest, a creditor should exercise a considerate discretion.—A man who has failed of paying his debts ought always to live with frugality, and carefully to economise such money as he gains. He should reflect that he is a trustee for his creditors, and that all the needless money which he expends is not his, but theirs.

45. The amount of property which the trading part of a commercial nation loses by insolvency, is great enough to constitute a considerable national evil. The fraud, too, that is practised under cover of insolvency, is doubtless the most extensive of all species of private robbery. The profligacy of some of these cases is well known to be extreme. He who is a bankrupt to-day, riots in the luxuries of affluence to-morrow; bows to the creditors whose money he is spending, and exults in the success and the impunity of his wickedness. Of such conduct, we should not speak or think but with detestation. We should no more sit at the table, or take the hand, of such a man, than if we knew he had got his money last night on the highway. There is a wickedness in some bankruptcies to which the guilt of ordinary robbers approaches but at a distance. Happy, if such wickedness could not be practised with legal impunity![1] Happy, if Public Opinion supplied the deficiency of the law, and held the iniquity in rightful abhorrence![2]

46. Perhaps nothing would tend so efficaciously to diminish the general evils of insolvency, as a sound state of public opinion respecting the obligation to pay our debts. The insolvent who, with the means of paying, retains the money in his own pocket, is, and he should be regarded as being, a dishonest man. If Public Opinion held such conduct to be of the same character as theft, probably a more powerful motive to avoid insolvency would be established than any which now exists. Who would not anxiously (and therefore, in almost all cases, successfully) struggle against insolvency, when he knew that it would be followed, if not by permanent poverty, by permanent disgrace? If it should be said that to act upon such a system would overwhelm an insolvent's energies, keep him in perpetual inactivity, and deprive his family of the benefit of his exertions,—I answer, that the evil, supposing it to impend, would be much less extensive than may be imagined. The calamity being foreseen, would prevent men from becoming insolvent; and it is certain that the majority might have avoided insolvency by sufficient care. Besides, if a man's principles are such that he would rather sink into inactivity than exert himself in order to be just, it is not necessary to mould public opinion to his character. The question too is, not whether some men would not prefer indolence to the calls of justice, but whether the public should judge accurately respecting what those calls are. The state, and especially a family, might lose occasionally by this reform of opinion—and so they do by sending a man to New South Wales; but who would think this a good reason for setting criminals at large? And after all, much more would be gained by preventing insolvency, than lost by the ill consequences upon the few who failed to pay their debts.

[1] See the 3rd Essay. [2] Ibid.

47. It is cause of satisfaction that, respecting this rectified state of opinion, and respecting integrity of private virtue, some examples are offered. There is one community of Christians which holds its members obliged to pay their debts whenever they possess the ability, without regard to the legal discharge.[1] By this means, there is thrown over the character of every bankrupt who possesses property, a shade which nothing but payment can dispel. The effect (in conjunction we may hope with private integrity of principle) is good good, both in instituting a new motive to avoid insolvency, and in inducing some of those who do become insolvent subsequently to pay all their debts.

48. Of this latter effect many honourable instances might be given : two which have fallen under my observation, I would briefly mention. -A man had become insolvent, I believe in early life ; his creditors divided his property amongst them, and gave him a legal discharge. He appears to have formed the resolution to pay the remainder, if his own exertions should enable him to do it. He procured employment, by which, however, he never gained more than twenty shillings a week ; and worked industriously and lived frugally for eighteen years. At the expiration of this time, he found he had accumulated enough to pay the remainder, and he sent the money to his creditors. Such a man, I think, might hope to derive, during the remainder of his life, greater satisfaction from the consciousness of integrity, than he would have derived from expending the money on himself. It should be told that many of his creditors, when they heard the circumstances, declined to receive the money, or voluntarily presented it to him again. One of these was my neighbour : he had been little accustomed to exemplary virtue, and the proffered money astonished him : he talked in loud commendation of what to him was unheard-of integrity ; signed a receipt for the amount, and sent it back as a present to the debtor. The other instance may furnish hints of a useful kind. It was the case of a female who had endeavoured to support herself by the profits of a shop. She, however, became insolvent, paid some dividend, and received a discharge. She again entered into business, and in the course of years had accumulated enough to pay the remainder of her debts. But the infirmities of age were now coming on, and the annual income from her savings was just sufficient for the wants of declining years. Being thus at present unable to discharge her obligations without subjecting herself to the necessity of obtaining relief from others ; she executed a will, directing that at her death the creditors should be paid the remainder of their demands : and when she died they were paid accordingly.

Wills, Legatees, and Heirs.

49. The right of a person to order the distribution of his property after death, is recommended by its Utility ; and were this less manifest than it is, it would be sufficient for us that the right is established by civil government.

It, however, happens in practice, that persons sometimes distribute their property in a manner that is both unreasonable and unjust. This evil the *law* cannot easily remedy ; and, consequently, the duty of remedying it devolves upon those to whom the property is bequeathed. If *they* do not prevent the injustice, it cannot be prevented. This indicates the propriety, on the part of a legatee or an heir, of considering, when property devolves to him in a manner or in a proportion that appears improper, how he may exercise upright integrity lest he should be the practical agent of injustice or oppression. Another cause for the exercise of this integrity consists in this circumstance:— When the right of a person to bequeath his property is admitted, it is evident that his *intention* ought in general to be the standard of his successor's conduct : and accordingly the law, in making enactments upon the subject, directs much of its solicitude to the means of ascertaining and of fulfilling the testator's *intentions*. These intentions must, according to the existing systems of Jurisprudence, be ascertained by some general rules—by a written declaration, perhaps, or a declaration of a specified kind, or made in a prescribed form, or attested in a particular manner. But in consequence of this it happens, that as through accident or inadvertency a testator does not always comply with these forms, the law, which adheres to its rules, frustrates his intentions, and therefore, in effect, defeats its own object in prescribing the forms. Here again the intentions of the deceased and the demands of equity cannot be fulfilled, except by the virtuous integrity of heirs and legatees.

50. I. If my father, who had one son besides myself, left nine-tenths of his property to me, and only the remaining tenth to my brother,

---

[1] "Where any have injured others in their property, the greatest frugality should be observed by themselves and their families ; and although they may have a legal discharge from their creditors, both equity and our Christian profession demand, that none, when they have it in their power, should rest satisfied until a just restitution be made to those who have suffered by them."

"And it is the judgment of this meeting, that monthly and other meetings ought not to receive collections or bequests for the use of the poor, or any other services of the Society, of persons who have fallen short in the payment of their just debts, though legally discharged by their creditors : for until such persons have paid the deficiency, their possessions cannot in equity be considered as their own."—Official Documents of the Yearly Meeting of the Society of Friends.

I should not think the will, however authentic, justified me in taking so large a proportion, unless I could discover some reasonable motive which influenced my father's mind. If my brother already possessed a fortune and I had none; if I were married and had a numerous family, and he were single and unlikely to marry; if he was incurably extravagant, and would probably in a few weeks or months squander his patrimony; in these or in such circumstances, I should think myself at liberty to appropriate my father's bequest; otherwise I should not. Thus if the disproportionate division was the effect of some unreasonable prejudice against my brother or fondness for me; or if it was made at the unfair instigation of another person, or in a temporary fit of passion or disgust; I could not, virtuously, enforce the will. The reason is plain. The will being unjust or extremely unreasonable, I should be guilty of injustice or extreme unreasonableness in enforcing it.

51. By the English law, the real estates of deceased persons are not available for the payment of debts of simple contract, unless they are made so by the will. The rule is, to be sure, sufficiently barbarous; and he who intentionally forbears to make the estates available, dies, as has been properly observed, with a deliberate fraud in his heart. But this fraud cannot be completed without the concurrence of a second person, the heir. *He* therefore is under a moral obligation to pay such debts out of the real estate, notwithstanding the deficiency of the will: for if the father was fraudulent in making such a will, the son is fraudulent in taking advantage of his parent's wickedness. He may act with strict legality in keeping the property, but he is condemned as dishonest by the Moral Law.

52. II. A person bequeaths five hundred pounds to some charity - for example, to the Foundling—and directs that the money shall be laid out in land. His intention is indisputably plain: but the law, with certain motives, says that the direction to lay out the money in land makes the bequest void; and it will not enforce the bequest. But, because the testator forgot this, can the residuary legatee honestly put the five hundred pounds into his own pocket? Assuredly he cannot. The money is as truly the property of the Foundling as if the will had been accurately framed. The circumstance that the law will not compel him to give it up, although it may exempt him from an action, cannot exempt him from guilt.

53. The law, either with reason or without it, prefers that an estate should descend to a brother's son rather than a sister's. Still it permits a man to leave it to his sister's son if he pleases; and only requires that, when he wishes to do this, he shall have three witnesses to his will instead of two. The reader will remark that the object of this legal provision is, that the *intention* of the party shall be indisputably known. The Legislature does not wish to control him in the disposition of his property, but only to ascertain distinctly what his intention is. A will then is made, leaving an estate to a sister's son, and is attested by two witnesses only. The omission of the third is a matter of mere inadvertence: no doubt exists as to the person's intention or its reasonableness. Is it then consistent with integrity for the brother's son to take advantage of the omission, and to withhold the estate from his cousin? I think the conscience of every man will answer no; and if this be the fact, we need inquire no further. Upon such a subject, the concurrent dictates in the minds of men can scarcely be otherwise than true and just. But even critically, the same conclusion appears to follow. The law required three witnesses *in order* that the person's intention should be known. Now it is known: and therefore the very object of the law is attained. To take advantage of the omission is, in reality, to misapply the law. It is insisting upon its letter in opposition to its motives and design. Dr. Paley has decided this question otherwise, by a process of reasoning of which the basis does not appear very sound. He says that such a person has no "right" to dispose of the property, because the law conferred the right upon condition that he should have three witnesses, with which condition he has not complied. But surely the "right" of disposing property is recognised *generally* by the law; the requisition of three witnesses is not designed to confer a right, but to adjust the mode of exercising it. Indeed, Paley himself virtually gives up his own doctrine; for he says he should hesitate in applying it, if "considerations of pity to distress, or duty to a parent, or of gratitude to a benefactor,"[1] would be disregarded by the application. Why should these considerations suspend the applicability of his doctrine? Because Christianity requires us to attend to them—which is the very truth we are urging—we say, the permission of the law is not a sufficient warrant to disregard the obligations of Christianity.

54. A man who possesses five thousand pounds has two sons, of whom John is well provided for and Thomas is not. With the privity of his sons he makes a will, leaving four thousand pounds to Thomas and one to John, explaining to both the reason of this division. A fire happens in the house and the

[1] Mor. and Pol. Phil., b. 3, p. 1, c. 23.

will is burnt; and the father, before he has the opportunity of making another, is carried off by a fever. Now the English law would assign a half of the money to each brother. If John demands his half, is he a just man? Every one I think will perceive that he is not, and that if he demanded it, he would violate the duties of benevolence. The law is not his sufficient rule.

55. A person whose near relations do not stand in need of his money, adopts the children of distant relatives, with the declared intention or manifest design of providing for them at his death. If, under such circumstances, he dies without a will, the heir-at-law could not morally avail himself of his legal privilege, to the injury of these expectant parties. They need the money, and he does not; which is one good reason for not seizing it: but the *intention* of the deceased invested them with a right; and so that the intention is known, it matters little to the moral obligation, whether it is expressed on paper or not.

56. Possibly some reader may say, that if an heir or legatee must always institute inquiries into the uncertain claims of others before he accepts the property of the deceased, and if he is obliged to give up his own claims whenever theirs seem to preponderate, he will be involved in endless doubts and scruples, and testators will never know whether their wills will be executed or not: the answer is, that no such scrupulousness is demanded. Hardheartedness, and extreme unreasonableness, and injustice, are *one* class of considerations; critical scruples, and uncertain claims, are *another*.

57. It may be worth a paragraph to remark, that it is to be feared some persons think too complacently of their *charitable* bequests, or what is worse, hope that it is a species of good works which will counterbalance the offence of some present irregularities of conduct. Such bequests ought not to be discouraged; and yet it should be remembered, that he who gives money after his death, parts with nothing of his own. He gives it only when he cannot retain it. The man who leaves his money for the single purpose of doing good, does right; but he who hopes that it is a work of merit, should remember that the money is given, that the privation is endured, not by himself but by his heirs. A man who has more than he needs, should dispense it whilst it is his own.

Minors' Debts.

58. A young man under twenty-one years of age purchases articles of a tradesman, of which some are necessary and some are not. Payment for *unnecessary* articles cannot be enforced by the English law—the reason with the Legislature being this, that thoughtless youths might be practised upon by designing persons, and induced to make needless and extravagant purchases. But is the youth who purchases unnecessary articles, with the promise to pay when he becomes of age, exempted from the obligation? Now it is to be remembered, generally, that this obligation is not founded upon the Law of the Land, and therefore that the law cannot dispense with it. But if the tradesman has actually taken advantage of the inexperience of a youth, to cajole him into debts of which he was not conscious of the amount or the impropriety, it does not appear that he is obliged to pay them: and for this reason, that he did not, in any proper sense of the term, come under an obligation to pay them. In other cases, the obligation remains. The circumstance that the law will not assist the creditor to recover the money, does not dispense with it. It is fit, no doubt, that these dishonourable tradesmen should be punished, though the mode of punishing them is exceptionable indeed. It operates as a powerful temptation to fraud in young men, and it is a bad system to discourage dishonesty in one person by tempting the probity of another. The youth, too, is of all persons the last who should profit by the punishment of the trader. He is reprehensible himself: young men who contract such debts are seldom so young or so ignorant as not to know that they are doing wrong.

59. A man's wife " runs him into debt" by extravagant purchases which he is alike unable to prevent or to afford. Many persons sell goods to such a woman, who are conscious of her habits and of the husband's situation, yet continue to supply her extravagance, because they know the law will enable them to enforce payment from the husband. These persons act legally, but they are legally wicked. Do they act as they would desire others to act towards them? Would one of these men wish another tradesman so to supply his own wife if she was notoriously a spendthrift? If not, morality condemns his conduct: and the laws, in effect, condemn it too; for the Legislature would not have made husbands responsible for their wives' debts any more than for their children's, *but for the presumption* that the wife generally buys what the husband approves. Debts of unprincipled extravagance are not debts which the law intended to provide that the husband should pay. If all women contracted such debts, the Legislature would instantly alter the law. If the Legislature could have made the distinction, perhaps it would have made it: since it did not or could not, the deficiency must be supplied by private integrity.

Bills of Exchange.

60. The law of England provides, that if the possessor of a Bill of Exchange fails to demand payment on the day on which it becomes due, he takes the responsibility, in case of its eventual non-payment, from the previous endorsers, and incurs it himself. This as a general rule may be just. A party may be able to pay to-day and unable a week hence; and if in such a case a loss arises by one man's negligence, it were manifestly unreasonable that it should be sustained by others. But if the acceptor becomes unable to pay a week or a month *before* the bill is due, the previous endorsers cannot in justice throw the loss upon the last possessor, even though he fails to present it on the appointed day. For *why* did the law make its provision? In order to secure persons from the loss of their property by the negligence of others over whom they had no control. But, in the supposed case, the loss is not occasioned by any such cause, and therefore the spirit of the law does not apply to it. You are insisting upon its literal, in opposition to its just, interpretation. Whether the bill was presented on the right day or the wrong, makes no difference to the previous endorsers, and for such a case the law was not made.

61. A similar rule of virtue applies to the case of *giving notice* of refusal to accept or to pay. If, in consequence of the want of this notice, the party is subjected to loss, he may avail himself of the legal exemption from the last possessor's claim. If the want of notice made no difference in his situation, he may not.

Shipments.

62. The same principles apply to a circumstance which not unfrequently occurs amongst men of business, and in which integrity is, I think, very commonly sacrificed to interest. A tradesman in Falmouth is in the habit of purchasing goods of merchants in London, by whom the goods are forwarded in vessels to Falmouth. Now it is a rule of law founded upon established custom, that goods when shipped are at the risk of the *buyer*. The law, however, requires that an account of the shipment shall be sent to the buyer by post, in order that, if he thinks proper, he may insure his goods; and in order to effect this object, the law directs, that if the account be not sent and the vessel is wrecked, it will not enforce payment from the buyer. All this as a general rule is just. But in the actual transactions of business, goods are very frequently sent by sea by an expressed or tacit agreement between the parties without notice by the post. The Falmouth tradesman then is in the habit of thus conducting the matter for a series of years. He habitually orders his goods to be sent by ship, and the merchant, as habitually, with the buyer's knowledge, sends the invoice with them. Of course the buyer is not in the habit of insuring. At length a vessel is wrecked and a package is lost. When the merchant applies for payment, the tradesman says—"No; you sent no invoice by post: I shall not pay you, and I know you cannot compel me by law." Now this conduct I think is condemned by morality. The man in Falmouth does not suffer any loss *in consequence* of the want of notice. He would not have insured if he had received it; and therefore the intention of the Legislature in withholding its assistance from the merchant was not to provide for such a case. Thus to take advantage of the law without regard to its intention is unjust. Besides, the custom of sending the invoice with the goods rather than by post, is for the advantage of the buyer only:—it saves him a shilling in postage. The understanding amongst men of business that the risk of loss at sea impends on buyers is so complete, that they habitually take that risk into account in the profits which they demand on their goods: sellers do not; and this again indicates the injustice of throwing the loss upon the seller when an accident happens at sea.—Yet tradesmen I believe rarely practise any other justice than that which the law will enforce; as if not to be compelled by law were to be exempt from all moral obligation. It is hardly necessary to observe, that if the man in Falmouth was actually prevented from insuring by the want of an invoice by post, he has a claim of justice as well as of law upon the merchant in London.

Distraints.

63. It is well known that, in distraints for rent, the law allows the landlord to seize whatever goods he finds upon the premises, without inquiring to whom they belong. And this rule, like many others, is as good as a general rule can be; since an unprincipled tenant might easily contrive to make it appear that none of the property was his own, and thus the landlord might be irremediably defrauded. Yet the landlord cannot always virtuously act upon the rule of law. A tenant who expects a distraint to-morrow, and of whose profligacy a lodger in the house has no suspicion, secretly removes his own goods in the night, and leaves the lodger's to be seized by the bailiff. The landlord ought not, as a matter of course, to take these goods, and to leave a family perhaps without a table or a bed. The law

indeed allows it; but benevolence, but probity, does not.

64. A man came to a friend of mine and proposed to take a number of his sheep to graze. My friend agreed with him, and sent the sheep. The next day these sheep were seized by the man's landlord for rent. It was an artifice, preconcerted between the landlord and the tenant in order that the rent might be paid out of my friend's pocket! Did this landlord act justly? The reader says, "No, he deserved a prison." And yet the seizure was permitted by the law; and if morality did not possess an authority superior to law, the seizure would have been just. Now, in less flagitious instances, the same regard to the dictates of morality is to be maintained notwithstanding the permissions of law.—The contrivers of this abandoned iniquity possessed the effrontery to come afterwards to the gentleman whom they had defrauded, to offer to compound the matter; to send back the sheep, which were of the value perhaps of fifty pounds, if he would give them thirty pounds in money. He refused to countenance such wickedness by the remotest implication, and sent them away to enjoy *all* their plunder.

65. *Theoretically*, perhaps no seizures are unjust when no fraud is practised by the landlord, because persons who entrust their property on the premises of another, are supposed to know the risk, and voluntarily to undertake it. But in practice, this risk is often not thought of and not known. Besides, mere *justice* is not the only thing which a landlord has to take into account. The authority which requires us to be just, requires us to be compassionate and kind. And here, as in many other cases, it may be remarked, that the *object* of the law in allowing landlords to seize whatever they find, was to protect them from fraud, and not to facilitate the oppression of under-tenants and others. If the first tenant has practised no fraud, it seems a violation of the *intention* of the law, to enforce it against those who happen to have entrusted their property in his hands.

Unjust Defendants.

66. It does not present a very favourable view of the state of private principle, that there are so many who refuse justice to plaintiffs unless they are compelled to be just by the law. It is indisputable that a multitude of suits are undertaken in order to obtain property or rights which the defendant knows he ought voluntarily to give up. Such a person is certainly a dishonest man. When the verdict is given against him, I regard him in the light of a convicted robber—differing from other robbers in the circumstance that he is tried at Nisi prius instead of the Crown bar. For what is the difference between him who takes what is another's and him who withholds it? This severity of censure applies to some who are sued for damages. A man who, whether by design or inadvertency, has injured another, and will not compensate him unless he is legally compelled to do it, is surely unjust. Yet many of these persons seem to think that injury to property, or person, or character, entails no duty to make reparation except it be enforced. Why, the law does not *create* this duty, it only compels us to fulfil it. If the minds of such persons were under the influence of integrity, they would pay such debts without compulsion.—This subject is one amongst the many upon which Public Opinion needs to be aroused and to be rectified. When our estimates of moral character are adjusted to individual *probity of principle*, some of those who now pass in society as creditable persons will be placed at the same point on the scale of morality as many of those who are consigned to a jail.

Extortion.

67. It is a very common thing for a creditor who cannot obtain payment from the person who owes him money, to practise a species of extortion upon his relations or friends. The man perhaps is insolvent and unable to pay, and the creditor threatens to imprison him in order to induce his friends to pay the money rather than allow him to be immured in a jail. This is not honest. Why should a person be deprived of his property because he has a regard for the reputation and comfort of another man? It will be said that the debtor's friends pay *voluntarily*; but it is only with that sort of willingness with which a traveller gives his purse to a footpad, rather than be violently assaulted or perhaps killed. Both the footpad and the creditor are extortioners—one obtains money by threatening mischief to the person, and the other by threatening pain to the mind. We do not say that their actions are equal in flagitiousness, but we say that both are criminal.—It is said that, after the death of Sheridan, and when a number of men of rank were assembled to attend his funeral, a person elegantly dressed, and stating himself to be a relation of the deceased, entered the chamber of death. He urgently entreated to be allowed to view the face of his departed friend, and the coffin lid was unscrewed. The stranger pulled a warrant out of his pocket and arrested the body. It was probably a concerted scheme to obtain a sum (which it is supposed was five hundred pounds) that had been owing by the deceased. The creditor doubtless expected that a number of

men of fortune would be present, who would prefer losing five hundred pounds to suffering the remains of their friend to be consigned to the police. The extortioner was successful; it is said that Lord Sidmouth and another gentleman paid the money. Was this creditor an honest man? If courts of Equity had existed adapted to such cases, and the man were prosecuted, the consciences of a jury would surely have impelled them to send him to Newgate.

Slaves.

68. If a person left me an estate in Virginia or the West Indies, with a hundred slaves, the law of the land allows me to keep possession of both; the Moral Law does not. I should therefore hold myself imperatively obliged to give these persons their liberty. I do not say that I would manumit them all the next day; but if I deferred their liberation, it ought to be for their sakes, not my own; just as if I had a thousand pounds for a minor, my motive in withholding it from him would be exclusively his own advantage. Some persons who perceive the flagitiousness of slavery, retain slaves. Much forbearance of thought and language should be observed towards the man, in whose mind perhaps there is a strong conflict between conscience and the difficulty or loss which might attend a regard to its dictates. I have met with a feeling and benevolent person who owned several hundred slaves, and who, I believe, secretly lamented his own situation. I would be slow in censuring such a man, and yet it ought not to be concealed, that if he complied with the requisitions of the Moral Law, he would at least hasten to prepare them for emancipation. To endeavour to extricate oneself from the difficulty by *selling* the slaves were self-imposition. A man may as well keep them in bondage himself as sell them to another who would keep them in it. A narrative has appeared in print of the conduct of a gentleman to whom a number of slaves had been bequeathed, and who acted towards them upon the principles which rectitude requires. He conveyed them to some other country, educated some, procured employment for others, and acted as a Christian towards all.

69. Upon similar grounds, an upright man should not accept a present of a hundred pounds from a person who had not paid his debts, nor become his legatee. If the money were not rightfully his, he cannot give it; if it be rightfully his creditors, it cannot be mine.

Privateers.

70. Although familiarity with war occasions many obliquities in the moral notions of a people, yet the silent verdict of public opinion is, I think, *against* the rectitude of privateering. It is not regarded as creditable and virtuous; and this public disapprobation appears to be on the increase. Considerable exertion at least has been made, on the part of the American government, to abolish it. — To this private plunderer himself I do not talk of the obligations of morality; he has many lessons of virtue to learn before he will be likely to listen to such virtue as it is the object of these pages to recommend: but to him who perceives the flagitiousness of the practice, I would urge the consideration that he ought not to receive the plunder of a privateer even at second hand. If a man ought not to be the legatee of a bankrupt, he ought not to be the legatee of him who gained his money by privateering. Yet it is to be feared that many who would not fit out a privateer, would accept the money which the owners had stolen. If it be stolen, it is not theirs to give; and what one has no right to give, another has no right to accept.

71. During one of our wars with France, a gentleman who entertained such views of integrity as these, was partner in a merchant vessel, and in spite of his representations, the other owners resolved to fit her out as a privateer. They did so, and she happened to capture several vessels. This gentleman received from time to time his share of the prizes and laid it by; till, at the conclusion of the war, it had amounted to a considerable sum. What was to be done with the money? He felt that as an upright man he could not retain the money; and he accordingly went to France, advertised for the owners of the captured vessels, and returned to them the amount. Such conduct, instead of being a matter for good men to admire, and for men of loose morality to regard as needless scrupulosity, ought, when such circumstances arise, to be an ordinary occurrence. I do not relate the fact because I think it entitles the party to any extraordinary praise. He was honest; and honesty was his duty. The praise, if praise be due, consists in this—that he was upright where most men would have been unjust. Similar integrity upon parallel subjects may often be exhibited again—upon *privateering* it cannot often be repeated: for when the virtue of the public is great enough to make such integrity frequent, it will be great enough to frown privateering from the world.

72. At the time of war with the Dutch, about forty years ago, an English merchant vessel captured a Dutch Indiaman. It happened that one of the owners of the merchantman was one of the Society of Friends or Quakers. This society, as it objects to war, does not permit its members to share in

such a manner in the profits of war. However, this person, when he heard of the capture, insured his share of the prize. The vessel could not be brought into port, and he received of the underwriters eighteen hundred pounds. To have retained this money would have been equivalent to quitting the Society, so he gave it to his friends to dispose of it as justice might appear to prescribe. The state of public affairs on the Continent did not allow the trustees immediately to take any active measures to discover the owners of the captured vessel. The money therefore was allowed to accumulate. At the termination of the war with France, the circumstances of the case were repeatedly published in the Dutch journals, and the full amount of every claim that has been clearly made out has been paid by the trustees.

Confiscations.

73. I do not know whether the history of confiscations affords any examples of persons who refused to accept the confiscated property. Yet, when it is considered under what circumstances these seizures are frequently made--of revolution, and civil war, and the like, when the vindictive passions overpower the claims of justice and humanity --it cannot be doubted that the acceptance of confiscated property has sometimes been an act irreconcilable with integrity. Look, for example, at the confiscations of the French Revolution. The government which at the moment held the reins, doubtless sanctioned the appropriation of the property which they seized; and in so far the acceptance was legal. But that surely is not sufficient. Let an upright man suppose himself to be the neighbour of another who, with his family, enjoys the comforts of a paternal estate. In the distractions of political turbulence this neighbour is carried off and banished, and the estate is seized by order of the government. Would such a man accept this estate when the government offered it, without inquiry or consideration? Would he sit down in the warm comforts of plenty, whilst his neighbour was wandering, destitute perhaps, in another land, and whilst his family were in sorrow and in want? Would he not consider whether the confiscation was consistent with justice and rectitude --and whether if it were right with respect to the man, it was right with respect to his children and his wife, who perhaps did not participate in his offences? It may serve to give clearness to our perception to consider, that if Louis XVII. had been restored to the throne soon after his father's death, it is probable that many of the emigrants would have been reinstated in their possessions. Louis's restoration might have been the result of some intrigue, or of a battle. Do, then, the obligations of mankind as to enjoying the property of another, depend on such circumstances as battles and intrigues? If the returning emigrant would have *rightfully* repossessed his estate if the battle was successful, can the present occupier *rightfully* possess it if the battle is not successful? Is the result of a political manœuvre a proper rule to guide a man's conscience in retaining or giving up the houses and lands of his neighbours? Politicians, and those who profit by confiscations, may be little influenced by considerations like these; but there are other men who, I think, will perceive that they are important, and who, though confiscated property may never be offered to them, will be able to apply the *principles* which these considerations illustrate, to their own conduct in other affairs.

74. It is worthy of observation that in our own country, "of all the persons who were enriched by the spoils of the religious houses, there was not one who suffered for his opinions during the persecution."[1] How can this be accounted for, except upon the presumption that those who were so willing to accept these spoils, were not remarkable for their fidelity to religion?

Public Money.

75. Some writers on political affairs declaim much against sinecures and "places;" not always remembering that these things may be only modes of paying, and of justly paying, the servants of the public. It would, no doubt, be preferable that he who is rewarded for serving the public should, be rewarded avowedly as such, and not by the salary of a nominal office, which is always filled whether the receiver deserves the money or not. Such a mode of remuneration would be more reasonable in itself, and more satisfactory to the people. However, if public men *deserve* the money they receive, the name by which the salary is designated is not of much concern. The great point is the *desert*. That this ought to be a great point with a government there can be no doubt; and it is indeed upon governments that writers are wont to urge the obligation.

76. But our business is with the receivers. May a person, morally, appropriate to his own use *any* amount of money which a government chooses to give him? No. Then, when the public money is offered to any man, he is bound in conscience to consider whether he is in equity entitled to it or not. If, not being entitled, he accepts it, he

[1] Southey's Book of the Church, vol.

is not an upright man. For who gives it to him? The government; that is, the trustee for the public. A government is in a situation not dissimilar to that of a trustee for a minor. It has no right to dispose of the public property according to its own will. Whatever it expends, except with a view to the public advantage, is to be regarded as so much fraud; and it is quite manifest that if the government has no right to give, the private person can have no right to receive. I know of no exception to the application of these remarks, except where the public have expressly delivered up a certain amount of revenue to be applied according to the *inclination* of the governing power.

77. Now, the equity of an individual's claims upon the public property must be founded upon his services *to the public:* not upon his services to a minister, not upon the partiality of a prince; but upon services actually performed or performing for the public.[1] The degree in which familiarity with an ill custom diminishes our estimate of its viciousness is wonderful. If you propose to a man to come to some understanding with a guardian, by which he shall get a hundred pounds out of a ward's estate, he starts from you with abhorrence. Yet that same man, if a minister should offer him ten times as much of the public property, puts it complacently and thankfully into his pocket. Is this consistency? Is it uprightness?

78. In estimating the recompense to which public men are entitled, let the principles by all means be liberal. Let them be well paid: but let the money be paid: not given; let it be the discharge of a debt, not the making of a present. And were I a servant of the public, I should not assume as of course, that whatever remuneration the government was disposed to give, it would be right for me to receive. I should think myself obliged to consider for myself; and without affecting a trifling scrupulousness, I could not with integrity receive two thousand a year, if I knew that I was handsomely remunerated by one. These principles of conduct do not appear to lose their application in respect of fixed salaries or perquisites that are attached to offices. If a man cannot uprightly take two thousand pounds when he knows he is entitled to but one, it cannot be made right by the circumstance that others have taken it before him, or that all take it who accept the office. The income may be exorbitantly disproportioned, not merely to the labour of the office, but to the total services of the individual. Nor, I think, do these principles lose their application, even when, as in this country, a sum is voted by the Legislature for the Civil List, and when it is out of this voted sum that the salaries are paid. You say—the representatives of the people gave the individual the money. Very well—yet even this may be true in theory rather than in fact. But who pretends that, when the votes for the Civil List are made in the House of Commons, its members actually consider whether the individuals to whom the money will be distributed are in equity entitled to it or not?—The question is very simple at last—whether a person may virtuously accept the money of the public, without having rendered proportionate services to the public? There have been examples of persons who have voluntarily declined to receive the whole of the sums allotted to them by the government; and when these sums were manifestly disproportionate to the claims of the parties, or unreasonable when compared with the privations of the people, such sacrifices approve themselves to the feelings and consciences of the public. We feel that they are just and right; and this feeling outweighs in authority a hundred arguments by which men may attempt to defend themselves in the contrary practice.

79. Those large salaries which are given by way of "supporting the dignity of public functionaries," are not I think reconcilable with propriety nor dictated by necessity. At any rate, there must be some sorrowful want of purity in political affairs, if an ambassador or a prime minister is indebted for any part of his efficiency to these dignities and splendours. If the necessity for them is not imaginary, it ought to be; and it may be doubted whether, even now, a minister of integrity who *could not afford* the customary splendours of his office, would not possess as much weight in his own country and amongst other nations, as if he were surrounded with magnificence. Who feels disrespect towards the great officers of the American government? And yet their salaries are incomparably smaller than those of some of the inferior ministers in Europe.

Insurance.

80. It is very possible for a man to act dishonestly every day and yet never to defraud another of a shilling. A merchant who conducts his business partly or wholly with borrowed capital, is not honest if he *endangers* the loss of an amount of property which, if lost, would disable him from paying his debts. He who possesses a thousand pounds of his own and borrows a thousand of some one else, cannot virtuously *speculate*

---

[1] It is not necessary that these services should have been personal. The widow or son of a man who had been inadequately remunerated during his life, may very properly accept a competent pension from the State.

so extensively as that, if his prospects should be disappointed, he would lose twelve hundred. The *speculation* is dishonest whether it succeeds or not: it is risking other men's property without their consent. Under similar circumstances it is unjust not to insure. Perhaps the majority of uninsured traders, if their houses and goods were burnt, would be unable to pay their creditors. The injustice consists not in the actual loss which may be inflicted (for whether a fire happens or not, the injustice is the same), but in *endangering* the infliction of the loss. There are but two ways in which, under such circumstances, the claims of rectitude can be satisfied—one is by not endangering the property, and the other by telling its actual owner that it will be endangered, and leaving him to incur the risk or not as he pleases.

81. "Those who hold the property of others are not warranted, on the principles of justice, in neglecting to inform themselves from time to time of the real situation of their affairs."[1] This enforces the doctrines which we have delivered. It asserts that injustice attaches to *not investigating:* and this injustice is often real whether creditors are injured or not.

82. During the seventeenth century, when religious persecution was very active, some beautiful examples of integrity were offered by its victims. It was common for officers to seize the property of conscientious and good men, and sometimes to plunder them with such relentless barbarity as scarcely to leave them the common utensils of a kitchen. These persons sometimes had the property of others on their premises ; and when they heard that the officers were likely to make a seizure, industriously removed from their premises all property but their own. At one period, a number of traders in the country who had made purchases in the London markets, found that their plunderers were likely to disable them from paying for their purchases, and they requested the merchants to take back, and the merchants did take back, their goods.

Improvements on Estates.

84. There are some circumstances in which the occupier of lands or houses, who has increased their value by erections or other improvements, cannot in justice be compelled to *pay* for the increased value if he purchases the property. A man purchases the lease of an estate, and has reason to expect, from the youth and health of the "lives," that he may retain possession of it for thirty or forty years. In consequence of this expectation, he makes many additions to the buildings ; and by other modes of improvement considerably increases the value of the estate. It, however, happens that in the course of two or three years all the lives drop. The landowner, when the person applies to him for a new lease, demands payment for all the improvements. This I say is not just. It will be replied, that all parties knew and voluntarily undertook the risk : so they did, and if the event had *approached* to the ordinary average of such risks, the owner would act rightly in demanding the increased value. But it does not ; and this is the circumstance which would make an upright man decline to avail himself of his advantages. Yet, if any one critically disputes the "justice" of the demand, I give up the word, and say that it is not considerate, and kind, and benevolent— in a word, it is not *Christian.* It is no light calamity upon such a tenant to be obliged so unexpectedly to repurchase a lease ; and to add to this calamity a demand which the common feelings of mankind would condemn, cannot be the act of a good man. Who doubts whether, within the last fourteen years, it has not been the *duty* of many landowners to return a portion of their rents ? The duty is the same in one case as in the other ; and it is founded on the same principles in both. To say that other persons would be willing to pay the *present* value of the property, would not affect the question of morality ; because, to sell it to another for that value when the former tenant was desirous of repurchasing, would not diminish the unkindness to him.

it be not the greater foundation of credit, is a great one. A person lives then at the rate of a thousand a year; he maintains a respectable establishment, and diffuses over all its parts indications of property. These appearances are relied upon by other men: they think they may safely entrust him, and they do entrust him, with goods or money; until, when his insolvency is suddenly announced, they are surprised and alarmed to find that five hundred a year is settled on his wife. Now this person has induced others to confide their property to him by holding out fallacious appearances. He has in reality *deceived* them; and the deception is as real, though it may not be as palpable, as if he had deluded them with verbal falsehoods. He has been *acting* a continued untruth. Perhaps such a man will say that he never denied that the greater part of his apparent property was settled on his wife. This may be true; but, when his neighbour came to him to lodge five or six hundred pounds in his hands; when he was conscious that this neighbour's confidence *was founded* upon the belief that his apparent property was really his own; when there was reason to apprehend, that if his neighbour had known his actual circumstances he would have hesitated in entrusting him with the money, then he does really and practically *deceive* his neighbour, and it is not a sufficient justification to say that he has *uttered* no untruth. The reader will observe that the case is very different from that of a person who conducts his business with borrowed money. This person must annually pay the income of the money to the lender. He does not expend it on his own establishment, and consequently does not hold out the same fallacious appearances. Some profligate spendthrifts take a house, buy elegant furniture, and keep a handsome equipage, in order by these appearances to deceive and defraud traders. No man doubts whether these persons act criminally. How then can he be innocent who knowingly practises a deception similar in kind though varying in degree?

Houses of Infamy.

86. If it were not that a want of virtue is so common amongst men, we should wonder at the coolness with which some persons of decent reputation are content to let their houses to persons of abandoned character, and to put periodically into their pockets the profits of infamy. Sophisms may easily be invented to palliate the conduct; but nothing can make it right. Such a landlord knows perfectly to what purposes his house will be devoted, and knows that he shall receive the wages, not perhaps of his own iniquity, but still the wages of iniquity. He is almost a partaker with them in their sins. If I were to sell a man arsenic or a pistol, *knowing* that the buyer wanted it to commit murder, should I not be a bad man? If I let a man a house, knowing that the renter wants it for purposes of wickedness, am I an innocent man?—Not that it is to be affirmed that no one may receive ill-gotten money. A grocer may sell a pound of sugar to a woman though he knows she is upon the town. But, if we cannot specify the point at which a lawful degree of participation terminates, we can determine, respecting some degrees of participation, that *they* are unlawful. To the majority of such offenders against the Moral Law, these arguments may be urged in vain; there are some of whom we may indulge greater hope. Respectable public brewers are in the habit of purchasing beer-houses in order that they may supply the publicans with their porter. Some of these houses are notoriously the resort of the most abandoned of mankind; the daily scenes of riot, and drunkenness, and of the most filthy debauchery. Yet these houses are purchased by brewers— perhaps there is a competition amongst them for the premises;—they put in a tenant of their own, supply him with beer, and regularly receive the profits of this excess of wickedness. Is there no such obligation as that of abstaining even from the appearance of evil? Is there no such thing as guilt without a *personal* participation in it? All pleas such as that, if one man did not supply such a house another would, are vain subterfuges. Upon such reasoning you might rob a traveller on the road, if you knew that at the next turning a footpad was waiting to plunder him if you did not. Selling such houses to be occupied as before, would be like selling slaves because you thought it criminal to keep them in bondage. The obligation to discountenance wickedness rests upon him who possesses the power. "To him who knoweth to do good and doeth it not, to him it is sin." To retain our virtue may in such cases cost us something; but he who values virtue at its worth will not think that he retains it at a dear rate.

Literary Property.

87. Upon similar grounds there are some of the profits of the press which a good man cannot accept. There are some periodical works and some newspapers from which, if he were offered an annual income, he would feel himself bound to reject it. Suppose there is a newspaper which is lucrative because it gratifies a vicious taste for slander or indecency—or suppose there is a magazine of which the profits result from the attraction of irreligious or licentious articles—I would

not put into my pocket, every quarter of a year, the money which was gained by vitiating mankind. In all such cases, there is one sort of obligation which applies with great force—the obligation not to discourage rectitude by our example. Upon this ground a man of virtue would hesitate even to contribute an article to such a publication, lest they who knew he was a contributor should think they had his example to justify improprieties of their own.

Rewards.

88. A person loses his pocket-book containing fifty pounds, and offers ten pounds to the finder if he will restore it. The finder ought not to demand the reward. It implies surely some imputation upon a man's integrity, when he accepts payment for being honest. For, for what else is he paid? If he retains the property he is manifestly fraudulent. To be paid for giving it up is to be paid for not committing fraud. The loser offers the reward in order to overpower the temptation to dishonesty. To accept the reward is therefore tacitly to acknowledge that you would have been dishonest if it had not been offered. This certainly is not maintaining an integrity that is "above suspicion." It will be said that the reward is offered *voluntarily*. This, in proper language, is not true. Two evils are presented to the loser, of which he is *compelled* to choose one. If men were honest, he would not offer the reward : he would make it known that he had lost his pocket-book, and the finder, if a finder there were, would restore it. The offered ten pounds is a tax which is imposed upon him by the want of uprightness in mankind, and he who demands the money actively promotes the imposition. The very word reward carries with it its own reprobation. As a reward, the man of integrity would receive nothing. If the loser requested it, he might if he needed it accept a donation ; but he would let it be understood that he accepted a present, not that he received a debt.

89. Perhaps examples enough, or more than enough, have been accumulated to illustrate this class of obligations. Many appeared needful, because it is a class which is deplorably neglected in practice. So strong is the temptation to think that we may rightfully possess whatever the law assigns to us —so insinuating is the notion, upon subjects of property, that whatever the law does not punish we may rightfully do, that there is little danger of supplying too many motives to habitual discrimination of our duties and to habitual purity of conduct. Let the reader especially remember, that the examples which are offered are not all of them selected on account of their individual importance, but rather as illustrations of the general principle. A man may meet with a hundred circumstances in life to which none of these examples are relevant, but I think he will not have much difficulty in estimating the principles which they illustrate. And this induces the observation, that although several of these examples are taken from British law or British customs, they do not, on that account, lose their applicability where these laws and customs do not obtain. If this book should ever be read in a foreign land, or if it should be read in this land when public institutions or the tenor of men's conduct shall be changed, the *principles* of its morality will, nevertheless, be applicable to the affairs of life.

CHAPTER III.

Inequality of Property.

Accumulation of Wealth : its proper limits—Provision for children : "Keeping up the family."

90. That many and great evils result from that inequality of property which exists in civilised countries, is indicated by the many propositions which have been made to diminish or destroy it. We want not indeed such evidence ; for it is sufficiently manifest to every man who will look round upon his neighbours. We join not with those who declaim against all inequality of property : the real evil is not that it is unequal, but that it is greatly unequal ; not that one man is richer than another, but that one man is so rich as to be luxurious, or imperious, or profligate, and that another is so poor as to be abject and depraved, as well as to be destitute of the proper comforts of life.

91. There are two means by which the pernicious inequality of property may be diminished ; by political institutions, and by the exertions of private men. Our present business is with the latter.

92. To a person who possesses and expends more than he needs, there are two reasonable inducements to diminish its amount—first, to benefit others, and next, to benefit his family and himself. The claims of benevolence towards others are often and earnestly urged upon the public, and for that reason they will not be repeated here. Not that there is no occasion to repeat the lesson, for it is very inadequately learnt ; but that it is of more consequence to exhibit obligations which are less frequently enforced. To insist upon diminishing the amount of a man's property *for the sake of his family and himself,*

may present to some men new ideas, and to some men the doctrine may be paradoxical.

93. Large possessions are in a great majority of instances injurious to the possessor—that is to say, those who hold them are generally less excellent, both as citizens and as men, than those who do not. The truth appears to be established by the concurrent judgment of mankind. Lord Bacon says—"Certainly great riches have sold more men than they have bought out. As baggage is to an army, so are riches to virtue.—It hindereth the march, yea, and the care of it sometimes loseth or disturbeth the victory."[1] —"It is to be feared that the general tendency of rank, and *especially of riches*, is to withdraw the heart from spiritual exercises."[1] "A much looser system of morals commonly prevails in the higher than in the middling and lower orders of society."[2] "The middle rank contains most virtue and abilities."[3]

"Wealth heaped on wealth nor truth nor safety buys, The dangers gather as the treasures rise."[4]

94. "There is no greater calamity than that of leaving children an affluent independence.—The worst examples in the Society of Friends are generally amongst the children of the rich."[5]

It was an observation of Voltaire's, that the English people were, like their butts of beer, froth at top, dregs at bottom—in the middle, excellent. The most rational, the wisest, the best portion of mankind, belong to that class who possess " neither poverty nor riches." Let the reader look around him. Let him observe who are the persons that contribute most to the moral and physical amelioration of mankind ; who they are that practically and personally support our unnumbered institutions of benevolence ; who they are that exhibit the worthiest examples of intellectual exertion ; who they are to whom he would himself apply if he needed to avail himself of a manly and discriminating judgment. That they are the poor is not to be expected : we appeal to himself whether they are the rich. Who then would make his son a rich man? Who would remove his child out of that station in society which is thus peculiarly favourable to intellectual and moral excellence?

95. If a man knows that wealth will in all probability be injurious to himself and to his children, injurious too in the most important points, the religious and moral character, it is manifestly a point of the soundest wisdom

[1] More's Moral Sketches, 3rd Ed., p. 446.
[2] Wilberforce : Pract. View.
[3] Wollestonecroft : Rights of Women, c. 4.
[4] Johnson : Vanity of Human Wishes.
[5] Clarkson : Portraiture.

and the truest kindness to decline to accumulate it. Upon this subject, it is admirable to observe with what exactness the precepts of Christianity are adapted to that conduct which the experience of life recommends. " The care of this world and the deceitfulness of riches choke the word :"—"choked with cares, and riches, and pleasures of this life, and bring no fruit to perfection :"—" How hardly shall they that have riches enter into the kingdom of God !" " They that will be rich fall into temptation and a snare, and into many foolish and hurtful lusts which drown men in destruction and perdition." Not that riches necessarily lead to these consequences, but that such is their tendency; a tendency so uniform and powerful that it is to be feared these are their very frequent results. Now this language of the Christian Scriptures does not contain merely statements of fact—it imposes duties ; and whatever may be the precise mode of regarding those duties, one point is perfectly clear ; that he who sets no other limit to his possessions or accumulations than inability or indisposition to obtain more, does not conform to the Will of God. Assuredly, if any specified thing is declared by Christianity to be highly likely to obstruct our advancement in goodness, and to endanger our final felicity, against that thing, whatever it be, it is imperative upon us to guard with wakeful solicitude.

96. And therefore, without affirming that no circumstance can justify a great accumulation of property, it may safely be concluded, that far the greater number of those who do accumulate it, do wrong : nor do I see any reason to be deterred from ranking the distribution of a portion of great wealth, or a refusal to accumulate it, amongst the imperative duties which are imposed by the Moral Law. In truth, a man may almost discover whether such conduct is obligatory, by referring to the motives which induce him to acquire great property or to retain it. The motives are generally impure ; the desire of splendour, or the ambition of eminence, or the love of personal indulgence. Are these motives fit to be brought into competition with the probable welfare, the virtue, the usefulness, and the happiness of his family and himself? Yet such is the competition, and to such unworthy objects, duty, and reason, and affection are sacrificed.

97. It will be said, a man should provide for his family, and make them, if he can, independent. That he should provide for his family is true ; that he should make them independent, at any rate that he should give them an affluent independence, forms no part of his duty, and is frequently a violation of it. As it respects almost all men, *he* will

best approve himself a wise and a kind parent, who leaves to his sons so much only as may enable them, by moderate engagements, to enjoy the conveniences and comforts of life; and to his daughters a sufficiency to possess similar comforts, but not a sufficiency to shine amongst the great, or to mingle with the votaries of expensive dissipation. If any father prefers other objects to the welfare and happiness of his children—if wisdom and kindness towards them are with him subordinate considerations, it is not probable that he will listen to reasonings like these. But where is the parent who dares to acknowledge this preference to his own mind?

98. It were idle to affect to specify any amount of property which a person ought not to exceed. The circumstances of one man may make it reasonable that he should acquire or retain much more than another who has fewer claims. Yet somewhat of a general rule may be suggested. He who is accumulating should consider *why* he desires more. If it really is that he believes an addition will increase the welfare and usefulness and virtue of his family, it is probable that further accumulation may be right. If no such belief is sincerely entertained, it is more than probable that it is wrong. He who already possesses affluence should consider its actual existing effects.—If he employs a competent portion of it in increasing the happiness of others, if it does not produce any injurious effect upon his own mind, if it does not diminish or impair the virtues of his children, if they are grateful for their privileges rather than vain of their superiority, if they second his own endeavours to diffuse happiness around them, he may remain as he is. If such effects are not produced, but instead of them others of an opposite tendency, he certainly has too much. — Upon this serious subject let the Christian parent be serious. If, as is proved by the experience of every day, great property usually inflicts great injuries upon those who possess it, what motive can induce a good man to lay it up for his children? What motive will be his justification, if it tempts them from virtue?

99. When children are similarly situated with respect to their probable wants, there seems no reason for preferring the elder to the younger, or sons to daughters. Since the proper object of a parent in making a division of his property is the comfort and welfare of his children, if this object is likely to be better secured by an equal than by any other division, an equal division ought to be made. It is a common, though not a very reasonable opinion, that a son needs a larger portion than a daughter. To be sure, if he is to live in greater affluence than she, he does. By why should he? There appears no motive in reason, and certainly there is none in affection, for diminishing one child's comforts to increase another's. A son too has greater opportunities of gain. A woman almost never grows rich except by legacies or marriage; so that, if her father do not provide for her, it is probable that she will not be provided for at all. As to marriage, the opportunity is frequently not offered to a woman; and a father, if he can, should so provide for his daughter as to enable her, in single life, to live in a state of comfort not greatly inferior to her brother's. The remark that the custom of preferring sons is *general*, and therefore that when a couple marry the inequality is adjusted, applies only to the case of those who do marry. The number of women who do not is great; and a parent cannot foresee his daughter's lot. Besides, since marriage is (and is reasonably) a great object to a woman, and is desirable both for women and for men, there appears a propriety in increasing the probability of marriage by giving to women such property as shall constitute an additional inducement to marriage in the men. I shall hardly be suspected of recommending persons to "marry for money." My meaning is this: A young man possesses five hundred a year, and lives on a corresponding scale. He is attached to a woman who has but one hundred a year. This young man sees that if he marries, he must reduce his scale of living; and the consideration operates (I do not say that it ought to operate) to deter him from marriage. But if the young man possessed three hundred a year and lived accordingly, and if the object of his attachment possessed three hundred a year also, he would *not* be prevented from marrying her by the fear of being obliged to diminish his system of expenditure. Just complaints are made of those half-concealed blandishments by which some women who need "a settlement" endeavour to procure it by marriage. Those blandishments would become more tempered with propriety if one great motive was taken away by the possession of a competence of their own.

100. An equal division of a father's property will be said to be incompatible with the system of primogeniture, and almost incompatible with hereditary rank. These are not subjects for the present Essay. Whatever the reader may think of the practical value of these institutions, it is manifest that far the greater number of those who have property to bequeath need not concern themselves with either: they may, in their own practice, contribute to diminish the general and the particular evils of unequal property. With respect to their own families, the result can hardly fail to be good. It is probable

that as men advance in intellectual, and especially in moral excellence, the desire of "keeping up the family" will become less and less an object of solicitude. That desire is not, in its ordinary character, recommended by any considerations which are obviously deducible from virtue or from reason. It is an affair of vanity; and vanity, like other weaknesses and evils, may be expected to diminish as sound habits of judgment prevail in the world.

101. Perhaps it is remarkable that the obligation not to accumulate great property for ourselves or our children is so little enforced by the writers on morality. None will dispute that such accumulation is both unwise and unkind. Every one acknowledges too that the general evils of the existing inequality of property are enormously great; yet how few insist upon those means by which, more than by any other private means, these evils may be diminished! If all men declined to retain, or refrained from acquiring, more than is likely to be beneficial to their families and themselves, the pernicious inequality of property would quickly be diminished or destroyed. There is a motive upon the individual to do this, which some public reformations do not offer. He who contributes almost nothing to diminish the general mischiefs of extreme poverty and extreme wealth, may yet do so much benefit to his own connections as shall greatly overpay him for the sacrifice of vanity or inclination. Perhaps it may be said that there is a claim too of justice. The wealth of a nation is a sort of common stock, of which the accumulations of one man are usually made at the expense of others. A man who has acquired a reasonable sufficiency, and who nevertheless retains his business to acquire more than a sufficiency, practises a sort of injustice towards another who needs his means of gain. There are always many who cannot enjoy the comforts of life, because others are improperly occupying the means by which those comforts are to be obtained. Is it the part of a Christian to do this?—even abating the consideration that he is injuring himself by withholding comforts from another.

CHAPTER IV.

Litigation—Arbitration.

Practice of early Christians—Evils of litigation—Efficiency of arbitration.

1. In the third Essay,[1] some inquiry will be attempted, as to whether justice may not often be administered between contending parties, or to public offenders, by some species of arbitration rather than by law;—whether a gradual substitution of Equity for fixed rules of decision, is not congruous alike with philosophy and morals. The present chapter, however, and that which succeeds it, proceed upon the supposition that the administration of justice continues in its present state.

2. The question for an individual, when he has some cause of dispute with another respecting property or rights, is, By what means ought I to endeavour to adjust it? Three modes of adjustment may be supposed to be offered: Private arrangement with the other party—Reference to impartial men—and Law. Private adjustment is the best mode; arbitration is good; law is good only when it is the sole alternative.

3. The litigiousness of some of the early Christians at Corinth gave occasion to the energetic expostulation, "Dare any of you, having a matter against another, go to law before the unjust, and not before the saints? Do ye not know that the saints shall judge the world? And if the world shall be judged by you, are ye unworthy to judge the smallest matters? Know ye not that we shall judge angels? How much more things that pertain to this life? If then, ye have judgments of things pertaining to this life, set them to judge who are least esteemed in the Church. I speak to your shame. Is it so that there is not a wise man among you? No, not one that shall be able to judge between his brethren? But brother goeth to law with brother, and that before the unbelievers. Now therefore there is utterly a fault among you, because ye go to law one with another. Why do ye not rather take wrong? Why do ye not rather suffer yourselves to be defrauded?"[1] Upon this, one observation is especially to be remembered: that a great part of its pointedness of reprehension is directed, not so much to litigation, as to litigation *before pagans*. "Brother goeth to law with brother, and that before the unbelievers." The impropriety of exposing the disagreements of Christians in pagan courts was manifest and great. They who had rejected the dominant religion for a religion of which one peculiar characteristic was goodwill and unanimity, were especially called upon to exhibit in their conduct an illustration of its purer principles. Few things, not grossly vicious, would bring upon Christians and upon Christianity itself so much reproach as a litigiousness which could not or would not find arbitration amongst themselves. The advice of the Apostle appears to have

[1] Chap. X.

[1] 1 Cor. vi.

been acted upon: "The primitive Church, which was always zealous to reconcile the brethren and to procure pardon for the offender from the person offended, did ordain, according to the Epistle of St. Paul to the Corinthians, that the saints or Christians should not maintain a process of law one against the other at the bar or tribunals of infidels."[1] The Christian of the present day is differently circumstanced, because, though he appeals to the law, he does not appeal to pagan judges; and therefore so much of the Apostle's censure as was occasioned by the paganism of the courts does not apply to us.

4. To this indeed there is an exception founded upon analogy. If at the commencement of the Reformation, two of the reformers had carried a dispute respecting property before Romish courts, they would have come under some portion of that reprobation which was addressed to the Corinthians. Certainly when persons profess such a love for religious purity and excellence that they publicly withdraw from the general religion of a people, there ought to be so much purity and excellence amongst them, that it would be needless to have recourse to those from whom they had separated to adjust their disputes. The Catholic of those days might reasonably have turned upon such reformers and said, "Is it so that there is not a wise man among you, no not one, that shall be able to judge between his brethren?" And if indeed no such wise man was to be found, it might safely be concluded that their reformation was an empty name.—For the same reasons, those who, in the present times, think it right to withdraw from other Protestant Churches in order to maintain sounder doctrines or purer practice, cast reproach upon their own community if they cannot settle their disputes amongst themselves. Pretensions to soundness and purity are of little avail if they do not enable those who make them to repose in one another such confidence as this. Were I a Wesleyan or a Baptist, I should think it discreditable to go to law with one of my own brotherhood.

5. But though the Apostle's *prohibition* of going to law appears to have been founded upon the paganism of the courts, his language evidently conveys disapprobation, generally, of appeals to the law. He insists upon the propriety of adjusting disputes by arbitration. Christians, he says, ought not to be unworthy to judge the smallest matters; and so emphatically does he insist upon the truth, that their religion ought to capacitate them to act as arbitrators, that he intimates that even a small advance in Christian excellence is sufficient for such a purpose as this:—"Set them to judge who are least esteemed in the Church." It will perhaps be acknowledged that when Christianity shall possess its proper influence over us, there will be little reason to recur, for adjustment of our disagreements, to fixed rules of law. And though this influence is so far short of universal prevalence, who cannot find amongst those to whom he may have access some who are capable of deciding rightly and justly? The state of that Christian country must indeed be bad if it contains not, even in every little district, one that is able to judge between his brethren.

6. Nevertheless, there are cases in which the Christian may properly appeal to the law. He may have an antagonist who can in no other manner be induced to be just or to act aright. Under some such circumstances Paul himself pursued a similar course: "I appeal unto Cæsar."—"Is it lawful for you to scourge a man that is a Roman and uncondemned?" And when he had been illegally taken into custody he availed himself of his legal privileges, and made the magistrates "come themselves and fetch him out." There are, besides, in the present condition of jurisprudence, some cases in which the rule of justice *depends* upon the rule of law—so that a thing is just or not just according as the law determines. In such cases neither party, however well disposed, may be able distinctly to tell what justice requires until the law informs them. Even then, however, there are better means of procedure than by prosecuting suits. The parties may obtain "Opinions."

7. Besides these considerations there are others which powerfully recommend arbitration in preference to law. The *evils* of litigation, from which arbitration is in a great degree exempt, are great.

8. *Expense* is an important item. A reasonable man desires of course to obtain justice as inexpensively as he can; and the great cost of obtaining it in courts of law is a powerful reason for preferring arbitration.

9. *Legal Injustice.*—He who desires that justice should be dispensed between him and another, should sufficiently bear in mind how much injustice is inflicted by the law. We have seen in some of the preceding chapters that law is often very wide of equity; and he who desires to secure himself from an inequitable decision, possesses a powerful motive to prefer arbitration. The technicalities of the law and the artifices of lawyers

---

[1] Rycaut's Lives of the Popes, fol. 2nd ed. 1688. Introd. p. 2.

are almost innumerable. Sometimes, when a party thinks he is on the eve of obtaining a just verdict, he is suddenly disappointed and his cause is lost by some technical defect —the omission of a word or the mis-spelling of a name ; matters which in no degree affect the validity of his claims. If the only advantage which arbitration offers to disagreeing parties was exemption from these deplorable evils, it would be a substantial and sufficient argument in its favour. There is no reason to doubt that justice would generally be administered by a reference to two or three upright and disinterested men. When facts are laid before such persons, they are seldom at a loss to decide what justice requires. Its principles are not so critical or remote as usually to require much labour of research to discover what they dictate. It might be concluded, therefore, even if experience did not confirm it, that an arbitration, if it did not decide absolutely aright, would at least come to as just a decision as can be attained by human means. But experience does confirm the conclusion. It is known that the Society of Friends *never* permits its members to carry disagreements with one another before courts of law. All, if they continue in the Society, must submit to arbitration. And what is the consequence? They find, practically, that arbitration is the best mode ; that justice is in fact administered by it, administered more satisfactorily and with fewer exceptions than in legal courts. No one pretends to dispute this. Indeed, if it were disputable, it may be presumed that this community would abandon the practice. They adhere to it because it is the most Christian practice and the best.

10. *Inquietude*. — The expense, the injustice, the delays and vexations which are attendant upon lawsuits, bring altogether a degree of inquietude upon the mind which greatly deducts from the enjoyment of life, and from the capacity to attend with composure to other and perhaps more important concerns. If to this we add the heart-burnings and ill-will which suits frequently occasion, a considerable sum of evil is in this respect presented to us : a sum of evil, be it remembered, from which arbitration is in a great degree exempt.

11. Upon the whole, arbitration is recommended by such various and powerful arguments, that when it is proposed by one of two contending parties and objected to by the other, there is reason to presume that, with that other, justice is not the paramount object of desire.

CHAPTER V.

The Morality of Legal Practice.

Complexity of law—Professional untruths—Defences of legal practice — Effects of legal practice : Seduction : Theft : Peculation—Pleading—The duties of the profession—Effects of legal practice on the profession and on the public.

12. If it should be asked why, in a book of general morality, the writer selects for observation the practice of a particular profession, the answer is simply this, that the practice of this particular profession peculiarly needs it. It peculiarly needs to be brought into juxtaposition with sound principles of morality. Besides this, an honest comparison of the practice with the principles will afford useful illustration of the requisitions of virtue.

13. That public opinion pronounces that there is, in the ordinary character of legal practice, much that is not reconcilable with rectitude, can need no proof. The public opinion could scarcely become general unless it were founded upon truth, and that it is general is evinced by the language of all ranks of men, from that of him who writes a treatise of morality, to that of him who familiarly uses a censorious proverb. It may reasonably be concluded that when the professional conduct of a particular set of men is characterised peculiarly with sacrifices of rectitude, there must be some general and peculiar cause. There appears nothing in the profession, as such, to produce this effect —nothing in taking a part in the administration of justice which necessarily leads men away from the regard to justice. How then are we to account for the fact as it exists, or where shall we primarily lay the censure? Is it the fault of the men or of the institution, of the lawyers or of the law? Doubtless the original fault is in the law.

14. This fault, as it respects our own country, and I suppose every other, is of two kinds ; one is necessary, and one accidental. First, wherever fixed rules of deciding controversies between man and man, or fixed rules of administering punishment to public offenders are established, there it is inevitable that equity will sometimes be sacrificed to rules. These rules are laws, that is, they must be uniformly, and for the most part literally, applied ; and this literal application (as we have already had manifold occasion to show) is sometimes productive of practical injustice. Since, then, the legal profession employ themselves in enforcing this literal application—since they habitually exert themselves to do this with little regard to the equity of the result, they cannot fail to deserve and to obtain the character of a profession that sacrifices rectitude. I know

not that this is evitable so long as numerous and *fixed* rules are adopted in the administration of justice.

15. The second cause of the evil, as it results from the law itself, is in its extreme complication—in the needless multiplicity of its forms, in the inextricable intricacy of its whole structure. This, which is probably by far the most efficient cause of the want of morality in legal practice, I call gratuitous. It is not necessary to law that it should be so extremely complicated. This, the public are beginning more and more to see and to assert. Simplification has indeed been in some small degree effected by recent Acts of the Legislature; and this is a sufficient evidence that it was needed. But whether needed or not, the temptation which it casts in the way of professional virtue is excessively great. A man takes a cause—a morally bad cause, we will suppose—to a barrister. The barrister searches his memory or his books for some one or more amongst the multiplicity of legal technicalities by which success may be obtained for his client. He finds them, urges them in court, shows that the opposing client cannot *legally* substantiate his claim, and thus inflicts upon him practical injustice. This is primarily the fault of the law. Take away or diminish this encumbering load of technicalities, and you take away, in the same proportion, the opportunity for the profession to sacrifice equity to forms, and by consequence diminish the immorality of its practice. There can be no efficient reform amongst lawyers without a reform of the law.

16. But whilst thus the original cause of the sacrifice of virtue amongst legal men is to be sought in legal institutions, it cannot be doubted that they are themselves chargeable with greatly adding to the evils which these institutions occasion. This is just what, in the present state of human virtue, we might expect. Lawyers familiarise to their minds the notion that whatever is legally right is right; and when they have once habituated themselves to sacrifice the manifest dictates of equity to law, where shall they stop? If a material informality in an instrument is to them a sufficient justification of a sacrifice of these dictates, they will soon sacrifice them because a word has been misspelt by an attorney's clerk. When they have gone thus far, they will go further. The practice of disregarding rectitude in courts of justice will become habitual. They will go onward from insisting upon legal technicalities to an endeavour to *pervert* the law, then to the giving a false colouring to facts, and then onward and still onward until witnesses are abashed and confounded, until juries are misled by impassioned appeals to their feelings, until deliberate untruths are solemnly averred, until, in a word, all the pitiable and degrading spectacles are exhibited which are now exhibited in legal practice.

17. But when we say that the original cause of this unhappy system is to be found in the law itself, is it tantamount to a justification of the system? No: if it were, it would be sufficient to justify any departure from rectitude—it would be sufficient to justify any crime to be able to show that the perpetrator possessed strong temptation. Strong temptation is undoubtedly placed before the legal practitioner. This should abate our censure, but it should not cause us to be silent.

18. We affirm that a lawyer cannot morally enforce the application of legal rules *without regard* to the claims of equity in the particular case.

19. If it has been seen in the preceding chapters that morality is paramount to law; if it has been seen that there are many instances in which private persons are morally obliged to forego their legal pretensions, then it is equally clear that a lawyer is obliged to hold morality as paramount to law in his own practice. If one man may not urge an unjust legal pretension, another may not assist him in urging it. No man, it may be hoped, will say that it is the lawyer's only business to apply the law. Men cannot so cheaply exempt themselves from the obligations of morality. Yet here the question is really suspended; for if *the business of the profession* does not justify a disregard of morality, it is not capable of justification. Suspended! It is lamentable that such a question can exist. For to what does the alternative lead us? Is a man, when he undertakes a client's business, at liberty to advance his interests by every method, good or bad, which the law will not punish? If he is, there is an end of morality. If he is not, *something* must limit and restrict him; and that something is the Moral Law.

20. Of every custom, however indefensible, some advocates offer themselves; and some accordingly have attempted to justify the practice of the bar.[1] Of that particular item in the practice which consists in uttering untruths in order to serve a client, Dr. Paley has been the defender. "There are falsehoods," says he, "which are *not criminal:* as where no one is deceived, which is the case with an advocate in asserting the justice, or his belief of the justice, of his client's cause." It is plain that in support of this position one argument, and only one, can be

[1] I speak of the *bar*, because that branch of the profession offers the most convenient illustration of the subject. The reasonings will generally apply to other branches.

urged, and that one has been selected. "No confidence is destroyed, because none was reposed; no promise to speak the truth is violated, because none was given or understood to be given."[1] The defence is not very creditable, even if it were valid: it defends men from the imputation of falsehood because their falsehoods are so habitual that no one gives them credit!

21. But the defence is not valid. Of this the reader may satisfy himself by considering why, if no one ever believes what advocates say, they continue to speak. They would not, year after year, persist in uttering untruths in our courts without attaining an object, and knowing that they would not attain it. If no one ever, in fact, believed them, they would cease to asseverate. They do not love falsehood for its own sake, and utter it gratuitously and for nothing. The custom itself, therefore, disproves the argument that is brought to defend it. Whenever that defence becomes valid—whenever it is really true that "*no* confidence is reposed" in advocates, they will cease to use falsehood, for it will have lost its motive. But the real practice is to mingle falsehood and truth together, and so to involve the one with the other that the jury cannot easily separate them. The jury know that some of the pleader's statements are true, and these they believe. Now he makes other statements with the same deliberate emphasis; and how shall the jury know whether these are false or true? How shall they discover the point at which they shall begin to "repose no confidence?" Knowing that a part is true, they cannot always know that another part is not true. That it is the pleader's design to persuade them of the truth of all he affirms is manifest. Suppose an advocate when he rose should say, "Gentlemen, I am now going to speak the truth;" and after narrating the facts of the case should say, "Gentlemen, I am now going to address you with fictions." Why would not an advocate do this? Because then no confidence would be reposed, which is the same thing as to say that he pursues his present plan because some confidence is reposed; and this decides the question. The decision should not be concealed—that the advocate who employs untruths in his pleadings, does really and most strictly *lie*.

22. And even if no one ever did believe an advocate, his false declarations would still be lies, because he always *professes* to speak the truth. This indeed is true upon the Archdeacon's own showing: for he says, "Whoever seriously addresses his discourse to another, tacitly *promises* to speak the

[1] Mor. and Pol. Phil., b. 3, p. 1, c. 15.

truth." The case is very different from others which he proposes as parallel—"parables, fables, jests." In these the speaker does not *profess* to state facts. But the pleader does profess to state facts. He intends and endeavours to mislead. His untruths, therefore, are lies to him whether they are believed or not; just as in vulgar life a man whose falsehoods are so notorious that no one gives him credit, is not the less a liar than if he were believed.

23. From one sort of legal falsehoods results one peculiar mischief, a mischief arising primarily out of an unhappy rule of law, but which is not on that account morally justifiable. "Decision is commanded by *pleadings* as by evidence, and that also to a vast extent and with a degree of certainty refused to evidence. Decision is produced by pleadings as if they were true, when they are known and acknowledged to be false; because they act as evidence and as true evidence in all cases where the opposed party cannot follow them by counter-declarations —a consequence which may and does result from poverty and other causes."[1] This is deplorable indeed. To employ false pleadings is sufficiently unjustifiable; but to employ them in order that a poor man, or that any man, may be debarred of his rights, is abominable. But why do we say that *this* peculiarly is abominable? For to what purpose is any falsehood urged at the bar but to impede or prevent the administration of justice between man and man? I make no pretensions to legal knowledge. Some false pleadings are legally "necessary" in order to give formality to a proceeding. In these cases the evil is attributable in a great degree to the law itself, though I presume the law is founded upon custom, which custom was introduced by lawyers. The evil, therefore, and the guilt lies at the door of the *system* of legal practice, although it may not all lie at the doors of existing practitioners.[2]

24. Gisborne is another defender of legal practice, and assumes a wider ground of justification. "The standard," says he, "to which the advocate refers the cause of his client, is not the law of reason nor the law of God, but the law of the land. His peculiar and proper object is not to prove the side of the question which he maintains

[1] West. Rev., No. 9.
[2] Some of these legal falsehoods are ridiculous to the last degree. A horse is sent to a farrier to be shod. Unhappily, and to the great regret of the farrier, his man accidentally lames the horse. What then says the legal form? That the farrier faithfully promised to shoe the horse properly: but that "he, not regarding his said promise and undertaking, but contriving and fraudulently intending, craftily, and subtilely to deceive and defraud the said plaintiff, did not nor would shoe the said horse, in a skilful, careful, and proper manner, &c.!"—See the Form, v, Chitty on Pleading, p. 154.

morally right, but legally right. The law offers its protection only on certain preliminary conditions; it refuses to take cognisance of injuries or to enforce redress, unless the one be proved in the specific manner and the other claimed in the precise form which it prescribes; and consequently, whatever be the pleader's opinion of his cause, he is guilty of no breach of truth and justice in defeating the pretensions of the persons whom he opposes, by evincing that they have not made good the terms on which alone they could be legally entitled, on which alone they could suppose themselves entitled, to success."[1] There is something specious in this reasoning, but what is its amount?—that if the laws of a country proceed upon such and such maxims, they exempt us from the authority of the laws of God. We arrive at this often-refuted doctrine at last. Either the Acts of a Legislature may suspend the obligations of morality or they may not. If they may, there is an end of that morality which is founded upon the Divine Will: if they may not, the argument of Gisborne is a fallacy. But in truth, he himself shows its fallaciousness: he says, "If a cause should present itself of an aspect so dark as to leave the advocate no reasonable doubt of its being founded in iniquity or baseness, or to justify extremely strong suspicions of its evil nature and tendency, he is bound in the sight of God to refuse all connection with the business." Why is he thus bound to refuse? *Because he will otherwise violate the Moral Law:* and this is the very reason why he is bound in other cases. Observe, too, the inconsistency: first we are told that whatever be the pleader's opinion of a cause, "he is guilty of no breach of truth and justice" in advocating it; and afterwards, that if the cause is of an "evil nature and tendency" he may *not* advocate it! That such reasoning does not prove what it is designed to prove is evident; but it proves something else—that the practice cannot be defended. Such reasoning would not be advanced if better could be found. Let us not, however, seem to avail ourselves of a writer's words without reference to his meaning. The meaning in the present instance is clearly this—that a pleader, generally, may undertake a vicious cause; but that if it be *very* vicious, he must refrain. You may abet an act of a certain shade of iniquity, but not if it be of a certain shade deeper: you may violate the Moral Law to a certain extent, but not to every extent. To him who would recommend rectitude in its purity, few reasonings are more satisfactory than such as these. They prove the truth which they assail by evincing that it cannot be disproved.

[1] Duties of Men. The Legal Profession.

25. Dr. Johnson tried a shorter course: "You do not know a cause to be good or bad till the judge determines it. An argument that does not convince you may convince the judge to whom you urge it, and if it does convince him, why then he is right and you are wrong." This is *satisfactory.* It is always satisfactory to perceive that a powerful intellect can find nothing but idle sophistry to urge against the obligations of virtue. One other argument is this: Eminent barristers, it is said, should not be too scrupulous, because clients might fear their causes would be rejected by virtuous pleaders, and might therefore go to "needy and unprincipled chicaners." Why, if their causes were good, virtuous pleaders would undertake them; and if they were bad, it matters not how soon they were discountenanced. In a right state of things, the very circumstance that only an "unprincipled chicaner" would undertake a particular cause, would go far towards procuring a verdict against it. Besides, it is a very loose morality that recommends good men to do improper things lest they should be done by the bad.

26. Seeing, therefore, that no tolerable defence can be adduced of the ordinary legal practice, let us consider for a moment what are its practical results.

27. A civil action is brought into court, and evidence has been heard which satisfies every man that the plaintiff is entitled in justice to a verdict. It is, on the part of the defendant, a clear case of dishonesty. Suddenly, the pleader discovers that there is some verbal flaw in a document, some technical irregularity in the proceedings—and the plaintiff loses his cause. The public are disappointed in their expectations of justice; the jury and the court are grieved, and the unhappy sufferer retires, injured and wronged, without redress or hope of redress. Can this be right? Can it be sufficient to justify a man in this conduct, to urge that such things are his business, the means by which he obtains his living? The same excuse would justify a corsair, or a troop of Arabian banditti which plunders the caravan. Yet indefensible, immoral, as this conduct is, it is the everyday practice of the profession, and the amount of injustice which is inflicted by this practice is enormous. The plea that such are the rules of the law is not admissible. Whatever utility we may be disposed to allow to the uniform application of the law, it will not justify such conduct as this. The integrity of the law would not have been violated though the pleader had not pointed out the mis-spelling, for example, of a

word. For a judge to refuse to allow the law to take its course after the mistake has been urged, is one thing; for a pleader to detect and to urge it, is another. The judge may not be able to regard the equity of the case without sacrificing the uniform operation of the law. But if the inadvertency is not pointed out, that uniform operation is perfect though equity be awarded. There is no excuse for thus inflicting injustice. It is an act of pure gratuitous mischief: an act not required by law, an act condemned by morality, an act possessing no apology but that the agent is tempted by the gains of his profession.

28. An unhappy father seeks, in a court of justice, some redress for the misery which a seducer has inflicted upon his family; a redress which, if he were successful, is deplorably inadequate, both as a recompense to the sufferers and as a punishment to the criminal. The case is established, and it is manifest that equity and the public good require exemplary damages. What then does the pleader do? He stands up and employs every contrivance to prevent the jury from awarding these damages. He eloquently endeavours to persuade them that the act involved little guilt; casts undeserved imputations upon the immediate sufferer and upon her family; jests, and banters, and sneers about all the evidence of the case; imputes bad motives (without truth or with it) to the prosecutor; expatiates upon the little property (whether it be little or much) which the seducer possesses: by these and by such means he labours to prevent this injured father from obtaining any redress, to secure the criminal from all punishment, and to encourage in other men the crime itself. Compassion, justice, morality, the public good, everything is sacrificed—to what? To that which, upon such a subject, it were a shame to mention.

29. In the criminal courts the same conduct is practised, and with the same indefensibility. Can it be necessary, or ought it to be necessary, to insist upon the proposition—" If it be right that offenders should be punished, it is not right to make them pass with impunity." If a police officer has seized a thief and carried him to prison, every one knows that it would be vicious in me to effect his escape. Yet this is the everyday practice of the profession. It is their regular and constant endeavour to prevent justice from being administered to offenders. Is it a sufficient justification of preventing the execution of justice, of preventing that which every good citizen is desirous of promoting, to say that a man is an advocate by profession? Is the circumstance of belonging to the legal profession a good reason for disregarding those duties which are obligatory upon every other man? He who wards off punishment from swindlers and robbers, and sends them amongst the public upon the work of fraud and plunder again, surely deserves worse of his country than many a hungry man who filches a loaf or a trinket from a stall. As to employing legal artifices or the tactics of declamation in order to obtain the conviction of a prisoner whom there is reason to believe to be innocent, or as to endeavouring to inflict upon him a punishment greater than his deserts, the wickedness is so palpable that it is wonderful that even the power of custom protects it from the reprobation of the world.

30. In Scotland, where the criminal process is in some respects superior to ours, the proportion of those prisoners who escape punishment on account of "technical niceties" is very great. "Of the persons acquitted in our courts, *at least one half* escape from technical niceties, or rules of evidence which give advantage to the prisoner, with which in the other part of the island they are wholly unacquainted."[1] Is not this a great public evil? And if we charge that evil originally upon the law, is it warrantable, is it *moral*, in the advocate actively to increase and extend it?

31. The plea that it is of consequence that law should be *uniformly* administered, does not suffice to justify the pleader in criminal any more than in civil courts. "A thief was caught coming out of a house in Highbury Terrace, with a watch he had stolen therein upon him. He was found guilty by the jury upon the clearest evidence of the theft; but his counsel having discovered that he was charged in the indictment with having stolen a watch, the property of the owner of the house, whereas the watch really belonged to his daughter, the prisoner got clear off."[2] The pretext of the value of a uniform operation of the law will not avail here. Suppose the counsel, though he did discover the watch was the daughter's, had not insisted upon the inaccuracy, no evil would have ensued. The integrity of the law would not have been violated. The act of a counsel, therefore, in such a case is simply and only a defeat of public justice, an injury to the State, an encouragement to thieves; and surely there is no reason, either in morals or in common-sense, why any particular class of men should be privileged thus to injure the community.

[1] Remarks on the Administration of Criminal Justice in Scotland, &c.
[2] West. Rev., No. 8, Art. 4.

32. The wife of a respectable tradesman in the town in which I live was left a widow with eight or ten children. She employed a confidential person to assist in conducting the business. The business was flourishing; and yet at the end of every year she was surprised and afflicted to find that her profits were unaccountably small. At length this confidential person was suspected of peculation. Money was marked and placed as usual under his care. It was soon missed, and found upon his person: and when the police searched his house, they found in his possession, methodically stowed away, five or six thousand pounds, the accumulated plunder of years! This cruel and atrocious robber found no difficulty in obtaining advocates, who employed every artifice of defence, who had recourse to every technicality of law, to screen him from punishment, and to secure for him the quiet possession of his plunder. They found in the indictment some word, of which the ordinary and the legal acceptation were different, and the indictment was quashed! Happily, another was proof against the casuistry, and the criminal was found guilty.

33. Will it be said that pleaders are not supposed to know, till the verdict is pronounced, whether a prisoner is guilty or not? If this were true, it would not avail as a justification; but, in reality, it is only a subterfuge. In this very case, after the verdict had been pronounced, after the prisoner's guilt had been ascertained, a new trial was obtained; not on account of any doubt in the evidence *that* was unequivocal —but on account of some irregularity in passing sentence. And now the same conduct was repeated. *Knowing* that the prisoner was guilty, advocates still exerted their talents and eloquence to procure impunity for him, nay, to *reward* him at the expense of public duty and of private justice. They did not succeed: the plunderer was transported; but their want of success does not diminish the impropriety, the *immorality*, of their endeavours. If, by the trickery of law, this man had obtained an acquittal, what would have been the consequence? Not merely that he would have possessed undisturbed his plundered thousands; not merely that he might have laughed at the family whose money he was spending; but that a hundred or a thousand other shopmen, taking confidence from his success and his impunity, might enter upon a similar course of treachery and fraud. They might think that if the hour of detection should arrive, nothing was wanting but a sagacious advocate to protect them from punishment and to secure their spoil. Will any man then say, as an excuse for the legal practice, that it is "usual," "customary," the "business of the profession"? It is preposterous.[1]

34. It really is a dreadful consideration that a body of men, respectable in the various relationships of life, should make, in consequence of the vicious maxims of a profession, these deplorable sacrifices of rectitude. To a writer upon such a subject it is difficult to speak with that plainness which morality requires without seeming to speak illiberally of men. But it is not a question of liberality, but of morals. When a barrister arrives at an assize town on the circuit, and tacitly publishes that (abating a few, and only a few cases) he is willing to take the brief of any client; that he is ready to employ his abilities, his ingenuity, in proving that any given cause is good or that it is bad; and when, having gone before a jury, he urges the side on which he happens to have been employed, with all the earnestness of seeming integrity and truth, and bends all the faculties which God has given him in promotion of its success; when we see all this, and remember that it was the toss of a die whether he should have done exactly the contrary, I think that no expression characterises the procedure but that of *intellectual and moral prostitution*. In any other place than a court of justice, every one would say that it was prostitution: a court of justice cannot make it less.

35. Perhaps the reader has heard of the pleader who, by some accident, mistook the side on which he was to argue, and earnestly contended for the opponent's cause. His distressed client at length conveyed an intimation of his mistake, and he, with forensic dexterity, told the jury that hitherto he had only been anticipating the arguments of the opposing counsel, and that now he would proceed to show they were fallacious. If the reader should imagine there is *peculiar* indecency in this, his sentiment would be founded upon habit rather than upon reason. There is really very little difference between contending for both sides of the same cause, and contending for either side, as the earliest retainer may decide. I lately read the report of a trial in which retainers from both parties had been sent to a counsel, and when the cause was brought into court, it was still undecided for whom he should appear. The scale was turned by the judgment of another

[1] Some obstacles in the way of this mode of defeating the ends of justice have been happily interposed by the admirable exertions of the late Secretary of State for the Home Department. Still such cases are applicable as illustrations of what the duties of the profession are; and, unfortunately, opportunities in abundance remain for sacrificing the duties of the profession to its "business." Here, without any advertence to political opinion, it may be remarked that one such statesman as ROBERT PEEL is of more value to his country than a multitude of those who take office and leave it without any endeavour to ameliorate the national institutions.

counsel, and the pleader instantly appeared on behalf of the client to whom his brother had allotted him. From the mistake which is mentioned at the head of this paragraph, let clients take a beneficial hint. I suggest to them, if their opponent has engaged the ablest counsel, to engage him also themselves. The arrangement might easily be managed, and would be attended with manifest advantages; clients would be sure of arraying against each other equal abilities; justice would be promoted by preventing the triumph of the more skilful pleader over the less; and the minds of juries might more quietly weigh the conflicting arguments, when they were all proved and all refuted by one man.

36. Probably it will be asked, What is a legal man to do? How shall he discriminate his duties, or know, in the present state of legal institutions, what extent of advocation morality allows? These are fair questions, and he who asks them is entitled to an answer. I confess that an answer is difficult: and why is it difficult? Because the whole system is unsound. He who would rectify the ordinary legal practice is in the situation of a physician who can scarcely prescribe with effect for a particular symptom in a patient's case unless he will submit to an entirely new regimen and mode of life. The conscientious lawyer is surrounded with temptations and with difficulties resulting from the general system of the law; difficulties and temptations so great that it may almost appear to be the part of a wise man to fly rather than to encounter them. There is, however, nothing *necessarily* incidental to the legal profession which makes it incompatible with morality. He who has the firmness to maintain his allegiance to virtue may doubtless maintain it. Such a man would consider, that law being *in general* the practical standard of equity, the pleader may properly illustrate and enforce it. He may assiduously examine statutes and precedents, and honourably adduce them on behalf of his client. He may distinctly and luminously exhibit his client's claims. In examining his witnesses, he may educe the whole truth: in examining the other party's, he may endeavour to detect collusion, and to elicit facts which they may attempt to conceal; in a word, he may lay before the court a just and lucid view of the whole question. But he may not quote statutes and adjudged cases which he really does not think apply to the subject, or if they do appear to apply, he may not urge them as possessing greater force or applicability than he really thinks they possess. He may not endeavour to mislead the jury by appealing to their feelings, by employing ridicule, and especially by unfounded insinuations or misrepresentation of facts. He may not endeavour to make his own witnesses affirm more than he thinks they know, or induce them, by artful questions, to give a colouring to facts different from the colouring of truth. He may not endeavour to conceal or discredit the truth by attempting to confuse the other witnesses, or by entrapping them into contradictions. Such as these appear to be the rules which rectitude imposes in ordinary cases. There are some cases which a professional man ought not to undertake at all. This is indeed acknowledged by numbers of the profession. The obligation to reject them is of course founded upon their contrariety to virtue. How then shall a legal man know whether he ought to undertake a cause at all, but by some previous consideration of its merits? This must really be done if he would conform to the requisitions of morality. There is not an alternative: and "absurd" or "impracticable" as it may be pronounced to be, we do not shrink from explicitly maintaining the truth. Impracticable! it is at any rate not impracticable to withdraw from the profession or to decline to enter it. A man is not compelled to be a lawyer; and if there are so many difficulties in the practice of professional virtue, what is to be said? Are we to say, Virtue must be sacrificed to a profession— or, The profession must be sacrificed to Virtue? The pleader will perhaps say that he cannot tell what the merits of a case are until they are elicited in court: but this surely would not avail to justify a disregard of morality in any other case. To defend one's-self for an habitual disregard of the claims of rectitude, because we cannot tell, when we begin a course of action, whether it will involve a sacrifice of rectitude or not, is an ill defence indeed. At any rate, if he connects himself with a cause of questionable rectitude, he needs not and he ought not to advocate it, whilst ignorant of its merits, as if he *knew that it was good*. He ought not to advocate it further than he thinks it is good. But if any apologist for legal practice should say that a pleader knows nothing, or almost nothing, of a brief till he is instructed in court by a junior counsel, or that he has too many briefs to be capable of any previous inquiry about them, the answer is at hand—Refuse them. It would only add one example to the many that virtue cannot always be maintained without cost. It is necessary that a man should adhere to virtue; it is not necessary that he should be overwhelmed with briefs.

37. There is one consideration under which a pleader may assist a client even with a bad cause, which is, that it is proper to prevent the client from suffering too far. I would acknowledge generally the justice of the opposite party's claims, or, if it were

a criminal case, I would acquiesce in the evidence which carried conviction to my mind; but still in both something may remain for the pleader to do. The plaintiff may demand a thousand pounds when only eight hundred are due, and a pleader, though he could not with integrity resist the whole demand, could resist the excess of the demand above the just amount. Or if a prosecutor urges the guilt of a prisoner, and attempts to procure the infliction of an undue punishment, a pleader, though he knows the prisoner's guilt, may rightly prevent a sentence too severe. Murray the grammarian had been a barrister in America: "I do not recollect," says he, "that I ever encouraged a client to proceed at law when I thought his cause was unjust or indefensible; but in such cases I believe it was my invariable practice to discourage litigation and to recommend a peaceable settlement of differences. In the retrospect of this mode of practice I have always had great satisfaction, and I am persuaded that a different procedure would have been the source of many painful recollections."[1]

38. One serious consideration remains—the effect of the immorality of legal practice upon the personal character of the profession. "The lawyer who is frequently engaged in resisting what he strongly suspects to be just, in maintaining what he deems to be in strictness untenable, in advancing inconclusive reasoning, and seeking after flaws in the sound replies of his antagonists, can be preserved by nothing short of serious and invariable solicitude from the risk of having the distinction between moral right and wrong almost erased from his mind."[2] Is it indeed so? Tremendous is the risk. Is it indeed so? Then the custom which entails this fearful risk must infallibly be bad. Assuredly no *virtuous* conduct tends to erase the distinctions between right and wrong from the mind.

39. It is by no means certain that if a lawyer were to enter upon life with a steady determination to act upon the principles of strict integrity, his experience would occasion any exception to the general rule that the path of virtue is the path of interest. The client who was conscious of the goodness of his cause would *prefer* the advocate whose known maxims of conduct gave weight to every cause that he undertook. When such a man appeared before a jury, they would attend to his statements and his reasonings with that confidence which integrity only can inspire. They would not make, as they now do, perpetual deductions from his averred facts; they would not be upon the watch, as they now are, to protect themselves from illusion and casuistry and misrepresentation. Such a man, I say, would have a weight of advocacy which no other qualification can supply; and upright clients, knowing this, would find it their interest to employ him. The majority of clients, it is to be hoped, are upright. Professional success, therefore, would probably follow. And if a few such pleaders, nay if one such p'eader, was established, the consequence might be beneficial and extensive to a degree which it is not easy to compute. It might soon become *necessary* for other pleaders to act upon the same principles, because clients would not intrust their interests to any but those whose characters would give weight to their advocacy. Thus even the profligate part of the profession might be reformed by motives of interest, if not from choice. Want of credit might be want of practice; for it might eventually be almost equivalent to the loss of a cause to intrust it to a bad man. The effects would extend to the public. If none but upright men could be efficient advocates, and if upright men would not advocate vicious causes, vicious causes would not be prosecuted. But if such be the probable or even the possible results of sterling integrity, if it might be the means of reforming the practice of a large and influential profession, and of almost exterminating wicked litigation from a people, the obligation to practise this integrity is proportionately great: the amount of depending good involves a corresponding amount of responsibility upon him who contributes to perpetuate the evil.

CHAPTER VI.

Promises—Lies.

PROMISES.—Definition of a promise—Parole—Extorted promises—John Fletcher.
LIES.—Milton's definition—Lies in war: to robbers: to lunatics: to the sick—Hyperbole—Irony—Complimentary untruths—"Not at home"—Legal documents.

40. A promise is a contract, differing from such contracts as a lawyer would draw up, in the circumstances that ordinarily it is not written. The motive for signing a contract is to give assurance or security to the receiver that its terms will be fulfilled. The same motive is the inducement to a promise. The general obligation of promises needs little illustration, because it is not disputed. Men are not left without the consciousness that what they promise they ought to perform; and thus thousands, who can give no philosophical account of the matter, know, with certain assurance, that if they violate their engagements they violate the law of God.

[1] Memoirs of Lindley Murray, p. 43. [2] Gisborne.

41. Some philosophers deduce the obligation of promises from the *expediency* of fulfilling them. Doubtless fulfilment is expedient, but there is a shorter and a safer road to truth. To promise and not to perform is to deceive; and deceit is peculiarly and especially condemned by Christianity. A lie has been defined to be "a breach of promise;" and since the Scriptures condemn lying, they condemn breaches of promise.

42. Persons sometimes deceive others by making a promise in a sense different from that in which they know it will be understood. They hope this species of deceit is less criminal than breaking their word, and wish to gain the advantage of deceiving without its guilt. They dislike the shame but perform the act. A son has abandoned his father's house, and the father promises that if he returns he shall be received with open arms. The son returns, the father "opens his arms" to receive him, and then proceeds to treat him with rigour. This father falsifies his promise as truly as if he had specifically engaged to treat him with kindness. The sense in which a promise binds a person is *the sense in which he knows it is accepted by the other party.*

43. It is very possible to promise without speaking. Those who purchase at auctions frequently advance on the price by a sign or a nod. An auctioneer, in selling an estate, says, "Nine hundred and ninety pounds are offered." He who makes the customary sign to indicate an advance of ten pounds *promises* to give a thousand.—A person who brings up his children or others in the known and encouraged expectation that he will provide for them, promises to provide for them. A shipmaster promises to deliver a pipe of wine at the accustomed port, although he may have made no written and no verbal engagement respecting it.

44. Parole, such as is taken of military men, is of imperative obligation. The prisoner who escapes by breach of parole ought to be regarded as the perpetrator of an aggravated crime: aggravated, since his word was accepted, as he knows, because *peculiar* reliance was placed upon it, and since he adds to the ordinary guilt of breach of promise that of casting suspicion and entailing suffering upon other men. If breach of parole were general, parole would not be taken. It is one of the anomalies which are presented by the adherents to the law of honour, that they do not reject from their society the man who impeaches their respectability and his own, whilst they reject the man who really impeaches neither the one nor the other.—To say I am a man of honour, and therefore you may rely upon my word;

and then, as soon as it is accepted, to violate that word, is no ordinary deceit. An upright man never broke parole.

45. Promises are not binding if performance is unlawful. Sometimes men promise to commit a wicked act—even to assassination; but a man is not required to commit murder because he has promised to commit it. Thus in the Christian Scriptures, the son who had said, "I will not" work in the vineyard, and "afterwards repented and went," is spoken of with approbation: his promise was not binding, because fulfilment would have been wrong. Cranmer, whose religious firmness was overcome in the prospect of the stake, recanted; that is, he promised to abandon the Protestant faith. Neither was his promise binding. To have regarded it would have been a crime. The offence both of Cranmer and of the son in the parable consisted not in violating their promises, but in making them.

46. Some scrupulous persons appear to attach a needless obligation to expressions which they employ in the form of promises. You ask a lady if she will join a party in a walk; she declines, but presently recollecting some inducement to go, she is in doubt whether her refusal does not oblige her to stay at home. Such a person should recollect that her refusal does not partake of the character of a promise: there is no other party to it; she comes under no engagement to another. She only expresses her present intention, which intention she is at liberty to alter.

47. Many promises are conditional though the conditions are not expressed. A man says to some friends, I will dine with you at two o'clock; but as he is preparing to go, his child meets with an accident which requires his attention. This man does not violate a promise by absenting himself, because such promises are in fact *made and accepted* with the tacit understanding that they are subject to such conditions. No one would *expect*, when his friend engaged to dine with him, that he intended to bind himself to come, though he left a child unassisted with a fractured arm. Accordingly, when a person means to exclude such conditions he says, "I will certainly do so and so if I am living and able."

48. Yet, even to *seem* to disregard an engagement is an evil. To an ingenuous and Christian mind there is always something painful in not performing it. Of this evil the principal source is gratuitously brought upon us by the habit of using unconditional terms for conditional engagements. That which is only intention should be expressed

as intention. It is better, and more becoming the condition of humanity, to say, I intend to do a thing, than, I will do a thing. The recollection of our dependency upon uncontrollable circumstances should be present with us even in little affairs—"Go to now, ye that say, To-day or to-morrow we will go into such a city and buy and sell and get gain: whereas ye know not what shall be on the morrow.—Ye ought to say, If the Lord will, we shall live, and do this or that." Not indeed that the sacred name of God is to be introduced to express the conditions of our little engagements; but the *principle* should never be forgotten that we know not what shall be on the morrow.

49. Respecting the often-discussed question whether *extorted* promises are binding, there has been, I suspect, a general want of advertence to one important point. What is an *extorted* promise? If by an extorted promise is meant a promise that is made involuntarily, without the concurrence of the will; if it is the effect of any ungovernable impulse, and made without the consciousness of the party—then it is *not* a promise. This may happen. Fear or agitation may be so great that a person really does not know what he says or does; and in such a case a man's promises do not bind him any more than the promises of a man in a fit of insanity. But if by an "extorted" promise it is only meant that very powerful *inducements* were held out to making it, inducements, however, which did not take away the power of choice —then these promises are in strictness voluntary, and, like all other voluntary engagements, they ought to be fulfilled. But perhaps fulfilment is itself unlawful. Then you may not fulfil it. The offence consists in making such engagements. It will be said, A robber threatened to take my life unless I would promise to reveal the place where my neighbour's money was deposited. Ought I not to make the promise in order to save my life? No. Here, in reality, is the origin of the difficulties and the doubts. To rob your neighbour is criminal; to enable another man to rob him is criminal too. Instead, therefore, of discussing the obligation of "extorted" promises, we should consider whether such promises may lawfully be made. The prospect of saving life is one of the utmost inducements to make them, and yet, amongst those things which we are to hold subservient to our Christian fidelity, is our "own life also." If, however, giving way to the weakness of nature, a person makes the promise, he should regulate his performance by the ordinary principles. Fulfil the promise unless fulfilment be wrong: and if, in estimating the propriety of fulfilling it, any difficulty arises, it must be charged not to the imperfection of moral principles, but to the entanglement in which we involve ourselves by having *begun* to deviate from rectitude. If we had not unlawfully made the promise, we should have had no difficulty in ascertaining our subsequent duty. The traveller who does not desert the proper road easily finds his way; he who once loses sight of it has many difficulties in returning.

50. The history of that good man John Fletcher (La Flechère) affords an example to our purpose. Fletcher had a brother, De Gons, and a nephew, a profligate youth. This youth came one day to his uncle De Gons, and holding up a pistol, declared he would instantly shoot him if he did not give him an order for five hundred crowns. De Gons in terror gave it; and the nephew then, under the same threat, required him solemnly to promise that he would not prosecute him; and De Gons made the promise accordingly. That is what is called an *extorted* promise, and an *extorted* gift. How, in similar circumstances, did Fletcher act? This youth afterwards went to him, told him of the "present" which De Gons had made, and showed him the order. Fletcher suspected some fraud, and thinking it right to prevent its success, he put the order in his pocket. It was at the risk of his life. The young man instantly presented his pistol, declaring that he would fire if he did not deliver it up. Fletcher did not submit to the extortion: he told him that his life was secure under the protection of God, refused to deliver up the order, and severely remonstrated with his nephew on his profligacy. The young man was restrained and softened; and before he left his uncle, gave him many assurances that he would amend his life.—De Gons might have been perplexed with doubts as to the obligation of his "extorted" promise: Fletcher could have no doubts to solve.

Lies.

51. The guilt of lying, like that of many other offences, has been needlessly founded upon its ill effects. These effects constitute a good reason for adhering to truth, but they are not the greatest nor the best. "Putting away lying, speak every man truth with his neighbour."[1] "Ye shall not steal, neither deal falsely, neither lie one to another."[2] "The law is made for unholy and profane, for murderers—for liars."[3] It may afford the reader some instruction to observe with what crimes lying is associated in Scripture —with perjury, and murder, and parricide. Not that it is necessary to suppose that the measure of guilt of these crimes is equal, but that the guilt of all is great. With respect to lying, there is no trace in these

[1] Eph iv. 25. [2] Lev. xix 11. [3] 1 Tim. i 9, 10.

passages that its guilt is *conditional upon its effects*, or that it is not always, and for whatever purpose, prohibited by the Divine Will.

52. A lie is, uttering what is not true when the speaker professes to utter truth, or when he knows it is expected by the hearer. I do not perceive that any looser definition is allowable, because every looser definition would permit deceit.

53. Milton's definition, considering the general tenor of his character, was very lax. He says, "Falsehood is incurred when any one, *from a dishonest motive*, either perverts the truth or utters what is false to one *to whom it is his duty to speak the truth.*"[1] To whom is it *not* our duty to speak the truth? What constitutes duty but the will of God? and where is it found that it is His will that we should sometimes lie?—But another condition is proposed: in order to constitute a lie, the *motive* to it must be *dishonest*. Is not all deceit dishonesty; and can any one utter a lie without deceit? A man who travels in the Arctic regions comes home and writes a narrative, professedly faithful, of his adventures, and decorates it with marvellous incidents which never happened, and stories of wonders which he never saw. You tell this man he has been passing lies upon the public. Oh no, he says, I had not "a dishonest motive." I only meant to make readers wonder.—Milton's mode of substantiating his doctrine is worthy of remark. He makes many references for authority to the Hebrew Scriptures, but *not one* to the Christian. The reason is plain, though perhaps he was not aware of it, that the purer moral system which the Christian Lawgiver introduced did not countenance the doctrine. Another argument is so feeble that it may well be concluded no valid argument can be found. If it had been discoverable, would not Milton have found it? He says, "It is universally admitted that feints and stratagems in war, when unaccompanied by perjury or breach of faith, do not fall under the description of falsehood.—It is scarcely possible to execute any of the artifices of war without openly uttering the greatest untruths with the indisputable intention of deceiving."[2] And so, because the "greatest untruths" are uttered in conducting one of the most flagitious departments of the most unchristian system in the world, we are told, in a system of Christian Doctrine, that untruths are lawful!

54. Paley's philosophy is yet more lax: he says that we may tell a falsehood to a person who "has no right to know the truth."[3]

[1] Christian Doctrine, p. 648.   [2] Ibid. 659.
[3] Mor. and Pol. Phil., b. 3, p. 1, c. 15.

What constitutes a right to know the truth, it were not easy to determine. But if a man has no right to know the truth—withhold it, but do not utter a lie. A man has no right to know how much property I possess. If, however, he impertinently chooses to ask, what am I to do? *Refuse to tell him*, says Christian morality. What am I to do? *Tell him it is ten times as great as it is*, says the morality of Paley.

55. To say that when a man is tempted to employ a falsehood, he is to consider the degree of "inconveniency which results from the want of confidence in such cases,"[1] and to employ the falsehood or not as this degree shall prescribe, is surely to trifle with morality. What is the hope that a man will decide aright, who sets about such a calculation at such a time? Another kind of falsehood which it is said is lawful, is that "to a robber, to conceal your property." A man gets into my house, and desires to know where he shall find my plate. I tell him it is in a chest in such a room, knowing that it is in a closet in another. By such a falsehood I might save my property or possibly my life; but if the prospect of doing this be a sufficient reason for violating the Moral Law, there is no action which we may not lawfully commit. May a person, in order to save his property or life, commit parricide? Every reader says, No. But where is the ground of the distinction? If you may *lie* for the sake of such advantages, why may you not *kill?* What makes murder unlawful but that which makes lying unlawful too? No man surely will say that we must make distinctions in the atrocity of such actions, and that, though it is not lawful for the sake of advantage to commit an act of a certain intensity of guilt, yet it is lawful to commit one of a certain gradation less. Such doctrine would be purely gratuitous and unfounded: it would be equivalent to saying that we are at liberty to disobey the Divine Laws when we think fit. The case is very simple: If I may tell a falsehood to a robber in order to save my property, I may commit parricide for the same purpose; for lying and parricide are placed together and jointly condemned[2] in the revelation from God.

56. Then we are told that we may "tell a falsehood to a madman for his own advantage," and this because it is beneficial. Dr. Carter may furnish an answer: he speaks of the Female Lunatic Asylum, Salpetrière, in Paris, and says, "The great object to which the views of the officers of La Salpetrière are directed, is to gain the confidence of the patients; and this object is generally attained by gentleness, by appearing to take an in-

[1] Mor. and Pol. Phil., b. 3, p. 1, c. 15.   [2] 1 Tim. i. 9, 10.

terest in their affairs, by a decision of character equally remote from the extremes of indulgence and severity, and by *the most scrupulous observance of good faith.* Upon this latter, *particular stress* seems to be laid by M. Pinel, who remarks 'that insane persons, like children, lose all confidence and all respect if you fail in your word towards them; and they immediately set their ingenuity to work to deceive and circumvent you.'"[1] What then becomes of the doctrine of "telling falsehoods to madmen *for their own advantage?*" It is pleasant thus to find the evidence of experience enforcing the dictates of principle, and that what morality declares to be right, facts declare to be expedient.

57. Persons frequently employ falsehoods to a sick man who cannot recover, lest it should discompose his mind. This is called kindness, although an earnest preparation for death may be at stake upon their speaking the truth. There is a peculiar inconsistency sometimes exhibited on such occasions: the persons who will not discompose a sick man for the sake of his interests in futurity, will discompose him without scruple if he has not made his will. Is a bequest of more consequence to the survivor than a hope full of immortality to the dying man?

58. It is curious to remark how zealously persons reprobate "pious frauds;" that is, lies for the religious benefit of the deceived party. Surely if any reason for employing falsehood be a good one, it is the prospect of effecting religious benefit. How is it then that we so freely condemn these falsehoods, whilst we contend for others which are used for less important purposes?

59. Still not every expression that is at variance with facts is a lie, because there are some expressions in which the speaker does not pretend, and the hearer does not expect, literal truth. Of this class are hyperboles and jests, fables and tales of professed fiction: of this class, too, are parables, such as are employed in the New Testament. In such cases affirmative language is used in the same terms as if the allegations were true, yet as it is known that it does not profess to narrate facts, no lie is uttered. It is the same with some kinds of irony: "Cry aloud," said Elijah to the priests of the idol, "*for he is a god*, peradventure he sleepeth." And yet, because a given untruth is not a lie, it does not therefore follow that it is innocent: for it is very possible to employ such expressions without any sufficient justification. A man who thinks he can best inculcate virtue through a fable, may write one: he who desires to discountenance an absurdity, may employ irony. Yet every one should use as little of such language as he can, because it is frequently dangerous language. The man who familiarises himself to a departure from literal truth is in danger of departing from it without reason and without excuse. Some of these departures are *like* lies; so much like them that both speaker and hearer may reasonably question whether they are lies or not. The lapse from untruths which can deceive no one, to those which are intended to deceive, proceeds by almost imperceptible gradations on the scale of evil: and it is not the part of wisdom to approach the verge of guilt. Nor is it to be forgotten that language, professedly fictitious, is not always understood to be such by those who hear it. This applies especially to the case of children—that is, of mankind during that period of life in which they are acquiring some of their first notions of morality. The boy who hears his father using hyperboles and irony with a grave countenance, probably thinks he has his father's example for telling *lies* amongst his schoolfellows.

60. Amongst the indefensible untruths which often are not lies, are those which factitious politeness enjoins. Such are compliments and complimentary subscriptions, and many other untruths of expression and of action which pass currently in the world. These are, no doubt, often estimated at their value: the receiver knows that they are base coin though they shine like the good. Now, although it is not to be pretended that such expressions, so estimated, are lies, yet I will venture to affirm that the reader cannot set up for them any tolerable defence; and if he cannot show that they are right, he may be quite sure that they are wrong. A defence has, however, been attempted: "How much is *happiness increased* by the general adoption of a system of concerted and limited deceit! He from whose doctrine it flows that we are to be in no case hypocrites, would, in mere manners, reduce us to a degree of barbarism beyond that of the rudest savage." We do not enter here into such questions as whether a man may *smile* when his friend calls upon him, though he would rather just then that he had stayed away. Whatever the reader may think of these questions, the "system of deceit" which passes in the world cannot be justified by the decision. There is no fear that "a degree of barbarism beyond that of the rudest savage" would ensue, if this system were amended. The first teachers of Christianity, who will not be charged with being in "any case hypocrites," both recommended and practised gentleness and courtesy.[1] And as to the increase of happiness which is assumed to result from this system of deceit, the fact is of a very questionable kind. No

[1] Account of the Principal Hospitals in France, &c.

[1] 1 Peter ii. 1; Tit. iii. 2; 1 Peter iii. 8.

society, I believe, sufficiently discourages it; but that society which discourages it probably as much as any other, certainly enjoys its full average of happiness. But the apology proceeds, and more seriously errs: "The employment of falsehood for the production of good cannot be more unworthy of the Divine Being than the acknowledged employment of rapine and murder for the same purpose."[1] Is it then not perceived that to *employ* the wickedness of man is a very different thing from *holding its agents innocent?* Some of those whose wickedness has been thus employed, have been punished for that wickedness. Even to show that the Deity has employed falsehood for the production of good, would in no degree establish the doctrine that falsehood is right.

61. The childish and senseless practice of requiring servants to "deny" their masters has had many apologists—I suppose because many perceive that it is wrong. It is not always true that such a servant does not in strictness *lie;* for, how well soever the folly may be understood by the gay world, some who knock at their doors have no other idea than that they may depend on the servant's word. Of this the servant is sometimes conscious, and to these persons, therefore, he who denies his master lies. An uninitiated servant suffers a shock to his moral principles when he is first required to tell these falsehoods. It diminishes his previous abhorrence of lying, and otherwise deteriorates his moral character. Even if no such ill consequences resulted from this foolish custom, there is objection to it which is short, but sufficient—*nothing* can be said in its defence.

62. Amongst the prodigious multiplicity of falsehoods which are practised in legal processes, the system of pleading not guilty is one that appears perfectly useless. By the rule, that all who refuse to plead were presumed to be guilty, prisoners were in some sort compelled to utter this falsehood before they could have the privilege of a trial. The law is lately relaxed, so that a prisoner, if he chooses, may refuse to plead at all. Still, only a part of the evil is removed, for even now to keep silent may be construed into a tacit acknowledgment of guilt, so that the temptation to falsehood is still exhibited. There is no other use in the custom of pleading guilty or not guilty, but that, if a man desires to acknowledge his guilt, he may have the opportunity; and this he may have without any custom of the sort.—It cannot be doubted that the multitude of falsehoods which obtain in legal documents during the progress of a suit at law have a powerful tendency to propagate habits of mendacity.

A man sells goods to the value of *twenty* pounds to another, and is obliged to enforce payment by law. The lawyer draws up for the creditor a Declaration in Assumpsit, stating that the debtor owes him *forty* pounds for goods sold, *forty* pounds for work done, *forty* pounds for money lent, *forty* pounds for money expended on his account, *forty* pounds for money received by the debtor for the creditor, and so on—and that two or three hundred pounds being thus due to the creditor, he has a just demand of *twenty* pounds upon the debtor! These falsehoods are not one half of what an everyday Declaration in Assumpsit contains. If a person refuses to give up a hundred head of cattle which a farmer has placed in his custody, the farmer declares that he "casually lost" them, and that the other party "casually found" them: and then, instead of saying he casually lost a hundred head of cattle, he declares that it was a thousand bulls, a thousand cows, a thousand oxen, and a thousand heifers![1] I do not think that the habits of mendacity which such falsehoods are likely to encourage are the *worst* consequences of this unhappy system, but they are seriously bad. No man who considers the influence of habit upon the mind, can doubt that an ingenuous abhorrence of lying is likely to be diminished by familiarity with these extravagant falsehoods.

CHAPTER VII.

Oaths.

Their Moral Character—Their Efficacy as Securities of Veracity—Their Effects.

A curse—Immorality of oaths—Oaths of the ancient Jews—Milton—Paley—The High Priest's adjuration—Early Christians—Inefficacy of oaths—Motives to veracity—Religious sanctions: Public opinion: Legal penalties—Oaths in evidence: Parliamentary evidence: Courts-martial—The United States—Effects of oaths: Falsehood—General obligations.

63. "An oath is that whereby we call God to witness the truth of what we say, with a curse upon ourselves, either implied or expressed, should it prove false."[2]

A Curse.

64. Now supposing the Christian Scriptures to contain no information respecting the moral character of oaths, how far is it reasonable, or prudent, or reverent for a man to stake his salvation upon the truth of what he says? To bring forward so tremendous an event as "everlasting destruction from the presence of the Lord," in attestation of the offence perhaps of a

---

[1] Edin. Rev., vol. 1, Art. Belsham's Philosophy of the Mind.

[1] See the Form, 2 Chitty on Pleading, p. 370.
[2] Milton, Christian Doctrine, p. 579.

poacher or of the claim to a field, is surely to make unwarrantably light of most awful things. This consideration applies, even if a man is sure that he speaks the truth: but who is, beforehand, sure of this? Oaths in evidence, for example, are taken before the testimony is given. A person swears that he will speak the truth. Who, I ask, is sure that he will do this? Who is sure that the embarrassment of a public examination, that the ensnaring questions of counsel, that the secret influence of inclination or interest, will not occasion him to utter one inaccurate expression? Who, at any rate, is so sure of this that it is rational, or justifiable, specifically to stake his salvation upon his accuracy? Thousands of honest men have been mistaken; their allegations have been sincere, but untrue. And if this should be thought not a legitimate objection, let it be remembered, that few men's minds are so sternly upright that they can answer a variety of questions upon subjects on which their feelings, and wishes, and interest are involved, without some little deduction from the truth, in speaking of matters that are against their cause, or some little over-colouring of facts in their own favour. It is a circumstance of constant occurrence, that even a well-intentioned witness adds to or deducts a little from the truth. Who then, amidst such temptation, would make, who ought to make, his hope of heaven dependent on his strict adherence to accurate veracity? And if such considerations indicate the impropriety of swearing upon subjects which affect the lives, and liberties, and property of others, how shall we estimate the impropriety of using these dreadful imprecations to attest the delivery of a summons for a debt of half-a-crown!

65. These are moral objections to the use of oaths independently of any reference to the direct Moral Law. Another objection of the same kind is this: To take an oath is to assume that the Deity will become a party in the case—that we can call upon Him, when we please, to follow up by the exercise of His almighty power, the contracts (often the very insignificant contracts) which men make with men. Is it not irreverent, and for that reason immoral, to call upon Him to exercise this power in reference to subjects which are so insignificant that other men will scarcely listen with patience to their details? The objection goes even further. A robber exacts an oath of the man whom he has plundered, that he will not attempt to pursue or to prosecute him. Pursuit and prosecution are duties; so then the oath assumes that the Deity will punish the swearer in futurity if he fulfils a duty. Confederates in a dangerous and wicked enterprise bind one another to secrecy and to mutual assistance by oaths—assuming that God will become a party to their wickedness, and if they do not perpetrate it, will punish them for their virtue.

66. Upon every subject of questionable rectitude that is sanctioned by habit and the usages of society, a person should place himself in the independent situation of an inquirer. He should not seek for arguments to defend an existing practice, but should simply inquire what our practice ought to be. One of the most powerful causes of the slow amendment of public institutions consists in this circumstance, that most men endeavour rather to justify what exists than to consider whether it ought to exist or not. This cause operates upon the question of oaths. We therefore invite the reader, in considering the citation which follows, to suppose himself to be one of the listeners at the Mount—to know nothing of the customs of the present day, and to have no *desire* to justify them.

67. "Ye have heard that it hath been said by them of old time, Thou shalt not forswear thyself, but shalt perform unto the Lord thine oaths. But I say unto you, Swear not at all: neither by heaven, for it is God's throne, nor by the earth, for it is His footstool, neither by Jerusalem, for it is the city of the Great King. Neither shalt thou swear by thy head, because thou canst not make one hair white or black. But let your communication be yea yea, nay nay; for whatsoever is more than these, cometh of evil." [1]

68. If a person should take a New Testament, and read these words to ten intelligent Asiatics who had never heard of them before, does any man believe that a single individual of them would think that the words did not prohibit *all* oaths? I lay stress upon this consideration: if ten unbiassed persons would, at the first hearing, say the prohibition was universal, we have no contemptible argument that that is the real meaning of the words. For to whom were the words addressed? Not to schoolmen, of whom it was known that they would make nice distinctions and curious investigations; not to men of learning, who were in the habit of cautiously weighing the import of words—but to a multitude—a mixed and unschooled multitude. It was to such persons that the prohibition was addressed: it was to such apprehensions that its form was adapted.

69. "It hath been said of old time, Thou shalt *not forswear* thyself." Why refer to what was said of old time? For this reason

[1] Matt. v. 33-37.

assuredly; to point out that the present requisitions were *different* from the former; that what was prohibited now was *different* from what was prohibited before. And what was prohibited before? Swearing *falsely*— swearing and *not performing*. What then could be prohibited now? Swearing *truly* swearing, even, and *performing:* that is, swearing at all; for it is manifest that if truth may not be attested by an oath, no oath may be taken. Of old time it was said, "Ye shall not swear by My name *falsely*."[1] "If a man swear an oath to bind his soul with a bond, he shall not *break* his word."[2] There could be no intelligible purpose in contradistinguishing the new precept from these, but to point out a characteristic difference; and there is no intelligible characteristic difference but that which denounces all oaths. Such were the views of the early Christians. "The old law," says one of them, "is satisfied with the honest *keeping* of the oath, but Christ cuts off the *opportunity* of perjury."[3] In acknowledging that this prefatory reference to the former law is in my view absolutely conclusive of our Christian duty, I would remark as an extraordinary circumstance, that Dr. Paley, in citing the passage, omits this introduction and takes no notice of it in his argument.

"I say unto you, Swear *not at all*." The words are absolute and exclusive.

70. "Neither by heaven, nor by the earth, nor by Jerusalem, nor by thy own head." Respecting this enumeration it is said that it prohibits swearing by certain objects, but not by all objects. To which a sufficient answer is found in the parallel passage in James: "Swear not," he says; "neither by heaven, neither by the earth, neither by *any other* oath."[4] This mode of prohibition, by which an absolute and universal rule is first proposed and then followed by certain *examples* of the prohibited things, is elsewhere employed in Scripture. "Thou shalt have no other gods before Me. Thou shalt not make unto thee any graven image, or any likeness of anything that is in heaven above, or that is in the earth beneath, or that is in the water under the earth."[5] No man supposes that this after-enumeration was designed to restrict the obligation of the law—Thou shalt have no other gods before Me. Yet it were as reasonable to say that it was lawful to make idols in the form of imaginary monsters because they were not mentioned in the enumeration, as that it is lawful to swear any given kind of oath because it is not mentioned in the enumeration. Upon this part of the prohibition

it is curious that two contradictory opinions are advanced by the defenders of oaths. The first class of reasoners says, The prohibition allows us to swear by the Deity, but disallows swearing by inferior things. The second class says, The prohibition allows swearing by inferior things, but disallows swearing by the Deity. Of the first class is Milton. The injunction, he says, "does not prohibit us from swearing by the name of God —We are only commanded not to swear by heaven, &c."[1] But here again the Scripture itself furnishes a conclusive answer. It asserts that to swear by heaven *is to swear by the Deity:* "He that shall swear by heaven, sweareth by the throne of God, and *by Him* that sitteth thereon."[2] To prohibit swearing by heaven is therefore to prohibit swearing by God. Amongst the second class is Dr. Paley. He says, "On account of the relation which these things [the heavens, the earth, &c.] bore to the Supreme Being, to swear by any of them was in effect and substance to swear by *Him;* for which reason our Saviour says, Swear not at all; that is, neither directly by God nor indirectly by anything related to Him."[3] But if we are thus prohibited from swearing by anything related to Him, how happens it that Paley proceeds to justify judicial oaths? Does not the judicial deponent swear by something related to God? Does he not swear by something much more nearly related than the earth or our own heads? Is not our hope of salvation more nearly related than a member of our bodies?—But after he has thus taken pains to show that swearing by the Almighty was especially forbidden, he enforces his general argument by saying that Christ *did* swear by the Almighty! He says that the high priest examined our Saviour upon oath, "by the living God;" which oath He took. This is wonderful; and the more wonderful because, of these two arguments, the one immediately follows the other. It is contended, within half a dozen lines, first that Christ forbade swearing by God, and next that He violated His own command.

71. "But let your communication be yea yea, nay nay." This is remarkable: it is positive superadded to negative commands. We are told not only what we ought not, but what we ought to do. It has indeed been said that the expression "your communication," fixes the meaning to apply to the ordinary intercourse of life. But to this there is a fatal objection: the whole prohibition *sets out* with a reference not to conversational language, but to solemn declarations on solemn occasions. Oaths,

---

[1] Lev. xix. 12. [2] Numb. xxx. 2. [3] Basil.
[4] James v. 12. [5] Exod. xx. 3. See also xx. 4.

[1] Christ. Doc., p. 58?. [2] Matt. xxiii. 22.
[3] Mor. and Pol. Phil., b. 3, p. 1, c. 16.

Oaths " to the Lord," are placed at the head of the passage; and it is too manifest to be insisted upon that solemn declarations, and not every-day talk, were the subject of the prohibition.

72. "Whatsoever is more than these cometh of evil." This is indeed most accurately true. Evil is the foundation of oaths: it is because men are bad that it is supposed oaths are needed: take away the wickedness of mankind, and we shall still have occasion for No and Yes, but we shall need nothing "more than these." And this consideration furnishes a distinct motive to a good man to decline to swear. To take an oath is tacitly to acknowledge that this "evil" exists in his own mind that with him Christianity has not effected its destined objects.

73. From this investigation of the passage, it appears manifest that all swearing upon all occasions is prohibited. Yet the ordinary opinion, or rather perhaps the ordinary defence, is that the passage has no reference to judicial oaths. "We explain our Saviour's words to relate not to judicial oaths, but to the practice of vain, wanton, and unauthorised swearing in common discourse." To this we have just seen that there is one conclusive answer: our Saviour distinctly and specifically mentions, as the subject of His instructions, *solemn oaths*. But there is another conclusive answer, even upon our opponents' own showing. They say, first, that Christ described particular forms of oaths which might be employed; and next, that His precepts referred to wanton swearing; that is to say, that Christ described what particular forms of wanton swearing He allowed and what He disallowed! You cannot avoid this monstrous conclusion. If Christ spoke only of vain and wanton swearing, and if He described the modes that were lawful, He sanctioned wanton swearing, provided we swear in the prescribed form.

74. With such distinctness of evidence as to the universality of the prohibition of oaths by Jesus Christ, it is not in strictness necessary to refer to those passages in the Christian Scriptures which some persons adduce in favour of their employment. If Christ have prohibited them, nothing else can prove them to be right. Our reference to these passages will accordingly be short.

75. "I adjure thee by the living God that thou tell us whether Thou be the Christ, the Son of God." To those who allege that Christ, in answering to this "Thou hast said," took an oath, a sufficient answer has already been intimated. If Christ then took an oath, He swore by the Deity, and this is precisely the very kind of oath which it is acknowledged He Himself forbade. But what imaginable reason could there be for examining Him upon oath? Who ever heard of calling upon a prisoner to *swear* that he was guilty? Nothing was wanted but a simple declaration that He was the Son of God. With this view the proceeding was extremely natural. Finding that to the less urgent solicitation He made no reply, the high priest proceeded to the more urgent. Schleusner expressly remarks upon the passage that the words, " I adjure," do not here mean, " I make to swear or put upon oath," but, " I solemnly and in the name of God exhort and enjoin." This is evidently the natural and the only natural meaning; just as it was the natural meaning when the evil spirit said, " I adjure thee by the living God that thou torment me not." The evil spirit surely did not administer an oath.

76. "God is my witness that without ceasing I make mention of you always in my prayers."[1] That the Almighty was witness to the subject of his prayers is most true; but to state this truth is not to swear. Neither this language nor that which is indicated below contains the characteristics of an oath according to the definitions even of those who urge the expressions. None of them contain, according to Milton's definition, "a curse upon ourselves;" nor, according to Paley's, "an invocation of God's vengeance." Similar language, but in a more emphatic form, is employed in writing to the Corinthian converts. It appears from 2 Cor. ii. that Paul had resolved not again to go to Corinth in heaviness, lest he should make them sorry. And to assure them *why* he had made this resolution he says, " I call God for a record upon my soul that *to spare you* I came not as yet unto Corinth." In order to show this to be an oath, it will be necessary to show that the Apostle imprecated the vengeance of God if he did not speak the truth. Who can show this? The expression appears to me to be only an emphatical mode of saying, God is witness; or, as the expression is sometimes employed in the present day, God knows that such was my endeavour or desire.

77. The next and the last argument is of a very exceptionable class: it is founded upon silence. "For men verily swear by the greater, and an oath for confirmation is to them an end of all strife."[2] Respecting this it is said that it "speaks of the

[1] Rom. i. 9. See also 1 Thess. ii. 5, and Gal. i. 20.
[2] Heb. vi. 16.

custom of swearing judicially without any mark of censure or disapprobation." Will it then be contended that whatever an Apostle mentions without reprobating he approves? The same Apostle speaks just in the same manner of the pagan games; of running a race for prizes and of " striving for the mastery." Yet who would admit the argument, that *because* Paul did not then censure the games, he thought them right? The existing customs both of swearing and of the games are adduced merely by way of *illustration* of the writer's subject.

78. Respecting the lawfulness of oaths, then, as determined by the Christian Scriptures, how does the balance of evidence stand? On the one side, we have plain emphatical prohibitions—prohibitions of which the distinctness is more fully proved the more they are investigated; on the other we have—counter precepts? No; it is not even pretended: but we have examples of the use of language, of which it is saying much to say that it is *doubtful* whether they are oaths or not. How, then, would the man of reason and of philosophy decide? "Many of the Christian fathers," says Grotius, " condemned *all* oaths without exception."[1] Grotius was himself an advocate of oaths. " I say nothing of perjury," says Tertullian, "since *swearing itself* is unlawful to Christians."[2] Chrysostom says, " Do not say to me, I swear for a just purpose ; it is no longer lawful for thee to swear either justly or unjustly."[3] " He who," says Gregory of Nysse, " has precluded murder by taking away anger, and who has driven away the pollution of adultery by subduing desire, has expelled from our life the curse of perjury by forbidding us to swear ; for where there is no oath, there can be no infringement of it."[4] Such is the conviction which the language of Christ conveyed to the early converts to His pure religion ; and such is the conviction which I think it would convey to us if custom had not familiarised us with the evil, and if we did not read the New Testament rather to find justifications of our practice, than to discover the truth and to apply it to our conduct.

Efficacy of Oaths as Securities for Veracity.

79. Men naturally speak the truth unless they have some inducements to falsehood. When they have such inducements, what is it that overcomes them and still prompts them to speak the truth?
Considerations of duty, founded upon religion :

[1] Rights of War and Peace.   [2] De Idol. cap. 11.
[3] In Gen. ii. Hom. xv.   [4] In Cant. Hom. 13.

The apprehension of the ill opinion of other men :
The fear of legal penalties.

80. 1. It is obvious that the intervention of an oath is designed to strengthen only the first of these motives—that is, the religious sanction. I say to *strengthen* the religious sanction. No one supposes it creates that sanction ; because people know that the sanction is felt to apply to falsehood as well as to perjury. The advantage of an oath. then, if advantage there be, is in the *increased power* which it gives to sentiments of duty founded upon religion. Now it will be our endeavour to show that this increased power is small ; that in fact the oath, as such, adds very little to the motives to veracity. What class of men will the reader select in order to illustrate its greatest power?

81. Good men? They will speak the truth, whether without an oath or with it. They know that God has appended to falsehood as to perjury the threat of His displeasure and of punishment in futurity. Upon them religion possesses its rightful influence without the intervention of an oath.

82. Bad men? Men who care nothing for religion ? They will care nothing for it though they take an oath.

83. Men of ambiguous character? Men on whom the sanctions of religion are sometimes operative and sometimes not? Perhaps it will be said that to these the solemnity of an oath is necessary to rouse their latent apprehensions, and to bind them to veracity. But these persons do not go before a legal officer or into a court of justice as they go into a parlour or meet an acquaintance in the street. Recollection of mind is forced upon them by the circumstances of their situation. The court, and the forms of law, and the audience, and the after publicity of the evidence, fix the attention even of the careless. The man of only occasional seriousness is serious then ; and if in their hours of seriousness such persons regard the sanctions of religion, they will regard them in a court of justice though without an oath.

84. Yet it may be supposed by the reader that the solemnity of a specific imprecation of the Divine vengeance would, nevertheless, frequently add stronger motives to adhere to truth. But what is the evidence of experience? After testimony has been given on affirmation, the parties are sometimes examined on the same subject upon oath. Now Pothier says, "In forty years of practice I have only met *two* instances where the parties, in the case of an oath offered after

evidence, have been prevented by a sense of religion from persisting in their testimonies." Two instances in forty years; and even with respect to these it is to be remembered, that one great reason why simple affirmations do not bind men is that their obligation is artificially diminished (as we shall presently see) by the employment of oaths. To the evidence resulting from these truths I know of but one limitary consideration; and to this the reader must attach such weight as he thinks it deserves—that a man on whom an oath had been originally imposed might then have been bound to veracity, who would not incur the shame of having lied by refusing afterwards to confirm his falsehoods with an oath.

85. II. The next inducement to adhere to truth is the apprehension of the ill opinion of others. And this inducement, either in its direct or indirect operation, will be found to be incomparably more powerful than that religious inducement which is applied by an oath as such. Not so much because religious sanctions are less operative than public opinion, as because public opinion applies or detaches the religious sanction. Upon this subject a serious mistake has been made; for it has been contended that the influence of religious motives is comparatively nothing—that unless men are impelled to speak the truth by fear of disgrace or of legal penalties, they care very little for the sanctions of religion. But the truth is, that the sanctions of religion are, in a great degree, either brought into operation, or prevented from operating, by these secondary motives. Religious sanctions necessarily follow the judgments of the mind: if a man by any means becomes convinced that a given action is wrong, the religious obligation to refrain from it follows. Now, the judgments of men respecting right and wrong are very powerfully affected by public opinion. It commonly happens that that which a man has been habitually taught to think wrong, he does think wrong. Men are thus taught by public opinion. So that if the public attach disgrace to any species of mendacity or perjury, the religious sanction will commonly apply to that species. If there are instances of mendacity or perjury to which public disapprobation does not attach, to those instances the religious sanction will commonly not apply, or apply but weakly. The power of public opinion in binding to veracity is therefore twofold. It has its direct influence arising from the fear which all men feel of the disapprobation of others, and the indirect influence arising from the fact that public opinion applies the sanctions of religion.

86. III. Of the influence of legal penalties in binding to veracity, little needs to be said. It is obvious that if they induce men to refrain from theft and violence, they will induce men to refrain from perjury. But it may be remarked, that the legal penalty tends to give vigour and efficiency to public opinion. He whom the law punishes as a criminal, is generally regarded as a criminal by the world.

87. Now that which we affirm is this—that unless public opinion or legal penalties enforce veracity, very little will be added by an oath to the motives to veracity more than would subsist in the case of simple affirmation. The observance of the Oxford statutes[1] is promised by the members on oath, yet no one observes them. They swear to observe them, they imprecate the Divine vengeance if they do not observe them, and yet they disregard them every day. The oath then is of no avail. An oath, as such, does not here bind men's consciences. And why? Because those sanctions by which men's consciences are bound are not applied. The law applies none: public opinion applies none: and therefore the religious sanction is weak; too weak with most men to avail. Not that no motives founded upon religion present themselves to the mind; for I doubt not there are good men who would refuse to take these oaths simply in consequence of religious motives; but constant experience shows that these men are comparatively few; and if any one should say that *upon them* an oath is influential, we answer, that they are precisely the very persons who would be bound by their simple promises without an oath.

88. The oaths of jurymen afford another instance. Jurymen swear that they will give a verdict according to the evidence, and yet it is perfectly well known that they often assent to a verdict which they believe to be contrary to that evidence. They do not all coincide in the verdict which the foreman pronounces, it is indeed often impossible that they should coincide. This perjury is committed by multitudes; yet what juryman cares for it, or refuses, in consequence of his oath, to deliver a verdict which he believes to be improper? The reason then that they do not care is, that the oath, as such, does not bind their consciences. It stands alone. The public do not often reprobate the violation of such oaths: the law does not punish it; jurymen learn to think that it is no harm to violate them; and the resulting conclusion is, that the form of an oath cannot and does not supply the deficiency;—it cannot and does not apply the religious sanction.

89. Step a few yards from the jury-box

[1] See p. 51.

to the witness-box, and you see the difference. There public opinion interposes its power— there the punishment of perjury impends— there the religious sanction is applied – and there, consequently, men regard the truth. If the simple intervention of an oath was that which bound men to veracity, they would be bound in the jury-box as much as at ten feet off; but it is not.

90. A custom-house oath is nugatory even to a proverb. Yet it is an oath : yet the swearer does stake his salvation upon his veracity : and still his veracity is not secured. Why? Because an oath, as such, applies to the minds of most men little or no motive to veracity. They do not in fact think that their salvation is staked, necessarily, by oaths. They think it is either staked or not, according to certain other circumstances quite independent of the oath itself. These circumstances are not associated with custom-house oaths, and therefore they do not avail. Churchwardens' oaths are of the same kind. Upon these Gisborne remarks :—" In the successive execution of the office of church-warden, almost every man above the rank of a day labourer, in every parish in the kingdom, learns to consider the strongest sanction of truth as a nugatory form." This is not quite accurate. They do not learn to consider the strongest *sanction of truth* as a nugatory form, but they learn to consider *oaths* as a nugatory form. The reality is, that the sanctions of truth are not brought into operation, and that oaths, as such, do not bring them into operation.

91. We return then to our proposition— Unless public opinion or legal penalties enforce veracity, very little is added by an oath to the motives to veracity, more than would subsist in the case of simple affirmation.

92. It is obvious that the Legislature might, if it pleased, attach the same penalties to falsehood as it now attaches to perjury ; and therefore all the motives to veracity which are furnished by the law in the case of oaths, might be *equally* furnished in the case of affirmation. This is in fact done by the Legislature in the case of the Society of Friends.

93. It is also obvious that public opinion might be applied to affirmation much more powerfully than it is now. The simple circumstance of disusing oaths would effect this. Even now, when the public disapprobation is excited against a man who has given false evidence in a court of justice, by what is it excited ? - by his having broken his oath, or by his having given false testimony? It is the falsehood which excites the disapprobation, much more than the circumstance that the falsehood was in spite of an oath. This public disapprobation is founded upon the general perception of the guilt of false testimony and of its perniciousness. Now if affirmation only was employed, this public disapprobation would follow the lying witness, as it now follows, or nearly as it now follows, the perjured witness. Everything but the mere oath would be the same—the fear of penalties, the fear of disgrace, the motives of religion would remain ; and we have just shown how little a mere oath avails. But we have artificially diminished the public reprobation of lying by establishing oaths. The tendency of instituting oaths is manifestly to diffuse the sentiment that there is a *difference* in the degree of obligation not to lie, and not to swear falsely. This difference is made, not so much by adding stronger motives to veracity by an oath, as by deducting from the motives to veracity in simple affirmations. Let the public opinion take its own healthful and unobstructed course, and falsehood in evidence will quickly be regarded as a flagrant offence. Take away oaths, and the public reprobation of falsehood will immediately increase in power, and will bring with its increase an increasing efficiency in the religious sanction. The present relative estimate of lying and perjury is a very inaccurate standard by which to judge of the efficiency of oaths. We have artificially reduced the abhorrence of lying, and then say that that abhorrence is not great enough to bind men to the truth.

94. Our reasoning then proceeds by these steps. Oaths are designed to apply a strong religious sanction: they, however, do not apply it unless they are seconded by the apprehension of penalties or disgrace. The apprehension of penalties and disgrace may be attached to *falsehood*, and with this apprehension the religious sanction will also be attached to it. Therefore, all those motives which bind men to veracity may be applied to falsehood as well as to oaths. In other words, oaths are needless.

95. But in reality we have evidence of this needlessness from every-day experience. In some of the most important of temporal affairs an oath is never used. The Houses of Parliament in their examinations of witnesses employ no oaths. They are convinced (and therefore they have proved) that the truth can be discovered without them. But if affirmation is thus a sufficient security for veracity in the great questions of a Legislature, how can it be insufficient in the little questions of private life ? There is a strange inconsistency here. That same Parliament which declares by its every-day practice that oaths are needless, continues by its every-day practice to impose them ! Even

more : those very men who themselves take oaths as a necessary qualification for their duties as legislators, proceed to the exercise of these duties upon the mere testimony of other men! Peers are never required to take oaths in delivering their testimony, yet no one thinks that a peer's evidence in a court of justice may not be as much depended upon as that of him who swears. Why are peers in fact bound to veracity though without an oath? Will you say that the religious sanction is more powerful upon lords than upon other men? The supposition were ridiculous. How then does it happen? You reply, Their honour binds them. Very well ; that is the same as to say that public opinion binds them. But then, he who says that honour, or anything else besides pure religious sanctions, binds men to veracity, impugns the very grounds upon which oaths are defended.

96. Oath evidence again is not required by courts-martial. But can any man assign a reason why a person who would speak the truth on affirmation before military officers would not speak it on affirmation before a judge? Arbitrations too proceed often, perhaps generally, upon evidence of parole. Yet do not arbitrators discover the truth as well as courts of justice? and if they did not, it would be little in favour of oaths, because a part of the sanction of veracity is, in the case of arbitrations, withdrawn.

97. But we have even tried the experiment of affirmations in our own courts of justice, and tried it for some ages past. The Society of Friends uniformly give their evidence in courts of law on their words alone. No man imagines that their words do not bind them. No legal court would listen with more suspicion to a witness because he was a Quaker. Here all the motives to veracity are applied: there is the religious motive, which in such cases all but desperately bad men feel: there is the motive of public opinion : and there is the motive arising from the penalties of the law. If the same motives were applied to other men, why should they not be as effectual in securing veracity as they are upon the Quakers?

98. We have an example even yet more extensive. In all the courts of the United States of America, no one is obliged to take an oath. What are we to conclude? Are the Americans so foolish a people that they persist in accepting affirmations knowing that they do not bind witnesses to truth? Or do the Americans really find that affirmations are sufficient? But one answer can be given :—They find that affirmations are sufficient ; they prove undeniably that oaths are needless. No one will imagine that virtue on the other side the Atlantic is so much greater than on this, that while an affirmation is sufficient for an American, an oath is necessary here.

99. So that whether we inquire into the moral lawfulness of oaths, they are not lawful ; or into their practical utility, they are of little use or of none.

Effects of Oaths.

100. There is a power and efficacy in our religion which elevates those who heartily accept it above that low moral state in which alone an oath can even be supposed to be of advantage. The man who takes an oath, virtually declares that his word would not bind him ; and this is an admission which no good man should make—for the sake both of his own moral character and of the credit of religion itself. It is the testimony even of infidelity, that "wherever men of uncommon energy and dignity of mind have existed, they have felt the degradation of binding their assertions with an oath."[1] This degradation, this descent from the proper ground on which a man of integrity should stand, illustrates the proposition that whatever exceeds affirmation "cometh of evil." The evil origin is so palpable that you cannot comply with the custom without feeling that you sacrifice the dignity of virtue. It is related of Solon that he said, "A good man ought to be in that estimation that he needs not an oath ; because it is to be reputed a lessening of his honour if he be forced to swear."[2] If to take an oath lessened a pagan's honour, what must be its effect upon a Christian's purity?

101. Oaths, at least the system of oaths which obtains in this country, tends powerfully to deprave the moral character. We have seen that they are continually violated —that men are continually referring to the most tremendous sanctions of religion with the habitual belief that those sanctions impose no practical obligation. Can this have any other tendency than to diminish the influence of religious sanctions upon other things? If a man sets light by the Divine vengeance in the jury box to-day, is he likely to give full weight to that vengeance before a magistrate to-morrow? We cannot prevent the effects of habit. Such things will infallibly deteriorate the moral character, because they infallibly diminish the power of those principles upon which the moral character is founded.

102. Oaths encourage falsehood. We

[1] Godwin : Political Justice, v 2, p. 633.
[2] Stobaeus : Serm. 3

have already seen that the effect of instituting oaths is to diminish the practical obligation of simple affirmation. The law says, You must speak the truth when you are upon your oath; which is the same thing as to say that it is less harm to violate truth when you are not on your oath. The court sometimes reminds a witness that he is upon oath, which is equivalent to saying, If you were not, we should think less of your mendacity. The same lesson is inculcated by the assignation of penalties to perjury and not to falsehood. What is a man to conclude, but that the law thinks light of the crime which it does not punish; and that since he may lie with impunity, it is not much harm to lie? Common language bears testimony to the effect. The vulgar phrase, I will take my oath to it, clearly evinces the prevalent notion that a man may lie with less guilt when he does not take his oath. No answer can be made to this remark, unless any one can show that the extra sanction of an oath is so much added to the obligation which would otherwise attach to simple affirmation. And who can show this? Experience proves the contrary: "Experience bears ample testimony to the fact that the prevalence of oaths among men (Christians not excepted) has produced a very material and very general effect in reducing their estimate of the obligation of plain truth in its natural and simple forms."[1]—" There is no cause of insincerity, prevarication, and falsehood more powerful than the practice of administering oaths in a court of justice."[2]

103. Upon this subject the legislator plays a desperate game against the morality of a people. He wishes to make them speak the truth when they undertake an office or deliver evidence. Even supposing him to succeed, what is the cost? That of diminishing the motives to veracity in all the affairs of life. A man may not be called upon to take an oath above two or three times in his life, but he is called upon to speak the truth every day.

104. A few, but a few serious, words remain. The investigations of this chapter are not matters to employ speculation, but to influence our practice. If it be indeed true that Jesus Christ has imperatively forbidden us to employ an oath, a duty, an imperative duty is imposed upon us. It is worse than merely vain to hear His laws unless we obey them. Of him, therefore, who is assured of the prohibition, it is indispensably required that he should refuse an oath. There is no other means of maintaining our allegiance to God. Our pretensions to Christianity are at stake: for he who, knowing the Christian law, will not conform to it, is certainly not a Christian. How then does it happen that, although persons frequently acknowledge they think oaths are forbidden, so few, when they are called upon to swear, decline to do it? Alas! this offers one evidence amongst the many of the want of uncompromising moral principles in the world—of such principles as it has been the endeavour of these pages to enforce—of such principles as would prompt us and enable us to sacrifice *every* thing to Christian fidelity. By what means do the persons of whom we speak suppose that the will of God respecting oaths is to be effected? To whose practice do they look for an exemplification of the Christian standard? Do they await some miracle by which the whole world shall be convinced and oaths shall be abolished without the agency of man? Such are not the means by which it is the pleasure of the Universal Lord to act. He effects His moral purposes by the instrumentality of faithful men. Where are these faithful men?—But let it be: if those who are called to this fidelity refuse, theirs will be the dishonour and the offence. But the work will eventually be done. Other and better men will assuredly arise to acquire the Christian honour and to receive the Christian reward.

CHAPTER VIII.

The Moral Character, Obligations, and Effects of Particular Oaths.

Oath of allegiance—Oath in evidence—Perjury—Military oath- Oath against bribery at elections —Oath against simony—University oaths—Subscription to Articles of Religion.—Meaning of the Thirty-Nine Articles literal—Refusal to subscribe.

Subscription to Articles of Religion.

1. In reading the paragraphs which follow respecting several of the specific oaths which are imposed in this country, the reader should remember that the evils with which they are attended would almost equally attend affirmations in similar circumstances. Our object, therefore, is less to illustrate their nature as oaths than as improper and vicious engagements. With respect to the interpretation of a particular oath, it is obviously to be determined by the same rule as that of promises. A man must fulfil his oath in that sense in which he knows the imposer designs and expects him to fulfil it. And he must endeavour to ascertain what the imposer's expectation is. To take an oath in voluntary ignorance of the obligations which it is intended to impose, and to excuse ourselves for disregarding

[1] Gurney: Observations, &c., c. x.
[2] Godwin: v. 2, p. 634.

them because we do not know what they are, cannot surely be right. Yet it is often difficult, sometimes impossible, to discover what an oath requires. The absence of precision in the meaning of terms, the alteration of general usages whilst the forms of oaths remain the same, and the original want of explicitness of the forms themselves, throw sometimes insuperable obstacles in the way of discovering, when a man takes an oath, what it is that he binds himself to do. This is manifestly a great evil: and it is chargeable primarily upon the custom of exacting oaths at all. It is in general a very difficult thing to frame an unobjectionable oath—an oath which shall neither be so lax as to become nugatory by easiness of evasion and uncertainty of meaning, nor so rigid as to demand in words more than the imposer wishes to exact, and thus to ensnare the consciences of those who take it. The same objections would apply to forms of affirmation. The only effectual remedy is to diminish, or, if it were possible, to abolish, the custom of requiring men to promise beforehand to pursue a certain course of action. How is non-fulfilment of these engagements punished? By fine, or imprisonment, or some other mode of penalty? Let the penalty, let the sanction remain, without the promise or the oath. A man swears allegiance to a prince: if he becomes a traitor, he is punished, not for the breach of his oath, but for his treason. Can you not punish his treason without the oath? A man swears he has not received a bribe at an election. If he does receive one, you send him to prison. You could as easily send him thither if he had not sworn. You reply—But by imposing the oath we bind the swearer's conscience. Alas! we have seen, and we shall presently again see, that this plan of binding men is of little effect. There is one kind of affirmation that appears to involve absurdity. I mean that by which a man affirms that he will speak the truth. Of what use is the affirmation? The affirmant is not bound to veracity more than he was before he made it. It is no greater lie to speak falsely after an affirmation than before.

Oath of Allegiance.

2. "I do sincerely promise and swear that I will be faithful and bear true allegiance to his Majesty King George." On the propriety of exacting these political oaths, we shall offer some observations in the next Essay.[1] At present we ask, What does the oath of allegiance mean? Set a hundred men each to write an exact account of what the party here promises to do, and I will undertake to affirm that not one in the hundred will agree with any other individual. "I will be faithful:" What is meant by being faithful? What is the extent of the obligation, and what are its limits? "I will bear true allegiance:" What does allegiance mean? Is it synonymous with fidelity? Or does it embrace a wider extent of obligation, or a narrower? And if either, how is the extent ascertained? The oath was, I believe, made purposely indefinite: the old oath of allegiance was more discriminative. But no form can discriminate the duty of a citizen to his rulers unless you make it consist of a political treatise; and no man can write a treatise with definitions to which all would subscribe. The truth is, that no one knows what the oath of allegiance requires. Paley attempts, in six separate articles, to define its meaning: one of which definitions is, that " the oath excludes all design, *at the time*, of attempting to depose the reigning prince."[1] At the time! Why, the oath is couched in the future tense. Its express purpose is to obtain a security for future conduct. The swearer declares, not what he then designs, but what, in time to come, he will do.—Another definition is, " it permits resistance to the king when his ill behaviour or imbecility is such as to make resistance beneficial to the community."[2] But how or in what manner "fidelity and true allegiance" means "resistance," casuistry only can tell. We may rest assured that, after all attempts at explanation, the meaning of the oath will be, at the least, as doubtful as before. Nor is there any remedy. The fault is not in the form, for no form can be good, but in the imposition of any oath of allegiance. The only means of avoiding the evil is by abolishing the oath. Besides, what do oaths of allegiance avail in those periods of disturbance in which princes are commonly displaced? What revolution has been prevented by oaths of allegiance?

3. Yet if the oath does no good, it does harm. It is always doing harm to exact promises from men, who cannot know beforehand whether they will fulfil them. And as to the ambiguity, it is always doing harm to require men to stake their salvation upon doing—they know not what.

Oath in Evidence.

4. "The truth, the whole truth, and nothing but the truth, touching the matter in question." Is the witness to understand by this that if he truly answers all questions that are put to him, he conforms to the requisitions of the oath? If he is, the terms of the oath are very exceptionable; for many a witness may give true answers to a counsel

---

[1] Essay III. chap. 5.   [1] Mor. and Pol. Phil., b. 3, p. 1, c. 18.   [2] Ib. 1, c. 16.

and yet not tell "the whole truth." Or does the oath bind him to give an exact narrative of every particular connected with the matter in question whether asked or not? If it does, multitudes commit perjury. How then shall a witness act? Shall he commit perjury by withholding all information but that which is asked? Or shall he be ridiculed and perhaps silenced in court for attempting to narrate all that he has sworn to disclose? Here again the morality of the people is injuriously affected. To take an oath to do a certain prescribed act, and then to do only just that which custom happens to prescribe, is to ensnare the conscience and practically to diminish the sanctions of veracity. The evil may be avoided either by disusing all previous promises to speak the truth, or to adapt the terms of the promise (if that can be done) to the duties which the law or which custom expects. "You shall true answer make to all such questions as shall be asked of you," is the form when a person is sworn upon a *voir dire;* and if this is all that the law expects when he is giving evidence, why not use the same form? If, however, in deference to the reasonings against the use of any oaths, the oath in evidence were abolished, no difficulty could remain; for to *promise* in any form to speak the truth, is, as we have seen, absurd.

5. Whilst the oath in evidence continues to be imposed, it is not an easy task to determine in what sense the witness should understand it. If you decide by the meaning of the Legislature which imposed the oath, it appears manifest that he should tell all he knows, whether asked or not. But what, it may be asked, is the meaning of a law, but that which the authorised expounders of the law determine? And if they habitually admit an interpretation at variance with the terms of the oath, is not their sanction an authoritative explanation of the Legislature's meaning? These are questions which I pretend not with confidence to determine. The mischiefs which result from the uncertainty are to be charged upon the Legislatures which do not remove the evil. I would, however, suggest that the meaning of a form in such cases is to be sought, not so much in the meaning of the original imposers, as in that of those who now sanction the form by permitting it to exist. This doubtless opens wide the door to extreme licentiousness of interpretation. Nor can that door be closed. There is no other remedial measure than an alteration of the forms or an abolition of the oath.

Military Oath.

6. "I swear to obey the orders of the officers who are set over me: so help me God." And suppose an officer orders him to do something which morality forbids, his oath then stands thus: "I swear to obey man rather than God." The profaneness is shocking. Will any extenuation be offered, and will it be said that the military man only swears to obey the *virtuous* orders of his superior? We deny the fact: the oath neither means nor is intended to mean any such thing. It may indeed by possibility happen that an officer may order his inferior to do a thing which a court-martial would not punish him for refusing to do. But if the law intends to allow such exceptions, what excuse is there for making the terms of the oath absolute? Is it not teaching military men to swear they care not what, thus to make the terms of the oath one thing and its meaning another? But the real truth is, that neither the law nor courts-martial allow any such limitations in the meaning of the oath as will bring it within the limits of morality, or of even a decent reverence to Him who commands morality to man. They do not intend to allow the Moral Law to be the primary rule to the soldier. They intend the contrary; and the soldier does actually swear that, if he is ordered so to do, he will violate the law of God. Of this impiety what is the use? Does any one imagine that a soldier obeys his superiors because he has sworn to obey them? It were ridiculous. When courts-martial inflict a punishment, they inflict it not for perjury, but for disobedience.

7. I would devote two or three sentences to the observation that the military oath is *sui generis.* So far at least as my information extends, no other oath is imposed which promises *unconditional* obedience to other men; no other oath exists by which a man binds himself to violate the laws of God. *Why* does the military oath thus stand alone, the explicit contemner of the obligations of morality? Because it belongs to a custom which itself contemns morality. Because it belongs to a custom which "repeals all the principles of virtue." Because it belongs to War. There is a lesson couched in this, which he who has ears to hear will find to be pregnant with instruction.

Oath against Bribery at Elections.

8. "I do swear I have not received, or had, by myself or any person whatsoever in trust for me, or for my use and benefit, directly or indirectly, any sum or sums of money: office, place, or employment; gift or reward: or any promise or security for any money, office, employment, or gift, in order to give my vote at this election." This is an attempt to secure incorruptness by extreme accuracy in framing the oath. With what success, public experience tells. No bribery oath

will prevent bribery. It wants efficient sanctions—punishment by the law or reprobation by the public. A man who possesses a vote in a close borough, and whose neighbours and their fathers have habitually pocketed a bribe at every election, is very little under the influence of public opinion. That public with which he is connected does not reprobate the act, and he learns to imagine it is of little moral turpitude. As to legal penalties, they are too unfrequently inflicted or too difficult of infliction to be of much avail. Why then is this nursery of perjury continued? Which action should we most deprecate, that of the voter who perjures himself for a ten-pound note, or that of the legislator who so tempts him to perjury by imposing an oath which he knows will be violated? If bribery be wrong, punish it; but it is utterly indefensible to exact oaths which everybody knows will be broken. Not indeed that anything in the present state of the representation will prevent bribery. We may multiply oaths and denounce penalties without end, yet bribery will still prevail. But though bribery be inseparable from the system, perjury is not. We should abolish one of the evils if we do not or cannot abolish both.

9. As to those endless contrivances by which electors avoid the arm of the law, and hope to avoid the guilt of perjury, they are, as it respects guilt, all and always vain. The intention of the Legislature was to prevent *bribery*, and he who is bribed violates his oath whether he violates its literal terms or not. The shopkeeper who *sells* a yard of cloth to a candidate for twenty pounds, is just as truly bribed, and he just as truly commits perjury, as if the candidate had said, I give you this twenty-pound note to tempt you to vote for me. These men may evade legal penalties; there is a power which they cannot evade.

Oath against Simony.

10. The substance of the oath is. "I do swear that I have made no simoniacal payment for obtaining this ecclesiastical place: so help me God through Jesus Christ!" The patronage of livings, that is, the legal right to give a man the ecclesiastical income of a parish, may, like other property, be bought and sold. But though a person may legally sell the power of giving the income, he may not sell the income itself; the reason it may be presumed being, that a person who can only *give* the income, will be more likely to bestow it upon such a clergyman as deserves it, than if he sold it to the highest bidder. It may, however, be observed in passing, that the security for the judicious presentation of church preferment is extremely imperfect: for the law, whilst it tries to take care that preferment shall be properly bestowed, takes no care that the power of bestowing it shall be intrusted to proper hands. The least virtuous man or woman in a district may possess this power; and it were vain to expect that they will be very solicitous to assign careful shepherds to the Christian flocks.

11. To prevent the income from being bought and sold, the law requires the acceptor of a living to swear that he has made no *simoniacal* payment for it. What then is simony? To answer this question the clergyman must have recourse to the definitions of the law. Simony is of various kinds, and the clergyman who is under strong temptation to make some contract with, or payment to the patron, is manifestly in danger of making them in the fearing, doubting hope that they are not simoniacal. And so he makes the arrangement, hardly knowing whether he has committed simony and perjury or not. This evil is seen and acknowledged. "The oath," says a dignitary of the Church, "lays a snare for the integrity of the clergy; and I do not perceive that the requiring of it, in cases of private patronage, produces any good effect sufficient to compensate for this danger."

University Oaths.

12. The various statutes of colleges, of which every member is obliged to promise the observance on oath, are become wholly or partly obsolete; some are needless and absurd, some illegal, and to some, perhaps, it is impossible to conform. Yet the oath to perform them is constantly taken. A man swears that he will speak within the college no language but Latin; and he speaks English in it every day. He swears he will employ so many hours out of every twenty-four in disputations; and does not dispute for days or weeks together. What remains, then, for those who take these oaths to do to show that this is not perjury? Here is the field for casuistry; here is the field in which ingenuity may exhibit its adroitness! in which sophistry may delight to range! in which Duns Scotus, if he were again in the world, might rejoice to be a combatant! And what do Ingenuity, and Casuistry, and Sophistry do? Oh! they discover consolatory truths; they discover that if the act which you promise to perform is unlawful, you may swear to perform it with an easy conscience; they discover that there is no harm in swearing to jump from Dover to Calais, because it is "impracticable;" they discover that it is quite proper to swear to do a foolish thing because it would be "manifestly inconvenient" and "prejudicial" to do it. In a word, they discover so many agreeable things, that if the book of Cervantes

were appended to the oath, they might swear to imitate all the deeds of his hero, and yet remain quietly and *innocently* in a college all their lives.

13. That nothing can be said in extenuation of those who take these oaths cannot be affirmed; yet that the taking them is wrong, every man who simply consults his own heart will know. Even if they were wrong upon no other ground they would be so upon this, that if men were conscientious enough to refuse to take them, the "necessity" for taking them would soon be withdrawn. No man questions that these oaths are a scandal to religion and to religious men; no man questions that their tendency is to make the public think lightly of the obligation of an oath. They *ought*, therefore, to be abolished. It is imperative upon the Legislature to abolish them, and it is imperative upon the individual, by refusing to take them, to evince to the Legislature the necessity for its interference. Nothing is wanted but that private Christians should maintain Christian fidelity. If they did do this, and refused to take these oaths, the Legislature would presently do its duty. It needs not be feared that it would suffer the doors of the colleges to be locked up because students were too conscientious to swear falsely. Thus, although the obligation upon the Legislature is manifest, it possesses some semblance of an excuse for refraining from reform, since those who are immediately aggrieved, and who are the immediate agents of the offence, are so little concerned that they do not address even a petition for interference. That some good men feel aggrieved is scarcely to be doubted: let these remember their obligations: let them remember that compliance entails upon posterity the evil and the offence, and sets, for the integrity of successors, a perpetual snare.

14. It is an unhappy reflection that men endeavour rather to pacify the misgiving voice of conscience under a continuance of the evil than exert themselves to remove it. Unschooled persons will *always* think that the usage is wrong. In truth, even after the licentious interpretations of the oaths have been resorted to—after it has been shown what he who takes them does *not* promise, what imaginable security is there that he will perform that which he does promise—that he will even know *what* he promises? None. Being himself the interpreter of the oath, and having resolved that the oath does not mean what it says, he is at liberty to think that it means anything; or, which I suppose is the practical opinion, that it means nothing. If we would remove the evil, we must abolish the oath.

Subscription to Articles of Religion.

15. Bishop Clayton said, "I do not only doubt whether the compilers of the Articles, but even whether any *two* thinking men, ever agreed exactly in their opinion not only with regard to all the Articles, but even with regard to any one of them."[1] Such is the character of that series of propositions in which a man is required to declare his belief before he can become a minister in a Christian community. The event may easily be foreseen; some will refuse to subscribe; some will subscribe though it violates their consciences; some will subscribe regardless whether it be right or wrong; and some of course will be found to justify subscription.

16. Of those who on moral grounds refuse to subscribe to that which they do not believe, it may be presumed that they are conscientious men—men who prefer sacrificing their interests to their duties. These are the men whom every Christian Church should especially desire to retain in its communion; and these are precisely the men whom the Articles exclude from the English Church.

17. As it respects those who perceive the impropriety of subscription and yet subscribe, whose consciences are wronged by the very act which introduces them into the Church—the evil is manifest and great. Chillingworth declared to Shelden that "if he subscribed, he subscribed his own damnation," yet not long afterwards Chillingworth was induced to subscribe. Unhappy, that they who are about to preach virtue to others should be initiated by a violation of the Moral Law.

18. With respect to those who subscribe heedlessly, and without regard to their belief or disbelief of the Articles—of what use is subscription? It is designed to operate as a test; but what test is it to him who would set his name to the Articles if they were exactly the contrary of what they are? If conscientiousness keeps some men out of the Church, the want of conscientiousness lets others in. The contrivance is admirably adapted to an end; but to what end? To the separation of the more virtuous from the less, and to the admission of the latter.

19. A reader who was a novice in these affairs would ask, in wonder, For what purpose is subscription exacted? If the Articles are so objectionable, and if subscription is productive of so much evil, why are not the Articles revised, or why is subscription required at all? These are reasonable questions. They involve, however, political

[1] Confessional, 3d ed., p. 246.

considerations; and in the Political Essay we hope to give such an inquirer satisfaction respecting them.

20. And with respect to the justifications that are offered of subscribing to doctrines which are not believed, it is manifest that they must set out with the assumption that the words of the Articles mean nothing that we are not to seek for their meaning in their terms, but in some other quarter. It is hardly necessary to remark, that when this assumption is made, the inquirer is launched upon a boundless ocean, and though he has to make his way to a port, possesses neither compass nor helm, and can see neither sun nor star. Who can assign any limit to license of interpretation, when it is once agreed that the words themselves mean nothing? The world is all before us, and we have to seek a place of rest from pyrrhonism wherever we can find it. We are told to go back to Queen Elizabeth's days, and to find out, if we can, what the Legislature who framed the Articles meant: always premising that we are not to judge of what they meant by what they said. How is it discovered that they did not mean what they said? By a process of most convincing argumentation; which argumentation consists in this, "It is difficult to conceive how" they could have meant it.[1] These are agreeable and convenient solutions; but they are not true.

21. "They who contend that nothing less can justify subscription to the Thirty-Nine Articles than the actual belief of each and every separate proposition contained in them, must suppose that the Legislature expected the consent of ten thousand men, and that in perpetual succession, not to one controverted proposition, but to many hundreds. *It is difficult to conceive* how this could be expected by any who observed the incurable diversity of human opinion upon all subjects short of demonstration."[2] Now it appears that the Legislature of Elizabeth actually did require uniformity of opinion upon these controverted points. Such has been the decision of the Judges. "One Smyth subscribed to the said Thirty-Nine Articles of Religion with this addition—*so far forth as the same were agreeable to the Word of God;*—and it was resolved by Wray, Chief-Justice in the King's Bench, and all the Judges of England, that this subscription was not according to the statute of 13th Eliz. Because the statute required an absolute subscription, and this subscription made it conditional: and that this act *was made for avoiding diversity of opinions*, &c.; and by this addition the party might,

[1] Mor. and Pol. Phil., b. 3, p. 1, c. 22.   [2] Ibid.

by his own private opinion, take some of them to be against the Word of God, and by this means *diversity of opinions* should not be avoided, *which was the scope of the statute*, and the very Act made touching subscription of none effect."[1]

22. This overthrows the convenient explanations of modern times. It is agreed by those who offer these explanations, that the meaning of Elizabeth's Legislature is that by which they are bound. That meaning then is declared by all the Judges of England to be, that subscribers should *believe* the propositions of the Articles. The modern explanations allow private opinion the liberty of thinking some of them to be "against the Word of God." This was precisely the liberty which the Legislature intended to preclude. The modern explanations affirm the Articles to be conditional, and, in fact, that they impose only a few general obligations; but unconditional subscription was the very thing which the Legislature required. If a person should now express the condition which Smyth, as reported by Coke, expressed, and should say, I believe the Articles so far as they are accordant with Christian truth—it appears that his subscription would not be accepted; and yet this is what is done by perhaps every clergyman in England with this difference only, that the reservation is secretly made and not frankly expressed. So that in reality, and according to the principles laid down by the apologists of subscription,[2] almost every subscriber subscribes falsely.

23. But what, it will be asked, is to be done? Refuse to subscribe. There is no other means of maintaining your purity, and perhaps no other means of procuring an abolition of the Articles. At least this means would be effectual. We may be sure that the Legislature would revise or abolish them if it was found that no one would subscribe. They would not leave the pulpits empty in compliment to a barbarous relic of the days of Elizabeth. Perhaps it will be said, that although men of virtue refused to subscribe, the pulpits would still be filled with unprincipled men. The effect would speedily be the same: the Legislature would not continue to impose subscription for the sake of excluding from the ministry all but bad men. Those who subscribe, therefore, bind the

[1] Coke: Instit. 4, cap. 74, p. 324.
[2] These principles are, that the meaning of a promise or an oath is to be determined by the meaning of those who impose it. This as a general rule is true; but I repeat the doubt whether, in the case of antiquated forms, a proper standard of their meaning is not to be sought in the intention of the Legislatures which now perpetuate those forms. This doubt, however, in whatever way it preponderates, will not afford a justification of subscribing to forms of which the terms are notoriously disregarded.

burden upon their own shoulders and upon the shoulders of posterity. The offence is great: the scandal to religion is great: and even if refusal to subscribe would not remove the evil, the question for the individual is not what may be the consequences of doing his duty, but what his duty is. We want a little more Christian fidelity, a little more of that spirit which made our forefathers prefer the stake to tampering with their consciences.

CHAPTER IX.
Immoral Agency.

Publication and circulation of books—Seneca—Circulating libraries – Public-houses – Prosecutions—Political affairs.

24. A great portion of the moral evil in the world is the result not so much of the intensity of individual wickedness, as of a general incompleteness in the practical virtue of all classes of men. If it were possible to take away misconduct from one half of the community and to add its amount to the remainder, it is probable that the moral character of our species would be soon benefited by the change. *Now*, the ill dispositions of the bad are powerfully encouraged by the want of upright examples in those who are better. A man may deviate considerably from rectitude, and still be as good as his neighbours. From such a man the motive to excellence which the constant presence of virtuous example supplies is taken away. So that there is reason to believe that if the bad were to become worse, and the reputable to become proportionably better, the average virtue of the world would speedily be increased.

25. One of the modes by which the efficacy of example in reputable persons is miserably diminished, is by what we have called Immoral Agency—by their being willing to encourage, at second hand, evils which they would not commit as principals. Linked together as men are in society, it is frequently difficult to perform an unwarrantable action without some sort of co-operation from creditable men. This co-operation is not often, except in flagrant cases, refused; and thus not only is the commission of such actions facilitated, but a general relaxation is induced in the practical estimates which men form of the standard of rectitude.

26. Since, then, so much evil attends this *agency* in unwarrantable conduct, it manifestly becomes a good man to look around upon the nature of his intercourse with others, and to consider whether he is not virtually promoting evils which his judgment deprecates, or re-

ducing the standard of moral judgment in the world. The reader would have no difficulty in perceiving that, if a strenuous opponent of the slave trade should establish a manufactory of manacles and thumbscrews and iron collars for the slave merchants, he would be grossly inconsistent with himself. The reader would perceive, too, that his labours in the cause of the abolition would be almost nullified by the viciousness of his example, and that he would generally discredit pretensions to philanthropy. Now that which we desire the reader to do is, to apply the principles which this illustration exhibits to other and less flagrant cases. Other cases of co-operation with evil may be less flagrant than this; but they are not, on that account, innocent. I have read, in the life of a man of great purity of character, that he refused to draw up a will or some such document because it contained a transfer of some slaves. He thought that slavery was absolutely wrong; and therefore would not, even by the remotest implication, sanction the system by his example.[1] I think he exercised a sound Christian judgment: and if all who prepare such documents acted upon the same principles, I know not whether they would not so influence public opinion as greatly to hasten the abolition of slavery itself. Yet where is the man who would refuse to do this, or to do things even less defensible than this?

Publication and Circulation of Books.

27. It is a very common thing to hear of the evils of pernicious reading, of how it enervates the mind, or how it depraves the principles. The complaints are doubtless just. These books could not be read, and these evils would be spared the world, if one did not write, and another did not print, and another did not sell, and another did not circulate them. Are those then, without whose agency the mischief could not ensue, to be held innocent in affording this agency? Yet, loudly as we complain of the evil, and carefully as we warn our children to avoid it, how seldom do we hear public reprobation of the writers? As to printers, and booksellers, and library keepers, we scarcely hear their offences mentioned at all. We speak not of those abandoned publications which all respectable men condemn, but of those which, pernicious as they are confessed to be, furnish reading-rooms and libraries, and are habitually sold in almost every bookseller's shop. Seneca says, " He that lends a man

---

[1] One of the publications of this excellent man contains a paragraph much to our present purpose: "In all our concerns, it is necessary that nothing we do may carry the appearance of approbation of the works of wickedness, make the unrighteous more at ease in unrighteousness, or occasion the injures committed against the oppressed to be more lightly looked over."—*Considerations on the True Harmony of Mankind*, c. 3, by John Woolman.

money to carry him to a bawdy-house, or a weapon for his revenge, makes himself a partner of his crime." He, too, who writes or sells a book which will, in all probability, injure the reader, is accessory to the mischief which may be done; with this aggravation, when compared with the examples of Seneca, that whilst the money would probably do mischief but to one or two persons, the book may injure a hundred or a thousand. Of the writers of injurious books, we need say no more. If the inferior agents are censurable, the primary agent must be more censurable. A printer or a bookseller should, however, reflect that to be not so bad as another is a very different thing from being innocent. When we see that the owner of a press will print any work that is offered to him, with no other concern about its tendency than whether it will subject him to penalties from the law, we surely must perceive that he exercises but a very imperfect virtue. Is it obligatory upon us not to promote ill principles in other men? He does not fulfil the obligation. Is it obligatory upon us to promote rectitude by unimpeachable example? He does not exhibit that example. If it were right for my neighbour to furnish me with the means of moral injury, it would not be wrong for me to accept and to employ them.

28. I stand in a bookseller's shop, and observe his customers successively coming in. One orders a lexicon, and one a work of scurrilous infidelity; one Captain Cook's Voyages, and one a new licentious romance. If the bookseller takes and executes all these orders with the same willingness, I cannot but perceive that there is an inconsistency, an incompleteness, in his moral principles of action. Perhaps this person is so conscious of the mischievous effects of such books, that he would not allow them in the hands of his children, nor suffer them to be seen on his parlour table. But if he thus knows the evils which they inflict, can it be right for him to be the agent in diffusing them? Such a person does not exhibit that consistency, that completeness of virtuous conduct, without which the Christian character cannot be fully exhibited. Step into the shop of this bookseller's neighbour, a druggist, and there, if a person asks for some arsenic, the tradesman begins to be anxious. He considers whether it is probable the buyer wants it for a proper purpose. If he does sell it, he cautions the buyer to keep it where others cannot have access to it; and, before he delivers the packet, legibly inscribes upon it "Poison." One of these men sells poison to the body, and the other poison to the mind. If the anxiety and caution of the druggist is right, the indifference of the bookseller must be wrong. Add to which, that the druggist would not sell arsenic at all if it were not sometimes useful; but to what readers can a vicious book be useful?

29. Suppose for a moment that no printer would commit such a book to his press, and that no bookseller would sell it, the consequence would be that nine-tenths of these manuscripts would be thrown into the fire, or rather that they would never have been written. The inference is obvious; and surely it is not needful again to enforce the consideration, that although *your* refusal might not prevent vicious books from being published, you are not therefore exempted from the obligation to refuse. A man must do his duty whether the effects of his fidelity be such as he would desire or not. Such purity of conduct might, no doubt, circumscribe a man's business, and so does purity of conduct in some other professions; but if this be a sufficient excuse for contributing to demoralise the world, if profit be a justification of a departure from rectitude, it will be easy to defend the business of a pickpocket.

30. I know that the principles of conduct which these paragraphs recommend lead to grave practical consequences; I know that they lead to the conclusion that the business of a printer or bookseller, as it is ordinarily conducted, is not consistent with Christian uprightness. A man may carry on a business in select works; and this, by some conscientious persons, is really done. In the present state of the press, the difficulty of obtaining a considerable business as a bookseller without circulating injurious works may frequently be great, and it is in consequence of this difficulty that we see so few booksellers amongst the Quakers. The few who do conduct the business generally reside in large towns, where the demand for all books is so great that a person can procure a competent income though he excludes the bad.

31. He who is more studious to justify his conduct than to act aright may say, that if a person may sell no book that can injure another, he can scarcely sell any book. The answer is, that although there must be some difficulty in discrimination, though a bookseller cannot always inform himself what the precise tendency of a book is—yet there can be no difficulty in judging, respecting numberless books, that their tendency is bad. If we cannot define the precise distinction between the good and the evil, we can, nevertheless, perceive the evil when it has attained to a certain extent. He who cannot distinguish day from evening can distinguish it from night.

32. The case of the proprietors of common circulating libraries is yet more palpable,

because the *majority* of the books which they contain inflict injury upon their readers. How it happens that persons of respectable character, and who join with others in lamenting the frivolity, and worse than frivolity, of the age, nevertheless daily and hourly contribute to the mischief, without any apparent consciousness of inconsistency, it is difficult to explain. A person establishes, perhaps, one of these libraries for the first time in a country town. He supplies the younger and less busy part of its inhabitants with a source of moral injury from which hitherto they had been exempt. The girl who, till now, possessed sober views of life, he teaches to dream of the extravagances of love ; he familiarises her ideas with intrigue and licentiousness ; destroys her disposition for rational pursuits ; and prepares her, it may be, for a victim of debauchery. These evils, or such as these, he inflicts, not upon one or two, but upon as many as he can ; and yet this person lays his head upon his pillow, as if, in all this, he was not offending against virtue or against man !

Inns.

33. When, in passing the door of an inn, I hear or see a company of intoxicated men in the "excess of riot," I cannot persuade myself that he who supplies the wine, and profits by the viciousness, is a moral man. In the private house of a person of respectability such a scene would be regarded as a scandal. It would lower his neighbour's estimate of the excellence of his character. But does it then constitute a sufficient justification of allowing vice in our houses that we *get* by it ! Does morality grant to a man an exemption from its obligations at the same time as he procures his license ? Drunkenness is immoral. If, therefore, when a person is on the eve of intoxication, the innkeeper supplies his demand for another bottle, he is accessory to the immorality. A man was lately found drowned in a stream. He had just left a public-house where he had been intoxicated during sixty hours ; and within this time the publican had supplied him (besides some spirits) with forty quarts of ale. Does any reader need to be convinced that this publican had acted criminally ? His crime, however, was neither the greater nor the less because it had been the means of loss of life ; no such accident might have happened ; but his guilt would have been the same.

34. Probity is not the only virtue which it is good policy to practise. The innkeeper, of whom it was known that he would not supply the means of excess, would probably gain by the resort of those who approved his integrity more than he would lose by the absence of those whose excesses that integrity kept away. An inn has been conducted upon such maxims. He who is disposed to make proof of the result might fix upon an established quantity of the different liquors, which he would not exceed. If that quantity were determinately fixed, the lover of excess would have no ground of complaint when he had been supplied to its amount. Such honourable and manly conduct might have an extensive effect, until it influenced the practice even of the lower resorts of intemperance. A sort of ill fame might attach to the house in which a man could become drunk ; and the maxim might be established by experience that it was necessary to the respectability, and therefore generally to the success of a public-house, that none should be seen to reel out of its doors.

Prosecutions.

35. It is upon principles of conduct similar to those which are here recommended that many persons are reluctant, and some refuse, to prosecute offenders when they think the penalty of the law is unwarrantably severe. This motive operates in our own country to a great extent ; and it ought to operate. I should not think it right to give evidence against a man who had robbed my house, if I knew that my evidence would occasion him to be hanged. Whether the reader may think similarly is of no consequence to the principle. The principle is, that if you think the end vicious and wrong, you are guilty of "Immoral Agency" in contributing to effect that end. Unhappily, we are much less willing to act upon this principle when our agency produces only moral evil, than when it produces physical suffering. He that would not give evidence which would take a man's life, or even occasion him loss or pain, would with little hesitation be an agent of injuring his moral principles ; and yet perhaps the evil of the latter case is incomparably greater than that of the former.

Political Affairs.

36. The amount of Immoral Agency which is practised in these affairs is very great. Look to any of the Continental governments, or to any that have subsisted there : how few acts of misrule, of oppression, of injustice, and of crime, have been prevented by the want of agents of the iniquity ! I speak not of notoriously bad men : of these, bad governors can usually find enough ; but I speak of men who pretend to respectability and virtue of character, and who are actually called respectable by the world. There is perhaps no class of affairs in which the agency of others is more indispensable to the accomplishment of a vicious act, than in the political. Very little—comparatively

very little—of oppression and of the political vices of rulers should we see, if *reputable* men did not lend their agency. These evils could not be committed through the agency of merely bad men; because the very fact that bad men only would abet them, would frequently preclude the possibility of their commission. It is not to be pretended that no public men possess or have possessed sufficient virtue to refuse to be the agents of a vicious government—but they are few. If they were numerous, especially if they were as numerous as they ought to be, history, even very modern history, would have had a far other record to frame than that which now devolves to her. Can it be needful to argue upon such things? Can it be needful to *prove* that neither the commands of ministers, nor "systems of policy," nor any other circumstance, exempts a public man from the obligations of the Moral Law? Public men often act as if they thought that to be a public man was to be brought under the jurisdiction of a new and a relaxed morality. They often act as if they thought that not to be the prime mover in political misdeeds was to be exempt from all moral responsibility for those deeds. A dagger, if it could think, would think it was not responsible for the assassination of which it was the agent. A public man may be a political dagger, but he cannot, like the dagger, be irresponsible.

37. These illustrations of Immoral Agency and of the obligation to avoid it might be multiplied, if enough had not been offered to make our sentiments, and the reasons upon which they are founded, obvious to the reader. Undoubtedly, in the present state of society, it is no easy task, upon these subjects, to wash our hands in innocency. But if we cannot avoid all agency, direct or indirect, in evil things, we can avoid much: and it will be sufficiently early to complain of the difficulty of complete purity when we have dismissed from our conduct as much impurity as we can.

CHAPTER X.

The Influence of Individuals upon Public Notions of Morality

Public notions of morality—Errors of public opinion: their effects—Duelling—Scottish Bench—Glory—Military virtues—Military talent—Bravery—Courage—Patriotism not the soldier's motive—Military fame—Public opinion of unchastity: In women: In men—Power of character—Character in Legal men—Fame—Faults of great men—The Press—Newspapers—History: Its defects: Its power.

38. That the influence of Public Opinion upon the practice of virtue is very great, needs no proof. Of this influence the reader has seen some remarkable illustrations in the discussion of the Efficacy of Oaths in binding to veracity.[1] There is, indeed, almost no action and no institution which Public Opinion does not affect. In moral affairs it makes men call one mode of human destruction murderous and one honourable; it makes the same action abominable in one individual and venial in another: in public institutions, from a village workhouse to the constitution of a state, it is powerful alike for evil or for good. If it be misdirected, it will strengthen and perpetuate corruption and abuse: if it be directed aright, it will eventually remove corruptions and correct abuses with a power which no power can withstand.

39. In proportion to the greatness of its power is the necessity of rectifying Public Opinion itself. To contribute to its rectitude is to exercise exalted philanthropy—to contribute to its incorrectness is to spread wickedness and misery in the world. The purpose of the present chapter is to remark upon some of those subjects on which the Public Opinion appears to be inaccurate, and upon the consequent obligation upon individuals not to perpetuate that inaccuracy and its attendant evils by their conduct or their language. Of the positive part of the obligation—that which respects the active correction of common opinions, little will be said. He who does not promote the evil can scarcely fail of promoting the good. A man often *must* deliver his sentiments respecting the principles and actions of others, and if he delivers them, so as not to encourage what is wrong, he will practically encourage what is right.

40. It might have been presumed of a people who assent to the authority of the Moral Law, that their notions of the merit or turpitude of actions would have been conformable with the doctrines which that law delivers. Far other is the fact. The estimates of the Moral Law and of public opinion are discordant to excess. Men have practised a sort of transposition with the moral precepts, and have assigned to them arbitrary and capricious, and therefore new and mischievous, stations on the moral scale. The order both of the vices and the virtues is greatly deranged.

41. Suppose, with respect to vices, the highest degree of reprobation in the Moral Law to be indicated by 20, and to descend by units, as the reprobation became less severe, and suppose, in the same manner, we put 20 for the highest offence according to popular opinion, and diminish the number as it accounts less of the offence, we should

[1] Essay 2, chap. 7.

probably be presented with some such graduation as this:

	Moral Law.	Public Opinion.	
Murder	20	20	
Human destruction under other names	18	0	
Unchastity, if of women	18	18	
Unchastity, if of men	18	2	
Theft	17	17	
Fraud and other modes of dishonesty	17	6—4 or 1	
Lying	17	17	
Lying for particular purposes or to particular classes of persons	17	2—or 0	
Resentment	16	6	and every inferior gradation.
Profaneness	15	12	and every inferior gradation.

42. We might make a similar statement of the virtues. This indeed is inevitable in the case of those virtues which are the opposites of some of these vices. Respecting others we may say—

	Moral Law.	Public Opinion.	
Forbearance	16	3	and lapsing into a vice.
Fortitude	16	10	
Courage	14	14	
Bravery	1	20	
Patriotism	2	20	
Placability	18	4	

43. How, it may reasonably be asked, do these strange incongruities arise? First, men practise a sort of voluntary deception on themselves: they persuade themselves to think that an offence which they desire to commit is not so vicious as the Moral Law indicates, or as others to which they have little temptation. They persuade themselves again, that a virtue which is easily practised is of great worth, because they thus flatter themselves with complacent notions of their excellences at a cheap rate. Virtues which are difficult they, for the same reason, depreciate. This is the dictate of interest. It is manifestly good policy to think lightly of the value of a quality which we do not choose to be at the cost of possessing; and who would willingly think there was much evil in a vice which he practised every day?—That which a man thus persuades himself to think a trivial vice or an unimportant virtue, he of course speaks of as such amongst his neighbours. They perhaps are as much interested in propagating the delusion as he: they listen with willing ears, and cherish and proclaim the grateful falsehood. By these and by other means the public notions become influenced; a long continuance of the general chicanery at length actually confounds the Public Opinion; and when once an opinion has become a public opinion, there is no difficulty in accounting for the perpetuation of the fallacy

44. If sometimes the mind of an individual recurs to the purer standard, a multitude of obstacles present themselves to its practical adoption. He hopes that under the present circumstances of society an exact obedience to the Moral Law is not required; he tries to think that the notions of a kingdom or a continent cannot be so erroneous; and at any rate trusts that as he deviates with millions, millions will hardly be held guilty at the bar of God. The misdirection of Public Opinion is an obstacle to the virtue even of good men. He who looks beyond the notions of others, and founds his moral principles upon the Moral Law, yet feels that it is more difficult to conform to that law when he is discountenanced by the general notions than if those notions supported and encouraged him. What then must the effect of such misdirection be upon those to whom acceptance in the world is the principal concern, and who, if others applaud or smile, seem to be indifferent whether their own hearts condemn them?

45. Now, with a participation in the evils which the misdirection of public opinion occasions, every one is chargeable who speaks of moral actions according to a standard that varies from that which Christianity has exhibited. Here is the cause of the evil, and here must be its remedy. "It is an important maxim in morals as well as in education to call things by their right names."[1] "To bestow good names on bad things, is to give them a passport in the world under a delusive disguise."[2] "The soft names and plausible colours under which deceit, sensuality, and revenge are presented to us in common discourse, weaken by degrees our natural sense of the distinction between good and evil."[3] Public notions of morality constitute a sort of line of demarcation, which is regarded by most men in their practice as a boundary between right and wrong. He who contributes to fix this boundary in the wrong place, who places evil on the side of virtue, or goodness on the side of vice, offends more deeply against the morality and the welfare of the world, than multitudes who are punished by the arm of law. If moral offences are to be estimated by their consequences, few wi'l be found so deep as that of habitually giving good names to bad things.[4] It is well indeed for the responsibility of individuals that their

[1] Rees's Encyclop., art. Philos. Moral.
[2] Knox's Essays, No. 34.   [3] Blair, Serm 9.
[4] Dr. Carpenter insists upon similar truths upon somewhat different subjects.— "If children hear us express as much approbation, and in the same terms, of the skill of a gentleman coach-driver, of the abilities of a philosophical lecturer, and of an individual who has just performed an elevated act of disinterested virtue, is it possible th t they should not feel great confusion of ideas? If each is termed a *n ble fellow*, with the same emphasis and animation, how can the youthful under t nding calculate with sufficient accuracy so as to appreciate the import of the expression in the same way that we should do?"—Principles of Education: Conscience.

contribution to the aggregate mischief is commonly small. Yet every man should remember that it is by the contribution of individuals that the aggregate is formed; and that it can only be by the deductions of individuals that it will be done away.

Duelling.

46. If two boys who disagreed about a game of marbles or a penny tart, should therefore walk out by the river-side, quietly take off their clothes, and when they had got into the water, each try to keep the other's head down until one of them was drowned, we should doubtless think that these two boys were mad. If, when the survivor returned to his schoolfellows, they patted him on the shoulder, told him he was a spirited fellow, and that, if he had not tried the feat in the water, they would never have played at marbles or any other game with him again, we should doubtless think that these boys were infected with a most revolting and disgusting depravity and ferociousness. We should instantly exert ourselves to correct their principles, and should feel assured that nothing could ever induce us to tolerate, much less to encourage, such abandoned depravity. And yet we do both tolerate and encourage such depravity every day. Change the penny tart for some other trifle; instead of boys put men, and instead of a river, a pistol—and we encourage it all. We virtually pat the survivor's shoulder, tell him he is a man of honour, and that, if he had not shot at his acquaintance, we would never have dined with him again. "Revolting and disgusting depravity" are at once excluded from our vocabulary. We substitute such phrases as "the course which a gentleman is obliged to pursue"—"it was necessary to his honour"—"one could not have associated with him if he had not fought." We are the schoolboys, grown up: and by the absurdity, and more than absurdity of our phrases and actions, shooting or drowning (it matters not which) becomes the practice of the national school.

47. It is not a trifling question that a man puts to himself when he asks, What is the amount of *my* contribution to this detestable practice? It is by individual contributions to the public notions respecting it that the practice is kept up. Men do not fire at one another because they are fond of risking their own lives or other men's, but because public notions are such as they are. Nor do I think any deduction can be more manifestly just, than that he who contributes to the misdirection of these notions is responsible for a share of the evil and the guilt. When some offence has given probability to a duel, every man acts immorally who evinces any disposition to coolness with either party until he has resolved to fight; and if eventually one of them falls, he is a party to his destruction. Every word of unfriendliness, every look of indifference, is positive guilt; for it is such words and such looks that drive men to their pistols. It is the same after a victim has fallen. "I pity his family, but they have the consolation of knowing that he vindicated his honour," is equivalent to urging another and another to fight. Every heedless gossip who asks, "Have you heard of this affair of honour?" and every reporter of news who relates it as a proper and necessary procedure, participates in the general crime.

48. If they who hear of an intended meeting amongst their friends hasten to manifest that they will continue their intercourse with the parties though they do not fight—if none talks of vindicating honour by demanding satisfaction—if he who speaks and he who writes of this atrocity, speaks and writes as reason and morals dictate, duelling will soon disappear from the world. To contribute to the suppression of the custom is therefore easy, and let no man, and let no woman, who does not, as occasion offers, express reprobation of the custom, think that their hands are clear of blood. They especially are responsible for its continuance whose station or general character gives peculiar influence to their opinions in its favour. What then are we to think of the conduct of a British judge who encourages it from the bench? A short time ago a person was tried on the Perth circuit for murder, having killed another in a duel. The evidence of the fact was undisputed. Before the verdict was pronounced, the judge is said to have used these words in his address to the jury: "The character you have heard testified by so many respectable and intelligent gentlemen this day, is *as high as is possible for man to receive*, and I consider that *throughout this affair the panel has acted up to it.*" So that it is laid down from the bench that the man who shoots another through the heart for striking him with an umbrella, acts up to the highest possible character of man! The prisoner, although every one knew he had killed the deceased, was acquitted, and the judge is reported to have addressed him thus: "You must be aware that the only duty I have to perform is to dismiss you from that bar with *a character unsullied.*"[1] If the judge's language be true, Christianity is an idle fiction. Who will wonder at the continuance of duelling, who will wonder that upon this subject the Moral Law is disregarded, if we are to be told that "unsullied character"—nay, that "the highest

[1] The trial is reported in the *Caledonian Mercury* of September 25, 1826.

possible character of man," is compatible with trampling Christianity under our feet?

49. How happy would it be for our country and for the world, how truly glorious for himself, if the king would act towards the duellist as his mother acted towards women who had lost their reputation. She rigidly excluded them from her presence. If the British monarch refused to allow the man who had fought a duel to approach him, it is probable that erelong duelling would be abolished, not merely in this country, but in the Christian world. Nor will true Christian respect be violated by the addition, that in proportion to the power of doing good is the responsibility for omitting it.

Glory: Military Virtues.

50. To prove that war is an evil were much the same as to prove that the light of the sun is a good. And yet, though no one will dispute the truth, there are few who consider, and few who know how great the evil is. The practice is encircled with so many glittering fictions, that most men are content with but a vague and inadequate idea of the calamities, moral, physical, and political, which it inflicts upon our species. But if few men consider how prodigious its mischiefs are, they see enough to agree in the conclusion, that the less frequently it happens the better for the common interests of man. Supposing then that some wars are lawful and unavoidable, it is nevertheless manifest, that whatever tends to make them more frequent than necessity requires, must be very pernicious to mankind. Now, in consequence of a misdirection of public notions, this needless frequency exists. Public opinion is favourable, not so much to war in the abstract or in practice, as to the profession of arms; and the inevitable consequence is this, that war itself is greatly promoted without reference to the causes for which it may be undertaken. By attaching notions of honour to the military profession, and of glory to military achievements, three wars probably have been occasioned where there otherwise would have been but one. To talk of the "splendours of conquest" and the "glories of victory," to extol those who "fall covered with honour in their country's cause," is to occasion the recurrence of wars, not because they are necessary, but because they are desired. It is in fact contributing, according to the speaker's power, to desolate provinces and set villages in flames, to ruin thousands and destroy thousands—to inflict, in brief, all the evils and the miseries which war inflicts. "Splendours,"—"Glories,"— "Honours!"—the listening soldier wants to signalise himself like the heroes who are departed; he wants to thrust his sickle into the fields of fame and reap undying laurels: How shall he signalise himself without a war, and on what field can he reap glory but in the field of battle? The consequence is inevitable: Multitudes desire war;—they are fond of war—and it requires no sagacity to discover, that to desire and to love it is to make it likely to happen. Thus a perpetual motive to human destruction is created, of which the tendency is as inevitable as the tendency of a stone to fall to the earth. The present state of public opinion manifestly promotes the recurrence of wars of all kinds, necessary (if such there are) and unnecessary. It promotes wars of pure aggression, of the most unmingled wickedness; it promoted the wars of the departed Louises and Napoleons. It awards "glory" to the soldier wherever be his achievements and in whatever cause.

51. Now, waiving the after consideration as to the nature of Glory itself, the individual may judge of his duties with respect to public opinion by its effects. To minister to the popular notions of glory is to encourage needless wars; it is therefore his duty not to minister to those notions. Common talk by a man's fireside contributes its little to the universal evil, and shares in the universal offence. Of the writers of some books it is not too much to suppose that they have occasioned more murders than all the clubs and pistols of assassins for ages have effected. Is there no responsibility for this?

52. But perhaps it will afford to some men new ideas if we inquire what the real nature of the military virtues is. They receive more of applause than virtues of any other kind. How does this happen? We must seek a solution in the seeming paradox that their pretensions to the characters of Virtues are few and small. They receive much applause because they merit little. They could not subsist without it; and if men resolve to practise war, and consequently to require the conduct which gives success to war, they must decorate that conduct with glittering fictions, and extol the military virtues though they be neither good nor great. Of every species of real excellence it is the general characteristic that it is not anxious for applause. The more elevated the virtue the less the desire, and the less is the public voice a motive to action. What should we say of that man's benevolence who would not relieve a neighbour in distress unless the donation would be praised in a newspaper? What should we say of that man's piety who prayed only when he was "seen of men"? But the military virtues live upon applause; it is their vital element and their food, their great pervading motive and reward. Are there, then, amongst the respective virtues

such discordances of character—such total contrariety of nature and essence? No, no. But how, then, do you account for the fact, that whilst all other great virtues are independent of public praise and stand aloof from it, the military virtues can scarcely exist without it?

53. It is again a characteristic of exalted Virtue that it tends to produce exalted virtues of other kinds. He that is distinguished by diffusive benevolence, is rarely chargeable with profaneness or debauchery. The man of piety is not seen drunk. The man of candour and humility is not vindictive or unchaste. Can the same things be predicated of the tendency of military virtues? Do they tend powerfully to the production of all other virtues? Is the brave man peculiarly pious? Is the military patriot peculiarly chaste? Is he who pants for glory and acquires it, distinguished by unusual placability and temperance? No, no. How then do you account for the fact that whilst other virtues thus strongly tend to produce and to foster one another,[1] the military virtues have little of such tendency, or none?

54. The simple truth, however veiled and however unwelcome, is this, that the military virtues will not endure examination. They are called what they are not, or what they are in a very inferior degree to that which popular notions imply. It would not serve the purposes of war to represent these qualities as being what they are; we therefore dress them with factitious and alluring ornaments; and they have been dressed so long that we admire the show, and forget to inquire what is underneath. Our applauses of military virtues do not adorn them like the natural bloom of loveliness; it is the paint of that which, if seen, would not attract, if it did not repel us. They are not like the verdure which adorns the meadow, but the greenness that conceals a bog. If the reader says that we indulge in declamation, we invite, we solicit him to investigate the truth. And yet, without inquiring further, there is conclusive evidence in the fact, that glory, that praise, is the vital principle of military virtue. Let us take sound rules for our guides of judgment, and it is not possible that we should regard any quality as possessing much virtue which lives only or chiefly upon praise. And who will pretend that the ranks of armies would be filled if no tongue talked of bravery and glory, and no newspaper published the achievements of a regiment?[2]

55. "Truth is a naked and open daylight, that doth not show the masques and mummeries and triumphs of the world half so stately and daintily as candlelights."[1] Let us dismiss, then, that candlelight examination which men are wont to adopt when they contemplate military virtues, and see what appearance they exhibit in the daylight of truth. Military *talent*, and *active courage*, and *patriotism*, or some other motive, appear to be the foundations and the subjects of our applause.

56. With respect to talent, little needs to be said, since few have an opportunity of displaying it. An able general may exhibit his capacity for military affairs; but of the mass of those who join in battles and participate in their "glories," little more is expected than that they should be obedient and brave. And as to the few who have the opportunity of displaying talent and who do display it, it is manifest that their claims to merit, independently of the purpose to which their talent is devoted, is little or none. A man deserves no applause for the possession or for the exercise of talent as such. One man may possess and exercise as much ability in corrupting the principles of his readers, as another who corrects and purifies them. One man may exhibit as much ability in swindling, as another in effectually legislating against swindlers. To applaud the *possession* of talent is absurd, and, like many other absurd actions, is greatly pernicious. Our approbation should depend on the objects upon which the talent is employed. Military talents, like all others, are only so far proper subjects of approbation as they are employed aright. Yet the popular notion appears to be, that the display of talent in a military leader is, *per se*, entitled to praise. You might as well applaud the dexterity of a corrupt minister of state. The truth is, that talent, as such, is not a proper subject of moral approbation any more than strength or beauty. But if we thus take away from the "glories" of military leaders all but that which is founded upon the causes in which their talents were engaged, what will remain to the Alexanders, and the Cæsars, and the Jenghizes, and the Louises, and the Charleses, and the Napoleons, with whose "glories" the idle voice of fame is filled? "Tout ce qui peut etre commun aux bons et aux méchans, ne le rend point véritablement estimable." Cannot military talents be exhibited indifferently by the good and the bad? Are they not in fact as often exhibited

than the love of riches:"[1] and it is pleasant to hear one of our then principal Reviews say, "Glory is the most selfish of all passions except love."[2] That which is selfish can hardly be very virtuous.
[1] Lord Bacon: Essays.

---

[1] "The virtues are nearly related, and live in the greatest harmony with each other."—OPIE.
[2] It is pleasant to hear an intelligent *woman* say, "I cannot tell how or why the love of glory is a less selfish principle

[1] Memoirs of late Jane Taylor. [2] West. Rev., No. 13.

by vicious men as by virtuous? They are, and therefore they are not really deserving of praise. But if any man should say that the circumstance of a leader's exerting his talents "for his king and country" is of itself a good cause, and therefore entitles him to praise, I answer that such a man is deluding himself with idle fictions. I hope presently to show this. Meanwhile it is to be remarked that if this be a valid claim to approbation, " king and country" must always be in the right. Who will affirm this? And yet, if it is not shown, you may as well applaud the brigand chief with his thirty followers as the greater marauder with his thirty thousand.

57. Valour and bravery, however, may be exhibited by the many—not by generals and admirals alone, but by ensigns and midshipmen, by seamen and by privates. What then is valour, and what is bravery? "There is nothing great but what is virtuous, nor indeed truly great but what is composed and quiet."[1] There is much of truth in this. Yet where then is the greatness of bravery, for where is the composure and quietude of the quality? " Valour or active courage is for the most part constitutional, and therefore can have no more claim to moral merit than wit, beauty, or health."[2] Accordingly, the question which we have just asked respecting military talent may be especially asked respecting bravery. Cannot bravery be exhibited in common by the good and the bad?—Yet further. " It is a great weakness for a man to value himself upon anything wherein he shall be outdone by fools and brutes." Is not the bravery of the bravest outdone even by brutes. When the soldier has vigorously assaulted the enemy, when though repulsed he returns to the conflict, when being wounded he still brandishes his sword, till it drops from his grasp by faintness or death—he surely is brave. What then is the moral rank to which he has attained? He has attained to the rank of a bull-dog. The dog, too, vigorously assails his enemy; when tossed into the air he returns to the conflict; when gored he still continues to bite, and yields not his hold until he is stunned or killed. Contemplating bravery as such, there is not a man in Britain or in Europe whose bravery entitles him to praise which he must not share with the combatants of a cockpit. Of the moral qualities that are components of bravery, the reader may form some conception from this language of a man who is said to be a large landed proprietor, a magistrate, and a member of Parliament. " I am one of those who think that *evil alone* does not result from poaching. The risk poachers run from the dangers that beset them, added to their occupation being carried on in cold dark nights, begets a hardihood of frame and contempt of danger that is not without its value. I never heard or knew of a poacher being a coward. They all make *good soldiers;* and military men are well aware that two or three men in each troop or company, of bold and enterprising spirits, are not without their effect on their comrades." The same may of course be said of smugglers and highwaymen. If these are the characters in whom we are peculiarly to seek for bravery, what are the moral qualities of bravery itself? All just, all rational, and I will venture to affirm all *permanent* reputation refers to the mind or to virtue; and what connection has animal power or animal hardihood with intellect or goodness? I do not decry *courage:* He who was better acquainted than we are with the nature and worth of human actions attached much value to courage, but He attached none to bravery.[1] Courage He recommended by His precepts and enforced by His example: bravery He never recommended at all. The wisdom of this distinction and its accordancy with the principles of His religion are plain. Bravery requires the existence of many of those dispositions which He disallowed. Animosity, the desire of retaliation, the disposition to injure and destroy— all this is necessary to the existence of bravery, but all this is incompatible with Christianity. The courage which Christianity requires is to bravery what fortitude is to daring—an effort of the mental principles rather than of the spirits. It is a calm steady determinateness of purpose, that will not be diverted by solicitation or awed by fear. " Behold, I go bound in the spirit unto Jerusalem, not knowing the things that shall befall me there; save that the Holy Ghost witnesseth in every city, saying that bonds and afflictions abide me. *But none of these things move me, neither count I my life dear unto myself.*"[2] What resemblance has bravery to courage like this? This courage is a virtue, and a virtue which it is difficult to acquire or to practise; and we have heedlessly or ingeniously transferred its praise to another quality which is inferior in its nature and easier to acquire, in order that we may obtain the reputation of virtue at a cheap rate.

58. Of those who thus extol the lower qualities of our nature, few perhaps are conscious to what a degree they are deluded. In exhibiting this delusion let us not forget the purpose for which it is done. The popular notion respecting bravery does not terminate in an innoxious mistake. The consequences are practically and greatly

[1] Seneca.
[2] Soame Jenyns: Internal Evid. of Christianity, Prop. 3.

[1] "Whatever merit valour may have assumed among Pagans, with Christians it can pretend to none."—Soame Jenyns: Internal Evid. of Christianity, Prop. 3.
[2] Acts xx. 22.

evil. He that has placed his hopes upon the praises of valour, desires of course an opportunity of acquiring them, and this opportunity he cannot find but in the destruction of men. That such powerful motives will lead to this destruction when even ambition can scarcely find a pretext, we need not the testimony of experience to assure us. It is enough that we consider the principles which actuate mankind.

59. And if we turn from actions to motives, from bravery to patriotism, we are presented with similar delusions, and with similar mischiefs as their consequence. To "fight nobly for our country," to "fall covered with glory in our country's cause," to "sacrifice our lives for the liberties and laws and religion of our country," are phrases in the mouth of multitudes. What do they mean, and to whom do they apply? We contend, that to say generally of those who perish in war that "they have died for their country," is simply untrue: and for this simple reason, that they did not fight for it. It is not true that patriotism is their motive. Why is a boy destined from school for the army? Is it that his father is more patriotic than his neighbour, who destines his son for the bar? Or if the boy himself begs his father to buy an ensigncy, is it because he loves his country, or is it because he dreams of glory, and admires scarlet and plumes and swords? The officer enters the service in order that he may obtain an income, not in order to benefit his fellow-citizens. The private enters it because he prefers a soldier's life to another, or because he has no wish but the wish for change. And having entered the army, what is the motive that induces the private or his superiors to fight? It is that fighting is part of their business; that it is one of the conditions upon which they were hired. Patriotism is *not* the motive. Of those who fall in battle, is there one in a hundred who even thinks of his country's good? He thinks perhaps of glory and of the fame of his regiment, he hopes perhaps that "Salamanca," or "Austerlitz" will henceforth be inscribed on its colours; but rational views of his country's welfare are foreign to his mind. He has scarcely a thought about the matter. He fights in battle as a horse draws in a carriage, because he is compelled to do it, or because he has done it before: but he probably thinks no more of his country's good than the same horse, if he were carrying corn to a granary, would think he was providing for the comforts of his master. The truth therefore is, that we give to the soldier that of which we are wont to be sufficiently sparing—a gratuitous concession of merit. If he but "fights bravely," he is a patriot and secure of his praise.

60. To sacrifice our lives for the liberties and laws and religion of our native land, are undoubtedly high-sounding words; but who are they that will do it? Who is it that will sacrifice his life for his country? Will the senator who supports a war? Will the writer who declaims upon patriotism? Will the minister of religion who recommends the sacrifice? Take away war and its fictions, and there is not a man of them who will do it. Will he sacrifice his life *at home?* If the loss of his life in London or at York would procure just so much benefit to his country as the loss of one soldier's in the field, would he be willing to lay his head upon the block? Is he willing, for such a contribution to his country's good, to resign himself without notice and without remembrance to the executioner? Alas for the fictions of war! where is such a man? Men will not sacrifice their lives at all unless it be in war; and they do not sacrifice them in war from motives of patriotism. In no rational use of language, therefore, can it be said that the soldier "dies for his country."

61. Not that there may not be, or that there have not been, persons who fight from motives of patriotism. But the occurrence is comparatively rare. There may be physicians who qualify themselves for practice from motives of benevolence to the sick, or lawyers who assume the gown in order to plead for the injured and oppressed; but it is an unusual motive, and so is patriotism to the soldier.

62. And after all, even if all soldiers fought out of zeal for their country, what is the merit of Patriotism itself? I do not say that it possesses no virtue, but I affirm, and hope hereafter to show, that its virtue is extravagantly overrated,[1] and that if every one who fought did fight for his country, he would often be actuated only by a mode of selfishness—of selfishness which sacrifices the general interests of the species to the interests of a part.

63. Such and so low are the qualities which have obtained from deluded and deluding millions fame, honours, glories. A prodigious structure, and almost without a base:—a structure so vast, so brilliant, so attractive, that the greater portion of mankind are content to gaze in admiration, without any inquiry into its basis or any solicitude for its durability. If, however, it should be that the gorgeous temple will be able to stand only till Christian truth and light become predominant, it surely will be wise of those who seek a niche in its apartments as their paramount and final good to pause ere they proceed. If they desire a reputation that

[1] Essay 3. c. 17.

shall outlive guilt and fiction, let them look to the basis of military fame. If this fame should one day sink into oblivion and contempt, it will not be the first instance in which wide-spread glory has been found to be a glittering bubble that has burst and been forgotten. Look at the days of chivalry. Of the ten thousand Quixotes of the middle ages, where is now the honour or the name? Yet poets once sang their praises, and the chronicler of their achievements believed he was recording an everlasting fame. Where are now the glories of the tournament? Glories

"Of which all Europe rang from side to side."

Where is the champion whom princesses caressed and nobles envied? Where are the triumphs of Scotus and Aquinas, and where are the folios that *perpetuated* their fame? The glories of war have indeed outlived these; human passions are less mutable than human follies; but I am willing to avow the conviction, that these glories are alike destined to sink into forgetfulness, and that the time is approaching when the applauses of heroism and the splendours of conquest will be remembered only as follies and iniquities that are past. Let him who seeks for fame other than that which an era of Christian purity will allow, make haste; for every hour that he delays its acquisition will shorten its duration. This is certain if there be certainty in the promises of Heaven.

64. But we must not forget the *purpose* for which these illustrations of the Military Virtues are offered to the reader;—to remind him not merely that they are fictions, but fictions which are the occasion of excess of misery to mankind—to remind him that it is his business, from considerations of humanity and of religion, to refuse to give currency to the popular delusions—and to remind him that, if he does promote them, he promotes, by the act, misery in all its forms and guilt in all its excesses. Upon such subjects, men are not left to exercise their own inclinations. Morality interposes its commands; and they are commands which, if we would be moral, we must obey.

Unchastity.

65. No portion of these pages is devoted to the enforcement of moral obligations upon this subject, partly because these obligations are commonly acknowledged how little soever they may be regarded, and partly because, as the reader will have seen, the object of these Essays is to recommend those applications of the Moral Law which are frequently neglected in the practice even of respectable men. But in reference to the influence of public opinion on offences connected with the sexual constitution, it will readily be perceived

that something should be said, when it is considered that some of the popular notions respecting them are extravagantly inconsistent with the Moral Law. The want of chastity in a woman is visited by public opinion with the severest reprobation—in men, with very little or with none. Now, morality makes no such distinction. The offence is frequently adverted to in the Christian Scriptures; but I believe there is no one precept which intimates that, in the estimation of its writer, there was any difference in the turpitude of the offence respectively in men and women. If it be in this volume that we are to seek for the principles of the Moral Law, how shall we defend the state of popular opinion? "If unchastity in a woman, whom St. Paul terms the glory of man, be such a scandal and dishonour, then certainly in a man, who is both the image and glory of God, it must, though commonly not so thought, be much more deflowering and dishonourable."[1] But this departure from the Moral Law, like all other departures, produces its legitimate, that is, pernicious effects. The sex in whom popular opinion reprobates the offences comparatively seldom commits them: the sex in whom it tolerates the offences commits them to an enormous extent. It is obvious, therefore, that to promote the present state of popular opinion is to promote and to encourage the want of chastity in men.

66. That some very beneficial consequences result from the strong direction of its current against the offence in a woman is certain. The consciousness that upon the retention of her reputation depends so tremendous a stake, is probably a more efficacious motive to its preservation than any other. The abandonment to which the loss of personal integrity generally consigns a woman is a perpetual and fearful warning to the sex. Almost every human being deprecates and dreads the general disfavour of mankind; and thus, notwithstanding temptations of all kinds, the number of women who do incur it is comparatively small.

67. But the fact that public opinion is thus powerful in restraining one sex is a sufficient evidence that it would also be powerful in restraining the other. Waiving for the present the question whether the popular disapprobation of the crime in a woman is not too severe—if the man who was guilty was forthwith and immediately consigned to infamy; if he was expelled from virtuous society, and condemned for the remainder of life to the lowest degradation, how quickly would the frequency of the crime be diminished! The reformation

[1] Milton, Christian Doctrine, p. 624.

amongst men would effect a reformation amongst women too; and the reciprocal temptations which each addresses to the other would in a great degree be withdrawn. If there were few seducers few would be seduced, and few therefore would in turn become the seducers of men.

68. But instead of this direction of public opinion, what is the ordinary language respecting the man who thus violates the Moral Law? We are told that "he is rather unsteady;" that "there is a little of the young man about him;" that "he is not free from indiscretions." And what is he likely to think of all this? Why, that for a young man to have a little of the young man about him is perfectly natural : that to be rather unsteady and a little indiscreet is not, to be sure, what one would wish, but that it is no great harm and will soon wear off. To employ such language is, we say, to encourage and promote the crime—a crime which brings more wretchedness and vice into the world than almost any other; and for which, if Christianity is to be believed, the Universal Judge will call to a severe account. If the immediate agent be obnoxious to punishment, can he who encouraged him expect to escape? I am persuaded that the frequency of this gross offence is attributable much more to the levity of public notions as founded upon levity of language than to passion; and perhaps, therefore, some of those who promote this levity may be in every respect as criminal as if they committed the crime itself.

69. Women themselves contribute greatly to the common levity and to its attendant mischiefs. Many a female who talks in the language of abhorrence of an offending sister, and averts her eye in contumely if she meets her in the street, is perfectly willing to be the friend and intimate of the equally offending man. That such women are themselves duped by the vulgar distinction is not to be doubted—but then we are not to imagine that she who practises this inconsistency abhors the crime so much as the criminal. Her abhorrence is directed, not so much to the violation of the Moral Law as to the party by whom it is violated. "To little respect has that woman a claim on the score of modesty, though her reputation may be white as the driven snow, who smiles on the libertine whilst she spurns the victims of his lawless appetites." No, no. If such women would convince us that it is the *impurity* which they reprobate, let them reprobate it wherever it is found : if they would convince us that morals or philanthropy is their motive when they spurn the sinning sister, let them give proof by spurning him who has occasioned her to sin.

70. The common style of narrating occurrences and trials of seduction, &c., in the public prints is very mischievous. These flagitious actions are, it seems, a legitimate subject of merriment; one of the many droll things which a newspaper contains. It is humiliating to see respectable men sacrifice the interests of society to such small temptation. They pander to the appetite of the gross and idle of the public : —they want to sell their newspapers.—Much of this ill-timed merriment is found in the addresses of counsel, and this is one mode amongst the many in which the legal profession appears to think itself licensed to sacrifice virtue to the usages which it has, for its own advantage, adopted. There is cruelty as well as other vices in these things. When we take into account the intense suffering which prostitution produces upon its victims and upon their friends, he who contributes, even thus indirectly, to its extension, does not exhibit even a tolerable sensibility to human misery. Even infidelity acknowledges the claims of humanity; and therefore, if religion and religious morals were rejected, this heartless levity of language would still be indefensible. We call the man *benevolent* who relieves or diminishes wretchedness : what should we call him who extends and increases it?

71. In connection with this subject, an observation suggests itself respecting the power of *Character* in affecting the whole moral principles of the mind. If loss of character does not follow a breach of morality, that breach may be single and alone. The agent's virtue is so far deteriorated, but the breach does not open wide the door to other modes of crime. If loss of character does follow one offence, one of the great barriers which exclude the flood of evil is thrown down; and though the offence which produced loss of character be really no greater than the offence with which it is retained, yet its consequences upon the moral condition are incomparably greater. The reason is, that if you take away a person's reputation you take away one of the principal motives to propriety of conduct. The labourer who, being tempted to steal a piece of bacon from the farmer, finds that no one will take him into his house or give him employment, and that wherever he goes he is pointed at as a thief, is almost as much *driven* as tempted to repeat the crime. His fellow-labourer, who has much more heinously violated the Moral Law by a flagitious intrigue with a servant girl, receives from the farmer a few reproaches and a few jests, retains his place,

never perhaps repeats the offence, and subsequently maintains a decent morality.

72. It has been said, "As a woman collects all her virtue into this point, the loss of her chastity is generally the destruction of her moral principle." What is to be understood by collecting virtue into one point it is not easy to discover. The truth is, that as popular notions have agreed that she who loses her chastity shall retain no reputation, a principal motive to the practice of other virtues is taken away:—she therefore disregards them; and thus by degrees her moral principle is utterly depraved. If public opinion was so modified that the world did not abandon a woman who has been robbed of chastity, it is probable that a much larger number of these unhappy persons would return to virtue. The case of men offers illustration and proof. The unchaste man retains his character, or at any rate he retains so much that it is of great importance to him to preserve the remainder. Public Opinion accordingly holds its strong rein upon other parts of his conduct, and by this rein he is restrained from deviating into other walks of vice. If the direction of Public Opinion were exchanged, if the woman's offence were held venial and the man's infamous, the world might stand in wonder at the altered scene. We should have worthy and respectable prostitutes, while the men whom we now invite to our tables and marry to our daughters would be repulsed as the most abandoned of mankind. Of this I have met with a curious illustration. Amongst the North American Indians "seduction is regarded as a despicable crime, and more blame is attached to the man than to the woman: hence the offence on the part of the female is *more readily forgotten* and *forgiven*, and she finds little or no difficulty in forming a subsequent matrimonial alliance when deserted by her betrayer, who is *generally regarded with distrust and avoided in social intercourse*."[1]

73. It becomes a serious question how we shall fix upon the degree in which diminution of character ought to be consequent upon offences against morality. It is not, I think, too much to say, that no single crime, once committed, under the influence perhaps of strong temptation, ought to occasion *such* a loss of character as to make the individual regard himself as abandoned. I make no exceptions—not even for murder. I am persuaded that some murders are committed with less of personal guilt than is sometimes involved in much smaller crimes: but however that may be, there is no reason why, even to the murderer, the motives and the avenues to amendment should be closed. Still less ought they to be closed against the female who is perhaps the victim—strictly the *victim*—of seduction. Yet if the public do not express, and strongly express, their disapprobation, we have seen that they practically encourage offences. In this difficulty I know of no better and no other guide than that system which the tenor of Christianity prescribes—Abhorrence of the evil and commiseration of him who commits it. The union of these dispositions will be likely to produce, with respect to offences of all kinds, that conduct which most effectually tends to discountenance them, while it as effectually tends to reform the offenders. These, however, are not the dispositions which actuate the public in measuring their reprobation of unchastity in women. Something probably might rightly be deducted from the severity with which their offence is visited: much may be rightly altered in the *motives* which induce this severity. And as to men, much should be added to the quantum of reprobation, and much correction should be applied to the principles by which it is regulated.

74. Another illustration of the power of character, as such, to corrupt the principles or to preserve them is furnished in the general respectability of the legal profession. We have seen that this profession, habitually and as a matter of course, violates many and great points of morality, and yet I know not that their character as men is considerably inferior to that of others in similar walks of life. Abating the *privileges* under which the profession is presumed to act, many of their legal procedures are as flagitious as some of those which send unprivileged professions to the bar of justice. How then does it happen that the moral offenders whom we imprison, and try, and punish are commonly in their general conduct depraved, whilst the equal offenders whom we do not punish are not thus depraved? The prisoner has usually lost much of his reputation before he becomes a thief, and at any rate he loses it with the act. But a man may enter the customary legal course with a fair name: Public Opinion has not so reprobated that course as to make it necessary to its pursuit that a man should already have become depraved. Whilst engaged in the ordinary legal practice he may be unjust at his desk or at the bar, he may there commit actions essentially and greatly wicked, and yet when he steps into his parlour his character is not reproached. A jest or two upon his adroitness is probably all the intimation that he receives that other men do not regard it with perfect complacency. Such a man will not pick your pocket the more readily because he has picked a hundred pockets at the bar. *This* were to sacrifice his character: the other does not; and accordingly all those

---

[1] Hunter's Memoirs.

motives to rectitude which the desire of preserving reputation supplies operate to restrain him from other offences. If public opinion were rectified, if character were lost by actual violations of the Moral Law, some of the ordinary processes of legal men would be practised only by those who had little character to lose. Not indeed that Public Opinion is silent respecting the habitual conduct of the profession. A secret disapprobation manifestly exists, of which sufficient evidence may be found even in the lampoons, and satires, and proverbs, which pass currently in the world. Unhappily, the disapprobation is too slight, and especially it is too slightly expressed. When it is thus expressed, the lawyer sometimes unites, with at least apparent good-humour, in the jest—feeling, perhaps, that conduct which cannot be shown to be virtuous, it is politic to keep without the pale of the vices by a joke.

Fame.

75. The observations which were offered respecting contributing to the passion for glory involve kindred doctrines respecting contributions generally to individual Fame. If the pretensions of those with whose applauses the popular voice is filled were examined by the only proper test, the test which Christianity allows, it would be found that multitudes whom the world thus honours must be shorn of their beams. Before Bacon's daylight of truth, Poets and Statesmen and Philosophers without number would hide their diminished heads. The mighty indeed would be fallen. Yet it is for the acquisition of this fame that multitudes toil. It is their motive to action, and they pursue that conduct which will procure fame whether it ought to procure it or not. The inference as to the duties of individuals in contributing to fame is obvious.

76. "The profligacy of a man of fashion is looked upon with much less contempt and aversion than that of a man of meaner condition."[1] It ought to be looked upon with much more. But men of fashion are not our concern. Our business is with men of talent and genius, with the eminent and the great. The profligacy of these, too, is regarded with much less of aversion than that of less gifted men. To be great, whether intellectually or otherwise, is often like a passport to impunity; and men talk as if we *ought* to speak leniently of the faults of a man who delights us by his genius or his talent. This precisely is the man whose faults we should be most prompt to mark, because he is the man whose faults are most seducing to the world. Intellectual superiority brings, no doubt, its congenial temptations. Let these affect our judgments of the man, but let them not diminish our reprobation of his offences. So to extenuate the individual as to apologise for his faults is to injure the cause of virtue in one of its most vulnerable parts. "Oh! that I could see in men who oppose tyranny in the state a disdain of the tyranny of low passions in themselves. I cannot reconcile myself to the idea of an immoral patriot, or to that separation of private from public virtue which some men think to be possible."[1] Probably it is possible : probably there may be such a thing as an immoral patriot : for public opinion applauds the patriotism without condemning the immorality. If men constantly made a fit deduction from their praises of public virtue on account of its association with private vice, the union would frequently be severed; and he who hoped for celebrity from the public would find it needful to be good as well as great. He who applauds human excellence and really admires it should endeavour to make its examples as pure and perfect as he can. He should hold out a motive to consistency of excellence, by evincing that nothing else can obtain praise unmingled with censure. This endeavour should be constant and uniform. The hearer should never be allowed to suppose that in appreciating a person's merits we are indifferent to his faults. It has been complained of one of our principal works of Periodical Literature, that amongst its many and ardent praises of Shakspeare, it has almost never alluded to his indecencies. The silence is reprehensible : for what is a reader to conclude but that indecency is a very venial offence? Under such circumstances, not to be *with* morality is to be *against* it. Silence is positive mischief. People talk to us of liberality, and of allowances for the aberrations of genius, and for the temptations of greatness. It is well. Let the allowances be made.—But this is frequently only affectation of candour. It is not that we are lenient to failings, but that we are indifferent to vice. It is not even enlightened benevolence to genius or greatness itself. The faults and vices with which talented men are chargeable deduct greatly from their own happiness ; and it cannot be doubted that their misdeeds have been the more willingly committed from the consciousness that apologists would be found amongst the admiring world. It is sufficient to make that world knit its brow in anger to insist upon the moral demerits of a Robert Burns. Pathetic and voluble extenuations are instantly urged. There are extenuations of such a man's vices, and they ought to be regarded; but no extenuations can remove the charge of voluntary and intentional violations of morality. Let us not

---

[1] Ad. Smith: Theo. Mor. Sent.   [1] Dr. Price: Revolution Serm.

hear of the enthusiasm of poetry. Men do not write poetry as they chatter with their neighbours: they sit down to a deliberate act; and he who in his verses offends against morals, intentionally and deliberately offends.

77. After all, posterity exercises some justice in its award. When the first glitter and the first applauses are past—when death and a few years of sobriety have given opportunity to the public mind to attend to truth, it makes a deduction, though not a due deduction, for the shaded portions of the great man's character. It is not forgotten that Marlborough was avaricious, that Bacon was mean; and there are great names of the present day of whom it will not be forgotten that they had deep and dark shades in their reputation. It is perhaps wonderful that those who seek for fame are so indifferent to these deductions from its amount. Supposing the intellectual pretensions of Newton and Voltaire were equal, how different is their fame! How many and how great qualifications are employed in praising the one! How few and how small in praising the other! Editions of the works of some of our first writers are advertised, " in which the exceptionable passages are expunged." How foolish, how uncalculating even as to celebrity, to have inserted these passages! To write in the hope of fame, works which posterity will mutilate before they place them in their libraries! Charles James Fox said, that if, during his administration, they could effect the abolition of the slave trade, it "would entail more true glory upon them, and more honour upon their country, than any other transaction in which they could be engaged."[1] If this be true (and who will dispute it?) ministers usually provide very ill for their reputation with posterity. How anxiously devoted to measures comparatively insignificant! How phlegmatic respecting those calls of humanity and public principle, a regard of which will *alone* secure the permanent honours of the world! It may safely be relied upon that "much more unperishable is the greatness of goodness than the greatness of power,"[2] or the greatness of talent. And the difference will progressively increase. If, as there is reason to believe, the moral condition of mankind will improve, their estimate of the *good* portion of a great man's character will be enhanced, and their reprobation of the bad will become more intense—until at length it will perhaps be found, respecting some of those who now receive the applauses of the world, that the balance of public opinion is against them, and that, in the universal estimate of merit and demerit, they will be ranked on the side of the latter. These motives to virtue in great men are not

[1] Fell's Memoirs.   [2] Sir R. K. Porter.

addressed to the Christian: he has higher motives and better: but since it is more desirable that a man should act well from imperfect motives than that he should act ill, we urge him to regard the integrity of his fame.

The Press.

78. It is manifest that if the obligations which have been urged apply to those who speak, they apply with tenfold responsibility to those who write. The man who, in talking to half a dozen of his acquaintance, contributes to confuse or pervert their moral notions, is accountable for the mischief which he may do to six persons. He who writes a book containing similar language is answerable for as much greater amount of mischief as the number of his readers may exceed six, and as the influence of books exceeds that of conversation, by the evidence of greater deliberation in their contents and by the greater attention which is paid by the reader. It is not a light matter, even in this view, to write a book for the public. We very insufficiently consider the amount of the obligations and the extent of the responsibility which we entail upon ourselves. Every one knows the power of the press in influencing the public mind. He that publishes five hundred copies of a book, of which any part is likely to derange the moral judgment of a reader, contributes materially to the propagation of evil. If each of his books is read by four persons, he endangers the infliction of this evil, whatever be its amount, upon two thousand minds. Who shall tell the sum of the mischief? In this country the periodical press is a powerful engine for evil or for good. The influence of the contents of one number of a newspaper may be small, but it is perpetually recurring. The editor of a journal, of which no more than a thousand copies are circulated in a week, and each of which is read by half a dozen persons, undertakes in a year a part of the moral guidance of thirty thousand individuals. Of some daily papers the number of readers is so great, that in the course of twelve months they may influence the opinions and the conduct of six or eight millions of men. To say nothing therefore of editors who intentionally mislead and vitiate the public, and remembering with what carelessness respecting the moral tendency of articles a newspaper is filled, it may safely be concluded that some creditable editors do harm in the world to an extent in comparison with which robberies and treasons are as nothing.

79. It is not easy to imagine the sum of advantages which would result if the periodical press not only excluded that which does harm, but preferred that which does good. Not that grave moralities, not, especially,

PUBLIC NOTIONS OF MORALITY.

that religious disquisitions are to be desired; but that every reader should see and feel that the editor maintained an allegiance to virtue and to truth. There is hardly any class of topics in which this allegiance may not be manifested, and manifested without any incongruous associations. You may relate the common occurrences of the day in such a manner as to do either good or evil. The trial of a thief, the particulars of a conflagration, the death of a statesman, the criticism of a debate, and a hundred other matters, may be recorded so as to exercise a moral influence over the reader for the better or the worse. That the influence is frequently for the worse needs no proof; and it is so much the less defensible because it may be changed to the contrary without a word directly respecting morals or religion.

80. However, newspapers do much more good than harm, especially in politics. They are in this country one of the most vigorous and beneficial instruments of political advantage. They effect incalculable benefit both in checking the statesman who would abuse power, and in so influencing the public opinion as to prepare it for, and therefore to render necessary, an amelioration of political and civil institutions. The great desideratum is enlargement of views and purity of principle. We want in editorial labours less of partisanship, less of petty squabbles about the worthless discussions of the day : we want more of the *philosophy* of politics, more of that grasping intelligence which can send a reader's reflections from facts to principles. Our journals are, to what they ought to be, what a chronicle of the Middle Ages is to a philosophical history. The disjointed fragments of political intelligence ought to be connected by a sort of enlightened running commentary. There is talent enough embarked in some of these ; but the talent too commonly expends itself upon subjects and in speculations which are of little interest beyond the present week.

81. And here we are reminded of that miserable direction to public opinion which is given in Historical Works.[1] I do not speak of party bias, though that is sufficiently mischievous ; but of the irrational selection by historians of comparatively unimportant things to fill the greater portion of their pages. People exclaim that the history of Europe is little more than a history of human violence and wickedness. But they confound history with that portion of history which historians record. That portion is doubtless written almost in blood—but it is a very small, and in truth a very subordinate portion.

The intrigues of cabinets ; the rise and fall of ministers ; wars and battles, and victories and defeats ; the plunder of provinces ; the dismemberment of empires ; these are the things which fill the pages of the historian, but these are not the things which compose the history of man. He that would acquaint himself with the history of his species must apply to other and to calmer scenes. " It is a cruel mortification, in searching for what is instructive in the history of past times, to find that the exploits of conquerors who have desolated the earth, and the freaks of tyrants who have rendered nations unhappy, are recorded with minute and often disgusting accuracy, while the discovery of useful arts and the progress of the most beneficial branches of commerce, are passed over in silence, and suffered to sink into oblivion."[1] Even a more cruel mortification than this is to find recorded almost nothing respecting the intellectual and moral history of man. You are presented with five or six weighty volumes which profess to be a History of England ; and after reading them to the end you have hardly found anything to satisfy that interesting question—How has my country been enabled to advance from barbarism to civilisation ; to come forth from darkness into light? Yes, by applying philosophy to facts yourself, you may attain some, though it be but an imperfect, reply. But the historian himself should have done this. The facts of history, simply as such, are of comparatively little concern. He is the true historian of man who regards mere facts rather as the *illustrations* of history than as its subject-matter. As to the history of cabinets and courts, of intrigue and oppression, of campaigns and generals, we can almost spare it all. It is of wonderfully little consequence whether they are remembered or not, except as lessons of instruction—except as proofs of the evils of bad principles and bad institutions. For any other purpose, Blenheim ! we can spare thee. And Louis, even Louis "*le grand!*" we can spare thee. And thy successor and his Pompadour ! we can spare ye all.

82. Much power is in the hands of the historian if he will exert it : if he will make the occurrences of the past subservient to the elucidations of the principles of human nature—of the principles of political truth—of the rules of political rectitude ; if he will refuse to make men ambitious of power by filling his pages with the feats or freaks of men in power ; if he will give no currency to the vulgar delusions about glory :—if he will do these things, and such as these, he will deserve well of his country and of man ; for he will contribute to that rectification of

---

[1] " Next to the guilt of those who commit wicked actions, is that of the historian who glosses them over and excuses them."—Southey: Book of the Church, c. 8.

[1] Robertson: Disq. on Anct. Comm. of India.

CHAPTER XI.
Intellectual Education.

Ancient Classics—London University—The Classics in boarding-schools—English grammar—Science and Literature—Improved system of education—Orthography: Writing: Reading: Geography: Natural History: Biography: Natural Philosophy: Political Science — Indications of a revolution in the system of education—Female education—The Society of Friends.

1. "It is no less true than lamentable, that hitherto the education proper for civil and active life has been neglected; that nothing has been done to enable those who are actually to conduct the affairs of the world to carry them on in a manner worthy of the age and country in which they live, by communicating to them the knowledge and the spirit of their age and country."¹—"Knowledge does not consist in being able to read books, but in understanding one's business and duty in life."—"Most writers have considered the subject of education as relative to that portion of it only which applies to learning; but the first object of all, in every nation, is to make a man a good member of society."—"Education consists in learning what makes a man useful, respectable, and happy, in the line for which he is destined."²

2. If these propositions are true, it is evident that the systems of Education which obtain need great and almost total reformation. What does a boy in the middle class of society learn at school of the knowledge and the spirit of his age and country? When he has left school, how much does he understand of the business and duty of life?

3. Education is one of those things which Lord Bacon would describe as having lain almost unaltered "upon the dregs of time." We still fancy that we educate our children when we give them, as its principal constituent, that same instruction which was given before England had a literature of its own, and when Greek and Latin contained almost the sum of human knowledge. Then the knowledge of Greek and Latin was called, and not unjustly called, Learning. It was the learning which procured distinction and celebrity. A sort of dignity and charm was thrown around the attainments and the word which designated them. That charm has continued to operate to the present hour, and

Public Opinion which, when it is complete and determinate, will be the most powerful of all earthly agents in ameliorating the social condition of the world.

we still call him a learned man who is skilful in Latin and Greek. Yet Latin and Greek contain an extremely small portion of that knowledge which the world now possesses; an extremely small portion of that which it is of most consequence to acquire. It would be well for society if this word *Learning* could be forgotten, or if we could make it the representative of other and very different ideas. But the delusion is continually propagated. The higher ranks of society give the tone to the notions of the rest; and the higher classes are educated at Westminster and Eton, and Cambridge and Oxford. At all these the languages which have ceased to be the languages of a living people—the authors which communicate, relatively, little knowledge that is adapted to the present affairs of man—are made the first and foremost articles of Education. To be familiar with these is still to be a "learned" man. Inferior institutions imitate the example; and the parent who knows his son will be, like himself, a merchant or manufacturer, thinks it almost indispensable that he should "learn Latin."

4. It may reasonably be doubted whether, to even the higher ranks of society, this preference of ancient learning is wise. It may reasonably be doubted whether, even at Oxford, a literary revolution would not be a useful revolution. Indeed the very circumstance that the system of education there is not essentially different from what it was centuries ago, is almost a sufficient evidence that an alteration is needed. If the circumstances and the contexture of human society are altered—if the boundaries of knowledge are very greatly extended, and if that knowledge which is now applicable to the affairs of life is extremely different from that which was applicable long ages ago—it surely is plain that a system which has not, or has only slightly, accommodated itself to the new condition and new exigencies of human affairs, cannot be a *good* system, cannot be a reasonable and judicious system. How stands the fact? When young men leave college to take part in the concerns of active life, how much assistance do they derive from classical literature? Look at the House of Commons. How much does this literature contribute to a member's legislating wisely upon questions of Political Economy, of Jurisprudence, of Taxation, of Reform? Or how much does it contribute to the capability of any other class of men to serve their families, their country, or mankind? I speak not of those professions to which a dead language may be necessary. A physician learns Latin as he attends the dissecting-room: it is a part of his system of preparation for his pursuits in life. Even with the professions, indeed, the need of a dead language is factitious. It is necessary only because usage has made it

¹ Art. 4, Education. West. Rev., No 1.
² Playfair: Causes of Decline of Nations, pp. 97, 98, 227.

INTELLECTUAL EDUCATION.

so. But I speak of that portion of mankind who, being exempt from the necessity for toil, fill the various gradations of society from that of the prince to the private gentleman. Select what rank or what class you please, and ask how much its members are indebted to ancient learning for their capability to discharge their duties as parents, as men, or as citizens of the state—the answer is literally, "Almost nothing." Now this is a serious answer, and involves serious consequences. A young man, when he enters upon the concerns of active life, has to set about acquiring new kinds of knowledge, knowledge totally dissimilar to the greater part of that which his "education" gave him; and the knowledge which education did give him he is obliged practically to forget—to lay it aside: it is something that is not adapted to the condition and the wants of society. But for what purpose are people educated unless it be to prepare them for this condition and these wants? Or how can that be a judicious system which does not effect these purposes?

5. That no advantages result from the study of ancient classics it would be idle to maintain. But this is not the question. The question is, Whether *so many* advantages result from this study as from others that might be substituted; and I am persuaded that we shall become more and more willing to answer, No. With respect to the sum of knowledge which the works of antiquity convey, as compared with that which is conveyed by modern literature, the disproportion is great in the extreme. To say that the modern is a hundred times greater than the ancient, is to keep far from the language of exaggeration. And, to say the truth, the majority of those who are educated at college leave it with but an imperfect acquaintance with those languages which they have spent years in professing to acquire. There are some men skilled in the languages; there are some "learned" men; but the very circumstance that great skill procures celebrity, is an evidence that great skill is rare. Amongst educated laymen, the number is very small of those whose knowledge of Latin bears any respectable proportion to their knowledge of their own language—of that language which they have hardly professed to learn at all. If the London University should be successfully established, it is probable that at least one collateral benefit will result from it. The wide range of subjects which it proposes to embrace in its system of education, will possess an influence upon other institutions; and the time may arrive when the impulse of public opinion shall reduce the mathematics of one of our Universities and the classics of both, to such a relative station amongst the objects of human study, as shall be better adapted to the purposes of human life.

6. If considerations like these apply to the *preference* of classical learning by those classes of society who can devote many years to the general purposes of education, much more do they apply to those who fill the middle ranks. Yet amongst these ranks the charm of the fiction has immense power. It has descended from Universities to boarding-schools of thirty pounds a year; and the parent complacently pays the extra "three guineas," in order that his boy may "learn Latin." We affirm that the knowledge of Latin and Greek is all but *useless* to these boys, and that if the knowledge were useful they do not acquire it. What are the stations which they are about to fill? One is to be a manufacturer, and one a banker, and one a merchant, and one a shipowner, and one will underwrite at Lloyd's, and one will be a consul at Toulon. Nay, we might go lower and say, one will be a tanner, and one a draper, and one a corn-factor. Yet these boys must learn Latin, and perhaps Greek too. And they do actually spend day after day, and perhaps year after year, upon "Hic hæc hoc,"—"Propria quæ maribus,"—"As in præsenti,"—"Et, *and;* cum, *when;*" and the like. What conceivable relationship do these things bear to making steam-engines, or discounting bills, or shipping cargoes, or making leather, or selling cloth? None. But it will be said, What relationship does any merely literary pursuit bear? Or why should a merchant's son read Paradise Lost? Such questions conduct us to the just view of the case; and accordingly we answer, Let these young persons attend to literature, but let it be literature of the most expedient kind. Let them read Paradise Lost. Why? Because it is delightful, and because they can do it *without learning a language in order to acquire the power*. If Paradise Lost existed only in Arabic, I should think it preposterous to teach young persons Arabic in order that they might read it. To those who are to fill the active stations of life, literature must always be a subordinate concern; and it would be vain to deny that our own language possesses a sufficient store for them without learning others to increase it.

7. But indeed the children of the middle classes do *not* learn the languages. They do not learn them so as to be able to appreciate the merits and the beauties of ancient literature. Ask the boys themselves. Ask them whether they could hold an hour's conversation with Cicero if he should stand before them. The very supposition is absurd. Or can they read and enjoy Cicero as they read and enjoy Addison? No. They do *not learn* the ancient languages. They pore over rules and exercises, and syntax and quantities; but as to learning the language, in the same sense as that in which it may be

said they learn English, there is not one in a hundred, nor probably in ten thousand, who does it. Yet unless a person does learn a language so as to read it, at least, with perfect facility, what becomes of the use of the study as a means of elevating the *taste?* This is one of the advantages which are attributed to the study of the classics. But without inquiring whether the taste might not be as well cultivated by other means, one short consideration is sufficient: that the taste is not cultivated by *studying* the classics but by *mastering* them—by acquiring such a familiarity with these works as enables us to appreciate their excellences. This familiarity, or anything that approaches to this familiarity, schoolboys do not acquire. Playfair makes a computation from which he concludes that in ordinary boarding-schools "not above one in a hundred learns to read even Latin decently well; that is, one good reader for every ten thousand pounds expended. As to speaking Latin," he adds, "perhaps one out of a thousand may learn that: so that there is a speaker for each sum of one hundred thousand pounds spent on the language."[1]

8. Then it is said that the act of studying the ancient languages exercises the memory, cultivates the habit of attention, and teaches, too, the art of reasoning. Grant all this. Cannot, then, the memory be exercised as well by acquiring valuable knowledge as by acquiring a mere knowledge of words? Would the memory lose anything by affixing ideas to the words it learnt? The same questions apply to those who urge the habit of attention, and to all those advocates of the study who insist upon the exercise which it gives to the mind. We do not question the utility of this exercise; we only say that *while* the mind is exercised it should also be fed. That such topics of advocacy are resorted to is itself an indication of the questionable utility of the study. No one thinks it necessary to adduce such topics as reasons for learning Addition and Subtraction.

9. The intelligent reader will perceive that the ground upon which these objections to classical studies are urged is, that they occupy time which might be more beneficially employed. If the period of education were long enough to learn the ancient languages *in addition* to the more beneficial branches of knowledge, our inquiry would be of another kind. But the period is not long enough: a selection must be made; and that which it has been our endeavour to show is, that in selecting the classics we make an *unwise* selection.

[1] Inq. Causes of Decline of Nations, p. 224.

10. The remarks which follow will be understood as applying to the middle ranks of society—that is, to the ranks in which the greatest sum of talent and virtue resides, and by which the business of the world is principally carried on. If we take up a card of terms of an ordinary boarding-school, we probably meet with an enumeration something like this:—" Reading, Writing, Arithmetic, English Grammar, Composition, History, Geography, Use of the Globes," &c. ; besides the "accomplishments," and French, Greek, and Latin. "Education consists in learning what makes a man useful, respectable, and happy in the line for which he is destined." Useful, respectable, and happy, not merely in his counting-house, but in his parlour; not merely in his own house, but amongst his neighbours, and as a member of civilised society. Now, surely the list of subjects which are set down above is, to say the least, very imperfect. Besides, reading, writing, and arithmetic, what is the amount of knowledge which it conveys? English grammar:—This is, in fact, *not learnt* by committing to memory lessons in the "grammar book." Composition :— This is of consequence; although, as school economy is now managed, it makes a better appearance on the master's card than on the boy's paper. History, geography, and the globe problems, are of great interest and value; and the great unhappiness is, that such studies are postponed to others of comparatively little worth.

11. Since human knowledge is so much more extensive than the opportunity of individuals for acquiring it, it becomes of the greatest importance so to economise the opportunity as to make it subservient to the acquisition of as large and as valuable a portion as we can. It is not enough to show that a given branch of education is useful ; you must show that it is the most useful that can be selected. Remembering this, I think it would be expedient to dispense with the formal study of English grammar—a proposition which, I doubt not, many a teacher will hear with wonder and disapprobation. We learn the grammar in order that we may learn English ; and we learn English whether we study grammars or not. Especially we shall acquire a competent knowledge of our own language if other departments of our education were improved. A boy learns more English grammar by joining in an hour's conversation with educated people than in poring for an hour over Murray or Horne Tooke. If he is accustomed to such society, and to the perusal of well-written books, he will learn English grammar though he never sees a word about syntax ; and if he is not accustomed to such society and such

reading, the "grammar books" at a boarding-school will not teach it. Men learn their own language by habit and not by rules; and this is just what we might expect; for the grammar of a language is itself formed from the prevalent habits of speech and writing. A compiler of grammar first observes these habits, and then makes his rules; but if a person is himself familiar with the habits, why study the rules? I say nothing of grammar as a general science, because, although the philosophy of language be a valuable branch of human knowledge, it were idle to expect that schoolboys should understand it. The objection is *to the system of attempting to teach children formally that which they will learn practically without teaching.* A grammar of Murray's lies before me, of which the leaves are worn into rags by being "learnt." I find the child is to learn that "words are articulate sounds, used by common consent as signs of our ideas." Now, I am persuaded that to nine out of every ten who "get this lesson by heart," it conveys little more information than if the sentence were in Esquimaux. They do not know, with any distinctness, what "articulate sounds" means —nor what the phrase "common consent" means—nor what "signs of ideas" means ; and yet they know, without learning, all that this formidable sentence proposes to teach. They know perfectly well that they speak to their brothers and sisters in order to convey their ideas. Again : "An improper diphthong has but one of the vowels sounded, as *ea* in eagle, *oa* in boat." Does not every child who can spell the words eagle and boat know this without hearing a word about improper diphthongs? This species of instruction is like that of a man who, seeing a boy running after a hoop, should stop him to make him learn by heart, that in order to run he must use, in a certain order, flexors and extensors and the tendon Achilles. A little girl runs to her mother and says, "Mary has given me Cowper's Task: This is *what* I wanted." But still the little girl must learn from her "grammar book" how to use the word *what*. And this is the process:—"*What* is a kind of compound relative, including both the antecedent and the relative, and is equivalent to that which, as, This is *what* I wanted !" It really is wonderful that such a system of instruction should be continued—a system which most laboriously attempts to teach that which a child will learn without teaching, and which is almost utterly abortive in itself. Children do not learn to speak and write correctly by learning lessons like these. A gentleman told me the other day, that he learnt one of Murray's grammars until he could actually repeat it from beginning to end ; and he does not recollect that one particle of knowledge was conveyed to his mind by it.

12. Whilst the attempt thus to teach grammar is so needless and so futile, it occupies a great deal of a boy's time ; and by doing this, it does great mischief, since his time is precious indeed. He might learn a great deal more of grammar by reading useful and interesting books, and by conversation respecting science and literature with an educated master, than by acquiring grammatical rules by rote. Grammar would be a collateral acquisition ; he would learn it *whilst* he was learning other important things.

13. In general, Science is preferable to Literature- the knowledge of things to the knowledge of words. It is not by literature, nor by merely literary men, that the business of human society is *now* carried on. "Directly and immediately we have risen to the station which we occupy, not by literature, not by the knowledge of extinct languages, but by the sciences of politics, of law, of public economy, of commerce, of mathematics ; by astronomy, by chemistry, by mechanics, by natural history. It is by these that we are destined to rise yet higher. These constitute the business of society, and in these ought we to seek for the objects of education."[1]

14. Yet at school how little do our children learn of these ! The reader will ask, what system of education we would recommend ; and although the writer of these pages can make no pretensions to accuracy of knowledge upon the subject, he thinks that an improved system would embrace, even in ordinary boarding-schools, such topics of instruction as these :

Reading — Writing — Common Arithmetic — Book-keeping.
Geography—Natural History, embracing Zoology, Botany, Mineralogy, &c.
History of Mankind, especially the History of recent times.
Biography, particularly of moderns.
Natural Philosophy, embracing Mechanics, Pneumatics, Optics, &c ; and illustrated by experiments; and embracing also Chemistry with experiments—Galvanism, &c.
Geology—Land Measuring—Familiar Geometry.
Elements of Political Science ; embracing Principles of Religious and Civil Liberty; of Civil Obedience ; of Penal Law and the general Administration of Justice ; of Political Economy, &c.

15. If the reader should think that boys under sixteen can acquire little or no knowledge of these multifarious subjects, he is

[1] Art. 9, Outlines of Philosophical Education, &c. West. Rev., No. 7

to remember what the enumeration excludes, and how vast a proportion of a boy's time the excluded subjects now occupy. The whole, perhaps, of all his forenoons is now devoted to Latin,—Latin is excluded. An hour before breakfast is probably spent in learning sentences in a book of Grammar :— *this* mode of learning Grammar is excluded. The amount of knowledge which a boy might acquire during these hours is very great. The formal learning of spelling does not appear in our enumeration. In many schools, this occupies a considerable portion of every week, if not of every day. Spelling may be learnt, and in fact is learnt, like grammar, by habit. A person reads a book, and without thinking of it, insensibly learns to spell: that is, he perceives, when he writes a word incorrectly, that it does not bear the same appearance as he has been accustomed to observe. Some persons, when they are in doubt as to the orthography of a word, *write* it in two or three ways, and their eye tells them which is correct. Here again is a considerable saving of time. Nor is this all. I would not *formally* teach boys to write. I would not give them a Copy Book to write hour after hour, *Reward sweetens Labour* and *Industry is praised;* but, since they would have occasion to write many things in the pursuit of their other studies, I would require them to write those things fairly:—that is, once more, they should learn to write *whilst* they are learning to think. Nor would I *formally* teach them to read; but since they would have many books to peruse, they should frequently read them audibly; and by degrees would learn to read them well. And they would be much more likely to read them well, when the books were themselves delightful than when they went up to the master's desk, to "read their lessons." Learning "words and meanings," as the schoolboy calls it, is another of the modes in which much time is wasted. The conversation to which a young person listens, the books which he reads, are the best teachers of words and meanings. He cannot help learning the meaning of words if they frequently and familiarly occur; and if they rarely occur, he will gain very little by learning columns of Entick.

16. With this exclusion of some subjects of study, and alteration of the mode of pursuing others, a schoolboy's time would really be much more than doubled. Every year would practically be expanded into two or three. Let us refer then to some of the subjects of Education which have been proposed.

17. In teaching Geography, too little use is made of maps and too much of books. A boy will learn more by examining a good map and by listening to a few intelligible explanations, than by wearying himself with pages of geographical lessons. Lesson-learning is the bane of education. It disgusts and wearies young persons; and, except with extreme watchfulness on the part of the teacher, is almost sure to degenerate into learning words without ideas. It is not an easy thing for a child to learn half a dozen paragraphs full of proper names, describing by what mountains and seas half a dozen countries are bounded. Yet with much less labour, he might learn the facts more perfectly by his eye, and with less probability of their passing from his memory. The lessons will not be remembered except as they convey ideas.

18. To most if not to all young persons, Natural History is a delightful study. Zoology, if accompanied by good plates, conveys permanent and useful knowledge. Such a book as Wood's Zoography is a more valuable medium of education than three-fourths of the professed school-books in existence.

19. History and Biography are, if it be not the fault of the teacher or his books, delightful also. Modern times should always be preferred; partly because the knowledge they communicate is more certain and more agreeable, and partly because it bears an incomparably greater relation to the present condition of men; and for that reason it is better adapted to prepare the young person for the part which he is to take in active life. If historical books even for the young possessed less of the character of mere chronicles of facts, and contained a few of those connecting and illustrating paragraphs which a man of philosophical mind knows how to introduce, History might become a powerful instrument in imparting sound principles to the mind, and thus in meliorating the general condition of society. Both Biography and History should be illustrated with good plates. The more we can teach through the eye the better. It is hardly necessary to add that a boy should not "learn lessons" in either. He should *read* these books, and means should afterwards be taken to ascertain whether he has read them to good purpose.

20. There is, according to my views, no study that is more adapted to please and improve young persons than that of Natural Philosophy. When I was a schoolboy I attended a few lectures on the Air Pump, Galvanism, &c., and I value the knowledge which I gained in three evenings more highly than any other that I gained at school in as many months. Whilst our children are poring over lessons which

disgust them, we allow that magazine of wonders which heaven has stored up to lie unexplored and unnoticed. There are multitudes of young men and women who are considered respectably educated, who are yet wonderfully ignorant of the first principles of natural science. Many a boy who has spent years upon Latin, cannot tell how it comes to pass that water rises in a pump; and would stare if he were told that the decanters on the table were not colder than the baize they stand on. I would rather that my son were familiar with the subjects of Paley's Theology, than that he should surpass Elizabeth Carter in a translation of Epictetus.

21. Respecting the propriety of attempting to convey any knowledge of Political Science, many readers will probably doubt. Yet why? Is it not upon the goodness or badness of political institutions that much of the happiness or misery of mankind depends? And what means are so likely to amend the bad, or to secure the continuance of the good, as the intelligent opinion of a people? We know that in all free states like our own, Public Opinion is powerful. What then can be more obviously true than that it should be made as just as we can? Nor would it be to much purpose to reply, that every master will teach his own political creed, and only nurse up ignorant and angry squabbles. The same reason would apply against inculcating *Religious* Principles: yet who thinks these principles should be neglected because there are many creeds? Besides, one of the best means of educing political truth is by inquiry and discussion, and these are likely to be rationally promoted by making the Elements of Political knowledge a subject of education. To say the truth, these elements are not really very abstruse or remote. Having once established the maxim—which no reasonable man disputes—that the proper purpose of government is to secure the happiness of the community, very little is wanted in applying the principle to particular questions but honest conscientious thought. The difficulties are occasioned not so much by the nature of the case, as by the interests and prejudices which habit and existing institutions introduce; and how shall these interests and prejudices be so effectually prevented from influencing the mind, as by the inculcation of simple truths before young persons mix in the business of the world?

22. These are general suggestions: details are foreign to our purpose; but from these general suggestions the intelligent parent will perceive the *kind* of education that is proposed. If such an education would convey to young persons some tolerable portion of "the knowledge and the spirit of their age and country," if it would tend to make them "useful, respectable, and happy" in the various relationships of life, the objects of Intellectual Education are, in the same degree, attained. So limited is the opportunity of the young for acquiring knowledge in comparison with the extent of knowledge itself, that, upon some subjects, little more is to be effected during the years that are professedly devoted to education, than to induce the desire of information, and the habit of seeking it. A boy cannot be expected to acquire very extensive information respecting the application of the mechanical powers; but if he sees the value and the pleasure of studying it, he may hereafter benefit his country and the world by his ingenuity. Or a boy cannot be expected to know more than the elements of chemistry; yet this knowledge may in future enable him to add greatly to the comforts and conveniences of human life.

23. There are indications of a revolution in the system of education which will probably lead both to great and beneficial results. Science is evidently gaining ground upon the judgments and affections of the public. Elementary books of Science are indeed the familiar companions of young persons *after they have left school*. They lay aside tenses and parsing for "Conversations on Chemistry." This is, so far, as it should be; and it would be better still if similar books had taken the place, *at school*, of accents and quantities, and cases and genders, and lesson-learning by rote. This revolution is also indicated by the topics which are introduced into Mechanics' Institutes. These Associations seem almost instinctively to prefer science to literature, simply as such. Perhaps it will be said that science is the branch of knowledge which is more peculiarly adapted to their employments in life. But the scientific information which an individual acquires usually produces little immediate effect upon his mode of working. The carpenter cannot put up a staircase the better for attending a lecture on Chemistry. No: they prefer science because it is preferable: preferable, not for mechanics merely, but for man. It is of less consequence to Man to know what Horace wrote, or to be able to criticise the Greek Anthology, than to know by what laws the Deity regulates the operations of nature, and by what means those operations are made subservient to the purposes of life.

24. A consideration of the kind of knowledge which education should impart is, however, but one division of the general subject. The consideration of the best mode of imparting it, is another. Various reasons induce the writer to say little respecting the last—of which reasons one is, that he does

not possess information that satisfies his own mind; and another, that it is not so immediately connected with the general purpose of the work. That great improvements have recently been made in the mode of conveying knowledge to large numbers, is beyond dispute. Whether, or to what extent, these improvements are applicable to schools of twenty children or to families of three or four, experience will be likely to decide. With the prodigious power of giving publicity and exciting discussion which men now possess, the best systems are likely ultimately to prevail.

25. One observation may, however, safely be made—that if two systems are proposed, each with apparently nearly equal claims, and one of which will be more pleasurable to the learner, that one is undoubtedly the best. That which a boy delights in he will learn; and if the subjects of instruction were as delightful as they ought to be, and the mode of conveying were pleasurable too, there would be an immense addition to the stock of knowledge which a schoolboy acquires. We complain of the aversion of the young to learning, and the young complain of their weariness and disgust. It is in a great degree our own faults. Knowledge is delightful to the human mind; but we may, if we please, select such kinds of knowledge, and adopt such modes of imparting it, as shall make the whole system not delightful, but repulsive. This, to a great extent, we actually do. We may do the contrary if we will.

26. There does not appear any reason why the education of women should differ, in its essentials, from that of men. The education which is good for human nature is good for them. They are a part—and they ought to be in a much greater degree than they are, a part—of the effective contributors to the welfare and intelligence of the human family. In intellectual as well as in other affairs, they ought to be fit helps to man. The preposterous absurdities of chivalrous times still exert a wretched influence over the character and allotment of women. Men are not polite but gallant: they do not act towards women as to beings of kindred habits and character, as to beings who, like the other portion of mankind, reason and reflect and judge, but as to beings who please, and whom men are bound to please. Essentially there is no kindness, no politeness in this; but selfishness and insolence. He is the man of politeness who evinces his respect for the female *mind*. He is the man of insolence who tacitly says, when he enters into the society of women, that he needs not to bring his intellects with him. I do not mean to affirm that these persons intend insolence, or are conscious always of the real character of their habits: they think they are attentive and polite; and habit has become so inveterate, that they really are not pleased if a woman, by the vigour of her conversation, interrupts the pleasant trifling to which they are accustomed. Unhappily, a great number of women themselves prefer this varnished and gilded contempt to solid respect. They would rather think themselves fascinating than respectable. They will not see, and very often they do not see, the practical insolence with which they are treated: yet what insolence is so great as that of half a dozen men who, having been engaged in an intelligent conversation, suddenly exchange it for frivolity if ladies enter.

27. For this unhappy state of intellectual intercourse, female education is in too great a degree adapted. A large class are taught less to think than to shine. If they glitter, it matters little whether it be the glitter of gilding or of gold. To be accomplished is of greater interest than to be sensible. It is of more consequence to this class to charm by the tones of a piano, than to delight and invigorate by intellectual conversation. The effect is reciprocally bad. An absurd education disqualifies them for intellectual exertion, and that very disqualification perpetuates the degradation. I say the degradation, for the word is descriptive of the fact. A captive is not the less truly bound because his chains are made of silver and studded with rubies. If any community exhibits, in the collective character of its females, an exception to these remarks, it is, I think, exhibited amongst the Society of Friends. Within the last twenty-five years the public have had many opportunities of observing the intellectual condition of quaker women. The public have not been dazzled:—who would wish it? but they have seen intelligence, sound sense, considerateness, discretion. They have seen these qualities in a degree, and with an approach to universality of diffusion, that is not found in any other class of women as a class. There are, indeed, few or no authors amongst them. The quakers are not a *writing* people. If they were, there is no reason to doubt that the intelligence and discretion which are manifested by their women's actions and conversation, would be exhibited in their books.

28. Unhappily some of the causes which have produced these qualities, are not easily brought into operation by the public. One of the most efficient of these causes consists in that economy of the society, by which its women have an extensive and a *separate* share in the internal administration of its affairs. In the exercise of this administration

they are almost inevitably taught to think and to judge. The instrument is powerful ; but how shall that instrument be applied— where shall it be procured—by the rest of the public?

29. Not, however, that the intellectual education of these females is what it ought to be, or what it might be. They, too, waste their hours over "grammar books," and "geography books," and lesson books over Latin sometimes, and Greek ; and, if the remark can be adventured on, over stitching and hemming too. *Something* must be amiss when a girl is kept two or three hours every day in acquiring the art of sewing. What that something is— whether it is practised like parsing because it is common, or whether more accurate proficiency is expected than reason would prescribe, I presume not to determine ; but it may safely be concluded, that if a portion equal to a fourth or a third part of those years which are afforded to that mighty subject, the education of the human mind, is devoted to the acquisition of one manual art like this—*more* is devoted than any one who reasons upon the subject can justify.

30. If then we were wise enough to regard women, and if women were wise enough to regard themselves, with that real practical respect to which they are entitled, and if the education they received was such as that respect would dictate, we might hereafter have occasion to say, not as it is now said, that "in England women are queens," but something higher and greater ; we might say that in everything social, intellectual, and religious, they were fit to co-operate with man, and to cheer and assist him in his endeavours to promote his own happiness, and the happiness of his family, his country, and the world.

CHAPTER XII.
Moral Education.

Union of moral principle with the affections—Society—Morality of the ancient classics—The supply of motives to virtue—Conscience—Subjugation of the will—Knowledge of our own minds—Offices of public worship.

31. To a good Moral Education, two things are necessary : that the young should receive *information* respecting what is right and what is wrong ; and, That they should be furnished with *motives* to adhere to what is right. We should communicate moral Knowledge and moral Dispositions.

1. In the endeavour to attain these ends, there is one great pervading difficulty, consisting in the imperfection and impurity of the actual moral condition of mankind. Without referring at present to that moral guidance with which all men, however circumstanced, are furnished,[1] it is evident that much of the practical moral education which an individual receives, is acquired by habit, and from the actions, opinions, and general example of those around him. It is thus that, to a great extent, he acquires his moral education. He adopts the notions of others, acquires insensibly a similar set of principles, and forms to himself a similar scale of right and wrong. It is manifest that the learner in such a school will often be taught amiss. Yet how can we prevent him from being so taught ? or what system of Moral Education is likely to avail in opposition to the contagion of example and the influence of notions insensibly, yet constantly, instilled ? It is to little purpose to take a boy every morning into a closet, and there teach him moral and religious truths for an hour, if, so soon as the hour is expired, he is left for the remainder of the day in circumstances in which these truths are not recommended by any living examples.

32. One of the first and greatest requisites, therefore, in Moral Education, is a situation in which the knowledge and the practice of morality is inculcated by the habitually virtuous conduct of others. The boy who is placed in such a situation is in an efficient moral school, though he may never hear delivered formal rules of conduct : so that, if parents should ask how they may best give their child a moral education, I answer, Be virtuous yourselves.

33. The young, however, are unavoidably subjected to bad example as to good : many who may see consistent practical lessons of virtue in their parents' parlours, must see much that is contrary elsewhere ; and we must, if we can, so rectify the moral perceptions and invigorate the moral dispositions, that the mind shall effectually resist the insinuation of evil.

34. Religion is the basis of Morality. He that would impart moral knowledge must begin by imparting a knowledge of God. We are not advocates of formal instruction —of lesson learning— in moral any more than in intellectual education. Not that we affirm it is undesirable to make a young person commit to memory maxims of religious truth and moral duty. These things may be right, but they are not the really efficient means of forming the moral character of the young. These maxims should recommend themselves to the judgment and affections, and this can

[1] See Essay 1, c. 6.

hardly be hoped whilst they are presented only in a didactic and insulated form to the mind. It is one of the characteristics of the times, that there is a prodigious increase of books that are calculated to benefit whilst they delight the young. These are effective instruments in teaching morality. A simple narrative (of *facts* if it be possible), in which integrity of principle and purity of conduct are recommended to the affections as well as to the judgment—without affectation, or improbabilities, or factitious sentiment, is likely to effect substantial good. And if these associations are judiciously renewed, the good is likely to be permanent as well as substantial. It is not a light task to write such books, nor to select them. Authors colour their pictures too highly. They must indeed interest the young, or they will not be read with pleasure: but the anxiety to give interest is too great, and the effects may be expected to diminish as the narrative recedes from congeniality to the actual condition of mankind.

35. A judicious parent will often find that the moral culture of his child may be promoted without seeming to have the object in view. There are many opportunities which present themselves for associating virtue with his affections—for throwing in amongst the accumulating mass of mental habits principles of rectitude which shall pervade and meliorate the whole.

36. As the mind acquires an increased capacity of judging, I would offer to the young person a sound exhibition, if such can be found, of the *Principles* of Morality. He should know, with as great distinctness as possible, not only his duty but the reasons of it. It has very unfortunately happened that those who have professed to deliver the principles of morality, have commonly intermingled error with truth, or have set out with propositions fundamentally unsound. These books effect, it is probable, more injury than benefit. Their truths, for they contain truths, are frequently deduced from fallacious premises — from premises from which it is equally easy to deduce errors. The fallacies of the Moral Philosophy of Paley are now in part detected by the public: there was a time when his opinions were regarded as more nearly oracular than now; and at that time, and up to the present time, the book has effectually confused the moral notions of multitudes of readers. If the reader thinks that the Principles which have been proposed in the present Essays are just, he might derive some assistance from them in conducting the moral education of his elder children.

37. There is negative as well as positive Education—some things to avoid, as well as some to do. Of the things which are to be avoided, the most obvious is unfit society for the young. If a boy mixes without restraint in whatever society he pleases, his education will in general be practically bad; because the world in general is bad: its moral condition is below the medium between perfect purity and utter depravation. Nevertheless, he must at some period mix in society with almost all sorts of men, and therefore he must be prepared for it. Very young children should be excluded if possible from *all* unfit association, because they acquire habits before they possess a sufficiency of counteracting principle. But if a parent has, within his own house, sufficiently endeavoured to confirm and invigorate the moral character of his child, it were worse than fruitless to endeavour to retain him in the seclusion of a monk. He should feel the necessity and acquire the power of resisting temptation, by being subjected, gradually subjected, to that temptation which *must* one day be presented to him. In the endlessly diversified circumstances of families, no suggestion of prudence will be applicable to all; but if a parent is conscious that the moral tendency of his domestic associations is good, it will probably be wise to send his children to day-schools rather than to send them wholly from his family. Schools, as moral instruments, contain much both of good and evil: perhaps no means will be more effectual in securing much of the good and avoiding much of the evil, than that of allowing his children to spend their evenings and early mornings at home.

38. In ruminating upon Moral Education, we cannot, at least in this age of reading, disregard the influence of books. That a young person should not read every book is plain. No discrimination can be attempted here; but it may be observed that the best species of discrimination is that which is supplied by a rectified condition of the mind itself. The best species of prohibition is not that which a parent pronounces, but that which is pronounced by purified tastes and inclinations in the mind of the young. Not that the parent or tutor can expect that all or many of his children will adequately make this judicious discrimination; but if he cannot do everything he can do much. There are many persons whom a contemptible or vicious book disgusts, notwithstanding the fascinations which it may contain. This disgust is the result of education in a large sense; and some portion of this disgust and of the discrimination which results from it, may be induced into the mind of a boy by having made him familiar with superior productions. He who is accustomed to good society feels little temptation to join in the vociferations of an alehouse.

39. And here it appears necessary to advert to the moral tendency of studying, without selection, the ancient classics. If there are objections to the study resulting from this tendency, they are to be superadded to those which were stated in the last chapter on intellectual grounds; and both united will present motives to hesitation on the part of a parent which he cannot, with any propriety, disregard. The mode in which the writings of the Greek and Latin authors operate is not an ordinary mode. We do not approach them as we approach ordinary books, but with a sort of habitual admiration which makes their influence, whatever be its nature, peculiarly strong. That admiration would be powerful alike for good or for evil. Whether the tendency be good or evil the admiration will make it great.

40. Now, previous to inquiring what the positive ill tendency of these writings is—what is *not* their tendency? They are Pagan books for Christian children. They neither inculcate Christianity, nor Christian dispositions, nor the love of Christianity. But their tendency is not negative merely. They do inculcate that which is adverse to Christianity and to Christian dispositions. They set up, as exalted virtues, that which our own religion never countenanced, if it has not specifically condemned. They censure as faults dispositions which our own religion enjoins, or dispositions so similar that the young will not discriminate between them. If we enthusiastically admire these works, who will pretend that we shall not admire the moral qualities which they applaud? Who will pretend that the mind of a young person accurately adjusts his admiration to those subjects only which Christianity approves? No: we admire them as a whole; not perhaps every sentence or every sentiment, but we admire their general spirit and character. In a word, we admire that which our own religion teaches us not to imitate. And what makes the effect the more intense is, that we do this at the period of life when we are every day *acquiring* our moral notions. We mingle them up with our early associations respecting right and wrong—with associations which commonly extend their influence over the remainder of life.[1]

41. A very able Essay, which obtained the Norrisian Medal at Cambridge for 1825, forcibly illustrates these propositions; and the illustration is so much the more valuable, because it appears to have been undesigned. The title is, "No valid argument can be drawn from the incredulity of the Heathen Philosophers against the truth of the Christian religion."[1] The object of the work is to show, by a reference to their writings, that the general system of their opinions, feelings, prejudices, principles, and conduct, was utterly incongruous with Christianity; and that, in consequence of these principles, &c., they actually did reject the religion. This is shown with great clearness of evidence; it is shown that a class of men who thought and wrote as these Philosophers thought and wrote, would be extremely indisposed to adopt the religion and morality which Christ had introduced. Now this appears to me to be conclusive of the question as to the present tendency of their writings. If the principles and prejudices of these persons indisposed them to the acceptance of Christianity, those prejudices and principles will indispose the man who admires and imbibes them in the present day. Not that they will now produce the effect in the same *degree*. We are now surrounded with many other media by which opinions and principles are induced, and these are frequently influenced by the spirit of Christianity. The study and the admiration of these writings may not therefore be expected to make men absolutely reject Christianity, but to indispose them, in a greater or less degree, for the hearty acceptance of Christian principles as their rules of conduct.

42. Propositions have been made to supply young persons with selected ancient authors, or perhaps with editions in which exceptionable passages are expunged. I do not think that this will greatly avail. It is not, I think, the broad indecencies of Ovid, nor any other insulated class of sentiments or descriptions, that effects the great mischief; it is the pervading spirit and tenor of the whole—a spirit and tenor from which Christianity is not only excluded, but which is actually and greatly adverse to Christianity. There is indeed one considerable benefit that is likely to result from such a selection, and from expunging particular passages. Boys in ordinary schools do not learn enough of the classics to acquire much of their general moral spirit, but they acquire enough to be influenced, and injuriously influenced, by being familiar with licentious language; and at any rate he essentially subserves the interests of morality, who diminishes the power of opposing influences though he cannot wholly destroy it.

43. Finally, the mode in which Intellectual Education generally is acquired, may be made either an auxiliary of Moral Education or the contrary. A young person may store his mind with literature and science, and together, with the acquisition, either corrupt his principles, or amend and invigorate them.

---

[1] "All education which inculcates Christian Opinions with Pagan Tastes, awakens conscience but to tamper with it." Schimmelpenninck: Biblical Fragments.

[1] By James Amiraux Jeremie.

The world is so abundantly supplied with the means of knowledge—there are so many paths to the desired temple, that we may choose our own and yet arrive at it. He that thinks he cannot possess sufficient knowledge without plucking fruit of unhallowed trees, surely does not know how boundless is the variety and number of those which bear wholesome fruit. He cannot indeed know everything without studying the bad; which, however, is no more to be recommended in literature than in life. A man cannot know all the varieties of human society without taking up his abode with felons and cannibals.

44. II. But, in reality, the second division of Moral Education is the more important of the two—*the supply of motives to adhere to what is right*. Our great deficiency is not in knowledge but in obedience. Of the offences which an individual commits against the Moral Law, the great majority are committed *in the consciousness* that he is doing wrong. Moral Education therefore should be directed, not so much to informing the young what they ought to do, as to inducing those moral dispositions and principles which will make them adhere to what they know to be right.

45. The human mind, of itself, is in a state something like that of men in a state of nature, where separate and conflicting desires and motives are not restrained by any acknowledged head. Government, as it is necessary to society, is necessary in the individual mind. To the internal community of the heart the great question is, Who shall be the legislator? Who shall regulate and restrain the passions and affections? Who shall command and direct the conduct?—To these questions the breast of every man supplies him with an answer. He knows, because he feels, that there is a rightful legislator in his own heart: he knows, because he feels, that he *ought* to obey it.

46. By whatever designation the reader may think it fit to indicate this legislator, whether he calls it the law written in the heart, or moral sense, or moral instinct, or conscience, we arrive at one practical truth at last; that to the moral legislation which does actually subsist in the human mind, it is right that the individual should conform his conduct.

The great point then is, to induce him to do this—to induce him, when inclination and this law are at variance, to sacrifice the inclination to the law: and for this purpose it appears proper. first to impress him with a high, that is, with an accurate estimate of the authority of the law itself. We have seen that this law embraces an actual expression of the Will of God; and we have seen that, even although the conscience may not always be adequately enlightened, it nevertheless constitutes to the individual an authoritative law. It is to the conscientious *internal apprehension* of rectitude that we should conform our conduct. Such appears to be the Will of God.

47. It should therefore be especially inculcated, that the dictate of conscience is never to be sacrificed; that whatever may be the consequences of conforming to it, they are to be ventured. Obedience is to be unconditional—no questions about the utility of the law—no computations of the consequences of obedience—no presuming upon the lenity of the divine government. " It is important so to regulate the understanding and imagination of the young, that they may be prepared to obey, even where they *do not see the reasons* of the commands of God." " We should certainly endeavour, where we can, to show them the reasons of the divine commands, and this more and more as their understandings gain strength; but let it be obvious to them that we do ourselves consider it as *quite sufficient* if God has commanded us to do or to avoid anything."[1]

48. Obedience to this internal legislator is not, like obedience to civil government, enforced. The law is promulgated, but the passions and inclinations can refuse obedience if they will. Penalties and rewards are indeed annexed; but he who braves the penalty, and disregards the reward, may continue to violate the law. Obedience therefore must be voluntary, and hence the paramount importance, in moral Education, of habitually subjecting the will. " Parents," says Hartley, should "labour from the earliest dawnings of understanding and desire, to check the growing *obstinacy of the will*, curb all sallies of passion, impress the deepest, most amiable, reverential, and awful impressions of God, a future state, and all sacred things."—" Religious persons in all periods, who have possessed the light of revelation, have in a particular manner been sensible that the habit of *self-control* lies at the foundation of moral worth."[2] There is nothing mean or mean-spirited in this. It is magnanimous in philosophy as it is right in morals. It is the subjugation of the lower qualities of our nature to wisdom and to goodness.

49. The subjugation of the will to the dictates of a higher law, must be endeavoured, if we would succeed, almost in infancy and in very little things; from the earliest dawnings, as Hartley says, of understanding and desire. Children must first obey their parents,

---

[1] Carpenter: Principles of Education.   [2] Ibid.

and those who have the care of them. The habit of sacrificing the will to another judgment being thus acquired, the mind is prepared to sacrifice the will to the judgment pronounced within itself. Show, in every practicable case, *why* you cross the inclinations of a child. Let obedience be as little blind as it may be. It is a great failing of some parents that they will not descend from the imperative mood, and that they seem to think it a derogation from their authority to place their orders upon any other foundation than their wills. But if the child sees—and children are wonderfully quick-sighted in such things—if the child sees that the *will* is that which governs his parent, how shall he efficiently learn that the will should *not* govern himself.

50. The internal law carries with it the voucher of its own reasonableness. A person does not need to be told that it is proper and right to obey that law. The perception of this rectitude and propriety is coincident with the dictates themselves. Let the parent, then, very frequently refer his son and his daughter to their own minds ; let him teach them to seek for instruction there. There are dangers on every hand, and dangers even here. The parent must refer them, if it be possible, not merely to conscience, but to enlightened conscience. He must unite the two branches of Moral Education, and communicate the knowledge whilst he endeavours to induce the practice of morality. Without this, his children may obey their consciences, and yet be in error, and perhaps in fanaticism. With it, he may hope that their conduct will be both conscientious, and pure, and right. Nevertheless, an habitual reference to the internal law is the great, the primary concern ; for the great majority of a man's moral perceptions are accordant with Truth.

51. There is one consequence attendant upon this habitual reference to the internal law which is highly beneficial to the moral character. It leads us to fulfil the wise instruction of antiquity, Know thyself. It makes us look within ourselves ; it brings us acquainted with the little and busy world that is within us, with its many inhabitants and their dispositions, and with their tendencies to evil or to good. This is valuable knowledge ; and knowledge for want of which, it may be feared, the virtue of many has been wrecked in the hour of tempest. A man's enemies are those of his own household ; and if he does not know their insidiousness and their strength, if he does not know upon what to depend for assistance, nor where is the probable point of attack, it is not likely that he will efficiently resist. Such a man is in the situation of the governor of an unprepared and surprised city. He knows not to whom to apply for effectual help, and finds perhaps that those whom he has loved and trusted are the first to desert or betray him. He feebly resists, soon capitulates, and at last scarcely knows why he did not make a successful defence.

52. It is to be regretted that, in the moral education which commonly obtains, whether formal or incidental, there is little that is calculated to produce this acquaintance with our own minds ; little that refers us to ourselves, and much, very much, that calls and sends us away. Of many it is not too much to say, that they receive almost no moral *culture*. The plant of virtue is suffered to grow as a tree grows in a forest, and takes its chance of storm or sunshine. This, which is good for oaks and pines, is not good for man. The general atmosphere around him is infected, and the juices of the moral plant are often themselves unhealthy.

53. In the nursery, formularies and creeds are taught ; but this does not refer the child to its own mind. Indeed, unless a wakeful solicitude is maintained by those who teach, the tendency is the reverse. The mind is kept from habits of introversion, even in the offices of religion, by practically directing its attention to the tongue. "Many, it is to be feared, imagine that they are giving their children religious principles, when they are only teaching them religious truths." You cannot impart moral education as you teach a child to spell.

54. From the nursery a boy is sent to school. He spends six or eight hours of the day in the schoolroom, and the remainder is employed in the sports of boyhood. Once, or it may be twice, in the day he repeats a form of prayer, and on one day in the week he goes to church. There is very little in all this to make him acquainted with the internal community ; and habit, if nothing else, calls his reflections away.

55. From school or from college the business of life is begun. It can require no argument to show, that the ordinary pursuits of life have little tendency to direct a man's meditations to the moral condition of his own mind, or that they have much tendency to employ them upon other and very different things.

56. Nay, even the offices of public devotion have almost a tendency to keep the mind without itself. What if we say that the self-contemplation which even natural religion is likely to produce, is obstructed by the forms of Christian worship? "The transitions from one office of devotion to another, are contrived, like scenes in the

drama, to supply the mind with a succession of diversified engagements."[1] This supply of diversified engagements, whatever may be its value in other respects, has evidently the tendency of which we speak. It is not designed to supply, and it does not supply, the opportunity for calmness of recollection. A man must abstract himself from the external service if he would investigate the character and dispositions of the inmates of his own breast. Even the architecture and decorations of churches come in aid of the general tendency. They make the eye an auxiliary of the ear, and both keep the mind at a distance from those concerns which are peculiarly its own; from contemplating its own weaknesses and wants; and from applying to God for that peculiar help which perhaps itself only needs, and which God only can impart. So little are the course of education and the subsequent engagements of life calculated to foster this great auxiliary of moral character. It is difficult, in the wide world, to foster it as much as is needful. Nothing but wakeful solicitude on the part of the parent can be expected sufficiently to direct the mind within; whilst the general tendency of our associations and habits is to keep it without. Let him, however, do what he can. The habitual reference to the dictates of conscience may be promoted in the very young mind. This habit, like others, becomes strong by exercise. He that is faithful in little things is intrusted with more; and this is true in respect of knowledge as in respect of other departments of the Christian life. Fidelity of obedience is commonly succeeded by increase of light; and every act of obedience and every addition to knowledge furnishes new and still stronger inducements to persevere in the same course. Acquaintance with ourselves is the inseparable attendant of this course. We know the character and dispositions of our own inmates by frequent association with them; and if this fidelity to the internal law, and consequent knowledge of the internal world, be acquired in *early* life, the parent may reasonably hope that it will never wholly lose its efficiency amidst the bustles and anxieties of the world.

57. Undoubtedly, this most efficient security of moral character is not likely fully to operate during the continuance of the present state of society and of its institutions. It is I believe true, that the practice of morality is most complete amongst those persons who peculiarly recommend a reference to the internal law, and whose institutions, religious and social, are congruous with the habit of this reference. Their history exhibits a more unshaken adherence to that which they conceived to be right—fewer sacrifices of conscience to interest or the dread of suffering—less of trimming between conflicting motives—more, in a word, of adherence to rectitude without regard to consequences. We have seen that such persons are likely to form *accurate* views of rectitude; but whether they be accurate or not, does not affect the value of their moral education as securing fidelity to the degree of knowledge which they possess. It is of more consequence to adhere steadily to conscience, though it may not be perfectly enlightened, than to possess perfect knowledge without consistency of obedience. But in reality they who obey most, know most; and we say that the general testimony of experience is, that those persons exhibit the most unyielding fidelity to the Moral Law whose Moral Education has peculiarly directed them to the law written in the heart.

CHAPTER XIII.
Education of the People.

Advantages of extended education—Infant schools—Habits of inquiry.

58. Whether the Education of those who are not able to pay for educating themselves ought to be a private or a national charge, it is not our present business to discuss. It is in this country, at least, left to the voluntary benevolence of individuals, and this consideration may apologise for a brief reference to it here.

59. It is not long since it was a question whether the poor should be educated or not. That time is past, and it may be hoped the time will soon be passed when it shall be a question, To what extent?—that the time will soon arrive when it will be agreed that no limit needs to be assigned to the education of the poor, but that which is assigned by their own necessities or which ought to be assigned to the education of all men. There appears no more reason for excluding a poor man from the fields of knowledge, than for preventing him from using his eyes. The mental and the visual powers were alike given to be employed. A man should, indeed, "shut his eyes from seeing *evil*," but whatever reason there is for letting him see all that is beautiful, and excellent, and innocent in nature or in art, there is the same for enabling his mind to expatiate in the fields of knowledge.

60. The objections which are urged against this extended education are of the same kind as those which were urged against any

[1] Paley, p. 3, b. 5, c. 5.

education. They insist upon the probability of abuse. It *was* said, They who can write may forge; they who can read may read what is pernicious. The answer was, or it might have been—They who can hear, may hear profaneness and learn it; they who can see, may see bad examples and follow them: —but are we therefore to stop our ears and put out our eyes? It is *now* said, that if you give extended education to the poor, you will elevate them above their stations: that a critic would not drive a wheelbarrow, and that a philosopher would not shoe horses or weave cloth. But these consequences are without the limits of possibility; because the question for a poor man is, whether he shall perform such offices or starve: and surely it will not be pretended that hungry men would rather criticise than eat. Science and literature would not solicit a poor man from his labour more irresistibly than ease and pleasure do now; yet in spite of these solicitations what is the fact? That the poor man works for his bread. This is the inevitable result.

61. It is not the positive but the relative amount of knowledge that elevates a man above his station in society. It is not because he knows much, but because he knows more than his fellows. Educate all, and none will fancy that he is superior to his neighbours. Besides, we assign to the possession of knowledge, effects which are produced rather by habits of life. Ease and comparative leisure are commonly attendant upon extensive knowledge, and leisure and ease disqualify men for the laborious occupations much more than the knowledge itself.

62. There are some collateral advantages of an extended education of the people, which are of much importance. It has been observed that if the French had been an educated people, many of the atrocities of their Revolution would never have happened, and I believe it. Furious mobs are composed, not of enlightened but of unenlightened men—of men in whom the passions are dominant over the judgment, because the judgment has not been exercised, and informed, and habituated to direct the conduct. A factious declaimer can much less easily influence a number of men who acquired at school the rudiments of knowledge, and who have subsequently devoted their leisure to a Mechanics' Institute, than a multitude who cannot write or read, and who have never practised reasoning and considerate thought. And as the Education of a People prevents political evil, it effects political good. Despotic rulers well know that knowledge is inimical to their power. This simple fact is a sufficient reason, to a good and wise man, to approve knowledge and extend it. The attention to public institutions and public measures which is inseparable from an educated population, is a great good. We all know that the human heart is such, that the possession of power is commonly attended with a desire to increase it, even in opposition to the general weal. It is acknowledged that a check is needed, and no check is either so efficient or so safe as that of a watchful and intelligent public mind: so watchful that it is prompt to discover and to expose what is amiss; so intelligent, that it is able to form rational judgments respecting the nature and the means of amendment. In all public institutions there exists, and it is happy that there does exist, a sort of *vis inertiæ* which habitually resists change. This, which is beneficial as a general tendency, is often injurious from its excess: the state of public institutions almost throughout the world, bears sufficient testimony to the truth that they need alteration and amendment faster than they receive it—that the internal resistance of change is greater than is good for man. Unhappily, the ordinary way in which a people have endeavoured to amend their institutions has been by some mode of violence. If you ask when a nation acquired a greater degree of freedom, you are referred to some era of revolution and probably of blood. These are not proper, certainly they are not Christian, remedies for the disease. It is becoming an undisputed proposition, that no bad institution can permanently stand against the distinct Opinion of a People. This opinion is likely to be universal, and to be intelligent only amongst an enlightened community. Now that reformation of public institutions which results from public opinion is the very best in kind, and is likely to be the best in its mode:—in its kind, because public opinion is the *proper measure* of the needed alteration; and in its mode, because alterations which result from such a cause, are likely to be temperately made.

63. It may be feared that some persons object to an extended education of the people on these very grounds which we propose as recommendations: that they regard the tendency of education to produce examination, and, if need be, alteration of established institutions, as a reason for withholding it from the poor. To these, it is a sufficient answer, that if increase of knowledge and habits of investigation tend to alter any established institution, it is fit that it should be altered. There appears no means of avoiding this conclusion, unless it can be shown that increase of knowledge is usually attended with depravation of principle, and that in proportion as the judgment is exercised it decides amiss.

64. Generally, that intellectual education

is good for a poor man which is good for his richer neighbours: in other words, that is good for the poor which is good for man. There may be exceptions to the general rule; but he who is disposed to doubt the fitness of a rich man's education for the poor, will do well to consider first whether the rich man's education is fit for himself. The children of persons of property can undoubtedly learn much *more* than those of a labourer, and the labourer must select from the rich man's system a part only for his own child. But this does not effect the general conclusion. The parts which he ought to select are precisely those parts which are most necessary and beneficial to the rich.

65. Great as have been the improvements in the methods of conveying knowledge to the poor, there is reason to think that they will be yet greater. Some useful suggestions for the instruction of older children may I think be obtained from the systems in Infant Schools. In a well-conducted infant school, children acquire much knowledge, and they acquire it with delight. This delight is of extreme importance: perhaps it may safely be concluded, respecting all innocent knowledge, that if a child acquired it with pleasure he is *well* taught. It is worthy observation, that in the infant system, lesson-learning is nearly or wholly excluded. It is not to be expected that in the time which is devoted professedly to education by the children of the poor, much extent of knowledge can be acquired; but something may be acquired which is of much more consequence than mere school-learning—the love and the habits of inquiry. If education be so conducted that it is a positive pleasure to a boy to learn, there is little doubt that this love and habit will be induced. Here is the great advantage of early intellectual culture. The busiest have some leisure, leisure which they may employ ill or well; and that they will employ it well may reasonably be expected when knowledge is thus attractive for its own sake. That this effect is in a considerable degree actually produced, is indicated by the improved character of the books which poor men read, and in the prodigious increase in the number of those books. The supply and demand are correspondent. Almost every year produces books for the labouring classes of a higher intellectual order than the last. A journeyman in our days can understand and relish a work which would have been like Arabic to his grandfather.

66. Of moral education we say nothing here, except that the principles which are applicable to other classes of mankind are obviously applicable to the poor. With respect to the inculcation of peculiar religious opinions on the children who attend schools voluntarily supported, there is manifestly the same reason for inculcating them in this case as for teaching them at all. This supposes that the supporters of the school are not themselves divided in their religious opinions. If they are, and if the adherents to no one creed are able to support a school of their own, there appears no ground upon which they can rightly refuse to support a school in which no religious peculiarities are taught. It is better that intellectual knowledge, together with imperfect religious principles, should be communicated, than that children should remain in darkness. There is indeed some reason to suspect the genuineness of that man's philanthropy, who refuses to impart any knowledge to his neighbours because he cannot, at the same time, teach them his own creed.

CHAPTER XIV.

Amusements.

The Stage—Religious amusements—Masquerades—Field sports—The turf—Boxing—Wrestling. Opinions of posterity—Popular amusements needless.

67. It is a remarkable circumstance, that in almost all Christian countries many of the public and popular Amusements have been regarded as objectionable by the more sober and conscientious part of the community. This opinion could scarcely have been general unless it had been just: yet *why* should a people prefer amusements of which good men feel themselves compelled to disapprove? Is it because no public recreation can be devised of which the evil is not greater than the good? or because the inclinations of most men are such, that if it were devised, they would not enjoy it? It may be feared that the desires which are seeking for gratification are not themselves pure; and pure pleasures are not congenial to impure minds. The real cause of the objectionable nature of many popular diversions is to be sought in the want of virtue in the people.

68. Amusement is confessedly a subordinate concern in life. It is neither the principal nor amongst the principal objects of proper solicitude. No reasonable man sacrifices the more important thing to the less, and that a man's religious and moral condition is of incomparably greater importance than his diversion, is sufficiently plain. In estimating the propriety or rather the lawfulness of a given amusement, it may safely be laid down, That none is lawful of which the aggregate consequences are injurious to morals:—nor, if its effects upon

the immediate agents are, in general, morally bad: - nor if it occasions needless pain and misery to men or to animals :—nor, lastly, if it occupies much time or is attended with much expense.—Respecting all amusements, the question is not whether, in their simple or theoretical character, they are defensible, but whether they are defensible in their actually existing state.

The Drama.

69. So that if a person, by way of showing the propriety of theatrical exhibitions, should ask whether there was any harm in a man's repeating a composition before others and accompanying it with appropriate gestures he would ask a very foolish question : because he would ask a question that possesses little or no relevancy to the subject.—What are the ordinary effects of the stage upon those who act on it? One and one only answer can be given—that whatever happy exceptions there may be, the effect is bad ;— that the moral and religious character of actors is lower than that of persons in other professions. " It is an undeniable fact, for the truth of which we may safely appeal to every age and nation, that the situation of the performers, particularly of the female sex, is remarkably unfavourable to the maintenance and growth of the religious and moral principle, and, of course, highly dangerous to their eternal interests."[1]

70. Therefore, if I take my seat in the theatre, I have paid three or five shillings as an inducement to a number of persons to subject their principles to extreme danger ; and the defence which I make is, that I am amused by it. Now, we affirm that this defence is invalid ; that it is a defence which reason pronounces to be absurd, and morality to be vicious. Yet I have no other to make: it is the sum total of my justification.

71. But this, which is sufficient to decide the morality of the question, is not the only nor the chief part of the evil. The evil which is suffered by performers may be more intense, but upon spectators and others it is more extended. The night of a play is the harvest time of iniquity, where the profligate and the sensual put in their sickles and reap. It is to no purpose to say that a man may go to a theatre or parade a saloon without taking part in the surrounding licentiousness. All who are there promote the licentiousness, for if none was there, there would be no licentiousness ; that is to say, if none purchased tickets there would be neither actors to be depraved, nor dramas to vitiate, nor saloons to degrade, and corrupt, and shock us.—The whole question of the lawfulness of the dramatic amusements, as they are ordinarily conducted, is resolved into a very simple thing : After the doors on any given night are closed, have the *virtuous* or the *vicious* dispositions of the attenders been in the greater degree promoted ? Every one knows that the balance is on the side of vice, and this conclusively decides the question - " Is it lawful to attend ? "

72. The same question is to be asked, and the same answer I believe will be returned, respecting various other assemblies for purposes of amusement. They do more harm than good. They please but they injure us ; and what makes the case still stronger is, that the pleasure is frequently such as ought not to be enjoyed. A tippler enjoys pleasure in becoming drunk, but he is not to allege the gratification as a set-off against the immorality. And so it is with no small portion of the pleasures of an assembly. Dispositions are gratified which it were wiser to thwart ; and, to speak the truth, if the dispositions of the mind were such as they ought to be, many of these modes of diversion would be neither relished nor resorted to. Some persons try to persuade themselves that *charity* forms a part of their motive in attending such places ; as when the profits of the night are given to a benevolent institution. They hope, I suppose, that though it would not be quite right to go if benevolence were not a gainer, yet that the end warrants the means. But if these persons are charitable, let them give their guinea without deducting half for purposes of questionable propriety. Religious amusements, such as Oratorios and the like, form one of those artifices of chicanery by which people cheat, or try to cheat, themselves. The music, say they, is sacred, is devotional ; and we go to hear it as we go to church : it excites and animates our religious sensibilities. This, in spite of the solemnity of the association, is really ludicrous. These scenes subserve religion no more than they subserve chemistry. They do not increase its power any more than the power of the steam-engine. As it respects Christianity, it is all imposition and fiction ; and it is unfortunate that some of the most solemn topics of our religion are brought into such unworthy and debasing alliance.[1]

Masquerades.

73. Masquerades are of a more decided character. If the pleasure which people derive from meeting in disguises consisted merely in the " fun and drollery " of the

[1] Wilberforce : Practical View. c. 4, s. 3.   [1] See also Essay 2, c. 1.

thing, we might wonder to see so many children of five and six feet high, and leave them perhaps to their childishness: but the truth is, that to many the zest of the concealment consists in the opportunity which it gives of covert licentiousness; of doing that in secret of which, openly, they would profess to be ashamed. Some men and some women who affect propriety when the face is shown, are glad of a few hours of concealed libertinism. It is a time in which principles are left to guard the citadel of virtue without the auxiliary of public opinion. And ill do they guard it! It is no equivocal indication of the slender power of a person's principles, when they do not restrain him any longer than his misdeeds will produce exposure. She who is immodest at a masquerade, is modest nowhere. She may affect the language of delicacy and maintain external decorum, but she has no purity of mind.

The Field.

74. If we proceed with the calculation of the benefits and mischiefs of Field Sports, in the merchant-like manner of debtor and creditor, the balance is presently found to be greatly against them. The advantages to him who rides after hounds and shoots pheasants, are—that he is amused, and possibly that his health is improved; *some* of the disadvantages are—that it is unpropitious to the influence of religion and the dispositions which religion induces; that it expends money and time which a man ought to be able to employ better; and that it inflicts gratuitous misery upon the inferior animals. The value of the *pleasure* cannot easily be computed, and as to *health* it may pass for nothing; for if a man is so little concerned for his health that he will not take exercise without dogs and guns, he has no reason to expect other men to concern themselves for it in remarking upon his actions. And then for the other side of the calculation. That field sports have any tendency to make a man better, no one will pretend; and no one who looks around him will doubt that their tendency is in the opposite direction. It is not necessary to show that every one who rides after the dogs is a worse man in the evening than he was in the morning: the influence of such things is to be sought in those with whom they are habitual. Is the character of the *sportsman*, then, distinguished by religious sensibility? No. By activity of benevolence? No. By intellectual exertion? No. By purity of manners? No. Sportsmen are not the persons who diffuse the light of Christianity, or endeavour to rectify the public morals, or to extend the empire of knowledge. Look again at the clerical sportsman. Is he usually as exemplary in the discharge of his functions as those who decline such diversions? His parishioners know that he is not. So, then, the religious and moral tendency of Field Sports is bad. It is not necessary to show *how* the ill effect is produced. It is sufficient that it actually is produced.

75. As to the expenditure of time and money, I dare say we shall be told that a man has a right to employ both as he chooses. We have heretofore seen that he has no such right. Obligations apply just as truly to the mode of employing leisure and property, as to the use which a man may make of a pound of arsenic. The obligations are not indeed alike enforced in a court of justice: the misuser of arsenic is carried to prison, the misuser of time and money awaits as sure an inquiry at another tribunal. But no folly is more absurd than that of supposing we have a right to do whatever the law does not punish. Such is the state of mankind, so great is the amount of misery and degradation, and so great are the effects of money and active philanthropy in meliorating this condition of our species, that it is no light thing for a man to employ his time and property upon vain and needless gratifications. It is no light thing to keep a pack of hounds, and to spend days and weeks in riding after them. As to the torture which field sports inflict upon animals, it is wonderful to observe our inconsistencies. He who has, in the day, inflicted upon half a dozen animals almost as much torture as they are capable of sustaining, and who has wounded perhaps half a dozen more, and left them to die of pain or starvation, gives in the evening a grave reproof to his child, whom he sees amusing himself with picking off the wings of flies! The infliction of pain is not that which gives pleasure to the sportsman (this were ferocious depravity), but he voluntarily inflicts the pain in order to please himself. Yet this man sighs and moralises over the cruelty of children! An appropriate device for a sportsman's dress would be a pair of balances, on which one scale was laden with "Virtue and Humanity," and the other with "Sport"; the latter should be preponderating and lifting the other into the air.

The Turf.

76. The Turf is still worse, partly because it is a stronghold of gambling, and therefore an efficient cause of misery and wickedness. It is an amusement of almost unmingled evil. But upon whom is the evil chargeable? Upon the fifty or one hundred persons only who bring horses and make bets? No; every man participates who attends the course. The great attraction of many public spectacles, and of this amongst others, consists more in the company than in the ostensible object of

amusement. Many go to a race-ground who cannot tell when they return what horse has been the victor. Every one, therefore, who is present must take his share of the mischief and the responsibility.

77. It is the same with respect to the gross and vulgar diversions of boxing, wrestling, and feats of running and riding. There is the same almost pure and unmingled evil—the same popularity resulting from the concourses who attend, and, by consequence, the participation and responsibility in those who do attend. The drunkenness, and the profaneness, and the debauchery, lie in part at the doors of those who are merely lookers-on; and if these lookers-on make pretensions to purity of character, their example is so much the more influential and their responsibility tenfold increased. Defences of these gross amusements are ridiculous. One tells us of keeping up the national spirit, which is the same thing as to say, that a human community is benefited by inducing into it the qualities of the bull-dog. Another expatiates upon invigorating the muscular strength of the poor, as if the English poor were under so little necessity to labour, and to strengthen themselves by labour, that artificial means must be devised to increase their toil.

78. The vicissitudes of folly are endless: the vulgar games of the present day may soon be displaced by others, the same in genus but differing in species. At the present moment, Wrestling has become the point of interest. A man is conveyed across the kingdom to try whether he can throw down another; and when he has done it, grave narratives of the feat are detailed in half the newspapers of the country! There is a grossness, a vulgarity, a want of mental elevation in these things, which might induce the man of intelligence to reprobate them even if the voice of morality were silent. They are remains of barbarism—evidences that barbarism still maintains itself amongst us—proofs that the higher qualities of our nature are not sufficiently dominant over the lower.

79. These grossnesses will pass away, as the deadly conflicts of men with beasts are passed already. Our posterity will wonder at the barbarism of us, their fathers, as we wonder at the barbarism of Rome. Let him, then, who loves intellectual elevation advance beyond the present times, and anticipate, in the recreations which he encourages, that period when these diversions shall be regarded as indicating one of the intermediate stages between the ferociousness of mental darkness and the purity of mental light.

80. These criticisms might be extended to many other species of amusement; and it is humiliating to discover that the conclusion will very frequently be the same—that the evil outbalances the good, and that there are no grounds upon which a good man can justify a participation in them. In thus concluding, it is possible that the reader may imagine that we would exclude enjoyment from the world, and substitute a system of irreproachable austerity. He who thinks this is unacquainted with the nature and sources of our better enjoyments. It is an ordinary mistake to imagine that pleasure is great only when it is vivid or intemperate, as a child fancies it were more delightful to devour a pound of sugar at once, than to eat an ounce daily in his food. It is happily and kindly provided that the greatest sum of enjoyment is that which is quietly and constantly induced. No men understand the nature of pleasure so well, or possess it so much, as those who find it within their own doors. If it were not that Moral Education is so bad, multitudes would seek enjoyment and find it here, who now fancy that they never partake of pleasure except in scenes of diversion. It is unquestionably true that no community enjoys life more than that which excludes all these amusements from its sources of enjoyment. We use therefore the language, not of speculation, but of experience, when we say, that none of them is, in any degree, necessary to the happiness of life.

CHAPTER XV.

Duelling.

Pitt and Tierney—Duelling the offspring of intellectual meanness, fear, and servility—"A fighting man"—Hindoo immolations—Wilberforce—Seneca.

1. It is not to much purpose to show that this strange practice is in itself wrong, because no one denies it. Other grounds of defence are taken, although, to be sure, there is a plain absurdity in conceding that a thing is wrong in morals, and then trying to show that it is proper to practise it.

2. Public notions exempt a clergyman from the "necessity" of fighting duels, and they exempt other men from the "necessity" of demanding satisfaction for a clergyman's insult. Now, we ask the man of honour whether he would rather receive an insult from a military officer or from a clergyman? Which would give him the greater pain, and cause him the more concern and uneasiness? That from the military officer, certainly. But why? Because the officer's affront

leads to a duel, and the clergyman's does not. So, then, it is preferable to receive an insult to which the "necessity" of fighting is *not* attached than one to which it *is* attached. Why then attach the necessity to any man's affront? You say, that demanding satisfaction is a remedy for the evil of an insult. But we see that the evil, *together with the remedy*, is worse than the evil alone. Why then institute the remedy at all? It is not indeed to be questioned that some insults may be forborne, because it is known to what consequences they lead. But, on the other hand, for what purpose does one man insult another? To give him pain; now, we have just seen that the pain is so much the greater *in consequence* of the "necessity" of fighting, and therefore the motives to insult another are increased. A man who wishes to inflict pain upon another, can inflict it more intensely in consequence of the system of duelling.

3. The truth is, that men fancy the system is useful, because they do not perceive how Public Opinion has been violently turned out of its natural and its usual course? When a military man is guilty of an insult, public disapprobation falls but lightly upon him. It reserves its force to direct against the insulted party if he does not demand satisfaction. But when a clergyman is guilty of an insult, Public disapprobation falls upon him with undivided force. The insulted party receives no censure. Now, if you take away the custom of demanding satisfaction, what will be the result? Why, that public opinion will revert to its natural course; it will direct all* its penalties to the *offending* party, and by consequence restrain him from offending. It will act towards all men as it now acts towards the clergy; and if a clergyman were frequently to be guilty of insults, his character would be destroyed. The reader will perhaps more distinctly perceive that the fancied utility of duelling in preventing insults, results from this misdirection of public opinion by this brief argument.

4. An individual either fears public opinion, or he does not. If he does not fear it, the custom of duelling cannot prevent him from insulting whomsoever he pleases; because public opinion is the only thing which makes men fight, and *he* does not regard it. If he does fear public opinion, then the most effectual way of restraining him from insulting others, is by directing that opinion against the act of insulting—just as it is now directed in the case of the clergy.[1]

5. Thus it is that we find—what he knows the perfection of Christian morality would expect that Duelling, as it is immoral, so it is absurd.

6. It appears to be forgotten that a *duel* is not more allowable to secure ourselves from censure or neglect than any other violation of the Moral Law. If these motives constitute a justification of a duel, they constitute a justification of robbery or poisoning. To advocate duelling is not to defend one species of offence, but to assert the general right to violate the laws of God. If, as Dr. Johnson reasoned, the "notions which prevail" make fighting right, they can make anything right. Nothing is wanted but to alter the "notions which prevail," and there is not a crime mentioned in the statute-book that will not be lawful and honourable to-morrow.

7. It is usual with those who do foolish and vicious things, or who do things from foolish or vicious motives, to invent some fiction, by which to veil the evil or folly, and to give it, if possible, a creditable appearance. This has been done in the case of duelling. We hear a great deal about honour, and spirit, and courage, and other qualities equally pleasant, and as it respects the duellist, equally fictitious. The *want* of sufficient honour, and spirit, and courage, is precisely the very reason why men fight. Pitt fought with Tierney; upon which Pitt's biographer writes —"A mind like his, cast in no common mould, should have risen superior to a *low and unworthy prejudice*, the folly of which it must have perceived, and the wickedness of which it must have acknowledged. Could *Mr. Pitt* be led away by that false shame which subjects the decisions of reason to the control of *fear*, and renders the admonitions of conscience subservient to the powers of ridicule?"[1] Low prejudice, folly, wickedness, false shame, and fear, are the motives which the complacent duellist dignifies with the titles of honour, spirit, courage. This, to be sure, is very politic: he would not be so silly as to call his motives by their right names. Others, of course, join in the chicanery. They reflect that they themselves may one day have "a meeting," and they wish to keep up the credit of a system which they are conscious they have not principle enough to reject.

8. Put Christianity out of the question— Would not even the philosophy of paganism have despised that littleness of principle which would not bear a man up in adhering to conduct which he knew to be right—that littleness of principle which sacrifices the dictates of the understanding to an unworthy fear?—When a good man, rather than conform to some vicious institution of the papacy, stood firmly against the frowns and

[1] See West. Rev., No. 7, Art. 2.   [1] Gifford's Life, vol. i. p. 263

persecutions of the world, against obloquy and infamy, we say that his mental principles were *great* as well as good. If they were, the principles of the duellist are *mean* as well as vicious. *He* is afraid to be good and great. He knows the course which dignity and virtue prescribe, but he will not rise above those lower motives which prompt him to deviate from that course. It does not affect these conclusions to concede, that he who is afraid to refuse a challenge may generally be a man of elevated mind. He may be such; but his refusal is an exception to his general character. It is an instance in which he impeaches his consistency in excellence. If it were consistent, if the whole mind had attained to the rightful stature of a Christian man, he would assuredly contemn in his practice the conduct which he disapproved in his heart. If you would show us a man of courage, bring forward him who will say, I will *not* fight. Suppose a gentleman who, upon the principles which Gifford says should have actuated Pitt and all great minds, had thus refused to fight, and suppose him saying to his withdrawing friends—" I have acted with perfect deliberation : I knew all the consequences of the course I have pursued : but I was persuaded that I should act most like a man of intellect, as well as like a Christian, by declining the meeting ; and therefore I declined it. I feel and deplore the consequences, though I do not deprecate them. I am not fearful, as I have not been fearful ; for I appeal to yourselves whether I have not encountered the more appalling alternative—whether it does not require a greater effort to do what I have done, and what I am at this moment doing, than to have met my opponent."—Such a man's magnanimity might not procure for him the *companionship* of his acquaintance, but it would do much more ; it would obtain the suffrages of their judgments and their hearts. Whilst they continued perhaps externally to neglect him, they would internally honour and admire. They would feel that his excellence was of an order to which they could make no pretensions ; and they would feel, as they were practising this strange hypocrisy of vice, that *they* were the proper objects of contempt and pity.

9. The species of slavery to which a man is sometimes reduced by being, as he calls it, " obliged to fight," is really pitiable. A British officer writes of a petulant and profligate class of men, one of whom is sometimes found in a regiment, and says, " Sensible that an officer *must* accept a challenge, he does not hesitate to deal them in abundance, and shortly acquires the name of a fighting man ; but as every one is not willing to throw away his life when called upon by one who is indifferent to his own, *many become condescending*, which this man immediately construes into fear ; and, presuming upon this, he acts as if he imagined *no one dare contradict him* but all *must yield obedience to his will.*" Here the servile bondage of which we speak is brought prominently out. Here is the crouching and unmanly fear. Here is the abject submission of sense and reason to the grossest vulgarity of insolence, folly, and guilt. The officer presently gives an account of an instance in which the whole mess were domineered over by one of these fighting men ;—and a pitiably ludicrous account it is. The man had invited them to dinner at some distance. " On the day appointed, there came on a most violent snowstorm, and in the morning we despatched a servant with an apology." But alas ! these poor men could not use their own judgments as to whether they should ride in a " most violent snowstorm " or not. The man sent back some rude message that he " expected them." They were afraid of what the fighting man would do next morning ; and so the whole mess, against their wills, actually rode "near four miles in a heavy snowstorm, and passed a day," says the officer, "that was, without exception, the most unpleasant I ever passed in my life !"[1] In the instance of these men, the motives to duelling as founded upon Fear, operated so powerfully that the officers were absolutely enslaved—driven against their will by Fear, as negroes are by a cartwhip.

10. We are shocked and disgusted at the immolation of women amongst the Hindoos, and think that, if such a sacrifice were attempted in England, it would excite feelings of the utmost repulsion and abhorrence. Of the custom of immolation, Duelling is the sister. Their parents are the same, and, like other sisters, their lineaments are similar. Why does a Hindoo mount the funeral pile ? To vindicate and maintain her honour. Why does an Englishman go to the heath with his pistols ? To vindicate and maintain his honour. What is the nature and character of the Hindoo's honour? Quite factitious. Of the duellist's ? Quite factitious. How is the motive applied to the Hindoo ? To her fears of reproach. To the duellist ? To his fears of reproach. What then is the difference between the two customs ? This—That one is practised in the midst of pagan darkness, and the other in the midst of Christian light. And yet these very men give their guineas to the Missionary Society, lament the degradation of the Hindoos, and expatiate upon the sacred duty of enlightening them with Christianity ! " Physician ! heal *thyself.*"

---

[1] Lieut. Aubrey : Travels in North America.

11. One consideration connected with duelling is of unusual interest. "In the judgment of that religion which requires purity of heart, and of that Being to whom thought is action, *he* cannot be esteemed innocent of this crime who lives in a settled, habitual determination to commit it, when circumstances shall call upon him so to do. This is a consideration which places the crime of duelling on a different footing from almost any other; indeed there is perhaps NO other, which mankind habitually and deliberately resolve to practise whenever the temptation shall occur. It shows also that the crime of duelling is far more general in the higher classes than is commonly supposed, and that the whole sum of the guilt which the practice produces, is great beyond what has perhaps been ever conceived."[1]

12. "It is the intention," says Seneca, "and not the effect which makes the wickedness:" and that Greater than Seneca who laid the axe to the root of our vices, who laid upon the mental disposition that guilt which had been laid upon the act, may be expected to regard this habitual willingness and intention to violate His laws as an actual and great offence. The felon who plans and resolves to break into a house, is not the less a felon because a watchman happens to prevent him; nor is the offence of him who happens never to be challenged, necessarily at all less than that of him who takes the life of his friend.

CHAPTER XVI.

Suicide.

Unmanliness of suicide—Forbidden in the New Testament—Its folly—Legislation respecting suicide—Verdict of *felo de se*.

13. There are few subjects upon which it is more difficult either to write or to legislate with effect than that of Suicide. It is difficult to a writer, because a man does not resolve upon the act until he has first become steeled to some of the most powerful motives that can be urged upon the human mind; and to the legislator, because he can inflict no penalty upon the offending party.

14. It is to be feared that there is little probability of diminishing the frequency of this miserable offence by urging the considerations which philosophy suggests. The voice of nature is louder and stronger than the voice of philosophy; and as nature speaks to the suicide in vain, what is the hope that philosophy will be regarded?—There appears

[1] Wilberforce: Practical View, c. 4, s. 3.

to be but one efficient means by which the mind can be armed against the temptations to suicide, because there is but one that can support it against *every* evil of life—practical religion—belief in the providence of God—confidence in His wisdom—hope in His goodness. The only anchor that can hold us in safety is that which is fixed "within the vail." He upon whom religion possesses its proper influence, finds that it enables him to endure, with resigned patience, every calamity of life. When patience thus fulfils its perfect work, suicide, which is the result of *impatience*, cannot be committed. He who is surrounded, by whatever means, with pain or misery, should remember that the present existence is strictly *probationary*—a scene upon which we are to be exercised, and tried, and tempted; and in which we are to manifest whether we are willing firmly to endure. The good or evil of the present life is of importance chiefly as it influences our allotment in futurity: sufferings are permitted for our advantage: they are designed to purify and rectify the heart. The universal Father "scourgeth every son whom He receiveth;" and the suffering, the scourging, is of little account in comparison with the prospects of another world. It is not worthy to be compared with the glory which shall follow—that glory of which an exceeding and eternal weight is the reward of a "*patient continuance* in well-doing." To him who thus regards misery, not as an evil but as a good; not as the unrestrained assault of chance or malice, but as the beneficent discipline of a Father; to him who remembers that the time is approaching in which he will be able most feelingly to say, "For all I bless Thee—most for the *severe*,"—every affliction is accompanied with its proper alleviation: the present hour may distress but it does not overwhelm him; he may be perplexed but is not in despair: he sees the darkness and feels the storm, but he knows that light will again arise, and that the storm will eventually be hushed with an efficacious, Peace, be still;—so that there shall be a great calm.

15. Compared with these motives to avoid the first promptings to suicide, others are likely to be of little effect; and yet they are neither inconsiderable nor few. It is more dignified, more worthy an enlightened and manly understanding, to meet and endure an inevitable evil than to sink beneath it. The case of him who feels prompted to suicide, is something like that of the duellist as it was illustrated in the preceding chapter. Each sacrifices his life to his fears. The suicide balances between opposing objects of dread (for dreadful self-destruction must be supposed to be), and chooses the alternative which he fears least. If his courage,

his firmness, his manliness, were greater, he who chooses the alternative of suicide, like him who chooses the duel, would endure the evil rather than avoid it in a manner which dignity and religion forbid. The lesson too which the self-destroyer teaches to his connections, of sinking in despair under the evils of life, is one of the most pernicious which a man can bequeath. The power of the example is also great. Every act of suicide tacitly conveys the sanction of one more judgment in its favour: frequency of repetition diminishes the sensation of abhorrence, and makes succeeding sufferers resort to it with less reluctance. "Beside which general reasons, each case will be aggravated by its own proper and particular consequences; by the duties that are deserted; by the claims that are defrauded; by the loss, affliction, or disgrace which our death, or the manner of it, causes our family, kindred, or friends; by the occasion we give to many to suspect the sincerity of our moral and religious professions, and, together with ours, those of all others;"[1] and lastly, by the scandal which we bring upon religion itself by declaring, practically, that it is not able to support man under the calamities of life.

16. Some men say that the New Testament contains no prohibition of suicide. If this were true, it would avail nothing, because there are many things which it does not forbid, but which every one knows to be wicked. But in reality it does forbid it. Every exhortation which it gives to be patient, every encouragement to trust in God, every consideration which it urges as a support under affliction and distress, is a virtual prohibition of suicide;—because, if a man commits suicide, he *rejects* every such advice and encouragement, and disregards every such motive.

17. To him who believes either in revealed or natural religion, there is a certain *folly* in the commission of suicide; for from what does he fly? From his present sufferings; whilst death, for aught that he has reason to expect, or at any rate for aught that he knows, may only be the portal to sufferings more intense. Natural religion, I think, gives no countenance to the supposition that suicide can be approved by the Deity, because it proceeds upon the belief that, in another state of existence, He will compensate good men for the sufferings of the present. At the best, and under either religion, it is a desperate stake. He that commits murder may repent, and we hope, be forgiven; but he that destroys himself, whilst he incurs a load of guilt, cuts off, by the act, the power of repentance.

[1] Mor. and Pol. Phil., b. 4, c. 3.

18. Not every act of suicide is to be attributed to excess of misery. Some shoot themselves or throw themselves into a river in rage or revenge, in order to inflict pain and remorse upon those who have ill-used them. Such, it is to be suspected, is sometimes a motive to self-destruction in disappointed love. The unhappy person leaves behind some message or letter, in the hope of exciting that affection and commiseration by the catastrophe, which he could not excite when alive. Perhaps such persons hope, too, that the world will sigh over their early fate, tell of the fidelity of their loves, and throw a romantic melancholy over their story. This needs not to be a subject of wonder: unnumbered multitudes have embraced death in other forms from kindred motives. We hear continually of those who die for the sake of glory. This is but another phantom, and the less amiable phantom of the two. It is just as reasonable to die in order that the world may admire our true love, as in order that it may admire our bravery. And the lover's hope is the better founded. There are too many aspirants for glory for each to get even his "peppercorn of praise." But the lover may hope for higher honours; a paragraph may record his fate through the existence of a weekly paper; he may be talked of through half a county; and some kindred spirit may inscribe a tributary sonnet in a lady's album.

19. To *legislate* efficiently upon the crime of suicide is difficult, if it is not impossible. As the legislator cannot inflict a penalty upon the offender, the act must pass with impunity unless the penalty is made to fall upon the innocent. I say the penalty; for such it would actually be, whatever were the provision of the law — whether, for instance, confiscation of property, or indignity to the remains of the dead. One would make a family poor, and the other perhaps unhappy. It does not appear just or reasonable that these should suffer for an offence which they could not prevent, and by which they, above all others, are already injured and distressed.

20. One thing appears to be clear, that it is vain for a legislature to attempt any interference of which the people do not approve. This is evident from the experience in our own country, where coroners' juries prefer perjuring themselves to pronouncing a verdict of *felo de se*, by which the remains would be subjected to barbarous indignities. Coroners' inquests seem to proceed rather upon the presupposition that he who destroys himself is insane, than upon the evidence which is brought before them; and thus, whilst the law is evaded, perjury, it is to be feared, is very frequent. That the public mind disapproves the existing law is a good reason for altering it; but, it is not

a good reason why coroners' juries should violate their oaths, and give encouragement to the suicide by telling him, that disgrace will be warded off from his memory and from his family by a generous verdict of insanity. It has been said that it is a common thing for a suicide's friends to *fee* the coroner in order to induce him to prevent a verdict of *felo de se*. If this be true, it is indeed time that the arm of the law should be vigorously extended. What punishment is due to the man who accepts a purse as a reward for inducing twelve persons to commit perjury? It is probable, too, that half-a-dozen just verdicts, by which the law was allowed to take its course, would occasion the abolition of the disgusting statute;[1] for the public would not bear that it should be acted upon.

21. The great object is to associate with the act of suicide ideas of guilt and horror in the public mind. This association would be likely to preclude, in individuals, that *first* complacent contemplation of the act which probably precedes, by a long interval, the act itself. The anxiety which the surviving friends manifest for a verdict of "insanity," is a proof how great is the power of imagination, and how much they are in dread of public opinion. They are anxious that the disgrace and reproach of conscious self-murder should not cling to their family. This is precisely that anxiety of which the legislator should avail himself, by enactments that would require satisfactory *proof* of insanity, and which, in default of such proof, would leave to its full force the stigma and the pain, and excite a sense of horror of the act, and a perception of its wickedness in the public mind. The point for the exercise of legislative wisdom is, to devise such an ultimate procedure as shall call forth these feelings, but as shall not become nugatory by being more dreadful than the public will endure. What that procedure should be, I pretend not to describe; but it may be observed that the simple circumstance of pronouncing a public verdict of *conscious self-murder*, would, amongst a people of good feelings, go far towards the production of the desired effect.—As the law now exists, and as it is now violated, the tendency is exactly the contrary of what it ought to be. By the almost universal custom which it generates, of declaring suicides to have been insane, it effectually diminishes that pain to individuals, and that horror in the public, which the crime itself would naturally occasion.

[1] This statute has been repealed; and the law now simply requires, when a verdict of *felo de se* is returned, that the body shall be interred privately, at night, and without the funeral service.—Ed.

CHAPTER XVII.

Rights of Self-Defence.

These rights not absolute—Their limits—Personal attack—Preservation of property—Much resistance lawful—Effects of forbearance—Sharpe—Barclay—Ellwood.

22. The right of defending ourselves against violence is easily deducible from the Law of Nature. There is, however, little need to deduce it, because mankind are at least *sufficiently* persuaded of its lawfulness.—The great question, which the opinions and principles that now influence the world makes it needful to discuss is, Whether the right of self-defence is absolute and unconditional—whether every action whatever is lawful, provided it is necessary to the preservation of life? They who maintain the affirmative maintain a great deal; for they maintain that whenever life is endangered, all rules of morality are, as it respects the individual, suspended, annihilated: every moral obligation is taken away by the single fact that life is threatened.

23. Yet the language that is ordinarily held upon the subject implies the supposition of all this. "If our lives are threatened with assassination or open violence from the hands of robbers or enemies, *any* means of defence would be allowed and laudable."[1] Again, "There is one case in which *all* extremities are justifiable, namely, when our life is assaulted, and it becomes necessary for our preservation to kill the assailant."[2]

24. The reader may the more willingly inquire whether these propositions are true, because most of those who lay them down are at little pains to *prove* their truth. Men are extremely willing to acquiesce in it without proof, and writers and speakers think it unnecessary to adduce it. Thus perhaps it happens that fallacy is not detected because it is not sought.—If the reader should think that some of the instances which follow are remote from the ordinary affairs of life, he is requested to remember that we are discussing the soundness of an alleged *absolute rule*. If it be found that there are or have been cases in which it is not absolute—cases in which *all* extremities are not lawful in defence of life—then the rule is not sound: then there are some limits to the Right of Self-Defence.

25. If "*any* means of defence are laudable," if "*all* extremities are justifiable," then they are not confined to acts of resistance to the

[1] Grotius: Rights of War and Peace.
[2] Paley: Mor. and Pol. Phil., p. 3, b. iv. c. 1.

assailing party. There may be other conditions upon which life may be preserved than that of violence towards *him*. Some ruffians seize a man in the highway, and will kill him unless he will conduct them to his neighbour's property and assist them in carrying it off. May this man unite with them in the robbery in order to save his life, or may he not? If he may, what becomes of the law, Thou shalt not steal? If he may not, then *not every means* by which a man may preserve his life is "laudable" or "allowed." We have found an exception to the rule. There are twenty other wicked things which violent men may make the sole condition of not taking our lives. Do all wicked things become lawful because life is at stake? If they do, Morality surely is at an end : if they do not, such propositions as those of Grotius and Paley are untrue.

26. A pagan has unalterably resolved to offer me up in sacrifice on the morrow, unless I will acknowledge the deity of his gods and worship them. I shall presume that the Christian will regard these acts as being, under every possible circumstance, unlawful. The night offers me an opportunity of assassinating him. Now I am placed, so far as the argument is concerned, in precisely the same situation with respect to this man, as a traveller is with respect to a ruffian with a pistol. Life in both cases depends on killing the offender. Both are acts of self-defence. Am I at liberty to assassinate this man? The heart of the Christian surely answers, No. Here then is a case in which I may not take a violent man's life in order to save my own.—We have said that the heart of the Christian answers, No : and this we think is a just species of appeal. But if any one doubts whether the assassination would be unlawful, let him consider whether one of the Christian apostles would have committed it in such a case. Here, at any rate, the heart of every man answers, No. And mark the reason—because every man perceives that the act would have been palpably inconsistent with the apostolic character and conduct ; or, which is the same thing, with a *Christian* character and conduct.

27. Or put such a case in a somewhat different form. A furious Turk holds a scimitar over my head, and declares he will instantly despatch me unless I abjure Christianity and acknowledge the divine legation of "the prophet." Now there are two supposable ways in which I may save my life ; one by contriving to stab the Turk, and one "by denying Christ before men." You say I am not at liberty to deny Christ, but I am at liberty to stab the man. *Why* am I not at liberty to deny Him? Because Christianity forbids it. Then we require you to show that Christianity does *not* forbid you to take his life. Our religion pronounces both actions to be wrong. You say that, under these circumstances, the *killing* is right. Where is your proof? What is the ground of your distinction?—But whether it can be adduced or not, our immediate argument is established—That there are *some* things which it is not lawful to do in order to preserve our lives. This conclusion has indeed been practically acted upon. A company of inquisitors and their agents are about to conduct a good man to the stake. If he could by any means destroy these men, he might save his life. It is a question, therefore, of self-defence. Supposing these means to be within his power—supposing he could contrive a mine, and by suddenly firing it, blow his persecutors into the air—would it be lawful and Christian thus to act ? No. The common judgments of mankind respecting the right temper and conduct of the martyr, pronounce it to be wrong. It is pronounced to be wrong by the language and example of the first teachers of Christianity. The conclusion, therefore, again is, that all extremities are *not* allowable in order to preserve life ;—that *there is a limit to the right of self-defence.*

28. It would be to no purpose to say that in some of the instances which have been proposed, *religious* duties interfere with and limit the rights of self-defence. This is a common fallacy. Religious duties and moral duties are identical in point of obligation, for they are imposed by one authority. Religious duties are not obligatory for any other reason than that which attaches to moral duties also ; namely, the Will of God. He who violates the Moral Law is as truly unfaithful in his allegiance to God, as he who denies Christ before men.

29. So that we come at last to one single and simple question, whether taking the life of a person who threatens ours, is or is not compatible with the Moral Law. We refer for an answer to the broad principles of Christian piety and Christian benevolence ; that piety which reposes habitual confidence in the Divine Providence, and an habitual preference of futurity to the present time ; and that benevolence which not only loves our neighbours as ourselves, but feels that the Samaritan or the *enemy* is a neighbour. There is no conjuncture in life in which the exercise of this benevolence may be suspended ; none in which we are not required to maintain and to practise it. Whether Want implores our compassion, or Ingratitude returns ills for our kindness ; whether a fellow-creature is drowning in a river or assailing us on the highway ; everywhere, and under all circumstances, the duty remains.

30. Is killing an assailant, then, *within* or *without* the limits of this Benevolence?—As to the man, it is evident that no good-will is exercised towards him by shooting him through the head. Who indeed will dispute that, before we can thus destroy him, benevolence towards him must be excluded from our minds? We not only exercise no benevolence ourselves, but preclude him from receiving it from any human heart; and, which is a serious item in the account, we cut him off from all possibility of reformation. To call sinners to repentance was one of the great characteristics of the mission of Christ. Does it appear consistent with this characteristic for one of His followers to take away from a sinner the power of repentance? Is it an act that accords, and is congruous, with Christian love?

31. But an argument has been attempted here. That we may "kill the assailant is evident in a state of nature, unless it can be shown that we are bound to prefer the aggressor's life to our own; that is to say, to love our enemy *better* than ourselves, which can never be a debt of justice, nor anywhere appears to be a duty of charity."[1] The answer is this: That although we may not be required to love our enemy *better* than ourselves, we are required to love him *as* ourselves; and therefore in the supposed case, it would still be a question equally balanced which life ought to be sacrificed; for it is quite clear that, if we kill the assailant, we love him *less* than ourselves, which does seem to militate against a duty of charity. But the truth is, that he who, from motives of obedience to the Will of God, spares the aggressor's life even to the endangering his own, does exercise love both to the aggressor and to himself, *perfectly:* to the aggressor, because by sparing his life we give him the opportunity of repentance and amendment: to himself, because every act of obedience to God is perfect benevolence towards ourselves; it is consulting and promoting our most valuable interests; it is propitiating the favour of Him who is emphatically "a rich rewarder." —So that the question remains as before, not whether we should love our enemy better than ourselves, but whether Christian principles are acted upon in destroying him; and if they are not, whether we should prefer Christianity to ourselves; whether we should be willing to lose our life for Christ's sake and the gospel's.

32. Perhaps it will be said that we should exercise benevolence to the public as well as to the offender, and that we may exercise more benevolence to them by killing than by sparing him. But very few persons, when they kill a man who attacks them, kill him out of benevolence to the public. That is not the motive which influences their conduct, or which they at all take into the account. Besides, it is by no means certain that the public would lose anything by the forbearance. To be sure, a man can do no more mischief after he is killed; but then it is to be remembered, that robbers are more desperate and more murderous from the apprehension of swords and pistols than they would be without it. Men are desperate in proportion to their apprehensions of danger. The plunderer who feels a confidence that his own life will not be taken, may conduct his plunder with comparative gentleness; whilst he who knows that his life is in immediate jeopardy, stuns or murders his victim lest he should be killed himself. The *great* evil which a family sustains by a robbery is often not the loss, but the terror and the danger; and these are the evils which, by the exercise of forbearance, would be diminished. So that, if some bad men are prevented from committing robberies by the fear of death, the public gains in other ways by the forbearance: nor is it by any means certain that the balance of advantages is in favour of the more violent course.—The argument which we are opposing proceeds on the supposition that our own lives are endangered. Now it is a fact that this very danger results, in part, from the want of habits of forbearance. We publicly profess that we would kill an assailant; and the assailant, knowing this, prepares to kill us when otherwise he would forbear.

33. And after all, if it were granted that a person is at liberty to take an assailant's life *in order to preserve his own,* how is he to know, in the majority of instances, whether his own would be taken? When a man breaks into a person's house, and this person, as soon as he comes up with the robber, takes out a pistol and shoots him, we are not to be told that this man was killed "in defence of life." Or go a step further, and a step further still, by which the intention of the robber to commit personal violence or inflict death is more and more probable:— you must at last shoot him in uncertainty whether your life was endangered or not. Besides, you can withdraw—you can fly. None but the predetermined murderer *wishes* to commit murder. But perhaps you exclaim—"Fly! Fly, and leave your property unprotected!" Yes—unless you mean to say that preservation of property, as well as preservation of life, makes it lawful to kill an offender. This were to adopt a new and a very different proposition; but a proposition which I suspect cannot be separated in practice from the former. He who affirms

---

[1] Paley: Mor. and Pol. Phil., p. 3, b. 4, c. 1.

that he may kill another in order to preserve his life, and that he may endanger his life in order to protect his property, does in reality affirm that he may kill another in order to preserve his property. But such a proposition, in an unconditional form, no one surely will tolerate. The laws of the land do not admit it, nor do they even admit the right of taking another's life simply because he is attempting to take ours. They require that we should be tender even of the murderer's life, and that we should fly rather than destroy it.[1]

34. We say that the proposition that we may take life in order to preserve our property is intolerable. To preserve how much? five hundred pounds, or fifty, or ten, or a shilling, or a sixpence? It has actually been declared that the rights of self-defence "justify a man in taking all forcible methods which are necessary, in order to procure the restitution of the freedom or the property of which he had been unjustly deprived."[2] All forcible methods to obtain restitution of property! No limit to the nature or effects of the force! No limit to the insignificance of the amount of the property! Apply, then, the rule. A boy snatches a bunch of grapes from a fruiterer's stall. The fruiterer runs after the thief, but finds that he is too light of foot to be overtaken. Moreover, the boy eats as he runs. "All forcible methods," reasons the fruiterer, "are justifiable to obtain restitution of property. I may fire after the plunderer, and when he falls regain my grapes." All this is just and right, if Gisborne's proposition is true. It is a dangerous thing to lay down maxims in morality.

35. The conclusion, then, to which we are led by these inquiries is, that he who kills another, even upon the plea of self-defence, does not do it in the predominance nor in the exercise of Christian dispositions ; and if this is true, is it not also true, that his life cannot be thus taken in conformity with the Christian law?

36. But this is very far from concluding that no resistance may be made to aggression. We may make, and we ought to make, a great deal. It is the duty of the civil magistrate to repress the violence of one man towards another, and by consequence it is the duty of the individual, when the civil power cannot operate, to endeavour to repress it himself. I perceive no reasonable exception to the rule—that whatever Christianity permits the magistrate to do in order to restrain violence, it permits the individual, under such circumstances, to do also. I know the consequences to which this rule leads in the case of the *punishment* of death, and of other questions. These questions will hereafter be discussed. In the meantime, it may be an act of candour to the reader to acknowledge, that our chief motive for the discussions of the present chapter, has been to pioneer the way for a satisfactory investigation of the Punishment of Death, and of other modes by which human life is taken away.

37. Many kinds of resistance to aggression come strictly within the fulfilment of the law of benevolence. He who, by securing, or temporarily disabling a man, prevents him from committing an act of great turpitude, is certainly his benefactor ; and if he be thus reserved for justice, the benevolence is great both to him and to the public. It is an act of much kindness to a bad man to secure him for the penalties of the law : or it *would be* such, if penal law were in the state in which it ought to be, and to which it appears to be making some approaches. It would then be very probable that the man would be reformed : and this is the greatest benefit which can be conferred upon him and upon the community.

38. The exercise of Christian forbearance towards violent men is not tantamount to an invitation of outrage. Cowardice is one thing ; this forbearance is another. The man of true forbearance is of all men the least cowardly. It requires courage in a greater degree and of a higher order to practise it when life is threatened, than to draw a sword or fire a pistol.—No : It is the peculiar privilege of Christian virtue to approve itself even to the bad. There is something in the nature of that calmness, and self-possession, and forbearance, that religion effects, which obtains, nay, which almost commands regard and respect. How different the effect upon the violent tenants of Newgate, the hardihood of a turnkey and the mild courage of an Elizabeth Fry! Experience, incontestable experience, has proved that the minds of few men are so depraved or desperate as to prevent them from being *influenced* by real Christian conduct. Let him therefore who advocates the taking the life of an aggressor, first show that all other means of safety are vain ; let him show that bad men, notwithstanding the exercise of true Christian forbearance, persist in their purposes of death : when he has done this he will have adduced an argument in favour of taking their lives which will not, indeed, be conclusive, but which will approach nearer to conclusiveness than any that has yet been adduced.

39. Of the consequences of forbearance,

[1] Blackstone: Com., v. 4, c. 4.
[2] Gisborne: Moral Philosophy.

even in the case of personal attack, there are some examples: Archbishop Sharpe was assaulted by a footpad on the highway, who presented a pistol and demanded his money. The Archbishop spoke to the robber in the language of a fellow-man and of a Christian. The man was really in distress, and the prelate gave him such money as he had, and promised that, if he would call at the palace, he would make up the amount to fifty pounds. This was the sum of which the robber had said he stood in the utmost need. The man called and received the money. About a year and a half afterwards, this man again came to the palace and brought back the same sum. He said that his circumstances had become improved, and that, through the "astonishing goodness" of the Archbishop, he had become "the most penitent, the most grateful, the happiest of his species."—Let the reader consider how different the Archbishop's feelings were, from what they would have been if, by his hand, this man had been cut off.[1]

40. Barclay, the Apologist, was attacked by a highwayman. He substituted for the ordinary modes of resistance a calm expostulation. The felon dropped his presented pistol, and offered no further violence. A Leonard Fell was similarly attacked, and from him the robber took both his money and his horse, and then threatened to blow out his brains. Fell solemnly spoke to the man on the wickedness of his life. The robber was astonished: he had expected, perhaps, curses, or perhaps a dagger. He declared he would not keep either the horse or the money, and returned both. "If thine enemy hunger, *feed him;* for in so doing thou shalt heap coals of fire upon his head."[2]—The tenor of the short narrative that follows is somewhat different. Ellwood, who is known to the literary world as the suggester to Milton of Paradise Regained,

[1] See Lond. Chron., Aug. 12, 1785. See also Life of Granville Sharpe, Esq., p. 13.
[2] "Select Anecdotes, &c.," by John Barclay.

was attending his father in his coach. Two men waylaid them in the dark and stopped the carriage. Young Ellwood got out, and on going up to the nearest, the ruffian raised a heavy club, "when," says Ellwood, "I whipt out my rapier and made a pass upon him. I could not have failed running him through up to the hilt," but the sudden appearance of the bright blade terrified the man so, that he stepped aside, avoided the thrust, and both he and the other fled. "At that time," proceeds Ellwood, "and for a good while after, I had no regret upon my mind for what I had done." This was whilst he was young, and when the forbearing principles of Christianity had little influence upon him. But afterwards, when this influence became powerful, "a sort of horror," he says, "seized on me when I considered how near I had been to the staining of my hands with human blood. And whensoever afterwards I went that way, and indeed as often since as the matter has come into my remembrance, my soul has blessed Him who preserved and withheld me from shedding man's blood."[1]

41. That those over whom, as over Ellwood, the influence of Christianity is imperfect and weak, should think themselves at liberty upon such occasions to take the lives of their fellow-men, needs to be no subject of wonder. Christianity, if we would rightly estimate its obligations, must be felt in the heart. They in whose hearts it is not felt, or felt but little, cannot be expected perfectly to know what its obligations are. I know not therefore that more appropriate advice can be given to him who contends for the lawfulness of taking another man's life in order to save his own, than that he would first inquire whether the influence of religion is dominant in his mind. If it is not, let him suspend his decision until he has attained to the fulness of the stature of a Christian man. Then, as he will be of that number who *do* the Will of Heaven, he may hope to "know of this doctrine whether it be of God."

[1] Ellwood's Life.

ESSAY III.*

POLITICAL RIGHTS AND OBLIGATIONS.

CHAPTER I.
Principles of Political Truth, and of Political Rectitude.

I.—"Political Power is rightly exercised only when it is possessed by consent of the community"—Governors officers of the public — Transfer of their rights by a whole people—The people hold the sovereign power — Right of Governors — A conciliating system.

II.—"Political Power is rightly exercised only when it subserves the welfare of the community"—Interference with other nations—Present expedients for present occasions—Proper business of Governments.

III.—"Political Power is rightly exercised only when it subserves the welfare of the community by means which the Moral Law permits"—The Moral Law alike binding on nations and individuals—Deviation from rectitude impolitic—"The Holy Alliance"—Durable fame.

The Fundamental principles which are deducible from the law of nature and from Christianity, respecting political affairs, appear to be these:—

1. Political Power is rightly *possessed* only when it is possessed by consent of the community;

2. It is rightly *exercised* only when it subserves the welfare of the community;

3. And only when it subserves this purpose, by *means* which the Moral Law permits.

I.—"Political Power is rightly possessed only when it is possessed by consent of the Community."

1. Perfect liberty is desirable if it were consistent with the greatest degree of happiness. But it is not. Men find that, by giving up a part of their liberty, they are more happy than by retaining, or attempting to retain, the whole. Government, whatever be its form, is the agent by which the *inexpedient* portion of individual liberty is taken away. Men institute government for their own advantage, and because they find they are more happy with it than without it. This is the sole reason, in principle, how little soever it be adverted to in practice.

Governors, therefore, are the officers of the public, in the proper sense of the word: not the *slaves* of the public; for if they do not incline to conform to the public will, they are at liberty, like other officers, to give up their office. They are servants, in the same manner, and for the same purpose, as a solicitor is the servant of his client, and the physician of his patient. These are employed by the patient or the client voluntarily for his own advantage, and for nothing else. A nation (not an *individual*, but a *nation*) is under no other obligation to obedience, than that which arises from the conviction that obedience is good for itself; —or rather, in more proper language, a nation is under no *obligation* to obedience at all. Obedience is voluntary. If they do not think it proper to obey—that is, if they are not satisfied with their officers—they are at liberty to discontinue their obedience, and to appoint other officers instead.

2. That which is thus true as an universal proposition, is asserted with respect to this country by the present king:[1]—"The powers and prerogatives of the crown are vested there *as a trust for the benefit of the people;* and they are sacred *only* as they are necessary to the preservation of that poise and balance of the constitution which experience has proved to be the best security of *the liberty of the subject.*"[2]

3. It is incidental to the office of the First public servants, that they should exercise authority over those by whom they are selected; and hence, probably, it has happened that the terms "public officer," "public servant," have excited such strange controversies in the world. Men have not maintained sufficient discrimination of ideas. Seeing that governors are great and authoritative, a man imagines it cannot be proper to say they are servants. Seeing that it is necessary and right that individuals should

[1] George IV.
[2] Letter when Prince of Wales to Wm. Pitt. Gifford's Life of Pitt, vol. 2.

[* This Essay the author did not live to revise, a circumstance which will account for a want of complete connection of the different parts of a subject which the reader will sometimes meet with. There occur also in this part of the manuscript numerous memoranda, which the author intended to make use of in a future revision. These are to be distinguished from the *Notes*, as the former refer, not to any particular passage, but only to the subject of the chapter or section. They were hastily, as the thought occurred, written in the margin or on a blank leaf of the manuscript, and they are here introduced at the bottom of the page, in those parts to which they appear to have the nearest reference.—ED.]

obey, he cannot entertain the notion that they are the servants of those whom they govern. The truth is, that governors are *not* the servants of individuals but of the community. They are the masters of individuals, the servants of the public; and if this simple distinction had been sufficiently borne in mind, much perhaps of the vehement contention upon these matters had been avoided.

4. But the idea of being a servant of the public, is quite consistent with the idea of exercising authority over them. The common language of a patient is founded upon similar grounds. He sends for a physician:—the physician comes at his desire—is paid for his services—and then the patient says, I am *ordered* to adopt a regimen, I am *ordered* to Italy;—and he obeys, not because he may not refuse to obey if he chooses, but because he confides in the judgment of the physician, and thinks that it is more to his benefit to be guided by the physician's judgment than by his own. But it will be said the physician cannot *enforce* his orders upon the patient against his will; neither, I answer, can the governor enforce his upon the public against theirs. No doubt Governors *do* sometimes so enforce them. What they do, however, and what they *rightfully* do, are separate considerations, and our business is only with the latter.

5. Grotius argues that sovereign power *may* be possessed by governors, so that it shall not rightfully belong to the community. He says, "From the Jewish as well as the Roman law it appears, that any one might engage himself in private servitude to whom he pleased. Now if an individual may do so, why may not a whole people, for the benefit of better government, and more certain protection, completely transfer their sovereign rights to one or more persons without reserving any portion to themselves?"[1] I answer, No individual *may* do this: and, If he might, it would not serve the doctrine in the case of nations.—It never can be *right* for a man to resign the absolute direction of his conduct to another, because he must then do actions *good or bad*, as that other might command—he must lie, or rob, or assassinate; and of this common sense would pronounce the impropriety, if the Moral Law did not. And if you say a man ought not *so* to resign himself to another, then I answer, he does not transfer sovereign power but retains it himself—which, in truth, ends the argument.

6. But if the doctrine were sound for the individual, it is unsound for a community.

What is meant by the "transfer of their sovereign rights by a *whole people*?" Is every man, woman, and child in the country formally to sign the transfer? If not, how shall a whole people transfer it? At any rate, if they did, their resignation could not bind their children or successors. Besides, there is the same objection to this transfer of the sovereign power on the part of a nation as on the part of an individual. The thing is absurd in reason, and criminal in morals.

7. Grotius illustrates his argument by " that authority to which a woman submits when she gives herself to her husband." But she does *not* submit to *sovereign* authority. He says again, "Some powers are conferred for the sake of the governor, as the right of a master over a slave." But such powers are never *justly* conferred.

8. After all, these arguments do but establish in reality the fundamental position. They assume that a people *can resign* the sovereign power; which is the same thing as to acknowledge that *they rightfully possess it*. Grotius himself says, "A state is a perfect body of free men, united together *in order to enjoy* common rights and advantages."[1]

9. It gives some anxiety to the mind of the writer, lest the reader should identify his principles with those of many who have asserted the "sovereignty of the people." This doctrine has been insisted upon by persons who have mingled with it, or deduced from it, principles which the writer not merely rejects, but abhors. A doctrine is not unsound because it has been advocated or perverted by bad men; and it is neither rational nor honest to reprobate a truth because it has been viciously associated. Gifford, in his Life of Pitt, complains of Fox, who by "a strange perversion of terms, and a confusion of intellect that would have disgraced even a schoolboy, called his sovereign the servant of the people." "This," says Gifford, "was a servile imitation of the French regicides, and a direct encouragement to all the theoretical reveries of all the disaffected in England." This is the species of association which I would deprecate: French regicides taught the doctrine, and disaffected theorists taught it. I am sorry that a truth should be so connected; but it is not the less a truth. The "confusion of intellect," of which Gifford speaks, probably subsisted more in the writer than in Fox— for reasons which the reader has just seen, and because the biographer had probably confounded the doctrine with the conduct of some who supported it. The reader should

---

[1] Rights of War and Peace, b. 1, c. 3, s. 8. [1] Rights of War and Peace.

practise a little of the power of abstraction, and detach accidental associations from truth itself.

10. In reality, it cannot be asserted that the people do not rightfully possess the supreme power, without asserting that governors may do what they will, and be as tyrannical as they will. Who may prevent them? The people? Then the people hold the sovereign power.

11. Many political constitutions have existed in which the governor was held to be absolutely the supreme power. The antiquity of such constitutions, or the regular succession of the existing governor, does not make his pretensions to this power just, because the principles on which it is ascertained that the people are supreme are antecedent to all questions of usage, and superior to them. No injustice, therefore, is done—nothing wrong is done—in diminishing or taking away the power of an absolute monarch, notwithstanding the regularity of his pretensions to it. Yet other principles have been held: and it was said of Louis the Sixteenth, that as he "was the sole maker and executor of the laws," and as this power "had been exercised by him and by his ancestors for centuries without question or control, it was not in the power of the states to deprive him of any portion of it without his own consent." So that we are told that many millions of persons ought to be subject for ever to the vices or caprices of one man, in compliment to the fact that their predecessors had been subject before them.[1] He who maintains such doctrine, surely forgets for what purpose government is instituted at all.

12. The rule that "Political Power is rightly possessed only when it is possessed by consent of the community," necessarily applies to the choice of the person who is to exercise it. No man, and no set of men, rightly govern unless they are preferred by the public to others. It is of no consequence that a people should formally select a president or a king. They continually act upon the principle without this. A people who are satisfied with their governor make, day by day, the choice of which we speak. They prefer him to all others ; they choose to be served by him rather than by any other ; and

[1] We do not here defend the conduct of the states, or censure that of Louis: we speak merely of the political Truth. That atrocious course of wickedness, the French Revolution, was occasioned by the abuses of the old government and its ramifications. The French p ople, unhappily, had neither virtue enough nor political knowledge enough, to reform these abuses by proper means. A revolution of some kind, and at some period, awaits, I doubt not, every despotic government in Europe and in the world. Happy wi'l it be for those rulers who timely and wisely regard the irresistible progress of Public Opinion! And happy for those communities which endeavour reformation only by virtuous means.

he, therefore, is virtually, though not formally, selected by the public. But when we speak of the *right* of a particular person or family to govern a people, we speak, as of all other rights, in conditional language. The right consists in the preference which is given to him ; and exists no longer than that preference exists. If any governor were fully conscious that the community preferred another man or another kind of government, he ought to regard himself in the light of an usurper if he nevertheless continues to retain his power. Not that every government ought to dissolve itself, or every governor to abdicate his office, because there is a general but temporary clamour against it. This is one thing—the steady deliberate judgment of the people is another.— Is it too much to hope that the time may come when governments will so habitually refer to the *purposes* of government, and be regulated by them, that they will not even *wish* to hold the reins longer than the people desire it ; and that nothing more will be needed for a quiet alteration than that the public judgment should be quietly expressed?

13. Political revolutions are not often favourable to the accurate illustration of political truth ; because, such is the moral condition of mankind, that they have seldom acted in conformity with it. Revolutions have commonly been the effect of the triumph of a party, or of the successes of physical power. Yet, if the illustration of these principles has not been accurate, the general position of the right of the people to select their own rulers has often been illustrated. In our own country, when James II. left the throne, the people filled it with another person, whose real title consisted in the choice of the people. James continued to talk of his rights to the crown ; but if William was preferred by the public, James was, what his son was afterwards called, a *Pretender*. The nonjurors appear to have acted upon erroneous principles (except indeed on the score of former oaths to James ; which, however, ought never to have been taken). If we acquit them of motives of party, they will appear to have entertained some notions of the rights of governors independently of the wishes of the people. At William's death, the nation preferred James's daughter to his son ; thus again elevating their judgments above all considerations of what the Pretender called his rights. Anne had then a *right* to the throne, and her brother had not. At the death of Anne, or rather in contemplation of her death, the public had again to select their governor ; and they chose, not the immediate representative of the old family, but the Elector of Hanover: and it is in virtue of the same choice, tacitly expressed

at the present hour, that the heir of the Elector now fills the throne.

14. [The habitual consciousness on the part of a legislature, that its authority is possessed in order to make it an efficient guardian and promoter of the general welfare and the general satisfaction would induce a more mild and conciliating system of internal policy than that which frequently obtains. Whether it has arisen from habit resulting from the violent and imperious character of international policy, or from that tendency to unkindness and overbearing which the consciousness of power induces, it cannot be doubted that measures of governments are frequently adopted and conducted with such a *high hand* as impairs the satisfaction of the governed, and diminishes, by example, that considerate attention to the claims of others, upon which much of the harmony, and therefore the happiness of society consists. Governments are too much afraid of conciliation. They too habitually suppose that mildness or concession indicates want of courage or want of power—that it invites unreasonable demands, and encourages encroachment and violence on the part of the governed. Man is not so intractable a being, or so insensible of the influence of candour and justice. In private life, *he* does not the most easily guide the conduct of his neighbours, who assumes an imperious, but he who assumes a temperate and mild demeanour. The best mode of governing, and the most *powerful* mode too, is to recommend state measures to the judgment and the affections of a people. If this had been sufficiently done in periods of tranquillity, some of those conflicts which have arisen between governments and the people had doubtless been prevented; and governments had been spared the mortification of conceding that to violence which they refused to concede in periods of quiet. We should not wait for times of agitation to do that which Fox advised even at such a time, because at other periods it may be done with greater advantage, and with a better grace. " It may be asked," said Fox, "what I would propose to do in times of agitation like the present? I will answer openly:—If there is a tendency in the Dissenters to discontent, what should I do? I would instantly repeal the Corporation and Test Acts, and take from them thereby all cause of complaint. If there were any persons tinctured with a republican spirit, I would endeavour to amend the representation of the Commons, and to prove that the House of Commons, though not chosen by all, should have no other interest than to prove itself the representative of all. If men were dissatisfied on account of disabilities or exemptions, &c., I would repeal the penal statutes, which are a disgrace to our law-books. If there were other complaints of grievance, I would redress them where they were really proved; but above all, I would *constantly, cheerfully, patiently* listen; I would make it known, that if any man felt, or thought he felt, a grievance, he might come freely to the bar of this House and bring his proofs. And it should be made manifest to all the world that where they did exist they should be redressed; where not, it should be made manifest."[1]

15. We need not consider the particular examples and measures which the statesman instanced. The *temper* and *spirit* is the thing. A government should do that of which every person would see the propriety in a private man; if misconduct was charged upon him, show that the charge was unfounded; or, being substantiated, amend his conduct.]

II.—" Political Power is rightly exercised only when it subserves the Welfare of the Community."

16. This proposition is consequent of the truth of the last. The community, which has the right to withhold power, delegates it, of course, for its own advantage. If in any case its advantage is not consulted, then the object for which it was delegated is frustrated; or, in simple words, the measure which does not promote the public welfare is not right. It matters nothing whether the community have delegated specifically so much power for such and such purposes; the power, *being possessed,* entails the obligation. Whether a sovereign derives absolute authority by inheritance, or whether a president is entrusted with limited authority for a year, the principles of their duty are the same. The obligation to employ it only for the public good, is just as real and just as great in one case as in the other. The Russian and the Turk have the same right to require that the power of their rulers shall be so employed as the Englishman or American. They may not be able to assert this right, but that does not affect its existence nor the ruler's duty, nor his responsibility to that *Almighty* Being before whom he must give an account of his stewardship. These reasonings, if they needed confirmation, derive it from the fact that the Deity imperatively requires us, according to our opportunities, to *do good* to man.

17. But, how ready soever men are to admit the truth of this proposition, as a proposition, it is very commonly disregarded in

[1] Fell's Memoirs of the Public Life of C. J. Fox.

practice; and a vast variety of motives and objects direct the conduct of governments which have no connection with the public weal. Some *pretensions* of consulting the public weal are, indeed, usual. It is not to be supposed that when public officers are pursuing their own schemes and interests, they will *tell* the people that they disregard theirs. When we look over the history of a Christian nation, it is found that a large proportion of these measures which are most prominent in it, had little tendency to subserve, and did not subserve, the public good. In practice, it is very often forgotten for what purpose governments are instituted. If a man were to look over twenty treaties, he would probably find that a half of them had very little to do with the welfare of the respective communities. He might find a great deal about Charles's rights, and Frederick's honour, and Louis's possessions, and Francis's interests, as if the proper subjects of international arrangements were those which respected rulers rather than communities. If a man looks over the state papers which inform him of the origin of a war, he will probably find that they agitate questions about Most Christian and Most Catholic Kings, and High Mightinesses, and Imperial Majesties — questions, however, in which Frenchmen, and Spaniards, and Dutch, and Austrians, are very little interested or concerned, or at any rate much less interested than they are in avoiding the quarrel.

18. Governments commonly trouble themselves unnecessarily and too much with the politics of other nations. A prince should turn his back towards other countries and his face towards his own—just as the proper place of a landholder is upon his own estates and not upon his neighbour's. If governments were wise, it would ere long be found that a great portion of the endless and wearisome succession of treaties, and remonstrances, and embassies, and alliances, and memorials, and subsidies, might be dispensed with, with so little inconvenience and so much benefit, that the world would wonder to think to what futile ends they had been busying, and how needlessly they had been injuring themselves.

19. No doubt, the immoral and irrational system of international politics which *generally* obtains, makes the path of one government more difficult than it would otherwise be; and yet it is probable that the most efficacious way of inducing another government to attend to its proper business, would be to attend to our own. It is not sufficiently considered, nor indeed is it sufficiently *known*, how powerful is the influence of uprightness and candour in conciliating the good opinion and the good offices of other men. Over-reaching and chicanery in one person, induce overreaching and chicanery in another. Men distrust those whom they perceive to be unworthy of confidence. Real integrity is not without its voucher in the hearts of others; and they who maintain it are treated with confidence, because it is seen that confidence can be safely reposed. Besides, he who busies himself with the politics of foreign countries, like the busybodies in a petty community, does not fail to offend. In the last century our own country was so much of a busybody, and had involved itself in such a multitude of treaties and alliances, that it was found, I believe, quite impossible to fulfil one, without, by that very act, violating another. This, of course, would offend. In private life, that man passes through the world with the least annoyance and the greatest satisfaction, who confines his attention to its proper business, that is, generally, to his own: and who can tell why the experience of nations should in this case be different from that of private men? In a rectified state of international affairs, half a dozen princes on a continent would have little more occasion to meddle with one another than half a dozen neighbours in a street.

20. But indeed, *Communities* frequently contribute to their own injury. If governors are ambitious, or resentful, or proud, so often are the people;—and the public good has often been sacrificed by the public, with astonishing preposterousness, to jealousy or vexation. Some merchants are angry at the loss of a branch of trade; they urge the government to interfere; memorials and remonstrances follow to the state of whom they complain;—and so, by that process of exasperation which is quite natural when people think that high language and a high attitude is politic, the nations soon begin to fight. The merchants applaud the spirit of their rulers, while in one year they lose more by the war than they would have lost by the want of the trade for twenty; and before peace returns, the nation has lost more than it would have lost by the continuance of the evil for twenty centuries. Peace at length arrives, and the government begins to devise means of repairing the mischiefs of the war. Both government and people reflect very complacently on the wisdom of their measures—forgetting that their conduct is only that of a man who wantonly fractures his own leg with a club, and then boasts to his neighbours how dexterously he limps to a surgeon.

21. Present expedients for present occasions, rather than a wide-embracing and far-seeing policy, is the great characteristic of European politics. We are hucksters who cannot resist the temptation of a present

sixpence, rather than merchants who wait for their profits for the return of a fleet. Si quæris monumentum, circumspice! Look at the condition of either of the continental nations, and consider what it might have been if even a short line of princes had attended to their proper business—had directed their solicitude to the improvement of the moral, and social, and political condition of the people. Who has been more successful in this huckster policy than France? and what is France, and what are the French people at the present hour?—Why, as it respects real welfare, they are not merely surpassed, they are left at an immeasurable distance by a people who sprung up but as yesterday—by a people whose land, within the memory of our grandfathers, was almost a wilderness—and which actually was a wilderness long since France boasted of her greatness. Such results have a cause. It is not possible that systems of policy can be good, of which the effects are so bad. I speak not of particular measures, or of individual acts of ill policy—these are not likely to be the result of the condition of man—but of the whole international system; a system of irritability, and haughtiness, and temporary expedients; a system of most unphilosophical principles, and from which Christianity is practically almost excluded. Here is the evidence of fact before us. We know what a sickening detail the history of Europe is; and it is obvious to remark, that the system which has given rise to such a history must be vicious and mistaken in its fundamental principles. The same class of history will continue to after generations unless these principles are changed—unless philosophy and Christianity obtain a greater influence in the practice of government; unless, in a word, governments are content to do their proper business, and to leave that which is not their business undone.

22. When such principles are acted upon, we may reasonably expect a rapid advancement in the whole condition of the world. Domestic measures, which are now postponed to the more stirring occupations of legislators, will be found to be of incomparably greater importance than they. A wise code of criminal law will be found to be of more consequence and interest than the acquisition of a million square miles of territory:—a judicious encouragement of general education will be of more value than all the "glory" that has been acquired from the days of Alfred till now. Of moral legislation, however, it will be our after business to speak; meanwhile the lover of mankind has some reason for gratulation, in perceiving indications that governments will hereafter direct their attention more to the objects for which they are invested with power. The statesman who promotes this improvement will be what many statesmen have been called—a great man. That government only is great which promotes the prosperity of its own people; and that people only are prosperous who are wise and happy.

III.—"Political Power is rightly exercised only when it subserves the welfare of the Community by means which the Moral Law permits."

23. It has been said by a Christian writer, that "the science of politics is but a particular application of that of morals;" and it has been said by a writer who rejected Christianity, that "the morality that ought to govern the conduct of individuals and of nations, is in all cases the same." If there be truth in the principles which are advanced in the first of these Essays, these propositions are indisputably true. It is the chief purpose of the present work to enforce the *supremacy* of the Moral Law; and to this supremacy there is no exception in the case of nations. In the conduct of nations this supremacy is practically denied, although, perhaps, few of those who make it subservient to other purposes would deny it in terms. With their lips they honour the doctrine, but in their works they deny it. Such procedures must be expected to produce much self-contradiction, much vacillation between truth and the wish to disregard it, much vagueness of notions respecting political rectitude, and much casuistry to educe something *like* a justification of what cannot be justified. Let the reader observe an illustration:—A moral philosopher says, " The Christian principles of love, and forbearance, and kindness, strictly as they are to be observed between man and man, are to be observed with *precisely the same strictness between nation and nation.*" This is an unqualified assertion of the truth. But the writer thinks it would carry him too far, and so he makes exceptions. " In reducing to practice the Christian principles of forbearance, &c., it will not be always feasible, nor always safe, to proceed to the *same extent* as in acting towards an individual." Let the reader exercise his skill in casuistry, by showing the difference between conforming to laws with "precise strictness," and conforming to them in their "full extent."—Thus far Christianity and Expediency are proposed as our *joint* governors.—We must observe the Moral Law, but still we must regulate our observance of it by considerations of what is feasible and safe. Presently afterwards, however, Christianity is quite dethroned, and we are to observe its laws only "so far as national ability and *national security* will permit."[1]—So that our rule of political con-

[1] Gisborne's Moral Philosophy.

duct stands at length thus : *obey Christianity with precise strictness—when it suits your interests.*

24. The *reasoning* by which such doctrines are supported, is such as it might be expected to be. We are told of the "caution requisite in affairs of such magnitude—the great uncertainty of the future conduct of the other nation,"—and of "patriotism."—So that, because the affairs are of great magnitude, the laws of the Deity are not to be observed ! It is all very well, it seems, to observe them in little matters, but for our more important concerns we want rules commensurate with their dignity- we cannot *then* be bound by the laws of God ! The next reason is, that we cannot foresee "the future conduct" of a nation.—Neither can we that of an individual. Besides this, inability to foresee inculcates the very lesson that we ought to observe the laws of Him who can foresee. It is a strange thing to urge the limitation of our powers of judgment, as a reason for substituting it for the judgment of Him whose powers are perfect. Then "patriotism" is a reason : and we are to be patriotic to our country at the expense of treason to our religion !

25. The principles upon which these reasonings are founded lead to their legitimate results : " In war and negotiation," says Adam Smith, "the laws of justice are very seldom observed. Truth and fair dealing are almost totally disregarded. Treaties are violated, and the violation, if some advantage is gained by it, sheds scarce any dishonour upon the violator. The ambassador who dupes the minister of a foreign nation is admired and applauded. The just man, the man who in all private transactions would be the most beloved and the most esteemed, in those public transactions is regarded as a fool and an idiot, who does not understand his business ; and he incurs always the contempt, and sometimes even the detestation of his fellow-citizens."[1]

26. Now, against all such principles— against all endeavours to defend the rejection of the Moral Law in political affairs, we would with all emphasis protest. The reader sees that it is absurd :—can he need to be convinced that it is unchristian ? Christianity is of paramount authority, or another authority is superior. He who holds another authority as superior rejects Christianity ; and the fair and candid step would be *avowedly* to reject it. He should say in distinct terms—Christianity throws some light on political principles ; but its laws are to be held subservient to our interests. This were far more satisfactory than the trimming system, the perpetual vacillation of obedience to two masters, and the perpetual endeavour to do that which never can be done—serve both.

27. Jesus Christ legislated for *man*—not for individuals only, not for families only, not for Christian churches only, but for man in all his relationships and in all his circumstances. He legislated for *states*. In his Moral Law we discover no indications that states were exempted from its application, or that any rule which bound social did not bind political communities. If any exemption were designed, the *onus probandi* rests upon those who assert it : unless they can show that the Christian precepts are *not* intended to apply to nations, the conclusion must be admitted that they *are*. But in reality, to except nations from the obligations is impossible ; for nations are composed of individuals, and if no individual may reject the Christian morality, a nation may not. Unless, indeed, it can be shown that when you are an agent for others you may do what neither yourself nor any of them might do separately—a proposition of which certainly the proof must be required to be very clear and strong.

28. But the truth is that those who justify a suspension of Christian morality in political affairs, are often unwilling to reason distinctly and candidly upon the subject. They satisfy themselves with a jest, or a sneer, or a shrug : being unwilling either to contemn morality in politics, or to practise it ; and it is to little purpose to offer arguments to him who does not need conviction, but virtue.

29. Expediency is the rock upon which we split—upon which, strange as it appears, not only our principles but our *interests* suffer continual shipwreck. It has been upon Expediency that European politics have so long been founded, with such lamentably inexpedient effects. We consult our interests so anxiously that we ruin them. But we consult them blindly : we do not know our interests, nor shall we ever know them whilst we continue to imagine that we know them better than He who legislated for the wor'd. Here is the perpetual folly as well as the perpetual crime. Esteeming ourselves wise, we have, emphatically, been fools—of which no other evidence is necessary than the present political condition of the Christian world. If ever it was true of any human being, that by his deviations from rectitude he had provided scourges for himself, it is true at this hour of every nation in Europe.

30. Let us attend to this declaration of a

---

[1] Theory of Moral Sentiments.

man who, whatever may have been the value of his general politics, was certainly a great statesman here : " I am one of those who firmly believe, as much indeed as a man can believe anything, that the greatest resource a nation can possess, the surest principle of power, is strict attention to the principles of justice. I firmly believe that the common proverb of honesty being the best policy, is as applicable to nations as to individuals." —" In all interference with foreign nations justice is the best foundation of policy, and moderation is the surest pledge of peace." —" If therefore we have been deficient in justice towards other states, we have been deficient in wisdom."[1]

31. Here, then, is the great truth for which we would contend—to be unjust is to be *unwise*. And since *justice* is not imposed upon nations more really than other branches of the Moral Law, the universal maxim is equally true—*to deviate from purity of rectitude is impolitic as well as wrong*. When will this truth be learnt and be acted upon? When shall we cast away the contrivances of a low and unworthy policy, and dare the venture of the consequences of virtue? When shall we, in political affairs, exercise a little of that confidence in the knowledge and protection of God, which we are ready to admire in individual life?—Not that it is to be assumed as certain that such fidelity would cost nothing. Christianity makes no such promise. But whatever it might cost it would be worth the purchase. And neither reason nor experience allows the doubt that a faithful adherence to the Moral Law would more effectually serve national interests, than they have ever yet been served by the utmost sagacity whilst violating that law.

32. The contrivances of expediency have become so habitual to measures of state, that it may probably be thought the dreamings of a visionary to suppose it possible that they should be substituted by purity of rectitude. And yet I believe it will be done—not perhaps by the resolution of a few cabinets—it is not from them that reformation is to be expected—but by the gradual advance of sound principles upon the minds of men ;—principles which will assume more and more their rightful influence in the world, until at length the low contrivances of a fluctuating and immoral policy will be substituted by firm, and consistent, and invariable integrity.

33. The convention of what is called the Holy Alliance was an extraordinary event ; and little as the contracting parties may have acted in conformity with it, and little as they or their people were prepared for such a change of principles, it is a subject of satisfaction that such a state paper exists. It contains a testimony at least to virtue and to rectitude ; and even if we should suppose it to be utterly hypocritical, the testimony is just as real. Hypocrisy commonly affects a character which it *ought* to maintain ; and the act of hypocrisy is homage to the character. In this view, I say, it is subject of some satisfaction that a document exists which declares that these powerful princes have come to a " fixed resolution, both in the administration of their respective states, and in their political relations with every other government, to take for their sole guide the precepts of the Christian religion —the precepts of Justice, Christian Charity, and Peace :" and which declares that these principles, "far from being applicable only to private concerns, must have an immediate influence on the councils of princes, as being the only means of consolidating human institutions, and remedying their imperfections."

34. The time, it may be hoped, will arrive when such a declaration will be the congenial and natural result of principles that are actually governing the Christian world. Meantime, let the philosopher and the statesman keep that period in their view, and endeavour to accelerate its approach. He who does this, will secure a fame for himself that will increase and still increase as the virtue of man holds its onward course, while multitudes of the *great*, both of past ages and of the present, will become beacons to warn, rather than examples to stimulate us.

CHAPTER II.
Civil Liberty.

Loss of Liberty—War—Useless laws.

35. Of *personal* liberty we say nothing, because its full possession is incompatible with the existence of society. All government supposes the relinquishment of a portion of personal liberty.

36. *Civil* Liberty may, however, be fully enjoyed. It is enjoyed, where the principles of political truth and rectitude are applied in practice, because there the people are deprived of that portion only of liberty which it would be pernicious to themselves to possess. If political power is possessed by consent of the community ; if it is exercised only for their good ; and if this welfare

---

[1] Fell's Memoirs of the Public Life of C. J. Fox.

is consulted by Christian means, the people are free. No man can define the particular enjoyments or exemptions which constitute civil liberty, because they are contingent upon the circumstances of the respective nations. A degree of restraint may be necessary for the general welfare of one community, which would be wholly unnecessary in another. Yet the first would have no reason to complain of their want of civil liberty. The complaint, if any be made, should be of the evils which make the restraint necessary. The single question is, whether any given degree of restraint is necessary or not. If it is, though the restraint may be painful, the civil liberty of the community may be said to be complete. It is useless to say that it is less complete than that of another nation; for complete civil liberty is a relative and not a positive enjoyment. Were it otherwise, no people enjoy, or are likely for ages to enjoy, full civil liberty; because none enjoy so much that they could not, in a more virtuous state of mankind, enjoy more. "It is not the rigour, but the inexpediency of laws and acts of authority, which makes them tyrannical."[1]

37. Civil liberty (so far as its present enjoyment goes) does not necessarily depend upon forms of government. All communities enjoy it who are properly governed. It may be enjoyed under an absolute monarch; as we know it may *not* be enjoyed under a republic. Actual, existing liberty, depends upon the actual, existing administration.

38. One great cause of diminutions of civil liberty is War; and if no other motive induced a people jealously to scrutinise the grounds of a war, this might be sufficient. The increased loss of personal freedom to a military man is manifest;—and it is considerable to other men. The man who now pays twenty pounds a year in taxes, would probably have paid but two if there had been no war during the past century. If he now gets a hundred and fifty pounds a year by his exertions, he is *obliged to labour* six weeks out of the fifty-two, to pay the taxes which war has entailed. That is to say, he is compelled to work two hours every day longer than he himself wishes, or than is needful for his support. This is a material deduction from personal liberty; and a man would feel it as such, if the coercion were directly applied if an officer came to his house every afternoon at four o'clock, when he had finished his business, and obliged him, under penalty of a distraint, to work till six. It is some loss of liberty, again, to a man to be unable to open as many windows in his house as he pleases—or to be forbidden to acknowledge the receipt of a debt without going to the next town for a stamp —or to be obliged to ride in an uneasy carriage unless he will pay for springs. It were to no purpose to say he may pay for windows and springs if he will, and if he can. A slave may, by the same reasoning, be shown to be free; because, if he will and if he can, he may purchase his freedom. There is a loss of liberty in being *obliged to submit to the alternative;* and we should feel it as a loss if such things were not habitual, and if we had not receded so considerably from the liberty of nature. A housewife on the Ohio would think it a strange invasion of her liberty, if she were told that henceforth the police would be sent to her house to seize her goods if she made any more soap to wash her clothes.

39. *Now,* indeed, that war has created a large public debt, it is necessary to the general good that its interest should be paid: and in this view a man's civil liberty is not encroached upon, though his personal liberty is diminished. The public welfare is consulted by the diminution. I may deplore the cause without complaining of the law. It may, upon emergency, be for the public good to suspend the Habeas Corpus Act. I should lament that such a state of things existed, but I should not complain that civil liberty was invaded. The lesson which such considerations teach is jealous watchfulness against wars for the future.

40. There are many other acts of governments by which civil liberty is needlessly curtailed—among which may be reckoned the *number* of laws. Every law implies restriction. To be destitute of laws is to be absolutely free: to multiply laws is to multiply restrictions, or which is the same thing, to diminish liberty. A great number of penal statutes lately existed in this country, by which the reasonable proceedings of a prosecutor were cramped, and impeded, and thwarted. A statesman to whom England is much indebted has supplied their place by *one* which is more rational and more simple; and prosecutors now find that they are so much more able to consult their own understandings in their proceedings, that it may, without extravagance, be said that our civil liberty is increased.

41. "A law being found to produce no sensible good effects, is a sufficient reason for repealing it."[1] It is not, therefore, sufficient to ask in reply, what harm does the law occasion? for you must prove that it does

[1] Paley: Mor. and Pol. Phil., p. 3, b. 6, c. 5.

[1] Paley: Mor. and Pol. Phil., p. 3, b. 6, c. 5.

good: because all laws which do no good, do harm. They encroach upon or restrain the liberty of the community, without that reason which *only* can make the deduction of any portion of liberty right—the public good. If this rule were sufficiently attended to, perhaps more than a few of the laws of England would quickly be repealed.

CHAPTER III.
Political Liberty.

Political Liberty the right of a community—Public satisfaction.

42. This is, in strictness, a branch of civil liberty. Political liberty implies the existence of such political institutions as *secure*, with the greatest practicable certainty, the future possession of freedom—the existence of which institutions is one of the requisites, in a general sense, of civil liberty; because it is as necessary to proper government that securities for freedom should be framed, as that present freedom should be permitted.

43. The possession of political liberty is of great importance. A Russian may enjoy as great a share of personal freedom as an Englishman—that is, he may find as few restrictions upon the exercise of his own will; but he has *no security for the continuance of* this. For aught that he knows, he may be arbitrarily thrown into prison to-morrow; and therefore, though he may live and die without molestation, he is politically enslaved. When it is considered how much human happiness depends upon *the security of enjoying happiness in future*, such institutions as those of Russia are great grievances; and Englishmen, though they may regret the curtailment of some items of civil liberty, have much comparative reason to think themselves politically free.

44. The possession of political liberty is unquestionably a right of a community. They may, with perfect reason, require it even of governments which actually govern well. It is not enough for a government to say, None but beneficial laws and acts of authority are adopted. It must, if it would fulfil the duties of a government, accumulate, to the utmost, *securities* for beneficial measures hereafter. In this view it may be feared that no government in Europe fulfils all its duty to the people.

45. And here considerations are suggested respecting the *representation* of a people—a point which, if some political writers were to be listened to, was a *sine qua non* of political liberty. "To talk of an abstract right of equal representation is absurd. It is to arrogate a right to one form of government, whereas Providence has accommodated the different forms of government to the different states of society in which they subsist."[1] If an inhabitant of Birmingham should come and tell me that he and his neighbours were debarred of political liberty because they sent no representatives to parliament, I should say that the justness of his complaint was problematical. It does not follow *because* a man is not represented, that he is not politically free. The question is, whether as good securities for liberty exist, without permitting him to vote, as with it. If it can be shown that the present legislative government affords as good a security for the future freedom of the people as any other that might be devised, the inhabitant of Birmingham enjoys, at present, political liberty. It is a very common mistake amongst writers to assume some particular privilege or institution as a test of this liberty —as something without which it cannot be enjoyed—and yet I suppose there is no one of their institutions or privileges under which it would not be possible to enslave a people. Simple republicanism, universal suffrage, and frequent elections, *might* afford no better security for civil liberty than absolute monarchy. In fine, political liberty is not a matter that admits of certain conclusions from theoretical reasoning; it is a question of facts; a question to be decided, like questions of philosophy, by reasoning founded upon experience. If the inhabitant of Birmingham can show, from relevant experience, good ground to conclude that greater security for liberty would be derived from extending the representation, he has reason to complain of an undue privation of political liberty if it is not extended.

46. But, then, it is always incumbent upon the legislature to prove the probable superiority of the existing institutions when any considerable portion of the people desire an alteration. That *desire* constitutes a claim to investigation; and to an alteration, too, unless the existing institutions appear to be superior to those which are desired. It is not enough to show that they are *as good;* for though in other respects the two plans were equally balanced, the present are *not so good* as the others if they give less satisfaction to the community. To be *satisfied* is one great ingredient in the welfare of a people; and in whatever degree a people are not satisfied, in the same degree civil government does not perfectly effect its proper ends. To deny satisfaction to a people without showing a reason, is to withhold from them the due portion of civil liberty.

[1] William Pitt: Gifford's Life, vol. 3.

CHAPTER IV.

Religious Liberty.

Civil disabilities—Interference of the Magistrate—Pennsylvania—Toleration—America—Creeds—Religious Tests—"The Catholic Question."

47. The magistrate may advert to subjects connected with religion so far as the public good requires and as Christianity permits ; or, upon these, as upon other subjects, he may endeavour to promote the welfare of the people by Christian means. What the public welfare *does* require, and what means for promoting it *are* Christian, are separate considerations.

48. Upon which grounds those advocates of religious liberty appear to assert too much, who assert, as a fundamental principle, that a government never has, nor can have, any just concern with religious opinions. Unless these persons can show that no advertence to them is allowed by Christianity, and that none can contribute to the public good, circumstances may arise in which an advertence would be right. No one perhaps will deny that a government may lawfully provide for the education of the people, and endeavour to diffuse just notions and principles, moral and religious, into the public mind. A government, therefore, may endeavour to discountenance unsound notions and principles. It may as reasonably discourage what is wrong as cherish what is right.

49. But by what means ? By influencing opinions, not by punishing persons who hold them. When a man publishes a book or delivers a lecture for the purpose of enlightening the public mind, he does well. A government may take kindred measures for the same purpose, and it does well. But this is all. If our author or lecturer, finding his opinions were not accepted, should proceed to *injure* those who rejected them, he would act, not only irrationally, but immorally. If a government, finding its measures do not influence or alter the views of the people, *injures* those who reject its sentiments, it acts immorally too. A man's opinions are not alterable at his own will ; and it is not right to injure a man for doing that which he cannot avoid. Besides, in religious matters especially, it is the Christian duty of a man, first, to seek truth, and next, to adhere to those opinions which truth, as he believes, teaches. And so again, it is not right to injure a man for doing that which it is his duty to do. When, therefore, it is affirmed, at the head of this chapter, that the magistrate may advert to subjects connected with religion, nothing more is to be understood than that he may endeavour to diffuse just sentiments, and to expose the contrary. To do more than this, although he may think his measures may promote the public welfare, would be to endeavour to promote it "by means which the Moral Law forbids."

50. To inflict civil disabilities is "to do more than this"- it is "to *injure* a man for doing that which he cannot avoid," and "that which it is his duty to do." Here, indeed, a sophism has been resorted to, in order to show that disabilities are not *injuries*. It is said of the dissenters of this country, that no penalty is inflicted upon them by excluding them from offices—that the state confers certain offices upon certain conditions, with which conditions a dissenter does not comply. And it is said that this is no more a penalty or a hardship than, when the law defines what pecuniary qualifications capacitate a man for a seat in parliament, it inflicts a penalty upon those who do not possess them. I answer, *Both* are penalties and hardships, and that the argument only attempts to justify one ill practice by the existence of another. It will be said that such regulations are necessary to the public good. Bring the proof. Here is a certain restraint : "The proof of the advantage of a restraint," says Dr. Paley, "lies upon the legislature." Unless, therefore, you can show- what to me is extremely problematical—that the public is benefited by a law that excludes a poor man from the legislature—the argument wholly fails. Consider for what purpose men unite in society—"in order," says Grotius, "to enjoy common rights and advantages," of which rights and advantages, eligibility to a representative body is one. Those principles of political rectitude which determine that a law which needlessly restrains natural liberty is wrong, determine that a law which needlessly restrains the enjoyment of the privileges of society, is wrong also. It is therefore not true that a dissenter suffers no hardship or penalty on account of his opinions. The only difference between disabilities and ordinary penalties is this, that one inflicts evil, and the other withholds good ; and both are, to all intents and purposes, *penalties*.

51. But even if the legislator thought he could show that the public were benefited by this penalty, upon conscientious dissidents, it would not be sufficient—for the penalty itself is wrong—it is not Christian ; and it is vain to argue that an unchristian act can be made lawful by prospects of advantage. Here, as everywhere else, we must maintain the supremacy of the Moral Law.

52. All these reasonings proceed upon the supposition that a man does not, in consequence of his opinions, disturb the peace of society by any species of violence. If he does, he is doubtless to be restrained. It may not be more necessary for the magistrate to inquire what are a man's opinions of religion, than for a rider to inquire what are the cogitations of his horse. So long as my horse carries me well, it matters nothing to me whether he be thinking of safe paces, or of meadows and corn-chests. So long as the welfare of the public is secured, it matters nothing to the magistrate what notion of Christianity a citizen accepts. But if my horse, in his anxiety to get into a meadow, leaps over a hedge, and impedes me in my journey, it is needful that I employ the whip and bridle : and if the citizen, in his zeal for opinions, violates the general good, it is needful that he should be punished or restrained. And even then, he is not restrained for his opinions, but for his conduct ; just as I do not apply the whip to my horse because he loves a meadow, but because he goes out of the road.

53. And even in the case of conduct, it is needful to discriminate accurately what is a proper subject of animadversion, and what is not. I perceive no truth in the ingenious argument, "that a man may entertain opinions however pernicious, but he may not be allowed to disseminate them ; as a man may keep poison in his house, but may not be allowed to give it to others as wholesome medicine." To support this argument you must have recourse to a *petitio principii*. How do you know that an opinion is pernicious? By reasoning and examination, if at all ; and that is the very end which the dissemination of an opinion attains. If the truth or falsehood of an opinion were demonstrable to the senses, as the mischief of poison is, there would be some justness in the argument ; but it is not : except, indeed, that there may be opinions so monstrous, that they immediately manifest their unsoundness by their effects on the conduct ; and, if they do this, these effects and not the dissemination of the opinion, are the proper subject of animadversion. The doctrine that a man ought not to be punished for disseminating whatever opinions he pleases, upon whatever subject, will receive some illustration in a future chapter. Meantime, the reader will, I hope, be prepared to admit, at least, that the religious opinions which obtain amongst Christian churches are not such as to warrant the magistrate in visiting those who disseminate them with any kind of penalty. What the magistrate may punish, and what an individual ought to do, are very different considerations : and though there is reason to think that no man should be punished by human laws for disseminating vicious notions, it is to be believed that those who consciously do it will be held far other than innocent at the bar of God.

54. All reference to creeds in framing laws for a general society is wrong. And it is somewhat humiliating that, in the present age, and in our country, it is necessary to establish this proposition by formal proof. It is humiliating, because it shows us how slow is the progress of sound principles upon the human mind, even when they are not only recommended by reason, but enforced by experience. It is now nearly a century and a half since one of our own colonies adopted a system of religious liberty, which far surpassed that of the parent state at the present hour. And this system was successful, not negatively, in that it produced no evil, but positively, in that it produced much good. One hundred and fifty years is a long time for a nation to be learning a short and plain lesson. In Pennsylvania, in addition to a complete toleration of "Jews, Turks, Catholics, and people of all persuasions in religion,"[1] there was no disability or test exacted of any professor of the Christian faith. "All persons," says Burke, "who profess to believe in one God, are freely tolerated. Those who believe in Jesus Christ, of whatever denomination, are not excluded from employments and posts."[2] The wisdom or justice of excluding those who were not Christians from employments and posts may be doubted. Penn, however, did much ; and far outstripped in enlightened institutions the general example of the world. If he had lived in the present day, it is not improbable that a mind like his would have seen no better reason for excluding those who disbelieved Christianity, than those who believed it imperfectly or by parts. The consequences, we say, were happy. Burke says again of Penn, "He made the most perfect freedom, both religious and civil, the basis of his establishment ; and this has done more towards the settling of the province, and towards the settling of it in a strong and permanent manner, than the wisest regulations could have done on any other plan."[3] "By the favourable terms," says Morse, " which Mr. Penn offered to settlers, and an unlimited toleration of all religious denominations, the population of the province was extremely rapid."[4] And yet England is, at this present hour, doubting and disputing whether tests are right !

55. Nor is example wanted at the present day. "In America, the question is not, What

[1] Clarkson's Life of Penn.
[2] Account of the European Settlements in America.
[3] Ibid.
[4] American Geography. See also Anderson's Deduction of the Origin of Commerce.

is his creed? but, What is his conduct? Jews have all the privileges of Christians. No religious test is required to qualify for public office; except, in some cases, a mere verbal assent to the truth of the Christian religion. While I was in New York," adds Duncan, "the sheriff of the city was a Jew."[1] It is vain to make any objection to the argument which these facts urge, unless we can show that the effect is not good. And where is the man who will even affect to do this? But if it should be said that what is wise and expedient with such national institutions as those of America would be unwise and inexpedient with such institutions as those of England or Spain, it will become a most grave inquiry whether the fault does not lie with the institutions that are not adapted to religious liberty:— for religious liberty is assuredly adapted to man.

56. Observe what absurdities this sacrifice of universal rectitude to particular institutions occasions. There may be ten nations on a continent, each of which selects a different creed for its preference, and excludes all others. The first excludes all but Catholics —the second all but Episcopalians—the third all but Unitarians—the fourth all but the Greek Church; and so on with the rest. If it be right that Unitarians should be intrusted with power on one side of a river, can it be right that they shall not be intrusted with it on the other? Or, if such an absurdity be really conducive to the support of the incongruous institutions of the several states, is it not an evidence that those institutions need to be amended? And are not the principles of perfect religious liberty nevertheless sound and true?

57. Englishmen have not to complain of a want of toleration. But *toleration* is a word which ought scarcely to be heard out of a Christian's mouth. I *tolerate* the religion of my brother! I might as well say I tolerate the continuance of his head upon his shoulders. I have no more right to hold his creed at my disposal, or his person in consequence of his creed, than his head. The idea of toleration is a relic of the effects of the Papal usurpation. That usurpation did not tolerate; and Protestants thought it was a great thing for them to do what the Papacy had thus refused. And so it was. It was a great thing *for them*. Very imperfectly, however, they did it; and it was a great thing for Penn, who was brought up in a land of intolerant Protestants, to declare universal toleration for all within his borders. But—(and we may reverently say, Thanks be to God!)— we live in happier times. We have advanced from intolerance to toleration; and now it is time to advance from toleration to *Religious Liberty*: to that religious liberty which excludes all reference to creeds from the civil institutions of a people.

58. The reader will perhaps have observed that Religious Liberty and Religious Establishments are incompatible things. An Establishment presupposes incomplete Religious Liberty. If an Establishment be right, Religious Liberty is not; and if Religious Liberty be right, an Establishment is not. Differently constituted religious establishments may, no doubt, impose greater or less restraint upon liberty; but every idea of an establishment —of a church preferred by the state— imposes some restraint. It is the same with Tests. A test of some kind is necessary to a church thus preferred by the state; for how else shall it be known who is a member of that church and who is not? Religious Liberty is incompatible with Religious Tests; for which reason again, all arguments by which this liberty is shown to be right, are so many proofs that religious tests are wrong. These considerations the reader will be pleased to bear in mind when he considers the question of Religious Establishments.

59. Tests are snares for the conscience. If their terms are so loose that *any* man can take them with a safe conscience, they are not tests. If their terms are definite, they make many hypocrites. Men are induced to assent, or subscribe, or perform (whatever the requisitions of the test may be) against their consciences, in order to obtain the advantages which are contingent upon it. An attempt was once made in England to introduce an unexceptionable test, by which the party was to declare "that the books of the Old and New Testament contained, in his opinion, a revelation from God." But whom did this exclude? *Perhaps* Deists, Mahometans, Pagans, Jews. But, as a snare, the operation was serious; for, simple as the test appears, it was liable to great uncertainty of meaning. Did it mean that *all* the books contained a revelation? Then some think that all the books are not authentic. Did it mean that there was a revelation in some of the books of the Bible? Then Jews, Mahometans, Pagans, and some Deists might, for aught that I know, conscientiously take it. No unexceptionable test is possible. There are, to be sure, gradations of impropriety; and in England we have not always resorted to the least objectionable. It was well observed by Charles James Fox, that "the idea of making a *religious rite* the qualification for holding a civil employment is more than absurd, and deserves to be considered as a profanation of a sacred institution."

60. A few, and only a few, sentences will

[1] Duncan's Travels in America.

be allowed to the writer upon the great, the very great question, of extending religious liberty to the Catholics of these kingdoms. I call it a very great question, not because of the difficulty of deciding it, if sound principles are applied, but because of the magnitude of the interests that are involved, and of the consequences which may follow if those principles are not applied. The reader will easily perceive, from the preceding contents of this chapter, the writer's conviction that full Religious Liberty ought to be extended to the Catholics, because it ought to be extended to *all* men. If a Catholic *acts* in opposition to the public welfare,—diminish or take away his freedom; if he only *thinks* amiss,—let him enjoy his freedom undiminished.

61. To this I know of but one objection that is worth noticing here—that they are harmless only because they have not the power of doing mischief, and that they wait only for the power to begin to do it. But they say, " This is not the case—we have no such intentions." Now, in all reason, you must believe them, or show that they are unworthy of belief. If you believe them, religious liberty follows of course. Can you then show that they are unworthy of belief? Where is your evidence?

62. You say their allegiance is divided between the king and a foreign power. They reply, "*It is not.* We hold ourselves bound in conscience to obey the civil government in all things of a temporal and civil nature, notwithstanding any dispensation to the contrary from the Pope or Church of Rome."

63. You say their declarations and oaths do not bind them, because they hold that they can be dispensed from the obligation of all oaths by the Pope. They reply, " *We do not.* We hold that the obligation of an oath is most sacred; that no power whatsoever can dispense with any oath, by which a Catholic has confirmed his duty of allegiance to his sovereign, or any obligation of duty to a third person."

64. You say they hold that faith is not to be kept with heretics. They reply, " *We do not.* British Catholics," say they, "have *solemnly sworn* that they *reject and detest* that unchristian and impious principle that faith is not to be kept with heretics or infidels." These declarations are taken from a "Declaration of the Catholic Bishops, the Vicars Apostolic, their coadjutors in Great Britain," 1825. They are signed by the Catholic Bishops of Great Britain, and are approved in an "address" signed by eight Catholic Peers and a large number of other persons of rank and character.

65. Now I ask of those who contend for the Catholic disabilities, What proof do you bring that these men are trying to deceive you? I can anticipate no answer because I have heard none. Will you, then, content yourselves by saying, We *will not* believe them? This would be at least the candid course, and the world might then perceive that our conduct was regulated not by reason, but by prejudice or the consciousness of power. " It is unwarrantable to infer, *à priori*, and contrary to the professions and declarations of the persons holding such opinions, that their opinions would induce acts injurious to the common weal." [1]

66. But if nothing can be said to show that the Catholic declarations do not bind them, something can be said to show that they do. If declarations be indeed so little binding upon their consciences, how comes it to pass that they do not make those declarations which would remove their disabilities, get a dispensation from the Pope, and so enjoy both the privileges and an easy conscience? Why if their oaths and declarations did not bind them, they would get rid of their disabilities to-morrow! Nothing is wanting but a few hypocritical declarations, and Catholic Emancipation is effected. Why do they not make these declarations? *Because their words bind them.* And yet (so gross is the absurdity), although it is their conscientiousness which keeps them out of office, we say they are to be kept out because they are not conscientious!

67. I forbear further inquiry: but I could not, with satisfaction, avoid applying what I conceive to be the sound principles of Political Rectitude to this great question; and let no man allow his prejudices or his fears to prevent him from applying them to this, as to every other political subject. Justice and Truth are not to be sacrificed to our weaknesses and apprehensions; and I believe that if the people and legislature of this country will adhere to justice and truth with regard to our Catholic brethren, they will find, erelong, that they have only been *delaying* the welfare of the Empire.

CHAPTER V.

Civil Obedience.

Expediency of Obedience—Obligations to Obedience—Extent of the duty—Resistance to the Civil Power—Obedience may be withdrawn—King James—America—Non-compliance—Interference of the Magistrate—Oaths of allegiance.

68. *Submission* to Government is involved in the very idea of the institution. None

[1] C. J. Fox: Gifford's Life of Pitt, vol. 2.

can govern, if none submit; and hence is derived the *duty* of submission, so far as it is independent of Christianity. Government being necessary to the good of society, submission is necessary also, and therefore it is right.

69. This duty is enforced with great distinctness by Christianity. "Be subject to principalities and powers."—"Obey magistrates."—"Submit to every ordinance of man." The great question, therefore, is whether the duty be absolute and unconditional; and if not, what are its limits, and how are they to be ascertained?

70. The *law of nature* proposes few motives to obedience except those which are dictated by expediency. The object of instituting government being the good of the governed, any means of attaining that object is, in the view of natural reason, right. So that, if in any case a government does not effect its proper objects, it may not only be exchanged, but exchanged by *any* means which will tend on the whole to the public good. Resistance —arms—civil war—every act is, in the view of natural reason, lawful if it is useful. But although good government is the *right* of the people, it is nevertheless not sufficient to release a subject from the obligation of obedience, that a government adopts *some* measures which he thinks are not conducive to the general good. A wise pagan would not limit his obedience to those measures in which a government acted expediently; because it is often better for the community that some acts of misgovernment should be borne, than that the general system of obedience should be violated. It is, as a general rule, more necessary to the welfare of a people that governments should be regularly obeyed, than that each of their measures should be good and right. In practice, therefore, even considerations of Utility are sufficient, generally, to oblige us to submit to the civil power.

71. When we turn from the law of nature to *Christianity*, we find, as we are wont, that the moral cord is tightened, and that *not every* means of opposing governments for the public good is permitted to us. The consideration of what modes of opposition Christianity allows, and what it forbids, is of great interest and importance.

72. "Let every soul be subject unto the higher powers. For there is no power but of God: the powers that be are ordained of God. Whosoever, therefore, resisteth the power, resisteth the ordinance of God. For rulers are not a terror to good works, but to the evil. He is the minister of God to thee for good—a revenger, to execute wrath upon him that doeth evil. Wherefore ye must needs be subject, not only for wrath, but also for conscience' sake."[1] Upon this often cited and often canvassed passage, three things are to be observed:—

73. 1. That it asserts the general duty of civil obedience, *because* government is an institution sanctioned by the Deity.

2. That it asserts this duty *under the supposition* that the governor is a minister of God *for good*.

3. That it gives but little other information respecting the *extent* of the duty of obedience.

74. I. The obligation to obedience is not founded, therefore, simply upon expediency, but upon the more satisfactory and certain ground, the expressed will of God. And here the superiority of this motive over that of fear of the magistrate's power is manifest. We are to be subject, not only for wrath, but for conscience' sake—not only out of fear of man, but out of fidelity to God. This motive, where it operates, is likely, as was observed in the first Essay, to produce much more consistent and conscientious obedience than that of expediency or fear.

75. II. The duty is inculcated under the supposition that the governor is a minister *for good*. It is upon this supposition that the Apostle proceeds: "*for* rulers are not a terror to good works, but to the evil;" which is tantamount to saying, that if they be not a terror to evil works but to good, the duty of obedience is altered. "*The power that is of God*," says an intelligent and Christian writer, "leaves neither ruler nor subject to the liberty of his own will, but limits both to the Will of God; so that the magistrate hath no power to command evil to be done because he is a magistrate, and the subject hath no liberty to do evil because a magistrate doth command it."[2] When, therefore, the Christian teacher says, "Let every soul be subject to the higher powers," he proposes not an absolute but a conditional rule—conditional upon the nature of the actions which the higher powers require. The expression, "There is *no* power but of God," does not invalidate this conclusion, because the Apostles themselves did not yield unconditional obedience to the powers that were. Similar observations apply to the parallel passage in 1st Peter: "Submit yourselves to every ordinance of man for the Lord's sake; whether it be to the king as supreme, or unto governors as unto them that are sent by him, *for the punishment of evil-doers and*

---
[1] Rom. xiii. 1–5.
[2] Crisp: "To the Rulers and Inhabitants in Holland, &c." Abt. Ann. 1670.

for the praise of them that do well. The supposition of the *just exercise of power* is still kept in view.

76. III. The precepts give little other information than this respecting the *extent* of the duty of obedience, " Whosoever resisteth the power, resisteth the ordinance of God," is, like the direction, to "be subject," a conditional proposition. What precise meaning was here attached to the word "resisteth," cannot perhaps be known : but there is reason to think that the meaning was not designed to be precise—that the proposition was *general.* "Magistrates are not to be resisted," without defining, or attempting to define, the limits of civil obedience.

77. Upon the whole, this often agitated portion of the Christian Scriptures does not appear to me to convey *much* information respecting the duties of civil obedience ; and although it explicitly asserts the general duty of obedience to the magistrate, it does not inform us how far that duty extends, nor what are its limits. To say this, however, is a very different thing from saying, with Dr. Paley, that " As to the *extent* of our civil rights and obligations, *Christianity hath left us where she found us;* that she hath neither altered nor ascertained it ; that the New Testament contains not one passage, which, fairly interpreted, affords either argument or objection applicable to any conclusions upon the subject that are deduced from the law and religion of nature."[1] Although the 13th chapter to the Romans may contain no such passage, yet I think it can be shown that the New Testament does. Indeed, it would be a strange thing if the Christian Scriptures, containing as they do manifold precepts for the regulation of human conduct, manifold precepts, of which the application is very wide, not to say universal—it would, I say, be a strange thing if none of these precepts threw *any* light upon duties of such wide embrace as those of citizens in relation to governors.

78. The error (assuming that there is an error) in the statement of Dr. Paley, results, probably, from the supposition, that because no passage specifically directed to civil obedience contained the rules in question, therefore no rules were to be found in the volume. This is an error of every day. There are numberless questions of duty which Christianity decides, yet respecting which, specifically, not a word is to be found in the New Testament. These questions are decided by general principles, which principles are distinctly laid down. These three words, " Love your enemies," are of greater practical application in the affairs of life, than twenty propositions which define exact duties in specific cases. It is for these exact definitions that men accustom themselves to seek ; and when they are not to be found, conclude that Christianity gives no directions upon the subject.

79. Thus it has happened with the question of Civil Obedience. Now, in considering the general principles of Christianity, I think very satisfactory knowledge may be deduced respecting *resistance* to the civil power. Those precepts to forbearance, to gentleness, to love, to mildness, which are iterated as the essence of the Christian morality, apply, surely, to the question of resistance. Surely there may be some degrees and kinds of resistance, which, being incompatible with the observance of these principles, Christianity distinctly forbids. If indeed the reader has given assent to our reasonings respecting self-defence (especially if he shall give his assent to the reasonings on *War*), he will readily admit that Christianity forbids an armed resistance to the civil power. Let me be distinctly understood. It forbids this armed resistance, not inasmuch as it is directed to the *civil power*, but inasmuch as such violence to *any power* is incompatible with the purity of the Christian character.

80. Concluding, then, that *specific* rules respecting the extent of Civil Obedience are not to be found in Scripture, we are brought to the position, that we must ascertain this extent by the general duties which Christianity imposes upon mankind, and by the general principles of political truth. In attempting, upon these grounds, to illustrate our civil duties, I am solicitous to remark, that the individual Christian who, regarding himself as a journeyer to a better country, thinks it best for him not to intermeddle in political affairs, may rightly pursue a path of simpler submission and acquiescence than that which I believe Christianity allows. Whatever may be the peculiar business of individuals, the business of *man* is to act as the Christian *citizen*—not merely to prepare himself for another world, but to do such good as he may, political as well as social, in the present. And yet, so fundamentally, so utterly incongruous with Christian rectitude, is the state of many branches of political affairs in the present day, that I know not whether he who is solicitous to adhere to this rectitude is not both wise and right in standing aloof. This consideration applies, especially, to circumstances in which the limits of Civil Obedience are brought into practical illustrations. The tumult and violence which ordinarily attend any approach to political revolutions are such, that the best and proper office of a good man

[1] Mor. and Pol. Phil., b. 6, c. 4.

may be rather that of a moderator of both parties than of a partisan with either. Nevertheless, it is fit that the obligations of Civil Obedience should be distinctly understood.

81. Referring, then, to political truth, it is to be remembered that governors are established, not for their own advantage, but for the people's. If they so far disregard this object of their establishment, as greatly to sacrifice the public welfare, the people (and consequently individuals) may rightly consider whether a change of governors is not dictated by utility; and if it is, they may rightly endeavour to effect such a change by recommending it to the public, and by transferring their obedience to those who, there is reason to believe, will better execute the offices for which government is instituted. I perceive nothing *unchristian* in this. A man who lived in 1688, and was convinced that it was for the general good that William should be placed on the throne instead of James, was at liberty to promote, by all Christian means, the accession of William, and consequently to withdraw his own, and to recommend others to withdraw their obedience, from James. The support of the Bill of Exclusion in Charles the Second's reign was nearly allied to a withdrawing of civil obedience. The Christian of that day who was persuaded that the bill would tend to the public welfare, was right in supporting it, and he would have been equally right in continuing his support if Charles had suddenly died, and his brother had suddenly stepped into the throne. If I had lived in America fifty years ago, and had thought the disobedience of the colonies wrong, and that the whole empire would be injured by their separation from England, I should have thought myself at liberty to urge these considerations upon other men, and otherwise to exert myself (always within the limits of Christian conduct) to support the British cause. I might, indeed, have thought that there was so much violence and wickedness on both sides, that the Christian could take part with neither: but this is an accidental connection, and in no degree affects the principle itself. But, when the colonies were actually separated from Britain, and it was manifestly the general will to be independent, I should have readily transferred my obedience to the United States, convinced that the new government was preferred by the people; that, therefore, it was the *rightful* government; and, being such, that it was my Christian duty to obey it.

82. Now the lawful means of discouraging or promoting an alteration of a government, must be determined by the general duties of Christian morality. There is, as we have seen, nothing in political affairs which conveys a privilege to throw off the Christian character; and whatever species of opposition or support involves a sacrifice or suspension of this character is, for that reason, wrong. Clamorous and vehement debatings and harangues—vituperation and calumny—acts of bloodshed and violence, or instigations to such acts, are, I think, measures in which the first teachers of Christianity would not have participated; measures which would have violated their own precepts; and measures, therefore, which a Christian is not at liberty to pursue. Objections to these sentiments will no doubt be at hand: we shall be told that such opposition would be ineffectual against the encroachments of power and the armies of tyranny—that it would be to no purpose to reason with a general who had orders to enforce obedience; and that the nature of the power to be overcome dictated the necessity of corresponding power to overcome it. To all which it is, in the first place, a sufficient answer, that the question is not what evils may ensue from an adherence to Christianity, but what Christianity requires. We renew the oft-repeated truth, that Christian rectitude is *paramount*. When the first Christians refused obedience to some of the existing authorities, *they did not resist.* They exemplified their own precepts—to prefer the Will of God before all; and if this preference subjected them to evils —to bear them without violating other portions of His Will in order to ward them off. But if resistance to the civil power was thus unlawful when the magistrate commanded actions that were morally *wrong*, much more clearly is it unlawful, when the wrongness consists only in political grievances. The inconveniences of bad governments cannot constitute a superior reason for violence to that which is constituted by the imposition of laws that are contrary to the laws of God. And if any one should insist upon the magnitude of political grievances, the answer is at hand—these evils cannot cost more to the community as a state than the other class of evils costs to the individual as a man. If fidelity is required in private life, through whatever consequences, it is required also in public. The national suffering can never be so great as the individual may be. The individual may lose his life for his fidelity, but there is no such thing as a *national* martyrdom. Besides, it is by no means certain that Christian opposition to misgovernment would be so ineffectual as is supposed. Nothing is so invincible as determinate non-compliance. He that resists by force may be overcome by greater force; but nothing can overcome a calm and fixed determination not to obey. Violence *might*, no doubt, slaughter those who practised it, but it were an unusual ferocity to destroy

such persons in cool malignity. In such inquiries we forget how much difficulty we entail upon ourselves. A regiment which, after endeavouring to the uttermost to destroy its enemies, refuses to yield, is in circumstances totally dissimilar to that which our reasonings suppose. Such a regiment might be cut to pieces; but it would be, I believe, a "new thing under the sun" to go on slaughtering a people of whom it was known not only that they had committed no violence, but that they would commit none.

83. Refer again to America: The Americans thought that it was best for the general welfare that they should be independent, but England persisted in imposing a tax. Imagine, then, America to have acted upon Christian principles, and to have refused to pay it, but without those acts of exasperation and violence which they committed. England might have sent a fleet and an army. To what purpose? Still no one paid the tax. The soldiery perhaps sometimes committed outrages, and they seized goods instead of the impost: still the tax could not be collected, except by a system of universal distraint. Does any man who employs his reason believe that England would have overcome such a people? does he believe that any government, or any army, would have gone on destroying them? especially does he believe this, if the Americans continually reasoned coolly and honourably with the other party, and manifested, by the unequivocal language of conduct, that they were actuated by reason and by Christian rectitude? No nation exists which would go on slaughtering such a people. It is not in human nature to do such things; and I am persuaded not only that American independence would have been secured, but that very far fewer of the Americans would have been destroyed: that very much less of devastation and misery would have been occasioned, if they had acted upon these principles instead of upon the vulgar system of exasperation and violence. In a word, they would have attained the same advantage with more virtue, and at less cost.—With respect to those voluble reasoners who tell us of *meanness of spirit*, of *pusillanimous submission*, of *base crouching before tyranny*, and the like, it may be observed that they do not know what mental greatness is. Courage is not indicated most unequivocally by wearing swords or by wielding them. Many who have courage enough to take up arms against a bad government have not courage enough to resist it by the unbending firmness of the mind—to maintain a tranquil fidelity to virtue in opposition to power, or to endure with serenity the consequences which may follow.

84. The Reformation prospered more by the resolute non-compliance of its supporters, than if all of them had provided themselves with swords and pistols. The most severely persecuted body of Christians which this country has in later ages seen, was a body who never raised the arm of resistance. They wore out that iron rod of oppression which the attrition of violence might have whetted into a weapon that would have cut them off from the earth; and they now reap the fair fruit of their principles in the enjoyment of privileges from which others are still debarred.

85. There is one class of cases in which obedience is to be refused to the civil power without any view to an alteration of existing institutions—that is, when the magistrate commands that which it would be immoral to obey. What is wrong for the Christian is wrong for the subject. "All human authority ceases at the point where obedience becomes criminal." Of this point of criminality every man must judge ultimately for himself; for the opinions of another ought not to make him obey when he thinks it is criminal, nor to refuse obedience when he thinks it is lawful. Some even appear to think that the nature of actions is altered by the command of the state; that what would be unlawful without its command is lawful with it. This notion is founded upon indistinct views of the extent of civil authority; for this authority can never be so great as that of the Deity, and it is the Deity who requires us not to do evil. The Protestant would not think himself obliged to obey if the state should require him to acknowledge the authority of the Pope; and why? Because he thinks it would be inconsistent with the Divine Will; and this precisely is the reason why he should refuse obedience in other cases. He cannot rationally make distinctions, and say, "I ought to refuse obedience in acknowledging the Pope, but I ought to obey in becoming the agent of injustice or oppression." If I had been a Frenchman, and had been ordered, probably at the instigation of some courtesan, to immure a man, whom I knew to be innocent, in the Bastile, I should have refused; for it never can be right to be the active agent of such iniquity.

86. Under an enlightened and lenient government like our own, the cases are not numerous in which the Christian is exempted from the obligation to obedience. When, a century or two ago, persecuting acts were passed against some Christian communities, the members of these communities were not merely at liberty, they were *required* to disobey them. One act imposed a fine of twenty pounds a month for absenting one's self from a prescribed form of worship. He

who thought that form less acceptable to the Supreme Being than another, ought to absent himself notwithstanding the law. So when, in the present day, a Christian thinks the profession of arms, or the payment of preachers whom he disapproves, is *wrong*, he ought, notwithstanding any laws, to decline to pay the money or to bear the arms.

87. *Illegal* commands do not appear to carry any obligation to obedience. Thus, when the Apostles had been "beaten openly and uncondemned, being Romans," they did not regard the directions of the magistracy to leave the prison, but asserted their right to legal justice, by making the magistrates "come themselves and fetch them out." When Charles I. made his demands of supplies upon his own illegal authority, I should have thought myself at liberty to refuse to pay them. This were not a disobedience to government. Government was broken. One of its constituent parts refused to impose the tax, and one imposed it. I might, indeed, have held myself in doubt whether Charles constituted the government or not. If the people had thought it best to choose him alone for their ruler, he constituted the government, and his demand would have been legal; for a law is but the voice of that governing power whom the people prefer. As it was, the people did not choose such a government: the demand was illegal, and might therefore be refused.

88. Promises or oaths of *Allegiance* to governors do not appear easily reconcilable with political reason. Promises are made for the advantage or security of the imposer; and to make them to governors seems an inversion of the order which just principles would prescribe. The security should be given by the employed party, not by the employer. A community should not be *bound* to obey any given officer whom they employ: because they may find occasion to exchange him for another. Men do not swear fidelity to their representatives in the senate. Promising fidelity to the *state* may appear exempt from these objections, but the promise is likely to be of little avail; for what is the state? or how is its will to be discovered but by the voice of the governing power? To promise fidelity to the state is not very different from promising it to a governor.

89. If it be said that promises of allegiance may be useful in periods of confusion, or when the public mind is divided respecting the choice of governors, such a period is peculiarly unfit for promising allegiance to *one*. The greater the instability of an existing government, the greater the unreasonableness of exacting an oath. If an oath should maintain a tottering government against the public mind, it does mischief; and if a government is secure, an oath is not needed.

90. The sequestered ministers in the time of Charles II. were required to take an oath, "declaring that they would not at any time endeavour an alteration in the government of the *church* or state."[1] One reason of their ejection was, that they would not declare their assent to everything in the Book of Common Prayer. Why should these persons be required to promise not to endeavour an alteration in Church Government, when, probably, some of them thought the endeavour formed a part of their Christian duty? Upon similar grounds, it may be doubted whether the Roman Catholics of our day ought to declare, as they do, that they will not endeavour any alteration in the religious establishments of the country. To promise this without limitation is surely promising more than a person who disapproves that establishment ought to promise. The very essence of peculiar religious systems tends to the alteration of all others. He who preaches the Romish creed and practice does practically oppose the Church of England, and practically endeavour an alteration in it. And if a man thinks his own system the best, he *ought*, by Christian means, to endeavour to extend it.

91. And even if these declarations were less objectionable in principle, their practical operation is bad. Some invasion or revolution places a new prince upon the throne—that very prince, perhaps, whom the people's oath of allegiance was expressly designed to exclude. What are such a people to do? Are they to refuse obedience to the ruler whom, perhaps, there are the best of reasons for obeying? Or are they to keep their oaths sacred, and thus injure the general weal? Such alternatives ought not to be imposed. But the truth is, that allegiance is commonly adjusted to a standard very distinct from the meaning of oaths. How many revolutions have oaths of allegiance prevented? In general a people will obey the power whom they prefer, whatever oaths may have bound them to another. In France, all men were required to swear "that they would be faithful to the Nation, the Law, and the *King*." A year after, these same Frenchmen swore an everlasting abjuration of *monarchy*. And now they are living quietly under a monarchy again! After the accession of William III., when the clergy were required to take oaths contrary to those which they

---

[1] Southey's Book of the Church.

had before taken to James, very few in comparison refused. The rest "took them with such reservations and distinctions as redounded very little to the honour of their integrity."[1]

92. Thus it is that these oaths which are objectionable in principle are so nugatory in practice. The mischief is radical. Men ought not to be required to engage to maintain, at a future period, a set of opinions which, at a future period, they may probably think erroneous: nor to maintain allegiance to any set of men whom, hereafter, they may perhaps find it expedient to replace by others.

CHAPTER VI.
Forms of Government.

Some general principles—Monarchy—Balance of interests and passions—Changes in a constitution—Popular government—The world in a state of improvement—Character of legislators.

1. There is one great cause which prevents the political moralist from describing, absolutely, what form of government is preferable to all others, which is, that the superiority of a form depends, like the proper degree of civil liberty, upon the existing condition of a community. Other doctrine has indeed been held: "Wherever men are competent to look the first duties of humanity in the face, and to provide for their defence against the invasions of hunger and the inclemencies of the sky, there they will, out of all doubt, be found equally capable of every other exertion that may be necessary to their security and welfare. Present to them a constitution which shall put them into a simple and intelligible method of directing their own affairs, adjudging their contests among themselves, and cherishing in their bosoms a manly sense of dignity, equality, and independence, and you need not doubt that prosperity and virtue will be the result."[2]

2. There is need to doubt and to disbelieve it—unless it can be shown from experience that uncultivated and vicious men require nothing more to make them wise and good than to be told the way. "Present to them a constitution." Who shall present it? Some foreign intelligence, manifestly; and if this foreign intelligence is necessary to *devise* a constitution, it will be necessary to keep it in operation and in order. But when this is granted, it is in effect granted that an uncultivated and vicious people are *not* "capable of every exertion that may be necessary to their security and welfare."

3. But if certain forms cannot be specified which shall be best for the adoption of every state, there are general principles to direct us.

4. It is manifest that the form of government, like the administration of power, should be conformable to the public wish. In a certain sense, and in a sense of no trifling import, that form is best for a people which the people themselves prefer: and this rule applies, even although the form may not be intrinsically the best; for public welfare and satisfaction are the objects of government, and this *satisfaction* may sometimes be ensured by a form which the public prefer, more effectually than by a form, essentially better, which they dislike. Besides, a nation is likely to prefer that form which accords best with what is called the national genius; and thus there may be a real adaptation of a form to a people which is yet not abstractedly the best, nor the best for their neighbours. But when it is said that that form of government ought to be adopted for a people which they themselves prefer, it is not to be forgotten that their preference is often founded upon their weaknesses or their ignorance. Men adhere to an established form because they think little of a better. Long prescription gives to even bad systems an obscure sanctity amongst unthinking men. No reasonable man can suppose that the government of Louis the Fourteenth was good for the French people, or that that form could be good which enabled him to trifle with or to injure the public welfare. And yet, when his ambition and tyranny had reduced the French to poverty and to wretchedness, they still clung to their oppressor, and made wonderful sacrifices to support his power. Now, though it might have been both improper and unjust to give a new constitution to the French when they preferred the old, yet such examples indicate the *sense* in which only it is true that the form which a people prefer is the best for them:—and they indicate, too, most powerfully, the duty of every citizen and of every legislator to diffuse just notions of political truth. The nature of a government contributes powerfully, no doubt, to the formation of this national genius; and thus an imperfect form sometimes contributes to its own duration.

5. In the present condition of mankind, it is probable that some species of monarchy is best for the greater part of the world. Republicanism opens more wide the gates of ambition. He who knows that the utmost

---
[1] Smollett's History of England.
[2] Godwin's Enq. Pol. Just., vol. 1, p. 69.

extent of attainable power is to be the servant of a prince, is not likely to be fired by those boundless schemes of ambition which may animate the republican leader. The virtue of the generality of mankind is not sufficiently powerful to prompt them to political moderation without the application of an external curb; and thus it happens that the order and stability of a government is more efficiently secured by the indisputable supremacy of one man. Now, order and stability are amongst the first requisites of a good constitution, for the objects of political institutions cannot be secured without them.

6. I accept the word Monarchy in a large sense. It is not necessary to the security of these advantages, even in the existing state of human virtue, that the monarch should possess what we call kingly power. By monarchy I mean a form of government in which one man is invested with power greatly surpassing that of every other. The peculiar means by which this power is possessed do not enter necessarily into the account. The individual may have the power of a Sultan, or a Czar, or a King, or a President; that is, he may possess various degrees of power, and yet the essential principle of monarchy and its practical tendencies may be the same in all—the same to repress violence by extent of power—the same to discountenance ambition by the hopelessness of gratifying unlimited desire.

7. It is usual to insist, as one of the advantages of monarchy, upon its *secrecy and despatch;* which secrecy and despatch, it is to be observed, would be of comparatively little importance in a more advanced state of human virtue. Where diplomatic chicanery and hostile exertions are employed, despatch and secrecy are doubtless very subservient to success; but take away the hostility and chicanery—take away, that is, such wickedness from amongst men, and secrecy and despatch would be of little interest or importance. We love darkness rather than light, *because our deeds are evil.* Thus it is that unnumbered usages and institutions find advocacy, rather in the immoral condition of mankind, than in direct evidences of their excellence.

8. "An *hereditary* monarchy is universally to be preferred to an *elective* monarchy. The confession of every writer on the subject of civil government, the experience of the ages, the example of Poland and of the Papal dominions, seem to place this amongst the few indubitable maxims which the science of politics admits of."[1] But, without attempting to decide upon the preferableness of hereditary or elective monarchy, it may be questioned whether this formidable array of opinion has not been founded upon the mischiefs which *actually have* resulted from electing princes, rather than from those which are inseparable from the election. The election of the kings of Poland convulsed that unhappy country, and sometimes embroiled Europe. The election of popes has produced similar effects; but this is no evidence that popes and kings *cannot* be elected by pacific means; cardinals and lords may embroil a nation, when other electors would not.

9. I call the President of the United States a monarch. He is not called, indeed, an emperor, or a king, or a duke, but he exercises much of regal power. Yet he is elected: and where is the mischief? The United States are not convulsed: civil war is not waged: foreign princes do not support with armies the pretensions of one candidate or another:—and yet he is elected. Who then will say that other monarchs might not be elected too? It will not be easy to show that the being invested with greater power than the President of America necessarily precludes the peaceable election of a prince. The power of the president differs, I believe, less from that of the king of England, than the power of the king differs from that of the Russian emperor. No man can define the maximum of power which might be conferred without public mischief by the election of the public. Yet I am attempting to elucidate a political truth, and not recommending a practice. It is, indeed, possible, that when the genius of a people, and the whole mass of their political institutions, are favourable to an election of the supreme magistrate, election would be preferable to hereditary succession. But election is not without its disadvantages, especially if the appointment be for a short time. When there are several candidates, and when the inclinations of the community are consequently divided, he who actually assumes the reins is the sovereign of the choice of only a *portion* of the people. The rest prefer another: which circumstance is not only likely to animate the hostilities of faction, but to make the elected party regard one portion of the people as his *enemies* and the other as his *friends.* But he should be the parent of *all* the people.

10. Fox observed with respect to the British Constitution, that "the safety of the whole depends on the jealousy which each retains against the others, not on the patriotism of any one branch of the legislature."[1] This is doubtless true; yet surely it is a

---

[1] Paley: Mor. and Pol. Phil., p. 3, b. 6, c. 6.

[1] Speech on the Regency Question.

melancholy truth. It is a melancholy consideration that, in constructing a constitution, it is found necessary not to encourage virtue but to repress vice, and to contrive mutual curbs upon ambition and licentiousness. It is a tacit, but a most emphatical acknowledgment, how much private inclination triumphs over public virtue, and how little legislators are disposed to keep in the right political path, unless they are restrained from deviation by walls and spikes.

11. Yet it is upon this lamentable acknowledgment that the great institutions of free states are frequently founded. A balance of interests and passions is contrived, something like the balance of power, of which we hear so much amongst the nations of Europe —a balance of which the necessity (if it be necessary) consists in the wickedness, the ambition, and the violence of mankind. If nations did not viciously desire to encroach upon one another, this balance of power would be forgotten; and in a purer state of human virtue, the jealousies of the different branches of a legislature will not need to be balanced against each other. Until the period of this advanced state of human excellence shall arrive, I know not how this balance can be dispensed with. It may still be needful to oppose power to power, to restrain one class of interests by the counteraction of others, and to procure general quiet to the whole by annexing inevitable evils to the encroachments of the separate parts. Thus, again, it happens that constitutions which are not abstractedly the best, or even good, may be the best for a nation *now*.

12. Whatever be the form of a government, one quality appears to be essential to practical excellence—that it should be susceptible of *peaceable* change. The science of government, like other sciences, acquires a constant accession of light. The intellectual condition of the world is advancing with onward strides. And both these considerations intimate that Forms of Government should be capable of admitting, without disturbance, those improvements which experience may dictate, or the advancing condition of a community may require. To reject improvement is absurd; to incapacitate ourselves for adopting it is absurd also. It surely is no unreasonable sacrifice of vanity to admit that those who succeed us may be better judges of what is good for themselves than we can be for them.

13. Upon these grounds no constitution should be regarded as absolutely and sacredly fixed, so that none ought and none have a right to alter it. The question of right is easily settled. It is inherent in the community, or in the legislature as their agents. It would be strange, indeed, if our predecessors, five or six centuries ago, had a right to make a constitution for us which we have no right to alter for ourselves. Such checks ought, no doubt, to be opposed to alterations, that they may not be lightly and crudely made. The exercise of political wisdom is to discover that point in which sufficient obstacles are opposed to hasty innovation, and in which sufficient facility is afforded for real improvement by virtuous means. The common disquisitions about the value of stability in governments, like those about the sacredness of forms, are frequently founded in inaccurate views. What confusion, it is exclaimed, and what anarchy and commotions would follow, if we were at liberty continually to alter political constitutions! But it is forgotten that these calamities result from the circumstance that constitutions are *not made easily alterable*. The interests which so many have in keeping up the present state of things make them *struggle* against an alteration; and it is this struggle which induces the calamities, rather than anything necessarily incidental to the alteration itself. Take away these interests, take away the motives to these struggles, and improvements may be peacefully made. Yet it must be acknowledged that to take away these interests is no light task. We must once again refer to "the present condition of mankind," and confess that it may be doubted whether any community would possess a stable or an efficient government, if no *interests* bound its officers to exertion. To such a government patronage is probably at present indispensable. They who possess patronage, and they who are enriched or exalted by its exercise, array themselves against those propositions of change which would diminish their eminence or their wealth. And I perceive no means by which the existence of these interests and their consequent operation can be avoided, except by that elevation of the moral character of our race which would bring with it adequate motives to serve the public without regard to honours or rewards. It is, however, indisputably true that these interests should be as much as is practicable diminished; and in whatever degree this is effected, in the same degree there will be a willingness to admit those improvements in the form of governments which prudence and wisdom may prescribe.

14. "Let no new practice in politics be introduced, and no old one anxiously superseded till called for by the public voice."[1]

---

[1] Godwin: Pol. Just., v. 2, p. 503. This doctrine is adverse to that which is quoted in the first page of this chapter, where to be able to provide for mere physical wants is stated to be a sufficient qualification for the reception of an entirely new system of politics.

The same advice may be given respecting the alteration of forms; because alterations which are not so called for may probably fail of a good effect from the want of a congenial temper in the people, and because, as the public wish is the natural measure of sound political institutions, even beneficial changes ought not to be forced upon them against their own consent. The public mind, however, should be enlightened by a government. The legislator who perceives that another form of government is better for his country, does not do all his duty if he declares himself willing to concur in the alteration when the country desires it: he should *create* that desire by showing its reasonableness. Unhappily there is a *vis inertiæ* in governments of which the tendency is opposite to this. The interests which prompt men to maintain things as they are, and dread of innovation, and sluggishness, and indifference, occasion governments to be amongst the last portion of the community to diffuse knowledge respecting political truth. But, when the public mind has by any means become enlightened, so that the public voice demands an alteration of an existing form, it is one of the plainest as well as one of the greatest duties of a government to make the alteration: not reluctantly, but joyfully, not urging the prescription of ages and what is called "the wisdom of our ancestors," but philosophically yet soberly accommodating present institutions to the present state of mankind.

15. If, then, it is asked by what general rule Forms of Government should be regulated, I would say— Accommodate the form to the opinion of the community, whatever that community may prefer; and, Adopt institutions such as will facilitate the peaceable admission of alterations, as greater light and knowledge become diffused. I would not say to the Sultan, Adopt the constitution of England to-morrow; because the sudden transition would probably effect, for a long time, more evil than good. I would not say to the King of France, Descend from the throne and establish a democracy; because I do not think, and experience does not teach us to think, that democracy, even if it were theoretically best, is best for France at the present day.

16. Turning, indeed, to the probable future condition of the world, there is reason to think that the popular branches of all governments will progressively increase in influence, and perhaps eventually predominate. This appears to be the natural consequence of the increasing power of public opinion. The public judgment is not only the proper, but almost the *necessary* eventual measure of political institutions; and it appears evident that, as that judgment becomes enlightened, it will be exercised, and that, as it is exercised, it will prevail. The expression of public opinion upon political affairs, and consequently the influence of that opinion, partakes obviously of the principles of popular government. If public opinion governs, it must govern by some agency by which public opinion is expressed; and this expression can in no way so naturally be effected as by some modification of *popular* authority. These considerations, which appear obvious to reasoning, are enforced by experience. There is a manifest tendency in the world to the increase of the power of the public voice; and the effect is seen in the new constitutions which have been established in the new world and in the old. Few permanent revolutions are effected in which the community do not acquire additional influence in governing themselves.

17. It will not perhaps be disputed, that if the world were wise and good, the best form of government would be that of democracy in a very simple state. Nothing would be wanting but to ascertain the general wish and to collect the general wisdom. If, therefore, the present propriety of other forms of government results from the present condition of mankind, there is reason to suppose that they may gradually lapse away, as that condition, moral and intellectual, is improved. Whether mankind are thus improving, readers may differently decide; and their various decisions will lead to various conclusions respecting the future predominance of the public voice: the writer of these pages is one who thinks that the world is improving, that virtue as well as knowledge is extending its power; and therefore that, as ages roll along, every form of government but that which consists in some organ of the general mind, will gradually pass away. It may be hoped, too, that this gradual lapse will be occasioned, without solicitude on the part of those who then possess privileges or power, to retain either to themselves. That same state of virtue and excellence which enabled the people almost *immediately* to govern themselves would prevent others from wishing to retain the reins. Purer motives than the love of greatness, of power, or of wealth, would influence them in the choice of their political conduct. They might have no motive so powerful as the promotion of the general weal.

18. As no limit can be assigned to that degree of excellence which it may please the Universal Parent eventually to diffuse through the world, so none can be assigned to the simplicity and purity of the form in which government shall be carried on. In truth, the mind, as it passes onward and still on-

ward in its anticipations of purity, stops not until it arrives at that period when all government shall cease; when there shall be no wickedness to require the repressing arm of power; when terror to the evil-doers and praise to them that do well, shall no longer be needed, because none will do evil though there be no ruler to punish, and all will do well from higher and better motives than the praise of man.

19. In speaking of political constitutions, it is not sufficiently remembered in how great a degree good government depends upon the character and the virtue of those who shall conduct it. There is much of truth in the political maxim, that "whatever is best administered is best." But how shall good administration be secured except by the good dispositions of the administrators? The great present concern of mankind, in the selection of their legislators, respects their political opinions rather than their moral and Christian character. This exclusive reference to political biasses is surely unwise, because it leaves the passions and interests to operate without that control which individual *virtue* only can impart. Thus we are obliged to contrive reins and curbs for the public servants, as the charioteer contrives them for an unruly horse; too much forgetting that the best means of securing the safety of the vehicle of state are found in the good dispositions of those who move it onward. Political tendencies are important; but they are not the most important point; moral tendencies are the first and the greatest. The question in England should be, less, "ministerialist or oppositionist?" in America, less, "federalist or republican?" than in both, "a good or a bad man?" Rectitude of intention is the primary requisite; and whatever preference I might give to superiority of talents and to political principles, above all and before all I should prefer the enlightened Christian, knowing that *his character* is the best pledge of political uprightness, and that political uprightness is the best security of good government.

CHAPTER VII.

Political Influence—Party—Ministerial Union.

Influence of the Crown—Effects of influence—Incongruity of public notions—Patronage—American States—Dependency on the mother country—Party—Ministerial union—"A party man"—The council board and the senate—Resignation of offices.

20. The system of governing by Influence appears to be a substitute for the government of force—an intermediate step between awing by the sword and directing by reason and virtue. When the general character of political measures is such that reason and virtue do not sufficiently support them to recommend them, on their own merits, to the public approbation—these measures must be rejected, or they must be supported by foreign means; and when, by the political institutions of a people, force is necessarily excluded, nothing remains but to have recourse to some species of Influence. There is another ground upon which Influence becomes, in a certain sense, necessary—which is, that there is so much imperfection of virtue in the majority of legislators—they are so much guided by interested or ambitious or party motives, that for a measure to be recommended by its own excellence is sometimes not sufficient to procure their concurrence; and thus it happens that Influence is resorted to, not merely because public measures are deficient in purity, but because there is a deficiency of uprightness in public men.

21. Whilst political affairs continue to be conducted on their present, or nearly on their present principles, I believe influence is necessary to the stability of almost all governments. How else shall they be supported? They are not sufficiently virtuous to bespeak the general and unbiassed support of the nations, and without support of some kind they must fall. That which Hume says of England is perhaps true of all civilised states—" The influence which the crown acquires from the disposal of places, honours, and preferments, may become too forcible, but it cannot altogether be abolished without the total destruction of monarchy, and even of *all regular authority*."[1] A mournful truth it is; because it necessarily implies one of two things—either that the acts "of authority" do not recommend themselves by their own excellences, or that subjects are too little principled to be influenced by such excellences alone.

22. Whilst the generality of subjects continue to be what they are, Influence is *inseparable* from the privilege of appointing to offices. With whomsoever that privilege is intrusted, *he* will possess influence, and consequently power. Multitudes are hoping for the gifts which he has to bestow; and they accommodate their conduct to his wishes, in order to propitiate his favour and to obtain the reward. When they have obtained it, they call themselves bound in gratitude to continue their deference; and thus the influence and the power is continually possessed. Now, there is no way of destroying this influence but by making men *good;* for until

[1] History of England.

they are good, they will continue to sacrifice their judgments to their interests, and support men or measures, not because they are right, but because the support is attended with reward. It matters little in morals *by whom* the power of bestowing offices is possessed, unless you can ensure the virtue of the bestower. Politicians may talk of taking the power from crowns and vesting it in senates : but it will be of little avail to change the hands who distribute, if you cannot change the hearts. If a man should ask whether the Influence of the crown in this country might not usefully be transferred to the House of Commons, I should answer, No. Not merely because it would overthrow (for it certainly would overthrow) the monarchy, but because I know not that any security would be gained for a better employment of this influence than is possessed already. In all but arbitrary governments it appears indispensable, that much of the privilege of appointing to offices should rest with the executive power. It is the peculiar source of its authority. In our own government, the peers possess power independently of their political character, and the commons possess it as representatives of the public mind ; but where, without *Influence*, would be the power of the king? So it is in America. They have two representative bodies, and a third estate in the office of their president. But that president could not execute the functions of a third estate, nor the office of an executive governor, without having the means of *influencing* the people. I do not know whether it was with the determinate object of giving to the president a competent share of power that the Americans invested him with the privilege of appointing to offices ; but it is not to be questioned, that if they had not done it, the fabric of their government would speedily have fallen.

23. The degree of this influence, which may be required to give stability to an executive body (and therefore to a constitution), will vary with the character of its own policy. The more widely that policy deviates from rectitude, the greater will be the demand for Influence to induce concurrence in its measures. The degree of influence that is actually exerted by a government is therefore no despicable criterion of the excellence of its practice. In the United States the degree is less than in England ; and it may therefore be feared that we are inferior to them in the purity of the general administration of the affairs of state.

24. But let it be constantly borne in mind, that when we thus speak of the "necessity" for influence to support governments, we speak only of governments as they are, and of nations as they are. There is no necessity for influence to support good government over a good people. All influence but that which addresses itself to the judgment is wrong—wrong in morals, and therefore indefensible upon whatever plea. Influence is in part necessary to a government in the same sense as oppression is necessary to a slave trader—not because the captain is a man, but because he has taken up the *trade in slaves*—not because the government is a government, but because it conducts so many political affairs upon unchristian principles or in an unchristian manner. The captain says, I cannot secure my slaves without oppression—*Let them go free.* The government says, I cannot conduct my system without Influence—*Make the system good.*

25. And here arises the observation, that if a government should faithfully act upon *moral* principles, that demand for influence which is occasioned by the ill principles of senators or the public would be diminished or done away. The opposition which governments are wont to experience—indefensible as that opposition frequently is—is the result, principally, of the general character of political systems. Men, seeing that integrity and purity are sacrificed by a government to other considerations, adopt kindred means of opposing it. If I reason with a man upon the impropriety of his conduct, he will probably listen ; if I use violence, he will probably use violence in return. There is no reason to doubt that if political measures were more uniformly conformable with the sober judgments of a community, respect and affection would soon become so general and powerful, that that clamorous opposition which it is now attempted to oppose by influence, would be silenced by the public voice. Besides, the very fact that Influence is exercised, animates opposition to measures of state. The possession of power—that is, in a great degree, of *Influence* —is a tempting bait ; and it cannot be doubted that some range themselves against an executive body, not so much from objections to its measures as from desire of its power. Take away the influence, therefore, and you take away one operative cause of opposition— one great obstacle to the free progress of the vessel of state.

26. "All influence but that which addresses itself to the judgment is *wrong.*" Of the moral offence which this influence implies, many are guilty who *oppose* governments, as well as those who support them, or as governments themselves. It is evidently not a whit more virtuous to exert influence in opposing governments than in supporting them ; nor, indeed, is it *so* virtuous. To

what is a man *influenced?* Obviously, to do that which, without the influence, he would not do ;—that is to say, he is induced to violate his judgment at the request or at the will of other men. It can need no argument to show that this is vicious. In truth, it is vicious in a very high degree ; for to conform our conduct to our *own* sober judgment, is one of the first dictates of the Moral Law : and the viciousness is so much the greater, because the express purpose for which a man is appointed to legislate, is that the community may have the benefit of his uninfluenced judgment. Breach of trust is added to the sacrifice of individual integrity. A nation can gain nothing by the knowledge or experience of a million of "influenced" legislators'. It is curious, that the submission to influence which men often practise as legislators, they would abhor as judges. What should we say of a judge or a juryman who accepted a place or a promise as a bribe for an unjust sentence ? We should prosecute the juryman and address the parliament for a removal of the judge. Is it then of so much less consequence in what manner *affairs of state* are conducted than the affairs of individuals, that that which would be disgraceful in one case, is reputable in another ? No account can be given of this strange incongruity of public notions, than that custom has in one case blinded our eyes, and in the other has taught us to see. Let the legislator who would abhor to accept a purse to bribe him to write Ignoramus upon a true bill, apply the principle upon which his abhorrence is founded to his political conduct. When our moral principles are *consistent* these incongruities will cease. When uniform truth takes the place of vulgar practice and opinion, these incongruities will become wonderful for their absurdity ; and men will scarcely believe that their fathers, who could see so clearly, saw so ill. The same sort of stigma which now attaches to Lord Bacon, will attach to multitudes who pass for honourable persons in the present day.

27. A man may lawfully, no doubt, take a more active part in political measures, in compliance with the wishes of another, than he might otherwise incline to do ; but to support the measures of an opposition or an administration because they are *their* measures can never be lawful.—Nor can it ever be lawful to magnify the advantages or to expatiate upon the mischiefs of a measure, beyond his secret estimate of its demerits or its merits. That legislator is viciously influenced, who says or who does anything which he would think it not proper to say or do if he were an independent man.

28. But it will be said, Since influence is inseparable from the possession of patronage, and since patronage must be vested somewhere, what is to be done? or how are the evils of Influence to be done away ?—a question which, like many other questions in political morality, is attended with accidental rather than essential difficulties. Patronage, in a virtuous state of mankind, would be small. There would be none in the church and little in the state. Men would take the oversight of the Christian flock, not for filthy lucre, but of a ready mind. If the ready mind existed, the influence of patronage would be needless ; and, as a needless thing, it would be done away. And as to the state, when we consider how much of patronage in all nations results from the vicious condition of mankind—especially for military and naval appointments—it will appear that much of this class of patronage is accidental also. Take away that wickedness and violence in which hostile measures originate, and fleets and armies would no longer be needed ; and with their dissolution there would be a prodigious diminution of Patronage and of Influence. So, if we continue the inquiry, how far any given source of influence arising from patronage is *necessary* to the institution of civil government, we shall find, at last, that the necessary portion is very small. We are little accustomed to consider how simple a thing civil government is—nor what an unnumbered multiplicity of offices and sources of patronage would be cut off, if it existed in its simple and rightful state.

29. Supposing this state of rectitude to be attained, and the little patronge which remained to be employed rather as an encouragement and reward of public virtue than of subserviency to purposes of party, we should have no reason to complain of the existence of Influence or of its effects. Swift said of our own country, that "while the prerogative of giving all employments continues in the crown, either immediately or by subordination, it is in the power of the prince to make piety and virtue become the fashion of the age, if, at the same time, he would make them necessary qualifications for favour and preferment."[1] But unhappily, in the existing character of political affairs in all nations, piety and virtue would be very poor recommendations to many of their concerns. "The just man," as Adam Smith says, " the man who, in all private transactions would be the most beloved and the most esteemed, in those public transactions is regarded as a fool and an idiot, who does not understand his business."[2] It would be as absurd to think of making "piety and

[1] Project for the Advancement of Religion.
[2] Theo. of Mor. Sent.

virtue, *qualifications*" for these offices, as to make idiocy a qualification for understanding the *Principia.*—But the position of Swift, although it is not true whilst politics remain to be what they are, contains truth if they were what they ought to be. We should have, I say, no reason to complain of the existence of influence or of its effects, if it were reduced to its proper amount, and exerted in its proper direction.

30. It has, I think, been justly observed that one of the principal causes of the separation of America from Britain, consisted in the little influence which the crown possessed over the American States. They had popular assemblies, guided, as such assemblies are wont to be, by impatience of control, as well as by zeal for independence ; and the government possessed no patronage that was sufficient to counteract the democratic principles. Occasion of opposition was ministered ; and the effect was seen. The American assemblies, and the corresponding temper of the people, were more powerful than the little influence which the crown possessed. What was to be done ? It was necessary either to relinquish the government, which could no longer be maintained without force, or to employ force to retain it. The latter was attempted ; and, as was to be expected, it failed. I say failure was to be expected ; because the state of America, and of England too, was such that a government of force could not be supposed likely to stand. Henry VIII. and Elizabeth governed England by a species of force. They induced parliamentary compliance by intimidation. This intimidation has given place to influence. But every man will perceive that it would be impossible to return to intimidation again. And it was equally impossible to adopt it permanently in the case of America.

31. And here it may be observed, in passing, that the separation from a mother country of extensive and remote dependencies, is always to be eventually expected. As the dependency increases in population, in intelligence, in wealth, and in the various points which enable it to be, and which practically constitute it, a nation of itself— it increases in the tendency to actual separation. This separation may be delayed by the peculiar nature of the parent's government, but it can hardly be in the end prevented. It is not in the constitution of the human species to remain under the supremacy of a foreign power, to which they are under no natural subordination, after the original causes of the supremacy have passed away. Accordingly, there is reason to expect that, in days to come, the possessions of the European powers on the other quarters of the globe will one after another lapse away.

Happy will it be for these powers and for the world, if they take counsel of the philosophy of human affairs, and of the experience of times gone by : if they are willing tranquilly to yield up a superiority of which the reasonableness and the propriety is passed —a superiority which no efforts can eventually maintain—and a superiority which really tends not to the welfare of the governing, of the governed, or of the world.

Party.

32. The system of forming *Parties* in governments is perfectly congruous with the general character of political affairs, but totally incongruous with political rectitude. Of this incongruity considerate men are frequently sensible ; and accordingly we find that defences of party are set up, and set up by men of respectable political character.[1] To defend a custom is to intimate that it is assailed.

33. What does the very nature of party imply? That he who adheres to it speaks and votes not always according to the dictates of his own judgment, but according to the plans of other men. This sacrifice of individual judgment violates one of the first and greatest duties of a legislator—to direct his separate and unbiassed judgment to the welfare of the state. There can be no proper accumulation of individual experience and knowledge amongst those who vote with a party.

34. But, indeed, the justifications which are attempted do not refer to the abstract rectitude of becoming one of a party, but to the unfailing ground of defending political evil—*Expediency.* An administration, it is said, would not be so likely to stand, or an opposition to prevail, when each man votes as he thinks rectitude requires, as when he ranges himself under a leader. The difference is like that which subsists in war between a body of irregular peasantry and a disciplined army : each man's arm is as strong in the one case as in the other, but each man's is not equally effective.

35. Very well. If we are to be told that it is fitting, or honest, or decent, that senates and cabinets should act upon the principles of conflicting armies, parties may easily be defended, but surely legislators have other business and other duties. It only exhibits the *wideness* of the general departure from the proper modes of conducting government and legislation, that such arguments are employed. It will be said, that there are no

[1] Fox, I believe, was one of them, and the present Lord John Russell, in his Life of Lord Russell, is another.

means of expelling a bad administration from office but by a systematic opposition to its measures. If this were true, it would be nothing to the question of rectitude, unless it can be shown that the end sanctions the means. The question is not whether we shall overthrow an administration, but whether we shall do what is right. But, even with respect to the success of political objects, it is not very certain that simple integrity would not be the most efficacious. The man who habitually votes on one side, loses, and he ought to lose, much of the confidence of other members and of the public. At what value ought we to estimate the mental principles of a man who foregoes the dictates of his own judgment, and acts in opposition to it in order to serve a party? What is the ground upon which we can place confidence in his integrity? Facts may furnish an answer. The speeches, and statements, and arguments of such persons are listened to with suspicion; and an habitual and large deduction is made from their weight. This is inevitable. Hearers and the public cannot tell whether the speaker is uttering his own sentiments or those of others: they cannot tell whether he believes his own statements, or is convinced by his own reasoning. So that, even when his cause is good and his advocacy just, he loses half his influence because men are afraid to rely upon him, and because they still do not know whether some illusion is not underneath. The mind is kept so constantly jealous of fallacies, that it excludes one half of the truth. But when the man stands up, of whom it is known that he is *sincere*, that what he says he thinks, and what he asserts he believes; the mind opens itself to his statements without apprehension of deceit. No deductions are made for the overcolourings of party. Integrity carries with it its proper sanction.

36. Now if, generally, the measures of a party are good, the *individual* support of upright men would probably more effectually recommend them to a senate and to a nation, than the ranked support of men whose uprightness must always be questionable and questioned. If the measures are not good, it matters not how inefficiently they are supported. Let those who now range themselves under political leaders of whatever party, throw away their unworthy shackles; let them convince the legislature and the public that they are absolutely sincere men; and it is probable that a vicious policy would not be able to stand before them. For other motives to opposition than actual viciousness of measures, I have nothing to say. He whose principles allow him to think that other motives justify opposition, may very well vote against his understanding. The principles and the conduct are congenial; but both are bad.

Ministerial Union.

37. The unanimous support or opposition which ordinarily is given to a measure by the members of an administration, whatever be their private opinions, is a species of party. Like other modes of party, it results from the impure condition of political affairs; like them, it is incongruous with sound political rectitude—and, like them, it is defended upon pleas of expediency. The immorality of this custom is easily shown; because it sacrifices private judgment, involves a species of hypocrisy, and defrauds the community of that uninfluenced judgment respecting public affairs for which all public men are appointed. "Ministers have been known, publicly and in unqualified terms, to applaud those very measures of a coadjutor which they have freely condemned in private."[1] Is this manly? Is it honest? Is it Christian? If it is not, it is vicious and criminal; and all arguments in its defence—all disquisitions about expediency—are sophistical and impertinent.

38. "The necessity for the co-operation" (I use political language) results from the general impurity of political systems—systems in which not reason, simply, and principle, direct, but influence also, and the spirit of party, and the love of power. Where influence is to be employed, union amongst a cabinet is likely to urge it in fuller force:— Where the spirit of party is to be employed, this union is necessary to the object:—Where the love of power is the guide, consistency and integrity must be sacrificed to its acquisition or retention. But take away this influence—which is bad; and this spirit of party —which is bad; and this love of power— which is bad; and the minister may speak and act like a consistent and a virtuous man. It is with this, as with unnumbered cases in life, that what is called the necessity for a particular vicious course of action is quite adventitious, resulting in no degree from the operation of sound principles, but from the diffused impurity of human institutions.

39. But, indeed, the necessity is not perhaps so obvious as is supposed. The same reasons as those which make the support of a partisan comparatively inefficient, operate upon the ministerial advocate. He is regarded as a party man; and as the exertions of a party man his arguments are received. People say or think, when such arguments are urged, as some men say and think of the labours of the clergy—" What they say

[1] Gisborne; Duties of Men.

is a matter of course;"—"It is their business; their trade." No one disputes that these feelings have a powerful effect in diminishing the practical effect of the labours of the pulpit; and they have the same effect with respect to the labours of a ministry. We listen to a minister rather as a pleader than as a judge; and every one knows what disproportionate regard is paid to these. Why should not ministers be judges? Why should not senates confide in their integrity, believe their statements, give candid attention to their reasonings—as we attend to, and believe, and confide in, what is uttered from the bench? And does any man think so ill of mankind as to believe that if an administration acted thus, they would not actually possess a greater influence upon the minds of men than they do now? Even now, when men are so habituated to the operation of influence and party, I believe that a minister is listened to with much greater confidence and satisfaction when he dissents from his colleagues, than when he makes common cause. We then insensibly reflect, that he is no longer the pleader but the judge. The independence of his judgment is unquestioned; and we regard it therefore as the judgment of an honest man.

40. Uniformity of opinion—or more properly, unity of exertion is not at all necessary to the stability of a cabinet. Several recent administrations in our own country have been divided in sentiment upon great questions of national policy, and their members have opposed one another in parliament. With what ill effects? Nay, has not that very contrariety recommended the reasonings of all, as those of sincere integrity? It is usual with some politicians to declaim vehemently against " unnatural coalitions in cabinets." As to individuals, they, no doubt, may be censurable for political tergiversation; but as to cabinets being composed of men of different sentiments of sentiments so different as their respective judgments may occasion—it is both allowable and expedient. It is just what a wise community would wish, because it affords a security for that *canvass* of public measures which is likely to illustrate their character and tendencies. But it is a sorrowful and a sickening sight to contemplate a number of persons frankly urging their various and disagreeing opinions at a council board, and as soon as some resolution is come to, *all* proceeding to a senate, and one half urging the very arguments against which they have just been contending, and by which they are not yet convinced. Is freedom of canvass for any reasons useful and right at the council board? Is it not, for the very same reasons, useful and right in a senate? The answer would be, *yes*, if public measures were regarded as the measures of the *community*, and not of the *administration;* because then the desire and judgment of the community would be sought by the public and independent discussion of the question. Here, then, at last is one great cause of the evil—that a large proportion of public acts are the measures of *administrations;* and, being such, administrations unitedly support them whatever be the individual opinions of their members. These things ought not so to be. I would not indeed say that, from the crown of the head to the sole of the foot, there is *no* soundness in the system—but the evil is mingled deplorably with the good. It is sometimes in practice almost forgotten, that an administration is an *Executive* rather than a Legislative body—that their original and natural business is rather to do what the legislature and constitution directs, than to direct the legislature themselves. I say *the original and natural business;* for, how congenial soever the great influence of administrations in public affairs may be with the present tenor of policy, and especially of international policy, it is not at all congenial with the original purpose and simple and proper objects of civil government—the welfare of the community, as determined by an enlightened survey of the national mind.

41. Of the want of advertence to these simple and proper objects, one effect has been that, in this country, administrations have frequently given up their offices when the senate has rejected their measures. This is an unequivocal indication of the wrong station in which cabinets are placed in the legislature—because it indicates, that if a cabinet cannot carry its point, it is supposed to be unfit for its office. All this is natural enough upon the present system, but it is very unnatural when cabinets are regarded, either in their ministerial capacity, as *executive officers*, or in their legislative capacity, as *ordinary members of the senate.* Executive officers are to do what the constitution and the legislature directs:—members of a senate are to assist that legislature in directing aright: in all which, no necessity is involved for ministers to resign their offices because the measures which they think best are not thought best by the majority. That a ministry should sometimes judge amiss is to be expected, because it is to be expected of all men: but surely in a sound state of political institutions, their fallibility would not be a necessary argument of unfitness for their offices, nor would the rejection of some of their opinions be a necessary evidence of a loss of the confidence of the public.

CHAPTER VIII.
British Constitution.

Influence of the crown—House of Lords—Candidates for a peerage—Sudden creation of peers—The bench of bishops—Proxies—House of Commons—The wishes of the people—Extension of the elective franchise—Universal suffrage—Frequent elections—Modes of election—Annual parliaments—Qualifications of voters and representatives—Of choosing the clergy—Duties of a representative—Systematic opposition—Placemen and pensioners—Posthumous fame.

42. That the British Constitution is relatively good, is satisfactorily indicated by its effects. Without indulging in the ordinary gratulations of our "own country being the first country in the world," it is unquestionably, in almost every respect, *amongst* the first—amongst the first in liberty, in intellectual and moral excellence, and in whatever dignifies and adorns mankind. A country which thus surpasses other nations, and which has, with little interruption, possessed a nearly uniform constitution for ages, may well rest assured that its constitution is good. To say that it is good is, however, very different from saying that it is theoretically perfect, or practically as good as its theory will allow. Under a King, Lords, and Commons, we have prospered ; but it does not therefore follow that under a King, Lords, and Commons, we might not have prospered more.

43. Whatever may be the future allotment of our country as to the form of its government, whether, at any period, or at what, the progressive advancement of the human species will occasion an alteration, we are not at present concerned to inquire. Of one thing, indeed, we may be assured, that if it should be the good pleasure of Providence that this advancement in excellence shall take place, the practical principles of the government and its constitutional form will be gradually moulded and modified into a state of adaptation to the then condition of mankind.

44. I. Of the regal part of the British Constitution I would say little. The sovereign is, in a great degree, identified with an administration ; and into the principles which should regulate ministerial conduct, the preceding chapters have attempted some inquiry.

45. Yet it may be observed that, supposing ministerial influence to be "necessary" to the constitution, there appears considerable reason to think that its amount may be safely and rightly diminished. As this influence becomes needless in proportion to the actual rectitude of political measures ; as there is some reason to hope that this rectitude is increasing ; and as the public capacity to judge soundly of political measures is manifestly increasing also ; it is probable that some portion of the influence of the crown might be given up, without any danger to the constitution or the public weal. And, waiving all reference to the essential *moral* character of influence, it is to be remembered, that no degree of it is defensible, even by the politician, but that which apparently subserves the reasonable purposes of government.

46. It is recorded that in 1741, in Scotland, "sixteen peers were chosen literally according to the list transmitted from court."[1] Such a fact would convince a man, without further inquiry, that there must have been something very unsound in the ministerial politics of the day ; or at any rate (which is nearly the same thing), something very discordant with the general mind.

47. In 1793, and whilst, of course, the Irish Parliament existed, a bill was brought into that parliament to repeal some of the Catholic disabilities. This bill the "parliament loudly, indignantly, and resolutely rejected." A *few months* afterwards, a similar bill was introduced under the auspices of the government. Pitt had taken counsel of Burke, and wished to grant the Catholics relief : and when the viceroy's secretary accordingly brought in a bill, *two* members only opposed it ; and at the second reading, it was opposed but by *one* vote. Now, whatever may be said of the "necessity" of ministerial influence for the purposes of state, nothing can be said in favour of such influence as this. Every argument which would show its expediency, would show even more powerfully the impurity of the system which could require it.

48. It is common to hear complaints of ministerial influence *in parliament*. "That kind of influence which the noble lord alludes to," said Fox in one of his speeches, "I shall ever deem unconstitutional ; for by the influence of the crown, he means the influence of the crown in parliament."[2] But, if it is concluded that influence is "necessary," it seems idle to complain of its exercise in the senate. Where should it be exerted with effect? Whether it be *constitutional* it is difficult to say, because it is difficult to define where constitutional acts end and unconstitutional acts begin. But, it may safely be concluded that in such matters, questions of *constitutional* rectitude are little relevant. Influence you say—and in

[1] Smollett : Hist. England, v. 3, p. 71.
[2] Fell's Public Life of C. J. Fox.

a certain sense you say it truly is necessary. To what purpose, then, can it be to complain of the exercise of that influence in those places in which only or principally it is effectual? It would be impossible for persons, with our views of political rectitude, to execute the office of minister upon any system that approached, in its character, to the present; but were it otherwise, I would advise a minister openly to avow the exercise of influence and to defend it. This were the frank, and I think the rational course. Why should a man affect secrecy or concealment about an act "politically necessary"? I would not talk about disinterestedness and independence; but tell the world that influence was needful, and that I exerted it. Not that such an avowal would stop, or ought to stop, the complaints of virtuous men. The morality of politics is not so obscure but that thousands will always perceive that the exertion of influence and the submission to it, is morally vicious. This conflict will continue. Artifice and deception are "necessary" to a swindler, but all honest men know and feel that the artifice and deception are wrong.

49. II. It appears to have been discovered, or assumed, in most free states, that it is expedient that there should be two deliberate assemblies, of which one shall, from its constitution, possess less of a democratical tendency than the other. Not that, in a purer state of society, two such assemblies would be necessary; but because, while separate individuals or separate classes of men pursue their peculiar interests, and are swayed by their peculiar prejudices, it is found needful to obstruct one class of interests and tendencies by another. Such a purpose is answered by the British House of Lords.

50. The privileges of the members of this house are such as to offer considerable temptation to their political virtue. A body of men, whose eminence *consists* in artificial distinctions between them and the rest of the community, are likely to desire to make these distinctions needlessly great; and for that purpose to postpone the public welfare to the interests of an order. We all know that there is a collective as well as an individual ambition. It is a truth which a peer should habitually inculcate upon himself, that however rank and title may be conferred for the gratification of the possessor, the *legislative* privileges of a peer are to be held exclusively subservient to the general good. I use the word "exclusively" in its strictest sense: so that, if even the question should come, whether any part or the whole of the privileges of the peerage should be withdrawn, or the general good should be sacrificed, I should say that no reasonable question could exist respecting the proper alternative. Were I a peer, I should not think myself at liberty to urge the privileges of my order in opposition to the public weal; for this were evidently to postpone the greater interests to the less. If rulers of all kinds, if civil government itself, are simply the officers of the nation, surely no one class of rulers is at liberty to put its pretensions in opposition to the national advantage.

51. The love of title and of rank constitutes one of the great temptations of the political man. He can obtain them only from the crown; and it is not usual to bestow them except upon those who support the administration of the day. The intensity of the desire which some men feel for these distinctions has a correspondently intense effect. Lord Chatham said, "that he had known men of great ambition for power and dominion, many whose characters were tarnished by glaring defects, some with many vices—who, nevertheless, could be prevailed upon to join in the best public measures; but the moment he found any man who had set himself down as a candidate for a peerage, he despaired of his ever being a friend to his country?"[1] This displays a curious political phenomenon. Can the reader give a better solution than the supposition that, in the *love itself* of title, there is something little and low, and that the minds which can be so anxious for it, are commonly too little and too low to sacrifice their hopes to friendship for their country?—Many who are not *candidates* for peerages, nevertheless look upon them with a wishing eye: and some who have attained to the lower honours of the order, are equally solicitous for advancement to the higher. So that even upon those on whom the temptation is not so powerful as that of which Chatham speaks —some temptation is laid; a temptation of which it were idle to dispute that the aggregate effect is great.

52. If, without reference to the existing state of Britain, a man should ask whether the legislators of a nation *ought* to be subjected to such temptation—whether it were a judicious political institution, I should answer, No; because I should judge that a legislative assembly ought to have *no* inducements or motives foreign to the general good. This appears to be so obviously true, that the necessity, if there be a necessity, for an assembly so constituted only evinces how imperfect the political character of a people is. There would be no need for having recourse to an objectionable species of assembly, if it were not wanted to counteract

[1] Quoted by Fox.—Fell's Memoirs.

or to effect purposes which a purely constituted assembly could not attain.

53. In estimating the relative worthiness of objects of human pursuit, a peerage does not appear to rank high. I know not, indeed, how it happens that men contemplate it with so much complacency; and that so few are found who appear to doubt whether it is one of the most reasonable and worthy objects of human desire. *A title!* Only think what a title is, and what it is not. It is a thing which philosophy may reasonably hold cheap; a thing which partakes of the character of the tinsel watch, for which the new-breeched urchin looks with anxious eyes, and by which, when he has got it, he thinks he is made a greater man than before. If such be the character of title when brought into comparison with the dignity of man, what is it when it is compared with the dignity of the Christian? Nothing. It may be affirmed, without any apprehension of error, that the greater the degree in which any man is a Christian, the less will be his wish to be called a lord; and that when he attains to the "fulness of the stature" of a Christian man, *no* wish will remain.—If additional motives can be urged to reduce our ambition of title, some, perhaps, may be found in considering the grounds upon which it has too frequently been conferred. Queen Anne, when once the ministry could not carry a measure in the upper house, made twelve new peers at once. These, of course, voted for the measure. What honourable and elevated mind would have purchased one of these titles at the expense of the caustic question which a member put when they were going to give their first vote —"Are you going to vote by your *foreman?*"

54. Whether the heads of a Christian church should possess seats in the legislature, is a question that has often been discussed. If a Christian bishop *can* attend to legislative affairs without infringing upon the time and attention which is due to his peculiar office, there appears nothing in that office which disqualifies him for legislative functions. The better a man is, the more, as a general rule, he is fit for a legislator; so that, assuming that bishops are peculiarly Christian men, it is not unfit that they should assist in the councils of the nation. Nevertheless, it must be conceded, that there is no peculiar congruity between the office of the Christian overseer and that of an agent in political affairs. They are not incompatible, indeed, but the connection is not natural. Politics do not form the proper business of a Christian shepherd. They are wholly foreign to his proper business; and that retirement from the things of the world which Christianity requires of her ministers, and which she must be supposed peculiarly to require of her more elevated ministers, indicates the impropriety of meddling but little in affairs of state. But, when it comes to be proposed that *all* the heads of a Christian church shall be selected for legislators, *because* they are heads of the church—the impropriety becomes manifest and great. To make a high religious office the *qualification* for a political office, is manifestly wrong. It may be found now and then that a good bishop is fit for a useful legislator—but because you have elevated a man to a more onerous and responsible office in the church, forthwith to superadd an onerous and responsible office in the state, is surely not to consult the dictates of Christianity or of reason. Nor is it rational or Christian forthwith to add a temporal peerage. If there be any one thing, not absolutely vicious, which is incongruous with the proper temper and character of an exalted shepherd of the flock, it is temporal splendour. Such splendour accords very well with the political character of the Romish Church—but with Protestantism, with Christianity, it has no accordance. The splendours of title are utterly dissimilar in their character to the character of the heads of the church, as that character is indicated in the New Testament. How preposterous is the association in idea of "My Lord" with a Paul or a Barnabas! The truth, indeed, is, that this species of fornication did not originate in religion nor in religious motives. It sprung up with the corruptions of the papacy; and in this, as in some other instances, we who have purified the vicious doctrine, have clung to the vicious practice.

55. To these considerations is to be added another: that the extent of jurisdiction which is assigned to the bishops of this country, is such as to occupy, if the office be rightly executed, a large portion of a bishop's time —a portion *so* large, that if he be exemplary as a bishop, he can hardly be exemplary as a legislator. If, as will perhaps be admitted, the diligent and conscientious pastor of an ordinary parish has a sufficient employment for his time, it cannot be supposed that a bishop has less. He who presides over hundreds of parishes and hundreds of pastors, and *rightly* presides over them, can surely find little time for attendance in the senate; especially when that attendance takes him, as it necessarily does, far away from the inferior shepherds and from the flocks.

56. But, when it comes to be considered that our bishops are the heads of an *established* church, we are presented with a very different field of inquiry. That which is not congruous with Christianity may be congruous with a religious establishment. Nor, in

a religious establishment like that which obtains in England, would there, perhaps, be any impropriety in dismissing bishops from the House of Lords. They have to watch over other interests than those of religion—political interests; and where shall they efficiently watch over them if they have no voice in political affairs? Bishops in this country have not merely to " feed the flock of God which is among them," but to take care that that flock and their shepherds retain their privileges and their supremacy: so that if I were asked whether bishops ought to have a seat in the legislature, I should answer— If you mean by a bishop a head of a Christian church, he has other and better business : —if by a bishop you mean the head of an *established* church, the question must be determined by the question of the rectitude of an established church itself.

57. Without stopping to decide this question, it may be observed that some serious mischiefs result from the institution as it exists. A bishop should be not only of unimpeachable, but, as far as may be, of *untempted* virtue. His office as a peer subjects him to great temptations. Bishops are more dependent upon the crown than any other class of peers, because vacancies for elevation in the church are continually occurring; and for these vacancies a bishop hopes. Since he cannot generally expect to obtain them by an opposition, however conscientious, to the minister of the day, he is placed in a situation which no good man ought to desire for himself; that of a powerful temptation to sacrifice his integrity to his interests. How frequently, or how far, that temptation prevails, I presume not to determine ; but it is plain, whatever be the cause, that the minister can count upon the support of the bishops more confidently than upon any other class of peers. This is not the experience of one minister, or of two, but, in general language, of all. History states informally, and as an unquestioned circumstance, that " from the bench of bishops the court usually expects the greatest complaisance and submission."[1] I perceive nothing in the nature of the Christian office to induce this support of the minister of the day. I do not see why a Christian pastor should do this rather than a legislator of another station; for it will hardly be contended that there is so much goodness and purity in ministerial transactions, that a Christian pastor must support them because they are so pure and so good. What conclusion then remains but that temptation is presented, and that it prevails? That this, simply regarded, is an evil no man can doubt : but let him remember that the evil is not necessarily incidental even to

[1] Hume's England.

the legislating bishop. There may be bishops without solicitude for translations, for there may be a church without dependence on the crown, or connection with the state. Whilst this connection and this dependence remains, I do not say that ecclesiastical peers *cannot* be exempt from unworthy influence, but there is no hope of exemption in the present condition of mankind.

58. The system which obtains in the House of Lords, of accepting *proxies* in divisions, appears strangely inconsistent with propriety and reason. It intimates utter contempt of the debates of the house, because it virtually declares that the arguments of the speakers are of no weight or concern. Who can tell, or who ought to tell, when he gives his proxy to another, whether the discussion might not alter his views and make him vote on the other side? Proxies are congruous enough with a system of legislation which is conducted upon maxims of interest and party ; but if we suppose legislation to proceed upon evidence and reasoning, they are a preposterous mockery of common sense.

59. The number of peers has rapidly increased. This may be a subject of regret to the peerage itself, because every addition to its number may be regarded as a reduction from the dignity of each. The dignity is relative, and consists in the *distinction* between them and other men, which distinction becomes less as peers become common. As the peerage is progressively increased in number, a lord will be progressively reduced in *practical* rank. The title remains the same, but the actual distinction between him and other men is waning away. But though this may cause regret to a peer, it ought to cause none to the man of reason or the patriot. As to reason, if our estimates of title be accurate, its distinctions are sufficiently vain ; and as to patriotism, if our country is increasing in knowledge and in excellence, it is increasing in its ability to direct its own policy without the intervention of an order of peers ; so that, supposing the cessation of that order to be hereafter desirable, the patriot may hope that its distinctions will be yielded up to the general weal more willingly when they have become insignificant by diffusion, than if they were great by being possessed but by a few.

60. In reflecting then upon the political character of the House of Lords, it is to be remembered that its utility appears to be *conditional*—conditional upon the state of the community. It may be needed to check intemperate measures—to restrain, for instance, the vicious encroachments of democracy ; but it is not needed in any other sense. It is like the physician's prescription or the

surgeon's knife—useful in an unhealthy state of the social body, but useless if it were sound. The reader will say that this is strong language, and so it is; but he has no reason to complain if it is the language of truth; and that it is true, he may perhaps be convinced by authority upon such a subject, less questionable than mine. "Were the voice of the people always *dictated by reflection*, did every man, or even one man in a hundred, *think for himself*, or *actually consider the measure* he was about to approve or censure, or even were the common people tolerably steadfast in the judgment which they formed, I should hold the interference of a superior order *not only superfluous, but wrong*."[1]

61. III. The House of Commons is constitutionally the representative of the people, and the degree in which it fulfils this, its constitutional office, is to be estimated by the degree in which the public wish is actually represented by its members. " It is essential to the happiness of the people, that they should be convinced that they, and the members of this house, feel an identity of interest; that the nation at large, and the representatives of the people, hold a conformity of sentiment. This is the essence of a proper representative assembly."[2] It is not necessary to the just fulfilment of this office, that every measure which a majority of the people desires, should be adopted by the house, because its members are often better able to judge what is good for the majority, than they are themselves; and because, sometimes, popular opinions are not, I think, *capricious*, but fluctuating, and unreasonably vehement. There was a time when the populace were in tumult, and almost in insurrection, because the legislature had erected turnpikes; but if three-fourths of the population of the country had joined in the outcry, it would not have been a good reason for repealing the act. But, if the public wish is not always to be gratified by the House of Commons, it is always to be *expressed* within its walls. The house should know what the people desire, though they are at liberty, if they think it needful, to reject that desire. This, it is obvious, is a right which the people may claim of the republican part of the constitution. It were neither decorous nor wise to show even impatience at the respectful petitions of the people;—not decorous, for it implies forgetfulness that the house is the servant of the public;—not wise, for a candid attention to the public representations, even when they are not acted upon, is one of the surest means of conciliating the esteem, and of administering to the satisfaction of the community.

[1] Paley: Mor. and Pol. Phil., b. vi. c. 7.
[2] William Pitt: Gifford's Life, v. iii.

62. In estimating the extent to which the decisions of the House of Commons ought actually to correspond with the public wishes, no narrow limits should be prescribed. It is here, if anywhere, that the people are to be heard. Both the other branches of the constitution tend naturally to their separate and privileged interests; so that, if in the senate of a republican government the people ought to be represented, much more emphatically ought they to be represented by the commons in a government like our own.

63. The most accurate test of the degree in which the British House of Commons fulfils this its primary office, is to be sought in the deliberate judgments of reasonable and thinking men; not of party men, or interested men, but of the temperate and the good. Now there is reason to think, that in the judgments of this portion of the community, there is not a just and sufficient identity between the public voice and the measures of this house.

64. But, supposing the practical representation to be defective, how is the defect to be repaired? A question this of far less easy solution than some politicians would persuade us! Not frequency of parliaments, not extensions of the franchise, not altering the modes of election, will be sufficient. The evil is seated primarily, and essentially, in the impure condition, in the imperfect virtue of man. To those who are imperfect and impure, temptation is offered: the temptation perhaps of party—perhaps of interest—perhaps of resentment—perhaps of ambition. You cannot make men proof against these temptations but by making them *good*; and modes of electing, or frequency of election, will not do this. The only reformation must result from the reformation of the heart. Electors themselves are not solicitous to elect good men: they are influenced by passion, and interest, and party. How then should they select those who are independent, and disinterested, and temperate?

65. But evils which cannot be removed may be diminished; and since the evil in question indicates an insufficient degree of liberty, both civil and political, it may be of advantage to inquire whether both cannot be, and ought not to be increased.

66. Now, remembering that it lies upon the legislature to prove that the present institutions are the *best*—what is the evidence that mischief would arise from an extension of the franchise and from an alteration of the modes of election? We are not required to evince that benefit would arise

from such measures; because their propriety is dictated by the principles of political truth, *unless* it is shown that they would be pernicious. Assuredly, in contemplating mere probabilities, it is more probable that a representative will be virtuously chosen, when he is chosen by a thousand men than when by only ten. The reason is simple, that it is much more difficult to offer vicious motives to the electors. If the probability of advantage in such an alteration is disputable, it must be by the production of very strong probabilities on the other side. And until those probabilities are adduced, I see not how it can be denied that from the public is withheld a portion of their civil *rights*. There is always one powerful reason for an extension of the legal right of election, which is, that it tends to *satisfy* the people. This satisfaction is of importance, whether the wish of the people be in itself desirable or not: so that of two measures which in other respects were equally eligible, *that* would become the best and the right one, which imparted the greatest satisfaction to the community. It cannot be hoped that this satisfaction will ever prevail during the continuance of the present state of the franchise. Its irregular and inconsistent character will always (even setting aside its consequences) give rise to uneasiness and complaints. A large county can never think political justice is exercised while it sends no more members than a little borough. Birmingham and Manchester will never think it is exercised, whilst Old Sarum sends two members and they send none.

67. There are, no doubt, many difficulties interposed in the way of the legislature in proceeding to a reformation—which difficulties, however, will generally be found to result from the existing impurity of the present system. It is not perhaps impossible that, if a House of Commons were selected by any approach to universal suffrage, it would ere long interfere with the established modes of governing. Many, it is probable, would feel that their prejudices were outraged, and their interests invaded, and their privileges diminished or taken away. These prospects interpose difficulties; and yet unless these prejudices are reasonable, and these interests virtuous, and these privileges dictated by the public good, it will be seen that the difficulties of reform result, not from any defect in the principles of Political Truth, but from the conflict between the operation of those principles and exceptionable systems.

68. Not, indeed, that a representative body, however elected, is to be concluded as necessarily temperate and wise. There is much reason to fear, in the present state of private virtue, that if the House of Commons were a purely popular assembly, it might both injudiciously and unjustifiably excite political distractions. If, on the one hand, they found that any existing institutions required amendment, they would probably, on the other hand, seek to establish popular power in opposition to the general good.

69. Nevertheless, there appears sufficient reason for thinking that some alteration, and considerable alteration, might be made in the system of representation, which would do good without doing evil. If the British empire is not prepared for a purely popular representation, it is, I think, prepared for a representation more popular than that which obtains. Mild and gradual alteration is perhaps the best. The franchise may be extended, one by one, to new districts or new towns, and taken away or modified, one by one, from places in which the electors are few, or in which they are corrupt. By such means the reformation might keep pace, and only keep pace, with the general progress of the nation. The prospect of successive amendment would tend to satisfy the public, and the general end be eventually answered by innoxious means.

70. Some want of enlargement of views appears to exist with respect to the propriety and the right of the legislature to remove the elective franchise. It seems to be thought that a borough ought not to be deprived of it, unless its corruption is both general and distinctly proved. But why? The franchise is not possessed for the gratification of the inhabitants of a particular spot, but for the national good. It might, no doubt, have originally been *given* for their gratification, but this was always an unreasonable motive for granting it. If the general advantage requires the transfer of the right of election, it were strange indeed if the inhabitants of a little town ought to prevent it by exclaiming, Do not encroach upon our *privileges!* As to the property vested in the privilege, it is founded, if not in corruption, in political impropriety. For a householder to say, I have given a hundred pounds more for my premises because they conveyed a right of voting, or for a patron to say, I have given an extra five thousand for a manor because it enabled me to nominate two representatives, is surely a very insufficient reason for continuing a franchise that is adverse to the common weal. However, it is probable that the great object is not to take away privileges but to extend them, and by that extension to secure the probability of uninfluenced elections.

71. *Universal suffrage* is a by-word of

political scorn; and yet it is probable that the country will one day be fit for the adoption of universal suffrage. The objections to it are founded, as, antecedently to inquiry, I should expect they would be founded—upon the ignorant and vicious state of mankind. If knowledge and virtue increase, universal suffrage may hereafter be rightly adopted.—If they are now increasing, *approaches* towards such suffrage are desirable now. Nor perhaps is the public preparation for these approaches so little as some men suppose. A part of our objections to it are quite fortuitous and accidental, and easily removable by legislative enactments. Nor again is it to be forgotten, that some of the states in the American Union do actually adopt universal suffrage, or something that is very much like it. Upon this subject it is always to be remembered, that unless the withholding of the privilege of election is necessary to the national welfare, the possession of it is, in strictness, a civil right. It can never be shown upon other grounds than expediency, why one man should possess the privilege whilst his neighbour should not.

72. The present modes of election are productive of much evil—evil by facilitating undue influence—evil by occasioning immorality and riot—and evil *by attaching to the idea of frequent elections ideas of national inquietude and confusion.* When we see, at the time of an election, a multitude of men brought together, many of them perhaps from a distance, and fed and lodged at the expense of one of the candidates, we certainly see that the door is opened wide for the entrance of corruption. In 1696 an Act was passed, "for voiding all the elections of parliament men, at which the elected had been at any expense in meat, drink, or money, to procure votes."[1] When we see the neighbouring tenantry of the several large landowners (petty freeholders though they be), classed in separate bodies, and voting, almost to a man, for the favourite of their landlord, we see either that improper influence is grossly employed, or that the exercise of private judgment is, with such voters, only a name. If indeed there were no possibility of obtaining more *considerate* votes from the population, I know not that much is to be hoped from a great extension of the franchise, or from an alteration of the modes of election.—The riot and confusion of elections is so great, that politicians find it needful to advise dissolutions of parliament, at periods when it is supposed that the excitement may be safely occasioned without endangering mischief to the general tranquillity. It would not be found a small item in the national guilt, if we were to compute the amount of private vice, of intemperance, profaneness, and debauchery, which a general election occasions.—These evils, again, are urged against proposals for increasing the frequency of elections! Thus one vicious system becomes an excuse for another. You are afraid to endeavour parliamentary integrity by frequent elections, because your bad system of elections produces so much mischief! The simple and obvious remedy is, to elect representatives on a less objectionable system. A few propositions respecting the *modes* of election, will probably not be rejected by reasonable men.

73. *That the elector should not be obliged to go to a distance from his own home:* because, if the place of election be distant, he will either refuse to go—which nullifies the institution with respect to him;—or he will go, and expect to be reimbursed his expenses and his loss of time—which leads, almost inevitably, to corruption.

74. *That candidates should be at no expense in conducting the election:*—because their payments will operate as bribes—because the necessity of expense precludes virtuous and able men, who cannot afford it, from being chosen—and because he who has, in this sense, *purchased* his seat, is in danger of thinking himself at liberty to repay himself by seeking the rewards of political subserviency.

75. *That it ought not to be known for what candidate an elector votes:*[1] because, if it is known, the elector will probably be afraid to vote for the man of his own choice, lest some friend of an adverse candidate, in whose good offices he is interested, should withdraw them.

76. These propositions tend to the recommendation of some species of *ballot* for securing secrecy; of *elections at the public expense,* for excluding the mischiefs of expenses to the candidate; and of the *visit, probably, of proper officers from house to house,* to exclude the mischiefs of requiring electors to leave their homes. Such institutions would, I believe, prevent many, at least, of the mischiefs, moral and political, of the present system; and would take away

---

[1] I am disposed to acknowledge that this *secrecy* of suffrages is not congruous with that manly independence which it were desirable to promote. In a better state of society open voting appears the more virtuous and honourable course; for why should a man desire to conceal that which he thinks it right to do? Besides, balloting endangers the practice of hypocrisy, by promising or pretending to vote according to the wish of another, and taking advantage of the secrecy to vote against it. Yet I see not that these consequences are such as to vitiate the system as applicable and as expedient in the present day.

---

[1] Smollett: Hist. England.

from the advocate of long-lived parliaments one popular reason in their favour.

77. ["Annual Parliaments" is another byword of contempt; and perhaps they will never be expedient. This is one question; the expediency of *septennial* parliaments is another. Nor is it a very philosophical nor a very honest mode of contemning an alteration, to assume that there is no practicable intermediate period between one year and seven. The American House of Representatives is elected for two years, and as their senate also is a representative body, whilst our House of Lords is not, it is probable that biennial parliaments, with a reformed mode of election, would be practicable and beneficial here.]

78. [The electors of a district choose a man of whom they hope rather than know the character. They find in the course of a year or two that he is unable or unwilling to discharge his public duty. To prevent such electors from making another choice —to oblige them, for seven years, to be, in effect, destitute of a representation, is a serious grievance, and it may be a serious evil.]

79. [A little before a dissolution there is sometimes a manifest endeavour to conciliate the public by the adoption of some measure which they approve. Can it be doubted that there would be an advantage in making such measures more frequently necessary?— or that more frequent parliaments would perceive the necessity, and act upon it?]

80. With respect to the *qualifications* for voting, no rule can be prescribed, because no rule can define how large a portion of the people, or whether the whole, ought to possess votes. The security of the virtuous exercise of the privilege is manifestly the object to be attained which security must be sought according to some general rule. It may be doubted whether (until *all* men are fit to become electors) any general rule is better than that of amount of property; not so much because the possession of property exempts men from vicious influence, as because, amongst the possessors of some competent property, is the largest portion of *thinking* men. We want not only an unbiassed, but a rational judgment. In the present state of property, the preference, in towns, of freeholders to renters, appears to be carried too far. The man who rents a house of forty pounds a year, is much more likely to give a free and considerate vote than he who possesses only a freehold of three or four pounds. Whatever qualification is required, it should be universally uniform. At any rate, it should vary only in compliance with the local necessities of a district. "Freedom" of burghs and cities, and the rules by which freedom is obtainable, are relics of a barbarous state of policy—relics which appear unworthy of the present age. They are like the local jurisdictions or chartered magistracy which one of our judges recently reprobated from the bench as blots in the constitution.

81. No qualifications should be required in a representative, but the single and sufficient one, that his constituents prefer him to any other man. It is a hardship upon them and upon him to thwart their choice—the best perhaps that could be made—because the candidate does not possess a certain amount of wealth. The case is different from that of the electors; for though the exaction of wealth in a representative may exclude some of the fittest men in the country to assist the councils of the state, yet from the eligibility of every man, there is no danger that such a *proportion* of poorer men would be elected, as to impede the legislature by their ignorance or vice.

82. The peculiar circumstances of a people may indeed occasion the propriety of requiring some qualification in their legislators. When the American colonies had separated themselves from England, and were anxious to perpetuate their independence, and when they observed that their country was continually replenishing with new adventurers, it was perhaps reasonable to enact, that the members of their government should have been American citizens a certain number of years. But local and temporary necessities do not affect the general truth.

83. *Canvassing* for votes is a vulgar and unworthy custom. I know not how it happens that a man of honourable mind is content to wander over the country, and call obeisantly at the doors of ignorant and low men, to solicit them to choose him for their representative. Why, if they prefer him, they ought to choose him without solicitation. If they do not, they ought not to choose him with it. I should not like the consciousness that I possessed my seat, not because I deserved it, but because I begged the voters to elect me. Gentlemen, I doubt not, often feel the humiliation, and experience the disgust, of these canvasses. It is one amongst the many sacrifices of manly dignity which are connected with political affairs.

84. To an inquirer who was uninformed of the national circumstances, it might appear an unaccountable absurdity to preclude Christian ministers from becoming the representative legislators of a Christian people. The *better* a man is, the better fitted he is for a

legislator; and assuming that Christian pastors are amongst the best men, there seems no rational motive to exclude them from the senate. Abating the *peculiar* circumstances of a people, I can perceive no reason for excluding them which would not hold in favour of excluding Christianity itself. To Christian legislators, Christianity is the primary rule; who then would refuse admittance to those of whom it may be presumed that they best understand the Christian law? But when we turn from the dictates of abstract reason and propriety to the state of a nation in which there is an established church —a church which assigns to one minister one specific spot for the exercise of its functions —we are presented with a very different scene. You cannot elect one of them (setting sinecures out of the question) without taking him away from his appointed charge, nor without leaving that charge to be as sheep without a shepherd. Nevertheless, since there are, in fact, more clergymen than parishes, it does not appear obvious why they should be refused eligibility. I would not, as in the case of the bishops, make any number, or any order, of clergy legislators *because* they were clergy; but neither would I, *because* they were clergy, refuse to admit them. Perhaps, if the institution were remodelled, clergy might be allowed to be eligible—for their exclusion, it may be presumed, is the result originally rather of accident than design. They once had a convocation of their own, with considerable political power; and when that convocation fell into disuse, no one perhaps thought of their reasonable claims for admissibility to the House of Commons. Let the writer be understood; he is not proposing that *Episcopal clergy, as such,* should be admitted into our House of Commons, but he is saying, that Christian ministers should not, as such, be excluded from the councils of a Christian nation. Penn was not the worse legislator because he was an active minister of the Gospel.

85. But, after all, it is disputed whether any alteration in the constitution of the House of Commons, or in the system of representation, would produce good effects—whether more virtue or more talent could be collected than is collected now. A question this, of which the negative has the advantage of experience, and the positive has not. We know that the present system has done good—the effect of another is involved in uncertainty. Now, let it be considered, first, that from the reign of Elizabeth, through several succeeding reigns down to the Revolution, the actual power of the House of Commons increased. Was not that increase productive, on the whole, and is it not at the present hour productive, of good effects? Granting that it was—will any man affirm that one hundred and forty years have added nothing to the capability of the British public to judge soundly respecting political affairs? If the capacity of sound judgment is increased, is it unreasonable —remembering the principles of political truth—that that judgment should possess a greater influence in the conduct of public affairs? If that influence ought, in reason, to be increased, how shall the increase be so judiciously contrived as by making the House of Commons a more accurate and immediate representative of the public mind?

86. As to the virtue, then, of the House of Commons, its peculiar and characteristic virtue *consists* in the accuracy of their representation; and no man, I think, will deny that a greater practical representation is possible than that which now obtains. It is asked, "If such a number of such men be liable to the influence of corrupt motives, what assembly of men will be secure from the same danger?"[1] But this is not the question: for even if six hundred and fifty-eight men could not be selected who would be more proof against corruption when elected for seven years, yet the same men might be found more proof against it if they were elected only for two. A minister, *then*, instead of having to provide the inducements of influence for six hundred and fifty-eight men, would have to provide them for nearly two thousand. Either he must augment three or four fold the aggregate *amount* of his influence, or he must, in the same proportion, diminish its power upon individuals. To think of so increasing the amount is absurd. He must, therefore, curtail its individual streams. It would, then, be much less *worth the while* of a member to submit to corruption. The temptation would be diminished, and with the diminution of temptation there would be an increase of practical *virtue*. Nor is this all. It is, I believe, an undisputed fact, that those who represent the largest number of electors are, in the aggregate, less subject to influence than those who represent a few. An altered mode of representation might increase the number of those whose constituents were numerous, or make them numerous to all— and thus that *scale* of virtuous independence which is now found amongst a part of the representatives, might then be found in all.

87. Then as to the accumulation of *talent*. I think it questionable whether the brilliancy of the House of Commons would not be diminished by such an alteration as that of which we speak: partly because, in the language of Dr. Paley, "when boroughs are set to sale, those men are likely to become purchasers, who are enabled, by their talents,

[1] Paley: Mor. and Pol. Phil., b. 6, c. 7.

to make the best of their bargain." Granting all this, the answer is at hand - that splendour of abilities is much less necessary than integrity of virtue. If the question is between talent and rectitude - rectitude is our choice. Unusual talents, how much soever they may amuse and delight the house, and how acceptably soever they may fill the columns of a newspaper, are greatly overrated in value —at least they are greatly overrated in reference to a sound state of political affairs. The tortuous and wily policy which obtains needs, no doubt, much sagacity and adroitness to conduct it successfully and with a fair face. What is really wanted in a legislator is not brilliancy of talent, but a sound, and an enlightened, and an upright mind. Nor is it to be forgotten, that the splendid talents of those who "seek to make the best of their bargain," may be an evil rather than a good. The bargain, it is to be feared, will be a losing one to the public; and by him who makes the *best*, the public may lose the *most*. After all, it needs not to be feared that six or seven hundred of such men as a House of Commons will always contain, will possess a sufficient aggregate of ability for all the needful and all the virtuous business of the house.

88. It has sometimes been inquired, What are the duties of a representative with respect to his constituents?—Generally, it is his duty to *represent* their opinions, and to *act* and *vote* upon his own. It has been well remarked, that a senator should consider himself not so much the representative of one portion of the community, as a legislator for all; and he can fulfil this superior duty only by exercising his individual judgment. Nevertheless, a man with a nice sense of justice and honour, if it be found that the majority of his votes were at variance with the desires of his constituents, ought to reflect that he is really no longer their representative, and to offer the resignation of their trust into their hands.

89. It is curious, that whilst it is thus made a question whether a man should follow his own judgment in opposition to that of his constituents, no question seems to be entertained whether a man should follow his own judgment in opposition to his *patrons*. There the elector's opinion is to prevail :—else, the representative is not a man of honour !—else, he does not fulfil the condition on which he was appointed ! At the contemplation of such things common sense is confounded, and purity turns away her eyes.[1]

[1] Some members who have owed their seats to patronage, have, I believe, had the virtue to stipulate for the freedom of their votes. Of this number it is said that the late Lord Chancellor Eldon was one.

90. Amongst the extraordinary doctrines which have arisen out of the impurity of political transactions, that of the "constitutional propriety of a systematic opposition" is one. To assert this, is to exhibit the political *disease* as he who has got the gout manifests the disorder to his visitors by his swathed and cushioned leg. You cannot frame a more preposterous proposition than that good government ought to be systematically opposed. If a government ought to be opposed, it is only because it is not good. If, being good, it is systematically opposed, there is viciousness in the opposition. In whatever way you defend an organised opposition, you assume the existence of evil. The motives in which the systematic opposition of some men is founded, correspond with the pervading impurity. Although there is reason to be assured that of some the very frequent opposition to a ministry is the result of political integrity, of others it cannot be doubted that the motives are kindred to those which are intimated in the humiliating note below.[1]

91. [The invective, and the ridicule, and retort, and personality, which are frequently indulged within the walls of parliament, and from which much amusement appears to be derived to the members and to the public, imply, to be sure, a sufficient degree of forgetfulness of the purpose for which parliaments meet. A spectator might sometimes imagine that the object of the assembly was to witness exhibitions of intellectual gladiators, rather than to debate respecting the welfare of a great nation. Nor can it be supposed that if this welfare were sufficiently, that is to say, *constantly*, dominant in the recollection, there would be so much solicitude to expose individual weaknesses and absurdity, or to obtain personal triumph.]

Much is said about "the exclusion of placemen and pensioners from parliament" —the propriety or impropriety of which is to be determined by the same rules as the question of political influence. If influence is necessary to the existence of the present form of government, and if that influence is necessary in parliament, I see little ground to declaim against the admission of placemen. In a purer state of society they would, no doubt, be improper members, because then none ought to be members who have any inducement to sacrifice the interests of the public to their own. By the Act of Settlement, indeed, it was provided, "that no person

[1] Opposition "had received a mortal wound by the death of the late Prince of Wales, some of whose adherents had prudently sung their palinodia to the ministry, and been gratified with profitable employments; while others, setting too great a price upon their own importance, kept aloof till the market was over, and were left to pine in secret over their disappointed ambition."—Smollett's England: v. 3, p. 391.

who has an office or place of profit under the king, or receives a pension from the crown, shall be capable of serving as member of the House of Commons." The spirit of this provision is practically superseded, though its letter so far operates that a king's counsel who receives a few pounds a year as a salary from the crown, is incapable of possessing a seat. However, subsequently to the Act of Settlement, various attempts were made really to exclude the possessors of offices and pensions. Bill after bill actually passed the house, but the measure was rejected and again rejected by the Lords.—To pass such a bill in the present day, and to act upon it, would probably be tantamount to an overthrow of the constitution.

92. It has sometimes been a subject of wonder to the writer, when reflecting upon the anxious solicitude of men for posthumous celebrity, that this single motive has not induced more vigorous attempts on the part of a minister to regulate his measures by a stricter regard to the dictates of everlasting rectitude. I have wondered, because it is manifest from experience that posterity will and does regard those dictates in its estimate of the honours of the dead. A very few years dismiss much of the false colouring which temporary interests and politics throw over a minister's conduct. It is ere long found that *he* obtains the largest share of posthumous celebrity, who has most constantly adhered to virtue. I propose not the hope of this celebrity as a motive to the Christian: he has higher inducements; but I propose it to the man of ambition. The simple love of fame would be, if he were rational with respect to his own interests, a sufficient inducement to prefer that conduct which will *for ever* recommend itself to the approbation of mankind. When we shall see the statesman who has, in private and in public, but one standard of rectitude, and that one the standard which is proposed in the Gospel; the statesman who is convinced, and acts upon the conviction, that everything is wrong in the minister which would be wrong in the man;—we shall see a statesman whom probably the clamour of to-day will call a fool or a traitor, but whom good men now, and all men hereafter, will regard as having attained almost to the pinnacle of virtue and honour and whom God will receive with the sentence of *Well done*.

93. In concluding these brief disquisitions upon the British government, I would be allowed to state the conviction, and to urge it upon those who complain of its defects in theory or in practice, that there is nothing in that theory or in that practice which warrants the attempt at amendment by any species of violence. I say this, even if I did not think,

as I do, that violence is unlawful upon other grounds. There are no evils which make violence politically *expedient*. The right way of effecting amendments is by enlightening the national mind—by enabling the public to think justly and temperately of political affairs. If to this temperate and just judgment, any part of the practice or of the form of our government should appear clearly and unquestionably adverse to the general good, it needs not to be feared that the corresponding alteration will be made—made by that best of all political agents, the power of deliberate public opinion. "The will of the people when it is determined, permanent, and general, almost always at length prevails."[1] And if it should appear to the lover of his country, that the prevalence of this will is too long delayed, let him take comfort in the recollection that less is lost by the postponement of reformation, than would be lost in the struggle consequent upon intemperate measures.

CHAPTER IX.
Moral Legislation.

Duties of a ruler—The two objects of moral legislation—Education of the people—Bible Society—Lotteries—Public-houses—Abrogation of bad laws—Primogeniture—Accumulation of property.

94. If a person who considered the general objects of the institution of civil government, were to look over the titles of the acts of a legislature during fifteen or twenty years, he would probably be surprised to find the proportion so small of those of which it was the express object to benefit the moral character of the people. He would find many laws that respected foreign policy, many perhaps that referred to internal political economy, many for the punishment of crime—but few that tended positively to promote the general happiness by increasing the general virtue. This, I say, may be a reasonable subject of surprise, when it is considered that the attainment of this happiness is the original and proper object of all government. There is a general want of advertence to this object, arising in part, perhaps, from the insufficient degree of conviction that *virtue is the best* promoter of the general weal.

95. To prevent an evil is always better than to repair it: for which reason, if it be in the power of the legislator to diminish temptation or its influence, he will find that *this* is the most efficacious means of diminishing the offences and of increasing the happiness of a people. He who vigilantly

[1] Paley: Mor. and Pol. Phil., b. 6, c. 7.

detects and punishes vicious men, does well; but he who prevents them from becoming vicious, does better. It is better, both for a sufferer, for a culprit, and for the community, that a man's purse should remain in his pocket, than that, when it is taken away, the thief should be sure of a prison.

96. So far as is practicable, a government ought to be to a people, what a judicious parent is to a family not merely the ruler, but the instructor and the guide. It is not perhaps so much in the power of a government to form the character of a people to virtue or to vice, as it is in the power of a parent to form that of his children. But much can be done if everything cannot be: and indeed, when we take into account the relative duration of the political body as compared with that of a family, we may have reason to doubt whether governments cannot effect as much in ages as parents can do in years.—Now, a judicious father adopts a system of moral *culture* as well as of restraint : he does not merely lop the vagrant branches of his intellectual plant, but he trains and directs them in their proper course. The second object is to punish vice—the *first* to promote virtue. You may punish vice without securing virtue ; but, if you secure virtue, the whole work is done.

97. Yet this primary object of moral legislation is that to which, comparatively, little attention is paid. Penalties are multiplied upon the doers of evil, but little endeavour is used to prevent the commission of evil by inducing principles and habits which overpower the tendency to the commission. In this respect, we begin to legislate at the secondary part of our office rather than at the first. We are political surgeons, who cut out the tumours in the state, rather than the prescribers of that wholesome regimen by which the diseases in the political body are prevented.

98. But here arises a difficulty—How shall that political parent teach virtue which is not virtuous itself? The governments of most nations, however they may inculcate virtue in their enactments, preach it very imperfectly by their example.—What then is to be done? "Make the tree good." The first step in moral legislation is to rectify the legislator. It holds of nations as of men, that the beam should be first removed out of our own eye. Laws, in their insulated character, will be but partially effectual, whilst the practical example of a government is bad. To this consideration sufficient attention is not ordinarily paid. We do not adequately estimate the influence of a government's example upon the public character. Government is an object to which we look up as to our superior ; and the many interests which prompt men to assimilate themselves to the character of the government, added to the natural tendency of subordinate parts to copy the example of the superior, occasions the *character* of a government, independently of its particular measures, to be of immense influence upon the general virtue. Illustrations abound. If, in any instance, political subserviency is found to be a more efficient recommendation than integrity of character, it is easy to perceive that subserviency is practically inculcated, and that integrity is practically discouraged.

99. Amongst that portion, then, of a legislator's office which consists in endeavouring the moral amelioration of a people, the amendment of political institutions is conspicuous. In proportion to the greatness of the influence of governments, is the obligation to direct that influence in favour of virtue. A government of which the principles and practice were accordant with rectitude, would very powerfully affect the general morals. He, therefore, who explodes one vicious principle, or who amends one corrupt practice, is to be regarded as amongst the most useful and honourable of public men.

100. If, however, in any state there are difficulties, at present insurmountable, in the way of improving political institutions, still let us do what we can. Precept without example may do *some* good : nor are we to forget, that if the public virtue is increased by whatever means, it will react upon the governing power. A good people will not long tolerate a bad government.

101. Amongst the most obvious means of rectifying the general morals by positive measures, one is the encouraging a judicious education of the people. Upon this *judiciousness* almost all its success depends. The great danger in undertaking a national system of education, is that some peculiar notions will be instilled for political purposes, and that it will be converted into a source of patronage. In a word, the great danger is, that national education should become, like national churches, an *ally* of the state ; and if this is done, the system will inevitably become, if not corrupt, lamentably alloyed with corruption. It does not seem as if the people of this country would countenance any endeavour to institute an education like this, because an attempt has been made, and the public voice was lifted successfully against it. A government, if it would rightly provide for the education of the community, must forget the peculiarities of creeds, political or religious. It must regard itself not as the

head of a party, but as the parent of the people.

102. We know that schools exist which impart an important and valuable education to the poor, and to which men of all principles and all creeds are willing to subscribe. Here is effected much good with little or no evil. The great defect is in the limited extent of the good. The public cannot or do not give enough of their money to provide education for all. Is there, then, any sufficient reason why a government should not supply the deficiency; or why it should not undertake the whole, and leave private bounty to flow in other channels? The great difficulty is to provide for the purity of the employment of the funds: for this employment may be made an ally of the petty politics of a town, as the whole institution may be made an ally of the state. However, as the annual grants to almost all such institutions would be small, it might perhaps escape that universal bane. One thing would be indispensable—to provide that the authority by which appointments to masterships, &c., are made, should be studiously constituted with a view to the exclusion of every motive but the single object of the institution. Whether it is possible to exclude improper motives may be doubted; but it is perhaps as possible to exclude them from those as from the many institutions which the public money now supports. There is one way indeed in which education may be promoted with little danger of this petty corruption—by the purchase of land and erection of school-houses. This, together with the supply of books and the like, forms a principal item in the expense of these schools: and it might be hoped that, if the government did this, the public would do the remainder.

103. But you say, All this will add to the national burdens. We need not be very jealous on this head, whilst we are so little jealous of more money worse spent. Is it known, or is it considered, that the expense of an ordinary campaign would endow a school in every parish in England and Ireland *for ever?* Yet how coolly (who will contradict me if I say—how needlessly?) we devote money to conduct a campaign!—Prevent, by a just and conciliating policy, one single war, and the money thus saved would provide, *perpetually*, a competent mental and moral education for every individual who needs it in the three kingdoms. Let a man for a moment indulge his imagination—let him rather indulge his reason, in supposing that one of our wars during the last century had been avoided, and that, fifty years ago, such an education had been provided. Of what comparative importance is the war to us now? In the one case, the money has provided the historian with materials to fill his pages with armaments, and victories, and defeats;—it has enabled us

To point a moral or adorn a tale;

—in the other, it would have effected, and would be now effecting, and would be destined for ages to effect, a great amount of solid good; a great increase of the virtue, the order, and the happiness of the people.

104. I suppose that the British and Foreign Bible Society, during the twenty or thirty years that it has existed, has done more direct good in the world—has had a greater effect in meliorating the condition of the human species—than all the measures which have been directed to the same ends, of all the prime ministers in Europe during a century. But suppose much less than this, suppose it has done more good than the moral measures of any one court, and will not this single and simple fact *prove* that much more is in the power of the legislator than he is accustomed to think; and prove, too, that there is an unhappy want of advertence amongst the conductors of governments to some of the most interesting and important duties of their office? With what means has this amount of moral good in all quarters of the earth been effected?—Why, with a revenue that never amounted to a hundred thousand pounds in any one year! A sum which, if we compare it with sums that are expended for measures of very questionable utility, is really trifling. Supposing that the legislature of this country had given an annual fifty thousand pounds to this institution, no man surely will dispute that the sums would have done incalculably more good in our own country—to say nothing of the world—than fifty thousand pounds of public money ordinarily effects. In passing, it may be observed too, that such an appropriation of money by a government, wou'd probably do much in propitiating the friendliness and good offices of other nations.

105. "No consideration of emolument can be put in competition with the morals of a nation; and no minister can be justified, either on civil or religious grounds, in rendering the latter subservient to the former."[1] Such a truth should be brought into practical operation. If it had been, lotteries in England had not been so long endured—if it were, the prodigious multitudes of public-houses would not be endured now. That these haunts and schools of vice are pernicious, no one doubts. Why is an excess of them permitted?— *They increase the revenue.* "Emolument is put in competition with morals," and it prevails. Even on grounds

[1] Gifford: Life of Pitt.

of political economy, however, the evil is great—for they materially diminish the effective labour of the population. If to this we add the multitudes whom the idleness of drunkards throws upon the parishes, perhaps as much is really lost in wealth by this penny-wise policy, as is lost in virtue. Besides, all needless alehouse-keepers are dead-weights upon the national industry. They contribute as little to the wealth of the state as he who lives upon the funds.

106. " It would be no injustice," says Playfair, "if publicans were prevented from legal recovery for beer or spirits consumed in their houses ; in the same manner that payment cannot be enforced of any person under twenty-one years of age, except for necessaries." [1] This, however, were to attempt to cure one evil by another. It were a practical encouragement of continual fraud. The short and simple way is to refuse licenses, and to take care that those who have the power of licensing shall exercise it justly.

107. This sound proposition, that neither on "civil nor religious grounds" is it right to consult policy at the expense of morals, is, as we have seen, at the basis of political truth. Here, then, let Political Truth be applied. It will be found, by the far-seeing legislator, to be expedient as well as right.

108. Bishop Warburton says. " Though a multiplication of good laws does nothing against a general corruption of manners, yet the abrogation of bad ones greatly promotes reformation." [2] The truth of the first clause is very disputable : the last is unquestionably true. This abrogation of bad laws forms a very important part of moral legislation ; and unhappily, it is a part which there are peculiar difficulties in effecting. There are few bad laws of which there are not some persons who are interested in the continuance. The interests of these persons, the supineness of others, the pride of a third class, and the superstitious attachment of a fourth to ancient things, occasion many laws to remain on the statute books of nations, long after their perniciousness has been ascertained.

109. Thus it has happened in our own country with respect to the game laws. It is perfectly certain that they greatly increase the vices of the people, and yet they remain unrepealed. Why? Voluble answers can no doubt be given, but they will generally be resolvable into vanity or selfishness. The legislator who shall thoroughly amend the game laws (perhaps thorough amendment will not be far from *abolition*), will be a greater benefactor to his country than multitudes who are rewarded with offices and coronets.

110. Thus, too, it has happened with the system of primogeniture. The two great effects of this system are, first, to increase the inequality of property, and next to perpetuate the artificial distinctions of rank.

111. That the existing inequality of property is a great political and moral evil, it was attempted in the third chapter of the preceding essay to show. The means of diminishing this inequality, which in that chapter were urged as an obligation of private life, are not likely to be fully effectual so long as the law encourages its continuance. A man who possesses an estate in land dies without a will. He has two sons. Why should the law declare that one of these should be rich and the other poor ? Is it reasonable ? Is it just ? As to its reasonableness, I discover no conceivable reason why, because one brother is born a twelvemonth before another, he should possess ten times as much property as the younger. Affection dictates equality ; and in such cases the dictate of affection is commonly the dictate of reason. We have seen, what antecedently to inquiry we might expect, that the practical effects are bad. Civil laws ought, as moral guides of the community, to discourage great inequality of property. How then shall we sufficiently deplore a system which expressly encourages and increases it ? Some time ago (and probably at the present day), the laws of Virginia did not permit one son to inherit the landed estates of his father to the exclusion of his brothers. The effect was beneficial, for it actually diminished the disparity of property.[1] We, however, not only do not forbid the descent of estates to one son, but we actually ordain it. It were sufficient, surely, to allow private vanity to have its own will in " keeping up a family " at the expense of sense and virtue, without encouraging it to do this by legal enactments when it might otherwise be more wise. The descent of intestates' estates in land to the elder son has the effect of an example, and of inducing vicious notions upon those who make their wills. That which is habitual to the mind as a provision of the law, acquires a sort of sanction and fictitious propriety, by which it is recommended to the public.

112. The partial distribution of intestates' estates is, however, only of casual operation.

---

[1] Causes of Decline of Nations, 4to, p. 226.
[2] Letters to Bishop Hurd, No. 32.

[1] The Virginians singularly confounded good moral legislation with bad, for they made a law declaring all landed property inviolable. The consequence was what might have been expected : many got into debt and remained quietly on their estates, laughing at their creditors.

Of the laws which make certain estates inalienable, or, which is not very different, allow the present possessor to entail them, the effect is constant and habitual. To prevent a reasonable and good man from making that division of his property which reason and goodness prescribe, is a measure which, if it be adopted, ought surely to be recommended by very powerful considerations. And what are they—except that they enable or oblige a man to keep up the splendour of his family? Splendour of family! Oh! to what an *ignis fatuus*, to what a pitiable scheme of vanity, are affection, and reason, and virtue, obliged to bow! Where is the man who will stand forward and affirm that this splendour is dictated by a regard to the proper dignity of our nature? Where is he who will affirm that it is dictated by sound principles of virtue?—Where, especially, is he who will affirm that it is dictated by religion? It has nothing to do with religion, nor virtue, nor human dignity: religion despises it as idly vain; morality reprobates it as sacrificing sense and affection to vanity; dignity rejects it as a fictitious and unworthy substitute for itself. Yet, perhaps, this humiliating motive of vanity is the most powerful of those which induce attachment to the system of primogeniture, or which would occasion opposition to attempts at reform. Perhaps it will be said, that to make the real estate of a man inalienable is really a kindness to his successors, by preventing him from squandering it away—to which the answer is, that there is no more reason for preventing the extravagance of those who possess much property than of those who possess little. No legislature thinks of enacting that a man who has two thousand pounds in the funds shall not sell it and spend it if he thinks fit. In general, men take care of their property without compulsion from the law; and if it is affirmed that the heads of great families are more addicted to this profusion and extravagance than other men, it will only additionally show the mischiefs of excessive possessions. Why should they be more addicted to it unless the temptations of greatness are unusually powerful and unusually prevail?

113. But it will be said, that the system is almost necessary to an order of nobility. I am sorry for it. If, as is probably at present the case, that order is expedient in the political constitution, and if its weight in the constitution must be kept up by the system of primogeniture, I do not affirm that, with respect to the peerage, this system should be at present abolished. But then let the enlightened man consider whither these considerations lead him. If a system essentially irrational and injurious is indispensable to a certain order of mankind, what is it but to show that, in the constitution of that order itself, there is something inherently wrong? Something that, if the excellence of mankind were greater, it would be found desirable to amend? Nor here, in accordance with that fearless pursuit of truth, whether welcome or unwelcome, which I propose to myself in these pages, can I refrain from the remark, that in surveying *from different points* the constituent principles of an order of peers, we are led to one and the same conclusion—that there is in these principles something really and inherently wrong; something which adapts the order to an imperfect, and only to an imperfect, state of mankind

114. If then we grant the propriety of an exception in the case of the peerage, we do not grant it with respect to other men. Much may be done to diminish the inequality of property, and with it to diminish the vices of a people, by abolishing the system of primogeniture *except* in the case of peers.

115. Of so great ill consequence is excessive wealth, and the effect to which it tends, excessive poverty, that a government might perhaps rightly discountenance the accumulation of extreme personal property. Probably there is no means of doing this, without an improper encroachment upon liberty, except by some regulations respecting wills. I perceive nothing either unreasonable or unjust in refusing a probate for an amount exceeding a certain sum. Supposing the law would allow no man to bequeath more than a given sum, what would be the ill effect? That it would discourage enterprising industry? *That* industry is of little use which extends its desires of accumulation to an amount that has no limit. The man of talent and application, after he had so far benefited himself and his country by his exertions or inventions, as to acquire such property as would procure for him all the accommodations of life which he could rationally enjoy, may retire from the accumulation of more, and leave the result of his talents to bring comfort and competence to other men. It may be said, that a man might still accumulate a larger sum to dispose of before his death :— So he might; but few would do it. Of those who are ambitious of so much more than conduces to the welfare of themselves and their children, few would continue to toil in order to give it away. Benevolence does not generally form a part of the motives to such accumulation. If once the law refused the bequest of more than a fixed sum, by appropriating the excess to the exigencies of the state, or to measures of public utility, men would learn to set limits to their desires. That restless pursuit of wealth which is pernicious to the pursuer and to other men, would be powerfully checked; and he who

had acquired enough, might habitually give place to the many who had too little. The writer of these pages makes no pretensions to a knowledge of the minute details of moral legislation. It is his business, in a case like this, whilst enforcing the end, only to *suggest* the means. Other and better means of diminishing the inequality of property than those which have just been alluded to, may probably be discovered by practical men. But of the end itself it becomes the writer of morality to speak with earnestness and with confidence.[1] It admits of neither dispute nor doubt, that in our own country, and in many others, there subsist extremes of wealth and poverty which are highly injurious to private virtue and to the public good; and therefore it admits neither of dispute nor doubt, that the endeavour to diminish these extremes is an important (unhappy—that it is also a *neglected*!) branch of moral legislation.

CHAPTER X.
Administration of Justice.

Substitution of justice for law—Court of Chancery—Of fixed laws—Their inadequacy—They increase litigation—Delays—Expenses—Informalities—Precedents—Verdicts—Legal proof—Courts of arbitration—An extended system of arbitration—Arbitration in criminal trials—Constitution of courts of arbitration—Their effects—Some alterations suggested—Technicalities—Useless laws.

1. In considering this great subject the inquirer after truth is presented, as upon some kindred subjects, with one great pervading difficulty. If he applies the conclusions of abstract truth, such is the imperfect condition of mankind, that it loses a portion of its practical adaptation to its object. If he deviates from this truth, where shall he seek for a director of his judgment? He is left to roam amongst endless speculations, where nothing is to be found with the impress of certain rectitude.

2. The dictate of simple truth respecting the Administration of Justice is, that if two men differ upon a question of property or of right, that decision should be made between them which Justice, in *that specific case*, requires; that if a person has committed a public offence, that punishment should be awarded which his *actual deserts* and the proper objects of punishment demand.

[1] The legal division of the personal property of intestates admits of easy amendment. Two men die, of whom each leaves six thousand pounds behind him. One has a wife and one child, and the other a wife and eight children. It can hardly be rational to give to the widow in both these cases the same share of the property. In one or two nations the law gives a third of the income of the real estates, in addition, to the widow; but better regulations even than this were easily devised.

3. But if this truth is applied in the present state of society, it is found so difficult to obtain judges who will apply the sound principles of equity, judges who will exercise absolute discretionary power without improper biasses, that the inquirer is fearful to pronounce a judgment respecting the rule which should regulate the administration of justice.

4. Men, seeing the difficulties to which an attempt to administer simple equity is exposed, have advanced as a fundamental maxim—that the law shall be made by one set of men and its execution entrusted to another—thus endeavouring, on the one hand, to prevent rules from being made under the bias resulting from the contemplation of particular cases, and on the other, to preclude the appliers of the rules from the influence of the same bias, by obliging them to decide according to a preconcerted law.

5. But, when we have gone thus far—when we have allowed that questions between man and man shall be decided by a rule that is independent of the merits of the present case, we have departed far from the pure dictate of rectitude. We have made the standard to consist not of justice but of law; and having done this, we have opened wide the door to the entrance of injustice. And it does enter indeed!

6. The consideration of this state of things indicates one satisfactory truth—that we should pursue the rule of abstract rectitude to the utmost of our power; that we should constantly keep in view, that whatever decision is made upon any other ground than that of simple justice, it is so far defeating the object for which Courts of Justice are established: and therefore, that in whatever degree it is practicable to find men who will decide every specific question according to the dictates of justice upon that question, in the same degree it is right to supersede the application of inferior principles.

7. Am I then sacrificing the fundamental principles upon which the morality of these Essays is founded? Am I, at last, conceding that expediency ought to take precedence of rectitude? No; but I am saying, that if the state of human virtue is such that not one *can* be found to judge justly between his brethren—men must judge as justly as they can, and a legislator must contrive such boundaries and checks for those who have to administer justice, as shall make the imperfection of human virtue as little pernicious as he may. If this virtue were perfect, courts of *law* might perhaps safely and rightly be shut up. There would be a rule of judgment preferable to law; and law itself, so

far as it consists of absolute rules for the direction of decisions between man and man, might almost be done away.

8. Now, in considering the degree in which this great desideratum—the substitution of justice for law—can be effected, let us be especially careful that we throw no other impediments in the way of justice than those which are interposed by the want of purity in mankind. Let us never regard a system of administering justice as fixed, so that its maxims shall not be altered whenever an increase of purity dictates that an alteration may be made. All the existing national systems of administering justice are imperfect and alloyed :—a mixture of evil and good. It were sorrowful indeed to assume that they cannot be, or to provide that they shall not be, amended.

9. The system in this country, like most systems which are the gradual accretion of the lapse of ages, is incongruous in its different parts. In the decisions that are founded upon legal technicalities, the method of applying absolute uniform law is adopted. In the assessment of damages there is exercised very great discretionary power. In pronouncing verdicts upon prisoners, juries are scarcely allowed any discretion at all. They say absolutely either not guilty or guilty.—Then again, discretion is entrusted to the judge, and he may pronounce sentences of imprisonment or of transportation, varying according to his judgment in their duration or circumstances. The reader should well observe this admission of discretionary power to the judicial court, because it is a practical acknowledgment that considerations of equity are indispensable to the administration of justice, whatever may be the multiplicity or precision of the laws. Our judges are entrusted, on the circuits, with the discretionary power of commuting capital punishments or leaving the offender for execution. This is equivalent to an acknowledgment, that even the most tremendous sanctions of the state are more safely applied upon principles of equity than upon principles of law. Let the reader bear this in his mind.

10. Of the general tendency and attendant evils of uniform law, some illustrations have been offered in the preceding Essay, and some observations have been offered in the chapter on Arbitration, on the advantages of administering justice upon principles of equity, that is, by a large discretionary power. *Now* it will be our business to inquire into some of the reasonings by which the application of uniform law is recommended—to illustrate yet further the moral claims of Courts of Equity, and to show if we can that some greater approximation to the adoption of these courts is practicable even in the present condition of mankind.

11. The administration of justice, according to a previously made rule, labours under this fundamental objection, that it assumes a knowledge in the maker of the rule which he does not possess. It assumes that he can tell beforehand, not only what is a good decision in a certain class of questions, but what is the best ; and the objection appears so much the more palpable, because it assumes that a party who judges a case before it exists, can better tell what is justly due to an offended or an offending person, than those who hear all the particulars of the individual case. This objection, which it is evident can never be got over, is practically felt and acknowledged. Every relaxation of a strict adherence to the law, every concession of discretionary power to juries or to courts, is an acknowledgment of the inherent inadequacy and impropriety of fixed rules. You perceive that no fixed rules *can* define and discriminate justly for specific cases. Multiply them as you may, the gradations in the demands for equitable decision will multiply yet faster ; so that you are forced at last to concede something to equity, though perhaps there has not hitherto been conceded enough. Our Court of Chancery was originally, and still is called, a Court of Equity, the erection of which court is paying a sort of tacit homage to equity as superior to law, and making a sort of tacit acknowledgment how imperfect and inefficient the fundamental principles of fixed law are. It is perhaps a subject of regret that this court is now a court of equity rather in name than in fact. It proceeds, in a great degree, according to the rule of precedent ; one of the principal differences between its practical character and that of legal courts being, that in one a jury decides questions, and in the other a judge.

12. And after all the fixedness of the law is much less in practice than in theory. We all know how various and contradictory are the "opinions" of legal men, so that a person may present his "case" to three or four able lawyers in succession, and receive from each a different answer. Nay, if several should agree when they are applied to as judges in the case, it is found, when a person comes into court, that counsel can find legal arguments, and unanswerable arguments too, on both sides of the question, till at last the question is decided, not by a fixed law, but by a preponderance of *weight* of conflicting precedents. Indeed the unfixedness of the law is practically so great, that common fame has made it a proverb.

13. Another inconvenience which is in-

separable from the use of fixed rules is, that they almost preclude a court from attending sufficiently to one very important point in the administration of justice, the *intention* of offending parties. Law says, if a man steals another person's watch under such and such circumstances, he shall receive such and such a punishment. Yet the guilt of two men who steal watches under the same *visible* circumstances, is often totally disproportionate ; and this disproportion indicates the propriety of corresponding gradations of penalty. Yet fixed law awards the same penalty to both. If it is said that a court may take intention and motives into the account in its sentence, so it may ; but in whatever degree it does this, in the same degree it acknowledges the incompetency and inaptitude of fixed laws.

14. "The motives and intentions of the parties." When we consider that the personal *guilt* of a man depends more upon these than upon his simple acts, and consequently that these rather than his acts indicate his *deserts*, it appears desirable that human tribunals should measure their punishments as much by a reference to actual deserts as is consistent with the public good. I would not undertake to affirm that the guilt of the offender is to us the ultimate standard of just punishment, because it may be necessary to the prevention of crimes, that of two offences equal in guilt, one should be punished more severely than another, on account of the greater facilities for its commission—that is, on account of the greater impracticability of guarding against the offence, or of detecting the offender after it is committed. But, in speaking of the propriety of adverting to *intention*, this is not the point in view. I speak not of the difference between two classes of crimes, but of the actual motives, inducements, and temptations of the individual offender. Stealing five pounds' worth of property in sheep, although it may be no more vicious, as an act, than stealing a five-pound note from the person, may perhaps be rightly visited with a severer punishment. This is one thing. But two men may each steal a sheep with very different degrees of personal guilt. This is another. And *this* is the point of which we speak. A man who is able to maintain himself in respectability, but will not apply himself to an honest occupation—who lives by artifices, or frauds, or thefts, or gambling, or contracting debts, watches night after night an opportunity to carry off sheep from an enclosure. He succeeds, and spends the value in drunkenness, or at a bagnio. A man of decent character who, in a period of distress, endeavours in vain to procure employment or bread—who pawns, day after day, his furniture, his clothing, his bed, to obtain food for his children and his wife—who finds at last that all is gone, and that hunger continues its demands—passes a sheep field. The thought of robbing starts suddenly before him, and he as suddenly executes it. He carries home the meat, and is found by the police hastily cutting slices for his voracious family. Ought these two men to receive the same punishment? It is impossible. Justice, common sense, Christianity forbid it. We cannot urge, in such cases, that human tribunals, being unable to penetrate the secret motives of action, must leave it to the Supreme Being to apportion punishment strictly to guilt. We can discover, though not the exact amount of guilt, a great deal of difference between its degrees. We do actually know, that of two persons who commit the same crime, one is often much more criminal than another ; and were it not that our jurisprudence habituates us so much to refer simply to *acts*, we might know much more than we do. We are often ignorant of motives only because we do not inquire for them. A law says, " If any person shall enter a field and steal a sheep or horse, he shall suffer death ;" and so, when a court comes to try a man charged with the act, they perhaps scarcely think of any other consideration than whether he stole the animal or not. Of ten who do thus steal, no two probably deserve exactly the same punishment, and some, undoubtedly, deserve *much* less than others.

15. Discrimination, then, is necessary to the demands alike of humanity, and reason, and religion. But how shall sufficient discrimination be exercised under a system of fixed laws ? If the decisions of courts must be regulated by the *acts* of the offender, how shall they take into account those endless gradations of personal desert, to refer to which is a *sine qua non* of the administration of *justice?* Now, in order to satisfy these demands, courts must by some means be entrusted with a greater discretionary power ; or, which is the same thing, decisions upon maxims of equity must, in a greater degree, take the place of decisions regulated by law.

16. The next great objection is, that to place, for example, men's property at the discretion of a court of equity that was not bound down by fixed rules, would make the possession of every man's property uncertain. Nobody would know whether the estate which he and his fathers enjoyed, might not to-morrow, by the decision of some court of equity, be taken away. But this supposes that the decisions of these courts would be arbitrary and capricious ; whereas, the supposition upon which we set out—the

supposition upon which alone we reason, is, that means can be devised by which their decisions shall be generally at least accordant with rectitude. They must deviate *very widely* from rectitude if they took away a man's estate without some reason which *appeared to them* to be good; and it could hardly *appear* to be good, on a full hearing of the case, unless the merits of that case were very questionable; but in proportion to that questionableness would be the smallness of the grievance if the estate were taken away. Let any man suppose a case for himself—he possesses a house, to which no one ever disputed his title, till some person chooses to bring his title before a court of equity—of the members of which court the possessor nominates one half; does any man in his senses suppose that the property would be endangered? or rather, does any man suppose that a person would be foolish enough to call the title in question? But we must repeat the other alternative. If a person holds an estate by a decision of *law* which he would *not* have held by a decision of rectitude, we do not listen to his complaints though it be taken away. It is just what we desire.

17. It has been contended, that to depart further from the system of deciding by law, would tend to the increase of litigation; that nothing prevents litigation so much as previous certainty of the rule of decision; and that if, instead of this certainty, the decision of a court were left to a species of chance, there would be litigation without end. But in this argument it is not sufficiently considered that previous certainty of the rule of decision is very imperfectly possessed—that, as we have just been observing, the law is *not* fixed; and, consequently, that that discouragement of litigation which would arise out of previously known rules, very imperfectly operates. Nor, again, is it enough considered, that the decision of a court of equity, if properly constituted, would not be a matter of chance, nor anything that is like it. Though a *legal* rule would not bind a court, still it would be bound—bound by the dictates—commonly the very intelligible dictates—of right and wrong. "Reason," it has been said, "is a thousand times more explicit and intelligible than law;" and if reason were not more intelligible, still the moral judgments in the mind assuredly are. Again, many causes are now brought into court, not because they are morally good, but legally good. Of this the contending parties are often conscious, and they would therefore be conscious that a court which regulated its decisions by the moral qualities of a case, would decide against them. *At present*, when a man contemplates a lawsuit, he has to judge as well as he can of the probability of success, by inquiring into the rules of law and decisions of former cases. *If a court of equity* were to be the judge, he would have to appeal to a much nearer and more determinate ground of probability—to *his own consciousness* of the justness of his cause. We are therefore to set the discouragement of litigation, which arises from this source, against that which arises from the supposed fixedness of law; and I am disposed to conclude, that in a well constituted court this discouragement would be practically the greater. Another point is this:—it is unhappily certain, that either the ignorance or the cupidity of some legal men prompts many to engage in lawsuits who have little even of legal reason to hope for success. This cause of litigation equity would do away; a lawyer would not be applied to, for a lawyer would have no better means of foreseeing the probable decision of a court of equity than another man.

18. Here, too, it is to be remembered that the great, what if I say the *crying* evils of the present state of legal practice, result from—the employment of fixed laws. It has indeed been acknowledged by an advocate of these laws, that they "erect the practice of the law into a separate profession."[1] Now, suppose all the evils, all the expenses, all the disposition to litigation and dispute, all the practical injustice, which results from this profession were done away—would not the benefit be very great? Would it not be a great advantage to the quiet, and the pockets, and the virtue of the nation? I regard this one circumstance as forming a recommendation of equity so powerful, that serious counterbalancing evils must be urged to overcome its weight. Even to the political economist the dissolution or great diminution of the profession is of some importance. I am no proficient in his science: but it requires little proficiency to discover, that the existence of a large number of persons who not only contribute little to the national prosperity, but often deduct from it, is no trifling evil in a state. But it is not simply as it respects the profession that fixed laws are thus injurious. They are the great ultimate occasion of those obstacles to the attainment of justice which are felt to be a grievance in almost all civilised nations. The delays and the expenses, and the undefined annoyances of vexation and disappointment, deter many from seeking their just rights. *Delays* are occasioned in a great degree by forms; and forms are a part of the system of fixed laws. *Expenses* are entailed by the necessity of complying with these forms, and of employing those persons whose knowledge is requisite to tell us what those forms are;

[1] Paley: Mor. and Pol. Phil., b. 6, c. 8.

and the acquisition of this knowledge requires so much time and care, that he who imparts it must be well paid. As to indeterminate vexations and disappointments, they too result principally from the fixedness of rules. A man with a cause of unquestioned rectitude is too often denied justice on account of the intervention of some absolute rule—that has little or no relevance to the question of rectitude. Persons fearing these various evils, decline to endeavour the attainment of their just rights, rights which, if equity were in a greater degree substituted for law, would be of comparatively easy attainment.

19. The reader can hardly too vigorously impress upon his mind the consideration, that the various sacrifices of rectitude which are made under colour of the legality of people's claims, result from the system of fixed laws. If to avail oneself of an informality in a will to defraud the claims of justice be wrong -the evil and the temptation is to be laid at the door of fixed law. If an undoubted criminal escapes justice merely because he cannot *legally* be convicted, the evil which is serious is to be laid at the door of fixed law. And so of a hundred other cases—cases of which the aggregate ill consequence is so great, as to form a weighty objection to whatever system may occasion them.

20. I make little distinction between deciding by fixed law and by precedents, because the principles of both are the same, and both, it is probable, will stand or fall together. Precedents are laws—but of somewhat less absolute authority; which indeed they ought to be, since they are made by courts of justice and not by the legislature. They are a sort of supplemental statutes, which attempt to supply (what, however, can never be supplied) the deficiencies of fixed laws. A statute is a general rule ; a precedent prescribes a case in which that rule shall be observed ; but a thousand cases still arise which neither statute nor precedent can reach.

21. So habitual is become our practice of judging questions rather by a previously made rule than by their proper merits, that even the House of Lords, which is the highest court of equity in the state, searches out, when a question is brought before it, its precedents ! Long debates ensue upon the parallelism of decisions a century or two ago ; when, if the merits of the case only were regarded, perhaps not an hour would be spent in the decision. Then the House is cramped and made jealous lest its present vote should be a precedent for another decision fifty years to come. New debates are started as to the bearing of the precedent upon some imagined question in after times ; and at last the decision is regulated perhaps as much by fears of distant consequences, as by a regard to present rectitude. Do away precedents, and the House might pursue unshackled the dictate of Virtue. And after all, when precedents are sought and found, the House usually acts upon the opinion of its *legal* members—thus subverting the very nature of a court of equity. It would seem the rational and consistent course that in the House of Lords, when it constitutes such a court, the law lords should be almost the last to give a sentiment ; for if it be to be decided by lawyers, to what purpose is it brought to the House of Peers?

22. And another inconvenience of fixed law -or at any rate of fixed laws such as ours are—is, that in cases of criminal trials the jury are bound down, as we have before noticed, to an absolute verdict either to acquit the prisoner of all crime and exempt him from all punishment, or to declare that he is guilty and leave him to the sentence of the court. Now since many verdicts are founded upon a balance of probabilities -- probabilities which leave the juror's mind uncertain of the prisoner's guilt, it would seem the dictate of reason that corresponding verdicts should be given. If it is quite certain that a man has stolen a watch, it seems reasonable that he should receive a greater punishment than he of whom it is only highly probable that he has stolen it. But the verdict in each case is the same—till, as the probability diminishes, the minds of the jury at last preponderate on the other side, and they pronounce an absolute verdict of acquittal. From this state of thing it happens that some are punished more severely than the amount of probability warrants, and that many are not punished at all, because there is no alternative to the jury between absolute acquittal and absolute conviction. Now the imperfection of human judgment, the impossibility of penetrating always into the real facts and motives of men, indicates that some penalties may justly be awarded, even though a court entertains doubts of a prisoner's guilt. Man must *doubt* because he cannot *know*. We may rightly therefore proceed upon probabilities and punish upon probabilities ; so that we should not wholly exempt a man from punishment because we are not sure that he is guilty, nor inflict a certain stipulated amount of it because we are only strongly persuaded that he is. Punishment may rightly then be regulated by probabilities : but how shall this be done without a large discretionary power in those who judge? And how shall such discretionary power be exercised whilst we act upon the maxims of fixed law?

23. The requisition of what is called *legal proof* is one result of fixed law that is attended with much evil. It not unfrequently happens, that a man who claims a right adduces such evidence of its validity that the court—that every man—is convinced he ought to possess it: but there is some deficiency in that precise *kind* of proof which the law prescribes; and so, in deference to law, justice is turned away. It is the same with crimes. Crimes are sometimes proved to the satisfaction of every one who hears the evidence; but because there is some want of strict legal proof, the criminal is again turned loose upon society. Such things, decisions founded upon equity would do away. All that the court would require would be a satisfactory conviction of the prisoner's guilt or of the claimant's rights; and having obtained that satisfaction it would decide accordingly.

24. Here, too, a consideration is suggested respecting the prerogative which is vested in the crown of pardoning offenders. The crown, if any, is doubtless the right repository of this prerogative; but it is not obvious upon principles of equity, that any repository is right. If an offender *deserves* punishment, he ought to receive it—and if he does *not* deserve it, no sentence ought to be passed upon him. This, of which the truth is very obvious, simply considered, is only untrue when you introduce fixed laws. These fixed laws require you to deliver a verdict, and when it is delivered, to pass a sentence;—and then, finding your sentence is improper or unjust, you are obliged to go to a court of equity to remedy the evil. Why should we pass a sentence if it is not deserved? Why is a sentence the indispensable consequence of a verdict? Why rather is a formal verdict pronounced at all? There appears in the view of equity no need for all these forms. What we want is to assign to an offender his *due* punishment;—and when no other is assigned, there is no need for prerogatives of pardon.

25. Proceeding, then, upon the conviction that law as distinguished from justice is attended with many evils, let us inquire whether the obstacles to decisions by considerations of justice are insuperable. Now I do believe that many of the objections which suggest themselves to an inquirer's mind are really adventitious—that the administration of simple justice may be detached from many of those inconveniences which attach no doubt to ill-constituted discretionary courts. So confident has been the objection to decisions upon rules of equity that Dr. Paley, in the eighth chapter of the Political division of his Philosophy, has these words: "The *first maxim* of a free state is, that the laws be made by one set of men and administered by another. When these offices are united in the same person or assembly, particular laws are made for particular cases, *springing oftentimes from partial motives, and directed to private ends.*" But if these partial motives and private ends can be wholly or in a great degree excluded, the objection which is founded upon them is in a great degree or wholly at an end. If these offices were united in any person or assembly, appointed or constituted as the administerers of justice *now are*, I doubt not that partial motives and private ends would prevail. But the necessity for this is merely assumed; and upon this assumption Paley proceeds: "Let it be supposed that the courts of Westminster Hall made their own laws, or that the two houses of parliament, with the king at their head, tried and decided causes at their bar"—then, he says, the inclinations of the judges would inevitably attach on one side or the other, and would interfere with the integrity of justice. No doubt this would happen; but because this would happen to the courts of Westminster Hall, or to the legislative assemblies, it does not follow that it would happen to all arbitrators, however appointed. Thus it is that the mind, habitually associating ideas which may reasonably be separated, founds its conclusions, not upon the proper and essential merits of the question, but upon the question as it is accidentally brought before it. The proper ground on which to seek objections to decision on rules of equity, is not in the want of adaptation of present judicial institutions, but on the impracticability of framing institutions in which these rules might safely prevail; and this impracticability has never, so far as the writer knows, been shown.

26. Now, without assigning the extent to which arbitration may eventually take place of law, or the degree in which it may be adopted in the present state of any country, it may be asked—Since a large number of disagreements are actually settled by arbitration, that is, by rules of equity, why may not that number be greatly increased? It is common in cases of partnership, and other agreements between several parties, to stipulate that if a difference arises it shall be settled by arbitrators. It must be presumed that this mode of settling is regarded as the best, else why formally stipulate for it? The superiority, too, must be discovered by experience. It is then in fact found that a great number of questions of property and other concerns, are settled more cheaply and more satisfactorily by equity than by law. Why then, we repeat, may not that number be indefinitely increased, or who will assign a limit to its increase? Now the constitution of these efficient courts of equity is not

permanent. They are not composed of judges previously appointed to decide all disputes. They are not composed, as the courts of Westminster Hall are, or as the houses of parliament are, or as benches of magistrates are. If they were, they would be open to the undue influence and private purposes of those who composed them. But the members of these courts are appointed by the disputants themselves, or by some party to whom they mutually agree to commit the appointment. Supposing then the worst, that the disputing parties appoint men who are interested in their favours; still the balance is equal:—both may do the same. The *court* is not influenced by undue motives, though its members are; and if, in consequence of such motives or of any other cause, the court cannot agree upon a verdict, what do they do? *They* appoint an umpire, or, which is the same thing, the disputants appoint one. This umpire must be presumed to be impartial; for otherwise the disputants would not both have assented to his appointment. At the *worst*, then, an impartial decision may be confidently hoped; and what may not be hoped under better circumstances? It is, I believe, common for disagreeing parties to nominate at once, disinterested and upright men; and if they do this, and take care, too, that they shall be intelligent men, almost everything is done which is in the power of man to secure a just decision between them.

27. Disinterestedness—uprightness—intelligence:—these are the qualities which are needed in an arbitrator. That he should be disinterested; that is, that he should possess no motive to prefer the interests of either party, is obviously indispensable. But this is not enough. Other motives than interest operate upon some men; and there is no sufficient security for the integrity of a decision, but in that habitual uprightness in the arbitrator by which the sanctions of morality are exercised and made influential. The requisiteness of intelligence, both as it implies competent talent and competent knowledge, is too manifest for remark.

28. Now one of the great objections which are made to a judicature appointed for the decision of one dispute, and that one only, is, "the want of legal science" "the ignorance of those who are to decide upon our rights."[1] This objection applies in great force to ordinary juries, but it scarcely applies at all to intelligent arbitrators properly selected—and not applying, we are at liberty to claim in favour of arbitration without abatement, that "indifferency," that "integrity," that "disinterestedness," which it is allowed that a casual judicature possesses.

[1] Paley: Mor. and Pol. Phil., b. 6, c. 7.

Men become skilful by habit and experience. The man who is now selected for the first time in his life to exercise the office of an arbitrator feels perhaps some difficulties. He is introduced into a new situation in society; and, like other novices, it is not unlikely that he will be under difficulties respecting his decision. But if the system of arbitration should become as common as lawsuits are now, men would soon learn expertness in the duties of arbitrators. If, in a moderate town, there were twelve or twenty men, whose characters and knowledge recommended them generally, and especially to the confidence of their neighbours—these are the men who would be selected to adjust their disputes. And even if the same individuals were not often employed, the habit of judging, a familiarity with such matters, becomes diffused, just as every other species of knowledge becomes diffused upon subjects that are *common* in the world.

29. Another ground of difficulty to an arbitrator in the present state of things, is the habit, which is so general in the community, of referring for justice to rules of law. A man when he enters an arbitration room, is continually referring in his mind to law-books and precedents. This is likely to confuse his principles of decision, to intermix foreign things with one another, and to produce sometimes perhaps a decision founded half upon law and half upon justice. This may indeed occasionally be in some sort imposed upon him—at least he would feel a hesitation, a sort of repugnance to deliver a decision which was absolutely *contrary* to the rule of law. But this inconvenience is in a great degree accidental and factitious. As the principles of equity assumed their proper dominance in the adjustment of disputes, fixed laws would proportionably decline in influence and in their practical hold upon the minds of men. Their judgments would gradually become emancipated from this species of shackle;—they would rise, disencumbered of arbitrary maxims, and decide according to those maxims of moral equity for the dictates of which no man has far to seek. The whole system tends to the invigoration and elevation of the mind. A man who is conscious of an absolute authority to decide—of an uncontrolled discretionary power, in a question perhaps of important interests, is animated by the moral eminence of his station to exert a vigorous and honourable endeavour to award sound justice. You are not to expect in such a man, what we find in *arbitrary* judges, that his very absoluteness will make him capricious and tyrannical; for the moment he has pronounced his decision, a calamity, if that decision have been unjust, awaits him;—the reprobation of his neighbours, of his friends, and of the

public. The exercise of his discretion is bound to the side of uprightness, though not by ordinary pains and penalties, yet by virtual pains and penalties, which to such men as are chosen for arbitrators are amongst the most powerful that can be applied.

30. One thing is indispensable to an extended system of arbitration, that the civil magistrate should sanction its decisions by a willing enforcement of the verdict. It is usual for disputants who refer to arbitrators to sign an agreement to abide by their decision; and this agreement may by some simple process of *law* be enforced. The law does indeed now sanction arbitrations; but then it is in a formal and expensive way. A deed is drawn up, and a stamp must be affixed, and a solicitor must be employed;— so that at last the disagreeing parties do but partly reap the benefits of arbitration. This should be remedied. The reader will observe that I say law is wanted to enforce the decisions of equity. No doubt it is. It is wanted for the same reason as government is wanted, to *exert power*, which power, it is evident, must be exercised by the government. But if any critic should say that this acknowledges the insufficiency of equity, I answer, that we are speaking of unconnected things. The business of equity is to decide between right and wrong, and to say what is right—with which the infliction of penalties or the enforcement of decisions has no concern. A court and jury say that a man shall be sent for six months to a prison, but it forms no part of their business to execute the sentence.

31. With respect to the applicability of courts of equity to criminal trials, I see nothing that necessarily prevents it. Men who can judge respecting matters of property and personal rights, can judge respecting questions of innocence and guilt. In one view, indeed, they can judge more easily; because moral desert is determinable upon more simple and obvious principles than claims of property. Many who would feel much difficulty in deciding involved disputes about money or land, would feel none in determining, with sufficient accuracy, the degree of an offender's guilt.

32. It being manifest, then, that offences against the peace of society may be as properly referred to courts of equity as questions of right—what should be the constitution of such a court? But here the reader is to remember, that the objection is not merely or principally to the constitution of present courts, but to the principles of fixed law upon which justice is administered. So that, if principles of equity were substituted, the constitution of the court would become a secondary concern; and courts consisting of a jury and a judge might not be bad, though they were not the best. If half a dozen intelligent and upright men could be appointed to examine the truth of charges against a prisoner, and if they were allowed to award a just punishment, I should have little fear, after making allowances for the frailties of humanity, that their penalties would generally be just;—at any rate, that they would be more accordant with justice than penalties which are regulated by fixed law. The difficulty is in procuring the arbitrators, a difficulty greater than that which obtains in cases of private right. For in the first place offenders against the peace of society generally excite the feelings of the public, and especially of the neighbourhood, against them. Men too often prejudge cases, and the prisoner is frequently condemned in the public mind before any evidence has been brought before a jury. This indicates a difficulty in selecting impartial men. And then, in the case of arbitrations, each party chooses one or more of the judges. Shall the same privilege be allowed to persons charged with crime? If it were, would they not select persons who would frustrate all the endeavours to administer justice? Besides, where is the conflicting party who shall be equally interested in appointing arbitrators of opposite dispositions? And if both did appoint such, what is the hope of a temperate and rational decision? Again, there are offences which are regarded with peculiar severity by particular classes of men. A court composed of country gentlemen would hardly award a fair verdict against a poacher.

33. These considerations and others indicate difficulty; and perhaps the difficulty cannot better be avoided than by a court selected by chance. In the selection of juries there have recently been introduced improvements. Still, if equity rather than law is to be regarded, something more is needed. *Now*, though a jury be ignorant, the judge is learned; and a learned judge is indispensable where law is to be applied. But if simple justice be the object, such a judge becomes comparatively little requisite; yet when we have dispensed with the intelligence of the judge, we must provide for greater intelligence in the jury. A jury from the lower classes of the community may serve with tolerable sufficiency the purposes of justice in the present system; but if they were converted from jurymen into arbitrators, much more of intelligence, and, we may add, much more of elevation of character, is required. To endeavour to obtain this intelligence and uprightness by a mode of chance selection, must always be very uncertain of success. If those who were

eligible for this species of jury, were obliged to possess a certain qualification in point of property: if, of those who were thus eligible, a competent number were selected by ballot, and if the prisoner and the prosecutor were allowed a large right of challenge, perhaps everything would be done which is in the power of man.

34. The number of arbitrators who form a court of equity should always be small. Large numbers effect less good by accumulating wisdom, than harm by putting off patient investigation to one another, and by "dividing the shame" of a partial decision.

35. The members of such courts, though capable of deciding with competent propriety on questions of right and wrong when facts are laid before them, may be incapable, from want of habit, of eliciting those facts from reluctant or partial witnesses. Now, I perceive no reason why, both in criminal and civil courts, a person could not be employed, whose profession it was to elicit the truth. Is he to be a *pleader* or an *advocate?* No. The very name is sufficient to discredit the office in the view of pure morality. One professional man only should be employed. That one should be employed by neither party separately, but by both, or by the state. It should be his simple and sole business to elicit the truth, and to elicit it from the witnesses of both sides. Securities against corruption in this man are obviously as easy as in arbitrators themselves. The judges of England evince, in general, an admirable example of impartiality; and as to corruptness, it is almost unknown. What reason is there for questioning that officers such as we speak of, may not be incorrupt and impartial too? If handsome remuneration be necessary to secure them from undue influence and to maintain the dignity of their office, let them by all means have it. Even in a present court of law or justice—suppose the examination of witnesses was taken from barristers and conducted by the judge, does not every man perceive that the truth might be elicited by one interrogator of the witnesses of both parties? And does not every one perceive that such an interrogator would elicit it in a far more upright and manly way than is now the case? *Pleading* is a thing which, in the administration of justice, ought not to be so much as named.

36. Bearing along in our minds, then, the inconveniences and the evils of Fixed Laws —let us suppose that a circuit was taken, and that courts were held from which the application of fixed law was, so far as is practicable, excluded. Suppose these courts to consist of three or five or seven men, selected according to the utmost skill of precautionary measures, for their intelligence and uprightness, and of one publicly authorised and dignified person, whose office it should be to assist the court in the discovery of the truth. Suppose that, when the facts of the case, and as far as possible the motives and intentions of the parties, were laid open, these three, or five, or seven men pronounced a decision as accordant as they could do with the immutable principles of right and wrong, and excluding almost all reference to fixed laws, and precedents, and technicalities;—is it not probable, is it not reasonable, to expect that the purposes of justice would be more effectually answered than they are at present? And even if justice was not *better* administered, would not such a system exclude various existing evils connected with legal institutions, evils so great as to be real calamities to the state?

37. Perhaps it is needless to remark, that all courts of equity which are recognised by the state should be *public*. Individuals who refer their disputes to private arbitrators, may have them privately adjusted if they please. But publicity is a powerful means of securing that impartiality which it is the first object in the administration of justice to secure.

38. There is one advantage, collateral indeed to the administration of equity, but not therefore the less considerable, that it would have a strong tendency to diffuse sound ideas of justice in the public mind. As it is, it may unhappily be affirmed that courts of judicature spread an habitual confusion of ideas upon the subject; and, what is worse, very frequently inculcate that as just which is really the contrary. Our notions of a court of judicature are, or they ought to be, that it is a place sacred to justice. But when, superinduced upon this notion, it is the fact, that by very many of its decisions justice is put into the background; that law is elevated into supremacy; that the technicalities of forms, and the finesse of pleaders, triumph over the decisions of rectitude in the mind—the effect cannot be otherwise than bad. It cannot do otherwise than confound, in the public mind, notions of good and evil, and teach them to think that everything is virtuous which courts of justice sanction.—If, instead of this, the public were habituated to a constant appeal to equity, and to a constant conformity to its dictates, the effect would be opposite, and therefore good. Justice would stand prominently forward to the public view as the object of reverence and regard. The distinctions between equity and injustice would become, by habit, broad and defined. Instead of confounding the public ideas of

morality, a court of judicature would teach, very powerfully teach, discrimination. A court, seriously endeavouring to discover the decision of justice, and uprightly awarding it between man and man, would be a spectacle of which the moral influence *could not* be lost upon the people.

39. In thus recommending the application of pure moral principles in the administration of justice, the writer does not presume to define *how far* the present condition of human virtue may capacitate a legislature to exchange fixed rules of decision for the impartial judgments of upright men. That it may be done to a much greater extent than it is now done, he entertains no doubt. A legislature might perhaps begin with that pernicious species of arbitrary rules which consists of technicalities and forms. To deny justice to a man because he has not claimed it in a specific form of words, or because some legal inaccuracy has been committed in the proceedings, must always disapprove itself to the plain judgments of mankind. Begin then with the most palpable and useless rules. Whatever *can* be dispensed with, it is a sacred duty to abolish, and every act of judicious abolition will facilitate the abolition of others:—it will prepare the public mind for the contemplation of purer institutions, and gradually enable it to adopt those institutions in the national practice.

As to the particular *modes* of securing the administration of simple justice, the writer would say, that those which he has suggested, he has suggested with deference. His business is rather with the *principles* of sound political institutions, than with the *form* and *mode* of applying them to practice. Other and better means than he has suggested are probably to be found. The candid reader will acknowledge, that in advocating institutions so different from those which actually obtain, the political moralist is under peculiar difficulties and disadvantages. The best *machinery* of social institutions is discovered rather from experience than from reasoning, and upon this machinery, in the present instance, experience has thrown little light.

Here, as in some other parts of this work, the reader will observe that alterations are proposed and improvements suggested which have been actually adopted since these Essays were written. Our courts, and also the legislature, have lately paid some attention to the modes in which public justice is administered. As yet the alterations which have been made are chiefly confined to the criminal Laws; but our judges are now beginning to exert the discretionary power which is vested in them, in preventing the course of justice from being so frequently as it heretofore has been, intercepted by technicalities and verbal inaccuracy. Of this the public had lately an instance in the cause of Gulley v. the Bishop of Exeter. A parliamentary commission has been appointed, and is now sitting, whose object it is to devise improvements in the practice of our courts of judicature.—ED.

CHAPTER XI.

Of the Proper Subjects of Penal Animadversion.

Crimes regarded by the Civil and the Moral Law—Created offences—Seduction—Duelling—Insolvents—Criminal debtors—Gradations of guilt in insolvency—Libels: mode of punishing—Effects of the laws respecting libels—Effects of public censure—Libels on the Government—Advantages of a free statement of the truth—Freedom of the press.

40. The man who compares the actions which are denounced as wrong in the Moral Law, with those which are punished by civil government, will find that they are far from an accordance. The Moral Law declares many actions to be wicked which human institutions do not punish; and there are some that these institutions punish, of which there is no direct reprehension in the communicated Will of God.

41. It is not easy to refer all these incongruities to the application of any one general principle of discrimination. You cannot say that the magistrate adverts only to those crimes which are pernicious to society, for *all* crimes are pernicious. Nor can you say that he selects the *greatest* for his animadversion, because he punishes many of which the guilt is incomparably less than others which he passes by. Nor again, can you say that he punishes only those in which there is an injured and complaining party; for he punishes some of which all the parties were voluntary agents. Lastly—and what seems at first view very extraordinary—we find that civil governments *create* offences which, simply regarded, have no existence in the view of morality, and punish them with severity, whilst others, unquestionably immoral, pass with impunity.

42. The practical rule which appears to be regarded in the selection of offences for punishment is founded upon the existing circumstances of the community.

43. Offences against which, from any cause, the public disapprobation is strongly directed, are usually visited by the arm of the civil magistrate, partly because that disapprobation implies that the offence disturbs the order of society, and partly because, in the case of such offences, penal animadversion is efficient and vigorous by the ready co-operation of the public. Thus it is with almost all offences against property, and with those which personally injure or alarm us. Every man is desirous of prosecuting a housebreaker, for he feels that his own house may be robbed. Every man is desirous of punish-

ing an assault or a threatening letter, because he considers that his peace may be disturbed by the one, and his person injured by the other. This general and strong reprobation makes detection comparatively easy, and punishment efficient.

44. Examples of the contrary kind are to be found in the crimes of drunkenness, of profane swearing, of fornication, of duelling. Not that we have any reason to expect, that at the bar of heaven some of these crimes will be at all less obnoxious to punishment than the former, but because, from whatever reason, the public very negligently co-operate with law in punishing them, and manifest little desire to see its penalties inflicted. An habitual drunkard does much more harm to his family and to the world, than he who picks my pocket of a guinea; yet we raise a hue and cry after the thief, and suffer the other to become drunk every day. So it is with duelling and fornication. The public know very well that these things are wrong, and pernicious to the general welfare; but scarcely any one will prosecute those who commit them. The magistrate may make laws, but in such a state of public feeling they will remain as a dead letter; or, which perhaps is as bad, be called out upon accidental and irregular occasions.

45. Another rule which appears to be practically, though not theoretically, adopted is, to punish those offences of which there is a natural prosecutor. Thus it is with every kind of robbery and violence. Some one especially is aggrieved: the sense of grievances induces a ready prosecution, and whatever is readily prosecuted by the people will generally be denounced in the laws of the state. The opposite fact is exhibited in the case of many offences against the public, such as smuggling, and generally in the case of all frauds upon the revenue. No individual is especially aggrieved (unless in the case of regular dealers whose business is injured by illicit trading), and the consequence is, either that numberless frauds of this kind are suffered to pass with impunity, or that the government is obliged to employ persons to detect the offenders, and to prosecute them itself. There are some crimes which seem in this respect of an intermediate sort; where there is a natural prosecutor, and yet where that prosecutor is not the most aggrieved person. This is instanced in the case of seduction. The father prosecutes, but he does not sustain one half the injury that is suffered by the daughter. There are obvious reasons why the most injured party should be at best an inefficient prosecutor; and the result is consonant—that this offence is frequently not punished at all, or, as is the case in our own country, it is punished very slightly—so slightly, that in no case does the person of the offender suffer. This lenity does not arise from the venialness of this crime, or of that of adultery. They are amongst the most enormous that can be perpetrated by man. Of the *less* flagitious of the two, it has been affirmed "that not one half of the crimes for which men suffer death by the laws of England are so flagitious as this."[1] This enormity is distinctly asserted in both the Old Testament and the New: in the first, adultery was punished with death; in the second, both this and fornication, which is less criminal than seduction, is repeatedly assorted with the greatest of crimes, and alike threatened with the tremendous punishments of religion.

46. Such considerations lead the inquirer to expect that the offences which are denounced in a statute book will bear some relation to the state of virtue in the people. The more virtuous the people are, the greater will be the number of crimes which can be efficiently visited by the arm of power. Thus, during some part of the seventeenth century, that is, during the interregnum, adultery was punished with death; and it may be remarked, without paying a compliment to the religion or politics of those times, that the actual practice of morality was then, amongst a large proportion of the nation, at a higher standard than it is now. No society exists without some species of penal justice—from that of a gang of thieves to that of a select and pious Christian community. The thieves will punish some crimes, but they will be *few*. The virtuous community will punish, or, which for our present purpose is the same thing, animadvert upon, *very many*. In a well-ordered family many things are held to be offences, and are noticed as such by the parent, which in a vicious family pass unregarded.

47. When therefore we contemplate the unnumbered offences against morality which the magistrate does not attempt to discourage, we may take comfort from hoping that, as the virtue of mankind increases, it may increase in more than a simple ratio. As the public become prepared for it, governments will lead their aid; and thus they who have now little restraint from some crimes but that which exists in their own minds, may hereafter be deterred by the fear of human penalty. And this induces the observation, that to throw obstacles in the way of increasing the subjects of penal animadversion, is both impolitic and wrong. This, unhappily, has frequently been done in our own country. Some public writers

[1] Paley: Mor. and Pol. Phil., b. 3, p. 3.—*Seduction.*

(writers not of great eminence to be sure) have taken great pains to *ridicule* legislation respecting cruelty to animals—and the endeavours on the part of well-disposed men to enforce almost obsolete statutes against some other common crimes. There are, surely, a sufficiency of obstacles to the extension of the subjects of penal legislation, without needlessly adding more. Besides, these men directly encourage the crimes. To sneer at him who prosecutes a ferocious man for cruelty to an animal, is to encourage cruelty. When a man is brought before a magistrate for profaneness—to joke about how the culprit swore in the court, is to teach men to be profane.

48. That which we have called, in the commencement of this chapter, the *creation* of offences, demands peculiar solicitude on the part of a government. By a created offence, I mean an act which, *but for the law*, would be no offence at all. Of this class are some offences against the game laws. He who on another continent was accustomed without blame to knock down hares and pheasants as he found occasion, would feel the force of this creation of offences when, on doing the same thing in England, he was carried to a jail. The most fruitful cause of these factitious offences is in extensive taxation. When a new tax is imposed the legislature endeavours to secure its due payment by requiring or forbidding certain acts. These acts, which antecedently were indifferent, become criminal by the legislative prohibition, or obligatory by the legislative command; and non-compliance is therefore punished as an offence by the civil power.[1] There is no more harm in a man's buying brandy in France and bringing it to England, than in buying a horse of his neighbour. The law lays a duty upon brandy, prohibits any man from bringing it to the country except through a customhouse, and treats as criminals those who do.

49. Now we do not affirm that those who commit these *created* offences do not absolutely offend against morality. They do offend; for in general every evasion or violation of the laws of the state is an immoral act. But this does not affect the truth, that such offences should be as few as they can be. The reasons are, first, that they are encroachments upon civil liberty, and secondly—which is our present concern—that they are pernicious to the public. Men perceive the distinction between moral crimes and legal crimes, without perhaps ever having inquired into its foundation. And they *act* upon this perception. He who has been convicted of killing hares, or evading taxes, or smuggling lace, is commonly willing to tell you of his exploits. He who has been convicted of stealing from his neighbour hangs down his head for shame. The sanctions of law ought to approve themselves to the common judgments of mankind. Whatever the state denounces, *that* the public ought to *feel* to be criminal, and to be willing to suppress. The penalties of the law ought to be accompanied in men's minds by the sanction of morality. They should feel that to be punished by a magistrate was tantamount to being a bad man. When, instead of this, there is an intricate admixture—when we see some things which are, simply regarded, innocent, visited by the same punishment as others that all men feel to be wicked, men are likely to feel a diminished respect for penal law itself. They learn to regard the requisitions of law as having little countenance from rectitude; and think that to violate them, though it may be dangerous, is not wrong. It does not approve itself, as a whole, to the public judgment; and there are many perhaps who feel, on this account, a diminished respect for penal institutions, without being able to assign the reason.

50. In the extension of this political and moral evil the greatest of all agents is war. With respect to the creation of offences, it stands *sui generis*, and converts a greater number of indifferent actions into punishable ones, than all other agents united. War produces the extensive taxation of which we speak; but the practical system has offences peculiar to itself—offences which the Moral Law of our Creator never denounced, but which the system of war visits with tremendous punishments. Adam Smith adverts to this deplorable circumstance. He says that the punishment of death to a sentinel who falls asleep upon his watch, "how necessary soever, always *appears to be excessively severe*. The natural atrocity of the crime seems to be so little, and the punishment so great, that *it is with great difficulty that our heart can reconcile itself to it*."[1] Nor *will* the heart, nor *ought* the heart, ever to be reconciled to it. It is, I know, perfectly easy to urge arguments in its favour from expediency and the like; but urge these arguments as you may, the uninitiated or unhardened heart will never be convinced; and it is vain to tell us that that is right which the immutable dictates in our minds pronounce to be wrong. There are, indeed, few spectacles more calculated to sicken the heart and to make it turn in disgust away from the monstrousness

---

[1] I have somewhere met with a book which contended that to commit these *created* offences was no breach of morality. This, however, is not true, because the obligation to obey civil government, in its innocent enactments, is clearly stated in the Moral Law.

[1] Theory of Moral Sentiments.

of human institutions, than a contemplation of martial law—a code which not only creates a multiplicity of offences that were never prohibited by our merciful Parent, but which visits the commission of those offences with inflictions that ought not to be so much as named amongst a Christian people.

51. Whilst then the philanthropist hopes that some of those intrinsically criminal actions to which human penalties are not attached, will one day become the object of their animadversion, he hopes that this other class, which are not intrinsically vicious, will gradually be expunged from amongst penal laws. Both the additions to, and the deductions from, the system which morality dictates, are the result of the impure or corrupt condition of society.

52. Meantime some approaches to a juster standard to regulate penal animadversion may be made, by transferring, in our own country, some offences from the civil to the criminal courts. An instance exists in the crime of seduction and its affinities. This crime, whether we regard it simply or in its consequences, or in the deliberation with which it is committed, is, as we have just seen, excessively flagitious. How then does it happen that its perpetration is regarded as a matter for the cognisance only of legal courts, and for the punishment only of a pecuniary fine? What should we say to that mode of justice which allowed the ruffian who assaults your person to escape by paying money? Yet even a severe assault does not approach, in enormity, to the crime of which we speak. I would punish seducers in their persons. I would send them to prison like other malefactors; and oblige them to labour, or subject them to that system of prison discipline which might give hope (if anything could give hope) of reformation. Alas! if there is no *reason* for not acting thus, there is a *motive*. That class of society to whom the framing of laws is entrusted regard the crime with but very ambiguous detestation. "The law of honour," it is said, "applauds the address of a successful intrigue." How should they who value themselves upon being the subjects of the law of honour, wish to consign a man to prison for that which the law of honour applauds? I doubt not that, if seduction were confined to low life, the legislature would quickly send seducers to the criminal courts. Would they were sent! The very idea of the punishment would, amongst gay men in the superior walks of life, often prevent the crime. To be seized by police! To be carried to a jail! To be brought to the bar with thieves and murderers! To be sentenced by the court! To be carried back to labour in a prison, or to be embarked for New South Wales!—The idea, I say, of this would go far to prevent the perpetration of this abandoned crime.

53. Duelling is another of the crimes which should be prosecuted in criminal courts. It is indeed prosecuted there if anywhere; but it is seldom prosecuted at all. The ultimate cause is easily discovered:—the crime is sanctioned by the law of honour. Like the preceding, if it were practised only by the poor,¹ it would quickly be visited by the arm of the law. Of the probability of this, we have an illustration in the case of boxing. One or more of the judges have recently declared, that if a man is convicted of having caused another's death in a boxing match, they will inflict the sentence which the law denounces upon manslaughter. The law of honour has no voice here; and here the voice of reason and common sense is regarded. Make boxing-matches, like duelling, a part of the system of the law of honour, and we shall hear very little about the punishment of manslaughter. The reader saw, in the last Essay, what an influence the law of honour had in a case of duelling on the mind, and on the charge of a judge on the Scotch bench.—These things suggest sorrowful reflections!

54. Much and very contradictory declamation is often employed respecting the treatment which is due to those who become insolvent. By our present law, the debtor may be arrested, that is, he may be imprisoned; on which account it may be allowable to range the discussion under the head of penal law. Imprisonment for debt is, in effect, a penalty, although it be not inflicted by a court of justice.

55. One class of persons declaims against the oppression of immuring men in a prison who have committed no crime; against the cruelty of the relentless creditor who, when misfortune has overtaken a fellow-creature, adds to his miseries the terrors of the law, and deprives him of the opportunity of exertion, and his family of the means of support; —and all this, it is said, is done without obtaining any other advantage to the persecutor than the gratification of his resentment or malignity. Another class expatiates upon the unprincipled fraud which is committed upon industrious traders by spendthrifts or villains—upon the hardship of leaving honest men at the mercy of every idle or profligate person who has address enough to obtain credit, and upon the absurdity

¹ In France, it is said, and in America, duelling is descending to the inferior classes of society. If this should become general, we may soon reckon upon an efficient diminution of the practice. The rich will forbear it on account of its vulgarity, and they will take care to punish it when it is practised only by the poor.

of that philanthropy which would prevent them from deterring him from his frauds by the terrors of a jail.

56. To determine between these vehement and conflicting opinions, the great question is, Whether a debtor is a *criminal?* If he is, there is no reason why he should not be treated as a criminal; and if he is not, there is no reason why an innocent man should meet the fate which is due only to the guilty. These contradictory opinions appear to result from the circumstance, that one set of persons regard insolvents as criminals, and the other as unfortunate men. The truth, however, is, that many are of one class and many of the other. It is therefore no subject of surprise, that when one set of persons view one side of the question, and another the opposite, they should involve themselves and the subject in conflict and contradiction.

57. From these considerations one conclusion appears plainly to follow—that no undiscriminating law upon the subject can be even tolerably just; that to concede the power of imprisoning all debtors, is to permit oppression: that to deny it to any, is to withhold punishment from guilt. In order therefore to attain the ends of justice, it is absolutely indispensable that discrimination should be made in every individual case.

58. Suppose, then, the first legal step towards enforcing payment from a debtor were, not to obtain a writ, but to summon him before a magistrate. If he refuses to attend to the summons a warrant might be granted for his arrest, since the reasonable inference would be, that his motives for withholding payment, or the causes by which he had become unable to pay, were such as he was afraid to acknowledge. If he attended, the case would be heard—not from lawyers but from the parties themselves. Supposing it appeared that the debtor was capable of paying but unwilling, or that, although then unable, his inability had been occasioned by manifest misconduct:—let him be committed to prison. And why? Because he is an offender against public justice, and, like other offenders, should await his punishment.

59. Supposing, again, it appeared that the debtor could not pay, and that his insolvency involved no fault:— let him be regarded as a man overtaken by misfortune, as a man whom it would be oppressive and wrong to punish, and who therefore should be set at large. His property of course would be secured.

Discrimination of this kind, whatever might be the mode of its exercise, appears to be a *sine quâ non* of the administration of justice.

It is exceedingly obvious, that when actions of which the external consequences may be the same, result some from innocent and some from criminal causes, they should not receive the same treatment at the hand of the law:—just as he who accidentally occasions a man's death should not receive the same treatment as he who commits murder. Now this manifest requisite of justice is in no other way attainable in the case of insolvency, than by investigating the conduct of every individual man.

60. When the *criminal* debtors are committed like other criminals to prison, they should be regarded as public offenders, and as such become amenable to penal animadversion. Courts of a simple construction might perhaps be erected for this class of offenders, which might possess the power of awarding such punishments for the various degrees of guilt as the law thought fit to prescribe. Nor does there appear any reason for deviating materially from those species of punishment which are properly employed for other offenders, because insolvency is occasioned by guilt in endless gradations, and sometimes by great crime. The number of insolvents who are entirely innocent is comparatively small, and of those who are not innocent the gradations of criminality are without end. Some are incautious or imprudent, some are heedlessly and some shamefully negligent, and some again are atrociously profligate. The whole amount of injury which is inflicted upon the people of this country by criminal insolvency, is much greater than that which is inflicted by any one other crime which is ordinarily punished by the law. Neither swindling, nor forgery, nor robbery, in their varieties, produces an equal amount of mischief. To every single individual who loses his property by theft or fraud, there are probably twenty who lose it by criminal debtors. Such facts evidently furnish weighty considerations for the legislator as the guardian of the public welfare; and that system of jurisprudence is surely defective which allows so much public mischief almost without restraint. Justice and policy alike indicate the necessity of more efficient security against the want of probity in debtors, than has hitherto been furnished by the law.

61. A man who begins business with a thousand pounds of his own, and who keeps a stock of goods to the value of fifteen hundred, is obliged in honesty to *insure*. If he does not insure, and a fire destroys his goods, so that his creditors lose five hundred pounds, he surely is chargeable with a moral offence. It cannot be just knowingly to endanger the loss of other men's property, which has been entrusted in the confidence of its repayment.

But if such a man commits injustice towards others, upon what grounds is he to be exempted from the rightful consequences of injustice? We would not speak of such a man as a criminal, nor affirm that he deserves severity of punishment; but we say that, since he has needlessly and negligently sacrificed the property of other men, it is fit that the penal legislator should notice and discountenance his offence.

62. Another trader, without any vicious intention, "neglects his business." His customers by degrees leave him. Year passes after year with an income continually diminishing, until at length he finds that his property is less than his debts. This man is more vicious than the former, and should be visited by a greater amount of punishment. Another, with a prosperous business and no great vices, allows a more expensive domestic establishment than his income warrants. His property gradually lapses away, and at last he cannot pay twenty shillings in the pound to his creditors. Can it be disputed that a man who knows that he is in a course of life which will probably end in defrauding others of their property, should be regarded in any other light than as an offender against justice? And can it be unreasonable for the jurisprudence of a community to act towards such an offender as if he were a dishonest man?

63. Another engages in speculations which endanger the property of his creditors, and which, if they do not succeed, will defraud them. Such speculations certainly are dishonest: and when they prove unsuccessful, he who makes them should be treated as the committer of voluntary fraud. The propriety of this is enforced by the consideration that it is nearly impossible for creditors to provide against such fraudulence; and laws should be severe in proportion as the facilities of wrong are great.

64. Such gradations might be multiplied indefinitely, until we arrived at those in which men contract debts without the probable prospect of payment; and thence up to the intentionally and voluntarily fraudulent. For such offenders the penalties should be severe. The guilt of some of them is at least as great as that of him who robs you of your purse or forges your signature. With respect, indeed, to those who pursue a deliberate course of fraud, and, under pretence of business, possess themselves of the property of others, and expend it or carry it off, there are few crimes connected with property that are equally atrocious. The law, indeed, appears to acknowledge this, for its penalty for a fraudulent bankrupt is desperately severe. Without stopping to inquire why it is so seldom inflicted, one truth appears to be plain, that a penal system which, like ours, scarcely adverts to crimes so extended and so great, must be greatly defective. Surely there are many persons who walk our streets every day, yet who are, in the view both of natural and of Christian justice, incomparably more guilty and more justly obnoxious to punishment, than the majority of those whom the law confines in jails or transports beyond the ocean.

65. We are persuaded, that if the penal law took cognisance of all insolvents, and regarded all who could not satisfactorily account for their insolvency as public delinquents—if these were prosecuted as systematically as thieves are now, and if by these means the idea of "crime" was associated with their conduct in the public mind, the deplorable mischiefs of bankruptcy would be quickly and greatly diminished. In the restraint of all crimes the power of public opinion is great. At present, unhappily, the man whose offence is justly worthy of imprisonment or transportation, obtains his certificate, and then becomes the accepted associate of virtuous men. But teach the public to connect with him the idea not of a bankrupt but of a prisoner; not of a man who has acted dishonourably towards his creditors, but of a convicted criminal and this association would cease. Who would admit a footpad to his table? And who would admit to his table a man who was just like a footpad? It requires little knowledge of the constitution of society to know, that when the offences of fraudulent and negligent insolvency are ranked in the public estimation with those of ordinary criminals, men will be influenced by a new, and a powerful, and an efficient motive to avoid them.

66. It is a question that involves some difficulties, whether the publication of statements injurious to individuals, to a government, or to religion, are proper subjects of penal animadversion. That the publishers of these statements frequently act criminally is certain, and they are therefore justly obnoxious to punishment: but still it is to be inquired, whether it can be efficiently punished; and whether, if they be, the punishment can be such as to attain the proper ends of all punishment—reformation, example, and redress.

67. And here we are presented, at the outset, with a great impediment resulting from the nature of fixed law. If a libeller is to be legally punished, the law must give some definition of what a libel is. Now it is actually impossible to frame any definition which shall not either on the one hand give license to injurious publications by its laxity,

or on the other prohibit a just publication of the truth by its rigour. The utmost sagacity of legislation cannot avoid one of these two consequences. They are not a Scylla and Charybdis which a wary helmsman may avoid: on the one or the other the legislator will infallibly find himself wrecked.

68. If libellers, like other offenders, were tried by courts of equity, which were guided in their award by the simple merits of the case, without any regard to the definitions of law—the case would be different. We might then expect that the publication of wholesome truths would receive no punishment though they constituted what is defined to be a libel now, and that the publication of gratuitous malignity *would* receive a punishment though lawyers now might say that the book was not a libel.

69. Yet even if these difficulties resulting from the vain attempt at legal definitions were surmounted, and equity alone were entrusted with the decision, it may still be greatly doubted whether, in the large majority of this class of publications, all attempts at direct punishment would not be better avoided.

70. Refer to the objects of punishment. Assume for the present that *reformation* is the first. Is it probable, from the motives and nature of the offence, that the reformation of the offender can often be hoped from any species of judicial penalties?

71. The second object we suppose to be *example*. Men may, no doubt, be deterred from publishing injurious statements by the fear of consequences; and thus far the end is attained. Supposing that the publishers could generally be discovered, and that the decisions of the courts were practically just, I should think the object of example would be a strong reason for inflicting judicial punishment upon the libeller:—still other considerations will presently be submitted, which induce the belief that such punishment is not the most effectual nor the most proper means of prevention.

72. Then as to *redress*. There is only one way in which rational redress can be attained by the aspersed party; and that is, by proving and making known the falsehood of the aspersion. But this can be done without applying to judicial courts.

73. The reader will ask, What then is it proposed to do? and, in furnishing a reply, I shall proceed upon the supposition that courts of law only exist.

74. A statement injurious to a private individual is published to the world. He prosecutes the libeller under the most favourable circumstances. He can prove that it is legally a libel, and he can prove also that it is false. What then does he gain by proceeding to law? Nothing individually, but that he proves the falsehood; and this he may do more satisfactorily, more cheaply, and more efficiently without a court of law than within it. If there are documents, or if there is testimony by which he can prove the falsehood, they can be adduced before the public without the intervention of courts, and juries, and pleaders. Besides, the verdict of law upon such cases is habitually received with a sort of suspicion and want of confidence in its foundation; because we know that verdicts are continually given against the publishers of libels *although the libel is true*. Now, in whatever degree the public doubts respecting the absolute falsehood of the libel, in the same degree its great private object of prosecuting the libeller is frustrated. The same evidence of falsehood adduced *without the intervention of law* would be much more effectual, because it would be exempted from the same suspicion.—I put other motives to prosecution, such as a regard to the public, out of the question, because these are not often the motives which operate. In such matters men usually act not from public but from private views.

75. But the prosecutor's circumstances may be less favourable. Suppose the statement, however injurious, is not legally a libel. Then, whatever evidence he produces, the verdict is against him, and the public, who do not trouble themselves with nice distinctions, perhaps think that the imputation upon his character is deserved. Again, it may be a libel, and yet he may fail of producing legal proof. The most mortifying and insignificant deficiencies in proof disappoint all his hopes. The publication of a libel which all the world has seen, and of which everybody knows the publisher, does not admit perhaps of legal proof. No man can be brought forward who has seen, with his own eyes, that a certain man did publish it. And here again the prosecutor obtains no redress. But further.—Many public statements are libellous, and are cruelly injurious to the sufferer, which, nevertheless, are true. To prosecute these statements is worse than merely vain. You only extend further and wider the reproach which was confined within narrower limits before. You make the evil to yourself more intense as well as more extended; for the prosecuted party will no doubt take care to bring proof of the *truth* of his statements. Thus the scandal which was accepted with doubt, and by a few, previous to the trial, is accepted with certainty and by a multitude afterwards.

76. What then is to be done? Is every man to be at liberty to say with impunity whatever he pleases, true or false, against other men? Not with impunity; but with *impunity from the law*. That this legal impunity may be productive of some evils is undoubtedly true. But the question is not whether evils exist, but whether they can be remedied. Let us suppose, then, that there was no such thing as libel law. I think it probable that if these laws were repealed to-morrow, the press would quickly inundate the public with torrents of vilification and slander. The malignity of bad men would, for a while, prevent them from perceiving the alteration which awaited the public habits. They would think that an aspersion would continue to have the same effect in practically injuring and blackening the character of others, as it has now, that it is comparatively unfrequent from the restraints of law. But what would be the result? Inevitably this: that the public would very quickly regard libels as they regard all other common things, with heedless indifference. They would not seize upon them as they now do with a vicious avidity. Published slander would become to the public what the abuse of fishwomen is to the inhabitants of Billingsgate, a thing which they do not regard — a thing about which they do not trouble themselves to consider whether the mutual vilifications be true or false, and for which they scarcely think either the worse or the better of the quarrellers. With respect to published slander, such a state of things could not last. Private malignity would often die for want of food. It would not publish the aspersion which, when published, no one would regard, and the flood of vituperation would soon subside.

77. But suppose, for a moment, that the contrary were possible. What would then happen? Why, the public would habituate themselves to discrimination. They would not, they could not, accept every libel as true; and in general they would accept *none* as true of which the truth was not proved. Here again the desire of virtue would be in a great degree fulfilled; for we need not trouble ourselves to repress libels by which no man's mind is influenced. In all suppositions, too, the proper means of redress are in the sufferer's power — to adduce proof of the falsehood and malignity of the assertion. And this is not only the greatest object to himself, but it would also be a positive punishment to the slanderer, whilst the custom would become a terror to other promulgators of slander. What punishment is so likely to be influential as to be *proved* to be a malicious and lying vilifier of innocent men? What motive so powerful to prevent this vilification, as the knowledge that this proof would be laid before the public?

78. If an innocent person, whose character had been in this manner publicly aspersed, should ask what I would advise him to do, I should say—Think nothing of law; go to those persons who have the means of testifying the falsehood of the aspersion; procure their explicit and attested allegations; or, if by any other means your innocence can be shown—avail yourself of them, and forthwith lay your exculpation before the public. Here the great end is attained. Your character is not injured; and as to the slanderer, he is punished by being made the subject of public reprobation and disgust. A few days previous to that on which I write, a wide extended daily newspaper published some insinuations against the character of a gentleman eminent in society. What was done? Why, the same day or the next, a nobleman who happened to know the truth, and whose word no one would dispute, sent a note to another paper saying, *the insinuation was unfounded*. Was not every object then attained? Would this gentleman have been further benefited by prosecuting the editor? or could this editor have been more appropriately punished than by this exposure of his malignity?

79. But it will be said, that there do not exist the means of disproving some aspersions, however false. This is correct; but what is to be done? If the sufferer cannot disprove it in a newspaper or pamphlet, neither can he in a court of law: and *unless it is disproved*, a prosecution, besides procuring little or no redress, publishes the aspersion to a tenfold number. Yet such a person may demand proof of the slanderer, and require that he come forward. This, and such things, may be done in a manner that so indicates integrity and innocence, that in failure of a justification of the slander it would recoil upon the author.

80. The most pitiable situation is that of a person, now perhaps virtuous and good, who is charged with some of the crimes or vices of which he was actually guilty in past times. Here the libel cannot be repelled, for it is true. To invite investigation is to publish and deepen the slander. It must therefore be borne: a painful alternative, but unavoidable; and he who endures it will, perhaps, if he be now a Christian, regard it with humility, as a not unjust retribution of his former sins.

81. But to allow the unrestrained publication of facts or falsehood, is not a matter purely evil. The statutes which prevent men from publishing libels, prevent them also from publishing truths — truths which all men ought to hear. There are some actions which can in no other way be punished or discountenanced than by exposing them to the public reprobation. I saw the other day, in a newspaper (I think these popular references much to the purpose), a narrative of the gross cruelty of some *gentleman* to his horse, by which a large part of the animal's tongue had been cut or torn from its mouth. The narrator said he was afraid to mention this man's name on account of the libel laws. Suppose the statement to have been true, and the name to have been made public; would it not have been a proper and a severe punishment for the inhumanity? Would it not have deterred others from such inhumanity? In a word, *ought* not such charges to be published?—And thus it would be with a multitude of other offences, for which scarcely any punishment is so effectual as the reprobation of the public. "There is no terror that comes home to the heart of vice, like the terror of being exhibited to the public eye." I am willing to acknowledge that if the publication of many species of vicious conduct was more frequent—so frequent as to be habitual, it would eventually tend to the extension of private and of public virtue. Men who were in any way ill-disposed, would find themselves under a constant apprehension of exposure, from which almost no vigilance could secure an escape. The writer from whom I have quoted the sentence above, holds much stronger language than mine. "If truth," says he, "were universally told of men's dispositions and actions, gibbets and wheels might be dismissed from the face of the earth. The knave unmasked, would be obliged to turn honest in his own defence. Nay, no man would have time to grow a knave. Truth would follow him in his first irresolute essays, and public disapprobation arrest him in the commencement of his career."[1] All this is not now to be hoped: yet when men knew that the exposure of their misdeeds was in the uncontrollable power of the press, and that there were no means of securing themselves from its punishment but by being virtuous, would not they be more anxious to practise virtue? Would not the dread of exposure operate upon some of the unpunished vices of private life, as the dread of public opinion operates upon more public vices now? The restraining power of public opinion we know is great :—by dispensing with libel laws we should extend that power.

82. Finally, the repeal of these laws would be attended with one of two consequences. If the consequence was, that these publications were not increased in number, no evil could be done. If they were increased, and

[1] Godwin: Enq. Pol. Just., v. 2, p. 643.

greatly increased in number, the public would soon learn to discriminate. Tales are believed now, because they are seldom told, and the public discrimination is not sufficiently habituated to distinguish the false from the true. If it were, the true only would pass current. These often *ought* to pass; and as to the false—who would publish what no one would believe?[1]

83. Publications to the discredit of government, or of its officers, assume a different character; but the difference appears to be such as still more strongly to argue against visiting them with legal penalties. Charles James Fox remarked upon this difference. He thought, however, that *private* libels, some of the true as well as the false, might rightly be punished by the state; but " in questions relating to public men," says he, " *verity* in respect of public measures ought to be regarded as a complete justification of a libel."[2] Whether truth be a *justification* of a political libel is one question,—whether such a libel ought to be punished by the law is another. But I think that no statement respecting public measures ought to be punished by the law—for this simple reason amongst others: if the statement be true, it is commonly right that the truth should be publicly known; if it be false, the mischief is better remedied by publicly *showing* the falsehood than by any other means. Surely to repel the aspersion upon public men, by showing that it is unfounded, is more consistent with the dignity of a government than to pursue the vituperator with fines and imprisonment. Surely this more dignified course would recommend the government and its measures to the judgments of all wise and judicious men.

84. To what purpose will you prosecute a *true* statement? If a hundred men hear of it before the prosecution, ten thousand perhaps will hear of it afterwards. Nor is this all: for I scarcely know an act which can more powerfully tend to weaken a government, than first to act amiss, and then vindictively to pursue him who mentions the misconduct. If the object of a government in instituting such a prosecution be to strengthen its own hands, surely it pursues the object by most inexpedient means; and as to suppressing truth by the mere influence of terror, it is a mode of governing

[1] I learn from a book which professes to give information respecting "Society and Manners in High and Low Life," that there existed (and perhaps there still exists) a House of Call in London, where he who had malice without ability might *bespeak* a libel upon any subject. The price was seven and sixpence. In a few hours he might hear the scandal, if such was his order, sung about the streets.— Such a fact may well affect our resolution to punish libellers by the grave power of the law.
[2] Fell's Memoirs.

for which no man in this country ought to lift his voice.

85. A very serious point in addition is this—that almost all political libels, whether true or false, are countenanced by a party. A prosecution, therefore, however seemingly successful, is sometimes totally defeated because the party recompenses the victim for his sufferings or his losses. The prosecution and those who conduct it become the laughing-stock of the party. In the days of Pitt, a person published a libel which that statesman declared in the House of Commons to be "the most infamous collection of sedition and treason that ever was published."[1] The man was prosecuted, found guilty, and sentenced to some imprisonment. What was the result? Why, *the party* made a subscription for him to the amount, it was said, of *four thousand pounds*. What bad man would not publish a libel to be so paid? What discreet government would prosecute a libel to be so defeated?

86. But if the *uses* of a free statement of the truth be so great in the case of private persons, much more is it desirable in the case of political affairs. To discuss, and, if needful, temperately to animadvert upon the conduct of governments, is the proper business of the public. How else shall the judgment of a people be called forth and expressed? How else shall they induce an amendment in public measures? The very circumstance that government is above the customary control of the laws, is a good reason for allowing the people freely to deliver their sentiments upon its conduct. Many ill actions of the private man may be punished by the law; but how shall the ill actions of public persons be discountenanced if it be not by the expression of the public mind? A people have sometimes no other means of promoting reformations in the conduct of government, than by exposing those parts in which reformation is needed. The argument then is short. To prosecute false political libels is unreasonable, for there are better and wiser means of procedure. To prosecute true statements is wrong, because truth ought to be freely told; and if it were not wrong, it would be absurd, because a government inflicts more injury upon itself by the prosecution than was inflicted by the statement itself.

87. As the subject maligned rises in dignity, we are presented with stronger and still stronger dissuasions to the legal prosecution of the maligner. There are more reasons against prosecuting a political than a private aspersion: there are more reasons against prosecuting aspersions upon religion than either.—Supposing, which we must suppose, that religion is true, then all libels upon it *must* be false; and, like other false libels, are better met by proving the truth than by punishing the liar. "Christianity is but ill defended," says Paley, "by refusing audience or toleration to the objections of unbelievers."[1] It is a scandal to religion to prosecute the man who makes objections to its truths: for what is the inference in the objector's mind but this, that we resort to force because we cannot produce arguments? Nor let me be misinterpreted if I ask, What is Christianity, or who shall define it? I may be of opinion, and in fact I am of opinion, that some of the doctrines which the professors of Christianity promulgate, are as much opposed to Christianity as some of the arguments of unbelievers. But this is not a good reason for making my judgment the standard of Truth. Yet, without a standard, how shall we prosecute him who impugns Christianity? How, rather, shall we know whether he impugns Christianity or something else?

88. Truth is an overmatch for falsehood. Where they are allowed fairly to conflict, truth is sure of the victory. Who then would rob her of the victory by silencing falsehood by force? It is by such contests that the cause of truth is promoted. The assailant calls forth defenders; and it has in fact happened, that the proofs and practical authority of religion have been strengthened by defences which, but for the assaults of error, might never have been made or sought.

89. If it be said that fair argument, however unsound, may be tolerated, and that you only mean to punish the authors of reproachful and scandalous attacks upon religion—we answer, that these attacks, like every other, are better repelled by exposure or by neglect than by force. You can scarcely prosecute these bad men (so experience teaches) without making them cry out about persecution, and without calling around them a party who might otherwise have held their peace. They exclaim, "The sufferer believed what he wrote, and thought that to publish it was for the general good!" All this may be false, but it is specious. At any rate you cannot disprove it. Sympathy for the man induces sympathy for his principles.—Another way in which a prosecution defeats its proper object is, that to prosecute a writing, whether scandalous or only false, is a sure way of making the book read. Thousands inquire for a profligate book because they hear it is of so much importance as to be prosecuted, who else would not have inquired because

[1] Gifford's Life.   [1] Mor. and Pol. Phil., b. 5, c 9.

they would not have heard of it. So it was about forty years ago with Paine's Works. What, says gaping curiosity, can this book be, which ministers and bishops are so anxious that we should not read? Multitudes have read the profligate later works of the unhappy Lord Byron, but probably unnumbered multitudes more would have read them, if they had been prosecuted by the Attorney-General and burned by the hangman. As it is, it may be hoped they will sink into oblivion by the weight of their own obscene profaneness.[1]

90. One objection applies to nearly all prosecutions of books—that it is almost impossible to restrain the licentiousness of the press without diminishing its wholesome freedom. The boundaries of freedom and licentiousness cannot be defined by law. No law can be devised which shall at once exclude the evil and permit the good. Now to restrain the freedom of the press is amongst the greatest mischiefs which can be inflicted upon mankind. The reader will be prepared to acknowledge the magnitude of the mischief, if he considers how powerful and how proper an agent public opinion is in promoting social and political reformations. There is no agent of reformation so desirable as the quiet influence of the public judgment; and in order to make this judgment sound and powerful, the press should be free.

91. The general conclusion that is suggested by the present chapter, is what the intelligent and Christian reader might expect —that the legislator should endeavour, so far as from time to time becomes practicable, to direct penal animadversion to those actions which are prohibited by the Moral Law; that he should endeavour this, both by addition and deduction; by ceasing to punish that which morality does not condemn, and by extending punishment to more of those actions which it does condemn.

92. As to the seeming exception in the case of libels, we do not contend so much for their impunity, as that the law is not the best means of punishment. By taking the care of restraining this offence from the law and placing it in the hands of the public, the punishment would sometimes be not only more effectual but more *severe*.

[1] This man affords an instance of that strange detraction from our own reputation with posterity to which we have before referred. He certainly wished that "dull oblivion" should not

"bar
His name from out the temple where the dead
Are honoured by the nations."—
How preposterous, then, to be the suicide of so large a portion of his hopes, by writing what experience might teach him the nations would not honour.

CHAPTER XII.
Of the Proper Ends of Punishment.

The three objects of punishment:—Reformation of the offender: Example: Restitution—Punishment may be increased as well as diminished.

1. Why is a man who commits an offence punished for the act? Is it for his own advantage, or for that of others, or for both? —For both, and primarily for his own;[1] which answer will perhaps the more readily recommend itself, if it can be shown that the good of others, that is, of the public, is best consulted by those systems of punishment which are most effectual in benefiting the offender himself.

2. When we recur to the precepts and the spirit of Christianity, we find that the one great pervading principle by which it requires us to regulate our conduct towards others, is that of operative, practical good-will—that good-will which, if they be in suffering, will prompt us to alleviate the misery, if they be vicious, will prompt us to reclaim them from vice. That the misconduct of the individual exempts us from the obligation to regard this rule, it would be futile to imagine. It is by him that the exercise of benevolence is peculiarly needed. He is the morally sick, who needs the physician; and such a physician he, who by comparison is morally whole, should be. If we adopt the spirit of the declaration, "I came not to call the righteous but sinners to repentance," we shall entertain no doubt that the *reformation* of offenders is the primary business of the Christian in devising punishments. There appears no reason why, in the case of public criminals, the spirit of the rule should not be acted upon—"If a brother be overtaken in a fault *restore* such an one." Amongst the Corinthians there was an individual who had committed a gross offence, such as is now punished by the law of England. Of this criminal Paul speaks in strong terms of reprobation in the first epistle. The effect proved to be good; and the offender having apparently become *reformed*, the Corinthians were directed in the second epistle to *forgive* and to comfort him.

3. When therefore a person has committed a crime, the great duty of those who in common with himself are candidates for the mercy of God, is to endeavour to meliorate and rectify the dispositions in which his crime originates; to subdue the vehemence of his passions—to raise up in his mind a

[1] "The end of all correction is either the amendment of wicked men or to prevent the influence of ill example." This is the rule of Seneca; and by mentioning amendment first, he appears to have regarded it as the *primary* object.

power that may counteract the power of future temptation. We should feel towards these mentally diseased, as we feel towards the physical sufferer—compassion; and the great object should be to cure the disease. No doubt, in endeavouring this object, severe remedies must often be employed. It is just what we should expect; and the remedies will probably be severe in proportion to the inveteracy and malignity of the complaint. But still the end should never be forgotten, and I think a *just* estimate of our moral obligations will lead us to regard the attainment of that end as paramount to every other.

4. There is one great practical advantage in directing the attention especially to this moral cure, which is this, that if it be successful, it prevents the offender from offending again. It is well known that the proportion of those who, having once suffered the stated punishment, again transgress the laws and are again convicted, is great. But to whatever extent reformation was attained, this unhappy result would be prevented.

5. The second object of punishment, that of example, appears to be recognised as right by Christianity, when it says that the magistrate is a "terror" to bad men; and when it admonishes such to be "afraid" of his power. There can be no reason for speaking of punishment as a terror, unless it were right to adopt such punishments as would deter. In the private discipline of the Church the same idea is kept in view:—" Them that sin rebuke before all, *that others also may fear.*"[1] The parallel of physical disease may also still hold. The offender is a member of the social body; and the physician who endeavours to remove a local disease, always acts with a reference to the health of the system.

6. In stating reformation as the first object, we also conclude, that if, in any case, the attainment of reformation and the exhibition of example should be found to be incompatible, the former is to be preferred. I say *if;* for it is by no means certain that such cases will ever arise. The measures which are necessary to reformation *must* operate as example; and in general, since the reformation of the more hardened offenders is not to be expected, except by severe measures, the influence of terror in endeavouring reformation will increase with the malignity of the crime. This is just what we need, and what the penal legislator is so solicitous to secure. The point for the exercise of wisdom is, to attain the second object in attaining the first. A primary regard to the first object is compatible with many modifications of punishment, in order more effectually to attain the second. If there are two measures, of which both tend alike to reformation, and one tends most to operate as example, that one should unquestionably be preferred.

7. There is a third object which, though subordinate to the others, might perhaps still obtain greater notice from the legislator than it is wont to do – Restitution or Compensation.[1] Since what are called criminal actions are commonly injuries committed by one man upon another, it appears to be a very obvious dictate of reason that the injury should be repaired ;—that he from whom the thief steals a purse should regain its value; that he who is injured in his person or otherwise, should receive such compensation as he may. When my house is broken into and a hundred pounds' worth of property is carried off, it is but an *imperfect* satisfaction to me that the robber will be punished. I *ought* to recover the value of my property. The magistrate, in taking care of the general, should take care of the individual weal. The laws of England do now award compensation in damages for some injuries. This is a recognition of the principle; although it is remarkable, not only that the number of offences which are thus punished is small, but that they are frequently of a sort in which *pecuniary* loss has not been sustained by the injured party.

8. I do not imagine that in the present state of penal law, or of the administration of justice, a general regard to compensation is practicable, but this does not prove that it ought not to be regarded. If in an improved state of penal affairs, it should be found practicable to oblige offenders to recompense by their labour those who had suffered by their crime, this advantage would attend, that while it would probably involve considerable punishment, it would approve itself to the offender's mind as the demand of reason and of justice. This is no trifling consideration; for in every species of coercion and punishment, public or domestic, it is of consequence that the punished party should feel the justice and propriety of the measures which are adopted.

9. The writer of these Essays would be amongst the last to reprobate a strict adherence to abstract principles, as such ; but some men, in their zeal for such principles, have proposed strange doctrines upon the subject of punishment. It has been said that when

---

[1] 1 Tim. v. 20.

[1] "The law of nature commands that reparation be made" (Mor. and Pol. Phil., b. 6, c. 8). And this dictate of nature appears to have been recognised in the Mosaic law, in which compensation to the suffering party is expressly required.

a crime has been committed it cannot be recalled; that it is a "past and irrevocable action," and that to inflict pain upon the criminal *because* he has committed it, "is one of the wildest conceptions of untutored barbarism." No one perhaps would affirm that, in strictness, such a motive to punishment is right; but how, when an offence is committed, can you separate the objects of punishment so as not *practically* to punish because the man has offended? If you regulate the punishment by its legitimate objects, you punish because the offender needs it; and as all offenders do need it, you punish all, which amounts in practice to nearly the same thing as punishing because they have committed a crime. However, as an abstract principle, there might be little occasion to dispute about it; but when it is made a foundation for such doctrine as the following, it is needful to recall the supreme authority of the Moral Law: "We are bound, under certain urgent circumstances, to deprive the offender of the liberty he has abused. *Further than this*, no circumstance can authorise us. The infliction of further evil, when his power to injure is removed, is the wild and unauthorised dictate of vengeance and rage." This is affirmative; and in turn I would affirm that it is the sober and authorised dictate of justice and goodwill. But indeed *why* may we even restrain him? Obviously for the sake of others; and for the sake of others we may also do more. Besides, this philosophy leaves the offender's reformation out of the question. If he is so wicked that you are obliged to confine him lest he should commit violence again, he is so wicked that you are obliged to confine him for *his own good*. And, in reality, the writer himself had just before virtually disproved his own position. "Whatever gentleness," he says, "the intellectual physician may display, it is not to be believed that men can part with rooted habits of injustice and vice without the sensation of considerable pain.[1] But, to occasion this pain in order to make them part with vicious habits, is to do something "further" than to take away liberty.

10. Respecting the relative utility of different modes of punishment and of prison discipline, we have little to say, partly because the practical recognition of *reformation* as a primary object affords good security for the adoption of judicious measures, and partly because these topics have already obtained much of the public attention. One suggestion may, however, be made, that as good consequences have followed from making a prisoner's confinement depend for its duration on his conduct, so that if it be exemplary the period is diminished, there

[1] Godwin: Enq. Pol. Just., v. II. pp. 748, 751.

appears no sufficient reason why the parallel system should not be adopted of increasing the original sentence if his conduct continue vicious. There is no breach of reason or of justice in this. For the reasonable object of punishment is to attain certain ends, and if, by the original sentence, it is found that these ends are not attained, reason appears to dictate that stronger motives should be employed. It cannot surely be less reasonable to add to a culprit's penalty if his conduct be bad, than to deduct from it if it be good. For a sentence should not be considered as a propitiation of the law, nor when it is inflicted should it be considered, as of necessity, that all is done. The sentence which the law pronounces is a general rule—good perhaps as a general rule, but sometimes inadequate to its end. And the utility of retaining the power of adding to a penalty is the same in kind, and probably greater in degree, than the power of diminishing it. In one case the culprit is influenced by hope, and in the other by fear. Fear is the more powerful agent upon some men's minds, and hope upon others. And as to the justice of such an institution, it appears easily to be vindicated; for what is the standard of justice? The sentence of the law? No; for if it were, it would be unjust to abate of it as well as to add. Is it the original crime of the offender? No; for if it were, the same crime, by whatever variety of conduct it was afterwards followed, must always receive an equal penalty. The standard of justice is to be estimated by the *ends* for which punishments are inflicted. Now, although it would be too much to affirm that any penalty, or duration of penalty, would be just until these ends were attained, yet surely it is not unjust to aim at their attainment by *some* additions to an original penalty when they cannot be attained without.

CHAPTER XIII.
Punishment of Death.

Of the three objects of punishment, the punishment of death regards but one—Reformation of minor offenders: Greater criminals neglected—Capital punishments not efficient as examples—Public executions—Paul—Grotius—Murder—The punishment of death irrevocable—Rousseau—Recapitulation.

11. I select for observation this peculiar mode of punishment on account of its peculiar importance.

12. And here we are impressed at the outset with the consideration, that of the three great objects which have just been proposed as the proper ends of punishment, the punishment of death regards but one,

and that one not the first and the greatest. The only end which is consulted in taking the life of an offender is that of example to other men. His own reformation is put almost out of the question. Now, if the principles delivered in the preceding chapter be sound, they present at once an almost insuperable objection to the punishment of death. If reformation be the primary object, and if the punishment of death precludes attention to that object, the punishment of death is wrong.

13. To take the life of a fellow-creature is to exert the utmost possible power which man can possess over man. It is to perform an action the most serious and awful which a human being can perform. Respecting such an action, then, can any truth be more manifest than that the dictates of Christianity ought especially to be taken into account? If these dictates are rightly urged upon us in the minor concerns of life, can any man doubt whether they ought to influence us in the greatest? Yet what is the fact? Why, that in defending capital punishments, these dictates are almost placed out of the question. We hear a great deal about security of property and life, a great deal about the necessity of making examples: but almost nothing about the Moral Law. It might be imagined that upon this subject our religion imposed no obligations: for nearly every argument that is urged in favour of capital punishments would be as valid and as appropriate in the mouth of a pagan as in our own. *Can* this be right? Is it conceivable that, in the exercise of the most tremendous agency which is in the power of man, it can be right to exclude all reference to the expressed will of God?

14. I acknowledge that this exclusion of the Christian law from the defences of the punishment, is to me almost a conclusive argument that the punishment is wrong. Nothing that is right can need such an exclusion; and we should not practise it if it were not for a secret perception, that to apply the pure requisitions of Christianity would not serve the purpose of the advocate. Look for a moment upon the capital offender and upon ourselves. *He*, a depraved and deep violator of the law of God one who is obnoxious to the vengeance of heaven one, however, whom Christ came peculiarly to call to repentance and to save—*Ourselves*, his brethren—brethren by the relationship of nature—brethren in some degree in offences against God brethren especially in the trembling hope of a common salvation. How ought beings so situated to act towards one another? Ought we to kill or to amend him? Ought we, so far as is in our power, to cut off his future hope, or, so far as is in our power, to strengthen the foundation of that hope? Is it the reasonable or decent office of one candidate for the mercy of God to hang his fellow-candidate upon a gibbet? I am serious, though men of levity may laugh. If such men reject Christianity, I do not address them. If they admit its truth, let them manfully show that its principles should not thus be applied.

15. No one disputes that the reformation of offenders is desirable, though some may not allow it to be the primary object. For the purposes of reformation we have recourse to constant oversight to classification of offenders to regular labour to religious instruction. For whom? For *minor* criminals. Do not the greater criminals need reformation too? If all these endeavours are necessary to effect the amendment of the less depraved, are they not necessary to effect the amendment of the more? But we stop just where our exertions are most needed; as if the reformation of a bad man was of the less consequence as the intensity of his wickedness became greater. If prison discipline and a penitentiary be needful for sharpers and pickpockets, surely they are necessary for murderers and highwaymen. Yet we reform the one and hang the other!

16. Since, then, so much is sacrificed to extend the terror of example, we ought to be indisputably certain that the terror of capital punishments is greater than that of all others. We ought not certainly to sacrifice the requisitions of the Christian law unless we *know* that a regard to them would be attended with public evil.[1] Do we know this? Are we indisputably certain that capital punishments are more efficient as examples than any others? *We are not.* We do not know from experience, and we cannot know without it. In England the experiment has not been made. The punishment therefore is wrong in us whatever it might be in a more experienced people. For it is wrong unless it can be *shown* to be right. It is not a neutral affair. If it is not indispensably necessary, it is unwarrantable. And since we do not know that it is indispensable, it is, so far as we are concerned, unwarrantable.

17. And with respect to the experience of other nations, who will affirm that crimes have been increased in consequence of the diminished frequency of executions? Who will affirm that the laws and punishments of America are not as effectual as our own? Yet they have abolished capital punishments for all private crimes except murder of the

[1] We ought not *for any reason* to do this; but I speak in the present paragraph of the *pretensions* of expediency.

first degree. Where, then, is our pretension to a justification of our own practice? It is a satisfaction that so many facts and arguments are before the public which show the inefficacy of the punishment of death in this country; and this is one reason why they are not introduced here. "There are no practical despisers of death like those who touch, and taste, and handle death daily, by daily committing capital offences. They make a jest of death in all its forms; and all its terrors are in their mouths a scorn."[1] "Profligate criminals, such as common thieves and highwaymen," "have always been accustomed to look upon the gibbet as a lot very likely to fall to them. When it does fall to them, therefore, they consider themselves only as not quite so lucky as *some* of their companions, and submit to their fortune without any other uneasiness than what may arise from the fear of death—a fear which even, by such worthless wretches, we frequently see can be so easily and so very completely conquered." A man some time ago was executed for uttering forged bank-notes, and the body was delivered to his friends. What was the effect of the example upon them? Why, with the corpse lying on a bed before them, they were themselves seized in the act of again *uttering forged bank-notes*. The testimony upon a subject like this, of a person who has had probably greater and better opportunities of ascertaining the practical efficiency of punishments than any other individual in Europe, is of great importance. "Capital convicts," says Elizabeth Fry, "pacify their conscience with the dangerous and most fallacious notion, that the violent death which awaits them will serve as a full atonement for all their sins."[2] It is their passport to felicity—the purchase-money of heaven! Of this deplorable notion the effect is doubly bad. First, it makes them comparatively *little afraid* of death, because they necessarily regard it as so much less an evil; and, secondly, it encourages them to go on in the commission of crimes, because they imagine that the number or enormity of them, however great, will not preclude them from admission into heaven. Of both these mischiefs, the punishment of death is the immediate source. Substitute another punishment, and they will not think that *that* is an "atonement for their sins," and will not receive their present encouragement to continue their crimes. But with respect to *example*, this unexceptional authority speaks in decided language. "The terror of example *is very generally rendered abortive* by the predestinarian notion, vulgarly prevalent among thieves, that 'if they are to be hanged they are to be hanged, and nothing can prevent it.'"[1] It may be said that the same notion might be attached to any other punishment, and that thus that other would become abortive; but there is little reason to expect this, at least in the same degree. The notion is now connected expressly with *hanging*, and it is not probable that the same notion would ever be transferred with equal power to another penalty. Where then is the overwhelming evidence of utility, which alone, even in the estimate of expediency, can justify the punishment of death? It cannot be adduced; it does not exist.

18. But if capital punishments do little good, they do much harm. "The frequent public destruction of life has a fearfully hardening effect upon those whom it is intended to intimidate. While it excites in them the spirit of revenge, it seldom fails to lower their estimate of the life of man, and renders them less afraid of taking it away in their turn by acts of personal violence."[2] This is just what a consideration of the principles of the human mind would teach us to expect. To familiarise men with the destruction of life, is to teach them not to abhor that destruction. It is the legitimate process of the mind in other things. He who blushes and trembles the first time he utters a lie, learns by repetition to do it with callous indifference. Now you execute a man in order to do good by the spectacle—while the practical consequence, it appears, is, that bad men turn away from the spectacle more prepared to commit violence than before. It will be said that this effect is produced only upon those who are already profligate, and that a salutary example is held out to the public. But the answer is at hand—The public do not usually begin with capital crimes. These are committed *after* the person has become depraved —that is, after he has arrived at that state in which an execution will harden rather than deter him. We "lower their estimate of the life of man." It cannot be doubted. It is the inevitable tendency of executions. There is much of justice in an observation of Beccaria's. "Is it not absurd that the laws which detect and punish homicide should, in order to prevent murder, publicly commit murder themselves?"[3] By the procedures of a court, we virtually and perhaps literally expatiate upon the sacredness of human life, upon the dreadful guilt of taking it away—and then forthwith take it away ourselves! It is no subject of wonder that this "lowers the estimate of the life of man."

---

[1] Irving's Orations.
[2] Observations on the Visiting, &c., of Female Prisoners, p. 73.

[1] Observations on the Visiting, &c., of Female Prisoners, p. 73.
[2] Ibid.
[3] Essay on Capital Punishments, c. 28.

The next sentence of the writer upon whose testimony I offer these comments, is of tremendous import:—"There is much reason to believe that our public executions have had *a direct and positive tendency to promote* both *murder and suicide.*" "Why, if a considerable time elapse between the trial and the execution, do we find the severity of the public changed into compassion? For the same reason that a master, if he do not beat his slave in the moment of resentment, often feels a repugnance to the beating him at all."[1] This is remarkable. If executions were put off for a twelvemonth, I doubt whether the public would bear them. But why if they were just and right? Respecting "the contempt and indignation with which every one looks on an executioner," Beccaria says the reason is, "that in a secret corner of the mind, in which the original impressions of nature are still preserved, men discover a sentiment which tells them that their lives are not lawfully in the power of any one."[2] Let him who has the power of influencing the legislature of the country or public opinion (and who has not?) consider the responsibility which this declaration implies, if he lifts his voice for the punishment of death!

19. But further: the execution of one offender excites in others "the spirit of revenge." This is extremely natural. Many a soldier, I dare say, has felt impelled to revenge the death of his comrades; and the member of a gang of thieves, who has fewer restraints of principle, is likely to feel it too. But upon whom is his revenge inflicted? Upon the legislature, or the jury, or the witnesses? No, but upon the public upon the first person whose life is in their power, and which they are prompted to take away. You execute a man, then, in order to save the lives of others; and the effect is, that you add new inducements to take the lives of others away.

20. Of a system which is thus unsound—unsound because it rejects some of the plainest dictates of the Moral Law—and unsound because so many of its effects are bad, I should be ready to conclude, with no other evidence, that it was utterly inexpedient and impolitic—that as it was bad in morals, it was bad in policy. And such appears to be the fact.—"It is *incontrovertibly proved* that punishments of a milder and less injurious nature are calculated to produce, for every good purpose, *a far more powerful effect.*"[3]

[1] Godwin: Enq. Pol. Just., v. 2, p. 726.
[2] Beccaria: Essay on Capital Punishments, chap. 28.
[3] Observations on the Visiting, &c., of Female Prisoners, p. 75.

21. Finally.—"The best of substitutes for capital punishment will be found in that judicious management of criminals in prison which it is the object of the present tract to recommend;"[1] which management is *Christian* management—a system in which reformation is made the first object, but in which it is found that in order to effect reformation *severity* to hardened offenders is needful. Thus then we arrive at the goal: —we begin with urging the system that Christianity dictates as *right;* we conclude by discovering that, as it is the right system, so it is practically the *best.*

22. But an argument in favour of capital punishments has been raised from the Christian Scriptures themselves.—"If I be an offender, or have committed anything worthy of death, I refuse not to die."[2] This is the language of an innocent person who was persecuted by malicious enemies. It was an assertion of innocence; an assertion that he had done nothing worthy of death. The case had no reference to the question of the lawfulness of capital punishment, but to the question of the lawfulness of inflicting it *upon him.* Nor can it be supposed that it was the design of the speaker to convey any sanction of the punishment itself, because the design would have been wholly foreign to the occasion. The argument of Grotius goes perhaps too far for his own purpose. "*If I be an offender,* or have done anything worthy of death, I refuse not to die." He refused not to die, then, *if he were an offender,* if he had done one of the "many and grievous things" which the Jews charged upon him. But will it be contended that he meant to sanction the destruction of every person who was thus "an offender"? His enemies were endeavouring to take his life, and he, in earnest asseveration of his innocence, says, If you can fix your charges upon me, take it.

23. Grotius adduces, as an additional evidence of the sanction of the punishment by Christianity, this passage, "Servants, be subject to your masters with all fear, &c. —What glory is it, if, when ye be buffeted for your faults, ye shall take it patiently? but if, when ye do well, and suffer for it, ye take it patiently, this is acceptable with God."[3] Some arguments disprove the doctrine which they are advanced to support, and this surely is one of them. It surely cannot be true that Christianity sanctions capital punishments, if this is the best evidence of the sanction that can be found.[4]

[1] Observations on the Visiting, &c., of Female Prisoners, p. 76.
[2] Acts xxv. 11; see Grotius: Rights of War and Peace.
[3] 1 Pet. ii. 18, 20.
[4] "Wickliffe," says Priestley, "seems to have thought it wrong to take away the life of man on any account."

24. Some persons, again, suppose that there is a sort of moral obligation to take the life of a murderer: "Whoso sheddeth man's blood, by man shall his blood be shed." This supposition is an example of that want of advertence to the supremacy of the *Christian* morality, which in the first Essay we had occasion to notice. Our law is the Christian law, and if Christianity by its precepts or spirit prohibits the punishment of death, it cannot be made right to Christians by referring to a commandment which was given to Noah. There is, in truth, some inconsistency in the reasonings of those who urge the passage. The fourth, fifth, and sixth verses of Genesis ix. each contains a law delivered to Noah. Of these three laws we habitually disregard two: how then can we with reason insist on the *authority* of the third?[1]

25. After all, if the command were in full force, it would not justify *our* laws; for they shed the blood of many who have not shed blood themselves.

26. And this conducts us to the observation, that the grounds upon which the United States of America still affix death to murder of the first degree, do not appear very clear; for if other punishments are found effectual in deterring from crimes of all degrees of enormity up to the last, how is it shown that they would not be effectual in the last also? There is nothing in the constitution of the human mind to indicate, that a murderer is influenced by passions which require that the counteracting power should be totally different from that which is employed to restrain every other crime. The difference too in the personal guilt of the perpetrators of some other crimes, and of murder, is sometimes extremely small. At any rate, it is not so great as to imply a necessity for a punishment totally dissimilar. The truth appears to be, that men entertain a sort of indistinct notion that murder is a crime which requires a peculiar punishment, which notion is often founded, not upon any process of investigation, by which the propriety of this peculiar punishment is discovered, but upon some vague ideas respecting the nature of the crime itself. But the dictate of *philosophy* is, to employ that punishment which will be most efficacious. Efficacy is the test of its propriety; and in estimating this efficacy, the character of the crime is a foreign consideration. Again, the dictate of *Christianity* is, to employ that punishment which, while it deters the spectator, reforms the man. Now, neither philosophy nor Christianity appears to be consulted in punishing murder with death. *because it is murder.* And it is worthy of especial remembrance, that the purpose for which Grotius defends the punishment of death is, that he may be able to defend the practice of war :—a bad foundation if this be its best!

27. It is one objection to capital punishment that it is absolutely irrevocable. If an innocent man suffers it is impossible to recall the sentence of the law. Not that this consideration alone is a sufficient argument against it, but it is one argument amongst the many. In a certain sense, indeed, all personal punishments are irrevocable. The man who by a mistaken verdict has been confined twelve months in a prison cannot be repossessed of the time. But if irrevocable punishments cannot be dispensed with, they should not be made needlessly common, and especially those should be regarded with jealousy which admit of no removal or relaxation in the event of subsequently discovered innocence, or subsequent reformation. It is not sufficiently considered that a jury or a court of justice never *know* that a prisoner is guilty.—A witness may know it who saw him commit the act, but others cannot know it who depend upon testimony, for testimony may be mistaken or false. All verdicts are founded upon probabilities—probabilities which, though they sometimes approach to certainty, never attain to it. Surely it is a serious thing for one man to destroy another upon grounds short of absolute certainty of his guilt. There is a sort of indecency attached to it—an assumption of a degree of authority which ought to be exercised only by Him whose knowledge is infallibly true. It is unhappily certain that some have been put to death for actions which they never committed. At one assizes, we believe, no less than six persons were hanged, of whom it was afterwards discovered that they were entirely innocent. A deplorable instance is given by Dr. Smollett :— " Rape and murder were perpetrated upon an unfortunate woman in the neighbourhood of London, and an innocent man suffered death for this complicated outrage, while the real criminals assisted at his execution, heard him appeal to Heaven for his innocence, and in the character of friends embraced him while he stood on the brink of eternity."[1] Others equally innocent, but whose innocence has never been made known, have doubtless shared the same fate. These are tremendous considerations, and ought to make men solemnly pause before, upon grounds necessarily uncertain, they take away that life which God has given, and which they cannot restore.

[1] Indeed it would almost appear from Genesis ix. 5, that even accidental homicide was thus to be punished with death; and if so, it is wholly disregarded in our present practice.

[1] Hist. of Eng., v. 3, p. 318.

28. Of the merely philosophical speculations respecting the rectitude of capital punishments, whether affirmative or negative, I would say little; for they in truth deserve little. One advantage indeed attends a brief review—that the reader will perceive how little the speculations of philosophers will aid us in the investigation of a Christian question.

29. The philosopher, however, would prove what the Christian cannot, and Mably accordingly says, " In the state of nature, I have a right to take the life of him who lifts his arm against mine. *This right, upon entering into society, I surrender to the magistrate.*" If we conceded the truth of the first position (which we do not), the conclusion from it is an idle sophism; for it is obviously preposterous to say, that because I have a right to take the life of a man who will kill me if I do not kill him, the state, which is in no such danger, has a right to do the same. That danger which constitutes the alleged right in the individual, does not exist in the case of the state. The foundation of the right is gone, and where can be the right itself? Having, however, been thus told that the state has a right to kill, we are next informed, by Filangieri, that the criminal has no right to live. He says, " If I have a right to kill another man, *he has lost his right to life.*"[1] Rousseau goes a little further. He tells us, that in consequence of the "social contract" which we make with the sovereign on entering into society, " Life is a conditional grant of the state:"[2] so that we hold our lives, it seems, only as " tenants at will," and must give them up whenever their owner, the state, requires them. The reader has probably hitherto thought that he retained his head by some other tenure.

30. The right of taking an offender's life being thus proved, Mably shows us how its exercise becomes expedient. " A murderer," says he, " in taking away his enemy's life, *believes he does him the greatest possible evil.* Death, then, in the murderer's estimation is the greatest of evils. *By the fear of death, therefore*, the excess of hatred and revenge must be restrained." If language wilder than this can be held, Rousseau, I think, holds it. He says, " The preservation of both sides (the criminal and the state) is incompatible ; one of the two must perish." How it happens that a nation " must perish," if a convict is not hanged, the reader, I suppose, will not know. Even philosophy, however, concedes as much : " *Absolute necessity alone*," says Pastoret, " can justify the punishment of death;" and Rousseau himself acknowledges that " we have no right to put to death, *even*

[1] Montagu on Punishment of Death.
[2] Contr. Soc., ii. 5, Montagu.

for the sake of example, any but those who cannot be permitted to live without danger." Beccaria limits the right to one specific case and in doing this he appears to sacrifice his own principle (deduced from that splendid fiction, the " social contract"), which is, that " the punishment of death is not authorised by any right :—no such right exists."

31. For myself, I perceive little value in such speculations to whatever conclusions they lead, for there are shorter and surer roads to truth; but it is satisfactory to find that, even upon the principles of such philosophers, the right to put criminals to death is not easily made out.

32. The argument, then, respecting the punishment of death, is both distinct and short.

It rejects, by its very nature, a regard to the first and greatest object of punishment.

It does not attain either of the other objects so well as they may be attained by other means.

It is attended with numerous evils peculiarly its own.

CHAPTER XIV.
Religious Establishments.

The primitive church—The established church of Ireland—America—Advantages and disadvantages of established churches—Alliance of a church with the state—An established church perpetuates its own evils—Persecution generally the growth of religious establishments—State religions injurious to the civil welfare of a people—Legal provision for Christian teachers—Voluntary payment—Advancement in the church—The appointment of religious teachers.

1. A large number of persons embark from Europe, and colonise an uninhabited territory in the South Sea. They erect a government—suppose a republic—and make all persons, of whatever creed, eligible to the legislature. The community prospers and increases. In process of time a member of the legislature, who is a disciple of John Wesley, persuades himself that it will tend to the promotion of religion that the preachers of Methodism should be supported by a national tax ; that their stipends should be sufficiently ample to prevent them from necessary attention to any business but that of religion ; and that accordingly they shall be precluded from the usual pursuits of commerce and from the professions. He proposes the measure. It is contended against by the Episcopalian members, and the Independents, and the Catholics, and the Unitarians — by all but the adherents to his own creed. They insist upon the equality of civil and religious rights, but in vain. The majority

prove to be Methodists; they support the measure: the law is enacted; and Methodism becomes, thenceforth, the religion of the state. This is a *Religious Establishment*.

2. But it is a religious establishment in its best form; and, perhaps, none ever existed of which the constitution was so simple and so pure. During one portion of the papal history, the Romish Church was indeed not so much an "establishment" of the state as a separate and independent constitution. For though some species of alliance subsisted, yet the Romanists did not acknowledge, as Protestants now do, that the power of *establishing* a religion resides in the state.

3. In the present day, other immunities are possessed by ecclesiastical establishments than those which are necessary to constitute the institution—such, for example, as that of exclusive eligibility to the legislature: and other alliances with the civil power exist than that which necessarily results from any preference of a particular faith—such as that of placing ecclesiastical patronage in the hands of a government, or of those who are under its influence. From these circumstances it happens, that in inquiring into the propriety of religious establishments, we cannot confine ourselves to the inquiry whether they would be proper in their simplest form, but whether they are proper as they usually exist. And this is so much the more needful, because there is little reason to expect that when once an ecclesiastical establishment has been erected—when once a particular church has been selected for the preference and patronage of the civil power—that preference and patronage will be confined to those circumstances which are necessary to the subsistence of an establishment at all.

4. It is sufficiently obvious that it matters nothing to the existence of an established church what the faith of that church is, or what is the form of its government. It is not the creed which constitutes the establishment, but the preference of the civil power: and accordingly the reader will be pleased to bear in mind, that neither in this chapter nor in the next have we any concern with religious opinions. Our business is not with churches, but with church *establishments*.

5. The actual history of religious establishments in Christian countries does not differ in essence from that which we have supposed in the South Sea. They have been erected by the influence or the assistance of the civil power. In one country a religion may have owed its political supremacy to the superstitions of a prince; and in another to his policy or ambition; but the effect has been similar. Whether superstition or policy, the contrivances of a priesthood, or the fortuitous predominance of a party, have given rise to the established church, is of comparatively little consequence to the fundamental principles of the institution.

6. Of the *divine right* of a particular church to supremacy I say nothing; because none with whom I am at present concerned to argue imagine that it exists.

7. The only ground upon which it appears that religious establishments can be advocated are, first, that of example or approbation in the primitive churches; and, secondly, that of public utility.

8. 1. The primitive church was not a religious establishment in any sense or in any degree. No establishment existed until the church had lost much of its purity. Nor is there any expression in the New Testament, direct or indirect, which would lead a reader to suppose that Christ or His apostles regarded an establishment as an eligible institution. "We find, in His religion, *no scheme of building up a hierarchy*, or *of ministering to the views of human governments*."—"Our religion, as it came out of the hands of its Founder and His apostles, exhibited *a complete abstraction from all views either of ecclesiastical or civil policy*."[1] The evidence which these facts supply respecting the moral character of religious establishments, whatever be its weight, tends manifestly to show that that character is not good. I do not say because Christianity exhibited this "complete abstraction," that it therefore necessarily *condemned* establishments; but I say that the bearing and the tendency of this negative testimony is against them.

9. In the discourses and writings of the first teachers of our religion, we find such absolute disinterestedness, so little disposition to assume political superiority, that to have become the members of an *established* church would certainly have been inconsistent *in them*. It is indeed almost inconceivable that they could ever have desired the patronage of the state for themselves or for their converts. No man conceives that Paul or John could have participated in the exclusion of any portion of the Christian church from advantages which they themselves enjoyed. Every man perceives that to have done this, would have been to assume a new character, a character which they had never exhibited before, and which was incongruous with their former principles and motives of action. But why is this incongruous with the apostolic character

[1] Paley: Evidences of Christianity, p. 2, c. 2.

unless it is incongruous with Christianity? Upon this single ground, therefore, there is reason for the sentiment of "many well-informed persons, that it seems extremely questionable whether the religion of Jesus Christ *admits* of any civil establishment at all."[1]

10. I lay stress upon these considerations. We all know that much may be learnt respecting human duty by a contemplation of the spirit and temper of Christianity as it was exhibited by its first teachers. When the spirit and temper is compared with the essential character of religious establishments, they are found to be incongruous—foreign to one another—having no natural relationship or similarity. I should regard such facts, in reference to any question of rectitude, as of great importance; but upon a subject so intimately connected with religion itself, the importance is peculiarly great.

11. II. The question of the *utility* of religious establishments is to be decided by a comparison of their advantages and their evils.

12. Of their advantages, the first and greatest appears to be that they provide, or are assumed to provide, religious instruction for the whole community. If this instruction be left by the state to be cared for by each Christian church as it possesses the zeal or the means, it may be supposed that many districts will be destitute of any public religious instruction. At least the state cannot be assured beforehand that every district will be supplied. And when it is considered how great is the importance of regular public worship to the virtue of a people, it is not to be denied, that a scheme which, by destroying an establishment, would make that instruction inadequate or uncertain, is so far to be regarded as of questionable expediency. But the effect which would be produced by dispensing with establishments is to be estimated, so far as is in our power, by facts. Now dissenters are in the situation of separate unestablished churches. If they do not provide for the public officers of religion voluntarily, they will not be provided for. Yet where is any considerable body of dissenters to be found who do not provide themselves with a chapel and a preacher? And if those churches which are not *established*, do in fact provide public instruction, how is it shown that it would not be provided although there were no established religion in a state? Besides, the dissenters from an established church provide this under peculiar disadvantages: for after paying, in common with others, their quota to the state religion, they have to pay in addition to their own. But perhaps it will be said that dissenters from a state religion are actuated by a zeal with which the professors of that religion are not; and that the legal provision supplies the deficiency of zeal. If this be said, the inquiry imposes itself How does this disproportion of zeal arise? Why should dissenters be more zealous than churchmen? What account can be given of the matter, but that there is something in the patronage of the state which induces apathy upon the church that it prefers? One other account may indeed be offered—that to be a dissenter is to be a positive religionist, whilst to be a churchman is frequently only to be nothing else; that an establishment embraces all who are not embraced by others; and that if those whom other churches do not include were not cared for by the state religion, they would not be cared for at all. This is an argument of apparent weight, but the effect of reasoning is to diminish that weight. For what is meant by "including," by "caring for," the indifferent and irreligious? An established church only *offers* them instruction; it does not "compel them to come in," and we have just seen that this offer is made by unestablished churches also. Who doubts whether in a district that is sufficient to fill a temple of the state religion, there would be found persons to offer a temple of public worship though the state did not compel it? Who doubts whether this would be the case if the district were inhabited by dissenters? and if it would not be done supposing the inhabitants to belong to the state religion, the conclusion is inevitable, that there is a tendency to indifference resulting from the patronage of the state.

13. Let us listen to the testimony of Archbishop Newcome. He speaks of Ireland, and says, " Great numbers of country parishes are *without churches*, notwithstanding the largeness and frequency of parliamentary grants for building them;" but meeting houses and Romish chapels, which *are built and repaired with greater zeal*, are in *sufficient numbers* about the country."[1] This is remarkable testimony indeed. That church which is patronised and largely assisted by the state, does not provide places for public worship : those churches which are not patronised and not assisted by the state, do provide them, and provide them in "sufficient numbers" and "with greater zeal." What then becomes of the argument, that a church establishment is necessary in order to provide

---

[1] Simpson's Plea for Religion and the Sacred Writings.

[1] See Gisborne's Duties of Men.

instruction which would not otherwise be provided?

14. Yet here one point must be conceded. It does not follow because one particular state religion is thus deficient, that none would be more exemplary. The fault may not be so much in religious establishments *as such*, as in that particular establishment which obtains in the instance before us.

15. Kindred to the testimony of the Irish primate is the more cautious language of the Archdeacon of Carlisle :—" I do not know," says he, " that it is in any degree true that the influence of religion is the greatest where there are the fewest dissenters." [1] This, I suppose, may lawfully be interpreted into positive language--that the influence of religion *is* the greatest where there are numerous dissenters. But if numerous adherents to unestablished churches be favourable to religion, it would appear that although there were *none* but unestablished churches in a country, the influence of religion would be kept up. If established churches are practically useful to religion, what more reasonable than to expect that where they possessed the more exclusive operation, their utility would be the greatest? Yet the contrary, it appears, is the fact. It may indeed be urged that it is the existence of a state religion which animates the zeal of the other churches, and that in this manner the state religion does good. To which it is a sufficient answer, that the benefit, if it is thus occasioned, is collateral and accidental, and offers no testimony in favour of establishments as such ; —and this is our concern. Besides, there are many sects to animate the zeal of one another, even though none were patronised by the state.

16. To estimate the relative influence of religion in two countries is no easy task. Yet, I believe, if we compare its influence in the United States with that which it possesses in most of the European countries which possess state religions, it will be found that the balance is in favour of the community in which there is no established church : at any rate, the balance is not so much against it as to afford any evidence in favour of a state religion. A traveller in America has remarked, " There is more religion in the United States than in England, and more in England than in Italy. The closer the monopoly, the less abundant the supply." [2] Another traveller writes almost as if he had anticipated the present disquisition—" It has been often said, that the disinclination of the heart to religious truth, renders a state establishment absolutely necessary for the purpose of Christianising the country. Ireland and America can furnish abundant evidence of the fallacy of such an hypothesis. In the one country we see an ecclesiastical establishment of the most costly description utterly inoperative in dispelling ignorance or refuting error ; in the other no establishment of any kind, and yet religion making daily and hourly progress, promoting inquiry, diffusing knowledge, strengthening the weak, and mollifying the hardened." [1]

17. In immediate connection with this subject is the argument that Dr. Paley places at the head of those which he advances in favour of religious establishments—that *the knowledge and profession of Christianity cannot be upholden without a clergy supported by legal provision, and belonging to one sect of Christians.* [2] *The justness of this proposition is founded upon the necessity of research.* It is said that " Christianity is an historical religion," and that the truth of its history must be investigated ; that in order to vindicate its authority and to ascertain its truths, leisure and education and learning are indispensable - so that such " an order of clergy is necessary to perpetuate the evidences of revelation, and to interpret the obscurity of those ancient writings in which the religion is contained." To all this there is one plain objection, that when once the evidences of religion are adduced and made public, when once the obscurity of the ancient writings is interpreted, the work, so far as discovery is concerned, is done ; and it can hardly be imagined that an established clergy is necessary in perpetuity to do that which in its own nature can be done but once. Whatever may have been the validity of this argument in other times, when few but the clergy possessed any learning, or when the evidences of religion had not been sought out, it possesses little validity now. These evidences are brought before the world in a form so clear and accessible to literary and good men, that, in the present state of society, there is little reason to fear they will be lost for want of an established church. Nor is it to be forgotten that, with respect to our own country, the best defences of Christianity which exist in the language, have not been the work either of the established clergy or of members of the established church. The expression, that such " an order of clergy is necessary to *perpetuate* the evidences of revelation," appears to contain an illusion. Evidences can in no other sense be perpetuated than by being again and again brought before the public. If this be the meaning, it belongs rather to the teaching of religious truths than to their discovery ; but it is upon the *discovery*, it is upon the opportunity of *research*, that the

---

[1] Paley : Evidences of Christianity. [2] Hall.

[1] Duncan's Travels in America.
[2] See Mor. and Pol. Phil., b. 6, c. 10.

argument is founded; and it is particularly to be noticed, that this is the primary argument which Paley adduces in deciding "the first and most fundamental question upon the subject."

18. It pleases Providence to employ human agency in the vindication and diffusion of His truth; but to employ the expression, "the knowledge and profession of Christianity" cannot be upholden without an established clergy, approaches to irreverence. Even a rejector of Christianity says, "If public worship be conformable to reason, reason without doubt will prove adequate to its vindication and support. If it be from God it is profanation to imagine that it stands in need of the alliance of the state."[1] And it is clearly untrue in fact; because, without such a clergy, it is actually upheld, and because, during the three first centuries, the religion subsisted and spread and prospered without any encouragement from the state. And it is remarkable, too, that the diffusion of Christianity in our own times in pagan nations, is effected less by the clergy of *established* churches than by others.[2]

19. Such are amongst the principal of the direct advantages of religious establishments as they are urged by those who advocate them. Some others will be noticed in inquiring into the opposite question of their disadvantages.

20. These disadvantages respect either the institution itself—or religion generally—or the civil welfare of a people.

21. I. The institution itself. "The single end we ought to propose by religious establishments is, the preservation and communication of religious knowledge. Every other idea, and every other end, that has been mixed with this, as the making of the church an engine, or even an ally, of the state; converting it into the means of strengthening or diffusing influence; or regarding it as a support of regal, in opposition to popular forms of government; *has served only to debase the institution, and to introduce into it numerous corruptions and abuses.*"[3] This is undoubtedly true. Now, we affirm that this "debasement of the institution," this "introduction of numerous corruptions and abuses," is *absolutely inseparable* from religious establishments as they ordinarily exist; that wherever and whenever a state so prefers and patronises a particular church, these debasements and abuses and corruptions will inevitably arise.

22. "An engine or ally of the state." How will you frame—I will not say *any* religious establishment, but—any religious establishment that approaches to the ordinary character, without making it an engine or ally of the state? Alliance is involved in the very idea of the institution. The state selects, and prefers, and grants privileges to, a particular church. The continuance of these privileges depends upon the continuance of the state in its present principles. If the state is altered, the privileges are endangered or may be swept away. The privileged church, therefore, is interested in supporting the state, in standing by it against opposition; or, which is the same thing, that church becomes an *ally* of the state. You cannot separate the effect from the cause. Wherever the state prefers and patronises one church, there will be an *alliance* between the state and that church. There may be variations in the strength of this alliance. The less the patronage of the state, the less strong the alliance will be. Or there may be emergencies in which the alliance is suspended by the influence of stronger interests; but still the alliance, as a general consequence of the preference of the state, will inevitably subsist. When, therefore, Dr. Paley says, that to make an establishment an ally of the state is to introduce into it numerous corruptions and abuses, he in fact says, that to make an establishment *at all* is to introduce into a church numerous corruptions and abuses.

23. It matters nothing what the doctrines or constitution of the church may be. The only point is, the alliance, and its degree. It may be Episcopal, or Presbyterian, or Independent; but wherever the degree of alliance—that is, of preference and patronage—is great, there the abuses and corruptions will be great. In this country during a part of the seventeenth century, Independency became, in effect, the established church. It became of course an ally of the state; and fought from its pulpits the battles of the state. Nor will any one, I suppose, deny that this alliance made Independency worse than it was before,—that it "introduced into it corruptions and abuses."

24. The less strict the alliance, the fewer the corruptions that spring from an alliance. One state may impose a test to distinguish the ministers of the preferred church, and leave the selection to the church itself: another may actually appoint some or all of the ministers. These differences in the closeness of the alliance will produce differences in the degree of corruption; but alli-

---

[1] Godwin's Pol. Just., 2, 608.
[2] In the preceding discussion, I have left out all reference to the proper qualification or appointment of Christian ministers, and have assumed (but without conceding) that the magistrate is at liberty to adjust those matters if he pleases.
[3] Paley: Mor. and Pol. Phil., b. 6. c. 10.

ance and corruption in both cases there will be. He who receives a legal provision from the minister of the day, will lend his support to the minister of the day. He who receives it by the operation of a general law, will lend his support to that political system which is likely to perpetuate that law.

25. "The means of strengthening or diffusing influence." This abuse of religious establishments is presupposed in the question of alliance. It is by the means of influence that the alliance is produced. There may be and there are gradations in the directness or flagrancy of the exercise of influence, but influence of some kind is inseparable from the selection and preference of a particular church.

26. "A support of regal in opposition to popular forms of government." This attendant upon religious establishments is accidental. An establishment will support that form, whatever it be, by which it is itself supported. In one country it may be the ally of republicanism, in another of aristocracy, and in another of monarchy; but in all it will be the ally of its own patron. The establishment of France supported the despotism of the Louises. The establishment of Spain supports at this hour the pitiable policy of Ferdinand. So accurately is alliance maintained, that in a mixed government it will be found that an establishment adheres to *that* branch of the government by which its own pre-eminence is most supported. In England the strictest alliance is between the church and the executive; and accordingly, in ruptures between the executive and legislative powers, the establishment has adhered to the former. There was an exception in the reign of James II.: but it was an exception which confirms the rule; for the establishment then found or feared that its alliance with the regal power *was about to be broken.*

27. Seeing, then, that the debasement of a Christian church—that the introduction into it of corruptions and abuses, is inseparable from religious establishments, what is this debasement and what are these abuses and corruptions?

28. Now, without entering into minute inquiry, many evils arise obviously from the nature of the case. Here is an introduction, into the office of the Christian ministry, of motives, and interests, and aims, foreign to the proper business of the office; and not only foreign but incongruous and discordant with it. Here are secular interests mixed up with the motives of religion. Here are temptations to assume the ministerial function in the church that is *established,* for the sake of its secular advantages.

Here are inducements, when the function is assumed, to accommodate the manner of its exercise to the inclinations of the state: to suppress, for example, some religious principles which the civil power does not wish to see inculcated; to insist for the same reason with undue emphasis upon others; in a word, to adjust the religious conduct so as to strengthen or perpetuate the alliance with the state. It is very easy to perceive that these temptations will and must frequently prevail: and wherever they do prevail, there the excellence and dignity of the Christian ministry are diminished, are depressed; there Christianity is not exemplified in its purity: there it is shorn of a portion of its beams. The extent of the evil will depend of course upon the vigour of the cause; that is to say, the evil will be proportionate to the alliance. If a religious establishment were erected in which the executive power of the country appointed all its ministers, there would, I doubt not, ensue an almost universal corruption of the ministry. As an establishment recedes in its constitution from this closeness of alliance, a corresponding increase of purity may be expected.

29. During the Reformation, and in Queen Elizabeth's time, "of nine thousand four hundred beneficed clergy" (adherents to Papacy), "only one hundred and seventy-seven resigned their preferment rather than acknowledge the Queen's supremacy,"[1] yet the Pope to them was head of the church. One particular manner in which the establishment of a church injures the character of the church itself is, by the temptation which it holds out to equivocation or hypocrisy. It is necessary to the preference of the teachers of a particular sect, that there should be some means of discovering who belong to that sect:—there must be some test. Before the man who is desirous of undertaking the ministerial office, there are placed two roads, one of which conducts to those privileges which a state religion enjoys, and the other does not. The latter may be entered by all who will: the former by those only who affirm their belief of the rectitude of some church forms or of some points of theology. It requires no argument to prove that this is to *tempt* men to affirm that which they do not believe: that it is to say to the man who does not believe the stipulated points, Here is money for you if you will violate your conscience. By some the invitation will be accepted;[2] and what is the result? Why that, just as they are going

---

[1] Southey: Book of the Church, Sir Thomas More.
[2] "Chillingworth declared in a letter to Dr. Sheldon, that if he subscribed he subscribed his own damnation, and yet in no long space of time, he actually did subscribe to the Articles of the Church again and again."—Simpson's Plea.

publicly to insist upon the purity and sanctity of the Moral Law, they violate that law themselves. The injury which is thus done to a Christian church by *establishing* it, is negative as well as positive. You not only tempt some men to equivocation or hypocrisy, but exclude from the office others of sounder integrity. Two persons, both of whom do not assent to the prescribed points, are desirous of entering the church. One is upright and conscientious, the other subservient and unscrupulous. An establishment excludes the good man and admits the bad. "Though some purposes of order and tranquillity may be answered by the establishment of creeds and confessions, yet they are at all times attended with serious inconveniences: they check inquiry; they violate liberty; they ensnare the consciences of the clergy, by holding out temptations to prevarication."[1]

30. And with respect to the habitual accommodation of the exercise of the ministry to the desires of the state, it is manifest that an enlightened and faithful minister may frequently find himself restrained by a species of political leading-strings. He has not the full command of his intellectual and religious attainments. He may not perhaps communicate the whole counsel of God.[2] It was formerly *conceded* to the English clergy that they might preach against the horrors and impolicy of war, *provided* they were not chaplains to regiments or in the navy. *Conceded!* Then if the state had pleased, it might have withheld the concession; and accordingly from some the state did withhold it. They were prohibited to preach against that against which apostles wrote! What would these apostles have said if a state had bidden them keep silence respecting the most unchristian custom in the world? They would have said, Whether we ought to obey God rather than man, judge ye. What would they have *done?* They would have gone away and preached against it as before. One question more should be asked—What would they have said to an alliance which thus brought the Christian minister under bondage to the state?

31. The next point of view in which a religious establishment is injurious to the church itself is, that it perpetuates any evils which happen to exist in it. The reason is this: the preference which a state gives to a particular church is given to it *as it is.* If the church makes alterations in its constitution, its discipline, or its forms, it cannot tell whether the state would continue to prefer and to patronise it. Besides, if alterations are begun, its members do not know whether the alacrity of some other church might not take advantage of the loosening alliance with the state, to supplant it. In short, they do not know what would be the consequences of amendments, nor where they would end. Conscious that the church *as it is* possesses the supremacy, they think it more prudent to retain that supremacy with existing evils, than to endanger it by attempting to reform them. Thus it is that whilst *unestablished* churches alter their discipline or constitution as need appears to require, established churches remain century after century the same.[1] Not to be free to alter, can only *then* be right when the church is at present as perfect as it can be; and no one perhaps will gravely say that there is any established church on the globe which needs no amendment. Dr. Hartley devoted a portion of his celebrated work to a discussion of the probability that all the existing church establishments in the world would be dissolved; and he founds this probability expressly upon the ground that they need so much reformation.

32. "In all exclusive establishments, where temporal emoluments are annexed to the profession of a certain system of doctrines, and the usage of a certain routine of forms, and appropriated to an order of men so and so qualified, that order of men will naturally think themselves *interested* that things should continue as they are. A reformation might endanger their emoluments."[2] This is the testimony of a dignitary of one of these establishments. And the fact being admitted, what is the amount of the evil which it involves? Let another dignitary reply: "He who, by a diligent and faithful examination of the original records, dismisses from the system *one article* which contradicts the apprehension, the experience, or the reasoning of mankind, does more towards recommending the belief, and with the belief the influence of Christianity, to the understandings and consciences of serious inquirers, and through them to universal reception and authority, than can be effected by a thousand contenders for creeds and ordinances of human establishments." If the benefits of dismissing such an article are so great, what must be the evil of continuing it? If the benefit of dismissing *one* such article be so great, what must be the evil of an established system which tends habitually and constantly to retain *many* of them? Yet these "articles, which thus contradict

[1] Paley: Mor. and Pol. Phil., b. 6, c. 10.
[2] "Honest and disinterested boldness in the path of duty is one of the first requisites of a minister of the gospel." —Gisborne. But how shall they be thus *disinterested?*—Mem. in the MS.

[1] It was not to religious establishments that Protestants were indebted for the first efforts of reformation. They have uniformly resisted reformation.—Mem. in the MS.
[2] Archdeacon Blackburn's Confessional: Pref.

the reasoning of mankind," are actually retained by established churches. "Creeds and confessions," says Dr. Paley, "however they may express the persuasion, or be accommodated to the controversies or to the fears of the age in which they are composed, in process of time, and by reason of the changes which are wont to take place in the judgment of mankind upon religious subjects, they come at length to *contradict the actual opinions* of the church whose doctrines they profess to contain."[1] It is then *confessed* by the members of an established church that religious establishments powerfully obstruct the belief, the influence, the universal reception and authority of Christianity. Great, indeed, must be the counter advantages of these establishments if they counterbalance *this* portion of its evils.

33. II. This last paragraph anticipates the second class of disadvantages attendant upon religious establishments : *their ill effects upon religion generally*. It is indisputable, that much of the irreligion of the world has resulted from those things which have been mixed up with Christianity, and placed before mankind as parts of religion. In some countries, the mixture has been so flagrant that the majority of the thinking part of the population have almost rejected religion altogether. So it was, and so it may be feared it still is, in France. The intellectual part of her people rejected religion, not because they had examined Christianity and were convinced that it was a fiction, but because they had examined what was proposed to them as Christianity and found it was absurd or false. So numerous were the "articles that contradicted the experience and judgment of mankind," that they concluded the whole was a fable, and rejected the whole.

34. Now that which the French church establishment did in an extreme degree, others do in a less degree. If the French church retained a hundred articles that contradicted the judgment of mankind, and thus made a nation of unbelievers, the church which retains ten or five such articles, *weakens* the general influence of religion although it may not destroy it.

35. Nor is it merely by unauthorised doctrinal articles or forms that the influence of religion is impaired, but by the general evils which affect the church itself. It is sufficiently manifest, that whatever tends to diminish the virtue, or to impeach the character, of the ministers of religion, must tend to diminish the influence of religion upon mankind. If the teacher is not good, we are not to expect goodness in the taught.

[1] Paley: Mor. and Pol. Phil., b. 6, c. 10.

If a man enters the church with impure or unworthy motives, he cannot do his duty when he is there. If he makes religion subservient to interest in his own practice, he cannot effectually teach others to make religion paramount to all. Men associate (they ought to do it less) the idea of religion with that of its teachers ; and their respect for one is frequently measured by their respect for the other. Now, that the effect of religious establishments has been to depress their teachers in the estimation of mankind, cannot be disputed. The effect is, in truth, inevitable. And it is manifest that whatever conveys disrespectful ideas of religion diminishes its influence upon the human mind. In brief, we have seen that to establish a religion is morally pernicious to its ministers ; and whatever is injurious to them diminishes the power of religion in the world.

36. Christianity is a religion of good-will and kind affections. Its essence, so far as the intercourse of society is concerned, is Love. Whatever diminishes good-will and kind affections amongst Christians, attacks the essence of Christianity. Now, religious establishments do this. They generate ill-will, heart-burnings, animosities- those very things which our religion deprecates more almost than any other. It is obvious that if a fourth or a third of a community think they are unreasonably excluded from privileges which the other parts enjoy, feelings of jealousy or envy are likely to be generated. If the minority are obliged to pay to the support of a religion they disapprove, these feelings are likely to be exacerbated. They soon become reciprocal ; attacks are made by one party and repelled by another, till there arises an habitual sense of unkindness or ill-will. I once met with rather a grotesque definition of religious dissent, but it illustrates our proposition :—"Dissenterism—that is, systematic opposition to the established religion." The deduction from the practical influence of religion upon the minds of men which this effect of religious establishments occasions, is great. The evil, I trust, is diminishing in the world ;[1] but then the diminution results, not from religious estab-

[1] "The placing all the religious sects (in America) upon an equal footing with respect to the government of the country has effectually secured the peace of the community, at the same time that it has essentially promoted the interests of truth and virtue."—Mem. Dr. Priestley, p. 175. Mem. in the MS.

Pennsylvania.—"Although there are so many sects and such a difference of religious opinions in this province, it is surprising the harmony which subsists among them ; they consider themselves as children of the same Father, and live like brethren because they have the liberty of thinking like men ; to this pleasing harmony, in a great measure, is to be attributed the rapid and flourishing state of Pennsylvania above all the other provinces."—Travels through the Interior Parts of North America, by an Officer. 1791. Lond. The officer was Thomas Anburey, who was taken prisoner by the Americans. Mem. in the MS.

lishments, but from that power of Christianity which prevails against these evils.

37. From these, and from other evidences of the injurious effects of religious establishments upon the religious condition of mankind, we shall perhaps be prepared to assent to the observations which follow: "The history of the last eighteen centuries does, indeed, afford, in various ways, a strong presumptive evidence, that the cause of true Christianity has very materially suffered in the world in consequence of the connection between the church and the state. It is probably in great measure the consequence of such an union that the church has assumed, in almost all Christian countries, so secular a character—that Christianity has become so lamentably mixed up with the spirit, maxims, motives, and politics of a vain and evil world. Had the union in question never been attempted, pure religion might probably have found a freer course; the practical effects of Christianity might have been more unmixed and more extensive; and it might have spread its influence in a much more efficient manner than is now the case, even over the laws and politics of kings and nations. Before its union with the state, our holy religion flourished with comparative incorruptness; afterwards it gradually declined in its purity and its power until all was nearly lost in darkness, superstition, and spiritual tyranny."[1] "Religion should remain distinct from the political constitution of a state. Intermingled with it, what purpose can it serve, except the baneful purpose of communicating and of receiving contamination?"[2]

38. III. Then as to the effect of religious establishments upon the civil welfare of a state—we know that the connection between religious and civil welfare is intimate and great. Whatever therefore diminishes the influence of religion upon a people, diminishes their general welfare. In addition, however, to this general consideration, there are some particular modes of the injurious effect of religious establishments which it may be proper to notice.

39. And, first, religious establishments are incompatible with complete religious liberty. This consideration we requested the reader to bear in mind when the question of religious liberty was discussed.[3] "If an establishment be right, religious liberty is not; and if religious liberty be right, an establishment is not." Whatever arguments therefore exist to prove the rectitude of complete religious liberty, they prove at the same time the

[1] J. J. Gurney; Peculiarities, c. 7.
[2] Charles James Fox; Fell's Life.
[3] Essay 3, c. 4.

wrongness of religious establishments. Nor is this all; for it is the manifest tendency of these establishments to withhold an increase of religious liberty, even when on other grounds it would be granted. The secular interests of the state religion are set in array against an increase of liberty. If the established church allows other churches to approach more nearly to an equality with itself, its own relative eminence is diminished; and i by any means the state religion adds to its own privileges, it is by deducting from the privileges of the rest. The state religion is, besides, afraid to dismiss any part even of its confessedly useless privileges, lest, when an alteration is begun, it should not easily be stopped. And there is no reason to doubt that it is temporal rather than religious considerations—interest rather than Christianity—which now occasions restrictions and disabilities and tests.

40. In conformity with these views, persecution has generally been the work of religious establishments. Indeed, some alliance or some countenance at least from the state is necessary to a systematic persecution. Popular outrage may persecute men on account of their religion, as it often has done; but fixed stated persecutions have perhaps always been the work of the religion of the state. It was the state religion of Rome that persecuted the first Christians.—"Who was it that crucified the Saviour of the world for attempting to reform the religion of His country? The Jewish priesthood. Who was it that drowned the altars of their idols with the blood of Christians for attempting to abolish Paganism? The Pagan priesthood. Who was it that persecuted to flames and death those who, in the time of Wickliffe and his followers, laboured to reform the errors of Popery? The Popish priesthood. Who was it, and who is it that, both in England and in Ireland since the Reformation but I check my hand, being unwilling to reflect upon the dead, or to exasperate, the living."[1] We also are unwilling to reflect upon or to exasperate, but our business is with plain truth. Who, then, was it that since the Reformation has persecuted dissentients from its creed, and who is it that at this hour thinks and speaks of them with unchristian antipathy? *The English Priesthood.* Not to mention that it was the state religion of Judea that put our Saviour Himself to death. It was, and it is, the state religion in some European countries that now persecutes dissenters from its creed. It was the state religion in this country that persecuted the Protestants; and since Protestantism has been established, it is the state religion which has persecuted Protestant

[1] Miscellaneous Tracts, by Richard Watson, D.D., Bishop of Llandaff, v. 2.

dissenters. Is this the fault principally of the faith of these churches, or of their alliance with the state? No man can be in doubt for an answer.

41. We are accustomed to attribute too much to bigotry. Bigotry has been very great and very operative; but bigotry alone would not have produced the disgraceful and dreadful transactions which fill the records of ecclesiastical history. Men have often been actuated by the love of supremacy or of money, whilst they were talking loudly of the sacredness of their faith. They have been less afraid for religion than for the dominance of a church. When the creed of that church was impugned, those who shared in its advantages were zealous to suppress the rising inquiry; because the discredit of the creed might endanger the loss of the advantages. The zeal of a Pope for the real presence was often quite a fiction. He and his cardinals cared perhaps nothing for the real presence, as they sometimes cared nothing for morality. But men might be immoral without encroaching upon the Papal power—they could not deny the doctrine without endangering its overthrow.

42. Happily, persecution for religion is greatly diminished; yet, whilst we rejoice in the fact, we cannot conceal from ourselves the consideration, that the diminution of persecution has resulted rather from the general diffusion of better principles than from the operation of religious establishments as such.

43. In most or in all ages, a great portion of the flagitious transactions which furnish materials for the ecclesiastical historian, have resulted from the political connections or interests of a church. It was not the interests of Christianity but of an establishment, which made Becket embroil his king and other sovereigns in distractions. It was not the interests of Christianity but of an establishment, which occasioned the monstrous impositions and usurpations of the Papal see. And I do not know whether there has ever been a religious war of which religion was the only or the principal cause. Besides all this, there has been an inextricable succession of intrigues and cabals—of conflicting interests—and clamour and distraction, which the world would have been spared if secular interests had not been brought into connection with religion.

44. Another mode in which religious establishments are injurious to the civil welfare of a people, is by their tendency to resist political improvements. That same cause which induces state religions to maintain themselves *as they are*, induces them to maintain the patron state *as it is*. It is the state in its present condition, that secures to the church its advantages; and the church does not know whether, if it were to encourage political reformation, the new state of things might not endanger its own supremacy. There are indeed so many other interests and powers concerned in political reformations, that the state religion cannot always prevent alterations from being effected. Nor would I affirm that they always endeavour to prevent it. And yet we may appeal to the general experience of all ages, whether established churches have not resisted reformation in those political institutions upon which their own privileges depended. Now, these are serious things. For after all that can be said, and justly said, of the mischiefs of political changes and the extravagances of political empiricism, it is sufficiently certain that almost every government that has been established in the world, has *needed* from time to time important reformations in its constitution or its practice. And it is equally certain, that if there be any influence or power which habitually and with little discrimination supports political institutions as they are, that influence or power must be very pernicious to the world.

45. We have seen that one of the requisites of a religious establishment is a "legal provision" for its ministers—that is to say, the members of all the churches which exist in a state must be obliged to pay to the support of one, whether they approve of that one or not.

46. Now in endeavouring to estimate the effects of this system, with a view to ascertain the preponderance of public advantages, we are presented at the outset with the inquiry—Is this compulsory maintenance *right?* Is it compatible with Christianity? If it is not, there is an end of the controversy: for it is nothing to Christians whether a system be politic or impolitic, if once they have discovered that it is wrong. But I waive for the present the question of rectitude. The reader is at liberty to assume that Christianity allows governments to make this compulsory provision if they think fit. I waive, too, the question whether a Christian minister *ought* to receive payment for his labours, whether that payment be voluntary or not.

47. The single point before us is, then, the balance of advantages. Is it more advantageous that ministers should be paid by a legal provision or by voluntary subscription?

48. *That* advantage of a legal provision which consists in the supply of a teacher to every district has already been noticed; so

that our inquiry is reduced to a narrow limit. Supposing that a minister would be appointed in every district although the state did not pay him, is it more desirable that he should be paid by the state or voluntarily by the people?

49. Of the legal provision some of the advantages are these: it holds out no inducement to the irreligious or indifferent to absent themselves from public worship lest they should be expected to pay the preacher. Public worship is conducted the preacher delivers his discourse, whether such persons go or not. They pay no more for going, and no less for staying away: and it is probable, in the present religious state of mankind, that some go to places for worship since it costs them nothing, who otherwise would stay away. But it is manifestly better that men should attend even in such a state of indifference than that they should not attend at all. Upon the voluntary system of payment, this good effect is not so fully secured; for though the doors of chapels be open to all, yet few persons of competent means would attend them constantly without feeling that they might be expected to contribute to the expenses. I do not believe that the non-attendance of indifferent persons would be greatly increased by the adoption of the voluntary system, especially if the payments were as moderate as they easily might be:

but it is a question rather of speculation than of experience, and the reader is to give upon this account to the system of legal provision, such an amount of advantage as he shall think fit.

50. Again.—Preaching, where there is a legal provision, is not "a mode of begging." If you adopt voluntary payment, that payment depends upon the good pleasure of the hearers, and there is manifestly a temptation upon the preacher to accommodate his discourses, or the manner of them, to the wishes of his hearers, rather than to the dictates of his own judgment. But the man who receives his stipend whether his hearers be pleased or not, is under no such temptation. He is at liberty to conform the exercise of his functions to his judgment without the diminution of a subscription. This, I think, is an undeniable advantage.

51. Another consideration is this:—That where there is a religious establishment with a legal provision, it is usual, not to say indispensable, to fill the pulpits only with persons who entertain a certain set of religious opinions. It would be obviously idle to assume that these opinions are true, but they are, or are in a considerable degree, *uniform*. Assuming, then, that one set of opinions is as sound as another, is it better that a district should always hear one set, or that the teachers of twenty different sets should successively gain possession of the pulpit, as the choice of the people might direct? I presume not to determine such a question; but it may be observed that, in point of fact, those churches which do proceed upon the voluntary system, are not often subjected to such fluctuations of doctrine. There does not appear much difficulty in constituting churches upon the voluntary plan, which shall in practice secure considerable uniformity in the sentiments of the teachers. And as to the bitter animosities and distractions which have been predicted if a choice of new teachers was to be left to the people—they do not, I believe, ordinarily follow. Not that I apprehend the ministers, for instance, of an Independent church are always elected with that unanimity and freedom from heart-burnings which ought to subsist, but that animosities do not subsist to any great extent. Besides, the prediction appears to be founded on the supposition, that a certain stipend was to be appropriated to one teacher or to another, according as he might obtain the greater number of votes—whereas every man is at liberty, if he pleases, to withdraw his contribution from him whom he disapproves, and to give it to another. And, after all, there may be voluntary support of ministers without an election by those who contribute, as is instanced by the Methodists in the present day.

52. On the other hand, there are some advantages attendant on the voluntary system which that of a legal provision does not possess.

53. And first it appears to be of importance that there should be an union, an harmony, a cordiality between the minister and the people. It is, in truth, an indispensable requisite. Christianity, which is a religion of love, cannot flourish where unkindly feelings prevail. Now, I think it is manifest that harmony and cordiality are likely to prevail more where the minister is chosen and voluntarily remunerated by his hearers, than where they are not consulted in the choice; where they are obliged to take him whom others please to appoint, and where they are compelled to pay him whether they like him or not. The *tendency* of this last system is evidently opposed to perfect kindliness and cordiality. There is likely to be a sort of natural connection, a communication of good offices induced between hearers and the man whom they themselves choose and voluntarily remunerate, which is less likely in the other case. If love be of so much consequence generally

to the Christian character, it is especially of consequence that it should subsist between him who assumes to be a dispenser, and them who are in the relation of hearers of the gospel of Christ.

54. Indeed the very circumstance that a man is *compelled* to pay a preacher, tends to the introduction of unkind and unfriendly feelings. It is not to be expected that men will pay him more graciously or with a better will than they pay a tax-gatherer; and we all know that the tax-gatherer is one of the last persons whom men wish to see. He who desires to extend the *influence* of Christianity, would be very cautious of establishing a system of which so ungracious a regulation formed a part. There is truth worthy of grave attention in the ludicrous verse of Cowper's—

" —A rarer man than you
In pulpit none shall hear;
But yet, methinks to tell you true,
You sell it plaguy dear."

It is easy to perceive that the influence of *that* man's exhortations must be diminished, whose hearers listen with the reflection that his advice is "plaguy dear." The reflection, too, is perfectly natural, and cannot be helped. And when superadded to this is the consideration, that it is not only sold "dear," but that payment is *enforced*—material injury must be sustained by the cause of religion. In this view it may be remarked, that the support of an establishment by a general tax would be preferable to the payment of each pastor by his own hearers. Nor is it unworthy of notice that some persons will always think (whether with reason or without it) that compulsory maintenance is not *right;* and in whatever degree they do this, there is an increased cause of dissatisfaction or estrangement.

55. Again.—The teacher who is *independent* of the congregation—who will enjoy all his emoluments whether they are satisfied with him or not—is under manifest temptation to remissness in his duty; not perhaps to remissness in those particulars on which his superiors would animadvert, but in those which respect the unstipulated and undefinable, but very important duties of private care, and of private labours. To mention this is sufficient. No man who reflects upon the human constitution, or who looks around him, will need arguments to prove that *they* are likely to labour negligently whose profits are not increased by assiduity and zeal. I know that the power of religion can, and that it often does, counteract this; but that is no argument for putting temptation in the way. So powerful indeed is this temptation, that with a very great number it is acknowledged to prevail. Even if we do not assert, with a clergyman, that a great proportion of his brethren labour only so much for the religious benefit of their parishioners as will screen them from the arm of the law, there is other evidence which is unhappily conclusive. The desperate extent to which non-residence is practised, is infallible proof that a large proportion of the clergy are remiss in the discharge of the duties of a Christian pastor. They do not discharge them *con amore;* and how should they? It was not the wish to do this which prompted them to become clergymen at first. They were influenced by another object, and that they have obtained—they possess an income: and it is not to be expected that, when this is obtained, the mental desires should suddenly become elevated and purified, and that they who entered the church for the sake of its emoluments, should commonly labour in it for the sake of religion.

56. Although to many the motive for entering the church is the same as that for engaging in other professions, it is an unhappiness peculiar to the clerical profession, that it does not offer the same stimulus to subsequent exertion; that advancement does not usually depend upon desert. The man who seeks for an income from surgery, or the bar, is continually prompted to pay exemplary attention to its duties. Unless the surgeon is skilful and attentive, he knows that practice is not to be expected: unless the pleader devotes himself to statutes and reports, he knows that he is not to expect cases and briefs. But the clergyman, whether he studies the Bible or not—whether he be diligent and zealous or not—still possesses his living. Nor would it be rational to expect, that where the ordinary stimulus to human exertion is wanting, the exertion itself should generally be found. So naturally does exertion follow from stimulus, that we believe it is an observation frequently made, that curates are more exemplary than beneficed clergymen. And if beneficed clergymen were more solicitous than they are to make the *diligence* of their curates the principal consideration in employing them, this difference between curates and their employers would be much greater than it is. Let beneficed clergymen employ and reward curates upon as simple principles as those are on which a merchant employs and rewards a clerk, and it is probable that nine-tenths of the parishes in England would wish for a curate rather than a rector.

57. But this very consideration affords a powerful argument against the present system. If much good would result from making clerical reward the price of desert, much evil results from making it independent of desert. This effect of the English Establishment is

not, like some others, inseparable from the institution. It would doubtless be possible, even with compulsory maintenance, so to appropriate it that it should form a constant motive to assiduity and exertion. Clergymen *might* be elevated in their profession according to their fidelity to their office ; and if this were done if, as opportunity offered, all were likely to be promoted who deserved it ; and if all who did not deserve it were sure to be passed by, a new face would soon be put upon the affairs of the church. The complaints of neglect of duty would quickly be diminished, and non-residence would soon cease to be the reproach of three thousand out of ten. We cannot, however, amuse ourselves with the hope that this will be done, because, in reference to the civil constitution of the church, there is too near an approach to that condition in which the whole head is sick, and the whole heart faint.

58. If then it be asserted, that it is one great advantage of the establishment that it provides a teacher for every parish, it is one great disadvantage that it makes a large proportion of those teachers negligent of their duty.

59. There may perhaps be a religious establishment in which the ministers shall be selected for their *deserts*, though I know not whether in any it is actually and sufficiently done. That it is one of the first requisites in the appointment of religious teachers is plain : and this point is manifestly better consulted by a system in which the people voluntarily pay and choose their pastors, than when they do not. Men love goodness in others, though they may be bad themselves ; and they especially like it in their religious teachers : so that, when they come to select a person to fill that office, they are likely to select one of whom they think at least that he is a good man.

60. The same observation holds of non-residence. Non-residence is not *necessary* to a state religion. By the system of voluntary payment it is *impossible*.

It has sometimes been said (with whatever truth) that in times of public discontent these persons have been disposed to disaffection. If this be true, compulsory support is in this respect a political evil, inasmuch as it is the cause of the alienation of a part of the community. We will not suppose so strong a case as that this alienation might lead to physical opposition ; but supposing the dissatisfaction only to *exist*, affords no inconsiderable topic of the statesman's inquiry. Happiness is the object of civil government, and this object is frustrated in part in respect of those who think themselves aggrieved by its policy. And when it is considered how numerous the dissenters are, and that they increase in number, the political impropriety and impolicy of keeping them in a state of dissatisfaction becomes increased.

61. The best security of a government is in the satisfaction and affection of the people ; which satisfaction is always diminished, and which affection is always endangered, in respect of those who, disapproving a certain church, are compelled to pay to its support. This is a consequence of a "legal provision" that demands much attention from the legislator. Every legislator knows that it is an evil. It is a point that no man disputes, and that every man knows should be prevented, unless its cause effects a counterbalance of advantages.

62. Lastly, upon the question of the comparative advantages of a legal provision, and a voluntary remuneration in securing the due discharge of the ministerial function, what is the evidence of facts ? Are the ministers of established, or of unestablished churches, the more zealous, the more exemplary, the more laborious, the more devoted ? Whether of the two are the more beloved by their hearers ? Whether of the two lead the more exemplary and religious lives ? Whether of the two are the more active in works of philanthropy ? It is a question of fact, and facts are before the world.

63. The discussions of the present chapter conduct the mind of the writer to these short conclusions : —

That of the two grounds upon which the propriety of Religious Establishments is capable of examination, neither affords evidence in their favour : That Religious Establishments derive no countenance from the nature of Christianity, or from the example of the primitive churches ; and, That they are not recommended by practical Utility.

CHAPTER XV.

The Religious Establishments of England and Ireland.

The English Church the offspring of the Reformation, the Church *establishment*, of Papacy— Alliance of Church and State :— The Priesthood averse from reformation"—Noble ecclesiastics —Purchase of advowsons—Non-residence—Pluralities—Parliamentary returns—The clergy fear to preach the truth—Moral preaching—Recoil from works of philanthropy—Tithes—" The Church is in danger" —The Church *establishment* is in danger—Monitory suggestion.

64. If the conclusions of the last chapter be just, it will now become our business to

inquire how far the disadvantages which are incidental to religious establishments actually operate in our own, and whether there subsist any additional disadvantages resulting from the peculiar constitution or circumstances of the English Church.

65. We have no concern with religious opinions or forms of church government, but *with the church as connected with the state*. It is not with an Episcopalian church, but with an established church, that we are concerned. If there must exist a religious establishment, let it by all means remain in its present hands. The experience which England has had of the elevation of another sect to the supremacy, is not such as to make us wish to see another elevated again.[1] Nor would any sect which takes a just view of its own religious interests desire the supremacy for itself.

66. The *origin* of the English establishment is papal. The political alliance of the church is similar now to what it was in the first years of Henry VIII. When Henry countenanced the preachers of the reformed opinions, when he presented some of them with the benefices which had hitherto been possessed by the Romish clergy; and when at length these benefices and the other privileges of the state religion were bestowed upon the "reformed" only—no essential change was effected in the political constitution of the church. In one point indeed the alliance with the state was made more strict, because the supremacy was transferred from the Pope to the monarch. So that the same or a kindred political character was put in connection with other men and new opinions. The church was altered, but the establishment remained nearly the same: or the difference that did obtain made the establishment more of a state religion than before. The origin, therefore, of the English establishment is papal. It was planted by papal policy, and nurtured by pervading superstition: and as to the transfer of the supremacy, but little credit is due to its origin or its motives. No reverence is due to our establishment on account of its parentage. The *church* is the offspring of the Reformation—the church *establishment* is not. It is not a daughter of Protestantism but of the Papacy brought into unnatural alliance with a better faith. Unhappily, but little anxiety was shown by some of the reformers to purify the political character of the church when its privileges came into their own hands. They declaimed against the corruptions of the former church, but were more than sufficiently willing to retain its profits and its power.

67. The *alliance* with the state of which we have spoken, as the inseparable attendant of religious establishments, is in this country peculiarly close. "Church and State," is a phrase that is continually employed, and indicates the intimacy of the connection between them. The question then arises, whether those disadvantages which result generally from the alliance, result in this country, and whether the peculiar intimacy is attended with peculiar evils.

68. Bishops are virtually appointed by the prince: and it is manifest that in the present principles of political affairs, regard will be had, in their selection, to the interests of the state. The question will not always be, when a bishopric becomes vacant, Who is the fittest man to take the oversight of the church? but sometimes What appointment will most effectually strengthen the administration of the day?—Bishops are temporal peers, and as such they have an efficient ability to promote the views of the government by their votes in parliament. Bishops in their turn are patrons; and it becomes also manifest that these appointments will sometimes be regulated by kindred views. He who was selected by the cabinet because he would promote their measures, and who cannot hope for advancement if he opposes those measures, is not likely to select clergymen who oppose them. Many ecclesiastical appointments, again, are in the hands of the individual officers of government—of the prime minister, for example, or the lord chancellor. That these officers will frequently regard political purposes, or purposes foreign to the *worth* of men, in making these appointments, is plain. Now, when we reflect that the *highest* dignities of the church are in the patronage of the king, and that the influence of their dignitaries upon the inferior clergy is necessarily great, it becomes obvious, that there will be diffused through the general whole of the hierarchy a systematic alliance with the ruling power. Nor is it assuming anything unreasonable to add, that

---

[1] The religious sect who are now commonly called Puritans, "prohibited the use of the Common Prayer, not merely in churches, chapels, and places of public worship, but in any private place or family as well, under a penalty of five pounds for the first offence, ten pounds for the second, and for the third a year's imprisonment."[1] These men did not understand, or did not practise the fundamental duties of toleration. For religious liberty they had still less regard. "They passed an ordinance by which eight heresies were made punishable with death upon the first offence, unless the offender abjured his errors, and irremissably if he relapsed. Sixteen other opinions were to be punished with imprisonment, till the offender should find sureties that he would maintain them no more."[2] And they quite abolished the episcopal rank and order, as if each church might not decide for itself by what form its discipline should be conducted! To have separated the civil privileges from the episcopal order was within the province of the legislature, and to have abolished those privileges would, we think, have been wise.

[1] Southey's Book of the Church. [2] Ibid.

whilst the ordinary principles that actuate mankind operate, the hierarchy will sometimes postpone the interests of religion to their own.

69. Upon the practical authority of cabinets over the church, Bishop Warburton makes himself somewhat mirthful :—"The rabbins make the giant Gog or Magog contemporary with Noah, and convinced by his preaching. So that he was disposed to take the benefit of the ark. But here lay the distress -it by no means suited his dimensions. Therefore, as he could not enter in, he contented himself to ride upon it astride. Image now to yourself this illustrious cavalier, mounted on his *hackney*, and see if he does not bring before you the church, bestrid by some lumpish minister of state, who turns and winds it at his pleasure. The only difference is, that Gog *believed* the preacher of righteousness and religion." [1]

70. If, then, to convert a religious establishment into " a means of strengthening or diffusing influence, serves only to debase it, and to introduce into it numerous corruptions and abuses." these debasements, corruptions, and abuses must necessarily subsist in the establishment of England.

71. And first as to the church itself.—It is not too much to believe that the honourable earnestness of many of the reformers to purify religion from the corruptions of the papacy, was cooled, and eventually almost destroyed, by the acquisition of temporal immunities. When they had acquired them, the unhappy reasoning began to operate—*Let us let well alone : if we encourage further changes our advantages will perhaps pass into other hands. We are safe as we are ; and we will not endanger the loss of present benefits by further reformation.* What has been the result?—That the church has never been fully reformed to the present hour. If any reader is disposed to deny this, I place the proposition not upon my feeble authority, but upon that of the members of the church and of the reformers themselves. The reader will be pleased to notice that there are few quotations in the present chapter except from members of the Church of England.

72. " If any person will seriously consider the low and superstitious state of the minds of men in general in the time of James I., much more in the reigns of his predecessors, he will not be surprised to find that *there are various matters in our ecclesiastical constitution which require some alteration.* Our forefathers did great things, and we cannot be sufficiently thankful for their labours, but much more remains to be done." [1] Hartley says of the ecclesiastical powers of the Christian world " They have *all* left the true, pure, simple religion, and teach for doctrines the commandments of men. They are *all* merchants of the earth, and have set up a kingdom of this world, abounding in riches, temporal power, and external pomp." [2] Dr. Henry More (he was zealous for the honour of the church) says of the reformed churches, they have " separated from the great Babylon to build those that are lesser and more tolerable, but yet not to be tolerated for ever." [3]

73. " It pleased God in His unsearchable wisdom to suffer the progress of this great work, the reformation, to be stopped in *the midway*, and the effects of it to be greatly weakened by many unhappy divisions among the reformed." [4]

74. " The innovations introduced into our religious establishment at the reformation, were great and glorious for those times : but *some further innovations are yet wanting* (would to God they may be quietly made !) to bring it to perfection." [5]

75. " I have always had a true zeal for the Church of England ; yet I must say—*there are many things in it that have been very uneasy to me.*" [6]

76. " Cranmer, Bucer, Jewel, and others, never considered the reformation which took place in their own times as complete." [7]

77. Long after Cranmer's days, some of the brightest ornaments of the church still thought a reformation was needed. Tillotson, Patrick, Tennison, Kidder, Stillingfleet, Burnet, and others,[8] endeavoured a further reformation, though in vain.

78. " We have been contented to suffer our religious constitution, our doctrines, and ceremonies, and forms of public worship, to remain nearly in the same *unpurged, adulterated*, and *superstitious state* in which the original reformers left them." [9]

79. I attribute this want of reformation

---

[1] Bishop Warburton's Letters to Bishop Hurd. Letter 47.

[1] Simpson's Plea, p. 147
[2] Essay on Man, 1749, v. 2, p. 370.
[3] Myst. of Iniquity, p. 553. This poor man found that his language laboured under the imputation of being unclerical, unguarded, and impolitic ; and he afterwards showed solicitude to retract it. See p. 476, &c., of same work.
[4] Dr. Louth, afterwards Bishop of London : *Visitation Sermon*, 1758.
[5] Dr. Watson, Bishop of Llandaff : Misc. Tracts v. 2, p. 17, &c.
[6] Bishop Burnet : Hist. Own Times, v. 2, p. 64.
[7] Simpson's Plea. [8] Ibid. [9] Ibid.

primarily to the political alliance of the church. Why should those who have the power refuse to effect it unless they feared some ill result? And what ill result could arise from religious reformation if it were not the endangering of temporal advantages?

80. "I would only ask," said Lord Bacon, two hundred years ago, "*why* the civil state should be purged and restored by good and wholesome laws, made every third or fourth year in parliament assembled, devising remedies as fast as time breedeth mischief; and *contrariwise*, the ecclesiastical state should still continue upon the dregs of time, and receive no alteration now for these five and-forty years and more.—If St. John were to indite an epistle to the Church of England, as he did to them of Asia, it would sure have the clause *habeo adversus te pauca*."[1] What would Lord Bacon have said if he had lived to our day, when two hundred years more have passed, and the establishment still continues "upon the dregs of time!"—But Lord Bacon's question should be answered; and though no *reason* can be given for refusing to reform, a *cause* can be assigned.

81. "Whatever truth there may be in the proposition which asserts that the multitude is fond of innovation, I think that the proposition which asserts that *the priesthood is averse from reformation, is far more generally true*."[2] This is the cause. They who have the power of reforming are afraid to touch the fabric. They are afraid to remove one stone however decayed, lest another and another should be loosened, until the fabric, as a political institution, should fall. Let us hear again episcopal evidence. Bishop Porteous informs us that himself with some other clergymen (amongst whom were Dr. Percy and Dr. Yorke, both subsequently bishops), attempted to induce the bishops to alter some things "which all reasonable persons agreed stood in need of amendment." The answer given by Archbishop Cornwallis was exactly to the purpose—"I have consulted, severally, my brethren the bishops; and it is the opinion of the bench in general, that nothing can in prudence be done in the matter."[3] Here is no attempt to deny the existence of the evils—no attempt to show that they ought not to be amended, but only that it would not "be prudent" to amend them. What were these considerations of prudence? Did they respect religion? Is it imprudent to purify religious offices? Or did they respect the temporal privileges of the church?—No man surely can doubt, that if the church had been a religious institution only, its heads would have thought it both prudent and right to amend it.

82. The matters to which Bishop Porteous called the attention of the bench were, " the liturgy, but especially the articles." These articles afford an extraordinary illustration of that tendency to resist improvement of which we speak.

83. "The requiring subscription to the Thirty-Nine Articles is a great imposition."[1] "Do the articles of the Church of England want a revisal?—Undoubtedly."[2]—In 1772, a clerical petition was presented to the House of Commons for relief upon the subject of subscription: and what were the sentiments of the house respecting the articles? One member said, "I am persuaded they are not warranted by scripture, and I am sure they cannot be reconciled to common sense."[3] Another—"They are contradictory, absurd, several of them damnable, not only in a religious and speculative light, but also in a moral and practical view."[4] Another—"The articles, I am sure, want a revisal; because several of them are heterodox and absurd, warranted neither by reason nor by scripture. Many of them seem calculated for keeping out of the church all but those who will subscribe anything, and sacrifice every consideration to the mammon of unrighteousness."[5] And a fourth said—"Some of them are, in my opinion, unfounded in, some of them inconsistent with, reason and scripture; and some of them subversive of the very genius and design of the gospel."[6] The articles found, it appears, in the House of Commons one, and one only defender; and that one was Sir Roger Newdigate, the member for Oxford.[7]—And thus a "Church of Christ" retains in its bosom that which is confessedly irrational, inconsistent with scripture, contradictory, absurd, subversive of the very genius and design of the gospel:—for what? Because the church *is allied to the state*: because it is a Religious *Establishment*.

84. There is such an interest, an importance, an awfulness in these things, resulting both from their effects and the responsibility which they entail, that I would accumulate upon the general necessity for reformation some additional testimonies.

---

[1] Works: Edit. 1803, v. 2, p. 527.
[2] Bishop Watson: Misc. Tracts, v. 2.
[3] Works of Bishop Porteous, vol. 1.

[1] Bishop Burnet: Hist. Own Times, v. 2, p. 634.
[2] Bishop Watson: Misc. Tracts, v. 2, p. 17.
[3] Lord George Germain.   [4] Sir William Meredith.
[5] Lord John Cavendish.   [6] Sir George Sackville.
[7] Parl. Hist., v. 17. The petition, after all this, was rejected by two hundred and seventeen votes against seventy-one. Can anything more clearly indicate the *fear* of reforming?—a fear that extends itself to the state, because the state thinks (with reason or without it) that to endanger the stability of the church were to endanger its own.

85. In 1746 was presented to the convocation, "Free and Candid Disquisitions by dutiful Sons of the Church," in which they say, "Our duty seems as clear as our obligations to it are cogent ; and is, in one word, to *reform*." Of this book Archdeacon Blackburn tells us that it was treated with "much contempt and scorn by those who ought to have paid the greatest regard to the subject of it ;" and that "it caused the *forms of the church* to be weighed in the balance of the sanctuary, where *they have been found greatly wanting*."[1]

86. "Our confirmations, and I may add even our ordinations for the sacred ministry, are dwindled into painful and disgusting ceremonies, as they are usually administered."[2]

87. Another archdeacon, who was not only a friend of the church but a public advocate of religious establishments, says, "Reflection, we hope, in some, and time we are sure in all, will reconcile men to alterations established in reason. If there be any danger it is *from some of the clergy*, who would *rather suffer the vineyard to be overgrown with weeds than stir the ground*: or, what is worse, call these weeds the fairest flowers in the garden." This is strong language : that which succeeds is stronger still. "If we are to wait for improvement till the cool, the calm, the discreet part of mankind begin it ; till *church governors* solicit, or *ministers of state* propose it, I will venture to pronounce, that (without *His* interposition with whom nothing is impossible) we may remain as we are till the renovation of all things."[3] Why "church governors" and "ministers of state" should be so peculiarly backward to improve, is easily known. Ministers of state are more anxious for the consolidation of their power than for the amendment of churches ; and church governors are more anxious to benefit themselves by consolidating that power, than to reform the system of which they are the heads. But let no man anticipate that we shall indeed remain as we are till the renovation of all things. The work will be done though these may refuse to do it. "If," says a statesman, "the friends of the church, instead of taking the lead in a mild reform of abuses, contend obstinately for their protection, and treat every man as an enemy who aims at reform, *they will certainly be overpowered at last, and the correction applied by those who will apply it with no sparing hand*."[4] If these declara-

[1] The Confessional. [2] Simpson's Plea.
[3] A Defence of the Considerations on the propriety of requiring a Subscription to Articles of Faith. By Dr. Paley, p. 35.
[4] Letters on the subject of the British and Foreign Bible Society, by the present Lord Bexley.

tions be true (and who will even question their truth?) we may be allowed, without any pretensions to extraordinary sagacity, to add another : that to these unsparing correctors the work will assuredly be assigned. How infatuated, then, the policy of refusing reformation even if policy only were concerned !

The next point in which the effect of the state alliance is injurious to the church itself, is by its effects upon the ministry.

88. It is manifest that where there are such powerful motives of *interest* to assume the ministerial office, and where there are such facilities for the admission of unfit men — unfit men will often be admitted. Human nature is very stationary ; and kindred results arose very many centuries ago. "The attainments of the clergy in the first ages of the Anglo-Saxon Church were very considerable. But a great and total degeneracy took place during the latter years of the Heptarchy, and for two generations after the union of its kingdoms." And why? Because "mere worldly views operated upon a great proportion of them ; no other way of life offered so fair a prospect of power to the ambitious, of security to the prudent, of tranquillity and ease to the easy-minded."[1] —Such views still operate, and they still produce kindred effects.

89. It is manifest, that if men undertake the office of Christian teachers not from earnestness in the cause, but from the desire of profit or power or ease, the office will frequently be ill discharged. Persons who possess little of the Christian minister but the name, will undertake to guide the flock ; and hence it is inevitable that the ministry, as a body, will become reduced in the scale of religious excellence. So habitual is the system of undertaking the office *for the sake* of its emoluments, that men have begun to avow the motive and to defend it. "It is no reproach to the church to say that it is supplied with ministers by the emoluments it affords."[2] Would it not have been a reproach to the first Christian churches, or could it have been said of them at all? Does he who enters the church for the sake of its advantages, enter it "of a ready mind"?—But the more lucrative offices of the church are talked of with much familiarity as "prizes," much in the same manner as we talk of prizes in a lottery. "The same fund produces more effect—when distributed into prizes of different value than when divided into equal shares."[3] This "effect" is de-

[1] Southey: Book of the Church, c. 6.
[2] Knox's Essays, No. 18.
[3] Mor. and Pol. Phil., b. 6, c. 10.

scribed as being "both an allurement to *men of talents* to enter into the church, and as a stimulus to the *industry* of those who are already in it." But every man knows that talent and industry are not the only nor the chief things which obtain for a person the prizes of the church. There is more of accuracy in the parallel passage of another moralist. "The medical profession does not possess so many *splendid prizes* as the church and the bar, and *on that account*, perhaps, is rarely, if ever, pursued by young men of noble families."[1] Here is the point: it is rather to noble families than to talent and industry, that the prizes are awarded. "There are, indeed, rich preferments, but these, it is observed, do not usually fall to merit as the reward of it, but are lavished where interest and family connection put in their irresistible claim."[2] That plain-speaking man Bishop Warburton writes to his friend Hurd, "Reckon upon it, that Durham goes to some *noble* ecclesiastic. 'Tis a morsel only for them."[3] It is manifest that when this language can be appropriate, the office of the ministry must be dishonoured and abused. Respecting the priesthood, it is acknowledged that "the characters of men are formed much more by the *temptations* than the duties of their profession."[4] Since, then, the temptations are worldly, what is to be expected but that the character should be worldly too?—Nor would anything be gained by the dexterous distinction that I have somewhere met with, that although the motive for "taking the oversight of the flock" be indeed "lucre," yet it does not come under the apostolical definition of "filthy."

90. Of the eventual consequences of thus introducing unqualified and perhaps irreligious nobles into the government of the church, Bishop Warburton speaks in strong language. "Our grandees have at last found their way back into the church. I only wonder they have been so long about it. But be assured that nothing but a new religious revolution, to sweep away the fragments that Harry the VIII. left after banqueting his courtiers, will drive them out again."[5] When that revolution shall come which will sweep away these prizes, it will prove not only to these but to other things to be a besom of destruction.

91. If the fountain be bitter, the current cannot be sweet. The principles which too commonly operate upon the dignitaries of the church, descend, in some degree, to the inferior ranks. I say in some degree, for I do not believe that the degree is the same, or so great. Nor is it to be expected. The temptation which forms the character, is diminished in its power, and the character therefore may rise.

92. I believe that (reverently be it spoken) *through the goodness of God*, there has been produced, since the age of Hartley, a considerable improvement in the general character (at least of the inferior orders) of the English clergy. In observing the character which he exhibited, let it be remembered that that character was the legitimate offspring of the *state* religion. The subsequent amendment is the offspring of another, and a very different, and a purer parentage. "The superior clergy are in general ambitious, and eager in the pursuit of riches: flatterers of the great, and subservient to party interest; negligent of their own immediate charges, and also of the inferior clergy and their immediate charges. The inferior clergy imitate their superiors, and, in general, take little more care of their parishes than barely what is necessary to avoid the censures of the law. I say this is the general case; that is, far the greater part of the clergy of all ranks in this kingdom are of this kind."[1]—These miserable effects upon the character of the clergy are the effects of a *Religious Establishment*. If any man is unwilling to admit the truth, let him adduce the instance of an *unestablished* church, in the past eighteen hundred years, in which such a state of things has existed. Of the times of Gregory Nazianzen, Bishop Burnet says—"The best men of that age, instead of pressing into orders or aspiring to them, fled from them, excused themselves, and judging themselves unworthy of so holy a character and so high a trust, were not without difficulty prevailed upon to submit to that which, in degenerate ages, men run to as a subsistence or the means of procuring it."[2]

93. It might almost be imagined that the right of *private patronage* was allowed for the express purpose of deteriorating the character of the ministers of religion—because it can hardly be supposed that any church would allow such a system without a perfect consciousness of its effects. To allow any man or woman, good or bad, who has money to spend, to purchase the power of assigning a Christian minister to a Christian flock, is one of those desperate follies and enormities which should never be spoken of

---

[1] Gisborne's Duties of Men.
[2] Knox's Essays, No. 53.
[3] Warburton's Letters to Hurd, No. 47.
[4] Mor. and Pol. Phil., p. 266.
[5] Warburton's Letters to Hurd, No. 47.

[1] Hartley: Observations on Man.
[2] Disc. of the Pastoral Care, 12th ed. p. 77. "Under Lanfranc's primacy no promotion in the church was to be obtained by purchase, neither was any unfit person raised to the episcopal rank."[1]

[1] Southey: Book of the Church, chap. 7.

but in the language of detestation and horror.[1] A man buys an advowson as he buys an estate, and for the same motives. He cares perhaps nothing for the religious consequences of his purchase, or for the religious assiduity of the person to whom he presents it. Nay, the case is worse than that of buying as you buy an estate; for land will not repay the occupier unless he cultivates it—but the living is just as profitable whether he exerts himself zealously or not. He who is unfit for the estate by want of industry or of talent, is nevertheless fit for the living! These are dreadful and detestable abuses. Christianity is not to be brought into juxtaposition with such things. It were almost a shame to allow a comparison. "Who is not aware that, in consequence of the prevalence of such a system, the holy things of God are often miserably profaned?"[2] "It is our firm persuasion, that the present system of bestowing church patronage is hastening the decay of morals, the progress of insubordination, and the downfall of the establishment itself." Morality and subordination have happily other supports:—the fate of the establishment is sealed. I say sealed. It cannot perpetually stand without thorough reformation; and it cannot be reformed while it remains an *establishment.*

94. Another mode in which the state religion of England is injurious to the character of its ministers is by its allowance and practical encouragement of non-residence and pluralities. These are the natural effects of the principles of the system. It is very possible that there should be a state religion without them; but if the alliance with the state is close—if a principal motive in the dispensation of benefices is the promotion of political purposes—if the prizes of the church are given where interest and family connections put in their claim—it becomes extremely natural that several preferments should be bestowed upon one person. And when once this is countenanced or done by the state itself, inferior patrons will as naturally follow the example. The prelate who receives from the state three or four preferments, naturally gives to his son or his nephew three or four if he can.

95. Pluralities and non-residence, whatever may be said in their favour by politicians or divines, will always shock the common sense and the virtue of mankind. Unhappily, they are evils which seem to have increased.

"Theodore, the seventh archbishop of Canterbury, restricted the bishops and secular clergy to their own dioceses;" and no longer ago than the reign of James I., "when pluralities were allowed, which was to be as seldom as possible, the livings were to be near each other."[1] But now we hear of one dignitary who possesses ten different preferments, and of another who, with an annual ecclesiastical revenue of fifteen thousand pounds, did not see his diocese for many years together.[2] And as to that proximity of livings which was directed in James's time, they are now held in plurality not only at a distance from each other, but so as that the duties *cannot* be performed by one person.

95*. Of the moral character of this deplorable custom, it is not necessary that we should speak. "I do not enter," says an eminent prelate, "into the scandalous practices of non-residence and pluralities. This is so shameful a profanation of holy things, that it ought to be treated with detestation and horror."[3] Another friend of the church says, "He who grasps at the revenue of a benefice, and studies to evade the personal discharge of the various functions which that revenue is intended to reward, and the performance of those momentous duties to God and man, which, by accepting the living, he has undertaken, evinces either a most reprehensible neglect of proper consideration, or a callous depravity of heart."[4] It may be believed that all are not thus depraved who accept pluralities without residence. Custom, although it does not alter the nature of actions, affects the character of the agent; and although I hold no man innocent in the sight of God who supports, in his example, this vicious practice, yet some may do it now with a less measure of guilt than that which would have attached to him who first, for the sake of money, introduced the scandal into the church.

96. The public has now the means of knowing, by the returns to Parliament, the extent in which these scandalous customs exist—an extent which, when it was first communicated to the Earl of Harrowby, "struck me," says he, "with surprise, I could almost say with horror." Alas, when temporal peers are horror-struck by the scandals that are tolerated and practised by their spiritual teachers!

97. By one of these returns it appears that

---

[1] Upon such persons "rests the awful responsibility (I might almost call it the divine prerogative) of assigning a flock to the shepherd, and of selecting a shepherd for the flock."- Gurney's Peculiar ties, 3d ed. p. 164.
[2] Christian Observer, v. 20, p. 11.

[1] Southey: Book of the Church, c. 6.
[2] For these examples see Simpson's Plea. I say nothing of *present* examples.
[3] Burnet: Hist. Own Times, v. 2, p. 646.
[4] Gisborne: Duties of Men.

the whole number of places[1] is ten thousand two hundred and sixty-one. Of the possessors of these livings, *more than one-half were non-resident.* The number of residents was only four thousand four hundred and twenty-one.—But the reader will perhaps say, What matters the residence of him who receives the money, so that a curate resides? Unfortunately, the proportion of absentee curates is still greater than that of incumbents. Out of three thousand six hundred and ninety-four who are employed, only one thousand five hundred and eighty-seven live in the parishes they serve; so that two thousand one hundred and seven parishes are left without even the residence of a curate. Besides this, there are nine hundred and seventy incumbents who neither live in their parishes themselves nor employ any curate at all! What is the result? That above one-half of those who receive the stipends of the church live away from their flocks; and that there are in this country three thousand and seventy-seven flocks amongst whom *no* shepherd is to be found!—When it is considered that all this is a *gratuitous* addition to the necessary evils of state religions, that there may be established churches without it, it speaks aloud of those mischiefs of our establishment which are peculiarly its own.

98. One other consideration upon this subject remains. An internal discipline in a church, both over its ministers and its members, appears essential to the proper exercise of Christian duty. From what cause does it happen that there is little exercise of discipline, or none, in the Church of England? The reader will perhaps answer the question to himself: "The exercise of efficient discipline in the church is *impossible;*" and he would answer truly. It is impossible. Who shall exercise it? The first Lord of the Treasury? He will not, and he cannot. The Bench of Bishops? Alas! *there* is the origin of a great portion of the delinquency. If they were to establish a discipline, the first persons upon whom they must exercise it would be themselves. Who ever heard of persons, so situated, instituting or re-establishing a discipline in the church? Who then shall exercise it? The subordinate clergy? If they have the will, they have not the power; and if they had the power, who can hope that they would use it? Who can hope that, whilst above half of these clergy are non-residents, they will erect a discipline by which residence shall be enforced?—I say, discipline, efficient discipline, is impossible; and I submit it to the reader whether *any* Establishment in which Christian Discipline is impossible, is not essentially bad.

99. From the contemplation of these effects of the English establishment upon its formularies, its ministers, and its discipline, we must turn to its effects generally upon the religious welfare of the people. This welfare is so involved with the general character of the establishment and its ministers, that to exhibit an evil in one is to illustrate an injury to the other. If the operation of the state religion prevents ministers from inculcating some portions of divine truth, its operation must indeed be bad. And how stands the fact? "Aspiring clergymen, wishing to avoid every doctrine which would retard their advancement, were very little inclined to preach the reality or necessity of divine influence."[1] The evil which this indicates is twofold: first, the vicious state of the heads of the church; for why else should "advancement" be refused to those who preached the doctrine of the gospel;—and next, the injury to religion; for religion must needs be injured if a portion of its truths are concealed. Another quotation gives a similar account: "Regular divines of great virtue, learning, and apparent piety, *feared* to preach the Holy Ghost and His operations, the main doctrines of the gospel, lest they should countenance the Puritan, the Quaker, or the Methodist, and lose the esteem of their own order or of the higher powers."[2] Did Paul or Barnabas ever "fear to preach the main doctrines of the gospel" from considerations like these, or from any considerations whatever? Did our Lord approve or tolerate such fear when He threatened with punishment any man who should take away from the words of His book? But why again should the clerical order or the higher powers disesteem the man who preached the main doctrines of the gospel, unless it were from motives of interest founded in the establishment?

100. And thus it is, that they who are assumed to be the religious leaders of the people, who ought, so far as in their power, to guide the people into *all* truth, conceal a portion of that truth from motives of interest! If this concealment is practised by men of great virtue, learning, and apparent piety, what are we to expect in the indifferent or the bad? We are to expect that not one but many doctrines of the gospel will be concealed. We are to expect that discourses not very different from those which Socrates might have delivered will be dispensed, instead of the whole counsel of God. What

---

[1] The diocese of St. David's is not included, and the return includes some dignities, sinecures, and dilapidated churches. It cites that of 1810. I do not know but that the details are substantially the same at the present time.

[1] Vicessimus Knox: Christian Philosophy, 3d edition, p. 24.
[2] Ibid. p. 23.

has been the fact? Of "moral preaching," Bishop Lavington says, "We have long been attempting the reformation of the nation by discourses of this kind. With what success? *None at all.* On the contrary, *we have dexterously preached the people into downright infidelity.*" Will any man affirm that this has not been the consequence of the *state* religion? Will any man, knowing this, affirm that a state religion is right or useful to Christianity?

101. But as to the tendency of the system to diffuse infidelity, we are not possessed of the testimony of Bishop Lavington alone. "It is evident that the worldly-mindedness and neglect of duty in the clergy is a great scandal to religion, and cause of infidelity."[1] Again : "Who is to blame for the spread of infidelity? The bishops and clergy of the land more than any other people in it. We, as a body of men, are almost solely and exclusively culpable."[2] Ostervald in his "Treatise concerning the causes of the present Corruption of Christians," makes the same remark of the clergy of other churches :—"The cause of the corruption of Christians is chiefly to be found in the clergy." Now, supposing this to be the language of exaggeration –supposing that they corrupt Christians only as much as men who make no peculiar pretensions to religion—how can such a fact be accounted for, but by the conclusion that there is something *corrupting* in the clerical system?

102. The refusal to amend the constitution or formularies of the church, is another powerful cause of injury to religion. Of one particular article- the Athanasian creed –a friend of the church, and one who mixed with the world, says, "I really believe that creed has made more deists than all the writings of all the oppugners of Christianity since it was first unfortunately adopted in our liturgy."[3] Would this deist-making document have been retained till now if the church were not allied to the state?—Bishop Watson uses language so unsparing, that, just and true as it is, I know not whether I would cite it from any other pen than a bishop's : "A motley monster of bigotry and superstition — a scarecrow of shreds and patches, dressed up of old by philosophers and popes to amuse the speculative and to affright the ignorant." Do I quote this because it is the unsparing language of truth? No ; but because of that which succeeds it : "*Now,*" says the bishop, "a butt of scorn, against which every unfledged witling of the age essays his wanton efforts, and before he has learned his catechism, is fixed *an infidel for life!* This I am persuaded is too frequently the case, for I have had too frequent opportunities to observe it."[1] If, by the church as it subsists, many are fixed infidels for life, how diffusively must be spread that minor, but yet practical disrespect for religion, which, though it amounts not to infidelity, makes religion an inoperative thing —inoperative upon the conduct and the heart — inoperative in animating the love and hope of the Christian inoperative in supporting under affliction, and in smoothing and brightening the pathway to the grave !

103. To these minor consequences also we have unambiguous testimony : "Where there is not this open and shameless disavowal of religion, few traces of it are to be found. Improving in every other branch of knowledge, we have become less and less acquainted with Christianity."[2]—"Two-thirds of the lower order of people in London," says Sir Thomas Bernard, "live as utterly ignorant of the doctrines and duties of Christianity, and are as errant and unconverted *pagans,* as if they had existed in the wildest part of Africa."—"The case," continues the *Quarterly Review,* "is *the same* in Manchester, Leeds, Bristol, Sheffield, and in all our large towns. The greatest part of the manufacturing populace, of the miners and colliers, are in the *same* condition ; and if they are not universally so, it is more owing to the zeal of the Methodists than to any other cause."[3] How is it accounted for, that in a country in which a teacher is appointed to diffuse Christianity in every parish, a considerable part of the population are confessed to be absolute *pagans?* How, especially, is it accounted for, that the few who are reclaimed from paganism, are reclaimed not by the established, but by an unestablished church ? It is not difficult to account for all this, if the condition of the established church is such as to make what follows the flippant language of a clergyman who afterwards was a bishop : "The person I engaged in the summer," as a curate, "is run away ; as you will think natural enough, when I tell you he was let out of jail to be promoted to this service."[4]

104. The ill effect of non-residence upon the general interests of religion is necessarily great. A conscientious clergyman finds that the offices of his pulpit are not the half of his business : he finds that he can often do more in promoting the religious welfare of his parishioners out of his pulpit than in it. It is out of his pulpit that he evinces and

---

[1] Hartley ; Observation on Man.
[2] Simpson's Plea, 3d edit. p. 76.
[3] Observations on the Liturgy, by an Under Secretary of State.

[1] Misc. Tracts by Watson, Bishop of Landaff, v. 2, p. 40.
[2] Wilberforce : Practical View, 6th edit. p. 389.
[3] *Quarterly Review,* April 1816, p. 233.
[4] Letters between Bishop Warburton and Bishop Hurd.

exercises the most unequivocal affection for his charge ; that he encourages or warns as *individuals* have need ; that he animates by the presence of his constant example ; that he consoles them in their troubles ; that he adjusts their disagreements ; that he assists them by his advice. It is by living amongst them, and by that alone, that he can be "instant in season and out of season," or that he can fulfil the duties which his station involves. How prodigious, then, must be the sum of mischief which the non-residence of three thousand clergymen inflicts upon religion ! How yet more prodigious must be the sum of mischief which results from that negligence of duty of which non-residence is but *one* effect ! Yet all this is occasioned by our religious establishment. "The total *absence of non-residence and pluralities* in the Church of Scotland, and the annual examination of all the inhabitants of the parish by its minister, *are circumstances highly advantageous to religion*."[1]

105. The minister in the English Church is under peculiar disadvantages in enforcing the truths or the duties of religion upon irreligious or sceptical men. Many of the topics which such men urge are directed, not against Christianity, but against *that exhibition* of Christianity which is afforded by the church. It has been seen that *this* is the cause of infidelity. How then shall the established clergyman efficiently defend our religion? He may indeed confine himself to the vindication of Christianity without reference to a church ; but then he does not defend that exhibition of Christianity which his own church affords. The sceptic presses him with those things which it is confessed are wrong. He must either defend them, or give them up as indefensible. If he defends them, he confirms the sceptic in his unbelief ; if he gives them up, he declares not only that the church is in the wrong, but that himself is in the wrong too ; and in either case, his fitness for an advocate of our religion is impaired.

106. Hitherto I have enforced the observations of this chapter by the authority of others. Now I have to appeal for confirmation to the experience of the reader himself. That peculiar mode of injury to the cause of virtue of which I speak, has received its most extensive illustrations during the present century ; and it has hitherto, perhaps, been the subject rather of private remark than of public disquisition. I refer to a sort of instinctive recoil from new measures that are designed to promote the intellectual, the moral, or the religious improvement of the public. I appeal to the experience of those philanthropic men who spend their time either in their own neighbourhoods, or in "going about doing good," whether they do not meet with a greater degree of this recoil from works of philanthropy amongst the teachers and members of the state religion than amongst other men—and whether this recoil is not the strongest amongst that portion who are reputed to be the most zealous friends of the church. Has not this been your experience with respect to the Slave Trade and to Slavery—with respect to the education of the people—with respect to scientific or literary institutions for the labouring ranks—with respect to sending preachers to pagan countries—with respect to the Bible Society? Is it not familiar to you to be in doubt and apprehension respecting the assistance of *these* members of the establishment, when you have no fear and no doubt of the assistance of other Christians ? Do you not call upon others, and invite their co-operation with confidence ? Do you not call upon these with distrust, and is not that distrust the result of your previous experience ?

107. Take, for example, that very simple institution, the Bible Society—simple, because its only object is, to distribute the authorised records of the dispensations of God. It is an institution upon which it may be almost said, that but one opinion is entertained—that of its great utility ; but one desire is felt—that of co-operation, *except* by the members of established churches. From this institution the most zealous advocates of the English Church stand aloof. Whilst Christians of other names are friendly almost to a man, the proportion is very large of *those* churchmen who show no friendliness. It were to no purpose to say that they have claims peculiarly upon themselves, for so have other Christians—claims which generally are complied with to a greater extent. Besides, it is obvious that these claims are not the grounds of the conduct that we deplore. If they were, we should still possess the cordial approbation of these persons—their personal, if not their pecuniary support. From such persons silence and absence are positive discouragement. How then are we to account for the phenomenon ? By the operation of a state religion. For when our philanthropist applies to the members of another church, their only question perhaps is, Will the projected institution be useful to mankind ? But when he applies to such a member of the state religion, he considers, How will it affect the establishment?—Will it increase the influence of dissenters?—May it not endanger the immunities of the church?—Is it countenanced by our superiors?—Is it agreeable to the administration ? And when

[1] Gisborne : Duties of Men.

all these considerations have been pursued, he very commonly finds something that persuades him that it is most "prudent" not to encourage the proposition. It should be remarked too, as an additional indication of the *cause* of this recoil from works of goodness, that where the genius of the state religion is most influential, there is commonly the greatest backwardness in works of mental and religious philanthropy. The places of peculiar frigidity are the places in which there are the greatest number of the dignitaries of the church.

108. Thus it is that the melioration of mankind is continually and greatly impeded, by the workings of an institution of which the express design is to extend the influence of religion and morality. Greatly impeded : for England is one of the principal sources of the current of human improvement, and in England the influence of this institution is great. These are fruits which are not borne by good and healthy trees. How can the tree be good of which these are the fruits ? Are these fruits the result of episcopacy ? No, but of *episcopacy wedded to the state*. Were this union dissolved (and the parties are not of that number whom *God* hath joined), not only would human reformation go forward with an accelerated pace, but Episcopalianism itself would in some degree arise and shake herself as from the dust of the earth. She would find that her political alliance has bound around her glittering but yet enslaving chains—chains which, hugged and cherished as they are, have ever fixed her, and ever will fix her, to the earth, and make her earthly.

109. The mode in which the legal provision for the ministry is made in this country, contains, like many other parts of the institution, evils superadded to those which are necessarily incidental to a state religion. If there be any one thing which, more than another, ought to prevail between a Christian minister and those whom he teaches, it is harmony and kindliness of feeling ; and this kindliness and harmony is peculiarly diminished by the system of tithes. There is no circumstance which so often "disturbs the harmony that should ever subsist between a clergyman and his parishioners as contentions respecting tithes."[1] Vicessimus Knox goes further : "One great cause of the clergy's losing their influence is, that the laity in this age of scepticism grudge them their tithes. The decay of religion and the contempt of the clergy arise in a great measure from this source."[2] What advantages can compensate for the contempt of Christian ministers and the decay of religion ? Or

[1] Gisborne: Duties of Men.   [2] Essays, No. 10.

who does not perceive that a legal provision might be made which would be productive, so far as the new system of itself was concerned, of fewer evils ?—Of the political ill consequences of the tithe system I say nothing here. If they were much less than they are, or if they did not exist at all, there is sufficient evidence against the system in its moral effects.

110. It is well known, and the fact is very creditable, that the clergy exact tithes with much less rigour, and consequently occasion far fewer heartburnings, than lay claimants. The want of cordiality often results, too, from the cupidity of the payers, who invent vexatious excuses to avoid payment of the whole claim, and are on the alert to take disreputable advantages.

111. But to the conclusions of the Christian moralist it matters little by what agency a bad system operates. The principal point of his attention is the system itself. If it be bad, it will be sure to find agents by whom its pernicious principles will be elicited and brought into practical operation. It is therefore no extenuation of the system, that the clergy frequently do not disagree with their parishioners : whilst it is a part of the system that tithes are sold, and sold to him, of whatever character, who will give most for them—he will endeavour to make the most of them again. So that the evils which result from the tithe system, although they are not chargeable upon religious establishments, are chargeable upon our own, and are an evidence against it. The animosities which tithe farmers occasion are attributable to the tithe system. Ordinary men do not make nice discriminations. He who is angry with the tithe farmer is angry with the rector, who puts the power of vexation into his hands, and he who is out of temper with the teacher of religion loses some of his complacency in religion itself. You cannot then prevent the loss of harmony between the shepherd and his flock, the loss of his influence over their affections, the contempt of the clergy, and the decay of religion, from tithes. You must amend the civil institution, or you cannot prevent the religious mischief.

112. Reviewing, then, the propositions and arguments which have been delivered in the present chapter — propositions which rest upon the authority of the parties concerned, what is the general conclusion ? If Religious Establishments are constitutionally injurious to Christianity, is not our establishment productive of superadded and accumulated injury ?— Let not the writer of these pages be charged with enmity to religion because he thus speaks. Ah ! they are the best

friends of the church who endeavour its amendment. I may be one of those who, in the language of Lord Bexley, shall be regarded as an enemy, because, in the exhibition of its evils, I have used great plainness of speech. But I cannot help it. I have other motives than those which are affected by these censures of men; and shall be content to bear my portion, if I can promote that purification of a Christian church, of which none but the prejudiced or the interested deny the need. They who endeavour to conceal the need may be the advocates, but they are not the *friends* of the church. The wound of the daughter of my people may not be slightly healed. It is vain to cry Peace, Peace, when there is no peace. What then will the reader, who has noticed the testimonies which have been offered in this chapter, think of the propriety of such statements as these? The "establishment is the firmest support and noblest ornament of Christianity."[1] It "presents the best security under heaven for the preservation of the true apostolical faith in this country."[2] "Manifold as are the blessings for which Englishmen are beholden to the institutions of their country—there is no part of those institutions from which they derive more important advantages than from its church establishment."[3] Especially what will the reader think of the language of Hannah More?—Hannah More says of the established church, "Here Christianity presents herself neither dishonoured, degraded, nor disfigured;" Bishop Watson says of its creed, that it is "a motley monster of bigotry and superstition." Hannah More says, "Here Christianity is set before us in all her original purity;" Archdeacon Blackburn says, that "the forms of the church, having been weighed in the balance of the sanctuary, are found greatly wanting." Hannah More says, "She has been *completely rescued* from that encumbering load under which she had so long groaned, and delivered from her heavy bondage by the labours of our blessed reformers;"[4] Dr. Lowth says, that the reformation from Popery "stopped in the midway." Hannah More says, "We here see Christianity in her whole consistent character—in all her fair and just proportions—as she came from the hands of her divine author;" Dr. Watson calls her creed "a scarecrow, dressed up of old by philosophers and Popes." To say that the language of this good woman is imprudent and improper, is to say very little. Yet I would say no more. Her own language is her severest censurer. When will it be sufficiently remembered that the evils of a system can neither be veiled nor defended

by praise? When will it be remembered that, if we "contend for abuses," the hour will arrive when "correction will be applied with no sparing hand?"

113. It has frequently been said, that "the church is in danger." What is meant by the church? Or what is it that is endangered? Is it meant that the episcopal form of church government is endangered —that some religious revolution is likely to take place, by which a Christian community shall be precluded from adopting that internal constitution which it thinks best? This surely cannot be feared. The day is gone by, in England at least, when the abolition of Prelacy could become a measure of state. One community has its conference, and another its annual assembly, and another its independency, without any molestation. Who, then, would molest the English Church because it prefers the government of bishops and deacons to any other? Is it meant that the *doctrines* of the church are endangered, or that its liturgy will be prohibited? Surely no. Whilst every other church is allowed to preach what doctrines it pleases, and to use what formularies it pleases, the liberty will not surely be denied to the Episcopal Church. If the doctrines and government of that church be Christian and true, there is no reason to fear for their stability. Its members have superabundant ability to defend the truth. What then is it that is endangered. Of what are those who complain of danger afraid? Is it meant that its civil immunities are endangered—that its revenues are endangered? Is it meant that its members will hereafter have to support their ministers without assistance from other churches? Is it feared that there will cease to be such things as rich deaneries and bishoprics? Is it feared that the members of other churches will become eligible to the legislature, and that the heads of this church will not be temporal peers? In brief, is it feared that this church will become merely one amongst the many, with no privileges but such as are common to good citizens and good Christians? These surely are the things of which they are afraid. It is not for religious truth, but for civil immunities: it is not for forms of church government, but for political preeminence: it is not for the church, but for the church *establishment*. Let a man, then, when he joins in the exclamation, The church is in danger! present to his mind distinct ideas of his meaning and of the object of his fears. If his alarm and his sorrow are occasioned, not for religion, but for politics—not for the purity and usefulness of the church, but for its immunities— not for the offices of its ministers, but for their splendours—let him be at peace.

[1] Dr. Howley, Bishop of London: Charge, 1814, p. 25.
[2] On the Nature of Schism, by C. Daubeny, Archdeacon of Sarum, p. 153.
[3] First words of Southey's Book of the Church.
[4] Moral Sketches, 3d edit. p. 9.

There is nothing in all this for which the Christian needs to be in sorrow or in fear.

114. And why? Because all that constitutes a church, as a Christian community, may remain when these things are swept away. There may be prelates without nobility; there may be deans and archdeacons without benefices and patronage; there may be pastors without a legal provision; there may be a liturgy without a test.

115. In the sense in which it is manifest that the phrase, "the church is in danger," is ordinarily to be understood—that is, "the *establishment* is in danger"—the fears are undoubtedly well founded: the danger is real and imminent. It may not be immediate perhaps: perhaps it may not be near at hand; but it is real, imminent, inevitable. The establishment is indeed in danger; and I believe that no advocacy, however zealous, that no support, however determined, that no power, however great, will preserve it from destruction. If the declarations which have been cited in this chapter be true—if the reasonings which have been offered in this and in the last be just, who is the man that, *as a Christian*, regrets its danger, or would delay its fall? He may wish to delay it as a politician; he may regret it as an expectant of temporal advantages; but as a Christian he will rejoice.

116. Supposing the doctrines and government of the church to be sound, it is probable that its stability would be increased by what is called its destruction. It would then only be detached from that alliance with the state which encumbers it, and weighs it down, and despoils its beauty, and obscures its brightness. Contention for this alliance will eventually be found to illustrate the proposition, that a man's greatest enemies are those of his own household. *He* is the practical enemy of the church who endeavours the continuance of its connection with the state: except indeed that the more zealous the endeavour, the more quickly, it is probable, the connection will be dissolved: and therefore, though such persons "mean not so, neither do their hearts think so," yet they may thus be the agents, in the hand of God, of hastening the day in which she shall be purified from every evil thing; in which she shall arise and shine, because her light is come, and because the glory of the Lord is risen upon her.

117. Let him, then, who can discriminate between the church and its alliances, consider these things. Let him purify and exalt his attachment. If his love to the church be the love of a Christian, let him avert his eye from everything that is political; let his hopes and fears be excited only by religion; and let his exertions be directed to that which alone ought to concern a Christian church, its purity and its usefulness.

118. In concluding a discussion in which it has been needful to utter with plainness unwelcome truths, and to adduce testimonies which some readers may wish to be concealed, I am solicitous to add the conviction, with respect to the *ministers* of the English Church, that there is happily a diminished ground of complaint and reprehension—the conviction that, whilst the liturgy is unamended and unrevised, the number of ministers is increased to whom temporal things are secondary motives, and who endeavour to be faithful ministers of one common Lord: the conviction too, with respect to other members of the church, that they are collectively advancing in the Christian path, and that there is an "evident extension of religion within her borders." Many of these, both of the teachers and of the taught, are persons with whom the writer of these pages makes no pretensions of Christian equality yet even to these he would offer one monitory suggestion— They are critically situated with reference to the political alliance of the church. Let them beware that they mingle not, with their good works and faith unfeigned, any confederacy with that alliance which will assuredly be laid in the dust. That confederacy has ever had one invariable effect —to diminish the Christian brightness of those who are its partisans. It will have the same effect upon them. If they are desirous of superadding to their Christianity the privileges and emoluments of a state religion—if they endeavour to retain in the church the interests of both worlds—if, together with their desire to serve God with a pure heart, they still cling to the advantages which this unholy alliance brings —and, contending for the faith, contend also for the establishment—the effect will be bad as the endeavour will be vain; bad, for it will obstruct their own progress and the progress of others in the Christian path: and vain, for the fate of that establishment is sealed.

119. In making these joyful acknowledgments of the increase of Christianity within the borders of the church, one truth, however, must be added; and it is a solemn truth—The increase is not attributable to the state religion, but has taken place *notwithstanding* it is a state religion. I appeal to the experience of good men: has the amendment been the effect of the establishment as such? Has the political connection of the church occasioned the amendment or promoted it? Nay—Has the amendment been encouraged by those on whom the political connection had the greatest influence? No : the reader, if he be an observer of religious affairs, knows that the state alliance is so far from having effected a reformation, that it does not even regard the instruments of that reformation with complacency.

CHAPTER XVI.

Of Legal Provision for Christian Teachers—Of Voluntary Payment and of Unpaid Ministry.

Compulsory payment—America—Legal provision for *one* church unjust—Payment of tithes by dissenters—Tithes a "property of the church"—Voluntary payment—The system of remuneration—Qualifications of a minister of the gospel—Unpaid ministry—Days of greater purity.

1. If some of the observations of the present chapter are not accurately classed with political subjects, I have to offer the apology that the intimacy of their connection with the preceding discussions appears to afford a better reason for placing them here than an adherence to system affords for placing them elsewhere. " The substance of method is often sacrificed to the exterior show of it." [1]

Legal Provision.

2. By one of those instances which happily are not unfrequent in the *progress* of human opinion from error to truth, the notion of a *divine right* on the part of any Christian teachers to a stated portion of the products of other men's labours, is now nearly given up.[2] There was a time when the advocate of the claim would have disdained to refer for its foundation to questions of expediency or the law of the land. And he probably as little thought that the divine right would ever have been given up by its advocates, as his successors now think that they have fallacious grounds in reasoning upon public utility. Thus it is that the labours of our predecessors in the cause of Christian purity

[1] Bishop Warburton.
[2] Yet let it not be forgotten that it is upon this exploded notion of the divine right that the legal right is founded. The law did not give tithes to the clergy because the provision was expedient, but because it was their divine right. It is upon this assumption that the law is founded. See Statutes at Large, 29 Hen. VIII. c. 20. Mem. in the MS. " The whole was received into a common fund, for the fourfold purpose of supporting the clergy, repairing the church, relieving the poor, and entertaining the pilgrim and the stranger."—" The payment of tithes had at first been voluntary, though it was considered as a religious obligation. King Ethelwolf, the father of Alfred, subjected the whole kingdom to it by a legislative act."—Southey's Book of the Church, c. 6. Mem. in the MS.
Wickliffe's followers asserted, "That tithes were purely eleemosynary, and might be withheld by the people upon a delinquency in the pastor, and transferred to another at pleasure."—Brodie's History of the British Empire, Introduction. Mem. in the MS.

have taken a large portion of labour out of our hands. They carried the outworks of the citadel ; and whilst its defenders have retired to some inner stronghold, it becomes the business of our day to essay the firmness of its walls. The writer of these pages may essay them in vain ; but he doubts not that before some power their defenders, as they have hitherto retired, will continue to retire, until the whole fortress is abandoned. Abandoned to the enemy? Oh no.—He is the *friend* of a Christian community who induces Christian principles into its practice.

3. In considering the evidence which Christianity affords respecting the lawfulness of making a legal provision for one Christian church, I would not refer to those passages of Scripture which appear to bear upon the question, whether Christian ministrations should be absolutely free : partly, because I can add nothing to the often urged tendency of those passages, and partly, because they do not all concern the question of legal provision. The man who thinks Christianity requires that those who labour in the gospel should live of the gospel, does not *therefore* think that a legal provision should be made for the ministers of one exclusive church.

4. One thing seems perfectly clear—that to receive from their hearers, and from those who heard them not, a compulsory payment for their preaching, is totally alien to all the practices of the apostles, and to the whole tenor of the principles by which they were actuated. Their one single and simple motive in preaching Christianity was to obey God, to do good to man ; nor do I believe that any man imagines it possible that they would have accepted of a compulsory remuneration from their own hearers, and especially from those who heard them not. We are therefore entitled to repeat the observation, that this consideration affords evidence against the moral lawfulness of instituting such compulsory payment. Why would not, and could not, the apostles have accepted such payment, except for the reason that it *ought* not to be enforced? No account, so far as I perceive, can be given of the matter, but that the system is contrary to the purity of Christian practice.

5. An English prelate writes thus : " It is a question which might admit of serious discussion, whether the majority of the members of any civil community *have a right* to compel all the members of it to pay towards the maintenance of a set of teachers appointed by the majority to preach a particular system of doctrines." [1] No discussion could be en-

[1] See *Quarterly Review*, No. 58.
" There was a party in the nation who conceived that every man should not only be allowed to choose his own religion, but contribute as he himself thought proper

tertained respecting this right, except on the ground of its Christian unlawfulness. A legislature has a right to impose a general tax to support a government, whether a minority approves the tax or not ; and the bishop here rightly assumes that there is an antecedent question—whether it is morally lawful to oblige men to pay teachers whom they disapprove? It is from the want of taking this question into the account, that inquirers have involved themselves in fallacious reasonings. It is not a question of the right of taxation, but of the right of the magistrate to oblige men to violate their consciences. Of those who have regarded it simply as a question of taxation, and who therefore have proceeded upon fallacious grounds, the author of the "Duties of Men in Society" is one. He says, "If a state thinks that national piety and virtue will be best promoted by consigning the whole sum raised by law to teachers of a particular description—it has the same right to adopt this measure, as it would have to impose a general tax for the support of a board of physicians, should it deem that step conducive to national health." Far other—No man's Christian liberty is evaded, no man's conscience is violated, by paying a tax to a board of physicians ; but many a man's religious liberty may be invaded, and many a man's conscience may be violated, by paying for the promulgation of doctrines which he thinks Christianity condemns. Whither will the argument lead us? If a Papal state thinks it will promote piety to demand contributions for the splendid celebration of an auto-da-fé, would Protestant citizens act rightly in contributing? Or would the state act rightly in demanding the contribution? Or has a Brahmin state a right to impose a tax upon Christian residents to pay for the faggots of Hindoo immolations? The antecedent question in all these cases is—Whether the immolations, and the auto-da-fé, and the system of doctrines, are consistent with Christianity? If they are not, the citizens ought not to contribute to their practice or diffusion ; and by consequence, the state ought not to compel him to contribute. Now, for the purposes of the present argument, the consistency of any set of doctrines with Christianity cannot be proved. It is to no purpose for the Unitarian to say, *My system is true;* nor for the Calvinist or Arminian or Episcopalian to say, *My system is true.* The Unitarian has no Christian right to compel me to pay him for preaching Unitarianism, nor has any religious community a right to compel the members of another to pay him for promulgating his own opinions.

6. If by any revolution in the religious affairs of this country, another sect was elevated to the pre-eminence, and its ministers supported by a legal provision, I believe that the ministers of the present church would think it an unreasonable and unchristian act to compel them to pay the preachers of the new state religion. Would not a clergyman think himself aggrieved, if he were obliged to pay a Priestley, and to aid in disseminating the opinions of Priestley?—That same grievance is now inflicted upon other men. The rule is disregarded, to do as we would be done by.

7. Let us turn to the example of America. In America the government does not oblige its citizens to pay for the support of preachers. Those who join themselves to any particular religious community commonly contribute towards the support of its teachers, but there is no law of the state which compels it. This is as it should be. The government which *obliged* its citizens to pay, even if it were left to the individual to say to what class of preachers his money should be given, would act upon unsound principles. It may be that the citizen does not approve of paying ministers at all ; or there may be no sect in a country with which he thinks it right to hold communion. How would the reader himself be situated in Spain perhaps, or in Turkey, or in Hindostan? Would he think it right to be obliged to encourage Juggernaut or Mahomet, or the Pope.

8. But passing from this consideration : it is after all said, that in our own country the individual citizen does not *pay* the ministers of the state religion. I am glad that this seeming paradox is advanced, because it indicates that those who advance it confess that to make them pay would be wrong. Why else should they deny it? It is said, then, that persons who pay tithes do not *pay* the established clergy ; that tithes are property held as a person holds an estate ; that if tithes were taken off, rents would advance to the same amount ; that the buyer of an estate pays so much the less for it because it is subject to tithes—and therefore that neither owner nor occupier pays anything. This is specious, but only specious. The landholder "pays" the clergyman just as he pays the tax-gatherer. If taxes were taken off, rents would advance just as much as if tithes were taken off ; and a person may as well say that he does not pay taxes as that he does not pay tithes—The simple fact is, that an order of clergy are, in this

---

towards the support of the pastor whose duties he exacted. The party, however, does not appear to have been great. Yet let us not despise the opinion, but remember that it has been taken up by Dr. Adam Smith himself as a sound one, and been acted upon successfully in a vast empire, the United States of America."—Brodie's History of the British Empire, v. 4. p. 365. Mem. in the MS.

respect, in the same situation as the body of stockholders who live upon their dividends. They are supported by the country. The people pay the stockholder in the form of taxes, and the clergyman in the form of tithes. Suppose every clergyman in England were to leave the country to-morrow, and to cease to derive any income from it, it is manifest that the income which they now derive would be divided amongst those who remain—that is, that those who now pay would cease to pay. Rent, and taxes, and tithes, are in these respects upon one footing. Without now inquiring whether they are right, they are all payments—something by which a man does not receive the whole of the product of his labour.

9. The argument, therefore, which affirms that dissenters from the state religion do not pay to that religion, appears to be wholly fallacious; and being such, we are at liberty to assume, that to make them pay is indefensible and unchristian. For we repeat the observation, that he who is anxious to prove they do not pay, evinces his opinion that to compel them to pay would be wrong.

10. There is some injustice in the legal provision for one church. The episcopalian, when he has paid his teacher, or rather when he has contributed that portion towards the maintenance of his teacher which by the present system becomes his share, has no more to pay. The adherent to other churches has to pay his own preacher and his neighbour's. This does not appear to be just. The operation of a legal provision is, in effect, to impose a double tax upon one portion of the community without any fault on their part. Nor is it to any purpose to say, that the dissenter from the Episcopalian Church imposes the tax on himself; so he does; but it is just in the same sense as a man imposes a penalty upon himself when he conforms to some prohibited point of Christian duty. A Papist, two or three centuries ago, might almost as well have said that a Protestant imposed the stake on himself, because he might have avoided it if he chose. It is a voluntary tax in no other way than as all other taxes are voluntary. It is a tax imposed by the state as truly as the window tax is imposed, because a man may, if he pleases, live in darkness; or as a capitation tax is imposed, because a man may, if he pleases, lose his head.

11. But what is he who conscientiously disapproves of a state religion to do? Is he, notwithstanding his judgment, to aid in supporting that religion, *because* the law requires it? No: for then, as it respects him, the obligation of the law is taken away. He is not to do what he believes Christianity forbids, because the state commands it. If public practice be a criterion of the public judgment, it may be concluded that the number of those who do thus believe respecting our state religion is very small; for very few decline actively to support it. Yet when it is considered how numerous the dissenters from the English establishment are, and how emphatically some of them disapprove the forms or doctrines of that establishment, it might be imagined that the number who decline thus to support it would, in consistency, be great. How are we to account for the fact as it is? Are we to suppose that the objections of these persons to the establishment are such as do not make it a case of conscience whether they shall support it or not? Or are we to conclude that they sacrifice their consciences to the terrors of a distraint? If no case of conscience is involved, the dissenter, though he may think the state religion inexpedient, can hardly think it wrong. And if he do not think it *wrong*, why should he be so zealous in opposing it, or why should he expect the church to make concessions in his favour? If, on the other hand, he sacrifices his conscience to his fears, it is obvious that, before he reprehends the establishment, he should rectify himself. He should leave the mote till he has taken out the beam.

12. Perhaps there are some who, seriously disapproving of the state religion, suspect that in Christian integrity they ought not to pay to its support—and yet are not so fully convinced of this, or do not so fully act upon the conviction, as really to decline to pay. If they are convinced, let them remember their responsibility, and not know their Master's will in vain. If these are not faithful, where shall fidelity be found? How shall the Christian churches be purified from their defilements, if those who see and deplore their defilements contribute to their continuance? Let them show that their principles are worthy a little sacrifice. Fidelity on their part, and a Christian submission to the consequences, might open the eyes and invigorate the religious principle of many more; and at length the objection to comply with these unchristian demands might be so widely extended, that the legislature would be induced to withdraw its legal provision; and thus one main constituent of an ecclesiastical system, which has grievously obstructed, and still grievously obstructs, the Christian cause, might be taken away.

13. As an objection to this fidelity of practice it has been said, that since a man rents or buys an estate for so much less

because it is subject to tithes, it is an act of dishonesty afterwards to refuse to pay them. The answer is this—that no dishonesty can be committed whilst the law exacts payment by distraint; and if the law were altered, there is no place for dishonesty. Besides, the desire of saving money does not enter into the refuser's motives. He does not decline to pay from motives of interest, but from motives of duty.

14. It is, however, argued that the legislature has no *right* to take away tithes any more than it has a right to deprive citizens of their lands and houses; and that a man's property in tithes is upon a footing with his property in an estate. Now, we answer that this is not true in fact; and that, if it were, it would not serve the argument.

15. It is not true in fact.—If tithes were a property, just *as* an estate is a property, why do men complain of the scandal of pluralities? Who ever hears of the scandal of possessing three or four estates? Why, again, does the law punish simoniacal contracts? Who ever hears of simoniacal contracts for lands and houses? The truth is, that tithes are regarded as religious property. The property is legally recognised, not for the sake of the individual who may possess it, but for the sake of religion. The law cares nothing for the men, except so far as they are ministers. Besides, tithes are a portion of the *produce* only of the land. The tithe-owner cannot walk over an estate, and say of every tenth acre, this is mine. In truth he has not, except by consent of the landholder, any property in it at all; for the landholder may, if he pleases, refuse to cultivate it—occasion it to produce nothing; and then the tithe-owner has no interest or property in it whatever. And in what sense can that be said to be property, the possession of which is at the absolute discretion of another man?

16. But grant for a moment that tithes are property. Is it affirmed that whatever property a man possesses cannot be taken from him by the legislature? Suppose I go to Jamaica and purchase a slave, and bring him to England, has the law no right to take this property away? Assuredly it has the right, and it exercises it too. Now, so far as the argument is concerned, the cases of the slave-holder and of the tithe-owner are parallel. Compulsory maintenance of Christian ministers, and compulsory retention of men in bondage, are *both inconsistent with Christianity*; and as such, the property which consists in slaves and in tithes may rightly be taken away—unless, indeed, any man will affirm that any property, however acquired, cannot lawfully be taken from the possessor. But when we speak of taking away the property in tithes, we do not refer to the consideration that it has been under the sanction of the law itself that that property has been purchased or obtained. The law has, in reality, been accessory to the offence, and it would not be decent or right to take away the possession which has resulted from that offence, without offering an equivalent. I would not advise a legislature to say to those persons who, under its own sanction, have purchased slaves, to turn upon them and say, I am persuaded that slavery is immoral, and therefore I command you to set your slaves at liberty;—and because you have no moral right to hold them, I shall not grant you a compensation. Nor, for the same reasons, would I advise a legislature to say so to the possessor of tithes.

17. But what sort of a compensation is to be offered? Not surely an amount equivalent to the principal money, computing tithes as interest. The compensation is for life interest only. The legislature would have to buy off, not a freehold but an annuity. The tithe-owner is not like the slave-holder, who can bequeath his property to another. When the present incumbent dies, the tithes, as property, cease to exist—until it is again appropriated to an incumbent by the patron of the living. This is true except in the instances of those deplorable practices, the purchase of advowsons, or of any other by which individuals or bodies acquire a pecuniary interest in the right of disposal.

18. The notion that tithes are a "property of the church" is quite a fiction. In this sense, what is the church? If no individual man has his property taken away by a legislative abolition of tithes, it is unmeaning to talk of "the church" having lost it.

19. It is, perhaps, a vain thing to talk of *how* the legislature might do a thing which perhaps it may not resolve, for ages, to do at all. But if it were to take away the right to tithes as the present incumbents died, or as the interests of the present owners ceased, there would be no reason to complain of injustice, whatever there might be of procrastinating the fulfilment of a Christian duty.

20. Whether a good man, knowing the inconsistency of forced maintenance with the Christian law, ought to accept a proffered equivalent for that maintenance, is another consideration. If it is wrong to retain it, it is not obvious how it can be right, or how at least it can avoid the appearance of evil, to accept money for giving it up. It is upon these principles that the religious community who decline to pay tithes, decline also to receive them. By legacy or otherwise, the

legal right is sometimes possessed by these persons, but their moral discipline requires alike a refusal to *receive* or to pay.

Voluntary Payment.[1]

21. That this system possesses many advantages over a legal provision we have already seen. But this does not imply that even voluntary payment is conformable with the dignity of the Christian ministry, with its usefulness, or with the requisitions of the Christian law.

22. And here I am disposed, in the outset, to acknowledge that the question of payment is involved in an antecedent question —the necessary qualifications of a Christian minister. If one of these necessary qualifications be, that he should devote his youth and early manhood to theological studies, or to studies or exercises of any kind, I do not perceive how the propriety of voluntary payment can be disputed; for, when a man who might otherwise have fitted himself, in a counting-house or an office, for procuring his after-support, employs his time necessarily in qualifying himself for a Christian instructor, it is indispensable that he should be paid for his instructions. Or if, after he has assumed the ministerial function, it be his indispensable business to devote all or the greater portion of his time to studies or other preparations for the pulpit, the same necessity remains. He must be paid for his ministry, because, in order to be a minister, he is prevented from maintaining himself.

23. But the necessary qualifications of a minister of the gospel cannot here be discussed. We pass on, therefore, with the simple expression of the sentiment, that how beneficial soever a theological education and theological inquiries may be in the exercise of the office, yet that they form no *necessary* qualifications ;—that men may be, and that some are, true and sound ministers of that gospel without them.

24. Now, in inquiring into the Christian character and tendency of payment for preaching Christianity, one position will perhaps be recognised as universally true —that if the same ability and zeal in the exercise of the ministry could be attained without payment as with it, the payment might reasonably and rightly be forborne. Nor will it perhaps be disputed, that if Christian teachers of the present day were possessed of some good portion of the qualifications, and were actuated by the motives, of the first teachers of our religion, stated remuneration would not be needed. If love for mankind, and "the ability which God giveth," were strong enough to induce and to enable men to preach the gospel without payment, the employment of money as a motive would be without use or propriety. Remuneration is a contrivance adapted to an imperfect state of the Christian church : nothing but imperfection can make it needful ; and, when that imperfection shall be removed, it will cease to be needful again.

25. These considerations would lead us to expect, even antecedently to inquiry, that some ill effects are attendant upon the system of remuneration. Respecting these effects, one of the advocates of a legal provision holds language which, though it be much too strong, nevertheless *contains* much truth. " Upon the voluntary plan," says Dr. Paley, " preaching, in time, would become a mode of begging. With what sincerity or with what dignity can a preacher dispense the truths of Christianity, whose thoughts are perpetually solicited to the reflection how he may increase his subscription ? His eloquence, if he possess any, resembles rather the exhibition of a player, who is computing the profits of his theatre, than the simplicity of a man who, feeling himself the awful expectations of religion, is seeking to bring others to such a sense and understanding of their duty as may save their souls.—He, not only whose success, but whose subsistence depends upon collecting and pleasing a crowd, must resort to other arts than the acquirement and communication of sober and profitable instruction. For a preacher to be thus at the mercy of his audience, to be obliged to adapt his doctrines to the pleasure of a capricious multitude, to be continually affecting a style and manner neither natural to him nor agreeable to his judgment, to live in constant bondage to tyrannical and insolent directors, are circumstances so mortifying not only to the pride of the human heart, but to the virtuous love of independency, that they are rarely submitted to, without a sacrifice of principle and a depravation of character ;—at least it may be pronounced, that a ministry so degraded would soon fall into the lowest hands ; for it would be found impossible to engage men of worth and ability in so precarious and humiliating a profession.[1]

26. To much of this it is a sufficient answer, that the predictions are contradicted by the fact. Of those teachers who are supported by voluntary subscriptions, it is *not true* that their eloquence resembles the exhibition of a player who is computing the

---

[1] " Thou shalt take no gift : for the gift blindeth the wise, and perverteth the words of the righteous."—Exod. xxiii. 8. Mem. in the MS.

[1] Mor. and Pol. Phil., b. 6, c. 10.

profits of his theatre; for the fact is, that a very large proportion of them assiduously devote themselves from better motives to the religious benefit of their flocks: it is *not true* that the office is rarely undertaken without what can be called the depravation of character; for the character, both religious and moral, of those teachers who are voluntarily paid, is at least as exemplary as that of those who are paid by provision of the state: it is *not true* that the office falls into the lowest hands, and that it is impossible to engage men of worth and ability in the profession, because very many of such men are actually engaged in it.

27. But although the statements of the Archdeacon are not wholly true, they are true in part. *Preaching will become a mode of begging.* When a congregation wants a preacher, and we see a man get into the pulpit, expressly and confessedly to show how he can preach, in order that the hearers may consider how they like him, and when *one* object of his thus doing is confessedly to obtain an income, there is reason—not certainly for speaking of him as a beggar—but for believing that the dignity and freedom of the gospel are sacrificed.—*Thoughts perpetually solicited to the reflection how he may increase his subscription.* Supposing this to be the language of exaggeration, supposing the increase of his subscription to be his subordinate concern, yet still it *is* his concern, and being his concern, it is his temptation. It is to be feared, that by the influence of this temptation his sincerity and his independence may be impaired, that the consideration of what his hearers *wish* rather than of what he thinks they need, may prompt him to sacrifice his conscience to his profit, and to add or to deduct something from the counsel of God. Such temptation necessarily exists; and it were only to exhibit ignorance of the motives of human conduct to deny that it will sometimes prevail.—*To live in constant bondage to insolent and tyrannical directors.* It is not necessary to suppose that directors will be tyrannical or insolent, nor by consequence to suppose that the preacher is in a state of constant bondage. But if they be not tyrants and he a slave, they may be masters and he a servant: a servant in a sense far different from that in which the Christian minister is required to be a servant of the church—in a sense which implies an undue subserviency of his ministrations to the will of men, and which is *incompatible* with the obligation to have *no* master but Christ.

28. Other modes of voluntary payment may be and perhaps they are adopted, but the effect will not be essentially different. Subscriptions may be collected from a number of congregations and thrown into a common fund, which fund may be appropriated by a directory or conference: but the objections still apply: for he who wishes to obtain an income as a preacher, has then to try to propitiate the directory instead of a congregation, and the temptation to sacrifice his independence and his conscience remains.

29. There is no way of obtaining emancipation from this subjection, no way of avoiding this temptation, but by a system in which the Christian ministry is absolutely free.

30. But the ill effects of thus paying preachers are not confined to those who preach. The habitual consciousness that the preacher is *paid,* and the notion which some men take no pains to separate from this consciousness, that he preaches *because* he is paid, have a powerful tendency to diminish the influence of his exhortations, and the general effect of his labours. The vulgarly irreligious think, or pretend to think, that it is a sufficient excuse for disregarding these labours to say, They are a matter of course—preachers must say something, because it is their trade. And it is more than to be feared that notions, the same in kind however different in extent, operate upon a large proportion of the community. It is not probable that it should be otherwise; and thus it is that a continual deduction is made by the hearer from the preacher's disinterestedness or sincerity, and a continual deduction therefore from the effect of his labours.

31. How seldom can such a pastor say, with full demonstration of sincerity, "I seek not yours, but you." The flock may indeed be, and happily it often is, his first and greatest motive to exertion; but the demonstrative evidence that it is so, can only be afforded by those whose ministrations are absolutely free. The deduction which is thus made from the practical influence of the labours of stipended preachers, is the same in kind (though differing in amount) as that which is made from a pleader's addresses in court. He pleads because he is paid for pleading. Who does not perceive, that if an able man came forward and pleaded in a cause without a retainer, and simply from the desire that justice should be awarded, he would be listened to with much more of confidence, and that his arguments would have much more weight, than if the same words were uttered by a barrister who was fee'd? A similar deduction is made from the *writings* of paid ministers, especially if they advocate their own particular faith. "He is interested evidence," says the reader—he has got a retainer, and of course argues for his client; and thus arguments that may be

invincible, and facts that may be incontrovertibly true, lose some portion of their effect, even upon virtuous men, and a large portion upon the bad, *because the preacher is paid*. If, as is sometimes the case, "the amount of the salary given is regulated very precisely by the frequency of the ministry required," --so that a hearer may possibly allow the reflection, The preacher will get half a guinea for the sermon he is going to preach—it is almost impossible that the dignity of the Christian ministry should not be reduced, as well as that the influence of his exhortations should not be diminished. "It is, however, more desirable," says Milton, "for example to be, and for the preventing of offence or suspicion, as well as more noble and honourable in itself, and conducive to our more complete glorying in God, to render an unpaid service to the church, in this as well as in all other instances; and after the example of our Lord, to minister and serve gratuitously."¹

32. Some ministers expend all the income which they derive from their office in acts of beneficence. To these we may safely appeal for confirmation of these remarks. Do you not find that the consciousness, in the minds of your hearers, that you gain nothing by your labour, greatly increases its influence upon them? Do you not find that they listen to you with more confidence and regard, and more willingly admit the truths which you inculcate and conform to the advices which you impart? If these things be so—and who will dispute it?—how great must be the aggregate obstruction which pecuniary remuneration opposes to the influence of religion in the world.

33. But indeed it is not practicable to the writer to illustrate the whole of what he conceives to be the truth upon this subject, without a brief advertence to the qualifications of the minister of the gospel: because, if his view of these qualifications be just, the stipulation for such and such exercise of the ministry, and such and such payment, is *impossible*. If it is "admitted that the ministry of the gospel is the work of the Lord, that it can be rightly exercised only in virtue of his appointment," and only when "a necessity is laid upon the minister to preach the gospel,"—it is manifest, that he *cannot* engage beforehand to preach when others desire it. It is manifest, that "the compact which binds the minister to preach on the condition that his hearers shall pay him for his preaching, assumes the character of absolute inconsistency with the spirituality of the Christian religion."²

¹ Christian Doctrine, p. 484.
² I would venture to suggest to some of those to whom these considerations are offered, whether the notion that a

34. Freely ye have received, freely give. When we contemplate a Christian minister who illustrates, both in his commission and in his practice, this language of his Lord; who teaches, advises, reproves, with the authority and affection of a commissioned teacher; who fears not to displease his hearers, and desires not to receive their reward; who is under no temptation to withhold, and does not withhold, any portion of that counsel which he thinks God designs for His church;—when we contemplate such a man, we may feel somewhat of thankfulness and of joy;—of thankfulness and joy that the Universal Parent thus enables His creatures to labour for the good of one another, in that same spirit in which He cares for them and blesses them himself.

35. I censure not, either in word or in thought, him who, in sincerity of mind, accepts remuneration for his labours in the church. It may not be inconsistent with the dispensations of Providence, that in the present imperfect condition of the Christian family, imperfect principles respecting the ministry should be permitted to prevail: nor is it to be questioned that some of those who do receive remuneration, are fulfilling *their* proper allotments in the universal church. But this does not evince that we should not anticipate the arrival, and promote the extension, of a more perfect state. It does not evince that a higher allotment may not await their successors—that days of greater purity and brightness may not arrive :—of purity, when every motive of the Christian minister shall be simply Christian; and of brightness, when the light of truth shall be displayed with greater effulgence. When the Great Parent of all shall thus turn His favour towards His people; when He shall supply them with teachers exclusively of His own appointment, it will be perceived that the ordinary present state of the Christian ministry is adapted only to the *twilight* of the Christian day; and some of those who now faithfully labour in this hour of twilight will be amongst the first to rejoice in the greater glory of the noon.

preacher is a *sine qua non* of the exercise of public worship, is not taken up without sufficient consideration of the principles which it involves. If, "where two or three are gathered together in the name" of Christ, there He, the minister of the sanctuary, is "in the midst of them," it surely cannot be *necessary* to the exercises of such worship that another preacher should be there. Surely, too, it derogates something from the excellence, something from the glory of the Christian dispensation, to assume that, if a number of Christians should be so situated as to be without a preacher, there the public worship of God cannot be performed. This may often happen in remote places, in voyages or the like; and I have sometimes been impressed with the importance of these considerations when I have heard a person say, "—— is absent, and *therefore* there will be no divine service this morning."

CHAPTER XVII.
Patriotism.

Patriotism as it is viewed by Christianity—A Patriotism which is opposed to general benignity—Patriotism not the soldier's motive.

36. We are presented with a beautiful subject of contemplation, when we discover that the principles which Christianity advances upon its own authority, are recommended and enforced by their practical adaptation to the condition and the wants of man. With such a subject I think we are presented in the case of Patriotism.

37. "Christianity does not encourage particular patriotism in opposition to general benignity."[1] If it did, it would not be adapted *for the world*. The duties of the subject of one state would often be in opposition to those of the subject of another, and men might inflict evil or misery upon neighbour nations in conforming to the Christian law. Christianity is designed to benefit, not a community, but the world. The promotion of the interests of one community by injuring another—that is, "patriotism in opposition to general benignity,"—it utterly rejects as wrong; and in doing this it does that which in a system of such wisdom and benevolence we should expect.—"The love of our country," says Adam Smith, "seems not to be derived from the love of mankind."[2]

38. I do not mean to say that the word patriotism is to be found in the New Testament, or that it contains any disquisitions respecting the proper extent of the love of our country; but I say that the universality of benevolence which Christianity inculcates, both in its essential character and in its precepts, is incompatible with that patriotism which would benefit our own community at the expense of general benevolence. Patriotism, as it is often advocated, is a low and selfish principle, a principle wholly unworthy of that enlightened and expanded philanthropy which religion proposes.

39. Nevertheless Christianity appears not to encourage the doctrine of being a "citizen of the world," and of paying no more regard to our own community than to every other. And why? Because such a doctrine is not rational; because it opposes the exercise of natural and virtuous feelings; and because, if it were attempted to be reduced to practice, it may be feared that it would destroy confined benignity without effecting a counterbalancing amount of universal philanthropy. This preference of our own nation is indicated in that strong language of Paul, "I could wish that myself were accursed from Christ for my brethren, my kinsmen according to the flesh, who are Israelites."[1] And a similar sentiment is inculcated by the admonition— "As we have, therefore, opportunity, let us do good unto *all* men, *especially* unto them who are of the household of faith."[2] In another place the same sentiment is applied to more private life :—" If any provide not *for his own, and especially for those of his own house*, he hath denied the faith."[3]

40. All this is perfectly consonant with reason and with nature. Since the helpless and those who need assistance must obtain it somewhere, where can they so rationally look for it, where shall they look for it at all except from those with whom they are connected in society? If these do not exercise benignity towards them, who will? And as to the dictate of nature, it is a law of nature that a man shall provide for his own. He is prompted to do this by the impulse of nature. Who, indeed, shall support, and cherish, and protect a child if his parents do not? That speculative philosophy is vain which would supplant these dictates by doctrines of general philanthropy. It cannot be applicable to human affairs until there is an alteration in the human constitution. Not only religion, therefore, but reason and nature, reject that philosophy which teaches that no man should prefer or aid another *because* he is his countryman, his neighbour, or his child :— for even this, the philosophy has taught us; and we have been seriously told that, in pursuance of general philanthropy, we ought not to cherish or support our own offspring in preference to other children. The effect of these doctrines, if they were reduced to practice, would be, not to diffuse universal benevolence, but to contract or destroy the charities of men for their families, their neighbours, and their country. It is an idle system of philosophy which sets out with extinguishing those principles of human nature which the Creator has implanted for wise and good ends. He that shall so far succeed in practising this philosophy as to look with indifference upon his parent, his wife, and his son, will not often be found with much zeal to exercise kindness and benevolence to the world at large.

41. Christianity rejects alike the extravagance of Patriotism and the extravagance of seeming philanthropy. Its precepts are ad-

---
[1] Bishop Watson.
[2] Theo. Mor. Sent. The limitation with which this opinion should be regarded we shall presently propose.

[1] Rom ix. 3.   [2] Gal. vi. 10.   [3] 1 Tim. v. 8.

dressed to us as men with human constitutions and as men in society. But to cherish and support my own child rather than others; to do good to my neighbours rather than to strangers; to benefit my own country rather than another nation, does not imply that we may *injure* other nations, or strangers, or their children, in order to do good to our own. Here is the point for discrimination—a point which vulgar patriotism and vulgar philosophy have alike overlooked.

42. The proper mode in which Patriotism should be exercised is that which does not necessarily respect other nations. He is the truest patriot who benefits his own country without diminishing the welfare of another. For which reason, those who induce improvements in the administration of justice, in the maxims of governing, in the political constitution of the state—or those who extend and rectify the education, or in any other manner amend the moral or social condition of a people, possess incomparably higher claims to the praise of patriotism than multitudes of those who receive it from the popular voice.

43. That patriotism which is manifested in political partisanship is frequently of a very questionable kind. The motives to this partisanship are often far other than the love of our country, even when the measure which a party pursues tends to the country's good; and many are called patriots, of whom both the motives and the actions are pernicious or impure. The most vulgar and unfounded talk of patriotism is that which relates to the agents of military operations. In general, the patriotism is of a kind which Christianity condemns; because it is "in opposition to general benignity." It does more harm to another country than good to our own. In truth, the merit often *consists* in the harm that is done to another country, with but little pretensions to benefiting our own. These agents, therefore, if they were patriotic at all, would commonly be so in an unchristian sense. And as to their being influenced by patriotism as a motive, the notion is ordinarily quite a fiction. When a Frenchman is sent with ten thousand others into Spain, or a Spaniard with an army into France, he probably is so far from acting the patriot that he does not know whether his country would not be more benefited by throwing down his arms; nor probably does he know about what the two nations are quarrelling. Men do not enter armies because they love their countries, but because they want a living, or are pleased with a military life: and when they have entered, they do not fight because they love their country, but because fighting is their business. At the very moment of fighting, the nation at home is perhaps divided in opinion as to the propriety of carrying on the war. One party maintains that the war is beneficial, and one that it is ruining the nation. But the soldier, for whatever he fights, and whether really in promotion of his country's good, or in opposition to it, is secure of his praise.

44. All this is sufficiently deceptive and absurd: the delusion would be ridiculous if the topic were not too grave for ridicule. It forms one amongst the many fictions by which the reputation of military affairs is kept up. *Why* such fictions are needful to the purpose, it may be wise for the reader to inquire. I suppose the cause is, that truth and reality would not serve the purposes of military reputation, and therefore that recourse is had to pleasant fictions. This may, however, have been done without a distinct consciousness, on the part of the inventors, of the delusions which they spread. I do not wholly coincide with the writer who says,—"The love of our country is one of those specious illusions which have been invented by impostors in order to render the multitude the blind instruments of their crooked designs."[1] The love of our country is a virtuous motive of action. The "specious illusion" consists in calling *that* "love of our country" which ought to be called by a far other name. As to those who have thus misnamed human motives and actions, I know not whether they have often been such wily impostors. The probable supposition is, that they have frequently been duped themselves. He whom ambition urged on to conquest, tried to persuade himself, and perhaps did persuade himself, that he was actuated by the love of his country. He persuaded, also, his followers in arms; and they, no doubt, were sufficiently willing to hope that they were influenced by such a motive. But, in whatever manner the fiction originated, a fiction it assuredly is; and the circumstance that it is still industriously imposed upon the world, is no inconsiderable evidence that the system which it is employed to encourage, would shrink from the eye of virtue and the light of truth.

45. Upon the whole, we shall act both safely and wisely in lowering the relative situation of patriotism in the scale of Christian virtues. It is a virtue; but it is far from the greatest or the highest. The world has given to it an unwarranted elevation—an elevation to which it has no pretensions in the view of truth; and if the friends of truth consign it to its proper station, it is probable that there will be fewer spurious pretensions to its praise.

[1] Godwin: Pol. Justice, v. 2, p. 514.

CHAPTER XVIII.

Slavery.

Requisitions of Christianity professedly disregarded—Persian law—The slave system a costly iniquity.

46. At a future day it will probably become a subject of wonder how it could have happened that upon such a subject as Slavery men could have inquired, and examined, and debated year after year; and that many years actually passed before the minds of a nation were so fully convinced of its enormity, and of their consequent duty to abolish it, as to suppress it to the utmost of their power. I say this will probably be a subject of wonder; because the question is so simple, that he who simply applies the requisitions of the Moral Law finds no time for reasoning or for doubt. The question, as soon as it is proposed, is decided. How, then, it will be asked, in future days, could a Christian Legislature argue and contend, and contend and argue again, and allow an age to pass without deciding?

47. The cause is, that men do not agree as to the rule of decision—as to the test by which the question should be examined. One talks of the rights to property—one of the interests of merchants—one of safety—one of policy—all which are valid and proper considerations; but they are not the primary consideration. The first question is, Is Slavery right? Is it consistent with the Moral Law? This question is in practice postponed to others, even by some who theoretically acknowledge its primary claim; and when to the indistinct principles of these is added the want of principle in others, it is easy to account for the delay and opposition with which the advocate of simple rectitude is met.

48. To him who examines Slavery by the standard to which all questions of human duty should be referred, the task of deciding, we say, is short. Whether it is consistent with the Christian law for one man to keep another in bondage without his consent, and to compel him to labour for that other's advantage, admits of no more doubt than whether two and two make four. It were humiliating, then, to set about the *proof* that the Slave System is incompatible with Christianity; because no man questions its incompatibility who knows what Christianity is, and what it requires. Unhappily, some who can estimate, with tolerable precision, the duties of morality upon other subjects, contemplate this through a veil—a veil which habit has suspended before them, and which is dense enough to intercept the view of the moral features of Slavery as they are presented to others who examine it without an intervening medium, and with no other light than the light of truth. To these the best counsel that we can offer is, to *simplify* their reasonings—to recur to first principles; and first principles are few. Look, then, at the foundation of all the relative duties of man—Benevolence—Love—that love and benevolence which is the fulfilling of the Moral Law—that "charity" which prompts to actions of kindness, and tenderness, and fellow-feeling for all men. Does he who seizes a person in Guinea, and drags him shrieking to a vessel, practise this benevolence? When three or four hundreds have been thus seized, does he who chains them together in a suffocating hold practise this benevolence? When they have reached another shore, does he who gives money to the first for his victims—keeps them as his property—and compels them to labour for his profit, practise this benevolence? Would either of these persons think, if their relative situations were exchanged with the African's, that the Africans used them kindly and justly? No. Then the question is decided. Christianity condemns the system, and no further inquiry about rectitude remains. The question is as distinctly settled as when a man commits a burglary it is distinctly certain that he has violated the law.

49. But of the flagitiousness of the system in the view of Christianity its defenders are themselves aware—for they tell us, if not with decency, at least with openness, that Christianity must be excluded from the inquiry. What does this exclusion imply? Obviously, that the advocates of slavery are *conscious* that Christianity condemns it. They take her away from the judgment-seat, because they know she will pronounce a verdict against them. Does the reader desire more than this? Here is the evidence, both of enemies and of friends, that the Moral Law of God condemns the slave system. If, therefore, we are Christians, the question is not merely decided, but *confessedly* decided: and what more do we ask?

It is, to be sure, a curious thing, that they who affirm they are Christians will not have their conduct examined by the Christian law; and whilst they baptize their children and kneel at the communion table, tell us that with one of the greatest questions of practical morality our religion has no concern.

50. Two reasons induce the writer to confine himself, upon this subject, to little more than the exhibition of fundamental principles;—first, that the details of the Slavery question are already laid, in unnumbered publications, before the public: and, secondly,

that he does not think it will long remain, at least in this country, a subject for discussion. That the system will, so far as the British Government is concerned, at no distant period be abolished, appears nearly certain; and he is unwilling to fill the pages of a book of general morality with discussions which, ere many years have passed, may possess no relevance to the affairs of the Christian world.

51. Yet one remark is offered as to a subordinate means of estimating the goodness or badness of a cause—that which consists in referring to the principles upon which each party reasons, to the general spirit, to the tone and the temper of the disputants. Now, I am free to confess, that, if I had never heard an argument against Slavery, I should find, in the writings of its defenders, satisfactory evidence that their cause is bad. So true is this, that if at any time I needed peculiarly to impress myself with the flagitiousness of the system, I should take up the book of a determined advocate. There I find the most unequivocal of all testimony against it—that which is unwittingly furnished by its advocates. There I find, first, that the fundamental principles of morality are given to the winds;—that the proper foundation of the reasoning is rejected and ridiculed. There I find that the temper and dispositions which are wont to influence the advocate of a good cause are scarcely to be found, and that those which usually characterise a bad one continually appear; and therefore, even setting aside inaccurate statements and fallacious reasonings, I am assured, from the general character of the defence and conduct of the defenders, that the system is radically vicious and bad.

52. The distinctions which are made between the original robbery in Africa, and the purchase, the inheritance, or the "breeding" of slaves in the colonies, do not at all respect the *kind* of immorality that attaches to the whole system. They respect nothing but the *degree*. The man who wounds and robs another on the highway is a more atrocious offender than he who plunders a hen-roost; but he is not more *truly* an offender, he is not more *certainly* a violator of the law. And so with the slave system. He who drags a wretched man from his family in Africa is a more flagitious transgressor than he who merely compels the African to labour for his own advantage; but the transgression, the immorality, is as real and certain in one case as in the other. He who has no right to steal the African can have none to sell him. From him who is known to have no right to sell, another can have no right to buy or to possess. Sale, or gift, or legacy imparts no right to me, because the seller, or giver, or bequeather had none himself. The sufferer has just as valid a claim to liberty at my hands as at the hands of the ruffian who first dragged him from his home.—Every hour of every day the present possessor is guilty of injustice. Nor is the case altered with respect to those who are born on a man's estate. The parents were never the landholder's property, and therefore the child is not. Nay, if the parents had been rightfully slaves, it would not justify me in making slaves of their children. No man has a right to make a child a slave but himself. What are our sentiments upon kindred subjects? What do we think of the justice of the Persian system, by which, when a state offender is put to death, his brothers and his children are killed or mutilated too? Or, to come nearer to the point, as well as nearer home, what should we say of a law which enacted that, of every criminal who was sentenced to labour for life, all the children should be sentenced so to labour also? And yet, if there is any comparison of reasonableness, it seems to be in one respect in favour of the culprit. *He* is condemned to slavery for his crimes: the African, for another man's profit.

53. That any human being, who has not forfeited his liberty by his crimes, has a right to be free, and that whosoever forcibly withholds liberty from an innocent man robs him of his right and violates the Moral Law, are truths which no man would dispute or doubt, if custom had not obscured our perceptions, or if wickedness did not prompt us to close our eyes.

54. The whole system is essentially and radically bad:—Injustice and oppression are its fundamental principles. Whatever lenity may be requisite in speaking of the agent, none should be shown, none should be expressed for the act. I do not affirm or imagine that every slaveholder is *therefore* a wicked man;—but if he be not, it is only upon the score of ignorance. If he is exempt from the guilt of violating the Moral Law, it is only because he does not perceive what it requires. Let us leave the *deserts* of the individual to Him who knoweth the heart; of his actions, *we* may speak; and we should speak in the language of reprobation, disgust, and abhorrence.

55. Although it could be shown that the slave system is expedient, it would not affect the question whether it ought to be maintained?—yet it is remarkable that it is shown to be impolitic as well as bad. We are not violating the Moral Law because it fills our pockets. We injure ourselves by our own transgressions. The slave system is a *costly* iniquity both to the nation and to individual men. It is matter of great satisfaction that

this is known and proved; and yet it is just what, antecedently to inquiry, we should have reason to expect. The truth furnishes one addition to the many evidences that, even with respect to temporal affairs, that which is right is commonly politic; and it ought, therefore, to furnish additional inducements to a fearless conformity of conduct, private and public, to the Moral Law.

56. It is quite evident that our slave system will be abolished, and that its supporters will hereafter be regarded with the same public feelings as he who was an advocate of the slave trade is now. How is it that legislators or that public men are so indifferent to their fame? Who would now be willing that biography should record of him—*This man defended the slave trade?* The time will come when the record—*This man opposed the abolition of slavery*—will occasion a great deduction from the public estimate of worth of character. When both these atrocities are abolished, and but for the page of history forgotten, that page will make a wide difference between those who aided the abolition, and those who obstructed it. The one will be ranked amongst the Howards that are departed, and the other amongst those who, in ignorance or in guilt, have employed their little day in inflicting misery upon mankind.

CHAPTER XIX.

War.

CAUSES OF WAR.—Want of inquiry—Indifference to human misery—National irritability—Interest—Secret motives of Cabinets—Ideas of glory—Foundation of military glory.
CONSEQUENCES OF WAR.—Destruction of human life—Taxation—Moral depravity—Familiarity with plunder—Implicit submission to superiors—Resignation of moral agency—Bondage and degradation—Loan of armies—Effects on the community.
LAWFULNESS OF WAR—Influence of habit—Of appealing to antiquity—The Christian Scriptures—Subjects of Christ's benediction—Matt. xxvii. 52—The Apostles and Evangelists—The Centurion—Cornelius—Silence not a proof of approbation—Luke xxii. 36—John the Baptist—Negative evidence—Prophecies of the Old Testament—The requisitions of Christianity of present obligation—Primitive Christians—Example and testimony of early Christians—Christian soldiers--Wars of the Jews—Duties of individuals and nations—Offensive and defensive war—Wars always aggressive—Paley—War *wholly* forbidden.
OF THE PROBABLE AND PRACTICAL EFFECTS OF ADHERING TO THE MORAL LAW IN RESPECT TO WAR.—Quakers in America and Ireland—Colonisation of Pennsylvania—Unconditional reliance on Providence—Recapitulation—General Observations.

1. It is one amongst the numerous moral phenomena of the present times that the inquiry is silently yet not slowly spreading in the world—*Is War compatible with the Christian religion?* There was a period when the question was seldom asked, and when War was regarded almost by every man both as inevitable and right. That period has certainly passed away; and not only individuals, but public societies, and societies in distant nations, are urging the question upon the attention of mankind. The simple circumstance that it is thus urged contains no irrational motive to investigation: for why should men ask the question if they did not doubt; and how, after these long ages of prescription, could they begin to doubt without a reason?

2. It is not unworthy of remark, that whilst disquisitions are frequently issuing from the press, of which the tendency is to show that War is not compatible with Christianity, few serious attempts are made to show that it is. Whether this results from the circumstance that no individual peculiarly is interested in the proof—or that there is a secret consciousness that proof cannot be brought—or that those who may be desirous of defending the custom rest in security that the impotence of its assailants will be of no avail against a custom so established and so supported—I do not know: yet the fact is remarkable, that scarcely a defender is to be found. It cannot be doubted that the question is one of the utmost interest and importance to man. Whether the custom be defensible or not, every man should *inquire* into its consistency with the Moral Law. If it is defensible, he may, by inquiry, dismiss the scruples which it is certain subsist in the minds of multitudes, and thus exempt himself from the offence of participating in that which, though pure, he "esteemeth to be unclean." If it is not defensible, the propriety of investigation is increased in a tenfold degree.

3. It may be a subject therefore of reasonable regret to the friends and the lovers of truth, that the question of the Moral Lawfulness of War is not brought *fairly* before the public. I say fairly: because though many of the publications which impugn its lawfulness advert to the ordinary arguments in its favour, yet it is not to be assumed that they give to those arguments all that vigour and force which would be imparted by a stated and an able advocate. Few books, it is probable, would tend more powerfully to promote the discovery and dissemination of truth than one which should frankly and fully and ably advocate, upon sound moral principles, the practice of War. The public would then see the whole of what can be urged in its favour without being obliged to seek for arguments, as they now must, in incidental or imperfect or scattered disquisitions: and possessing in a distinct form the evidence of both

parties, they would be enabled to judge justly between them. Perhaps if, invited as the public are to the discussion, no man is hereafter willing to adventure in the cause, the conclusion will not be unreasonable, that no man is destitute of a consciousness that the cause is not a good one.

4. Meantime it is the business of him whose inquiries have conducted him to the conclusion that the cause is not good, to exhibit the evidence upon which the conclusion is founded. It happens upon the subject of War, more than upon almost any other subject of human inquiry, that the individual finds it difficult to contemplate its merits with an uninfluenced mind. He finds it difficult to examine it as it would be examined by a philosopher to whom the subject was new. He is familiar with its details; he is habituated to the idea of its miseries; he has perhaps never doubted, because he has never questioned, its rectitude; nay, he has associated with it ideas not of splendour only, but of honour and of merit. That such an inquirer will not, without some effort of abstraction, examine the question with impartiality and justice, is plain; and therefore the first business of him who would satisfy his mind respecting the lawfulness of War is to divest himself of all those habits of thought and feeling which have been the result, not of reflection and judgment, but of the ordinary associations of life. And perhaps he may derive some assistance in this necessary but not easy dismissal of previous opinions by referring first to some of the ordinary Causes and Consequences of War. The reference will enable us also more satisfactorily to estimate the moral character of the practice itself; for it is no unimportant auxiliary, in forming such an estimate of human actions or opinions, to know how they have been produced and what are their Effects.

Causes of War.

5. Of these Causes one undoubtedly consists in the want of inquiry. We have been accustomed from earliest life to a familiarity with its "pomp and circumstance;" soldiers have passed us at every step, and battles and victories have been the topic of every one around us. It therefore becomes familiarised to all our thoughts and interwoven with all our associations. We have never inquired whether these things should be: the question does not even suggest itself. We acquiesce in it, as we acquiesce in the rising of the sun, without any other idea than that it is a part of the ordinary processes of the world. And how are we to feel disapprobation of a system that we do not examine, and of the nature of which we do not think? Want of inquiry has been the means by which long-continued practices, whatever has been their enormity, have obtained the general concurrence of the world, and by which they have continued to pollute or degrade it, long after the few who inquire into their nature have discovered them to be bad. It was by these means that the Slave Trade was so long tolerated by this land of humanity. Men did not *think* of its iniquity. We were induced to think, and we soon abhorred, and then abolished it. Of the effects of this want of inquiry we have indeed frequent examples upon the subject before us. Many who have all their lives concluded that War is lawful and right have found, when they began to examine the question, that their conclusions were founded upon no evidence:—that they had believed in its rectitude not because they had possessed themselves of proof, but because they had never inquired whether it was capable of proof or not. In the present moral state of the world, one of the first concerns of him who would discover pure morality should be to question the purity of that which now obtains.

6. Another cause of our complacency with War, and therefore another cause of War itself, consists in that callousness to human misery which the custom induces. They who are shocked at a single murder on the highway, hear with indifference of the slaughter of a thousand on the field. They whom the idea of a single corpse would thrill with terror, contemplate that of heaps of human carcases mangled by human hands, with frigid indifference. If a murder is committed, the narrative is given in the public newspapers, with many adjectives of horror—with many expressions of commiseration, and many hopes that the perpetrator will be detected. In the next paragraph, the editor, perhaps, tells us that he has hurried a second

edition to the press, in order that he may be the first to glad the public with the intelligence, that in an engagement which has just taken place, *eight hundred and fifty of the enemy were killed*. Now, is not this latter intelligence eight hundred and fifty times as deplorable as the first? Yet the first is the subject of our sorrow, and this—of our joy! The inconsistency and disproportionateness which has been occasioned in our sentiments of benevolence offers a curious moral phenomenon.[1]

7. The immolations of the Hindoos fill us with compassion or horror, and we are zealously labouring to prevent them. The sacrifices of life by our own criminal executions are the subject of our anxious commiseration, and we are strenuously endeavouring to diminish their number. We feel that the life of a Hindoo or a malefactor is a serious thing, and that nothing but imperious necessity should induce us to destroy the one, or to permit the destruction of the other. Yet what are these sacrifices of life in comparison with the sacrifices of War? In the late campaign in Russia, there fell, during one hundred and seventy-three days in succession, an average of two thousand nine hundred men per day: more than five hundred thousand human beings in less than six

[1] Part of the Declaration and Oath prescribed to be taken by Catholics is this: "I do solemnly declare before God, that I believe that no act in itself unjust, immoral, or wicked, can ever be justified or excused by or under pretence or colour that it was done either for the good of the Church or in obedience to any ecclesiastical power whatsoever." This declaration is required as a solemn act, and is supposed, of course, to involve a great and sacred principle of rectitude. We propose the same declaration to be taken by military men, with the alteration of two words. "I do solemnly declare before God, that I believe that no act in itself unjust, immoral, or wicked, can ever be justified or excused by or under pretence or colour that it was done either for the good of the State or in obedience to any military power whatsoever." How would this declaration assort with the customary practice of the soldier? Put *state* for *church*, and *military* for *ecclesiastical*, and then the world thinks that acts in themselves most unjust, immoral, and wicked, are not only justified and excused, but very meritorious : for in the whole system of warfare, justice and morality are utterly disregarded. Are those who approve of this Catholic declaration conscious of the grossness of their own inconsistency? Or will they tell us that the interests of the State are so paramount to those of the Church, that what would be wickedness in the service of one, is virtue in the service of the other? The truth we suppose to be, that so intense is the power of public opinion, that of the thousands who approve the Catholic declarations and the practices of War, there are scarcely tens who even perceive their own inconsistency.—Mem. in the MS.

months! And most of these victims expired with peculiar intensity of suffering. We are carrying our benevolence to the Indies, but what becomes of it in Russia or at Leipsic? We are labouring to save a few lives from the gallows, but where is our solicitude to save them on the field? Life is life wheresoever it be sacrificed, and has everywhere equal claims to our regard. I am not now saying that War is wrong, but that we regard its miseries with an indifference with which we regard no others : that if our sympathy were *reasonably* excited respecting them, we should be powerfully prompted to avoid War ; and that the want of this reasonable and virtuous sympathy is one cause of its prevalence in the world.

8. And *another* consists in national irritability. It is assumed (not indeed upon the most rational grounds) that the best way of supporting the dignity and maintaining the security of a nation is, when occasions of disagreement arise, to assume a high attitude and a fearless tone. We keep ourselves in a state of irritability which is continually alive to occasions of offence ; and he that is prepared to be offended readily finds offences. A jealous sensibility sees insults and injuries where sober eyes see nothing ; and nations thus surround themselves with a sort of artificial tentacula, which they throw wide in quest of irritation, and by which they are stimulated to revenge by every touch of accident or inadvertency. They who are easily offended will also easily offend. What is the experience of private life? The man who is always on the alert to discover trespasses on his honour or his rights, never fails to quarrel with his neighbours. Such a person may be dreaded as a torpedo. We may fear, but we shall not love him ; and fear without love easily lapses into enmity. There are, therefore, many feuds and litigations in the life of such a man, that would never have disturbed its quiet if he had not captiously snarled at the trespasses of accident and savagely retaliated insignificant injuries. The viper that we chance to molest, we suffer to live if he continue to be quiet ; but if he raise himself in menaces of destruction, we knock him on the head.

9. It is with nations as with men. If on every offence we fly to arms, we shall of

necessity provoke exasperation; and if we exasperate a people as petulant as ourselves, we may probably continue to butcher one another, until we cease only from emptiness of exchequers or weariness of slaughter. To threaten War is therefore often equivalent to beginning it. In the present state of men's principles, it is not probable that one nation will observe another levying men, and building ships, and founding cannon, without providing men, and ships, and cannon themselves; and when both are thus threatening and defying, what is the hope that there will not be a War?

10. If nations fought only when they could not be at peace, there would be very little fighting in the world. The wars that are waged for "insults to flags," and an endless train of similar motives, are perhaps generally attributable to the irritability of our pride. We are at no pains to appear pacific towards the offender: our remonstrance is a threat; and the nation which would give satisfaction to an *inquiry*, will give no other answer to a menace than a menace in return. At length we begin to fight, not because we are aggrieved, but because we are angry. One example may be offered. In 1789 a small Spanish vessel committed some violence in Nootka Sound, under the pretence that the country belonged to Spain. This appears to have been the principal ground of offence; and with this both the Government and the people of England were very angry. The irritability and haughtiness which they manifested were unaccountable to the Spaniards, and "the peremptory tone was imputed by Spain, not to the feelings of offended dignity and violated justice, but to some lurking enmity, and some secret designs which we did not choose to avow."[1] If the tone had been less peremptory and more rational, no such suspicion would have been excited, and the hostility which was consequent upon the suspicion would, of course, have been avoided. Happily the English were not so passionate, but that before they proceeded to fight they negotiated, and settled the affair amicably. The *preparations* for this foolish War cost, however, three millions one hundred and thirty-three thousand pounds!

[1] Smollett's England.

11. So well indeed is national irritability known to be an efficient cause of War, that they who from any motive wish to promote it, endeavour to rouse the temper of a people by stimulating their passions—just as the boys in our streets stimulate two dogs to fight. These persons talk of the insults, or the encroachments, or the contempts of the destined enemy, with every artifice of aggravation; they tell us of foreigners who want to trample upon our rights, of rivals who ridicule our power, of foes who will crush, and of tyrants who will enslave us. They pursue their object, certainly, by efficacious means: they desire a War, and therefore irritate our passions; and when men are angry they are easily persuaded to fight.

12. That this cause of War is morally bad —that petulance and irritability are wholly incompatible with Christianity, these pages have repeatedly shown.

13. Wars are often promoted from considerations of interest, as well as from passion. The love of gain adds its influence to our other motives to support them; and without other motives, we know that this love is sufficient to give great obliquity to the moral judgment, and to tempt us to many crimes. During a War of ten years there will always be many whose income depends on its continuance; and a countless host of commissaries, and purveyors, and agents, and mechanics, commend a War because it fills their pockets. And unhappily, if money is in prospect, the desolation of a kingdom is often of little concern: destruction and slaughter are not to be put in competition with a hundred a year. In truth, it seems sometimes to be the system of the conductors of a War, to give to the sources of gain endless ramifications. The more there are who profit by it, the more numerous are its supporters; and thus the projects of a cabinet become identified with the wishes of the people, and both are gratified in the prosecution of War.

14. A support more systematic and powerful is however given to War, because it offers to the higher ranks of society a profession which unites gentility with profit, and which, without the *vulgarity* of trade, maintains or enriches them. It is of little consequence to

inquire whether the distinction of vulgarity between the toils of War and the toils of commerce be fictitious. In the abstract, it is fictitious; but of this species of reputation public opinion holds the *arbitrium et jus et norma;* and public opinion is in favour of War.

15. The army and the navy, therefore, afford to the middle and higher classes a most acceptable profession. The profession of arms is like the profession of law or physic —a regular source of employment and profit. Boys are educated for the army as they are educated for the bar; and parents appear to have no other idea than that War is part of the business of the world. Of *younger sons,* whose fathers, in pursuance of the unhappy system of primogeniture, do not choose to support them at the expense of the heir, the army and the navy are the common resource. They would not know what to do without them. To many of these the news of a peace is a calamity; and though they may not *lift their voices* in favour of new hostilities for the sake of gain, it is unhappily certain that they often secretly desire it.

16. It is in this manner that much of the rank, the influence, and the wealth of a country become interested in the promotion of wars; and when a custom is promoted by wealth, and influence, and rank, what is the wonder that it should be continued? It is said if my memory serves me, by Sir Walter Raleigh), "he that taketh up his rest to live by this profession shall hardly be an honest man."

17. By depending upon War for a subsistence, a powerful inducement is given to desire it; and when the question of War is to be decided, it is to be feared that the whispers of Interest will prevail, and that humanity, and religion, and conscience will be sacrificed to promote it.

18. Of those Causes of War which consist in the ambition of princes or statesmen or commanders, it is not necessary to speak, because no one to whom the world will listen is willing to defend them.

19. Statesmen however have, besides ambition, many purposes of nice policy which make wars convenient; and when they have such purposes, they are sometimes cool speculators in the lives of men. They who have much patronage have many dependents, and they who have many dependents have much power. By a War, thousands become dependent on a minister; and if he be disposed, he can often pursue schemes of guilt, and entrench himself in unpunished wickedness, because the War enables him to silence the clamour of opposition by an office, and to secure the suffrages of venality by a bribe. He has therefore many motives to War—in ambition, that does not refer to conquest; or in fear, that extends only to his office or his pocket: and fear or ambition are sometimes more interesting considerations than the happiness and the lives of men. Cabinets have, in truth, many secret motives to wars of which the people know little. They talk in public of invasions of right, or breaches of treaty, or the support of honour, of the necessity of retaliation, when these motives have no influence on their determinations. Some untold purpose of expediency, or the private quarrel of a prince, or the pique or anger of a minister, are often the real motives to a contest, whilst its promoters are loudly talking of the honour or the safety of the country.

20. But perhaps the most operative cause of the popularity of War, and of the facility with which we engage in it, consists in this; that an idea of Glory is attached to military exploits, and of Honour to the military profession. The glories of battle, and of those who perish in it, or who return in triumph to their country, are favourite topics of declamation with the historian, the biographer, and the poet. They have told us a thousand times of *dying heroes,* who "resign their lives amidst the joys of conquest, and, filled with their country's glory, smile in death;" and thus every excitement that eloquence and genius can command is employed to arouse that ambition of fame which can be gratified only at the expense of blood.

21. Into the nature and principles of this fame and glory we have already inquired; and in the view alike of virtue and of intellect, they are low and bad.[1] "Glory is the most selfish of all passions except love."[2]—" I can-

[1] See Essay 2, c. 10.
[2] *West. Rev.* No. 1, for 1827.

not tell how or why the love of glory is a less selfish principle than the love of riches."[1] Philosophy and intellect may therefore well despise it, and Christianity silently, yet emphatically, condemns it. "Christianity," says Bishop Watson, "quite annihilates the disposition for martial glory." Another testimony, and from an advocate of War, goes further—*No part* of the heroic character is the subject of the "commendation, or precepts, or example of Christ;" but the character the most opposite to the heroic is the subject of them all.[2]

22. Such is the foundation of the glory which has for so many ages deceived and deluded multitudes of mankind! Upon this foundation a structure has been raised so vast, so brilliant, so attractive, that the greater portion of mankind are content to gaze in admiration, without any inquiry into its basis or any solicitude for its durability. If, however, it should be, that the gorgeous temple will be able to stand only till Christian truth and light become predominant, it surely will be wise of those who seek a niche in its apartments as their paramount and final good, to pause ere they proceed. If they desire a reputation that shall outlive guilt and fiction, let them look to the basis of military fame. If this fame should one day sink into oblivion and contempt, it will not be the first instance in which wide-spread glory has been found to be a glittering bubble, that has burst and been forgotten. Look at the days of chivalry. Of the ten thousand Quixotes of the Middle Ages, where is now the honour or the name? yet poets once sang their praises, and the chronicler of their achievements believed he was recording an everlasting fame. Where are now the glories of the tournament? glories

"Of which all Europe rang from side to side."

Where is the champion whom princesses caressed and nobles envied? Where are now the triumphs of Duns Scotus, and where are the folios that *perpetuated* his fame? The glories of War have indeed outlived these: human passions are less mutable than human follies; but I am willing to avow my conviction, that these glories are alike destined to sink into forgetfulness; and that the time is approaching when the applauses of heroism and the splendours of conquest will be remembered only as follies and iniquities that are past. Let him who seeks for fame, other than that which an era of Christian purity will allow, make haste; for every hour that he delays its acquisition will shorten its duration. This is certain, if there be certainty in the promises of Heaven.

23. Of this factitious glory as a cause of War, Gibbon speaks in the "Decline and Fall." "As long as mankind," says he, "shall continue to bestow more liberal applause on their destroyers than on their benefactors, the thirst of military glory will ever be the vice of the most exalted characters." "'Tis strange to imagine," says the Earl of Shaftesbury, "that War, which of all things appears the most savage, should be the passion of the most heroic spirits." But he gives us the reason. "By a small *misguidance of the affection*, a lover of mankind becomes a ravager; a hero and deliverer becomes an oppressor and destroyer."[1]

24. These are amongst the great perpetual causes of War. And what are they? First, That we *do not inquire* whether War is right or wrong. Secondly, That we are habitually *haughty* and *irritable* in our intercourse with other nations. Thirdly, That War is a source of *profit* to individuals, and establishes *professions which are very convenient* to the middle and higher ranks of life. Fourthly, That it gratifies the *ambition* of public men, and *serves the purposes of state policy*. Fifthly, That *notions of glory* are attached to Warlike affairs; which glory is factitious and impure.

25. In the view of reason, and especially in the view of religion, what is the character of these Causes? Are they pure? Are they honourable? Are they, when connected with their effects, compatible with the Moral Law? Lastly, and especially, Is it probable that a system of which these are the great ever-during Causes can itself be good or right?

---

[1] Mem. and Rem. of the late Jane Taylor.
[2] Paley, Evidences of Christianity, p. 2, c. 2.

[1] Essay on the Freedom of Wit and Humour.

Consequences of War.

26. To expatiate upon the miseries which War brings upon mankind appears a trite and a needless employment. We all know that its evils are great and dreadful. Yet the very circumstance that the knowledge is familiar may make it inoperative upon our sentiments and our conduct. It is not the intensity of misery, it is not the extent of evil alone, which is necessary to animate us to that exertion which evil and misery should excite: if it were, surely we should be much more averse than we now are to contribute, in word or in action, to the promotion of War.

27. But there are mischiefs attendant upon the system which are not to every man thus familiar, and on which, for that reason, it is expedient to remark. In referring especially to some of those moral consequences of War which commonly obtain little of our attention, it may be observed, that social and political considerations are necessarily involved in the moral tendency: for the happiness of society is always diminished by the diminution of morality; and enlightened policy knows that the greatest support of a state is the virtue of the people.

28. And yet the reader should bear in mind—what nothing but the frequency of the calamity can make him forget—the intense sufferings and irreparable deprivations which one battle inevitably entails upon private life. These are calamities of which the world thinks little, and which, if it thought of them, it could not remove. A father or a husband can seldom be replaced; a void is created in the domestic felicity which there is little hope that the future will fill. By the slaughter of a War, there are thousands who weep in unpitied and unnoticed secrecy, whom the world does not see; and thousands who retire in silence to hopeless poverty, for whom it does not care. To these, the conquest of a kingdom is of little importance. The loss of a protector or a friend is ill repaid by empty glory. An addition of territory may add titles to a king, but the brilliancy of a crown throws little light upon domestic gloom. It is not my intention to insist upon these calamities, intense, and irreparable, and unnumbered as they are; but those who begin a War without taking them into their estimates of its consequences must be regarded as, at most, half-seeing politicians. The legitimate object of political measures is the good of the people; —and a great sum of good a War must produce, if it outbalances even *this* portion of its mischiefs.

29. Nor should we be forgetful of that dreadful part of all warfare, the destruction of mankind. The frequency with which this destruction is represented to our minds, has almost extinguished our perception of its awfulness and horror. Between the years 1141 and 1815, an interval of six hundred and seventy years, our country has been at War, with France alone, *two hundred and sixty-six years*. If to this we add our wars with other countries, probably we shall find that one-half of the last six or seven centuries has been spent by this country in War? A dreadful picture of human violence! How many of our fellow-men, of our fellow-Christians, have these centuries of slaughter cut off! What is the sum total of the misery of their deaths?[1]

30. When political writers expatiate upon the extent and the evils of taxation, they do not sufficiently bear in mind the reflection that almost all our taxation is the effect of War. A man declaims upon national debts. He ought to declaim upon the parent of those debts. Do we reflect that if heavy taxation entails evils and misery upon the community, that misery and those evils are inflicted upon us by War? The amount of supplies in Queen Anne's reign was about seventy millions;[2] and of this about sixty-six millions[3] was expended in War. Where is our equivalent good?

31. Such considerations ought, undoubtedly, to influence the conduct of public men in their disagreements with other states, even if higher considerations do not influence it. They ought to form part of the calculations

---

[1] "Since the peace of Amiens more than *four millions* of human beings have been sacrificed to the personal ambition of Napoleon Buonaparte."—*Quarterly Review*, 25 Art. 1, 1825.
[2] The sum was £69,815,457.
[3] The sum was £65,853,799. "The nine years' war of 1739 cost this nation upwards of sixty-four millions without gaining any object."—Chalmers' Estimate of the Strength of Great Britain.

of the evil of hostility. I believe that a greater mass of human suffering and loss of human enjoyment are occasioned by the pecuniary distresses of a War, than any ordinary advantages of a War compensate. But this consideration seems too remote to obtain our notice. Anger at offence or hope of triumph overpowers the sober calculations of reason, and outbalances the weight of after and long-continued calamities. The only question appears to be, whether taxes enough for a War can be raised, and whether a people will be willing to pay them. But the great question ought to be (setting questions of Christianity aside), whether the nation will gain as much by the War as they will lose by taxation and its other calamities.

32. If the happiness of the people were, what it ought to be, the primary and the ultimate object of national measures, I think that the policy which pursued this object would often find that even the pecuniary distresses resulting from a War make a greater deduction from the quantum of felicity than those evils which the War may have been designed to avoid.

33. "But War does more harm to the morals of men than even to their property and persons."[1] If, indeed, it depraves our morals more than it injures our persons and deducts from our property, how enormous must its mischiefs be!

34. I do not know whether the greater sum of moral evil resulting from War is suffered by those who are immediately engaged in it, or by the public. The mischief is most extensive upon the community, but upon the profession it is most intense.

"Rara fides pietasque viris qui castra sequuntur."
—LUCAN.

No one pretends to applaud the morals of an army, and for its religion, few think of it at all. The fact is too notorious to be insisted upon, that thousands who had filled their stations in life with propriety, and been virtuous from principle, have lost, by a military life, both the practice and the regard of morality; and when they have become habituated to the vices of War, have laughed at their honest and plodding brethren, who are

[1] Erasmus.

still spiritless enough for virtue or stupid enough for piety.

35. Does any man ask, What occasions depravity in military life? I answer in the words of Robert Hall:[1] "War reverses, with respect to its objects, all the rules of morality. It is nothing less than a temporary repeal of all the principles of virtue. It is a system out of which almost all the virtues are excluded, and in which nearly all the vices are incorporated." And it requires no sagacity to discover that those who are engaged in a practice which reverses all the rules of morality, which repeals all the principles of virtue, and in which nearly all the vices are incorporated, cannot, without the intervention of a miracle, retain their minds and morals undepraved.

36. Look for illustration to the familiarity with the plunder of property and the slaughter of mankind which War induces. He who plunders the citizen of another nation without remorse or reflection, and bears away the spoil with triumph, will inevitably lose something of his principles of probity.[2] He who is familiar with slaughter, who has himself often perpetrated it, and who exults in the perpetration, will not retain undepraved the principles of virtue. His moral feelings are blunted; his moral vision is obscured; his principles are shaken; an inroad is made upon their integrity, and it is an inroad that makes after inroads the more easy. Mankind do not generally resist the influence of habit. If we rob and shoot those who are "enemies" to-day, we are in some degree prepared to shoot and rob those who are not enemies to-morrow. Law may indeed still restrain us from violence: but the power and efficiency of Principle is diminished: and this alienation of the mind from the practice, the love, and the perception of Christian purity, therefore, of necessity extends its influence to the other circumstances of life. *The whole evil* is imputable to War; and we say that this evil forms a powerful evidence against it, whether we direct that evidence

[1] Sermon, 1822.
[2] See Smollett's England, vol. iv. p. 376. "This terrible truth, which I cannot help repeating, must be acknowledged:—indifference and selfishness are the predominant feelings in an army."—Miot's Mémoires de l'Expédition en Egypte, &c. Mem. in the MS.

to the abstract question of its lawfulness, or to the practical question of its expediency. *That* can scarcely be lawful which necessarily occasions such wide-spread immorality. *That* can scarcely be expedient which is so pernicious to virtue, and therefore to the state.

37. The economy of War requires of every soldier an implicit submission to his superior; and this submission is required of every gradation of rank to that above it. " I swear to obey the orders of the officers who are set over me : so help me God." This system may be necessary to hostile operations, but I think it is unquestionably adverse to intellectual and moral excellence.

38. The very nature of unconditional obedience implies the relinquishment of the use of the reasoning powers. Little more is required of the soldier than that he be obedient and brave. His obedience is that of an animal, which is moved by a goad or a bit, without judgment of his own ; and his bravery is that of a mastiff that fights whatever mastiff others put before him.[1] It is obvious that in such agency the intellect and the understanding have little part. Now I think that this is important. He who, with whatever motive, resigns the direction of his conduct implicitly to another, surely cannot retain that erectness and independence of mind, that manly consciousness of mental freedom, which is one of the highest privileges of our nature. A British captain declares that " the tendency of strict discipline, such as prevails on board ships of war, where almost every act of a man's life is regulated by the orders of his superiors, is to weaken the faculty of independent thought."[2] Thus the rational being becomes reduced in the intellectual scale : an encroachment is made upon the integrity of its independence. God has given us, individually, capacities for the regulation of our individual conduct. To resign its direction, therefore, to the absolute disposal of another, appears to be an unmanly and unjustifiable relinquishment of the privileges which He has granted to us. And the

[1] By one article of the Constitutional Code even of republican France, " the army were expressly prohibited from deliberating on any subject whatever."
[2] Captain Basil Hall : Voyage to Loo Choo, c. 2. We make no distinction between the military and naval professions, and employ one word to indicate both.

effect is obviously bad ; for although no character will apply universally to any large class of men, and although the intellectual character of the military profession does not result *only* from this unhappy subjection ; yet it will not be disputed that the honourable exercise of intellect amongst that profession is not relatively great. It is not from them that we expect, because it is not from them that we generally find, those vigorous exertions of intellect which dignify our nature and which extend the boundaries of human knowledge.

39. But the intellectual effects of military subjection form but a small portion of its evils. The great mischief is, that it requires the relinquishment of our moral agency ; that it requires us to do what is opposed to our consciences, and what we know to be wrong. A soldier must obey, how criminal soever the command, and how criminal soever he knows it to be. It is certain, that of those who compose armies, many commit actions which they believe to be wicked, and which they would not commit but for the obligations of a military life. Although a soldier determinately believes that the War is unjust, although he is convinced that his particular part of the service is atrociously criminal, still he must proceed—he must prosecute the purposes of injustice or robbery ; he must participate in the guilt, and be himself a robber.

40. To what a situation is a rational and responsible being reduced, who commits actions, good or bad, at the word of another? I can conceive no greater degradation. It is the lowest, the final abjectness of the moral nature. It is *this* if we abate the glitter of War, and if we add this glitter it is nothing more.

41. Such a resignation of our moral agency is not contended for, or tolerated in any one other circumstance of human life. War stands upon this pinnacle of depravity alone. She, only, in the supremacy of crime, has told us that she has abolished even the obligation to be virtuous.

42. Some writers who have perceived the monstrousness of this system have told us that a soldier should assure himself, before

he engages in a War, that it is a lawful and just one; and they acknowledge that, if he does not feel this assurance, he is a "murderer." But how is he to know that the War is just? It is frequently difficult for the people distinctly to discover what the objects of a War are. And if the soldier knew that it was just in its commencement, how is he to know that it will continue just in its prosecution? Every War is, in some parts of its course, wicked and unjust; and who can tell what that course will be? You say —When he discovers any injustice or wickedness, let him withdraw: we answer, He cannot; and the truth is, that there is no way of avoiding the evil, but by avoiding the army.

43. It is an inquiry of much interest, under what circumstances of *responsibility* a man supposes himself to be placed who thus abandons and violates his own sense of rectitude and of his duties. Either he is responsible for his actions or he is not; and the question is a serious one to determine.¹ Christianity has certainly never stated any cases in which personal responsibility ceases. If she admits such cases, she has at least not told us so; but she has told us, explicitly and repeatedly, that she does require individual obedience and impose individual responsibility. She has made no exceptions to the imperativeness of her obligations, whether we are required by others to neglect them or not; and I can discover in her sanctions no reason to suppose that in her final adjudications she admits the plea *that another required us to do that which she required us to forbear.*—But it may be feared, it may be *believed*, that how little soever religion will abate of the responsibility of those who obey, she will impose not a little upon those who command. They, at least, are answerable for the enormities of War : unless, indeed, any one shall tell me that responsibility attaches nowhere; that that which would be wickedness in another man, is innocence in a soldier; and that Heaven has granted to the directors of War a privileged immunity, by virtue of which crime incurs no guilt and receives no punishment.

44. And here it is fitting to observe, that the obedience to arbitrary power which War exacts, possesses more of the character of servility, and even of slavery, than we are accustomed to suppose. I will acknowledge that when I see a company of men in a stated dress, and of a stated colour, ranged, rank and file, in the attitude of obedience, turning or walking at the word of another, now changing the position of a limb and now altering the angle of a foot, I feel that there is something in the system that is wrong—something incongruous with the proper dignity, with the intellectual station of man. I do not know whether I shall be charged with indulging in idle sentiment or idler affectation. If I hold unusual language upon the subject, let it be remembered that the subject is itself unusual. I will retract my affectation and sentiment if the reader will show me any case in life parallel to that to which I have applied it.

45. No one questions whether military power *be* arbitrary. And what are the customary feelings of mankind with respect to a subjection to arbitrary power? How do we feel and think when we hear of a person who is obliged to do whatever other men command, and who, the moment he refuses, is punished for attempting to be free? If a man orders his servant to do a given action, he is at liberty, if he think the action improper, or if, from any other cause, he choose not to do it, to refuse his obedience. Far other is the nature of military subjection. The soldier is compelled to obey, whatever be his inclination or his will. It matters not whether he have entered the service voluntarily or involuntarily. Being in it, he has but one alternative—submission to arbitrary power or punishment— the punishment of death perhaps—for refusing to submit. Let the reader imagine to himself any other cause or purpose for which freemen shall be subjected to such a condition, and he will then see that condition in its proper light. The influence of habit and the gloss of public opinion make situations that would otherwise be

---

¹ Vattel indeed tells us that soldiers ought to "submit their judgment." "What," says he, "would be the consequence, if at every step of the sovereign the subjects were at liberty to weigh the justice of his reasons, and refuse to march to a War which, to them, might appear unjust?"—Law of Nat. b. 3, c. 11, sec. 187. Gisborne holds very different language. "It is," he says, "at all times the duty of an Englishman steadfastly to decline obeying any orders of his superiors, which his conscience should tell him were in any degree impious or unjust."—Duties of Men.

loathsome and revolting, not only tolerable but pleasurable. Take away this influence and this gloss from the situation of a soldier, and what should we call it? We should call it a state of degradation and of bondage. But habit and public opinion, although they may influence notions, cannot alter things. It *is* a state intellectually, morally, and politically of bondage and degradation.

46. But the reader will say that this submission to arbitrary power is necessary to the prosecution of War. I know it; and that is the very point for observation. It is *because* it is necessary to War that it is noticed here: for a brief but clear argument results:—That custom to which such a state of mankind is necessary must inevitably be bad; —it must inevitably be adverse to rectitude and to Christianity. So deplorable is the bondage which War produces, that we often hear, during a War, of subsidies from one nation to another, for the loan, or rather for the purchase of an army. To borrow ten thousand men who know nothing of our quarrel and care nothing for it, to help us to slaughter their fellows! To pay for their help in guineas to their sovereign! Well has it been exclaimed—

"War is a game, that, were their subjects wise, Kings would not play at."

A prince sells his subjects as a farmer sells his cattle; and sends them to destroy a people, whom, if they had been higher bidders, he would perhaps have sent them to defend. The historian has to record such miserable facts as that a potentate's troops were, during one War, "hired to the King of Great Britain and his enemies alternately, as the scale of convenience happened to preponderate!"[1] That a large number of persons, with the feelings and reason of men, should coolly listen to the bargain of their sale, should compute the guineas that will pay for their blood, and should then quietly be led to a place where they are to kill people towards whom they have no animosity, is simply wonderful. To what has inveteracy of habit reconciled mankind! I have no capacity of supposing a case of slavery, if slavery be denied in this. Men have been sold in another continent, and philanthropy has been shocked and aroused to interference; yet these men were sold, not to be slaughtered, but to work: but of the purchases and sales of the world's political slave-dealers, what does philanthropy think or care? There is no reason to doubt that, upon other subjects of horror, similar familiarity of habit would produce similar effects; or that he who heedlessly contemplates the purchase of an army, wants nothing but this familiarity to make him heedlessly look on at the commission of parricide.

47. Yet I do not know whether, in its effects on the military character, the greatest moral evil of War is to be sought. Upon the community its effects are indeed less apparent, because they who are the secondary subjects of the immoral influence are less intensely affected by it than the immediate agents of its diffusion. But whatever is deficient in the degree of evil, is probably more than compensated by its extent. The influence is like that of a continual and noxious vapour: we neither regard nor perceive it, but it secretly undermines the moral health.

48. Every one knows that vice is contagious. The depravity of one man has always a tendency to deprave his neighbours; and it therefore requires no unusual acuteness to discover that the prodigious mass of immorality and crime which are accumulated by a War must have a powerful effect in "demoralising" the public. But there is one circumstance connected with the injurious influence of War which makes it peculiarly operative and malignant. It is, that we do not hate or fear the influence, and do not fortify ourselves against it. Other vicious influences insinuate themselves into our minds by stealth: but this we receive with open embrace. Glory, and patriotism, and bravery, and conquest are bright and glittering things. Who, when he is looking, delighted, upon these things, is armed against the mischiefs which they veil?

49. The evil is, in its own nature, of almost universal operation. During a War, a whole people become familiarised with the utmost excesses of enormity—with the utmost intensity of human wickedness—and they rejoice and exult in them; so that there is probably not an individual in a hundred who

[1] Smollett's England, v. 4, p. 330.

does not lose something of his Christian principles by a ten years' War.

50. "It is, in my mind," said Fox, "no small misfortune to live at a period when scenes of horror and blood are frequent."— "One of the most evil consequences of War is, that it tends to render the hearts of mankind callous to the feelings and sentiments of humanity."[1]

51. Those who know what the Moral Law of God is, and who feel an interest in the virtue and the happiness of the world, will not regard the animosity of Party and the restlessness of resentment which are produced by a War as trifling evils. If anything be opposite to Christianity, it is retaliation and revenge. In the obligation to restrain these dispositions, much of the characteristic placability of Christianity consists. The very essence and spirit of our religion are abhorrent from resentment. The very essence and spirit of War are promotive of resentment; and what, then, must be their mutual adverseness? That War excites these passions, needs not to be proved. When a war is in contemplation, or when it has been begun, what are the endeavours of its promoters? They animate us by every artifice of excitement to hatred and animosity. Pamphlets, Placards, Newspapers, Caricatures—every agent is in requisition to irritate us into malignity. Nay, dreadful as it is, the pulpit resounds with declamations to stimulate our too sluggish resentment, and to invite us to slaughter. And thus the most unchristianlike of all our passions, the passion which it is most the object of our religion to repress, is excited and fostered. Christianity cannot be flourishing under circumstances like these. The more effectually we are animated to War, the more nearly we extinguish the dispositions of our religion. War and Christianity are like the opposite ends of a balance, of which one is depressed by the elevation of the other.

52. These are the consequences which make War dreadful to a state. Slaughter and devastation are sufficiently terrible, but their collateral evils are their greatest. It is *the immoral feeling* that War diffuses—it is

[1] Fell's Life of C. J. Fox.

the depravation of Principle, which forms the mass of its mischief.

53. To attempt to pursue the consequences of War through all their ramifications of evil were, however, both endless and vain. It is a moral gangrene, which diffuses its humours through the whole political and social system. To expose its mischief, is to exhibit all evil; for there is no evil which it does not occasion, and it has much that is peculiar to itself.

54. That, together with its multiplied evils, War produces some good, I have no wish to deny. I know that it sometimes elicits valuable qualities which had otherwise been concealed, and that it often produces collateral and adventitious, and sometimes immediate advantages. If all this could be denied, it would be needless to deny it; for it is of no consequence to the question whether it be proved. That any wide extended system should not produce *some* benefits, can never happen. In such a system, it were an unheard-of purity of evil, which was evil without any mixture of good. But to compare the ascertained advantages of War with its ascertained mischiefs, and to maintain a question as to the preponderance of the balance, implies, not ignorance, but disingenuousness, not incapacity to decide, but a voluntary concealment of truth.

55. And *why* do we insist upon these consequences of War? Because the review prepares the reader for a more accurate judgment respecting its lawfulness. Because it reminds him what War is, and because, knowing and remembering what it is, he will be the better able to compare it with the standard of rectitude.

Lawfulness of War.

1. I would recommend to him who would estimate the moral character of War, to endeavour to forget that he has ever presented to his mind the idea of a battle, and to endeavour to contemplate it with those emotions which it would excite in the mind of a being who had never before heard of human slaughter. The prevailing emotions of such a being would be astonishment and horror. If he were shocked by the horribleness of the

scene, he would be amazed at its absurdity. That a large number of persons should assemble by agreement, and deliberately kill one another, appears to the understanding a proceeding so preposterous, so monstrous, that I think a being such as I have supposed would inevitably conclude that they were mad. Nor is it likely, if it were attempted to explain to him some motives to such conduct, that he would be able to comprehend how any possible circumstances could make it reasonable. The ferocity and prodigious folly of the act would, in his estimation, outbalance the weight of every conceivable motive, and he would turn unsatisfied away—

"Astonished at the madness of mankind."

2. There is an advantage in making suppositions such as these; because when the mind has been familiarised to a practice, however monstrous or inhuman, it loses some of its sagacity of moral perception; the practice is perhaps veiled in glittering fictions, or the mind is become callous to its enormities. But if the subject is, by some circumstance, presented to the mind unconnected with any of its previous associations, we see it with a new judgment and new feelings; and wonder, perhaps, that we have not felt so or thought so before. And such occasions it is the part of a wise man to seek; since, if they never happen to us, it will often be difficult for us accurately to estimate the qualities of human actions, or to determine whether we approve them from a decision of our judgment, or whether we yield to them only the acquiescence of habit.

3. It may properly be a subject of wonder that the arguments which are brought to justify a custom such as War receive so little investigation. It must be a studious ingenuity of mischief which could devise a practice more calamitous or horrible; and yet it is a practice of which it rarely occurs to us to inquire into the necessity, or to ask whether it cannot be, or ought not to be avoided. In one truth, however, all will acquiesce—that the arguments in favour of such a practice should be unanswerably strong.

4. Let it not be said that the experience and the practice of other ages have superseded the necessity of inquiry in our own; that there can be no reason to question the lawfulness of that which has been sanctioned by forty centuries, or that he who presumes to question it is amusing himself with schemes of visionary philanthropy. "There is not, it may be," says Lord Clarendon, "a greater obstruction to the investigation of truth or the improvement of knowledge, than the too frequent appeal, and the too supine resignation of our understanding, to antiquity."[1] Whosoever proposes an alteration of existing institutions will meet from some men with a sort of instinctive opposition, which appears to be influenced by no process of reasoning, by no considerations of propriety or principles of rectitude, which defends the existing system because it exists, and which would have equally defended its opposite if that had been the oldest. "Nor is it out of modesty that we have this resignation, or that we do, in truth, think those who have gone before us to be wiser than ourselves; we are as proud and as peevish as any of our progenitors; but it is out of laziness; we will rather take their words than take the pains to examine the reason they governed themselves by."[2] To those who urge objections from the authority of ages, it is, indeed, a sufficient answer to say, that they apply to *every* long-continued custom. Slave-dealers urged them against the friends of the abolition; Papists urged them against Wickliffe and Luther; and the Athenians probably thought it a good objection to an apostle that "he seemed to be a setter forth of *strange* gods."

5. It is some satisfaction to be able to give, on a question of this nature, the testimony of some great minds against the lawfulness of War, opposed, as these testimonies are, to the general prejudice and the general practice of the world. It has been observed by Beccaria, that "it is the fate of great truths to glow only like a flash of lightning amidst the dark clouds in which error has enveloped the universe;" and if our testimonies are few or transient, it matters not, so that their light be the light of truth. There are, indeed, many, who in describing the horrible particulars of a siege or a battle, indulge in some declamation on the horrors of War, such as has been often repeated, and often

[1] Lord Clarendon's Essays. [2] Ibid.

applauded, and as often forgotten. But such declamations are of little value and of little effect; he who reads the next paragraph finds, probably, that he is invited *to follow the path to glory and to victory;—to share the hero's danger and partake the hero's praise;* and he soon discovers that the moralising parts of his author are the impulse of feelings rather than of principles, and thinks that though it may be very well to write, yet it is better to forget them.

6. There are, however, testimonies, delivered in the calm of reflection, by acute and enlightened men, which may reasonably be allowed at least so much weight as to free the present inquiry from the charge of being wild or visionary. Christianity indeed needs no such auxiliaries; but if they induce an examination of her duties, a wise man will not wish them to be disregarded.

7. "They who defend War," says Erasmus, "must defend the dispositions which lead to War: *and these dispositions are absolutely forbidden by the gospel.* Since the time that Jesus Christ said, Put up thy sword into its scabbard, *Christians ought not to go to War.* Christ suffered Peter to fall in to an error in this matter, on purpose that, when He had put up Peter's sword, it might remain *no longer a doubt that War was prohibited*, which, before that order, had been considered as allowable."—"Wickliffe seems to have thought it was wrong to take away the life of man on any account, and that War was utterly unlawful."[1]—" I am persuaded," says the Bishop of Landaff, "*that when the spirit of Christianity shall exert its proper influence, War will cease throughout the whole Christian world.*"[2] "War," says the same acute prelate, "has practices and principles peculiar to itself, *which but ill quadrate with the rule of moral rectitude, and are quite abhorrent from the benignity of Christianity.*"[3] A living writer of eminence bears this remarkable testimony:—"There is but one community of Christians in the world, and that unhappily of all communities one of the smallest, enlightened enough to understand the *prohibition of War by our Divine Master*, in its plain, literal, and undeniable sense, and con- scientious enough to obey it, subduing the very instinct of nature to obedience."[1]

8. Dr. Vicessimus Knox speaks in language equally specific:—"*Morality and religion forbid War, in its motives, conduct, and consequences.*"[2]

9. Those who have attended to the mode in which the Moral Law is instituted in the expressions of the Will of God, will have no difficulty in supposing that it contains no *specific* prohibition of War. Accordingly, if we be asked for such a prohibition, in the manner in which *Thou shalt not kill* is directed to murder, we willingly answer that no such prohibition exists;—and it is not necessary to the argument. Even those who would require such a prohibition are themselves satisfied respecting the obligation of many negative duties on which there has been no specific decision in the New Testament. They believe that suicide is not lawful: yet Christianity never forbade it. It can be shown, indeed, by implication and inference, that suicide could not have been allowed, and with this they are satisfied. Yet there is, probably, in the Christian Scriptures, not a twentieth part of as much indirect evidence against the lawfulness of suicide as there is against the lawfulness of War. To those who require such a command as *Thou shalt not engage in War*, it is therefore sufficient to reply, that they require that which, upon this and upon many other subjects, Christianity has not seen fit to give.

10. We have had many occasions to illustrate, in the course of these disquisitions, the characteristic nature of the Moral Law as a law of *Benevolence*. This benevolence, this good-will and kind affections towards one another, is placed at the basis of practical morality—it is "the fulfilling of the law"—it is the test of the validity of our pretensions to the Christian character. We have had occasion, too, to observe that this law of Benevolence is universally applicable to public affairs as well as to private, to the intercourse of nations as well as of men. Let us refer, then, to some of those requisitions of this law

---

[1] Priestley.   [2] Life of Bishop Watson.   [3] Ibid.

[1] Southey's History of Brazil.
[2] Essays. The Paterines or Gazari of Italy in the 11th, 12th, and 13th centuries, "held that it was not lawful to bear arms or to kill mankind."

which appear peculiarly to respect the question of the moral character of War.

11. *Have peace one with another.—By this shall all men know that ye are My disciples, if ye have love one to another.*

Walk with all lowliness and meekness, with long-suffering, forbearing one another in love.

Be ye all of one mind, having compassion one of another; love as brethren, be pitiful, be courteous: not rendering evil for evil, or railing for railing.

Be at peace among yourselves. See that none render evil for evil unto any man.—God hath called us to peace.

Follow after love, patience, meekness.—Be gentle, showing all meekness unto all men.—Live in peace.

Lay aside all malice.—Put off anger, wrath, malice.—Let all bitterness, and wrath, and anger, and clamour, and evil-speaking, be put away from you, with all malice.

Avenge not yourselves.—If thine enemy hunger, feed him; if he thirst, give him drink.—Recompense to no man evil for evil. —Overcome evil with good.

12. Now we ask of any man who looks over these passages, What evidence do they convey respecting the lawfulness of War? Could any approval or allowance of it have been subjoined to these instructions without obvious and most gross inconsistency? But if War is obviously and most grossly inconsistent with the general character of Christianity; if War could not have been permitted by its teachers without an egregious violation of their own precepts, we think that the evidence of its unlawfulness, *arising from this general character alone*, is as clear, as absolute, and as exclusive as could have been contained in any form of prohibition whatever.

13. But it is not from general principles alone that the law of Christianity respecting War may be deduced.—" Ye have heard that it *hath* been said, An eye for an eye, and a tooth for a tooth : but *I* say unto you, That ye resist not evil : but whosoever shall smite thee on thy right cheek, turn to him the other also."—" Ye have heard that it *hath* been said, Thou shalt love thy neighbour, and hate thine enemy : but *I* say unto you, Love your enemies, bless them that curse you, do good to them that hate you, and pray for them which despitefully use you, and persecute you ; for if ye love them which love you, what reward have ye?"[1]

14. Of the precepts from the Mount the most obvious characteristic is greater moral excellence and superior purity. They are directed, not so immediately to the external regulation of the conduct, as to the restraint and purification of the affections. In another precept it is not enough that an unlawful passion be just so far restrained as to produce no open immorality—the passion itself is forbidden. The tendency of the discourse is to attach guilt not to action only, but also to *thought*. It has been said, " Thou shalt not kill ; and whosoever shall kill shall be in danger of the judgment ; but *I* say unto you, that whosoever is *angry* with his brother without a cause, shall be in danger of the judgment."[2] Our Lawgiver attaches guilt to some of the violent feelings, such as resentment, hatred, revenge ; and by doing this, we contend that he attaches guilt to War. War cannot be carried on without those passions which He prohibits. Our argument, therefore, is syllogistical :—War cannot be allowed, if that which is necessary to War is prohibited. This, indeed, is precisely the argument of Erasmus :—" They who defend War must defend *the dispositions which lead to War; and these dispositions are absolutely forbidden.*"

15. Whatever might have been allowed under the Mosaic institution as to retaliation or resentment, Christianity says, " If ye love them only which love you, what reward have ye?— Love your *enemies.*" Now what sort of love does that man bear towards his enemy who runs him through with a bayonet ? We repeat, that the distinguishing duties of Christianity must be sacrificed when War is carried on. The question is between the abandonment of these duties and the abandonment of War, for both cannot be retained.[3]

---
[1] Matt. v. 38, &c.   [2] Matt. v. 21, 22.
[3] Yet the retention of both has been, unhappily enough, attempted. In a late publication, of which a part is devoted to the defence of War, the author gravely recom-

16. It is however objected, that the prohibitions, "Resist not evil," &c., are figurative; and that they do not mean that no injury is to be punished, and no outrage to be repelled. It has been asked, with complacent exultation, What would these advocates of peace say to him who struck them on the right cheek? Would they turn to him the other? What would these patient moralists say to him who robbed them of a coat? Would they give a cloak also? What would these philanthropists say to him who asked them to lend a hundred pounds? Would they not turn away? This is *argumentum ad hominem*; one example amongst the many, of that low and dishonest mode of intellectual warfare, which consists in exciting the feelings instead of convincing the understanding. It is, however, some satisfaction that the motive to the adoption of this mode of warfare is itself an indication of a bad cause; for what honest reasoner would produce only a laugh, if he were able to produce conviction?

17. We willingly *grant* that not all the precepts from the Mount were designed to be literally obeyed in the intercourse of life. But what then? To show that their meaning is not literal, is not to show that they do not forbid War. We ask in our turn, What *is* the meaning of the precepts? What *is* the meaning of "Resist not evil"? Does it mean to allow bombardment—devastation—slaughter? If it does not mean to allow all this, it does not mean to allow War. What, again, do the objectors say is the meaning of, "Love your enemies," or of, "Do good to them that hate you?" Does it mean, "ruin their commerce"—"sink their fleets"—"plunder their cities"—"shoot through their hearts?" If the precept does not mean to allow all this, it does not mean to allow War. It is, therefore, not at all necessary here to discuss the precise signification of some of the precepts from the Mount, or to define what limits Christianity may admit in their application, since, whatever exceptions she may allow, it is manifest what she does *not* allow:[1] for if we give to our objectors whatever license of interpretation they may desire, they cannot, without virtually rejecting the precepts, *so* interpret them as to make them allow War.

18. Of the injunctions that are contrasted with, "eye for eye, and tooth for tooth," the entire scope and purpose is the suppression of the violent passions, and the inculcation of forbearance and forgiveness, and benevolence and love. They forbid, not specifically, the act, but the *spirit* of War; and this method of prohibition Christ ordinarily employed. He did not often condemn the individual doctrines or customs of the age, however false or however vicious; but He condemned the passions by which only vice could exist, and inculcated the truth which dismissed every error. And this method was undoubtedly *wise*. In the gradual alterations of human wickedness, many new species of profligacy might arise which the world had not yet practised: in the gradual vicissitudes of human error, many new fallacies might obtain which the world had not yet held: and how were these errors and these crimes to be opposed, but by the inculcation of principles that were applicable to every crime and to every error?—principles which define not always what is wrong, but which tell us what always is right.

19. There are two modes of censure or condemnation; the one is to reprobate evil, and the other to enforce the opposite good; and both these modes were adopted by Christ.—He not only censured the passions that are necessary to War, but inculcated the affections which are most opposed to them. The conduct and dispositions upon which He pronounced his solemn benediction are exceedingly remarkable. They are these, and in this order: Poverty of spirit;—Mourning;—Meekness;—Desire of righteousness;—Mercy;—Purity of heart;—

[1] It is manifest, from the New Testament, that we are not required to give a "cloak," in *every* case, to him who robs us of a "coat;" but I think it is equally manifest that we are required to give it *not the less*, because he has robbed us: the circumstance of his having robbed us, does not entail an obligation to give; but it also does not impart a permission to withhold. If the necessities of the plunderer require relief, it is the business of the plundered to relieve them.

---

mends soldiers, whilst shooting and stabbing their enemies, to maintain towards them a feeling of "good-will!"— Tracts and Essays by the late William Hey, Esq., F.R.S. And Gisborne, in his Duties of Men, holds similar language. He advises the soldier "never to forget the common *ties of human nature* by which he is inseparably *united* to his enemy!"

Peace-making;—Sufferance of persecution. Now let the reader try whether he can propose eight other qualities, to be retained as the general habit of the mind which shall be more incongruous with War.

20. Of these benedictions, I think the most emphatical is that pronounced upon the *Peace-makers*. "Blessed are the peace-makers: for they shall be called the children of God."[1] Higher praise or a higher title no man can receive. Now, I do not say that these benedictions contain an absolute proof that Christ prohibited War, but I say they make it clear that He did not approve it. He selected a number of subjects for His solemn approbation; and not one of them possesses any congruity with War, and some of them cannot possibly exist in conjunction with it. Can any one believe that He who made this selection, and who distinguished the peace-makers with peculiar approbation, could have sanctioned His followers in destroying one another? Or does any one believe that those who were mourners and meek and merciful and peace-making, could at the same time perpetrate such destruction? If I be told that a temporary suspension of Christian dispositions, although necessary to the prosecution of War, does not imply the extinction of Christian principles; or that these dispositions may be the general habit of the mind, and may both precede and follow the acts of War, I answer that this is to grant all that I require, since it grants that, when we engage in War, we abandon Christianity.

21. When the betrayers and murderers of Jesus Christ approached Him, His followers asked, "Shall we smite with the sword?" and without waiting for an answer, one of them drew "his sword, and smote the servant of the high priest, and cut off his right ear."—"Put up again thy sword into his place," said his Divine Master, "for all they that take the sword shall perish with the sword."[2] There is the greater importance in the circumstances of this command, because it prohibited the destruction of human life in a cause in which there were the best of possible reasons for destroying it. The question, "Shall we smite with the sword?" obviously refers to the defence of the Redeemer from His assailants by force of arms. His followers were ready to fight for Him; and if any reason for fighting could be a good one, they certainly had it. But if, in defence of Himself from the hands of bloody ruffians, His religion did not allow the sword to be drawn, for what reason can it be lawful to draw it? The advocates of War are at least bound to show a better reason for destroying mankind than is contained in this instance in which it was forbidden.

22. It will, perhaps, be said, that the reason why Christ did not suffer Himself to be defended by arms was, that such a defence would have defeated the purpose for which He came into the world, namely, to offer up His life; and that He Himself assigns this reason in the context.—He does indeed assign it; but the *primary* reason, the *immediate* context is,—"for all they that take the sword shall perish with the sword." The reference to the destined sacrifice of His life is an after reference. This destined sacrifice might, perhaps, have formed a reason why His followers should not fight *then*, but the first, the principal reason which He assigned, was the reason why they should not fight *at all*. —Nor is it necessary to define the precise import of the words, "for all they that take the sword shall perish with the sword;" since it is sufficient for us all, that they imply reprobation.

23. It is with the apostles as with Christ Himself. The incessant object of their discourses and writings is the inculcation of peace, of mildness, of placability. It might be supposed that they continually retained in prospect the reward which would attach to "Peace-makers." We ask the advocate of War, whether he discovers in the writings of the apostles or of the evangelists anything that indicates they approved of War. Do the tenor and spirit of their writings bear any congruity with it? Are not their spirit and tenor entirely discordant with it? We are entitled to renew the observation, that the pacific nature of the apostolic writings proves, presumptively, that the writers disallowed War. *That* could not be allowed by them as sanctioned by Christianity, which outraged all the principles that they inculcated.

---

[1] Matt. v. 9.   [2] Matt. xxvi. 52.

24. "Whence come wars and fightings among you?" is the interrogation of one of the apostles, to some whom he was reproving for their unchristian conduct: and he answers himself by asking them, "Come they not hence, even of your lusts that war in your members?"[1] This accords precisely with the argument that we urge. Christ forbade the passions which lead to War; and now, when these passions had broken out into actual fighting, His apostle, in condemning War, refers it back to their passions. We have been saying that *the passions are condemned, and therefore War;* and now, again, the apostle James thinks, like his Master, that the most effectual way of eradicating War is to eradicate the passions which produce it.

25. In the following quotation we are told, not only what the arms of the apostles were not, but what they were. "The weapons of our warfare are *not carnal*, but mighty through God to the pulling down of strongholds; and bringing into captivity *every thought to the obedience of Christ.*"[2] I quote this, not only because it assures us that the apostles had nothing to do with military weapons, but because it tells us the object of their warfare — the bringing every *thought* to the obedience of Christ: and this object I would beg the reader to notice, because it accords with the object of Christ Himself in His precepts from the Mount—the reduction of the *thoughts* to obedience. The apostle doubtless knew that, if he could effect this, there was little reason to fear that his converts would slaughter one another. He followed the example of his Master. He attacked wickedness in its root; and inculcated those general principles of purity and forbearance, which, in their prevalence, would abolish War, as they would abolish all other crimes. The teachers of Christianity addressed themselves not to communities but to men. They enforced the regulation of the passions and the rectification of the heart; and it was probably clear to the perceptions of apostles, although it is not clear to some species of philosophy, that whatever duties were binding upon one man, were binding upon ten, upon a hundred, and upon the state.

26. War is not often directly noticed in the writings of the apostles. When it is noticed, it is condemned, just in that way in which we should suppose anything would be condemned that was *notoriously* opposed to the whole system—just as murder is condemned at the present day. Who can find, in modern books, that murder is formally censured? We may find censures of its motives, of its circumstances, of its degrees of atrocity; but the act itself no one thinks of censuring, because *every one knows* that it is wicked. Setting statutes aside, I doubt whether, if an Otaheitan should choose to argue that Christians allow murder because he cannot find it formally prohibited in their writings, we should not be at a loss to find direct evidence against him. And it arises, perhaps, from the same causes, that a formal prohibition of War is not to be found in the writings of the apostles. I do not believe they *imagined* that Christianity would ever be charged with allowing it. They write as if the idea of such a charge never occurred to them. They did, nevertheless, virtually forbid it; unless any one shall say that they disallowed the passions which occasion War, but did not disallow War itself; that Christianity prohibits the cause but permits the effect; which is much the same as to say, that a law which forbade the administering arsenic did not forbid poisoning.

27. But although the general tenor of Christianity and some of its particular precepts appear distinctly to condemn and disallow War, it is certain that different conclusions have been formed; and many, who are undoubtedly desirous of performing the duties of Christianity, have failed to perceive that War is unlawful to them.

28. In examining the arguments by which War is defended, two important considerations should be borne in mind—first, that those who urge them are not simply defending War, they are also defending *themselves.* If War be wrong, their conduct is wrong; and the desire of self-justification prompts them to give importance to whatever arguments they can advance in its favour. Their decisions may, therefore, with reason, be regarded as in some degree the decisions of a party in the cause. The other consideration is, that the defenders of War come to the discussion prepossessed in its favour. They are attached to it by their

[1] James iv. 1.   [2] 2 Cor. x. 4.

earliest habits. They do not examine the question as a philosopher would examine it, to whom the subject was new. Their opinions had been already formed. They are discussing a question which they had already determined: and every man, who is acquainted with the effects of evidence on the mind, knows that under these circumstances a very slender argument in favour of the previous opinions possesses more influence than many great ones against it. Now all this cannot be predicated of the advocates of peace; they are *opposing* the influence of habit; they are contending *against* the general prejudice; they are, perhaps, dismissing their own previous opinions: and I would submit it to the candour of the reader, that these circumstances ought to attach, in his mind, *suspicion* to the validity of the arguments against us.

29. The narrative of the centurion who came to Jesus at Capernaum to solicit Him to heal his servant, furnishes one of these arguments. It is said that Christ found no fault with the centurion's profession; that if He had disallowed the military character, He would have taken this opportunity of censuring it; and that, instead of such censure, He highly commended the officer, and said of him, "I have not found so great faith, no, not in Israel."[1]

30. An obvious weakness in this argument is this, that it is founded not upon an approval, but upon silence. Approbation is indeed expressed, but it is directed, not to his arms, but to his "faith;" and those who will read the narrative, will find that no occasion was given for noticing his profession. He came to Christ, not as a military officer, but simply as a deserving man. A censure of his profession *might* undoubtedly have been pronounced, but it would have been a gratuitous censure, a censure that did not naturally arise out of the case. The objection is, in its greatest weight, presumptive only; for none can be supposed to countenance everything that he does not condemn. To observe *silence*[2] in such cases was indeed the ordinary practice of Christ.

He very seldom interfered with the civil or political institutions of the world. In these institutions there was sufficient wickedness around Him; but some of them, flagitious as they were, He never, on any occasion, even noticed. His mode of condemning and extirpating political vices was by the inculcation of general rules of purity, which, in their eventual and universal application, would reform them all.

31. But how happens it that Christ did not notice the centurion's *religion?* He surely was an idolater. And is there not as good reason for maintaining that Christ approved idolatry because He did not condemn it, as that He approved War because He did not condemn it? Reasoning from analogy, we should conclude that idolatry was likely to have been noticed rather than War; and it is therefore peculiarly and singularly inapt to bring forward the silence respecting War as an evidence of its lawfulness.

32. A similar argument is advanced from the case of Cornelius, to whom Peter was sent from Joppa, of which it is said, that although the gospel was imparted to Cornelius by the especial direction of heaven, yet we do not find that he therefore quitted his profession, or that it was considered inconsistent with his new character. The objection applies to this argument as to the last—that it is built upon silence, that it is simply negative. *We do not find* that he quitted the service: I might answer, Neither do we find that he continued in it. We only know nothing of the matter; and the evidence is therefore so much less than proof, as silence is less than approbation. Yet that the account is silent respecting any disapprobation of War, might have been a reasonable ground of argument under different circumstances. It might have been a reasonable ground of argument, if the primary object of Christianity had been the reformation of political institutions, or, perhaps, even if her primary object had been the regulation of the external conduct; but her *primary* object was neither of these. She directed herself to the reformation of the heart, knowing that all other reformation

---

[1] Matt. viii. 10.
[2] "Christianity, soliciting admission into all nations of the world, abstained, as behoved it, from intermeddling with the civil institutions of any. But does it follow, from the silence of Scripture concerning them, that all the civil institutions which then prevailed were right, or that the bad should not be exchanged for better?"—PALEY.

would follow. She embraced, indeed, both morality and policy, and has reformed, or will reform, both—not so much immediately as consequently—not so much by filtering the current as by purifying the spring. The silence of Peter, therefore, in the case of Cornelius, will serve the cause of War but little: that little is diminished when urged against the positive evidence of commands and prohibitions, and it is reduced to nothingness when it is opposed to the *universal tendency* and *object* of the revelation.

33. It has sometimes been urged that Christ paid taxes to the Roman government at a time when it was engaged in War, and when, therefore, the money that He paid would be employed in its prosecution. This we shall readily grant; but it appears to be forgotten by our opponents, that if this proves War to be lawful, they are proving too much. These taxes were thrown into the exchequer of the state, and a part of the money was applied to purposes of a most iniquitous and shocking nature—sometimes, probably, to the gratification of the emperor's personal vices, and to his gladiatorial exhibitions, &c., and certainly to the support of a miserable idolatry. If, therefore, the payment of taxes to such a government proves an approbation of War, it proves an approbation of many other enormities. Moreover, the argument goes too far in relation even to War: for it must necessarily make Christ approve of all the Roman wars, without distinction of their justice or injustice—of the most ambitious, the most atrocious, and the most aggressive—and these, even our objectors will not defend. The payment of tribute by our Lord was accordant with His usual system of avoiding to interfere in the civil or political institutions of the world.

34. "He that hath no sword, let him sell his garment and buy one."[1] This is another passage that is brought against us. "For what purpose," it is asked, "were they to buy swords, if swords might not be used?" It may be doubted whether, with some of those who advance this objection, it is not an objection of words rather than of opinion. It may be doubted whether they themselves think there is any weight in it. To those, however, who may be influenced by it, I would observe that, as it appears to me, a sufficient answer to the objection may be found in the immediate context: "Lord, behold, here are two swords," said they, and He immediately answered, "It is enough." How could two be enough when eleven were to be supplied with them? That swords in the sense, and for the purpose, of military weapons, were even intended in this passage, there appears much reason for doubting. This reason will be discovered by examining and connecting such expressions as these: "The Son of Man is not come to destroy men's lives, but to save them," said our Lord. Yet, on another occasion, He says, "I came not to send peace on earth, but a *sword.*" How are we to explain the meaning of the latter declaration? Obviously by understanding "sword" to mean something far other than steel. There appears little reason for supposing that physical weapons were intended in the instruction of Christ. I believe they were not intended, partly because no one can imagine His apostles were in the habit of using such arms, partly because they declared that the weapons of their warfare were *not* carnal, and partly because the word "*sword*" is often used to imply "dissension," or the religious warfare of the Christian. Such an use of language is found in the last quotation; and it is found also in such expressions as these: "*shield* of faith,"—"*helmet* of salvation,"—"*sword* of the Spirit,"—"I have *fought* the good *fight* of faith."

35. But it will be said that the apostles did provide themselves with swords, for that on the same evening they asked, "Shall we smite with the sword?" This is true, and it may probably be true also, that some of them provided themselves with swords in *consequence* of the injunction of their Master. But what then? It appears to me that the

---

[1] Luke xxii. 36. Upon the interpretation of this passage of Scripture, I would subjoin the sentiments of two or three authors. Bishop Pearce says, "It is plain that Jesus never intended to make any resistance, or suffer a sword to be used on this occasion." And Campbell says, "We are sure that He did not intend to be understood literally, but as speaking of the weapons of their spiritual warfare." And Beza: "This whole speech is allegorical: My fellow-soldiers, you have hitherto lived in peace, but now a dreadful war is at hand; so that, omitting all other things, you must think only of *arms*. But when He prayed in the garden, and reproved Peter for smiting with the sword, He himself showed *what these arms were.*"—See Peace and War, an Essay. Hatchard, 1824.

apostles acted on this occasion upon the principles on which they had wished to act on another, when they asked, "Wilt Thou that we command fire to come down from heaven, and consume them?" And that their Master's principles of action were also the same in both.—" Ye know not what manner of spirit ye are of; for the Son of Man is not come to destroy men's lives, but to save them." *This* is the language of Christianity; and I would seriously invite him who now justifies " destroying men's lives," to consider what manner of spirit he is of.

36. I think, then, that no argument arising from the instruction to buy swords can be maintained. This, at least, we know, that when the apostles were *completely* commissioned, they neither used nor possessed them. An extraordinary imagination he must have, who conceives of an apostle, preaching peace and reconciliation, crying " forgive injuries,"—" love your enemies,"—" render not evil for evil ; " and at the conclusion of the discourse, if he chanced to meet violence or insult, promptly drawing his sword and maiming or murdering the offender. We insist upon this consideration. If swords were to be worn, swords were to be used ; and there is no rational way in which they could have been used, but some such as that which we have been supposing. If, therefore, the words, " He that hath no sword, let him sell his garment and buy one," do not mean to authorise *such an use* of the sword, they do not mean to authorise its use at all : and those who adduce the passage, must allow its application in such a sense, or they must exclude it from any application to their purpose.

37. It has been said, again, that when soldiers came to John the Baptist to inquire of him what they should do, he did not direct them to leave the service, but to be content with their wages. This, also, is at best but a negative evidence. It does not prove that the military profession was wrong, and it certainly does not prove that it was right. But in truth, if it asserted the latter, Christians have, as I conceive, nothing to do with it : for I think that we need not inquire what John allowed, or what he forbade. He, confessedly, belonged to that system which required " an eye for an eye,

and a tooth for a tooth ; " and the observations which we shall by and by make on the authority of the law of Moses, apply, therefore, to that of John the Baptist. Although it could be proved (which it cannot be) that he allowed wars, he acted not inconsistently with his own dispensation ; and with that dispensation we have no business. Yet, if any one still insists upon the authority of John, I would refer him for an answer to Jesus Christ Himself. What authority *He* attached to John on questions relating to His own dispensation, may be learnt from this—" The *least* in the kingdom of heaven is *greater* than he."

38. It is perhaps no trifling indication of the difficulty which writers have found in discovering in the Christian Scriptures arguments in support of War, that they have had recourse to such equivocal and far-fetched arguments. Grotius adduces a passage which he says is " *a leading point of evidence*, to show that the right of War is not taken away by the law of the gospel." And what is this leading evidence ? That Paul, in writing to Timothy, exhorts that prayer should be made "for kings !"[1]—Another evidence which this great man adduces is, that Paul suffered himself to be protected on his journey by a guard of soldiers, without hint ng any disapprobation of repelling force by force. But how does Grotius know that Paul did not hint this ? And who can imagine that to suffer himself to be guarded by a military escort, in the appointment of which he had no control, was to approve War?

39. But perhaps the real absence of sound Christian arguments in favour of War is in no circumstance so remarkably intimated as in the citations of Milton in his Christian Doctrine. " With regard to the duties of War," he quotes or refers to thirty-nine passages of Scripture—thirty-eight of which are from the Hebrew Scriptures : and what is the individual *one* from the Christian ? —" What king going to war with another king ! " &c.[2]

40. Such are the arguments which are adduced from the Christian Scriptures by the advocates of War. In these five passages,

[1] See Rights of War and Peace. [2] Luke xiv. 31

the principal of the New Testament evidences in its favour unquestionably consist: they are the passages which men of acute minds, studiously seeking for evidence, have selected. And what are they? Their evidence is in the majority of instances negative at best. A "NOT" intervenes. The centurion was *not* found fault with: Cornelius was *not* told to leave the profession: John did *not* tell the soldiers to abandon the army: Paul did *not* refuse a military guard. I cannot forbear to solicit the reader to compare these objections with the pacific evidence of the gospel which has been laid before him; I would rather say, to compare it with the gospel itself; for the sum, the tendency, of the *whole revelation* is in our favour.

41. In an inquiry whether Christianity allows of War, there is a subject that always appears to me to be of peculiar importance—the prophecies of the Old Testament respecting the arrival of a period of universal peace. The belief is perhaps general amongst Christians, that a time will come when vice shall be eradicated from the world, when the violent passions of mankind shall be repressed, and when the pure benignity of Christianity shall be universally diffused. That such a period will come we indeed know assuredly, for God has promised it.

42. Of the many prophecies of the Old Testament respecting this period, we refer only to a few from the writings of Isaiah. In his predictions respecting the "last times," by which it is not disputed that he referred to the prevalence of the Christian religion, the prophet says—"They shall beat their swords into ploughshares, and their spears into pruning-hooks: nation shall not lift up sword against nation, neither shall they learn war any more."[1] Again, referring to the same period, he says—"They shall not hurt nor destroy in all my holy mountain: for the earth shall be full of the knowledge of the Lord, as the waters cover the sea."[2] And again, respecting the same era—"Violence shall no more be heard in thy land, wasting nor destruction within thy borders."[3]

43. Two things are to be observed in relation to these prophecies; 1st, that it is the Will of God that War should eventually be abolished. This consideration is of importance; for if War be not accordant with His Will, War cannot be accordant with Christianity, which is the revelation of His Will. Our business, however, is principally with the second consideration—*that Christianity will be the means of introducing this period of Peace*. From those who say that our religion sanctions War, an answer must be expected to questions such as these:— By what instrumentality and by the diffusion of what principles, will the prophecies of Isaiah be fulfilled? Are we to expect some new system of religion, by which the imperfections of Christianity shall be removed and its deficiencies supplied? Are we to believe that God sent His only Son into the world to institute a religion such as this—a religion that, in a few centuries, would require to be altered and amended? If Christianity allows of War, they must tell us what it is that is to extirpate War. If she allows "violence, and wasting, and destruction," they must tell us what are the principles that are to produce gentleness, and benevolence, and forbearance. —I know not what answer such inquiries will receive from the advocate of War, but I know that Isaiah says the change will be effected by *Christianity*: and if any one still chooses to expect another and a purer system, an apostle may, perhaps, repress his hopes:—"Though we or an angel from heaven," says Paul, "preach any other gospel unto you, than that which we have preached unto you, let him be accursed."[1]

44. Whatever the principles of Christianity will require hereafter, they require now. Christianity, *with its present principles and obligations*, is to produce universal peace. It becomes, therefore, an absurdity, a simple contradiction, to maintain that the principles of Christianity allow of War, when they, and they only, are to eradicate it. If we have no other guarantee of Peace than the existence of our religion, and no other hope of Peace than in its diffusion, how can that religion sanction War?

45. The case is clear. A more perfect obedience to that same gospel, which, we are told, sanctions slaughter, will be the means, and the only means, of exterminating

[1] Isa ii. 4. [2] Ibid. xi 9. [3] Ibid. lx. 18.   [1] Gal. i. 8.

slaughter from the world. It is not from an alteration of Christianity, but from an assimilation of Christians to its nature, that we are to hope. It is because we violate the principles of our religion, because we are not what they require us to be, that Wars are continued. If we will not be peaceable, let us then, at least, be honest, and acknowledge that we continue to slaughter one another, not because Christianity permits it, but because we reject her laws.

46. The opinions of the earliest professors of Christianity upon the lawfulness of War are of importance, because they who lived nearest to the time of its Founder were the most likely to be informed of His intentions and His will, and to practise them without those adulterations which we know have been introduced by the lapse of ages.

47. During a considerable period after the death of Christ, it is certain, then, that His followers believed he had forbidden War, and that, in consequence of this belief, many of them refused to engage in it whatever were the consequence, whether reproach, or imprisonment, or death. These facts are indisputable. "It is as easy," says a learned writer of the seventeenth century, "to obscure the sun at mid-day, as to deny that the primitive Christians renounced all revenge and War." Christ and His apostles delivered general precepts for the regulation of our conduct. It was necessary for their successors to apply them to their practice in life. And to what did they apply the pacific precepts which had been delivered? They applied them to War; they were assured that the precepts absolutely forbade it. This belief they derived from those very precepts on which we have insisted; they referred, expressly, to the same passages in the New Testament, *and from the authority and obligation of those passages*, they refuse to bear arms. A few examples from their history will show with what undoubting confidence they believed in the unlawfulness of War, and how much they were willing to suffer in the cause of Peace.

48. Maximilian, as it is related in the Acts of Ruinart, was brought before the tribunal to be enrolled as a soldier. On the proconsol's asking his name, Maximilian replied, "I am a Christian, and cannot fight." It was, however, ordered that he should be enrolled, but he refused to serve, still alleging *that he was a Christian*. He was immediately told that there was no alternative between bearing arms and being put to death. But his fidelity was not to be shaken: —"I cannot fight," said he, "if I die." He continued steadfast to his principles, and was consigned to the executioner.

49. The primitive Christians not only refused to be enlisted in the army, but when they embraced Christianity, whilst already enlisted, they abandoned the profession at whatever cost. Marcellus was a centurion in the legion called Trajana. Whilst holding this commission, he became a Christian; and believing, in common with his fellow-Christians, that War was no longer permitted to him, he threw down his belt at the head of the legion, declaring, that he had become a Christian, and that he would serve no longer. He was committed to prison; but he was still faithful to Christianity. "It is not lawful," said he, "for a Christian to bear arms for any earthly consideration;" and he was, in consequence, put to death. Almost immediately afterwards, Cassian, who was notary to the same legion, gave up his office. He steadfastly maintained the sentiments of Marcellus, and like him was consigned to the executioner. Martin, of whom so much is said by Sulpicius Severus, was bred to the profession of arms, which, on his acceptance of Christianity, he abandoned. To Julian the Apostate, the only reason that we find he gave for his conduct was this:— "I am a Christian, and therefore I cannot fight."

50. These were not the sentiments, and this was not the conduct, of insulated individuals who might be actuated by individual opinion, or by their private interpretations of the duties of Christianity. Their principles were the principles of the body. They were recognised and defended by the Christian writers, their cotemporaries. Justin Martyr and Tatian talk of soldiers and Christians as distinct characters; and Tatian says that the Christians declined even military commands. Clemens of Alexandria calls his Christian cotemporaries the "Followers of Peace," and expressly tells us that "the followers of

peace used none of the implements of War." Lactantius, another early Christian, says expressly, "It can *never* be lawful for a righteous man to go to War." About the end of the second century, Celsus, one of the opponents of Christianity, charged the Christians *with refusing to bear arms even in case of necessity.* Origen, the defender of the Christians, does not think of denying the fact; he admits the refusal, and justifies it, *because War was unlawful.* Even after Christianity had spread over almost the whole of the known world, Tertullian, in speaking of a part of the Roman armies, including more than one-third of the standing legions of Rome, distinctly informs us, that "not a Christian could be found amongst them."

51. All this is explicit. The evidence of the following facts is, however, yet more determinate and satisfactory. Some of the arguments which, at the present day, are brought against the advocates of peace, were then urged against these early Christians; and *these arguments they examined and repelled.* This indicates investigation and inquiry, and manifests that their belief of the unlawfulness of war was not a vague opinion, hastily admitted and loosely floating amongst them, but that it was the result of deliberate examination, and a consequent firm conviction that Christ had forbidden it. The very same arguments which are brought in defence of War at the present day, were brought against the Christians sixteen hundred years ago; and sixteen hundred years ago, they were repelled by these faithful contenders for the purity of our religion. It is remarkable, too, that Tertullian appeals to the precepts from the Mount, in proof of those principles on which this chapter has been insisting:—*that the dispositions which the precepts inculcate are not compatible with War, and that War, therefore, is irreconcilable with Christianity.*

52. If it be possible, a still stronger evidence of the primitive belief is contained in the circumstance, that some of the Christian authors *declared that the refusal of the Christians to bear arms* was a fulfilment of ancient prophecy. The peculiar strength of this evidence consists in this—that the fact of a refusal to bear arms is assumed as notorious and unquestioned. Irenæus, who lived about the year 180, affirms that the prophecy of Isaiah, which declared that men should turn their swords into ploughshares and their spears into pruning-hooks, *had been fulfilled in his time;* "for the Christians," says he, "have changed their swords and their lances into instruments of peace, and *they know not how to fight.*" Justin Martyr, his cotemporary, writes—"That the prophecy is fulfilled you have good reason to believe, for we, who in times past killed one another, *do not now fight with our enemies.*" Tertullian, who lived later, says, "You must confess that the prophecy has been accomplished, as far as *the practice of every individual is concerned,* to whom it is applicable."

53. It has been sometimes said, that the motive which influenced the early Christians to refuse to engage in War, consisted in the *idolatry* which was connected with the Roman armies.—*One* motive this idolatry unquestionably afforded; but it is obvious, from the quotations which we have given, that their belief of the unlawfulness of *fighting,* independent of any question of idolatry, was an insuperable objection to engaging in War. Their words are explicit: "I cannot *fight,* if I die."—"I am a Christian, and therefore I cannot *fight.*"—"Christ," says Tertullian, "*by disarming Peter,* disarmed every soldier;" and Peter was not about to fight in the armies of idolatry. So entire was their conviction of the incompatibility of War with our religion, that they would not even *be present* at the gladiatorial fights, "lest," says Theophilus, "we should become partakers of the murders committed there." Can any one believe that they, who would not *even witness* a battle between two men, would themselves fight in a battle between armies? And the destruction of a gladiator, it should be remembered, was authorised by the state, as much as the destruction of enemies in War.

54. It is therefore indisputable, that the Christians who lived nearest to the time of our Saviour, believed with undoubting confidence, that He had unequivocally forbidden War; that they openly avowed this belief; and that, in support of it, they were willing to sacrifice, and did sacrifice, their fortunes and their lives.

55. Christians, however, afterwards became soldiers: and when?—When their general fidelity to Christianity became relaxed;—when, *in other respects*, they violated its principles;—when they had begun "to dissemble," and "to falsify their word," and "to cheat;"—when "Christian casuists" had persuaded them that they might "*sit at meat in the idol's temple;*"—when Christians accepted even *the priesthoods of idolatry*. In a word, they became soldiers when they had ceased to be Christians.

56. The departure from the original faithfulness was, however, not suddenly general. Like every other corruption, War obtained by degrees. During the first two hundred years, not a Christian soldier is upon record. In the third century, when Christianity became partially corrupted, Christian soldiers were common. The number increased with the increase of the general profligacy; until at last, in the fourth century, Christians became soldiers without hesitation, and perhaps without remorse. Here and there, however, an ancient father still lifted up his voice for Peace; but these, one after another, dropping from the world, the tenet that *War is unlawful*, ceased at length to be a tenet of the Church.

57. Let it always be borne in mind, by those who are advocating War, that they are contending for a corruption which their forefathers abhorred; and that they are making Jesus Christ the sanctioner of crimes, which His purest followers offered up their lives because they would not commit.

58. An argument has sometimes been advanced in favour of War, from the divine communications to the Jews under the administration of Moses. It has been said, that as wars were allowed and enjoined to that people, they cannot be inconsistent with the Will of God.

59. The reader who has perused the First Essay of this work, will be aware that to the present argument our answer is short:— If *Christianity* prohibits War, there is, to Christians, an end of the controversy. War cannot then be justified by the referring to any antecedent dispensation. One brief observation may, however, be offered, that those who refer, in justification of our present practice, to the authority by which the Jews prosecuted their wars, must be expected to produce the same authority for our own. Wars were *commanded* to the Jews, but are they commanded to us? War, in the abstract, was never commanded: and surely those specific wars which were enjoined upon the Jews for an express purpose, are neither authority nor example for us, who have received no such injunction, and can plead no such purpose.

60. It will perhaps be said, that the commands to prosecute wars, even to extermination, are so positive, and so often repeated, that it is not probable, if they were inconsistent with the will of heaven, that they would have been thus peremptorily enjoined. We answer, that they were not inconsistent with the will of heaven *then*. But even then, the prophets foresaw that they were not accordant with the universal Will of God, since they predicted, that when that Will should be fulfilled, War should be eradicated from the world. And by what dispensation was this Will to be fulfilled? By that of the "Rod out of the stem of Jesse." It is worthy of recollection, too, that David was forbidden to build the temple *because* he had shed blood. "As for me, it was in my mind to build an house unto the name of the Lord my God: but the word of the Lord came to me, saying, Thou hast shed blood abundantly, and hast made great *wars:* thou shalt not build an house unto my name, *because* thou hast shed much blood upon the earth in my sight."[1] So little accordancy did War possess with the purer offices even of the Jewish Dispensation.

61. Perhaps the argument to which the greatest importance is attached by the advocates of War, and by which thinking men are chiefly induced to acquiesce in its lawfulness, is this—*That a distinction is to be made between rules which apply to us as individuals, and rules which apply to us as subjects of the state; and that the pacific injunctions of Christ from the Mount, and all the other kindred commands and prohibitions of the Christian Scriptures, have no reference to our conduct as members of the political body.*

[1] 1 Chron. xxii. 7, 8.

62. If there be soundness in the doctrines which have been delivered at the commencement of the Essay upon the "Elements of Political Rectitude," this argument possesses no force or application.

63. When persons make such broad distinctions between the obligations of Christianity on private and on public affairs, the proof of the rectitude of the distinction must be expected of those who make it. General rules are laid down by Christianity, of which, in some cases, the advocate of War denies the applicability. *He*, therefore, is to produce the reason and the authority for the exception. And that authority must be a *competent* authority—the authority mediately or immediately of God. It is to no purpose for such a person to tell us of the magnitude of political affairs—of the greatness of the interests which they involve—of " necessity," or of expediency. All these are very proper considerations *in subordination* to the Moral Law:—otherwise they are wholly nugatory and irrelevant. Let the reader observe the manner in which the argument is supported. —If an individual suffers aggression, there is a power to which he can apply that is above himself and above the aggressor; a power by which the bad passions of those around him are restrained, or by which their aggressions are punished. But amongst nations there is no acknowledged superior or common arbitrator. Even if there were, there is no way in which its decisions could be enforced, but by the sword. War, therefore, is the only means which one nation possesses of protecting itself from the aggression of another. The reader will observe the fundamental fallacy upon which the argument proceeds.—It *assumes*, that the reason why an individual is not permitted to use violence is, *that the laws will use it for him.* Here is the error; for the foundation of the duty of forbearance in private life is *not* that the laws will punish aggression, but *that* Christianity requires forbearance.

64. Undoubtedly, if the existence of a common arbitrator were the foundation of the duty, the duty would not be binding upon nations. But that which we require to be proved is this—that Christianity exonerates nations from those duties which she has imposed upon individuals. This the present argument does not prove; and, in truth, with a singular unhappiness in its application, it assumes, in effect, that she has imposed these duties upon neither the one nor the other.

65. If it be said, that Christianity allows to individuals some degree and kind of resistance, and that some resistance is therefore lawful to states, we do not deny it. But if it be said, that the degree of lawful resistance extends to the slaughter of our fellow-Christians—that it extends to War—we do deny it: we say that the rules of Christianity cannot, by any possible latitude of interpretation, be made to extend to it. The duty of forbearance, then, is *antecedent* to all considerations respecting the condition of man; and whether he be under the protection of laws or not, the duty of forbearance is imposed.

66. The only truth which appears to be elicited by the present argument is, that the difficulty of obeying the forbearing rules of Christianity is *greater* in the case of nations than in the case of individuals: *The obligation to obey them is the same in both.* Nor let any one urge the difficulty of obedience in opposition to the duty; for he who does this, has yet to learn one of the most awful rules of his religion—a rule that was enforced by the precepts, and more especially by the final example, of Christ, of apostles and of martyrs—the rule which requires that we should be "obedient even unto death."

67. Let it not, however, be supposed that we believe the difficulty of forbearance would be great in practice as it is great in theory. Our interests are commonly promoted by the fulfilment of our duties; and we hope hereafter to show, that the fulfilment of the duty of forbearance forms no exception to the applicability of the rule.

68. The intelligent reader will have perceived that the "War" of which we speak is all War, without reference to its objects, whether offensive or defensive. In truth, respecting any other than defensive War, it is scarcely worth while to entertain a question, since no one with whom we are concerned to reason will advocate its opposite.

Some persons indeed talk with much complacency of their reprobation of offensive War. Yet to reprobate no more than this, is only to condemn that which wickedness itself is not wont to justify. Even those who practise offensive War, affect to veil its nature by calling it by another name.

69. In conformity with this, we find that it is to *defence* that the peaceable precepts of Christianity are directed. *Offence* appears not to have even suggested itself. It is, "Resist not *evil:*" it is, "Overcome *evil* with good:" it is, "Do good to them that *hate* you:" it is, "Love your *enemies:*" it is, "Render not evil for *evil:*" it is, "Unto him that *smiteth thee on the one cheek.*" All this supposes previous offence, or injury, or violence; and it is *then* that forbearance is enjoined.

70. It is common with those who justify defensive War to identify the question with that of individual self-defence; and although the questions are in practice sufficiently dissimilar, it has been seen that we object not to their being regarded as identical. The Rights of Self-Defence have already been discussed, and the conclusions to which the Moral Law appears to lead, afford no support to the advocate of War.

71. We say the questions are practically dissimilar; so that if we had a right to kill a man in self-defence, very few wars would be shown to be lawful. Of the wars which are prosecuted, some are simply wars of aggression; some are for the maintenance of a balance of power; some are in assertion of technical rights; and some, undoubtedly, to repel invasion. The last are perhaps the fewest; and of these only it can be said that they bear any analogy whatever to the case which is supposed; and even in these, the analogy is seldom complete. It has rarely indeed happened that wars have been undertaken simply for the preservation of life, and that no other alternative has remained to a people than to kill, or to be killed. And let it be remembered, that *unless this alternative alone remains*, the case of individual self-defence is irrelevant: it applies not, practically, to the subject.

72. But indeed you cannot in practice make distinctions, even moderately accurate, between defensive War and War for other purposes.

73. Supposing the Christian Scriptures had said, *An army may fight in its own defence, but not for any other purpose.*—Whoever will attempt to apply this rule in practice, will find that he has a very wide range of justifiable warfare; a range that will embrace many more wars than moralists, laxer than we shall suppose him to be, are willing to defend. If an army may fight in defence of their own lives, they may, and they must fight in defence of the lives of others: if they may fight in defence of the lives of others, they will fight in defence of their property: if in defence of property, they will fight in defence of political rights: if in defence of rights, they will fight in promotion of interests: if in promotion of interests, they will fight in promotion of their glory and their crimes. Now let any man of honesty look over the gradations by which we arrive at this climax, and I believe he will find that, *in practice,* no curb can be placed upon the conduct of an army until they reach that climax. There is, indeed, a wide distance between fighting in defence of life and fighting in furtherance of our crimes; but the steps which lead from one to the other will follow in inevitable succession. I know that the letter of our rule excludes it, but I know that the rule will be a letter only. It is very easy for us to sit in our studies, and to point the commas, and semicolons, and periods of the soldier's career: it is very easy for us to say, he shall stop at defence of life, or at protection of property, or at the support of rights: but armies will never listen to us: we shall be only the Xerxes of morality, throwing our idle chains into the tempestuous ocean of slaughter.

74. What is the testimony of experience? When nations are mutually exasperated, and armies are levied, and battles are fought, does not every one know that with whatever motives of defence one party may have begun the contest, both, in turn, become aggressors? In the fury of slaughter, soldiers do not attend, they cannot attend, to questions of aggression. Their business is destruction, and their business they will per-

form. If the army of defence obtains success, it soon becomes an army of aggression. Having repelled the invader, it begins to punish him. If a War has once begun, it is vain to think of distinctions of aggression and defence. Moralists may *talk* of distinctions, but soldiers will *make* none; and none can be made; it is without the limits of possibility.

75. Indeed, some of the definitions of defensive or of *just* War which are proposed by moralists, indicate how impossible it is to confine warfare within any assignable limits. "The objects of *just* War," says Paley, "are precaution, defence, or reparation."—"Every *just* War supposes an injury perpetrated, attempted, or feared."

76. I shall acknowledge, that if these be justifying motives to War, I see very little purpose in talking of morality upon the subject.

77. It is in vain to expatiate on moral obligations, if we are at liberty to declare War whenever an "injury is feared:"—an injury, without limit to its insignificance! a fear, without stipulation for its reasonableness! The judges, also, of the reasonableness of fear, are to be they who are under its influence; and who so likely to judge amiss as those who are afraid? Sounder philosophy than this has told us, that "he who has to reason upon his duty when the temptation to transgress it is before him, is almost sure to reason himself into an error."

78. Violence, and Rapine, and Ambition are not to be restrained by morality like this. It may serve for the speculations of a study; but we will venture to affirm, that mankind will never be controlled by it. Moral rules are useless, if from their own nature they cannot be, or will not be applied. Who believes that if kings and conquerors may fight when they have fears, they will not fight when they have them not? The morality allows too much latitude to the passions, to retain any practical restraint upon them. And a morality that will not be practised, I had almost said, that cannot be practised, is an useless morality. It is a *theory* of morals. We want clearer and more exclusive rules; we want more obvious and immediate sanctions. It were in vain for a philosopher to say to a general who was burning for glory, "You are at liberty to engage in the War provided you have suffered, or fear you will suffer an injury—otherwise Christianity prohibits it." He will tell him of twenty injuries that have been suffered, of a hundred that have been attempted, and of a thousand that he fears. And what answer can the philosopher make to him?

79. If these are the proper standards of just War, there will be little difficulty in proving any War to be just, except, indeed, that of simple aggression; and by the rules of this morality, the aggressor is difficult of discovery, for he whom we choose to "fear," may say that he had previous "fear" of us, and that his "fear" prompted the hostile symptoms which made us "fear" again. The truth is, that to attempt to make any distinctions upon the subject is vain. War must be wholly forbidden, or allowed without restriction to defence; for no definitions of lawful and unlawful War will be, or can be, attended to. If the principles of Christianity in any case, or for any purpose, allow armies to meet and to slaughter one another, her principles will never conduct us to the period which prophecy has assured us they shall produce. There is no hope of an eradication of War but by an absolute and total abandonment of it.

OF THE PROBABLE AND PRACTICAL EFFECTS OF ADHERING TO THE MORAL LAW IN RESPECT TO WAR.

1. We have seen that the duties of the religion which God has imparted to mankind require irresistance; and surely it is reasonable to hope, even without a reference to experience, that He will make our irresistance subservient to our interests: that if, for the purpose of conforming to His Will, we subject ourselves to difficulty or danger, He will protect us in our obedience, and direct it to our benefit: that if He requires us not to be concerned in War, He will preserve us in peace: that He will not desert those who have no other protection, and who have abandoned all other protection because they confide in His alone.

2. This we may reverently *hope*; yet it is never to be forgotten that our apparent interests in the present life are sometimes, in the economy of God, made subordinate to our interests in futurity.

3. Yet, even in reference only to the present state of existence, I believe we shall find that the testimony of experience is, that forbearance is most conducive to our interests. There is practical truth in the position, that "When a man's ways please the Lord," He "maketh even his *enemies to be at peace with him.*"

4. The reader of American history will recollect, that in the beginning of the last century a desultory and most dreadful warfare was carried on by the natives against the European settlers; a warfare that was provoked—as such warfare has almost always originally been—by the injuries and violence of the Christians. The mode of destruction was secret and sudden. The barbarians sometimes lay in wait for those who might come within their reach, on the highway or in the fields, and shot them without warning: and sometimes they attacked the Europeans in their houses, "scalping some, and knocking out the brains of others." From this horrible warfare the inhabitants sought safety by abandoning their homes, and retiring to fortified places, or to the neighbourhood of garrisons; and those whom necessity still compelled to pass beyond the limits of such protection, provided themselves with arms for their defence. But amidst this dreadful desolation and universal terror, the *Society of Friends*, who were a considerable proportion of the whole population, were steadfast to their principles. They would neither retire to garrisons, nor provide themselves with arms. They remained openly in the country, whilst the rest were flying to the forts. They still pursued their occupations in the fields or at their homes, without a weapon either for annoyance or defence. And what was their fate? They lived in security and quiet. The habitation which, to his armed neighbour, was the scene of murder and of the scalping-knife, was to the unarmed Quaker a place of safety and of peace.

5. *Three* of the Society were, however, killed. And who were they? They were three who abandoned their principles. Two of these victims were men who, in the simple language of the narrator, "used to go to their labour without any weapons, and trusted to the Almighty, and depended on His providence to protect them (it being their principle not to use weapons of War to offend others, or to defend themselves); *but a spirit of distrust* taking place in their minds, they took weapons of War to defend themselves, and the Indians, who had seen them several times without them and let them alone, saying they were peaceable men and hurt nobody, therefore they would not hurt them—now seeing them have guns, and supposing they designed to kill the Indians, they therefore shot the men dead." The third whose life was sacrificed was a woman, who "had remained in her habitation," not thinking herself warranted in going "to a fortified place for preservation, neither she, her son, nor daughter, nor to take thither the little ones; but the poor woman after some time began to let in a slavish fear, and advised her children to go with her to a fort not far from their

dwelling." She went;—and shortly afterwards "the bloody, cruel Indians, lay by the way, and killed her."[1]

6. The fate of the Quakers during the Rebellion in Ireland was nearly similar. It is well known that the Rebellion was a time not only of open War but of cold-blooded murder; of the utmost fury of bigotry, and the utmost exasperation of revenge. Yet the Quakers were preserved even to a proverb; and when strangers passed through streets of ruin and observed a house standing uninjured and alone, they would sometimes point and say—"That, doubtless, is the house of a Quaker."[2] So complete indeed was the preservation which these people experienced, that in an official document of the Society they say—"No member of our Society fell a sacrifice but one young man;"—and that young man had assumed regimentals and arms.[3]

7. It were to no purpose to say, in opposition to the evidence of these facts, that they form an exception to a general rule.—The exception to the rule consists in the *trial* of the experiment of non-resistance, not in its *success*. Neither were it to any purpose to say, that the savages of America or the desperadoes of Ireland, spared the Quakers because they were *previously* known to be an unoffending people, or because the Quakers had *previously* gained the love of these by forbearance or good offices:—we concede all this; it is the very argument which we maintain. We say, that an *uniform, undeviating* regard to the peaceable obligations of Christianity, *becomes the safeguard of those who practise it*. We venture to maintain, that no reason whatever can be assigned, why the fate of the Quakers would not be the fate of *all* who should adopt their conduct. No reason can be assigned why, if their number had been multiplied ten-fold or a hundred-fold, they would not have been preserved. If there be such a reason, let us hear it. The American and Irish Quakers were, to the rest of the community, what one nation is to a continent. And we must require the advocate

[1] See Select Anecdotes, &c., by John Barclay, pages 71, 79.
[2] The Moravians, whose principles upon the subject of War are similar to those of the Quakers, experienced also similar preservation.
[3] See Hancock's Principles of Peace Exemplified.

of War to produce (that which has never yet been produced) a reason for believing, that although individuals exposed to destruction were preserved, a nation exposed to destruction would be destroyed. We do not, however, say, that if a people, in the customary state of men's passions, should be assailed by an invader, and should, on a sudden, choose to declare that they would try whether Providence would protect them—of such a people we do not say that they would experience protection, and that none of them would be killed: but we say, that the evidence of experience is, that a people who habitually regard the obligations of Christianity in their conduct towards other men, and who steadfastly refuse, through whatever consequences, to engage in acts of hostility, *will experience protection in their peacefulness:*—And it matters nothing to the argument, whether we refer that protection to the immediate agency of Providence, or to the influence of such conduct upon the minds of men.[1]

8. Such has been the experience of the unoffending and unresisting in individual life. A *National* example of a refusal to bear arms has only once been exhibited to the world: but that one example has proved, so far as its political circumstances enabled it to prove, all that humanity could desire and all that scepticism could demand, in favour of our argument.

9. It has been the ordinary practice of those who have colonised distant countries, to force a footing, or to maintain it, with the sword. One of the first objects has been to build a fort and to provide a military. The adventurers became soldiers, and the colony

[1] Ramond, in his "Travels in the Pyrenees," tell in from time to time with those desperate marauders who infest the boundaries of Spain and Italy—men who are familiar with danger and robbery and blood. What did *experience* teach him was the most efficient means of preserving himself from injury? To go "*unarmed*." He found that he had "little to apprehend from men whom we inspire with no distrust or envy, and everything to expect in those from whom we claim only what is due from man to man. The laws of nature still exist for those who have long shaken off the law of civil government."—"The assassin has been my guide in the defiles of the boundaries of Italy; the smuggler of the Pyrenees has received me with a welcome in his secret paths. *Armed,* I should have been the enemy of both: *unarmed,* they have alike respected me. In such expectation I have long since laid aside all menacing apparatus whatever. Arms irritate the wicked and intimidate the simple: the man of peace amongst mankind has a much more sacred defence—his character."

18

was a garrison. Pennsylvania was, however, colonised by men who believed that War was absolutely incompatible with Christianity, and who therefore resolved not to practise it. Having determined not to fight, they maintained no soldiers and possessed no arms. They planted themselves in a country that was surrounded by savages, and by savages who knew they were unarmed. If easiness of conquest, or incapability of defence, could subject them to outrage, the Pennsylvanians might have been the very sport of violence. Plunderers might have robbed them without retaliation, and armies might have slaughtered them without resistance. If they did not give a temptation to outrage, no temptation could be given. But these were the people who possessed their country in security, whilst those around them were trembling for their existence. This was a land of peace, whilst every other was a land of War. The conclusion is inevitable, although it is extraordinary: —they were in no need of arms, *because they would not use them.*

10. These Indians were sufficiently ready to commit outrages upon other States, and often visited them with desolation and slaughter; with that sort of desolation, and that sort of slaughter, which might be expected from men whom civilisation had not reclaimed from cruelty, and whom religion had not awed into forbearance. "But whatever the quarrels of the Pennsylvanian Indians were with others, they uniformly respected and held as it were sacred, the territories of William Penn.[1] The Pennsylvanians never lost man, woman, or child by them; which neither the colony of Maryland nor that of Virginia could say, no more than the great colony of New England."[2]

11. The security and quiet of Pennsylvania was not a transient freedom from war, such as might accidentally happen to any nation. She continued to enjoy it "for more than seventy years,"[3] and "subsisted in the midst of six Indian nations, without so much as a militia for her defence."[4] "The Pennsylvanians became armed, though without arms; they became strong, though without strength; they became safe, without the ordinary means of safety. The constable's staff was the only instrument of authority amongst them for the greater part of a century, and never, during the administration of Penn, or that of his proper successors, was there a quarrel or a war."[1]

12. I cannot wonder that these people were not molested—extraordinary and unexampled as their security was. There is something so noble in this perfect confidence in the Supreme Protector, in this utter exclusion of "slavish fear," in this voluntary relinquishment of the means of injury or of defence, that I do not wonder that even ferocity could be disarmed by such virtue. A people, generously living without arms, amidst nations of warriors! Who would attack a people such as this? There are few men so abandoned as not to respect such confidence. It were a peculiar and an unusual intensity of wickedness that would not even revere it.

13. And when was the security of Pennsylvania molested, and its peace destroyed?— When the men who had directed its counsels, and *who would not engage in war,* were *outvoted in its legislature:* when *they who supposed that there was greater security in the sword than in Christianity, became the predominating body.* From that hour the Pennsylvanians transferred their confidence in Christian Principles to a confidence in their arms;—and from that hour to the present they have been subject to War.

14. Such is the evidence, derived from a national example, of the consequences of a pursuit of the Christian policy in relation to War. Here are a people who absolutely refused to fight, and who incapacitated themselves for resistance by refusing to possess arms; and these were the people whose land, amidst surrounding broils and slaughter, was selected as a land of security and peace. The only national opportunity which the virtue of the Christian world has afforded us, of ascertaining the safety of relying upon God for defence, has determined that it is safe.

15. If the evidence which we possess do not satisfy us of the expediency of confiding in God, what evidence do we ask, or what

[1] Clarkson. [2] Oldmixon, anno 1708.
[3] Proud. [4] Oldmixon.

[1] Clarkson: Life of Penn.

can we receive? We have His promise that He will protect those who abandon their seeming interests in the performance of His Will; and we have the testimony of those who have confided in Him, that He has protected them. Can the advocate of War produce one single instance in the history of man, of a person who had given an unconditional obedience to the will of heaven, and who did not find that his conduct was *wise* as well as virtuous, that it accorded with his *interests* as well as with his duty. We ask the same question in relation to the peculiar obligations to irresistance. Where is the man who regrets, that, in observance of the forbearing duties of Christianity, he consigned his preservation to the superintendence of God?—And the solitary national example that is before us, confirms the testimony of private life; for there is sufficient reason for believing, that no nation, in modern ages, has possessed so large a portion of virtue or of happiness, as Pennsylvania before it had seen human blood. I would therefore repeat the question—What evidence do we ask or can we receive?

16. *This* is the point from which we wander:—WE DO NOT BELIEVE IN THE PROVIDENCE OF GOD. When this statement is formally made to us, we think, perhaps, that it is not true; but our practice is an evidence of its truth; for if we did believe, we should also *confide* in it, and should be willing to stake upon it the consequences of our obedience.[1] We can talk with sufficient fluency of "trusting in Providence;" but in the application of it to our conduct in life we know wonderfully little. Who is it that confides in Providence, and for what does he trust Him? Does his confidence induce him to set aside his own views of interest and safety, and simply to obey precepts which appear inexpedient and unsafe? This is the confidence that is of value, and of which we know so little. There are many who believe that War is disallowed by Christianity, and who would rejoice that it were for ever abolished; but there are few who are willing to maintain an undaunted and unyielding stand against it. They can talk of the loveliness of peace, ay, and argue against the lawfulness of War; but when difficulty or suffering would be the consequence, they will not refuse to do what they know to be unlawful, they will not practise the peacefulness which they say they admire. Those who are ready to sustain the consequences of undeviating obedience, are the supporters of whom Christianity stands in need. She wants men who are willing to *suffer* for her principles.

1 "The dread of being destroyed by our enemies if we do not go to War with them, is a plain and unequivocal proof of our disbelief in the superintendence of Divine Providence."—*The Lawfulness of Defensive War impartially considered. By a Member of the Church of England.*

17. The positions, then, which we have endeavoured to establish are these—

    I. That those considerations which operate as general Causes of War, are commonly such as Christianity condemns:

    II. That the Effects of War are, to a very great extent, prejudicial to the moral character of a people, and to their social and political welfare:

    III. That the General Character of Christianity is wholly incongruous with War, and that its General Duties are incompatible with it:

    IV. That some of the express Precepts and Declarations of the Christian Scriptures virtually forbid it:

    V. That the Primitive Christians believed that Christ had forbidden War; and that some of them suffered death in affirmance of this belief:

    VI. That God has declared, in Prophecy, that it is His Will that War should eventually be eradicated from the earth; and that this eradication will be effected by Christianity, by the influence of its *present* Principles:

    VII. That those who have refused to engage in War, in consequence of their belief of its inconsistency with Christianity, have found that Providence has protected them.

18. Now, we think that the establishment of any considerable number of these positions is sufficient for our argument. The establishment of the whole forms a body of Evidence to which I am not able to believe that an inquirer, to whom the subject was new, would be able to withhold his assent. But since such an inquirer cannot be found, I would invite the reader to lay prepossession aside, to suppose himself to have now first heard of battles and slaughter, and dispassionately to examine whether the evidence in favour of Peace be not very great, and whether the objections to it bear any proportion to the evidence itself. But whatever may be the determination upon this question, surely it is reasonable to try the experiment, whether security cannot be maintained without slaughter. Whatever be the reasons for War, it is certain that it produces enormous mischief. Even waiving the obligations of Christianity, we have to choose between evils that are certain and evils that are doubtful; between the actual endurance of a great calamity, and the possibility of a less. It certainly cannot be proved that Peace would not be the best policy; and since we know that the present system is bad, it were reasonable and wise to try whether the other is not better. In reality I can scarcely conceive the possibility of a greater evil than that which mankind now endure; an evil, moral and physical, of far wider extent, and far greater intensity, than our familiarity with it allows us to suppose. If a system of Peace be not productive of less evil than the system of War, its consequences must indeed be enormously bad; and that it would produce such consequences, we have no warrant for believing, either from reason or from practice—either from the principles of the moral government of God, or from the experience of mankind. Whenever a people shall pursue, steadily and uniformly, the pacific morality of the gospel, and shall do this from the pure motive of obedience, there is no reason to fear for the consequences: there is no reason to fear that they would experience any evils such as we now endure, or that they would not find that Christianity understands their interests better than themselves; and that the surest, and the only rule of wisdom, of safety, and of expediency, is to maintain her spirit in every circumstance of life.

19. "There is reason to expect," says Dr. Johnson, "that as the world is more enlightened, policy and morality will at last be reconciled."[1] When this enlightened period shall arrive, we shall be approaching, and we shall not till then approach, that era of purity and of peace, when "violence shall no more be heard in our land—wasting nor destruction within our borders;"—that era in which GOD has promised that "they shall not hurt nor destroy in all His holy mountain." That a period like this will come, I am not able to doubt: I believe it, because it is not credible that He will always endure the butchery of man by man; because He has declared that He will not endure it; and because I think there is a perceptible approach of that period in which He will say—" It is enough."[2] In this belief the Christian may rejoice; he may rejoice that the number is increasing of those who are asking—" Shall the sword devour for ever?" and of those who, whatever be the opinions or the practice of others, are openly saying, "I am for Peace."[3]

20. It will perhaps be asked, what then are the duties of a subject who believes that all War is incompatible with his religion, but whose governors engage in a War and demand his service? We answer explicitly, *It is his duty mildly and temperately, yet firmly, to refuse to serve.*—Let such as these remember, that an honourable and an awful duty is laid upon them. It is upon their fidelity, so far as human agency is concerned, that the Cause of Peace is suspended. Let them then be willing to avow their opinions and to defend them. Neither let them be contented with words, if more than words, if suffering also, is required. It is only by the unyielding fidelity of virtue that corruption can be extirpated. If you believe that Jesus Christ has prohibited slaughter, let not the opinions or the commands of a world induce you to join in it. By this "steady and determinate pursuit of virtue," the benediction which attaches to those who hear the sayings of God and *do* them, will rest upon you; and the time will come when even the world will honour you, as contributors to the work of Human Reformation.

[1] Falkland's Islands. [2] 2 Sam. xxiv. 16. [3] Ps. cxx. 7.

CONCLUSION.

21. That hope which was intimated at the commencement of this volume—that a period of greater moral purity would eventually arrive—has sometimes operated as an encouragement to the writer, in enforcing the obligations of morality to an extent which few who have written such books have ventured to advocate. In exhibiting a standard of rectitude such as that which it has been attempted to exhibit here—a standard to which not many in the present day are willing to conform, and of which many would willingly dispute the authority, some encouragement was needed; and no human encouragement could be so efficient as that which consisted in the belief that the principles would *progressively* obtain more and more of the concurrence and adoption of mankind.

22. That there are indications of an advancement of the human species towards greater purity in principle and in practice, cannot, I think, be disputed. There is a manifest advancement in intellectual concerns:—Science of almost every kind is extending her empire; Political Institutions are becoming rapidly ameliorated;[1]—and Morality and Religion, if their progress be less perceptible, are yet advancing with an onward pace.[2]

Lamentations over the happiness or excellence of other times have generally very little foundation in justice or reason.[1] In truth they cannot be just, because they are perpetual. There has probably never been an age in which mankind have not bewailed the good times that were departed, and made mournful comparisons of them with their own. If these regrets had not been ill-founded, the world must have perpetually sunk deeper and deeper in wickedness, and retired further and further towards intellectual night. But the intellectual sun has been visibly advancing towards its noon; and I believe there never was a period in which, speaking collectively of the species, the power of religion was greater than it is now: at least there never was a period in which greater efforts were made to diffuse the influence of religion amongst mankind. Men are to be judged of by their fruits; and why should men thus more vigorously exert themselves to make others religious, if the power of religion did not possess increased influence upon their own minds? The increase of crime—even if it increased in a progression more rapid than that of population, and the state of society which gives rise to crime—is a very imperfect standard of judgment. Those offences of which civil laws take cognisance, form not an hundredth part of the wickedness of the world. What multitudes are there of bad men who never yet were amenable to the laws! How extensive may be the additional purity without any diminution of legal crimes!

23. And assuredly there is a perceptible advance in the sentiments of good men towards a higher standard of morality. The lawfulness is frequently questioned now of actions of which, *a few* ages ago, *few* or none doubted the rectitude. Nor is it to be disputed, that these questions are resulting more and more in the conviction, that this

---

[1] "The degree of scientific knowledge which would once have conferred celebrity and immortality, is now, in this country, attained by thousands of obscure individuals."—*Fox's Lectures.* "To one who considers coolly of the subject, it will appear that human nature in general really enjoys more liberty at present, in the most arbitrary governments of Europe, than it ever did during the most flourishing period of ancient times."—*Hume.*

[2] Not that the present state, or the prospects of the world, afford any countenance to the speculations—favourite speculations with some men—respecting "human perfectibility." In the sense in which this phrase is usually employed, I fear there is little hope of the perfection of man; at least there is little hope, if Christianity be true. Christianity declares that man is *not* perfectible except by the immediate assistance of God; and this immediate assistance the advocates of "human perfectibility" are not wont to expect. The question, in the sense in which it is ordinarily exhibited, is in reality a question of the truth of Christianity.

[1] "This humour of complaining proceeds from the frailty of our natures; it being natural for man to complain of the present, and to commend the times past."—*Sir Josiah Child,* 1665. This was one hundred and fifty years ago. The same frailty appears to have subsisted two or three thousands of years before: "Say not thou what is the cause that the former days were better than these? for thou dost not inquire wisely concerning this."—Eccles. vii. 10.

higher standard is proposed and enforced by the Moral Law of God. Who that considers these things will hastily affirm, that doctrines in morality which refer to a standard that to him is new, are unfounded in this Moral Law? Who will think it sufficient, to say that strange things are brought to his ears? Who will satisfy himself with the exclamation, These are hard sayings, who can hear them? Strange things *must* be brought to the ears of those who have not been accustomed to hear the truth. Hard sayings *must* be heard by those who have not hitherto practised the purity of morality.

24. Such considerations, I say, have afforded encouragement in the attempt to uphold a standard which the majority of mankind have been little accustomed to contemplate;—and *now*, and in time to come, they will still suffice to encourage, although that standard should be, as by many it undoubtedly will be, rejected and contemned.

25. I am conscious of inadequacy—what if I speak the truth and say, I am conscious of *unworthiness*—thus to attempt to advocate the Law of God. Let no man identify the advocate with the Cause, nor imagine, when he detects the errors and the weaknesses of the one, that the other is therefore erroneous or weak. I apologise for myself: especially I apologise for those instances in which the character of the Christian may have been merged in that of the exposer of the evils of the world. There is a Christian love which is paramount to all;—a love which he only is likely sufficiently to maintain, who remembers that he who exposes an evil and he who partakes in it, will soon stand *together* as suppliants for the mercy of God.

26. And finally, having written a book which is devoted almost exclusively to disquisitions on *Morality*, I am solicitous lest the reader should imagine that I regard the practice of morality as all that God requires of Man. I believe far other; and am desirous of here expressing the conviction, that although it becomes not us to limit the mercy of God, or curiously to define the conditions on which He will extend that mercy—yet that the true and safe foundation of our Hope is in "the redemption that it is in Christ Jesus."

APPENDIX.

ARBITRATION, ARMAMENTS, WAR.

OPINIONS OF EMINENT MEN.

Right Hon. W. E. Gladstone, speaking in Parliament upon the efforts which the Government were making to settle the "Alabama Difficulty," said :—" Both sides of this House are animated by one sentiment, that we should make progress in gradually establishing in Europe a state of opinion which should favour a common action of the Powers to avert the terrible calamity of War." Speaking again upon the same subject at the Guildhall, London, in November 1871, Mr. Gladstone said :—" But differences will occur, quarrels will arise ; honour—not merely visionary sentiments of honour, but sound principles of honour—will forbid the absolute surrender of the points for which the contest is waged. How are these contests to be settled ? 'By blood,' has been the unfortunate reply almost invariably in former times. A great experiment is now being tried : it may be no more than an experiment. The vision may be too bright and too happy to be capable of being realised in this wayward and chequered world in which we live ; but it is an experiment worth the trial, at any rate, whether it is possible to bring the conflicts of opinion between nations to the adjudication of a tribunal of reason instead of to the bloody arbitrament of arms."

. . . "I am fully convinced that there is reserved for this country a great and honourable destiny in connection with this subject. If we are to become effective missionaries of these principles, we can only derive authority by making them our own, and by giving to them practical effect by acting on the principles of moderation, goodwill, and justice. If we do so, then every year will add more and more weight to the abstract doctrines we preach."

. . . "I cannot question the fact that Militarism is a tremendous scourge, a tremendous curse to civilisation."

Sir Robert Peel (1841).—" Is not the time come when the powerful countries of Europe should reduce those military armaments which they have so sedulously raised ? Is not the time come when they should be prepared to declare that there is no use in such overgrown establishments ? What is the advantage of one Power greatly increasing its army and navy ? Does it not see that other Powers will follow its example ? The consequence of this must be that no increase of relative strength will accrue to any one Power ; but there must be a universal consumption of the resources of every country in military preparations. . . . The true interest of Europe is to come to some one common accord so as to enable every country to reduce those military armaments which belong to a state of War rather than of peace. . . ." (1850).—" There was a current maxim, 'If you wish for peace, prepare for War.' That was regarded as an axiom which could not be contradicted, but he believed that one which must be received with greater qualification and reserve had never fallen from the lips of any man."

OPINIONS OF EMINENT MEN (Continued)

Earl of Aberdeen (1849).—I am disposed to dissent from that maxim which has been so generally received, that 'If you wish for peace you must be prepared for War.' It may have been applied to the nations of antiquity, and to society in a comparatively barbarous and uncivilised state, when warlike preparations cost but little; but in the state of society in which we now live, and when the warlike preparations of Great Powers are made at an enormous expense, I say that so far from their being any security for peace, they are directly the contrary, and tend at once to War; for it is natural that men having adopted means they think efficient to any end, should desire to put their efficiency to the test, and to have some result from their labours and expense."

General Grant, President of the United States.—"An Arbitration between two nations may not satisfy either party at the time, but it satisfies the conscience of mankind, and it must commend itself more and more as a means of adjusting differences. Though I have been trained as a soldier, and have participated in many battles, there never was a time when, in my opinion, some way could not have been found of preventing the drawing of the sword. I look forward to an epoch when a court, recognised by all nations, will settle International differences, instead of keeping large standing armies, as they do in Europe."

The Emperor Alexander of Russia.—A distinguished Quaker, "Stephen Grellet," who was accorded an interview with the Emperor in 1819, says:—" The Emperor conversed very freely upon War, and his desire to establish a Congress of Nations to prevent a resort to the sword. He stated: 'His soul's anxiety had been that Wars and bloodshed might cease for ever from the earth; that he had passed sleepless nights on account of it, deeply deploring the woes brought on humanity by War; and that whilst his mind was bowed before the Lord in prayer, the plan of all the Crowned Heads joining in the conclusion to submit to Arbitration whatever differences might arise among them, instead of resorting to the sword, had presented itself to his mind in such a manner, that he rose from bed and wrote what he had so sensibly felt; that his intentions had been misunderstood or misrepresented by some, but that love to God and to man was his only motive in the Divine sight.'"

John Bright (1853).—" It is only a few years since duelling was believed to be as indispensable for the settlement of private quarrels, and to cause a gentleman to be gentlemanly in his conduct to another gentleman, as Wars are now believed to be indispensable between communities and nations. I believe, in spite of all the ridicule some parties bestow on this which we believe to be reasonable and Christian, that the time will come—and much faster than some believe—when War between nations will be considered as brutal and idiotic as duelling is now considered amongst all classes of the community."

Richard Cobden (1848).—" I cordially approve of the expediency of recommending the insertion of an Arbitration clause in all International treaties, by which questions of dispute shall be settled by mediation; but it will be better to recommend that treaties be entered into for the express purpose of binding the contracting nations to submit their future quarrels to the decision of Arbitrators. I do not think that it would be easy to find an object more worthy of a separate treaty than that which is contemplated in the clause."

Lord Rosebery.—" All War is odious. There is something, to my mind, even puerile in settling the differences of great nations by warfare. We do not settle difficulties in private life by personal combat, and it seems strange that when we cease to be individuals and become an aggregation we should think it necessary to do so. I go further, and say that every War is deplorable, because it means a step backward in that civilisation which it has cost so many centuries and so many noble lives to earn."

ON ARBITRATION—ARMAMENTS—WAR.

Sir Stafford Northcote (when Secretary of State).—"It is our sincere and earnest belief that the interests of this country and of the whole world lie in the direction of a *peaceful* instead of a *warlike* policy. We firmly believe that the differences between nations may best be settled by the counsels that prevail in time of peace, and not amidst the excitement and clash of War."

. . . "National honour does not consist in refusing to acknowledge wrong, in always insisting that what has been done has been right. True national honour, like true personal honour, consists in being ready to do justice in all things ; and when the point of justice is doubtful, to give it against yourself rather than for yourself."

Earl of Beaconsfield (1859).—"Let us terminate this disastrous system of wild expenditure by mutually agreeing, with no hypocrisy, but in a manner and under circumstances which admit of no doubt, by the reduction of Armaments, that peace is really our policy ; and then the Chancellor of the Exchequer may look forward with no apprehension to his next budget, and England may then witness the termination of the income-tax."

Henry Richard.—"I will venture to say this, that if all the ministers of Christ's Gospel were with one voice, constantly, courageously, earnestly, to preach to the nations the Truce of God, and were to denounce War, not merely as costly, and cruel, and barbarous, but as essentially and eternally unchristian, another War in the civilised world would become impossible."

Lord Russell.—"On looking at all the Wars which have been carried on during the last century, and examining into the causes of them, *I do not see one of these Wars, in which, if there had been proper temper between the parties, the questions in dispute might not have been settled without recourse to arms.*"

Hon. Rev. S. T. Lyttelton, M.A. (Master of Selwyn College).—"It is a profanation of the sacred name of justice to apply it to the blind and brutal arbitrament of War ; for though there is nothing in the world, except love, more God-like than the justice which controls and wields the force of society, and thereby avenges wrong and punishes the sinner, there is nothing less God-like than force, which usurps the place of justice, and constitutes itself both judge and executioner ; and such a force is War."

Canon Freemantle.—"When men speak of the horrors of War they are apt to dwell far too much on the physical sufferings which are witnessed, and far too little upon the moral evil. It is not suffering in itself, if we are followers of Christ, that we must chiefly dread, either for ourselves or others, but the evil disposition, the cruelty, or the callousness which causes the suffering. . . . As the real evil of War is the moral not the material, so the remedy for it is the remedy for moral evil ; that is, the application of the Gospel of Jesus Christ."

John Stuart Mill.—"The Tribunals of the United States, which act as umpires between the Federal and State Governments, naturally also decide all disputes between two States. The usual remedies between nations, War and Diplomacy, being precluded by the Federal Union, it is necessary that a judicial remedy should supply their place. The Supreme Court of the Federation dispenses International Law, and is the first great example of what is now one of the most prominent wants of civilised society, a real International Tribunal."

Professor Seeley (1871).—"If War between individuals, between townships, between counties can be prevented without eradicating the passions from which it springs, why not in nations ? . . . England and Scotland fought like cat and dog for centuries, and now they are bound together in an indissoluble concord. Here is a great political achievement. . . . When we hear it said that Englishmen and Frenchmen, or Frenchmen and Germans, will not for hundreds of years lose their antipathies sufficiently to be united, let us remember the case of England and Scotland."

OPINIONS OF EMINENT MEN (Continued)

Brougham.—"I abominate War as unchristian. I hold it the greatest of human crimes. I deem it to include all others—violence, blood, rapine, fraud; everything which can deform the character, alter the nature, and debase the name of man."

Victor Hugo.—"If to kill is a crime, to kill much cannot be an extenuating circumstance. If to steal is a disgrace, to rob a nation cannot be a glory. *Te Deums* are of small significance; homicide is homicide; bloodshed is bloodshed; it alters nothing to call one's self Cæsar or Napoleon; in the eyes of the Eternal God, a murderer is not changed in character because, instead of a hangman's cap, there is placed on his head an emperor's crown. Kings are for to-day, peoples for to-morrow. A day will come when War between Paris and London, Petersburg and Berlin, Vienna and Turin, will seem as impossible as between Rouen and Amiens; when bullets and bombs will be replaced by votes, by the universal suffrage of peoples, by the Arbitrage of a great sovereign assembly which shall be to Europe what the legislative assembly is to France: when cannons will be exhibited in museums, as are to-day the instruments of torture of past generations; when the United States of America will join hands across the seas with the United States of Europe."

General Sheridan (1886).—"At a banquet in Philadelphia, the general said:—"There is one thing you should appreciate, and that is, that the improvement in guns and in the material of War, in dynamite and other explosives, and in breech-loading guns is rapidly bringing us to a period when War will be eliminated from history, when we can no longer stand up and fight each other, and when we shall have to resort to something else. Now, what will that 'something else' be? It will be Arbitration. I mean what I say when I express the belief that any who may live to the next centennial (in 1987) will find that Arbitration will rule the whole world."

Vattel.—"These large armies, maintained at all times, deprive the earth of its cultivators, arrest the progress of population, and can answer no purpose but to oppress the liberties of the people who nourish them. Arbitration is a very reasonable mode, and one that is perfectly conformable to the law of nature for the decision of every dispute which does not directly interest the safety of nations. Though the claims of justice may be mistaken by the Arbitrators, it is still more to be feared that it will be overpowed by an appeal to the sword. The Swiss have had the precaution in all their alliances among themselves, and even in those they have contracted with the neighbouring Powers, to agree beforehand on the manner in which their disputes were to be submitted to Arbitrators, in case they could not adjust them in an amicable manner. This wise precaution has not a little contributed to maintain the Swiss Republic in that flourishing state which secures her liberty and renders her respected throughout Europe."

Bishop Fraser.—"War is not the triumph of righteousness. It is the triumph of brute force. Can anything be conceived more unchristian, more irrational, than the present mode by which international quarrels are commonly adjusted?"

Dr. Chalmers.—"The mere existence of the prophecy, 'They shall learn War no more,' is a sentence of condemnation on War."

Robert Hall.—"War is nothing less than a temporary repeal of the principles of virtue."

Sydney Smith.—"God is forgotten in War: every principle of Christianity is trampled upon."

John Wesley.—"Shall Christians assist the Prince of Hell, who was a murderer from the beginning, by telling the world of the *benefit or the need of War?*"

Dr. Adam Clarke.—"War is as contrary to the spirit of Christianity as murder."

ON ARBITRATION—ARMAMENTS—WAR.

Lord Carnarvon.—" You have no right to divorce your system of politics from your system of morals. There are no two sides to that silver shield."

Duke of Wellington (to Lord Shaftesbury).—"War is a most detestable thing. If you had seen but one day of War, you would pray God that you might never see another."

Grotius, in his great work, *De Jure Belli ac Pacis*, says of Arbitration :—" Christian kings and States are bound, above all others, to adopt this expedient to prevent War. Therefore, it would be useful, and in some sort necessary, that the Christian Powers should appoint some body in which the disputes of any States might be settled by the judgment of the others which are not interested."

William Penn says :—" The Princes of Europe should establish one Sovereign Assembly, before which all International differences should be brought, which cannot be settled by the Embassies."—*Essay on the Peace of Europe.*

Earl Derby (when Secretary of State for Foreign Affairs, 1867).—" Unhappily there is no International Tribunal to which cases can be referred, and there is no International Law by which parties can be required to refer their disputes. *If such a Tribunal existed, it would be a great benefit to the civilised world.*"

Dr. Clifford.—" Let us distinctly teach that War is wrong, a falling short of Christ's ideal for the nations, an outrage on the principles and spirit of the Christianity of our Divine Lord."

John Bright.—" As to War, in a short sentence it may be summed up to be the combination and concentration of all the horrors, atrocities, crimes, and sufferings of which human nature on the globe is capable."

Baboo Reshub Chunder Sen.—" As a Hindoo, I cannot understand. . . . I really cannot tell how the followers of the Prince of Peace can ever go to War. I cannot for one moment believe that men can live and die true Christians without doing all in their power to check and arrest the growth and spirit of War."

Speech by Signor Bonghi.—" Allow me to remind you of a Christian conception, of grand and deep mystic import, accepted by all Christian sects. Humanity, they affirm, is the very body of Christ. All men are His members. Hence every War between Christian nations has been with good reason called a Civil War ; and there is no friend or partisan of War who does not think Civil War accursed."

Baron de Courcel.—" No aspiration is more ideal, no effort more noble, than the endeavour to effect 'the gradual abolition of the custom of resorting to brute force for the settlement of the differences between nations.' Every Arbitration affords fresh proof of the practicability of what was so lately regarded as merely an idle dream."

Charles H. Spurgeon.—" If there be anything clear in Scripture, it does seem to me that it is for a Christian to have nothing to do with carnal weapons; and how it is that the great mass of Christendom do not see this, I cannot understand ; surely it must be through the blinding influences of the society in which the Christian Church is cast."

Montesquieu.—" A new disease has spread itself through Europe ; it has taken hold of our princes, and led them to maintain an inordinate number of troops. It has its paroxysms, and becomes necessarily contagious ; for as soon as one State augments its troops, the others forthwith augment theirs ; so that they gain nothing by it but a common ruin. Each monarch keeps on foot as many armed men as he could have if their people were in danger of being exterminated ; and they call this rivalry of all against all—Peace."

OPINIONS OF EMINENT MEN (Continued).

A French Journalist, following the same course of reasoning as Professor Seeley, says :—" Not many years since in France, counties, duchies, marquisates, baronies made war against each other—fought for the most trivial causes. A few families could not live in peace near a few others. To be born a Norman and to be born a Breton sufficed to be born enemies. Well, this barbarous state is so astonishingly changed that to-day forty millions of people live under the same law, the same social bond uniting them."

Jeremy Bentham.—" Whatsoever nation should get the start of the other in making the proposal to reduce and fix the amount of its armed force would crown itself with everlasting honour. The risk would be nothing, the gain certain. The gain would be, the giving incontrovertible demonstration of its own disposition to peace, and of the opposite disposition in the other nation in case of its rejecting the proposal. . . . It would sound the heart of the nation addressed. It would discover its intentions, and proclaim them to the world."

F. E. Willard.—" Happy are we who see the days of gentleness begin to dawn, and who may ourselves, in steady and practical fashion, help on the time when the Prince of Peace shall reign in government, and the flags of War shall all be furled."

Professor Newman.—" When men, not for justice, but as a trade, habitually expose their own lives to deadly risk, very few indeed of them will sustain in their hearts much tender humanity or horror at slaying and starving innocent thousands."

Channing.—" The death-groan on the battlefield is awful. How much more appalling the spirit of murder which extorts it."

The Marquis of Salisbury.—" After all, the great triumph of civilisation in the past has been in the substitution of judicial determination for the cold, cruel, crude arbitrament of War."
. . . " We are going back to a very rudimentary stage of the world's history if nothing but material force is to decide a question between two civilised countries."

Count L. N. Tolstoi.—" In one hundred years, I think, Wars will cease, and men will look back at War as we now look back at torture, wondering how mankind could be so stupid as to tolerate it."

Arthur Helps.—" The measure of civilisation in a people is to be found in its just appreciation of the wrongfulness of War."

M. Siccardi.—" War cannot be the instrument of civilisation, because it is the negation of morality. of justice, and of liberty. Civilisation is the residuum of that which War has been unable to destroy."

The Times.—" At present the real quarrel is a rivalry of Armaments. The only check on so foolish a competition is a general agreement to reduce these excessive preparations. The path of peace once entered, there may soon be a rivalry in this direction as great as that which is hurrying myriads to a cruel and fratricidal War."

Washington.—" How much more delightful to an undebauched mind is the task of making improvements in the earth than all the vainglory which can be acquired by the most uninterrupted career of conquests ! "

Jefferson.—" Will nations never devise a more rational umpire of differences than force ? War is an instrument entirely inefficient towards redressing wrong. and multiplies instead of indemnifying losses."

The President of the Chili Republic.—" The principle of Arbitration has been tested : it provides for the honourable settlement of International disputes, for the equality of nations in the practice of International Law, and for the legitimate satisfaction of claims based upon justice."

ON ARBITRATION—ARMAMENTS—WAR.

Earl de Grey and Ripon.—"Nations, like men, are bad judges of their own quarrels. Anything which will remove International disputes from the fatal arbitrament of the sword is indeed a great advance in the march of progress."

Michel Chevalier.—"Is it not, indeed, evident that an essential condition of the progress and preservation of Europe must be sought in a permanent Congress, resembling that which sits at Washington, elective in its constitution, and carrying on its deliberations in public?"

King Louis Philippe (1843).—"The sentiment, or rather the principle, that in peace you must prepare for War, is one of difficulty and danger ; for while we keep armies on hand to preserve peace, they are at the same time incentives and instruments of War."

Lamartine.—"War, very far from being the progress of humanity, is only murder in mass, which retards it, afflicts it, decimates it, dishonours it. The nations who sport in blood are instruments of ruin, not instruments of life to the world. Unlawful murder is not less a crime in a nation than in an individual."

Benjamin Franklin.—"There never has been, nor ever will be, any such thing as a good War or a bad peace. All Wars are follies—very expensive and very mischievous ones. When will mankind be convinced of this, and agree to settle their differences by Arbitration? Were they to do it by the cast of a die it would be better than by fighting and destroying each other."

M. Drouyn d' l'Huys, French Minister for Foreign Affairs, said in 1867 :—"If any difference were to arise between two nations, what sovereign, what assembly, would dare to refer the decision to the terrible chances of battle when there would be a law which had foreseen the case, and a tribunal of Arbitration, the composition of which should be indicated or described?"

The King of Portugal (1864). "Congresses after War are ordinarily the consecration of the advantages of the strongest ; and the treaties which result therefrom, resting rather on facts than on rights, create forced positions, resulting in that general uneasiness which give rise to violent protests and armed demands. A Congress before War, with the object of preventing it, is, in my opinion, a noble idea of progress."

Judge Williams, of the United States (one of the High Commissioners for arranging the Treaty of Arbitration between Great Britain and the United States).—" We have read and heard much of the 'pomp and circumstance of glorious War,' but in all history there is not a spectacle more sublime than two great nations not afraid of each other, or of any power upon earth, submitting themselves with questions of International right and duty to the arbitrament of three or five individuals, and pledging to each other their national faith and honour to abide by that decision, whatever it may be. The distinguishing feature of the Treaty, as it appears to me, is, that it provides for the peaceful adjustment of those questions that have heretofore been considered as within the exclusive jurisdiction of the sword.'

President Hayes, in his inaugural address, 1877, said :—"The policy inaugurated by my honoured predecessor, President Grant, of submitting to Arbitration grave questions in dispute between ourselves and Foreign Powers, points to a new, and comparatively the best, instrumentality for the preservation of peace, and will, as I believe, become a beneficent example, to be pursued in similar emergencies by other nations."

Since the Peace of 1815 there have been about sixty instances of Arbitration for the settlement of International disputes, some of them involving great and difficult questions. In all of these cases a satisfactory and permanent settlement was effected.

SOME OF THE DISPUTES BETWEEN NATIONS WHICH HAVE BEEN DECIDED BY ARBITRATION.

DISPUTES BETWEEN GREAT BRITAIN AND THE UNITED STATES.

Date.	Nature of Dispute.	Arbitrators Appointed.	Result.
1816	Boundaries—River St. Croix.	Three Commissioners—one chosen by each nation, and another by agreement.	Decision accepted by both nations.
1818	Obligation to Restore Slaves in British possession at Treaty of Ghent.	Emperor of Russia.	Decision in favour of United States. Great Britain paid 1,204,000 dollars.
1827	North-East Boundary of United States.	King of Netherlands.	Decision not accepted. Afterwards settled by a compromise.
1853	All outstanding Claims, and for Slaves captured.	Two Commissioners, and Mr. Joshua Bates, of London, Umpire.	Decision accepted.
1871	Alabama Claims. United States claimed 17,900,000 dollars.	Commission, which met at Geneva. Count E. Sclopis, named by King of Italy. Jacob Staempfli, named by President of Swiss Federation. Viscount D'Itajuba, named by the Emperor of Brazil. Mr. C. F. Adams, named by the President of United States. Sir Alex. Cockburn, named by the Queen of England.	Decision accepted. England to pay a sum of 15,500,000 dollars for losses of ships and cargoes and interest.
1871	Outstanding Claims by Great Britain upon United States, amounting to 498, and contra claims 19 by United States upon Great Britain.	A mixed Commission, consisting of— Mr. Russell Gurney, for Great Britain. Hon. J. S. Fraser, for United States. And Count Corti, Italian Minister at Washington.	Decision accepted. The United States to pay to Great Britain a sum of £386,000.
1871	The San Juan dispute.	Emperor of Germany.	Decision accepted. American claim sustained.
1871	Nova Scotia Fisheries.	Three Commissioners. Sir Alex. Galt. Mr. Ensign H. Kellog. Mr. Maurice Belford.	Decision accepted. Award in favour of England.
1888	Fisheries Question between Great Britain and Canada and the United States.	Joint Commission.	Not accepted by the United States. American Senate refused to ratify decision.
1891	Behring Sea Fisheries.	Referred to a Joint Commission of seven persons.	Decision accepted. Award in favour of Britain.

DISPUTES BETWEEN GREAT BRITAIN AND OTHER COUNTRIES.

Date.	Nature of Dispute.	Arbitrators.	Result.
1835	**Great Britain and France.** Portendic claims.	King of Prussia.	Decision accepted. France to pay 42,000 francs.
1863	**Great Britain and Brazil.** Imprisonment of British naval officer.	King of the Belgians.	Decision accepted. Brazil was justified.
1864	**Great Britain and Peru.** Compensation for false imprisonment of British subject.	Senate of Hamburg.	Decision accepted. Claim inadmissible.
1867	**Great Britain and Spain.** The *Mermaid* difficulty.	—	—
1870	**Great Britain and Portugal.** Rival claims to Island of Bulama.	President of United States.	Decision accepted. Award in favour of Portugal.
1873	**Great Britain and Brazil.** Dundonald claims.	United States Minister at Rio. Italian Minister at Rio.	Decision accepted. Award against Brazil nearly £40,000.
1875	**Great Britain and Portugal.** Delagoa Bay.	President of French Republic.	Decision accepted. Portuguese title accepted.
1879	**Great Britain and Nicaragua.** Sovereignty over the Mosquito Indians.	Emperor of Austria, who appointed three assessors.	Decision accepted. Award in favour of Great Britain.
1884	**Great Britain and Chili.** Damages to British subjects in war between Chili and Peru.	Commission of three members.	—
1885	**Great Britain and Germany.** Claims of German subjects in Fiji.	Two Commissioners.	Decision accepted. Award £10,620.

Many other disputes have been settled by arbitration. The following countries and states may be named: Denmark, France, Germany, Holland, Italy, Persia, Russia, Spain, Turkey, &c. Thus the principle of arbitration in disputes may be said to have received a general adoption by the countries of the world.

SOME OF THE CONSEQUENCES OF THE MODERN WAR SYSTEM.

DESTRUCTION OF LIFE FROM WAR IN TWENTY-FIVE YEARS (1855-80), AND COST OF RECENT WARS (1855-80).

	Killed in Battle, or Died of Wounds and Disease.	Cost of recent War
CRIMEAN WAR	750,000	£340,000,000
Italian War, 1859	45,000	60,000,000
War of Schleswig-Holstein	3,000	7,000,000
AMERICAN CIVIL WAR—the North	280,000	940,000,000
" " the South	520,000	460,000,000
War between Prussia, Austria, and Italy in 1866	45,000	66,000,000
Expeditions to Mexico, Cochin China, Morocco, Paraguay, &c.	65,000	40,000,000
FRANCO-GERMAN WAR OF 1870-71—		
FRANCE	155,000 ⎫	500,000,000
GERMANY	60,000 ⎭	
RUSSIAN AND TURKISH WAR OF 1877	225,000	210,000,000
ZULU AND AFGHAN WARS, 1879	40,000	30,000,000
Total	2,188,000 *	£2,653,000,000 †

Killed in twenty-five years of nineteenth century "civilisation!"

* If the execution of two or three criminals justly excites horror, what should be the feeling produced by the contemplation of such an awful sacrifice of human life in millions upon millions, and often amid circumstances of unimaginable horror!

† This vast sum is equal to £2 for every man, woman, and child in the world! It represents a mass of wasted labour and money, which might, if wisely directed, have been an untold blessing to the nations.

It has been computed that the actual workers in Great Britain, even in time of Peace, work every day of the year to pay the interest of the National Debt, twenty-six minutes : for the maintenance of our armaments, thirty minutes a day ; for the cost of collecting the taxes, four minutes a day ; for the relief of the poor, nine minutes a day ; for local taxes, nine minutes a day ; for the cost of civil government, twelve minutes a day. Adding these together, we find our labourers working every day of the year one hour and thirty minutes, or nine hours per week, for the payment of our national and local taxes. Very nearly two-thirds of this time is occupied in producing the cost of our War system, that is, of our National Debt and of our Armaments.

INDEX.

	Paragraph	Page
ACCOMPLISHMENTS in female education	27	116
Accumulation, proper limits of	92-94	64
—— silence of moralists in relation to	101	66
Advowsons	93	224
Alliance of State and Church	113-116	230
Amusements, masquerades	73	125
—— on Sundays	16-19	46
—— public	67, 68	124
—— the drama	69 72	125
—— the field and the turf	74-80	126
Antiquity, of appealing to	4	256
ARBITRATION:—		
Cases settled by rules of equity	26	186
Change from jurymen to arbitrators	33	188
Courts to consist of three, five, or seven members	36	189
Deliberations to be public	37	189
Diffuse the principles of justice	38	189
Instead of strikes		
International—cases of success		286
Legal officers to assist in arbitrations	35	189
Not to be governed by rules of fixed law	23, 29	186
Opinions of statesmen and eminent men		279
Qualities needed in arbitrators	27	187
Substitution of, for war		
To replace litigation	3-11	66
Armies, loan of, by one State to another	46	254
Army and navy as respectable professions	50	100
Articles of Religion, subscription to	15 23	92
AXIOMS:—		
Freely ye have received, freely give	34	238
I seek not yours but you	31	237
Not to do evil that good may come	87	17
That the end justifies the means	88	17
The obligation of every law depends upon its ultimate utility	30	6
Whatever is expedient is right	30, 40	6
BAD influence of classics in education	39 42	119
Ballot, the	75	172
Bankrupts and insolvents	41	51
—— need of a sound state of opinion as to	46	52
—— obligation to pay all debts—Society of Friends acknowledges this rule	47	53

	Paragraph	Page
Bequests, charitable	52	54
Bible Society	107	228
Bills of exchange	60	56
Bishops, bench of	56	168
Books, circulating libraries	32	95
—— often injurious in education	38	118
—— publication of	27	94
—— responsibility for the circulation of	28, 29	95
Boxing and wrestling	77, 78	127
Bribery, oath against	8	90
British constitution, the	42	166
CANDIDATES should be elected by ballot	75	172
—— should be elected free of expense	74	172
Canvassing for votes	83	173
Catholic question, the	64	150
Ceremonial institution	22	47
—— and ritual	31	49
Children, provision for the wants of	97-100	64
Christian ministers: axiom, I seek not yours but you	31	237
—— ministers, legal provision for	1-5	232
—— ,, qualifications of	33	238
—— ,, voluntary provision for	33-35	238
Christianity, benevolence of	90	18
Christ's teachings - law of love	63	11
CHURCH AND STATE:—		
Alliance with State weakens episcopacy	113-116	230
Cry of Church in danger	113	230
Effect of State Church on religious welfare of the people	99	226
Effect of State Church upon internal discipline	98	226
Evil from pluralities and non-residence	95	225
,, of payments by tithes	110	229
Influence upon preaching	101	227
Non-residence a great injury to religion	104	227
Opposition of sceptics	105	228
Produces inactivity in social progress	106, 107	228
Refusal to alter constitution and creed	103	227
Return of livings and non-residents	97	225
State religion injurious to Christianity	112	229
,, ,, to ministers	94	225
Tithes as property	14-18	235
Tithes the legal provision for the clergy	109	229

INDEX.

	Paragraph	Page
Church, see also Religious Establishments.		
—— alliance with the State	21-23	211
—— an established	1, 2, 3	207
—— the primitive	8	208
Civil government	94	176
—— obedience, duty of Christians	68, 69	150
Classics, ancient, see Education.		
Clergy, see also Church and State.		
Commons, House of	61	170
—— modes of election	72	172
—— no canvassing should be allowed	83	173
—— no qualification should be required	81	173
—— the house of the people	62	170
—— universal suffrage	71	171
Confiscations of property and estates immoral	73	59

	Paragraph	Page
CONSCIENCE:—		
A discussion of opinions	118-124	25
Authority of	109	21
its nature and authority	99	20
Scripture teaching about	109	21
Conversation, religious	10	44
Courage	57	102
Courts martial, the military oath	6	90
—— of equity	33	188
Creeds and confessions	32	213
—— the Athanasian refusal to amend	102	227
Crime in the eyes of the civil law and the moral law	47	191
—— in the eyes of the moral law and public opinion	39	97
Curse, a, in the form of an oath	64	80

	Paragraph	Page
DAYS, non-sanctity of	2	43
Death punishment, see Punishments.		
Debtor, a, engages in speculations	63	195
—— a, neglects his business	62	195
—— discrimination belongs to the law	59	194
—— is a debtor a criminal	56	194
—— is it right to imprison some	57	194
—— law should take cognisance of all insolvent	65	195
—— who shall say when debtors become criminal	60	194
Debts, minors', and a wife's	58	55
—— payment of, a perpetual obligation	46, 47	52
Defendants, unjust	66	57
Devotion, factitious semblance of	1	43
Divine attributes, the	53	10
Drama, the	69	125
Duelling should be punished	53	193
—— general remarks	1	127

	Paragraph	Page
Duty, the source of	53	10
—— mode of applying Scripture	75	14
—— different forms to express the idea of	79	15
—— two modes of teaching	83	61
—— the golden rule	84	16
—— discussion is needful	85, 86	17
—— love the great test of character	91	18

	Paragraph	Page
EDUCATION:—		
A preparation for the duties of life	4, 5	110
Bacon's views on Latin and Greek	3	110
Bad influence of Latin and Greek authors	39-42	119
Change of method in teaching	23	115
Essentials of, to be taught to men and women	26	116
Female accomplishments in	27	116
Geography in	17	114
History and biography in	19	114
Influence of books in, often evil	38	118
Moral and religious	31-37	117
Natural History in	18	114
Natural Philosophy	20	114
No formal study of English required in	11	112
Object of, to make a man a good member of society	1	110
Of the middle classes	10	112
Of the people, reasons for	59	122
Of the Society of Friends	27-30	116
Political science	21	115
Practice of copy-writing	15	113
Should train the character in morals and religion	46-49	120
Study of the classics discussed	7-9	112
,, science preferable to literature	13	113
Executions, public, do great harm	18	204
Expediency, general experience	38, 39	7
—— Paley's axiom	30	6
—— silence of Scripture on	37	7
—— the foundation of European politics	29	143
Extortion	67	57

	Paragraph	Page
FALSEHOODS, see also Lies.		
—— in legal documents	62	80
Fame	75	107
—— military, not durable	63	103
Family, keeping up the	100	65
—— provision for	97	64
—— splendour	115	180
Faults of great men	76	107
Field sports, see Amusements.		
Forms of government: elective	9	157
—— general principles	1	156
—— hereditary	8	157
—— monarchy	6	157
—— should be susceptible of peaceable change	12	158
—— should follow opinion of community	15	159

INDEX.

	Paragraph	Page
Formularies, *see* Ceremonial Institutions.		
FRIENDS:—		
Education of Society of	27 30	116
Glory, military, *see* under War.		
Government by ministerial union	37	161
—— by political influence	20	160
—— parties	32	163
Grammar, English, *see also* under Education	11	112
Heirs of estates	53	54
Historical works, defective	81	109
Holy alliance	33	144
—— days	21	47
Houses of Infamy	86	62
Hyperbole and lies	59	79
Immoral agency	24 26	94
Imprisonment for crime, *see* Punishment.		
Improvement on estates	84	61
Infanticide	147	30
Inns a cause of drunkenness	33	96
Insolvency	41	51
—— imprisonment for debt	54	193
—— losses to the nation from	45	52
—— need of sound opinions as to	46	52
Institutions, *see* Ceremonial.		
Insurance against fire a moral duty	80	60
INTEMPERANCE:—		
Publicans' licenses should be refused	106	179
Intestates: primogeniture	110, 111	179
Irony dangerous, leading to untruth	59, 60	79
Justice, change of law may tend to increase litigation	17	184
—— considers the motives and intentions	14	183
—— courts of arbitration	26, 27	186
—— courts of equity, their rules and conditions	35 38	189
—— distinction between known and probable crime	22	185
—— effects of the prerogative of pardon	24	186
—— evil effects of having laws too fixed	18	184
—— evil effects of precedents	21	185
—— left in the hands of the judges	9	182
—— principles of administration	1, 4, 5	181
—— pure moral principles should rule in courts	39	190

	Paragraph	Page
Land, Primogeniture, &c.	110, 111	179
Law and precedents	20	185
—— intention of the law *v.* its expression	14	34
—— of the land, its authority	1	32
—— useless laws should be repealed	41	145
—— *v.* Equity	18	69
—— what is legally right, may not be morally right	10, 11	33
LAW OF HONOUR:—		
Authority	50	41
Character	53	42
Effects upon society	55	42
LAW OF NATURE:—		
Definitions	16	34
Natural rights	17	34
Political duties arising from	29	36
Subordinate to moral law	20	35
Laws, nugatory	45	40
—— obligatory	42	39
—— of nations, definitions	41	39
—— subordinate to moral law	48	40
Legal customs permitting falsehood wrong	23	70
—— effect of, on the profession	38	75
Legal proof	23	70
Libel, cases of	74 77	196
—— disproof of the best remedy	74	196
—— general conclusion	91	200
—— hardship of, when mixed with truth	80	197
—— on governments	83	198
—— party libels on opponents	85	199
—— power of public opinion over vicious	81	197
—— prosecution of libellous books excites demand	89	199
—— settled by a court of equity	68	196
—— some definition required	67	195
—— use of a free statement of truth	86	199
Liberty, Catholic allegiance	62 64	150
—— civil	36	144
—— effect of war upon	38	145
—— political, definition	42	146
—— ,, a right of the community	44	146
—— religious, opposed to civil disabilities	50	147
—— ,, ,, religious establishments	58	149
—— religious, opposed to tests, oaths, and formularies of belief	59	149
—— restrained by unnecessary laws	40	145
Libraries, circulating, duty of restraining issue of some books	32	95
Lies and promises	40	75
—— defended for particular purposes	54-58	78
—— definition of	52	78
Litigation, Christian condemnation of	1-3	66
Lords, Christian bishops in	54	168
—— House of, the privileges	50	167
—— increase in numbers	59	169
Lotteries condemned	105	178

INDEX.

	Paragraph	Page
MINISTERIAL union	37	164
Ministers, Christian, legal provision for	47-51	216
—— voluntary payment of	52, 53	217
Monarchy, hereditary and elective	8, 9	157
Moral sense, opinions respecting it	113	23

MORAL LAW :—

	Paragraph	Page
Benevolence of the	90	18
Every person possesses	118	24
Foundation of the	1-4	1
No formal moral system in Scripture	75	14
Obedience to the, in respect of war	51	255
Obligance of nations to obey it	27	143
Spirit of the	83	16
Superiority of the Christian	68, 71	12
The law of limitations and the precepts of Scripture	77-81	15
Two modes of enforcing it in Scripture	83	16
Variations in the	73	13
War reverses the rules of	35	251

	Paragraph	Page
Moral character of actions, intentions	60	11
—— legislation	94	176
Morality of legal practice	12	68
—— of Patriarchal, Mosaic, and Christian dispensations	61-74	11
—— professional lies	16	69

	Paragraph	Page
Motives of actions, *see* Justice.		
Murder	26	206
—— life destroyed under other names	41-42	98

	Paragraph	Page
PARLIAMENT, candidates should be at no expense	74	172
—— election should be secret ballot	75	172
—— extension and privilege of the franchise	69	171
—— House of Commons, duration of	77	173
—— ,, ,, duty of members in voting	88	175
—— ,, ,, moral qualification of members	87	174
—— House of Lords not needed	60	169
—— ,, ,, bishops objectionable	54-57	168
—— ,, ,, proxies wrong	58	169
—— is the representative of the people	61	170
—— universal suffrage	71	171
Party, in politics injurious	32-34	163
Patriotism as viewed by Christianity	36	239
Patronage an influence frequently immoral	27, 28	162
Pennsylvania, colonisation of	9	273
Pensioners and placemen	91	175

	Paragraph	Page
Pleadings in courts of justice, not guilty	62	80
Pluralities	95	225
Political influence	28	162
Political power, possession of	1	137
—— rightly exercised	16	140
Prayer, forms of	29	49
Press, obligations of the	78	108
—— special duties of the historian	82	109
Primogeniture	110, 111	179
Promises, *see* Lies.		

PROPERTY :—

	Paragraph	Page
Bad distribution, illustrations of	51 57	54
Confiscations	73	59
Defects in the law of, bills of exchange	60	56
Distraints	63	56
Distribution of property at death	50	53
Duty of parents	95	64
Extortion	67	57
Founded on the law of the land	37, 38	51
Houses of infamy	86	62
Improvement on estates	84	61
Inequality of distribution	90	63
,, ,, remedy for	92	63
Insurance against fire	80	60
Literary, vicious	87	62
Minor's debts	58	55
Privateers	70	58
Rewards for finding lost	88	63
Riches injure the possessor of	93	64
Settlements of estates	85	61
Shipments	62	56
Slaves	68	58
Unjust defendants	66	57
Wife's debts	59	55
Prosecutions sometimes refused	35	96
Providence of God, duty of reliance upon the	15-17	275
Public money	75, 76	59
—— opinion, influence of	{ 85-87 38, 39	85 97
Punishment of death	11	202

PUNISHMENT :—

	Paragraph	Page
Capital punishment, death	12, 13	202
,, ,, does harm	18	204
,, ,, sometimes a mistake	27	206
,, the argument summarised	32	207
Christian aim in	3	200
General conclusions	91, 92	200
Inflicted for actions not condemned by moral law	40	190
Inflicted a measure of the virtue of the people	46	191
In reference to created offences	48	192
Insolvents should be subjects of penal law	65	195
It may be right to punish debtors	57	194
Libels against governments not proper subjects of	83	198
Modes of carrying punishment into effect	10	202

INDEX.

	Paragraph	Page
PUNISHMENT (Continued)—		
Proper ends of punishment	1	200
Should apply in some instances to libels	74	106
Should follow certain offences against morals	52	193
To compensate for the wrong done	7	201
To restrain evil doers	5	201
RELIGIOUS OBLIGATIONS:—		
Ceremonial institutions	22	47
Divine power in prayer	30	49
Establishments opposed to religious liberty	1, 39	207, 215
„ the primitive church	8, 9	208
Feelings, the	8	44
Forms of prayer	29	49
Identical authority of moral and religions	51	9
Inward devotion	3	43
Outward worship	1	43
Sabbatical institutions	11	45
Scepticism	32	49
Sunday newspapers	18	47
Travelling habits on Sunday	17	46
Rewards, the evil of, for restoring lost property	88	63
Rights and religious obligations	1	43
—— of self-defence	22, 35	132
—— political obligations	1	137
Rituals, ceremonial institutions	22	47
SABBATH as an institution	11	45
—— temporal occupations on the	16, 17	46
Scepticism on religion	32, 35	49
Schools, public, the	3	110
—— see Education.		
Scripture	61	11
Seduction, a father seeks redress for	28	72
—— should be treated as a crime	52	193
Self-defence	22, 35	132
Sermon on the Mount, principles of the	14	258
Settlements of property on wife	85	61
Slavery	46	241
Standard of right and wrong	5	1
—— the will of God	7	1
Subordinate standards of right and wrong	45–50	8
Subscription to articles of religion	15	92

	Paragraph	Page
TAXES: Christ paid taxes	33	263
Tests, reasons for imposing them by Elizabeth	29	212
—— religious, in the Colonies	64	148
Toleration a usurpation in thought	57	149
UNCHASTITY	65	104
Unpaid minority, axiom	34	238
Untruth, see also Lies	51	77
UTILITY:—		
Another name for expediency	30	6
Axiom, not to do evil that good may come	87	17
„ the end justifies the means	88	17
„ whatever is expedient is right	30	6
Discussion of the principle	34, 40	6
Further discussion of this topic	32, 40	37
Obligation of every law depends upon its ultimate utility	30	6
VERDICTS	32	188
Vices, national	152	31
Virtue as defined by the moral law	58	11
—— as practised by the community	57	10
—— as regarded by public opinion	38	97
—— as respects the agents	59	11
—— definitions of	57	10
—— military, depends upon public praise	52	100
—— military, is hollow and deceitful	54	101
WAR:—		
Anger and irritation a cause of	10	247
Christians declined to be soldiers	48	266
Conclusions from the argument	17	275
Discussion has been evaded	3	244
Does Christianity sanction it	1	244
Duty of every one to inquire	2	244
Favourable public opinion makes the soldier's life genteel	14, 15	247
Gives employment in troubled times	19	248
Implies unbelief in the Providence of God	16	275
Incompatible with Christian religion	63	269
Loss of life fails to awaken horror against it	6	245
Love of gain influences to	13	247
Moravians hold same views as Quakers on	note	273
Pomp and glitter of the soldier's life blunts our feelings to the evil of	5	245

INDEX.

	Paragraph	Page
WAR (Continued)—		
Russian war of Napoleon I., loss of life	7	246
Safety of Quakers in Ireland	6	273
,, ,, America	7	273
Unlawfulness of war, a belief of the early Christians	48-54	266
Wealth, evils of great accumulation of	115	180

	Paragraph	Page
WILL OF GOD :—		
Conscience, authority of	109	21
,, Scripture teaching	138-141	29
,, the	{ 96-100	19
	113-124	23
Given to the heathen, pagans, &c.	127	27
Immediate communication of	125	27
The final law	20	3
The Scriptures communicate the	22	4
The standard of moral law or duty	7	1
What it is—*not*—why it is	56	10
Wills, legatees, heirs	50	53

THE END.

Printed by BALLANTYNE, HANSON & CO.
Edinburgh and London

www.ingramcontent.com/pod-product-compliance
Lightning Source LLC
Chambersburg PA
CBHW022058230426
43672CB00008B/1210